图解工程机械英汉词汇

吴永平 陈波 赵利军 编著

Illustrated
English-Chinese
Vocabulary
of Construction
Machinery

化学工业出版社
·北京·

图书在版编目（CIP）数据

图解工程机械英汉词汇/吴永平，陈波，赵利军编著.
北京：化学工业出版社，2009.10
ISBN 978-7-122-06599-5

Ⅰ.图… Ⅱ.①吴…②陈…③赵… Ⅲ.工程机械-词汇-英、汉 Ⅳ.TU6-61

中国版本图书馆CIP数据核字（2009）第154404号

责任编辑：贾　娜　　　　　　　装帧设计：史利平
责任校对：顾淑云

出版发行：化学工业出版社（北京市东城区青年湖南街13号　邮政编码100011）
印　　刷：北京永鑫印刷有限责任公司
装　　订：三河市万龙印装有限公司
850mm×1168mm　1/32　印张18¼　字数389千字
2010年1月北京第1版第1次印刷

购书咨询：010-64518888（传真：010-64519686）　售后服务：010-64518899
网　　址：http://www.cip.com.cn
凡购买本书，如有缺损质量问题，本社销售中心负责调换。

定　价：49.00元　　　　　　　　　　　　版权所有　违者必究

前　言

　　工程机械是集机、电、液一体化和信息、激光等高新技术以及审美艺术于一身的现代机电产品，正在向着自动化、远距离控制和智能化等方向发展。现代工程机械产品的技术水平在一定程度上代表了一个国家的工业化水平。近 20 年来，我国工程机械产品得到了很大的发展。然而，到目前为止，现代工程机械产品的核心技术仍为发达国家所垄断，发达国家的产品技术仍然代表着相应的技术发展方向。

　　我国仍有不少工程机械产品要从国外进口，在使用维修和进口贸易的过程中，常常会用到工程机械的专业术语，掌握一定的专业词汇逐渐成为工程机械领域从业人员的必备技能。考虑到机械专业的专业特点，辅以图形会使专业内容更加直观、具体、形象、生动，基本可以达到"望图知意"的程度，更易于读者理解，所以本书以"看图识字"的方式编写专业英语，内容紧扣工程机械领域，采用图文并举、英汉同步跟随的编写形式，对工程机械的相关知识做了新形式的表达。这种方式可使读者在学会某个名词、动词英语表达的同时，进一步巩固、加强对工程机械本身专业术语的理解。

　　考虑到近年来工程机械的发展情况，本书以英汉对照的方式，对工程机械的通用结构及工程施工中应用较多的工程机械做了详细讲述，内容包括发动机、传动系统、转向系统、行驶系、制动系统，以及液压挖掘机、装载机、自行式平地机、推土机、沥青摊铺机、压路机、沥青混合料搅拌设备、公路养护机械等。本书内容系统新颖、实用性强，可供工程机械领域的技术人员作为简明的图解工程机械词汇手册使用，也可作为工程机械及相关专业的教材供师生查阅参考。

　　本书由长安大学吴永平、陈波、赵利军共同编著。其中，

Unit1、Unit7~Unit10 由吴永平编写，Unit2~Unit6 由陈波编写，Unit11~Unit14 由赵利军编写。本书在编写过程中，得到了各界同仁和朋友的大力支持、鼓励和帮助，在此表示衷心的感谢！

由于编者水平所限，书中不妥之处在所难免，敬请广大读者和专家批评指正。

编　者

目 录

Unit 1 Generality of Construction Machinery 工程机械概述 …… 1
1.1 Basic Concept 基本概念 …… 1
1.2 Application Fields 应用领域 …… 2
 Fig. 1.1 Application fields of construction machinery 工程机械的应用领域 …… 3
1.3 Classification 分类 …… 4
 Fig. 1.2 Earthmoving machinery 铲土运输机械 …… 4
 Fig. 1.3 Rock machinery 石方机械 …… 6
 Fig. 1.4 Compactors 压实机械 …… 6
 Fig. 1.5 Pavement machinery 路面机械 …… 7
 Fig. 1.6 Hoisting machinery 起重机械 …… 8
 Fig. 1.7 Pile driving machinery 桩工机械 …… 10
 Fig. 1.8 Bridge and tunnel machinery 桥梁和隧道机械 …… 10
 Fig. 1.9 Pavement maintenance machinery 路面养护机械 …… 13
 Fig. 1.10 Concrete machinery 混凝土机械 …… 14
1.4 Components of Construction Machinery 工程机械组成 …… 14
 Fig. 1.11 Basic components of self-propelled construction machinery 自行工程机械基本组成 …… 14
 Fig. 1.12 Basic components of wheeled chassis 轮式底盘基本组成 …… 15
 Fig. 1.13 Basic components of tracked chassis 履带底盘基本组成 …… 16

Unit 2 Engine 发动机 …… 17
2.1 General 概述 …… 17
 Fig. 2.1 Gasoline engine 汽油机 …… 21
 Fig. 2.2 Diesel Engine 柴油机 …… 25
2.2 Crank Connecting Rod Mechanism 曲柄连杆机构 …… 27
 Fig. 2.3 Cylinder liner (Cylinder sleeve) 汽缸套 …… 27

Fig. 2.4	Oil pan 油底壳	27
Fig. 2.5	Piston (1) 活塞 (1)	28
Fig. 2.6	Piston (2) 活塞 (2)	30
Fig. 2.7	Piston ring technical terms 活塞环专门术语	32
Fig. 2.8	Piston ring 活塞环形式	33
Fig. 2.9	Connecting rod 连杆	35
Fig. 2.10	Crankshaft and flywheel 曲轴和飞轮	36
Fig. 2.11	Crankshaft 曲轴	37
Fig. 2.12	Built-up crankshaft 组合式曲轴	37

2.3 Valve Mechanism 配气机构 ……………………………………… 38

Fig. 2.13	Single overhead camshaft 单顶置凸轮轴	38
Fig. 2.14	Underneath camshaft overhead valve 下置凸轮轴顶置式气门	39
Fig. 2.15	Valve 气门	40
Fig. 2.16	Rocker-arm mounting structure 摇臂支架结构	41

2.4 Fuel System 供油系统 ……………………………………… 42

Fig. 2.17	Fuel system principle 燃油供给系统原理	42
Fig. 2.18	Hole type nozzle 孔式喷嘴	43
Fig. 2.19	Pintle type nozzle 轴针式喷嘴	44
Fig. 2.20	Jerk fuel injection pump 柱塞式喷油泵	45
Fig. 2.21	Delivery valve 出油阀	46
Fig. 2.22	Distributor-type injection pump 分配式喷油泵	47
Fig. 2.23	Fuel control mechanism 油量调节机构	48
Fig. 2.24	RQ and RSV types governor RQ 和 RSV 型调速器	49
Fig. 2.25	RAD minimum-maximum-speed governor RAD 型两极式减速器	50
Fig. 2.26	Mechanical add-on equipments of governor (1) 调速器机械式附加装置 (1)	51
Fig. 2.27	Mechanical Add-on Equipments of Governor (2) 调速器机械式附加装置 (2)	52
Fig. 2.28	Diesel electronic control system 柴油机电子控制系	53
Fig. 2.29	Electronically controlled unit-injector injection system 电子控制泵-喷嘴喷射系统	54

Fig. 2.30　Electronically controlled unit injector common-rail injection system 电子控制式泵-喷嘴共轨喷射系统 …………… 56
Fig. 2.31　Common-rail (fuel) injection system (accumulator concept) 共轨燃油喷射系统（蓄压器原理）……………… 58
Fig. 2.32　Injector for common rail injection system 共轨燃油喷射系统喷油器 …………………………………………… 59
Fig. 2.33　Gasoline engine fuel system 汽油机供油泵 ………… 60
Fig. 2.34　Schematic for a carburetor fuel system 化油器式供给系统简图 ……………………………………………………… 61
Fig. 2.35　Air cleaner 纸质空气滤清器（空气滤清器）……… 62
Fig. 2.36　Fuel system-gasoline injection 汽油喷射式燃油系统 ……… 63
Fig. 2.37　Injector 喷油器 ……………………………………… 65
Fig. 2.38　Fuel pressure regulator 燃油压力调节器 …………… 66
2.5　Spark-Ignition System 火花塞点火系统 …………………… 67
Fig. 2.39　Classical (conventional) ignition system 传统线圈点火系统 …………………………………………………… 67
Fig. 2.40　Ignition coil 点火线圈 ……………………………… 68
Fig. 2.41　Spark (ing) plug 火花塞 …………………………… 69
Fig. 2.42　Battery (accumulator) 蓄电池 ……………………… 70
2.6　Cooling System 冷却系统 ………………………………… 71
Fig. 2.43　Liquid cooling system 水冷系统 …………………… 71
Fig. 2.44　Radiator 散热器 ……………………………………… 72
Fig. 2.45　Cooling fan 风扇 …………………………………… 73
Fig. 2.46　Coolant pump 水泵 ………………………………… 74
Fig. 2.47　Viscous fan coupling (clutch) 黏液风扇离合器 …… 75
2.7　Lubrication System 润滑系统 …………………………… 76
Fig. 2.48　Fundamental principle 基本原理 …………………… 76
Fig. 2.49　Oil pump 机油泵 …………………………………… 77
Fig. 2.50　Full-flow (oil) filter 全流式（机油）滤清器 ……… 78
2.8　Starting System 启动系统 ………………………………… 79
Fig. 2.51　Gasoline starting engine 汽油启动机 ……………… 79
Fig. 2.52　Starting switch 启动开关 …………………………… 80
Fig. 2.53　Starter 启动机 ……………………………………… 81

Fig. 2.54　Alternator 交流发电机 ……………………………… 82
Fig. 2.55　Heater plug 电热塞 ………………………………… 83
Fig. 2.56　Roller-type overruning clutch 滚柱式单向离合器 ……… 84
Fig. 2.57　Multi-disc overruning clutch 摩擦片式单向离合器 …… 85

Unit 3　Power Train System 传动系统 ……………………… 86

3.1　General 概述 …………………………………………… 86
3.2　Mechanical Transmission System 机械传动系统 ………… 87
　　Fig. 3.1　Mechanical transmission system 机械传动系统 ……… 87
　　Fig. 3.2　Main clutch 主离合器 ………………………………… 88
　　Fig. 3.3　Clutch driven plate 离合器从动盘 …………………… 90
　　Fig. 3.4　Clutch operation 离合器操纵机构 …………………… 91
　　Fig. 3.5　Clutch rod-operated mechanism 离合器杠杆操纵机构 …… 92
　　Fig. 3.6　Transmission case 变速箱 …………………………… 93
　　Fig. 3.7　Self-locking and interlocking device 自锁和互锁装置 ……… 95
　　Fig. 3.8　Gearshift mechanism 换挡机构 ……………………… 96
　　Fig. 3.9　Drive shaft structure and types 传动轴结构和类型 ……… 98
　　Fig. 3.10　Drive axle assembly 驱动桥总成 …………………… 100
　　Fig. 3.11　Main drive 主传动 …………………………………… 101
　　Fig. 3.12　Track drive and steering clutch 履带驱动与转向离合器 …… 102
3.3　Hydromechanical Transmission System 液力机械传动系统 …… 103
　　Fig. 3.13　Hydromechanical transmission system 液力机械传动系统 … 103
　　Fig. 3.14　Torque converter 变矩器 …………………………… 104
　　Fig. 3.15　Power shifting transmission case 动力换挡变速箱 ……… 105
　　Fig. 3.16　Automatic transmission 自动换挡变速箱 …………… 107
3.4　Hydraulic Transmission System（Track Paver）液压传动系统
　　（履带摊铺机）…………………………………………… 108
　　Fig. 3.17　Hydraulic transmission system（track paver）液压传动
　　　　　　系统（履带摊铺机）…………………………………… 108

Unit 4　Steering System 转向系统 ………………………… 109

4.1　General 概述 …………………………………………… 109
4.2　Wheeled Steering System 轮式转向系统 ………………… 110
　　Fig. 4.1　Steering types 转向类型 ……………………………… 110
　　Fig. 4.2　Steering linkage (mechanism) 转向传动机构 ………… 112

Fig. 4.3　Steering axle 转向桥 …………………………………………… 114
Fig. 4.4　Steering gear 转向器 …………………………………………… 115
Fig. 4.5　Articulated steering system 铰接式转向系统 ………………… 116
Fig. 4.6　Hydraulic steering system 液压转向系统 …………………… 117
4.3　Crawler Steering Mechanism 履带车辆转向机构 ……………………… 118
Fig. 4.7　Crawler steering axle 履带车辆转向桥 ……………………… 118
Fig. 4.8　Double action steering clutch 双作用转向离合器 ………… 119

Unit 5　Running Gear 行驶系 …………………………………………… 120
5.1　Overview 概述 ………………………………………………………… 120
5.2　Wheeled Running Gear 轮式行驶系 ……………………………………… 121
Fig. 5.1　Wheeled running mechanism 轮式行走机构 ………………… 121
Fig. 5.2　Tire (tyre) type 轮胎类型 ……………………………………… 122
Fig. 5.3　Tire tread 胎面 ………………………………………………… 124
Fig. 5.4　Rim 轮辋 ………………………………………………………… 125
Fig. 5.5　Tire valve 气门嘴 ……………………………………………… 126
5.3　Crawler Unit 履带行走装置 …………………………………………… 127
Fig. 5.6　Crawler 履带式车辆 …………………………………………… 127
Fig. 5.7　TY220 crawler dozer frame TY220 推土机机架 …………… 128
Fig. 5.8　SD7 crawler dozer frame SD7 推土机机架 ………………… 129
Fig. 5.9　Track assembly 履带总成 ……………………………………… 130
Fig. 5.10　Track roller 履带支重轮 ……………………………………… 131
Fig. 5.11　Carrier roller 托链轮 ………………………………………… 132
Fig. 5.12　Track idler 引导轮 …………………………………………… 133
Fig. 5.13　Tension device 张紧装置 …………………………………… 134
Fig. 5.14　Track frame 台车架 …………………………………………… 135
5.4　Suspension 悬架 ……………………………………………………… 136
Fig. 5.15　Suspension spring element 悬架弹性元件 ………………… 137
Fig. 5.16　Leaf spring suspension 板簧式悬架 ………………………… 138
Fig. 5.17　Hydraulic compensating axle suspension 液压平衡
悬架 ………………………………………………………… 140
Fig. 5.18　Tractor suspension 拖拉机悬架 …………………………… 141
Fig. 5.19　Semi-rigid suspension 半刚性悬架 ………………………… 142
Fig. 5.20　Rigid suspension (swing axle) 刚性悬架（摆动桥）…… 142

Fig. 5.21　Telescopic shock absorber 筒式减振器 ……………………… 143

Unit 6　Braking System 制动系统 ……………………………… 145
6.1　General 概述 ……………………………………………………… 145
6.2　Types of Brake 制动器类型 …………………………………… 146
Fig. 6.1　Types of brake 制动器类型 ……………………………… 146
Fig. 6.2　Cam brake 凸轮张开式制动器 …………………………… 148
Fig. 6.3　Oil pressure brake 油压张开式制动器 ………………… 149
Fig. 6.4　Drum brake structural components 鼓式制动器结构零件 …… 150
Fig. 6.5　Caliper disk brake 钳盘式制动器 ……………………… 152
Fig. 6.6　Automatic clearance compensator 自动间隙补偿装置 …… 153
Fig. 6.7　Structural components 结构零件 ……………………… 154
Fig. 6.8　Dry-type complete disc brake 干式全盘式制动器 ……… 156
Fig. 6.9　Band brake (1) 带式制动器（1） ……………………… 157
Fig. 6.10　Band brake (2) 带式制动器（2） …………………… 158
Fig. 6.11　Parking brake 驻车制动器 …………………………… 159
6.3　Basic Components of Braking System 制动系统基本组成 …… 160
Fig. 6.12　Basic components of braking system 制动系统基本组成 …… 160
6.4　Braking Control System 制动操纵系统 …………………… 161
Fig. 6.13　Manpower brake system 人力制动系统 ……………… 161
Fig. 6.14　Typical air brake system 典型气制动系统 …………… 162
Fig. 6.15　Double pipeline air boost brake system 双管路空气增压制动系统 ……………………………………………………… 163
Fig. 6.16　Electronic brake system (EBS) 电子制动系统 ……… 164
6.5　Antilock Brake System (ABS) 防抱死制动系统 ……………… 165
Fig. 6.17　Antilock brake system (ABS) 防抱死制动系统 ……… 165

Unit 7　Hydraulic Excavators 液压挖掘机 ……………………… 166
7.1　Overview 概述 ……………………………………………………… 166
Fig. 7.1　Applications of excavator 挖掘机的应用 ……………… 169
Fig. 7.2　Types of excavator 挖掘机的类型 ……………………… 171
7.2　Components and Features 组成与特点 ……………………… 172
Fig. 7.3　Overall structure 总体结构 …………………………… 172
Fig. 7.4　Diesel engine and hydraulic system 柴油机及液压系统 … 173
Fig. 7.5　Undercarriage 行走支承机构 ………………………… 173

Fig. 7.6	Work equipment assembly 工作装置总成	174
Fig. 7.7	General purpose bucket 通用铲斗	175
Fig. 7.8	Steering and operating system 转向操纵系统	175
Fig. 7.9	General arrangement of large type excavator 大型挖掘机总体布置	176
Fig. 7.10	Typical hydraulic system 典型液压系统	177
Fig. 7.11	APC system 自动功率控制系统	178
Fig. 7.12	Dimensions 尺寸规格	181
Fig. 7.13	Working ranges 工作范围	182
Fig. 7.14	Small excavator features 小型挖掘机	183
7.3	Working Attachments 工作附件	185
Fig. 7.15	Working attachments 工作附件	187
7.4	New Technology of Hydraulic Excavator 液压挖掘机新技术	187
Fig. 7.16	Common rail type fuel injection system 共轨型燃油喷射系统	189
Fig. 7.17	Cooled EGR system 冷却废气再循环系统	190
Fig. 7.18	Enhanced boom recirculation system 加速型动臂再循环系统	191
Fig. 7.19	Boom mode selector 动臂工作模式选择	192
Fig. 7.20	ON comfortable mode 舒适工作模式	192
Fig. 7.21	OFF powerful mode 重型工作模式	192
Fig. 7.22	Combined operation of boom and arm 动臂与杆臂的组合作业	193
Fig. 7.23	Strengthened general-purpose bucket 增强型通用铲斗	196
Fig. 7.24	Strengthened H-bucket for heavy-duty H 形重型强化铲斗	196
Fig. 7.25	Ample foot space 宽敞的足下空间	197
Fig. 7.26	Comfort-designed operator seat 设计舒适的驾驶员座椅	198
Fig. 7.27	Monitor 监视器	199
Fig. 7.28	Rear view camera 后视摄像头	199
Fig. 7.29	Arrangement of engine 发动机的布置	200
Fig. 7.30	Dual main fuel filters provided standard 标准化双主燃油	

		滤清器 …………………………………………………	201
Fig. 7.31		Easy draining 排油方便 …………………………	201
Fig. 7.32		New Pilot Control shut-off lever 新型驾驶操纵锁定杆 …	204

Unit 8　Loaders 装载机 ……………………………………… 206

8.1　Overview 概述 …………………………………………… 206
- Fig. 8.1　Applications of loader 装载机的应用 ………… 210
- Fig. 8.2　Types of loader 装载机的类型 ……………… 212

8.2　Components and Features 组成与特点 …………… 213
- Fig. 8.3　Basic components 基本部件 ………………… 213
- Fig. 8.4　Hydromechanical transmission system 液力机械传动系统 ………………………………………………… 215
- Fig. 8.5　Transmission system arrangement 传动系统布置 …… 216
- Fig. 8.6　Torque converter 液力变矩器 ………………… 217
- Fig. 8.7　Performance characteristic 工作特性 ………… 219
- Fig. 8.8　Hydro-mechanical series drive 液压机械组合传动 …… 219
- Fig. 8.9　Hystat power train system 静液传动系统 ……… 220
- Fig. 8.10　Operator station of track loader 履带式装载机驾驶员操作台 ………………………………………………… 221
- Fig. 8.11　Wheel loader 轮式装载机 …………………… 225
- Fig. 8.12　Track-type loader 履带式装载机 …………… 226

8.3　Working Attachments 工作附件 …………………… 229
- Fig. 8.13　Bucket types 铲斗类型 ……………………… 229
- Fig. 8.14　Working attachments of skid-steer loader 滑移装载机工作附件 ……………………………………………… 231

8.4　New Technology of Wheel Loader 轮式装载机新技术 …… 232
- Fig. 8.15　Digging operations 铲装作业 ………………… 234
- Fig. 8.16　Lifting operations 提升作业 ………………… 235
- Fig. 8.17　Komatsu components 小松部件 …………… 235
- Fig. 8.18　Flat face-to-face O-ring seals 扁平面对面O形圈密封 …… 236
- Fig. 8.19　Cylinder buffer rings 液压缸缓冲密封圈 …… 236
- Fig. 8.20　Wet multi-disc brakes and fully hydraulic braking system 湿式多片制动器与全液压制动系统 ……… 237
- Fig. 8.21　High-rigidity frames 大刚度车架 …………… 238

Unit 9　Motor Graders 自行式平地机 ……………………………… 239
9.1　Overview 概述 …………………………………………………… 239
　　Fig. 9.1　Applications of grader 平地机的应用 ………………… 241
　　Fig. 9.2　Types of grader 平地机的类型 ………………………… 242
9.2　Components and Features 组成与特点 ………………………… 243
　　Fig. 9.3　Overall structure 总体结构 …………………………… 243
　　Fig. 9.4　Power train 传动装置 …………………………………… 244
　　Fig. 9.5　Operation mechanism 工作机构 ……………………… 245
　　Fig. 9.6　Typical drive line system 典型传动系统 …………… 246
　　Fig. 9.7　Typical hydraulic control system 典型液压控制系统 ……… 247
　　Fig. 9.8　Dimensions 尺寸规格 …………………………………… 248
　　Fig. 9.9　Blade operating space 铲刀工作范围 ………………… 248
　　Fig. 9.10　Activity types 作业类型 ……………………………… 249
　　Fig. 9.11　Laser grade control system 激光找平系统 ………… 252
　　Fig. 9.12　Transmission 变速箱 ………………………………… 252
　　Fig. 9.13　Powertrain 传动系 …………………………………… 253
　　Fig. 9.14　Hydraulic system 液压系统 ………………………… 254
　　Fig. 9.15　Duramide bearings 嵌入耐磨支承垫 ……………… 254
　　Fig. 9.16　Circle 回转圈 …………………………………………… 255
　　Fig. 9.17　Front frame 前机架 …………………………………… 256
　　Fig. 9.18　Drive circle 驱动回转圈 ……………………………… 256
　　Fig. 9.19　Moveable blade control system 可移动铲刀控制系统 …… 257
　　Fig. 9.20　Articulation 铰接连接 ………………………………… 258
　　Fig. 9.21　Front axle mobility 前桥机动性 …………………… 259
　　Fig. 9.22　Brakes 制动装置 ……………………………………… 260
　　Fig. 9.23　Controls 操作控制装置 ……………………………… 260
　　Fig. 9.24　Smart shifter 灵巧变速器 …………………………… 261
9.3　Working Attachments 工作附件 ……………………………… 262
　　Fig. 9.25　Working attachments 工作附件 …………………… 262
9.4　New Technology of Motor Grader 平地机新技术 …………… 263
　　Fig. 9.26　Power train 传动系 …………………………………… 263
　　Fig. 9.27　Front axle 前桥 ………………………………………… 264
　　Fig. 9.28　Hydraulic brakes 液压制动器 ……………………… 265

- Fig. 9.29　Top-adjust drawbar wear strips 顶部调节牵引架耐磨垫 …… 268
- Fig. 9.30　Shimless moldboard retention system 无垫片铲刀板外伸系统 …… 269
- Fig. 9.31　Cat comfort series seat 卡特舒适型系列驾驶座椅 …… 270
- Fig. 9.32　Left joystick functions 左操纵杆功能 …… 271
- Fig. 9.33　Right joystick functions 右操纵杆功能 …… 272
- Fig. 9.34　Visibility 驾驶视野 …… 273

Unit 10　Bulldozer 推土机 …… 274

10.1　Overview 概述 …… 274
- Fig. 10.1　Applications of bulldozer 推土机的应用 …… 277
- Fig. 10.2　Types of bulldozer 推土机类型 …… 278

10.2　Components and Features 组成与特点 …… 279
- Fig. 10.3　Overall structure 总体结构 …… 279
- Fig. 10.4　Hydrodynamic drive 液力传动装置 …… 280
- Fig. 10.5　Typical hydrodynamic drive system 典型液力传动系统 …… 281
- Fig. 10.6　Typical hydraulic control system 典型液压控制系统 …… 282
- Fig. 10.7　Hydrostatic drive dozer 静液传动推土机 …… 283
- Fig. 10.8　Wheel dozer power train 轮式推土机传动装置 …… 284
- Fig. 10.9　Electronic control system 电控系统 …… 285
- Fig. 10.10　Operator station 驾驶员操作台 …… 286
- Fig. 10.11　Monitoring system 监控系统 …… 287
- Fig. 10.12　Dimensions 尺寸规格 …… 290
- Fig. 10.13　Fundamental operation 基本作业 …… 290

10.3　Principal Assembly and Attachments 主要总成与附件 …… 291
- Fig. 10.14　Principal assembly and attachments 主要总成与附件 …… 292

10.4　New Technology of Crawler Dozer 履带推土机新技术 …… 293
- Fig. 10.15　Controller's automatical adjustment 控制器自动调节 …… 293
- Fig. 10.16　Dozing and turning 推土与转弯作业 …… 294
- Fig. 10.17　Dozing downhill 下坡推土作业 …… 294
- Fig. 10.18　Preset travel speed selection function 行驶速度预置选择功能 …… 295

Fig. 10.19　Automatic torque converter lockup system 液力变矩器自动闭锁系统 ……… 296

Fig. 10.20　K-bogie undercarriage system K 形台车架行走系统 …… 297

Fig. 10.21　Track shoe slip control system 履带板滑移控制系统 …… 298

Fig. 10.22　Rippers 松土器 ……… 299

Fig. 10.23　Hexagonal pressurized cab 六边形压力密封驾驶室 ……… 300

Fig. 10.24　New cab damper mounting 新型减振安装形式 ……… 301

Fig. 10.25　Monitor with self-diagnostic function 具有自诊断功能的监视器 ……… 302

Fig. 10.26　Track link with wedge ring 楔形环履带链 ……… 303

Fig. 10.27　VHMS (Vehicle Health Monitoring System) 车辆正常工作状况监视系统 ……… 304

Unit 11　Asphalt Paver 沥青摊铺机 ……… 305

11.1　Overview 概述 ……… 305

Fig. 11.1　Routine paving 常规摊铺 ……… 308

Fig. 11.2　Continuous paving 不间断摊铺 ……… 308

Fig. 11.3　Types of asphalt paver 沥青摊铺机的类型 ……… 309

11.2　Components and Features 组成与特点 ……… 310

Fig. 11.4　Basic components 基本部件 ……… 311

Fig. 11.5　Mechanical transmission system 机械式传动系统 ……… 312

Fig. 11.6　Hydraulic-mechanical transmission system 液压机械式传动系统 ……… 313

Fig. 11.7　Hydraulic transmission system (wheel paver) 液压传动系统（轮式摊铺机）……… 314

Fig. 11.8　Hydraulic transmission system (track paver) 液压传动系统（履带摊铺机）……… 315

Fig. 11.9　Control panel 操纵控制台 ……… 316

Fig. 11.10　Tracked pavers 履带式摊铺机 ……… 320

Fig. 11.11　Wheeled pavers 轮胎式摊铺机 ……… 321

11.3　Working Equipment and Attachments 工作装置与附件 ……… 322

Fig. 11.12　Tamper configuration of screed units 熨平板振捣配置 … 322

Fig. 11.13　Components of mechanical extension screed 机械加宽式熨平板组成 ……… 323

Fig. 11.14　Extensions 加宽段 …………………………………… 324
Fig. 11.15　Components of hydraulic extension screed 液压伸缩式熨平板组成 ……………………………………………… 325
Fig. 11.16　The different extensions with the bolts 不同尺寸的加宽段熨平板 …………………………………………………… 326
Fig. 11.17　Components of auto leveling device 自动找平装置的组成 ………………………………………………………… 327
Fig. 11.18　Types of auto leveling device 自动找平装置的类型 …… 328
11.4　New Technology of Asphalt Paver 沥青摊铺机新技术 ………… 328
Fig. 11.19　High ambient temperature cooling system 高温环境下的冷却系统 ……………………………………………… 329
Fig. 11.20　Dual operator stations 双操作台 ……………………… 330
Fig. 11.21　Mobil-trac undercarriage 移动式履带行走机构 ……… 331
Fig. 11.22　Steel track undercarriage 钢履带行走机构 …………… 331
Fig. 11.23　Hydrostatic drive system 液压驱动系统 ……………… 332
Fig. 11.24　Exclusive material delivery system 独特的材料传输系统 ……………………………………………………… 333
Fig. 11.25　Gateless feeders 无门送料器 ………………………… 334
Fig. 11.26　Feeder 送料器 ………………………………………… 335
Fig. 11.27　Auger assembly 螺旋器组件 ………………………… 336

Unit 12　Rollers 压路机 …………………………………………… 338
12.1　Overview 概述 ………………………………………………… 338
Fig. 12.1　Application of rollers 压路机的应用 …………………… 342
Fig. 12.2　Types of roller 压络机的类型 …………………………… 344
12.2　Components and Features 组成与特点 ……………………… 344
Fig. 12.3　Basic components of single drum vibratory roller 单钢轮振动压路机基本部件 ………………………………… 344
Fig. 12.4　Basic components of tandem vibratory roller 双钢轮振动压路机基本部件 ………………………………………… 345
Fig. 12.5　Mechanical transmission system 机械式传动系统 ……… 346
Fig. 12.6　Hydraulic transmission system (one-wheel drive) 液压式传动系统（单轮驱动）………………………………… 347
Fig. 12.7　Hydraulic transmission system (two-wheel drive) 液压式

      传动系统（双轮驱动） ·············· 348
 Fig. 12.8 Hydraulic traveling system 行走液压系统 ·············· 349
 Fig. 12.9 Hydraulic vibration system 振动液压系统 ·············· 350
 Fig. 12.10 Hydraulic steering system 转向液压系统 ············· 351
 Fig. 12.11 Rigid frame 刚性（整体式）车架 ·················· 351
 Fig. 12.12 Articulated frame 铰接式车架 ···················· 352
 Fig. 12.13 Integral-pin articulated frame 整体铰销式铰接车架 ····· 352
 Fig. 12.14 Two-pins articulated frame 双铰销式铰接架 ········· 353
 Fig. 12.15 Gross-pins articulated frame 十字轴式链接车架 ······ 354
 Fig. 12.16 None drive mode 非驱动型 ······················ 355
 Fig. 12.17 Drive mode 驱动型 ···························· 356
 Fig. 12.18 Dual amplitude mechanism of reversible eccentric weight
      逆转偏心块式双幅机构 ························ 357
 Fig. 12.19 Dual amplitude mechanism of reversible steel shot 逆转流
      球式双幅机构 ································ 358
 Fig. 12.20 Five amplitude vibratory system 5 振幅振动系统 ······ 358
 Fig. 12.21 Control panel 操纵控制台 ······················· 359
 Fig. 12.22 Water spray system 喷水系统 ···················· 361
 Fig. 12.23 Single drum vibratory rollers 单钢轮振动压路机 ······ 366
 Fig. 12.24 Tandem vibratory rollers 双钢轮振动压路机 ········ 366
12.3 Automatic Amplitude Compaction System 自动调幅压实系统 ··· 367
 Fig. 12.25 Single drum vibratory rollers 单钢轮振动压路机 ······ 367
 Fig. 12.26 Tandem vibratory rolles 双钢轮振动压路机 ········· 367
12.4 Oscillation Compaction Technology 振荡压实技术 ············ 369
 Fig. 12.27 Components of oscillation roller 振荡轮结构 ········· 369
 Fig. 12.28 The principle of oscillation compaction 振荡压实原理 ··· 370
 Fig. 12.29 The compaction level 压实效果 ··················· 371

Unit 13 Asphalt Mixing Plant 沥青混合料搅拌设备 ·············· 373
 13.1 Overview 概述 ·································· 373
  Fig. 13.1 Types of asphalt mixing plant 沥青混合料搅拌设备的
      类型 ······································ 376
  Fig. 13.2 Productive processes of batch forced mixing plant 间歇强
      制式搅拌设备的生产工艺 ······················ 377

Fig. 13.3　Productive processes of continuous drum mixing plant 连续滚筒式搅拌设备的生产工艺 …… 377

13.2　Components and Features 组成与特点 …… 378

　　Fig. 13.4　Basic components of batch forced mixing plant 间歇强制式搅拌设备基本部件 …… 378

　　Fig. 13.5　Basic components of continuous drum mixing plant 连续滚筒式搅拌设备基本部件 …… 379

　　Fig. 13.6　Reciprocating feeder 往复式给料器 …… 379

　　Fig. 13.7　Electromagnetic vibrating feeder 电磁振动式给料器 …… 380

　　Fig. 13.8　Belt feeder 带式给料器 …… 380

　　Fig. 13.9　Slat feeder 板式给料器 …… 381

　　Fig. 13.10　Forced batch mixing plant 强制间歇式搅拌设备 …… 382

　　Fig. 13.11　Continuous drum mixing plant 连续滚筒式搅拌设备 …… 383

　　Fig. 13.12　Screening drum technology 筛网烘干筒技术 …… 384

　　Fig. 13.13　Driving type of drum 干燥滚筒驱动形式 …… 385

　　Fig. 13.14　Burner 燃烧器 …… 385

　　Fig. 13.15　Hot aggregate elevator 热骨料提升机 …… 386

　　Fig. 13.16　Underneath vibrator 下置式振动器 …… 387

　　Fig. 13.17　Overhead vibrator 上置式振动器 …… 387

　　Fig. 13.18　Hot aggregate bins 热骨料储仓 …… 388

　　Fig. 13.19　Filler storage and conveying device 粉料储存和输送装置 …… 389

　　Fig. 13.20　Weigh system of batch forced mixing plant 间歇强制式搅拌设备称量系统 …… 390

　　Fig. 13.21　Positive displacement asphalt weigh system 容积式沥青称量装置 …… 391

　　Fig. 13.22　Gravity asphalt weigh system 重力式沥青称量装置 …… 392

　　Fig. 13.23　Low speed side synchronous mixer 低速端同步式搅拌器 …… 393

　　Fig. 13.24　High speed side synchronous mixer 高速端同步式搅拌器 …… 394

　　Fig. 13.25　Underneath mixed material storage silo 底置式成品料储仓 …… 395

　　Fig. 13.26　Offset mixed material storage silo 旁置式成品料储仓 … 396

- Fig. 13.27　Cyclone dust filter 旋风式除尘器 …… 397
- Fig. 13.28　Venturi scrubbing dust filter 文丘里除尘器 …… 397
- Fig. 13.29　Bag dust filter 袋式除尘器 …… 398
- 13.3　Standard Equipment Specifications 标准装置规格类型与性能参数 …… 399
- 13.4　Double Barrel Dryer/drum Mixer Technology 双滚筒拌和技术 …… 403
  - Fig. 13.30　Three different types of flights 三种不同类型的叶片 …… 403
  - Fig. 13.31　Basic structure 基本结构 …… 405

Unit 14　Highway Maintenance Machinery 公路养护机械 …… 406

- 14.1　Asphalt Distributor 沥青洒布车 …… 406
  - Fig. 14.1　Application of highway maintenance machinery 公路养护机械的应用 …… 407
  - Fig. 14.2　Components of highway maintenance machinery 公路养护机械的组成 …… 408
  - Fig. 14.3　Asphalt storage tank 沥青箱 …… 410
  - Fig. 14.4　Heating system 加热系统 …… 411
  - Fig. 14.5　Fuel tank 燃料箱 …… 412
  - Fig. 14.6　Circulating and distributing system 循环、洒布系统 …… 413
  - Fig. 14.7　Operating mechanism 操纵机构 …… 414
  - Fig. 14.8　Asphalt pump 沥青泵 …… 415
- 14.2　Slurry Seal Machine 稀浆封层车 …… 416
  - Fig. 14.9　Slurry seal machine 稀浆封层车 …… 416
  - Fig. 14.10　Components of slurry seal machine 稀浆封层车的组成 …… 417
  - Fig. 14.11　Mixing system 拌和系统 …… 418
  - Fig. 14.12　Spreader box 摊铺箱 …… 420
- 14.3　Pavement Recyclers 道路再生机 …… 421
  - Fig. 14.13　Hot-in-place recycling train 就地热再生机组 …… 421
  - Fig. 14.14　Concentrated combustion preheater 集中燃烧式加热机 …… 422
  - Fig. 14.15　Decentralized combustion preheater 分散燃烧式加热机 …… 422
  - Fig. 14.16　Preheater/Miller 加热/铣刨机 …… 423

Fig. 14.17	Postheater/Dryer/Mixer 后加热/烘干/搅拌机	424
Fig. 14.18	Heating system 加热系统	425
Fig. 14.19	Hot-in-place remixer 就地热再生重铺机	426
Fig. 14.20	Operating principle of hot-in-place remixer 就地热再生重铺机工作原理	427
Fig. 14.21	Components of hot-in-place remixer 就地热再生重铺机的组成	428
Fig. 14.22	Cold-in-place recycler 就地冷再生机	429
Fig. 14.23	Components of cold-in-place recycler 就地冷再生机的组成	430
Fig. 14.24	Components of the milling drum 铣刨转子的组成	431
Fig. 14.25	Components of the twin-shaft mixer 双轴搅拌器的组成	432
Fig. 14.26	Operating principle 工作原理	433
Fig. 14.27	Basic operation process 基本作业过程	433
Fig. 14.28	Stabilizer/Recycler 稳拌/再生机	434
Fig. 14.29	Components of stabilizer/recycler 稳拌/再生机的组成	435
Fig. 14.30	Application of stabilizing soils 稳定土壤功用	436
Fig. 14.31	Application of cold recycling 冷再生功用	436
Fig. 14.32	Micro-processor control for the injection systems 喷洒系统微机控制	437
Fig. 14.33	Basic operation process 基本作业过程	437

14.4　Pothole Patcher 坑槽修补车 ……………………………… 438

Fig. 14.34	Combined maintenance truck 综合养护车	438
Fig. 14.35	Components of combined maintenance truck 综合养护车的组成	439
Fig. 14.36	Spray patching road maintenance vehicle 喷射式道路修补车	441
Fig. 14.37	Trailer-mounted pothole patcher 拖挂喷射式坑槽修补机	442
Fig. 14.38	Working procedure 作业工序	443

Vocabulary Index 词汇索引（英中对照）……………………… 444

Vocabulary Index 词汇索引（中英对照）……………………… 503

参考文献 ……………………………………………………………… 562

Unit 1　Generality of Construction Machinery
工程机械概述

1.1　Basic Concept 基本概念

　　Construction Machinery, known by the other terms: engineering vehicles, construction equipment, earth movers, heavy equipment or just plain equipment, are machines, specifically designed to execute civil engineering and construction engineering tasks. The scope of the specialized manufacturing industries covered by the previously mentioned engineering fields is broad, encompassing in no order: construction, logging, mining, waste management, military engineering and agriculture. These machines are most often associated with earthworks. These engineering vehicle machines, in the most basic form, are compound machines composed of simple machines. These components make up the five equipment systems: implement, traction, structure, power train, control and information. Currently most equipment use hydraulics as a primary source of transferring power. The use of heavy equipment has a long history. Vitruvius, a 1st century B.C. engineer, gave detailed descriptions of Roman heavy equipment and Roman cranes in his treatise De Architectura.

　　工程机械是指各种专门用于完成土木工程和建筑工程任务的机械设备。工程机械又被称为工程车辆、建筑设备、铲土运输机械、重型机械设备，或简称为设备。上述工程领域所涵盖的专门制造业范围广泛，其中包括建筑、伐木、采矿、废物处理、军事工程和农业。工程机械常与土方工程有关。大部分工程机械的基本形式是一些简单机械的组合。工程机械的组成分为五个设备系统：工作装置、牵引装置、结构件、传动系统、控制及信息系统。目前，大部分工程机械以液压动力作为主要的传动动力源。重型机械的应用历史悠久。作为公元前一世纪的工程师维特鲁威在其著作《建筑十书》中就对罗马重型设备和起重机械进行了详细的描述。

1.2 Application Fields 应用领域 (Fig. 1.1)

(a) earthmoving work 土方工程

(b) rock breaking work 石方工程

(c) road construction 道路建设

(d) bridge work 桥梁工程

Fig. 1.1

(e) tunnel construction 隧道工程

(f) architectural engineering 建筑工程

(g) agricultural and hydraulic engineering
农业与水利工程

(h) habour and riverbank protective construction
港口及河岸防护工程

(i) mining industry 采矿业

(j) forest engineering 林业工程

(k) environmental engineering 环境工程

(l) pile foundation work 桩基工程

Fig. 1.1 Application fields of construction machinery
工程机械的应用领域

1.3 Classification 分类

1.3.1 Earthmoving Machinery 铲土运输机械 (Fig. 1.2)

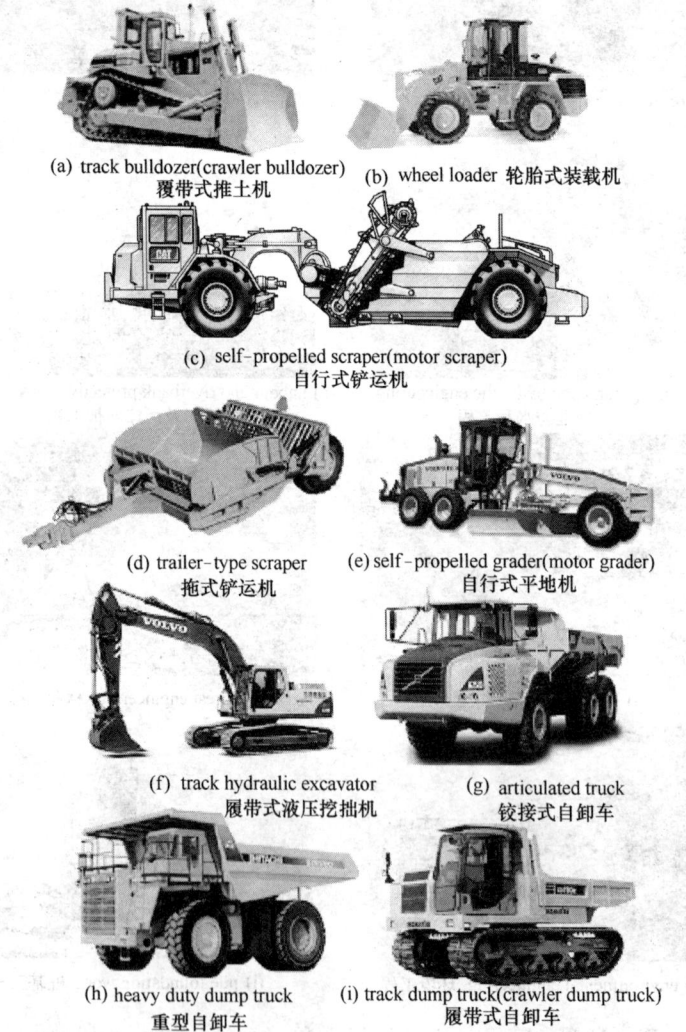

(a) track bulldozer(crawler bulldozer) 覆带式推土机
(b) wheel loader 轮胎式装载机
(c) self-propelled scraper(motor scraper) 自行式铲运机
(d) trailer-type scraper 拖式铲运机
(e) self-propelled grader(motor grader) 自行式平地机
(f) track hydraulic excavator 履带式液压挖掘机
(g) articulated truck 铰接式自卸车
(h) heavy duty dump truck 重型自卸车
(i) track dump truck(crawler dump truck) 履带式自卸车

Fig. 1.2 Earthmoving machinery 铲土运输机械

1.3.2 Rock Machinery 石方机械（Fig. 1.3）

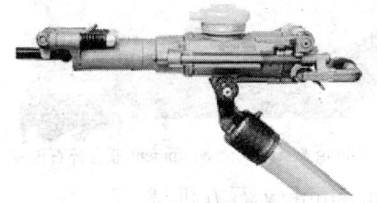
(a) air-leg rock drill 气腿式凿岩机

(b) in-the-hole drill 潜孔钻机

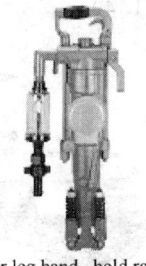
(c) air leg hand-hold rock drill 气腿手持式凿岩机

(d) crawler hydraulic drill rig 履带式全液压凿岩钻车

(e) jaw crusher 鄂式碎石机

(f) hammer crusher 锤式碎石机

(g) cone crusher 圆锥式碎石机

(h) impact crusher 反击式碎石机

Fig. 1.3

(i) vibrating screen 振动筛　　(j) crushing & screening equipment 联合碎石设备

Fig. 1.3　Rock machinery 石方机械

1.3.3　Compactors 压实机械（Fig. 1.4）

(a) single drum vibratory roller
单钢轮振动压路机

(b) double drum vibratory compactor
(tandem vibratory roller)
双钢轮振动压路机
（串联式振动压路机）

(c) pneumatic tire compactor(pneumatic tyred roller)
轮胎压路机

(d) walk behind roller
手扶压路机

(e) vibratory plate 振动平板夯

(f) impacting rammer 冲击夯

Fig. 1.4　Compactors 压实机械

1.3.4 Pavement Machinery 路面机械（Fig. 1.5）

Fig. 1.5 Pavement machinery 路面机械

1.3.5　Hoisting Machinery 起重机械（Fig. 1.6）

(a) mobile crane 汽车起重机

(b) all terrain crane 全路面起重机

(c) crawler crane 履带起重机

(d) telescopic crawler crane 伸缩臂履带起重机

(e) lorry-mounted crane 随车起重机

(f) column crane(tower crane) 塔式起重机

Fig. 1.6　Hoisting machinery 起重机械

1.3.6 Pile driving Machinery 桩工机械 (Fig. 1.7)

(a) track rotary drilling rig 履带式旋挖钻机

(b) step-type hydraulic pile driving machine 液压步履式桩机

(c) step-type multi-function hydraulic driller 液压步履式多功能钻机

(d) continuous flight auger drilling machine 长螺旋钻机

(e) horizontal directional drilling machine 水平定向钻机

(f) jet grouting drilling machine 旋喷钻机

(g) continuous wall grab 连续墙抓斗

(h) hydraulic pile-driver 全液压打桩机

Fig. 1.7

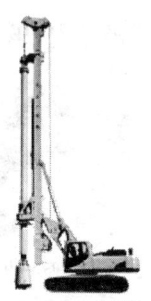

(i) hydrostatic pressure pile driver 液压静力压桩机   (j) reverse circulation drilling rig 反循环钻机

Fig. 1.7　Pile driving machinery 桩工机械

1.3.7　Bridge and Tunnel Machinery 桥梁和隧道机械 (Fig. 1.8)

(a) bridge girder erection equipment 架桥机　　(b) transporting girder vehicle 运梁车

(c) bridge inspection vehicle 桥梁检测车　　(d) step-type bridge erection equipment 步履式架桥机

(e) tunnel borer, tunnel boring machine 隧道掘进机　　(f) tunnel shield machine 盾构机

Fig. 1.8　Bridge and tunnel machinery 桥梁和隧道机械

1.3.8 Pavement Maintenance Machinery 路面养护机械 (Fig. 1.9)

(a) asphalt pavement combined maintenance vehicle 沥青路面综合养护车

(b) pavement repairing vehicle 路面修补车

(c) grooving machine 开槽机

(d) crack pouring machine 灌缝机

(e) paint line marker 划线机

(f) pavement heating repairing vehicle 路面加热修补车

(g) asphalt slurry seal machine 稀浆封层机

(h) synchronous chip seal vehicle 同步碎石封层车

Fig. 1.9

(i) multifunctional vehicle
多功能工程车

(j) snow plough 犁式除雪机

(k) broom sweeper 滚刷式清扫车

(l) salt-sand spreader
盐沙防滑材料洒布机

(m) stone chip spreader
碎石洒布机

(n) road stabilizer/reclaimer
稳定土拌和 / 道路再生机

(o) asphalt pavement-hot-in-place recycling machine set
沥青路面就地热再生机组

(p) asphalt pavement heater
沥青路面加热机

(q) track cold milling machine, track cold planer
履带式冷铣刨机

Fig. 1.9

(r) asphalt distributor
沥青洒布车

(s) small wheel cold planer
小型轮式冷铣刨机

(t) pavement breaker
路面破碎机

(u) pavement high pressure cleaning vehicle
路面高压清洗车

Fig. 1.9　Pavement maintenance machinery 路面养护机械

1.3.9　Concrete Machinery 混凝土机械（Fig. 1.10）

(a) concrete mixer truck
混凝土搅拌车

(b) trailer concrete pump
混凝土拖泵

(c) truck-mounted concrete pump
混凝土泵车

(d) concrete placing boom
混凝土布料机

Fig. 1.10

(e) truck-mounted concrete line pump
混凝土车载泵

(f) concrete mixing plant
混凝土搅拌设备

Fig. 1.10 Concrete machinery 混凝土机械

1.4 Components of Construction Machinery 工程机械组成

1.4.1 Basic Components of Self-propelled Construction Machinery 自行工程机械基本组成（Fig. 1.11）

Fig. 1.11 Basic components of self-propelled construction machinery 自行工程机械基本组成

1　engine assembly 发动机总成
2　wheeled chassis 轮式底盘
3　work equipment assembly 工作装置总成
4　tracked chassis 履带底盘

14

1.4.2 Basic Components of Wheeled Chassis 轮式底盘基本组成
(Fig. 1.12)

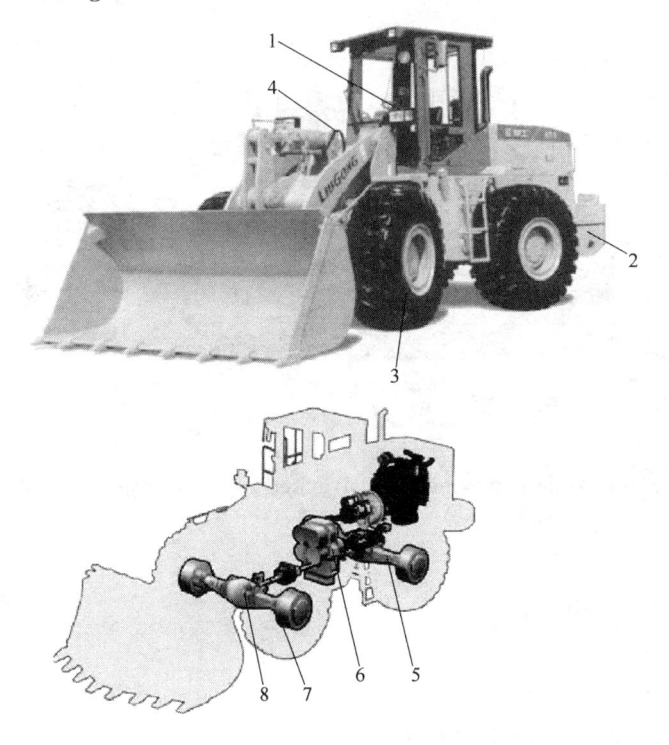

Fig. 1.12　Basic components of wheeled chassis
轮式底盘基本组成

1　steering and operating system 转向操纵系统
2　frame and suspension system 车架与悬挂系统
3　wheeled chassis travel system 轮式底盘行走系统
4　hydraulic system 液压系统
5　rear axle 后桥
6　power train system 传动系统
7　brake system 制动系统
8　front axle 前桥

1.4.3 Basic Components of Tracked Chassis 履带底盘基本组成
(Fig. 1.13)

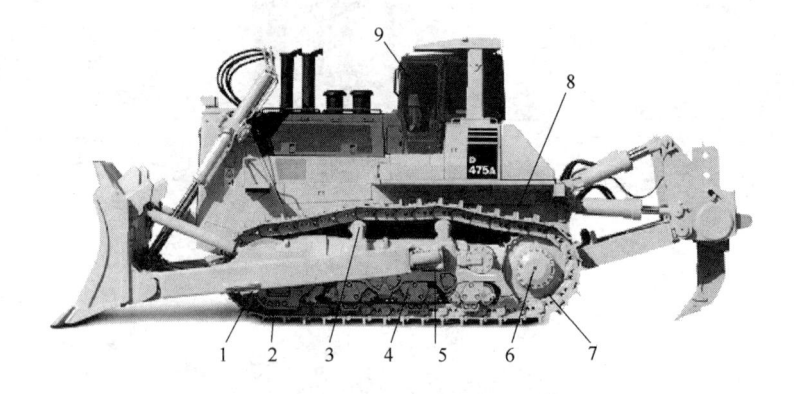

Fig. 1.13 Basic components of tracked chassis 履带底盘基本组成
1　track idler 引导轮
2　track 履带
3　carrier roller 托链轮
4　track roller 支重轮
5　track roller frame 台车架
6　final drive 最终传动装置
7　drive sprocket 驱动链轮
8　main frame 主机架
9　steering and operating system 转向操纵系统

Unit 2 Engine 发动机

2.1 General 概述

The engine which is called the "heart" of a vehicle is used to supply power for an automobile. It includes the fuel, lubricating, cooling, ignition and starting systems. Generally, an automobile is operated by internal combustion engine. The internal combustion engine burns fuel within the cylinders and converts the expanding force of the combustion or "explosion" into rotary force used to propel the vehicle.

发动机是车辆的心脏，用于为其提供动力。发动机包含燃料系统、润滑系统、冷却系统、点火系统和启动系统。车辆一般依靠内燃发动机驱动。内燃发动机在汽缸里燃烧燃料，并将燃烧所产生的膨胀力转变成旋转力，用以推动车辆前进。

The engine is a self-contained power unit which converts the heat energy of fuel into mechanical energy for moving the vehicle. Because fuel is burned within the engine, it is known as an internal combustion engine. In the internal combustion engine, air/fuel mixture is introduced into a closed cylinder where it is compressed and then ignited. The burning of the fuel causes a rapid rise in cylinder pressure which is converted to useful mechanical energy by the piston and crankshaft. The most common engine is the four-stroke piston engine. These four strokes are intake, compression stroke, power stroke and exhaust stroke.

发动机是独立的动力装置，能够将燃料的热能转换成推动车辆前进的机械能。由于燃料在发动机内部燃烧，因此这种发动机被称为内燃机。在内燃机里，可燃混合气被引入到封闭的汽缸内，并在汽缸内被压缩以及点燃。燃料燃烧引起汽缸内压力迅速上升，并通过活塞和曲轴被转换成有用的机械能。最常见的发动机是四冲程活塞式发动机。四冲程包括进气冲程、压缩冲程、做功冲程和排气冲程。

The reciprocating engines can be classified according to: ①number of cylinders: single-cylinder engine and multiple-cylinder engine; ②arrangement of cylinders: in-line engine、vee engine、radial engine and opposed-cylinder engine; ③type of cooling: air-cooled engine and liquid-cooled engine; ④number of cycles: two-stroke engine and four-stroke engine; ⑤type of ignition, there are two types of engine: gasoline (also called a spark-ignition engine) and diesel (also called a compression-ignition engine).

往复式发动机可以按以下几种情况分类：①按汽缸的数量：单缸发动机和多缸发动机；②按汽缸排列的方式：直列发动机、V形发动机、星形发动机和对置发动机；③按冷却形式：空气冷却式发动机和水冷却式发动机；④按工作循环的行程数：二冲程发动机和四冲程发动机；⑤按点火方式，有两种类型的发动机：汽油机（也称为火花塞点火式发动机）和柴油机（也称为压燃式发动机）。

The single-cylinder engine provides only one power stroke during every two crankshaft revolutions or delivers power only one-fourth of the time (four-stroke engine). To provide a more even and continuous flow of power, vehicle have engines with four, six or eight cylinders. These engines have power strokes arranged so as to follow one another closely or overlap one another.

单缸发动机在两个曲轴旋转周期内产生一个做功冲程或在四分之一时间内输出动力（四冲程发动机）。为使动力传递变得更加平滑和连续，车辆上采用四缸、六缸甚至八缸发动机。这种多缸发动机使各个做功冲程紧密相连或者彼此重叠。

The fundamental difference between gasoline and diesel engines is that in the gasoline engine the source of the heat for igniting the charge, namely, an electric spark, is generated outside the engine, and is taken, as it were, into the waiting charge at the required instant. In the diesel engine the source of heat for igniting the charge is created within the engine by compressing pure air to a degree that will initiate combustion and then injecting the fuel at right time in relation to the movement of the crankshaft.

汽油发动机与柴油发动机的基本区别在于，在汽油机中点燃混合气的热源是电火花。电火花是在发动机外面产生的。按照实际情况来说，电火花总是在需要的瞬间进入等待燃烧的混合气中。在柴油发动机中，使燃油点火的热源是靠将空气压缩到可以引燃的程度来产生的，并在对应于曲轴转动的恰当时刻喷入燃料。

2.1.1 Gasoline Engine 汽油机（Fig. 2.1）

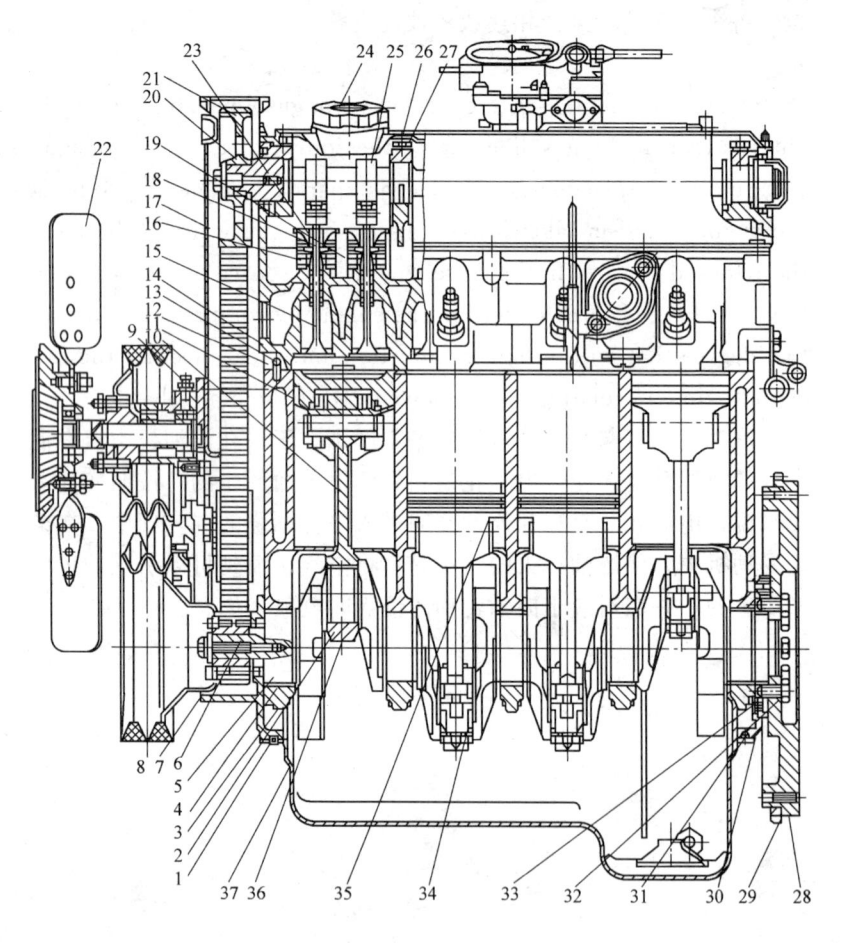

Fig. 2.1

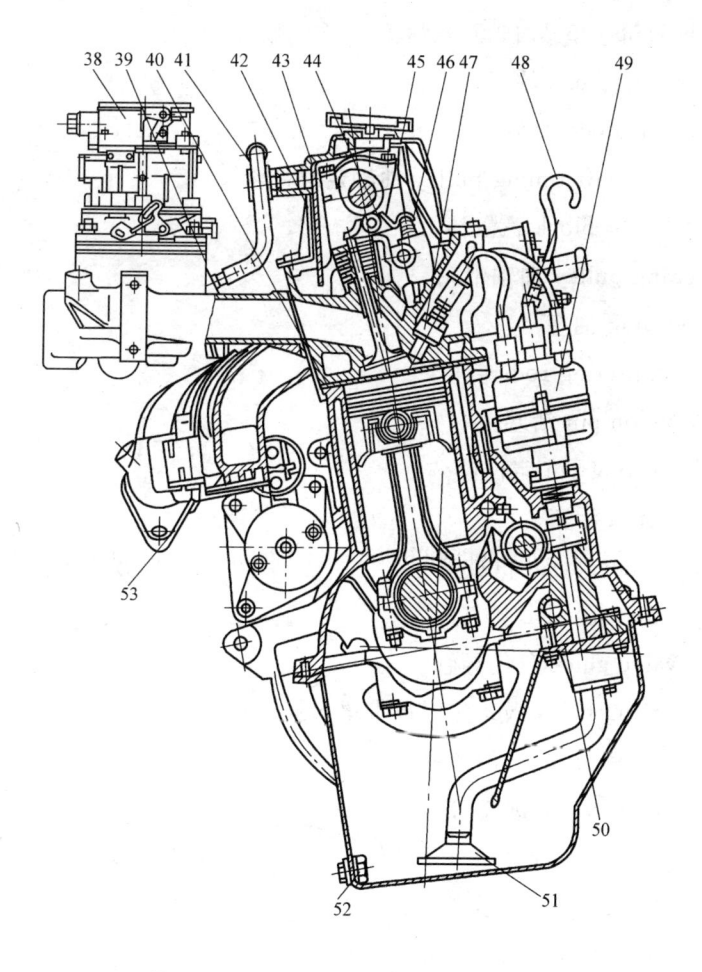

Fig. 2.1 Gasoline engine 汽油机

1,31,33　sealing element 密封件

2　connecting rod bearing cap 连杆盖

3　bearing cap（曲轴）轴承盖

4　bearing bush 轴瓦

5　crank shaft 曲轴

6　crankshaft timing pulley 曲轴定时带轮

7　cylinder block 汽缸体

8　crank pulley 曲轴带轮

9　oil plug 油塞

10　connecting rod 连杆

11　piston pin 活塞销

12　locating pin 定位销

13　piston 活塞

14　cylinder head 汽缸盖

15　exhaust valve 排气门

16　valve guide 气门导管

17　timing belt cover 定时齿带罩

18　valve spring 气门弹簧

19　intake valve 进气门

20　timing belt pulley（凸轮轴）定时带轮

21　toothed belt 齿形带

22　fan 风扇

23　valve spring retainer 气门弹簧座

24　filler cap（机油）加油口盖

25　cam shaft 凸轮轴

26　camshaft bearing cap 凸轮轴轴承盖

27 bolt 螺栓
28 flywheel 飞轮
29 ring gear （飞轮）齿圈
30 rear end cover 后端盖
32 compression bolt 压紧螺栓
34 thrust bearing shell 止推轴瓦
35 oil ring 油环
36 connecting rod bearing shell 连杆轴瓦
37 oil pan 油底壳
38 carburetor 化油器
39 intake tube 进气管
40 cylinder head gasket 汽缸衬垫
41 breather tube 通风管
42 oil baffle 挡油罩板
43 cylinder head cover 汽缸盖罩
44 bearing 轴承
45 rocker arm 摇臂
46 gap adjuster （气门）间隙调节器
47 spark plug 火花塞
48 oil rule 油标尺
49 distributor 分电器
50 oil pump 机油泵
51 oil strainer 机油集滤器
52 drain pulley 放油螺塞
53 exhaust pipe 排气管

23

2.1.2 Diesel Engine 柴油机 (Fig. 2.2)

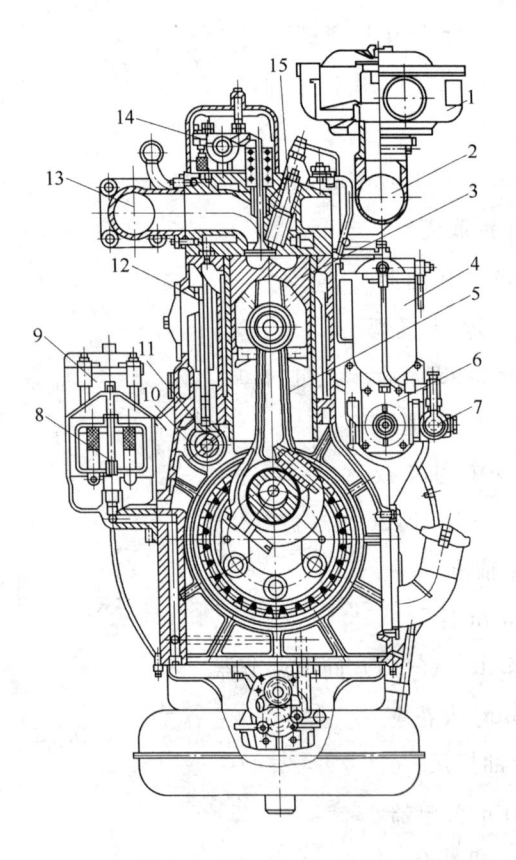

Fig. 2.2

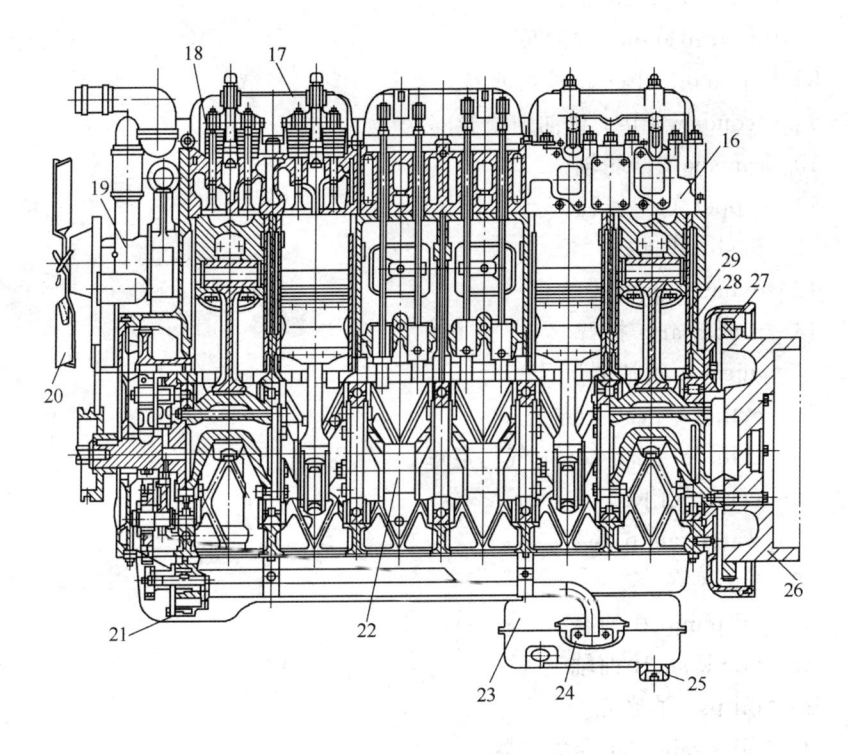

Fig. 2.2 Diesel Engine 柴油机

1　air cleaner 空气滤清器

2　intake tube 进气管

3　piston 活塞

4　oil cleaner 机油滤清器

5　connecting rod 连杆

6　injection pump 喷油泵

7　fuel feed pump 输油泵

8　coarse oil filter 机油粗滤器

9　secondary filter 机油细滤器

10　camshaft 凸轮轴

11　tappet（s）挺柱

12　pushrod 推杆

13　exhaust pipe 排气管

14　rocker arm 摇臂

15　injector 喷油器

16　cylinder head 汽缸盖

17　cylinder head cover 气门室罩

18　valve 气门

19　water pump 水泵

20　fan 风扇

21　oil pump 机油泵

22　crank shaft 曲轴

23　oil pan 油底壳

24　oil strainer 机油集滤器

25　drain pulley 放油螺塞

26　flywheel 飞轮

27　ring gear （飞轮）齿圈

28　cylinder block 机体

29　cylinder liner 汽缸套

2.2 Crank Connecting Rod Mechanism 曲柄连杆机构

2.2.1 Cylinder Liner (Cylinder Sleeve) 汽缸套 (Fig. 2.3)

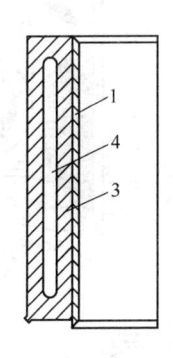

(a) dry sleeve(liner) type 干式缸套 (b) wet sleeve(liner) type 湿式缸套

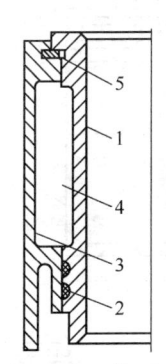

Fig. 2.3 Cylinder liner (Cylinder sleeve) 汽缸套

1 cylinder liner (cylinder sleeve) 汽缸套
3 engine blok, block 汽缸体
4 water jacket 水套
2,5 sleeve seal 缸套密封圈

2.2.2 Oil Pan 油底壳 (Fig. 2.4)

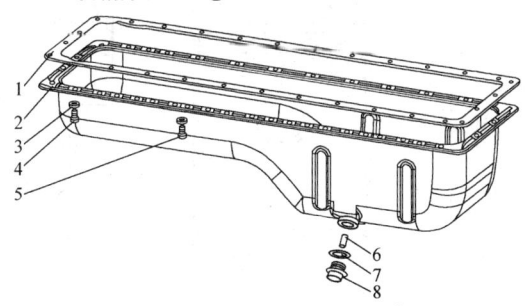

Fig. 2.4 Oil pan 油底壳

1 gasket 密封垫
2 oil pan 油底壳
3 washer 垫圈
4,5 bolt 螺栓
6 magnetic (drain) plug 磁性放油塞
7 gasket 衬垫
8 drain pulley 放油螺塞

27

2.2.3 Piston 活塞 (Fig. 2.5 and Fig. 2.6)

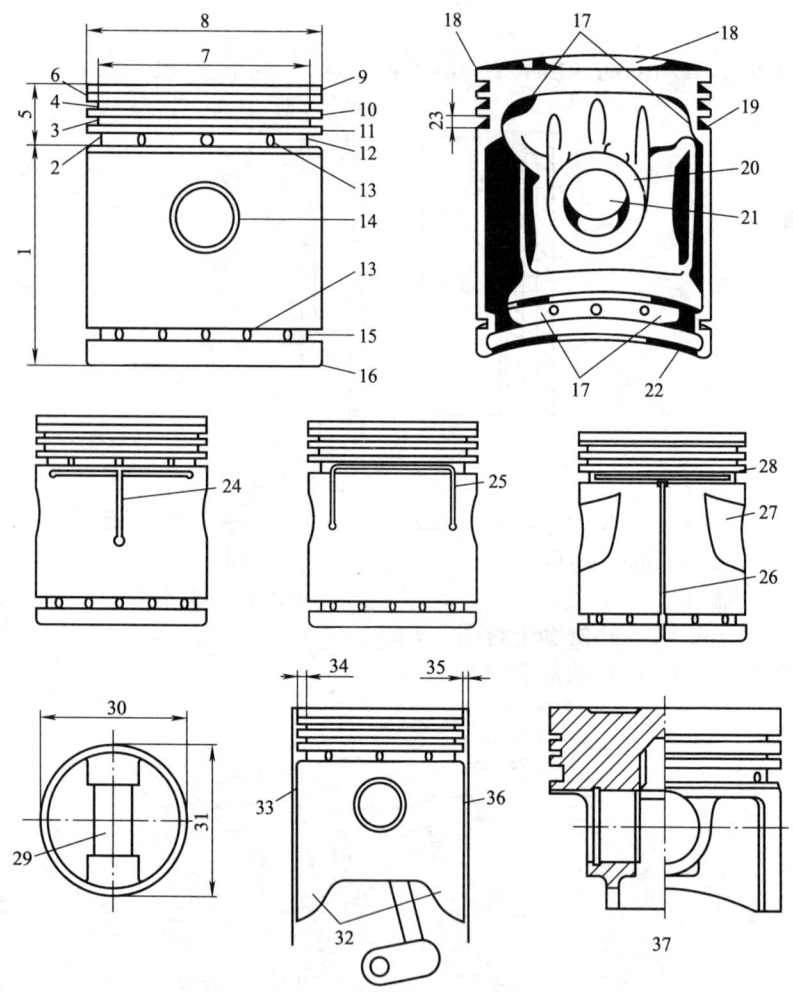

Fig. 2.5 Piston (1) 活塞 (1)

1 piston skirt (body, barrel) 活塞裙部
2 oil ring groove (slot) 油环槽
3 second (No. 2) ring groove (slot) 第二道环槽
4 top (No. 1) ring groove (slot) 第一道环槽

5	ring belt, ring zone	活塞环（分布）带
6	heat dam	热坝，隔热槽
7	groove-bottom diameter	槽底直径
8	land diameter, ring land diameter	环岸直径
9	top (No. 1) land, fire (head) land	第一环岸，火力岸
10	second (NO. 2) land	第二环岸
11	third land	第三环岸
12	ring groove bottom	槽底
13	oil drain (return) hole, oil return passage	回油孔
14	bevel	斜角
15	skirt ring groove (slot)	（活塞）裙部环槽
16	chamfer	圆角，倒角
17	ring-groove pad	环槽加厚部，环槽基底
18	head, crown, top, roof	顶（部），头（部），piston head (crown, top, roof) 活塞顶
19	ring-groove side	环槽侧面
20	pin boss	活塞销孔凸台
21	pin hole, gudgeon (piston, wrist) hole	活塞销孔
22	bottom rib	（活塞裙部）底肋
23	groove width	（活塞）槽高
24	T-slot, T-shaped slot	T形槽，T-slot piston T形槽活塞
25	U-slot	U形槽
26	vertical slot	直槽
27	skirt relief	裙部凹口
28	horizontal slot	水平切槽
29	piston pin, gudgeon pin, wrist pin, pin	活塞销
30	major diameter	大直径
31	minor diameter	小直径
32	slipper, slipper skirt	（活塞）拖板，滑座
33	major thrust face	主承推面
34	groove depth, depth of groove	（活塞环）槽深
35	land clearance	岸隙
36	minor thrust face	次承推面（传递小侧压力面）
37	full slipper piston, slipper (-skirt) piston	全拖板式活塞

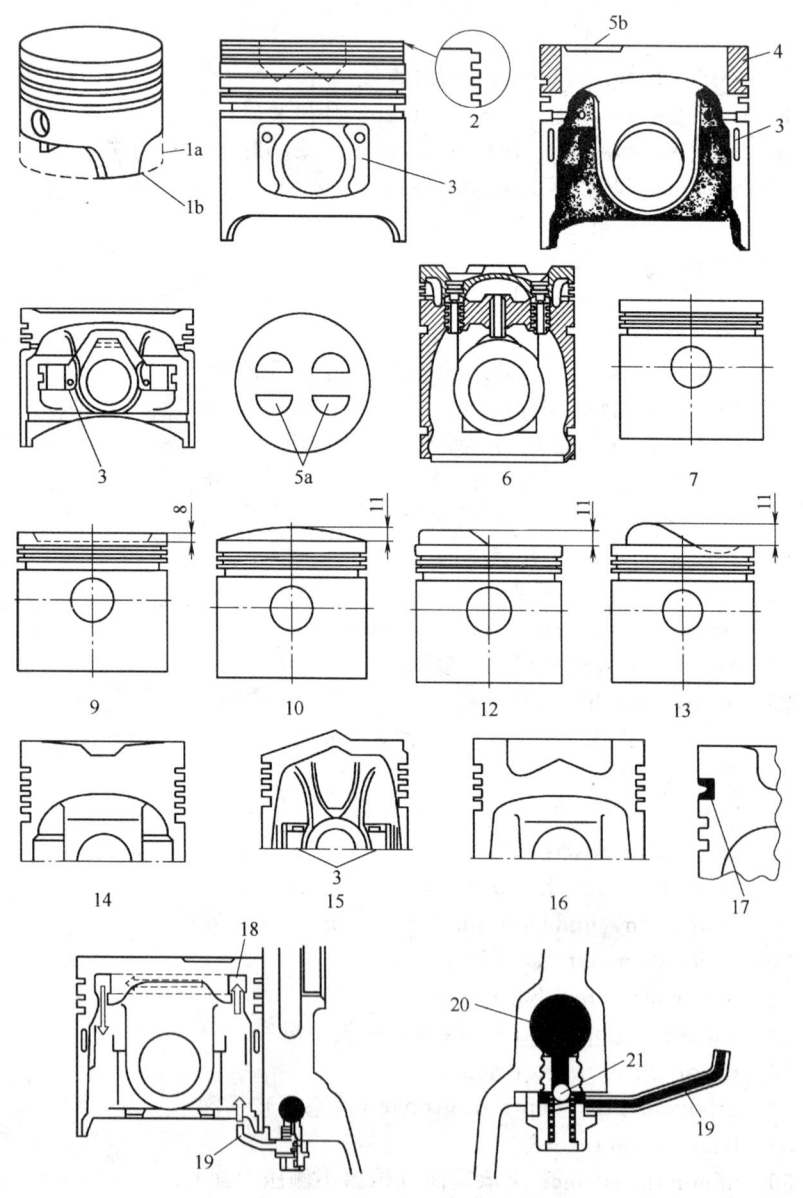

Fig. 2.6 Piston (2) 活塞(2)

1a full-skirt piston 全裙式活塞
1b half-slipper piston 半拖板式活塞
2   heat-proof slots 隔热槽
3   fiber reinforced metal 纤维增强金属
4   steel insert 钢镶片，steel piston insert 活塞钢镶片，invar insert 恒范钢镶片，殷钢镶片，strip inserts for expansion control 控制膨胀镶片，invar strut piston 恒范钢镶片活塞，autothermic piston 热膨胀自动调节式活塞（此时镶片为低碳钢）
5a valve relief （活塞上防干涉）气门凹坑
5b piston relief (recess) 活塞凹坑
6   multi-piece oil-cooled piston 多件式油冷活塞
7   flat head (top, crown, poof) 平顶
8   cup depth 杯深
9   cup (dish) head (top, crown, roof) 杯形顶，dish piston 皿形（顶）活塞
10 home head (top, crown, roof) 圆顶
11 home height 圆顶高度，凸高
12 hump head (top, crown, roof), convex head (top, crown, roof), hump (convex) piston head (top, crown, roof) 凸顶
13 contour head (top, crown, roof) 异形顶
14 concave head (top, crown, roof) 凹顶
15 step head (top, crown, roof) 台阶顶
16 piston head with combustion chamber 带燃烧室的活塞顶
17 piston insert 活塞环槽镶圈，top ring insert 头道环槽镶圈，Ni-resist insert 耐蚀高镍铸铁镶圈
18 cooling gallery, cooling passage 冷却槽（通道）
19 oil nozzle 机油喷嘴
20 main oil gallery (channel) 主油道
21 check valve 单向阀

2.2.4 Piston Ring Technical Terms 活塞环专门术语 (Fig. 2.7)

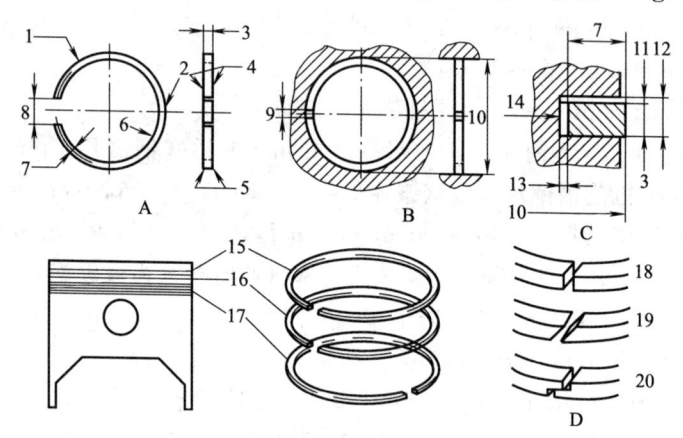

Fig. 2.7 Piston ring technical terms 活塞环专门术语

A free ring, unstressed ring 自由状态环
B closed ring 工作状态环
C ring clearance 环间隙
D types of ring gap, joint ring end gap types 环的切口形式
1 ring face, ring periphery, ring working face 环（工作）表面，环外表面
2 back of the ring 环后部
3 ring width 环高度
4 side face 侧面
5 peripheral edge 外棱
6 inside surface 内表面
7 radial wall thickness, radial thickness 径向宽度
8 total free gap 总自由间隙
9 closed gap, end clearance, end play, compressed gap 开口间隙，端隙
10 nominal ring diameter 环标称直径
11 side clearance, side play, land clearance 侧隙
12 groove width 槽高
13 radial clearance, back clearance 背隙
14 groove root diameter 槽底直径
15 top (upper) compression ring, top ring, No.1 compression ring 第一道气环，上压缩环
16 second (compression) ring, 2nd (compression) ring, lower compression ring 第二道气环，第二道压缩环
17 oil (control) ring 油环
18 butt joint 平切口
19 beveled joint, diagonal joint 斜切口，45° angle joint 45°切口
20 step joint 阶梯状切口

2.2.5 Piston Ring 活塞环形式 (Fig. 2.8)

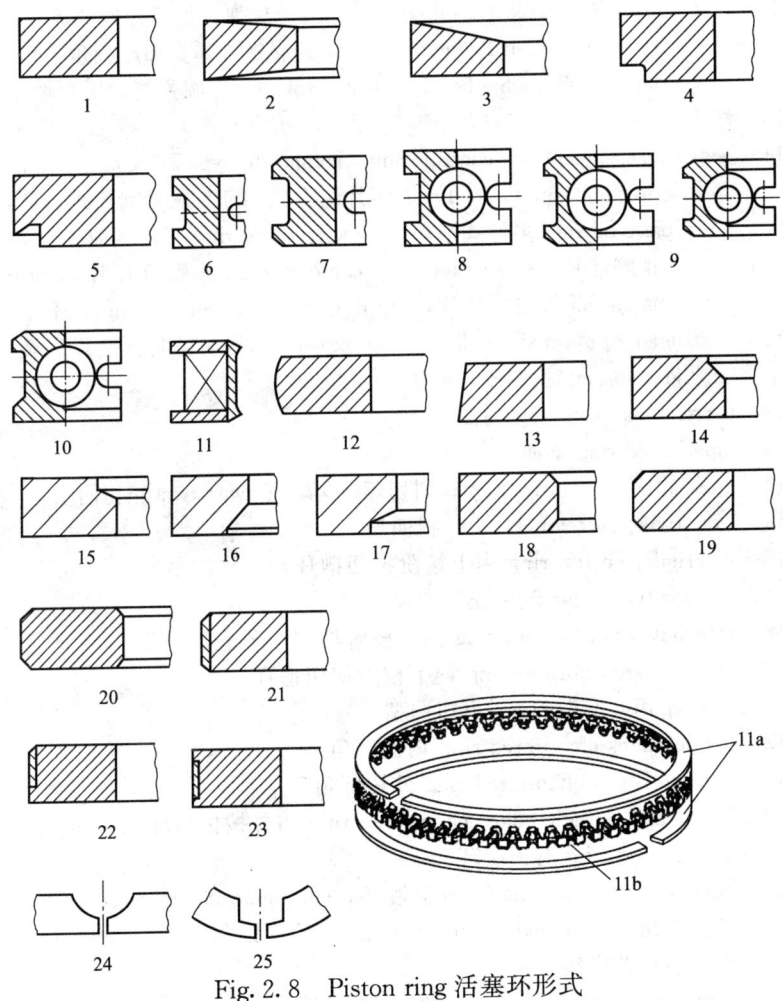

Fig. 2.8　Piston ring 活塞环形式

1　rectangular ring, plain (piston) ring 矩形环, uncoated ring 无镀层环
2　keystone ring, wedge section ring, full keystone ring 梯（楔）形环
3　half keystone ring 半梯（楔）形环
4　stepped scraper ring 阶梯状切口刮油环
5　Napier ring, Napier scraper ring 鼻型环、纳尔比环
6　slotted oil ring 开槽油环

33

7 bevelled edge oil control ring 倒角油环

8 coil (spring) loaded slotted oil control ring 螺旋弹簧加压开槽油环

9 coil spring loaded beveled edge oil control ring 螺旋弹簧加压倒角油环

10 coil spring loaded double beveled oil control ring 螺旋弹簧加压双倒角油环

11 expander/segment oil control ring, composite type oil control ring, steel strip composite type oil ring 钢片组合式油环，胀簧刮片式油环，multi-piece oil ring 多件式油环，three piece oil ring 三件式油环

11a side rail 侧环片，segment 挂片，conformable rail 贴合环片，chromium-plated rail 镀铬的环片，top ring 上环片，bottom ring 下环片

11b expander 衬簧，axial-radial spring expander 轴向-径向弹簧式胀簧，expander-spacer 轴向-径向胀簧

12 barrell (ed) face ring 桶面环

13 taper faced ring 锥面环

14 internal bevel top ring 内上棱斜切环，positive twist type 正扭曲型

14～17 twist (torsional) ring 扭曲型

15 internal step top ring 内上棱阶梯切槽环

14,15 positive twist type 正扭曲型

16 internal bevel bottom ring 内上棱阶梯切槽环

17 internal step bottom ring 内下棱阶梯切槽环

16,17 negative twist type 反扭曲型

18 inside edges chamfered ring 内棱倒角环

19 outside edges chamfered ring 外棱倒角环

20 inside and outside edges chamfered ring 内外棱倒角环

21～23 coated ring 有镀层环

21 coated fully faced ring 表面全镀环，chromium-plated ring, chrome-plated ring, chromed (piston) ring 表面镀铬气环，porous-chrome ring 多孔镀铬环

22 semi-inlaid (filled) ring 两半填充环，molybdenum-filled inlay ring, molybdenum coated ring, molybedeum ring 表面填（镶）钼环，喷钼环

23 inlaid ring 填充环

24 joint with side notch 带侧切口开口

25 joint with internal notch 带内切口开口

2.2.6 Connecting Rod 连杆 (Fig. 2.9)

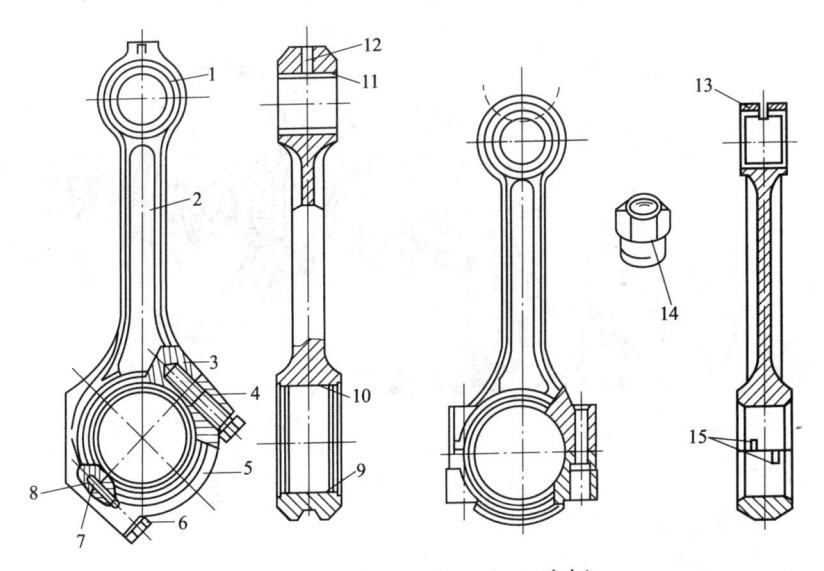

Fig. 2.9　Connecting rod 连杆

1　small end, top end（连杆）小头
2　connecting rod shank 连杆杆身
3　big end, bottom end（连杆）大头
4,6　connecting rod bolt 连杆螺栓
5　connecting rod cap 连杆大头盖
6　retaining member 锁紧件，锁止装置
7　serrated joint 锯齿式切口
8　locating pin 定位销
9,10　connecting rod bearing shell 连杆轴瓦
11　piston pin bush (ing) 活塞销衬套
12　oil hole 油孔
13　annular oil groove 环形油槽
14　connecting rod nut 连杆螺母
15　locking lip, locating lug (tang) 定位凸键

2.2.7 Crankshaft and Flywheel 曲轴和飞轮 (Fig. 2.10)

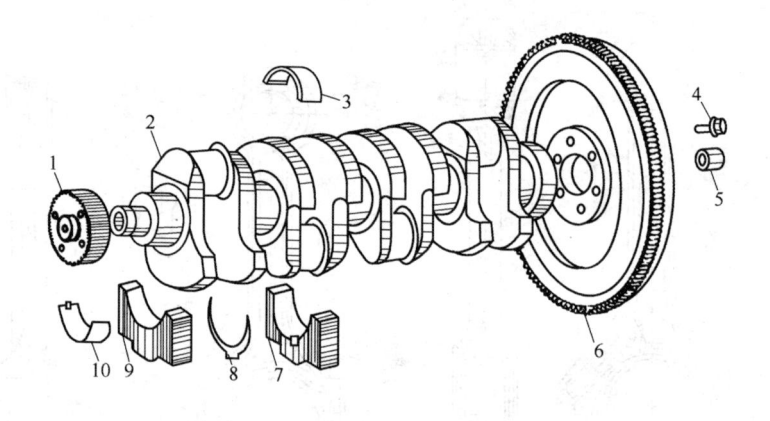

Fig. 2.10　Crankshaft and flywheel 曲轴和飞轮

1　timing gear 正时齿轮
2　crankshaft 曲轴
3,10　main bearing shell (upper, lower) 主轴承（上、下）轴瓦
4　bolt 螺栓
5　nut 螺母
6　flywheel gear ring 飞轮齿圈
7,9　mainshaft bearing cap 主轴承盖
8　thrust washer 止推垫圈

2.2.8 Crankshaft 曲轴 (Fig. 2.11)

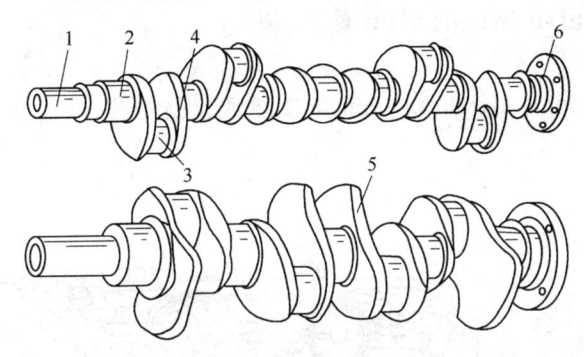

Fig. 2.11 Crankshaft 曲轴

1　crankshaft front end 曲轴前端
2　main journal 主轴颈
3　crank pin 曲柄销
4　crank web 曲柄臂
5　balance weight 平衡重块
6　retainer oil seal groove 挡油环油槽

2.2.9 Built-up Crankshaft 组合式曲轴 (Fig. 2.12)

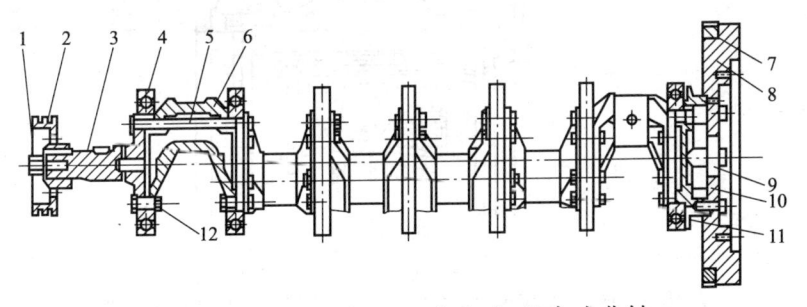

Fig. 2.12 Built-up crankshaft 组合式曲轴

1　starting jaw 启动爪
2　crankshaft pulley 曲轴带轮
3　crankshaft front end 曲轴前端
4　rolling bearing 滚动轴承
5　retaining bolt 固定螺栓
6　crank 曲柄
7　gear ring 齿圈
8　flywheel 飞轮
9　back end collar 后端凸缘
10　lock plate 锁片
11　oil baffle 挡油圈
12　locating pin 定位销

37

2.3 Valve Mechanism 配气机构

2.3.1 Single Overhead Camshaft 单顶置凸轮轴（Fig. 2.13）

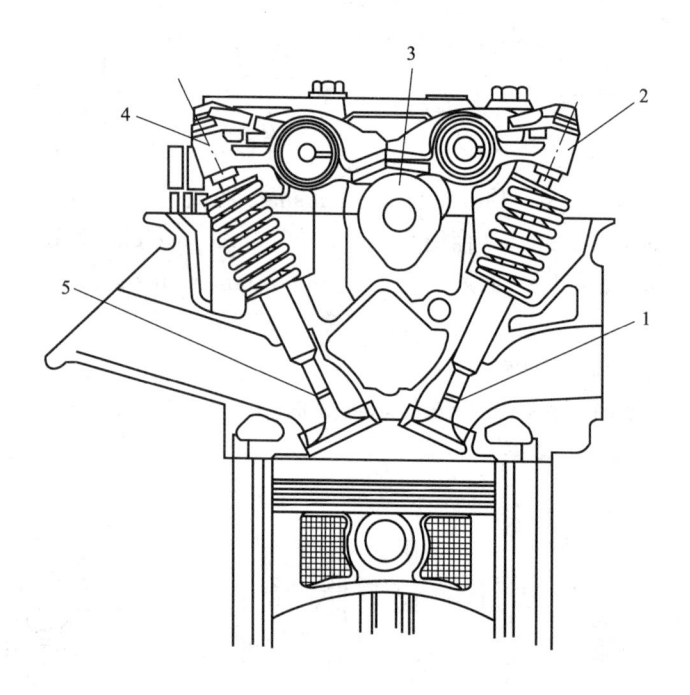

Fig. 2.13 Single overhead camshaft 单顶置凸轮轴
1 exhaust valve 排气门
2,4 rocker arm 摇臂
3 cam 凸轮
5 intake valve 进气门

2.3.2 Underneath Camshaft Overhead Valve 下置凸轮轴顶置式气门 (Fig. 2.14)

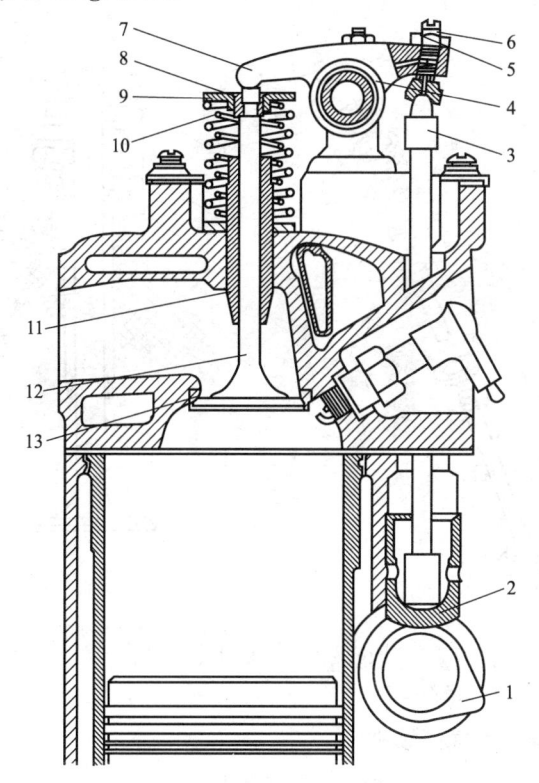

Fig. 2.14 Underneath camshaft overhead valve
下置凸轮轴顶置式气门

1 camshaft 凸轮轴
2 tappet (s) 挺杆
3 pushrod 推杆
4 rocker shaft 摇臂轴
5 check nut 锁紧螺母
6 adjusting screw 调整螺钉
7 rocker arm 摇臂
8 valve collet 气门锁夹
9 valve spring retainer 气门弹簧座
10 valve spring 气门弹簧
11 valve guide 气门导管
12 valve 气门
13 valve seat 气门座

2.3.3 Valve 气门 (Fig. 2.15)

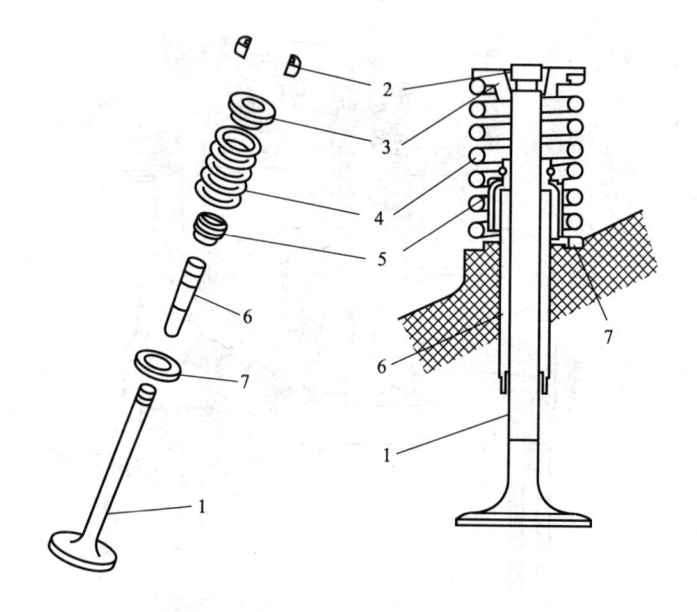

Fig. 2.15 Valve 气门

1   valve 气门
2   valve collet 气门锁夹
3,7   valve spring retainer 气门弹簧座
4   valve spring 气门弹簧
5   oil seal 油封
6   valve guide 气门导管

2.3.4 Rocker-arm Mounting Structure 摇臂支架结构 (Fig. 2.16)

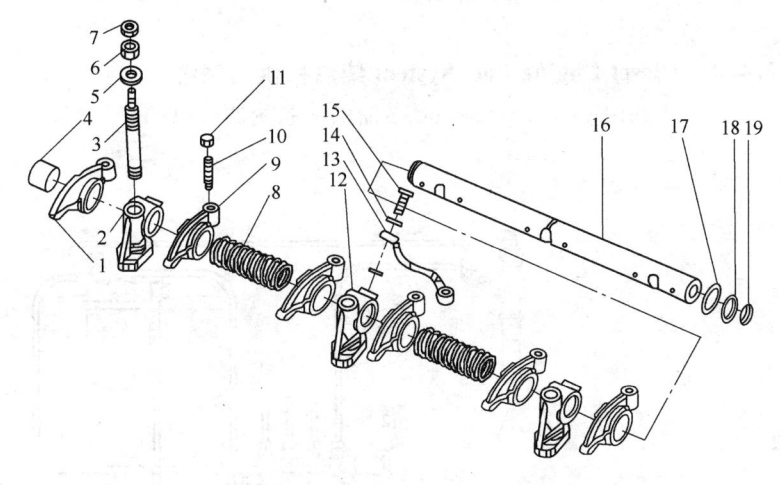

Fig. 2.16　Rocker-arm mounting structure 摇臂支架结构

1,9　rocker arm 摇臂
2,12　rocker-arm support 摇臂轴座
3　rocker support screw 摇臂轴座螺杆
4　rocker bush (ing) 摇臂衬套
5　spring washer 弹簧垫圈
6,7　nut 螺母
8　rocker-arm spring 定位弹簧
10　adjust screw 调整螺钉
11　locknut 锁止螺母
13　oil gallery 油道
14　oil seal 油封
15　bolt 螺栓
16　rocker shaft 摇臂轴
17　washer 垫圈
18　retaining ring 挡圈
19　bowl cap 碗形盖

41

2.4 Fuel System 供油系统

2.4.1 Diesel Engine Fuel System 柴油机供油系统
（1）Fuel System Principle 燃油供给系统原理（Fig. 2.17）

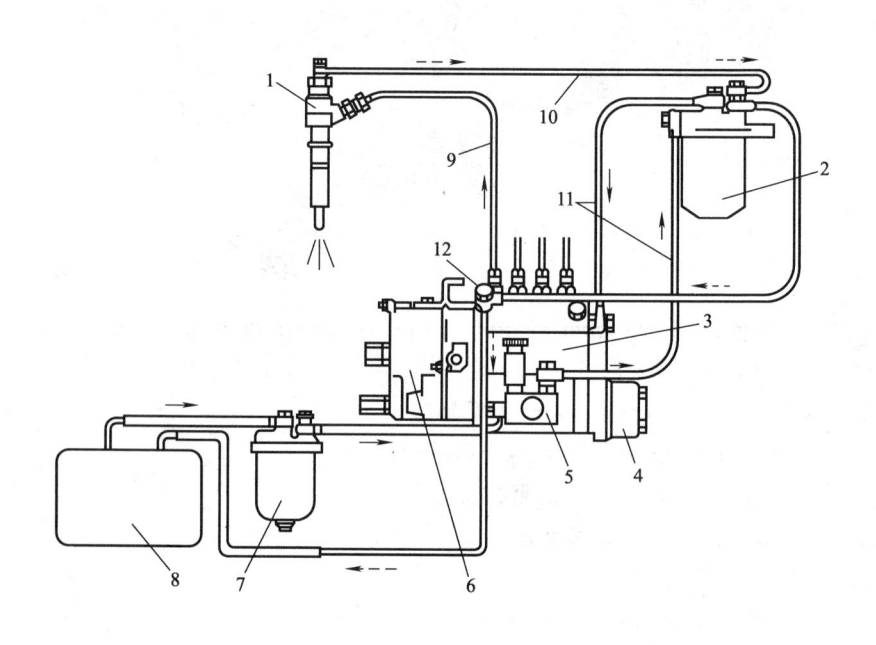

Fig. 2.17 Fuel system principle 燃油供给系统原理

1　injector 喷油器
2　fuel fine 柴油细滤器
3　injection pump 喷油泵
4　injection timing device 喷油提前器
5　fuel feed pump 输油泵
6　governor 调速器
7　oil water separator 油水分离器
8　fuel tank 燃油箱
9　pressure pipe 高压油管
10　return pipe 回油管
11　leak-off pipe 溢流回油管
12　pressure regulator 压力调节器

(2) Hole Type Nozzle 孔式喷嘴 (Fig. 2.18)

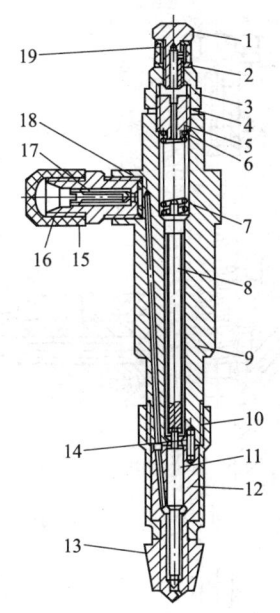

Fig. 2.18 Hole type nozzle 孔式喷嘴
1   leak-off connection 回油接头
2,18 shim 垫片
3   protective nut 保护螺母
4,6 washer 垫圈
5   adjust screw 调整螺钉
6   pressure-adjusting shim 调压垫片
7   pressure spring 调压弹簧
8   tappet 挺杆
9   nozzle holder 喷油器体
10 nozzle (retaining) nut 喷油嘴固定螺母
11 needle valve 喷油器针阀
12 nozzle body 针阀体
13 nozzle holder body 喷油嘴体
14 locating pin (plug) 定位销
15 inlet adaptor 进油管接头
16 high pressure pipe connection 高压油管接头
17 edge filter 缝隙式滤清器
19 protective sleeve 保护套

（3）Pintle Type Nozzle 轴针式喷嘴 (Fig. 2.19)

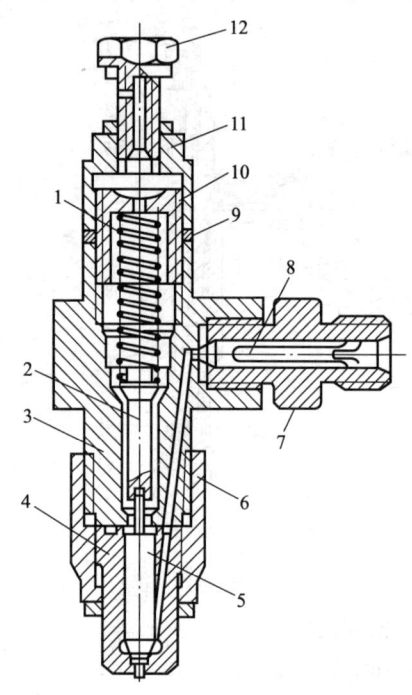

Fig. 2.19 Pintle type nozzle 轴针式喷嘴

1 pressure spring 调压弹簧
2 tappet 挺杆
3 nozzle holder 喷油器体
4 nozzle body 针阀体
5 needle 针阀
6 nozzle (retaining) nut 喷油嘴固定螺母
7 inlet adaptor 进油管接头
8 edge filter 缝隙式滤清器
9 washer 垫圈
10 adjust screw 调整螺钉
11 protective nut 保护螺母
12 leak-off connection 回油接头

(4) Jerk Fuel Injection Pump 柱塞式喷油泵 (Fig. 2.20)

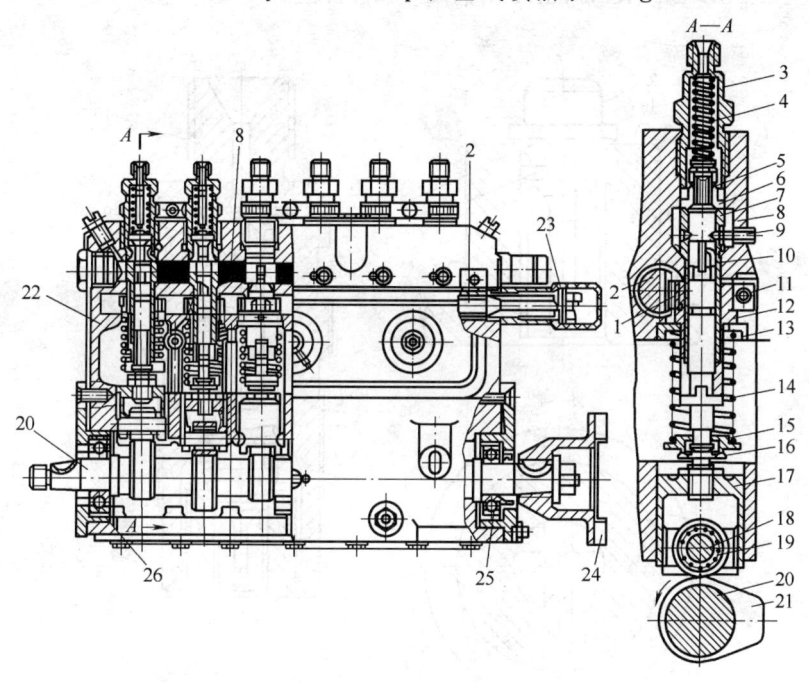

Fig. 2.20 Jerk fuel injection pump 柱塞式喷油泵

1　control pinion 调节齿圈
2　control rack（供油量）调节齿杆
3　delivery valve holder 出油阀压紧座
4　delivery valve spring 出油阀弹簧
5　delivery valve 出油阀
6　delivery valve seat 出油阀座
7　barrel 柱塞套
8　slight pressure chamber 低压油腔
9　locating screw 定位螺钉
10　plunger 柱塞
11　tightening screw（齿圈）紧固螺钉
12　control sleeve（油量）调节套筒
13,15　spring seat 弹簧座
14　plunger spring 柱塞弹簧
16　adjusting screw（供油定时）调节螺钉
17　roller tappet 滚轮式挺柱
18　roller pin 滚轮销
19　roller 滚轮
20　camshaft 凸轮轴
21　cam 凸轮
22　pump body 泵体
23　protective cap 保护帽
24　joint slack 联轴器
25,26　bearing 轴承

45

(5) Delivery Valve 出油阀 (Fig. 2.21)

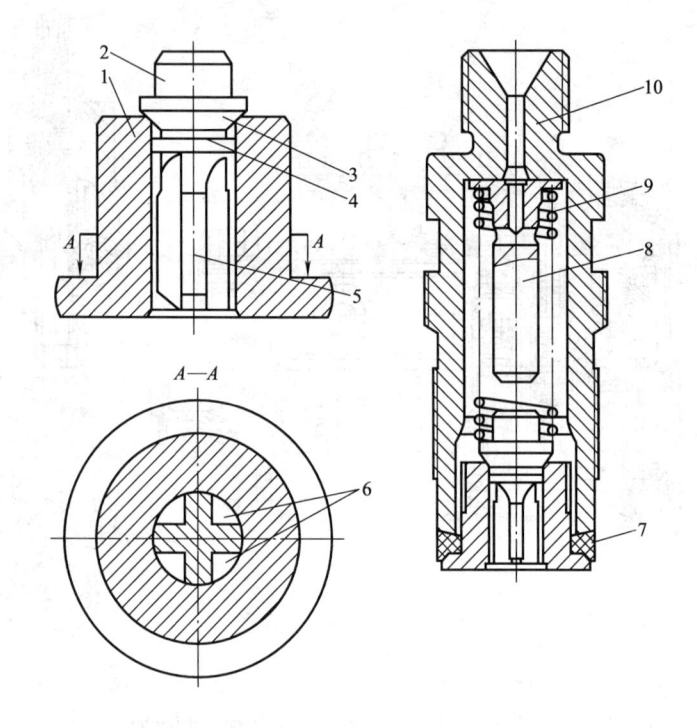

Fig. 2.21 Delivery valve 出油阀

1 delivery valve seat 出油阀座
2 delivery valve 出油阀
3 sealing cone 密封锥面
4 retraction piston 减压环带
5 guide 导向体
6 delivery valve flute 出油阀切槽
7 seal ring 密封垫
8 delivery valve volume reducer 减容体
9 delivery valve spring 出油阀弹簧
10 delivery valve holder (carrier, support) 出油阀紧座

(6) Distributor-type Injection Pump 分配式喷油泵 (Fig. 2.22)

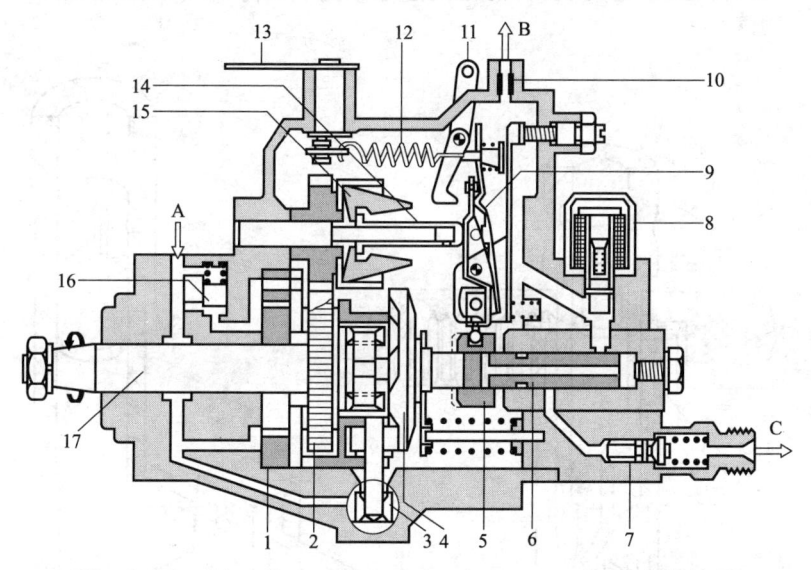

Fig. 2.22 Distributor-type injection pump 分配式喷油泵

A fuel supply 燃油供给
B return line to fuel tank 至燃油箱的回油管
C to injection nozzle 至喷油器
1 vane-type supply pump 滑片式输油泵
2 governor drive 调速器驱动装置
3 timing device, timing control, injection advance mechanism (device) 喷油提前器，正时装置
4 cam disc, plate cam, disk cam 凸轮盘
5 spill ring 溢流环
6 distributor plunger, distributor-pump 分配柱塞
7 delivery valve, check valve 出油阀
8 fuel shutoff solenoid 电磁断油阀
9 governor lever mechanism (drive) 调速器杠杆机构
10 overflow throttle 溢流节流孔
11 mechanical shutoff device 机械式断油装置
12 governor spring 调速器弹簧
13 speed-control lever（发动机）转速控制杆，control lever 控制杆
14 control sleeve 控制套筒，timing sleeve (collar) 正时套筒
15 flyweight, centrifugal weight 提前器飞锤，离心重块
16 pressure-control valve 压力调节阀
17 drive shaft 驱动轴

(7) Fuel Control Mechanism 油量调节机构 (Fig. 2.23)

(a) rack control mechanism
齿杆式油量调节机构

(b) fork control mechanism
拨叉式油量调节机构

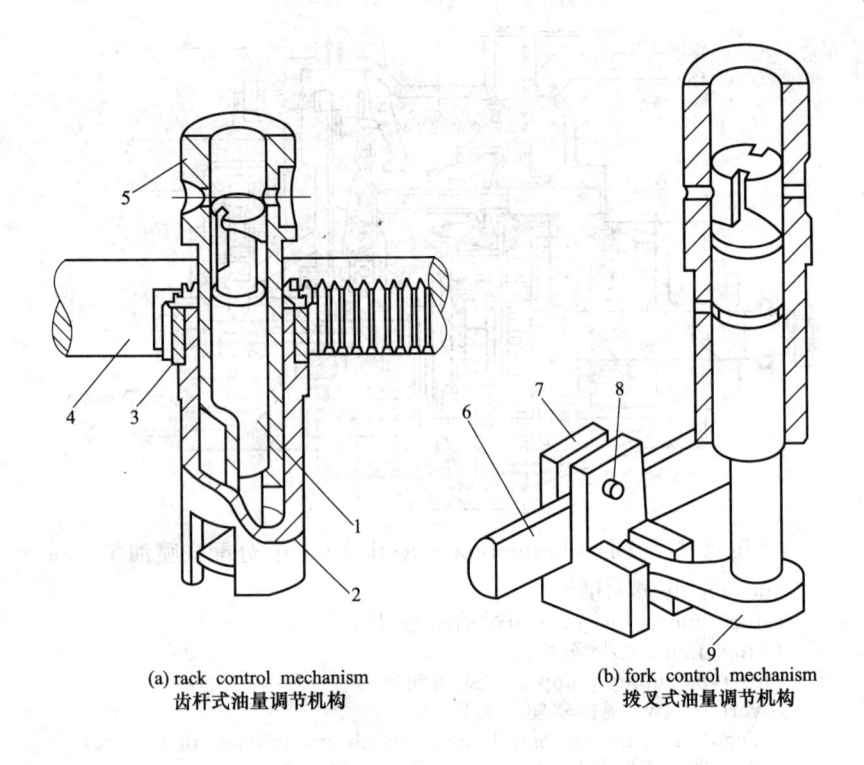

Fig. 2.23　Fuel control mechanism 油量调节机构

1　plunger 柱塞
2　control sleeve 控制套筒
3　control pinion 调节齿圈
4　control rack 调节齿杆
5　barrel 柱塞套
6　control rod 调节拉杆
7　control fork 调节叉
8　tightening screw 紧固螺钉
9　control arm 调节臂

(8) RQ and RSV Types Governor RQ 和 RSV 型调速器 (Fig. 2.24)

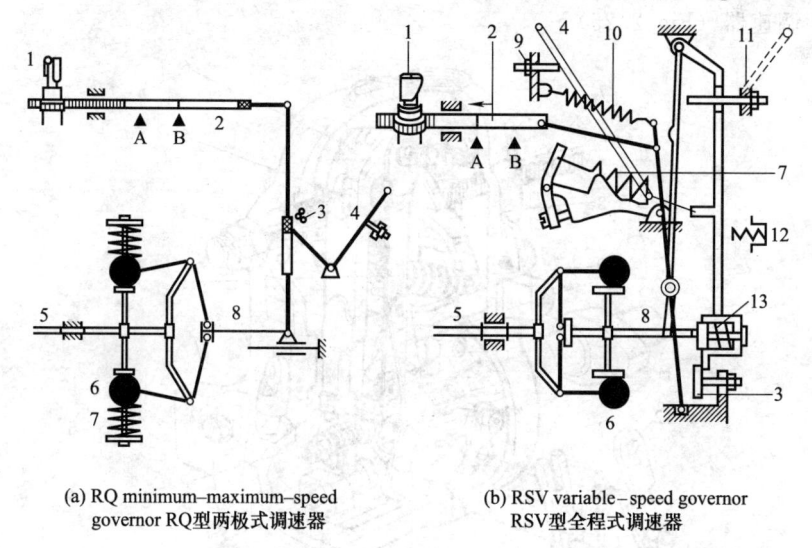

Fig. 2.24　RQ and RSV types governor RQ 和 RSV 型调速器

A　start 启动
B　stop 停止
1　pump plunger 柱塞
2　control rack 调节齿杆
3　full-load stop 全负荷限制器
4　control lever 控制杠杆
5　injection-pump camshaft 喷油泵凸轮轴
6　flyweight 提前器飞锤
7　governor spring 调速弹簧
8　sliding rod 滑动杆
9　maximum-speed stop 最高转速限制器
10　start (ing) spring 启动弹簧
11　stop or idle stop 断油或怠速限制器
12　auxiliary idle spring 怠速辅助弹簧
13　torque-control spring 转矩控制弹簧

(a) RQ minimum–maximum–speed governor RQ型两极式调速器
(b) RSV variable–speed governor RSV型全程式调速器

(9) RAD Minimum-maximum-speed Governor RAD 型两极式调速器 (Fig. 2.25)

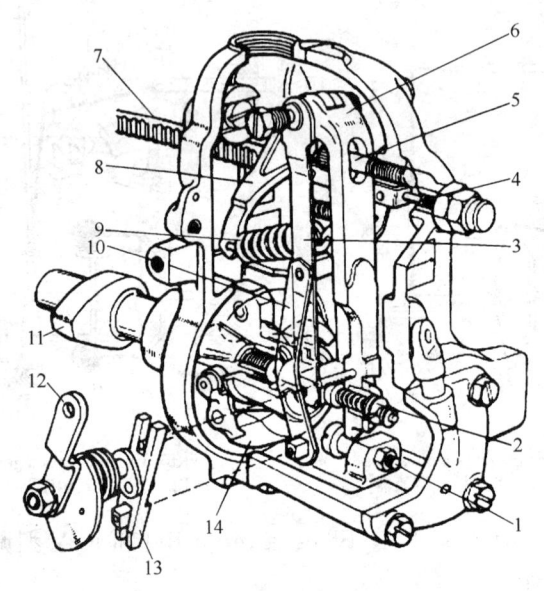

Fig. 2.25 RAD minimum-maximum-speed governor
RAD 型两极式减速器

1　stroke adjusting screw 行程调节螺钉
2　idle spring, idling spring 怠速弹簧
3　guide lever 导向杠杆
4　adjusting spring 调节弹簧
5　adjusting speed bolt 调速螺栓
6　drag rod, drag link, pull-rod 拉杆
7　control rack 调节齿杆
8　speed control lever, adjusting speed lever 调速杠杆
9　governor spring 调速弹簧
10　floating lever 浮动杠杆
11　injection-pump camshaft 喷油泵凸轮
12　control lever 控制杠杆
13　support lever 支承杆
14　flyweight 提前器飞锤，飞锤

(10) Mechanical Add-on Equipments of Governor 调速器机械式附加装置 (Fig. 2.26 and Fig. 2.27)

(a) manifold–pressure compensator
增压补偿器

(b) altitude–pressure compensator
海拔(高度)补偿器

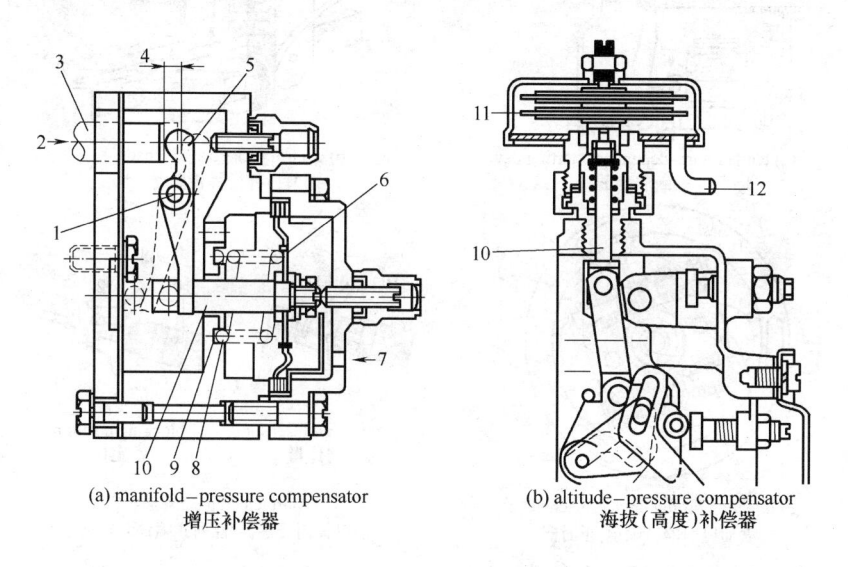

Fig. 2.26　Mechanical add-on equipments of governor (1)
调速器机械式附加装置 (1)

1　supporting point 支点
2　feed increment direction 增加供给方向
3　control rack 调节齿杆
4　boost feed fuel stroke 增压供油行程
5　lever arm 杠杆臂
6　diaphragm 膜片
7　boost pressure connection 增压进气压力接头
8　spring 弹簧
9　adjusting washer 调节垫片
10　push rod 推杆
11　pressure capsule 压力膜盒
12　altitude-pressure connection 大气压力接头

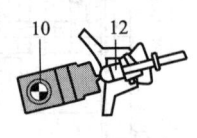

Fig. 2.27 Mechanical Add-on Equipments of Governor (2)
调速器机械式附加装置（2）

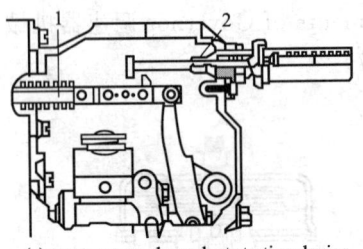

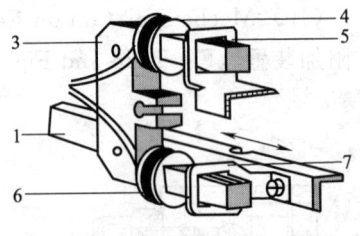

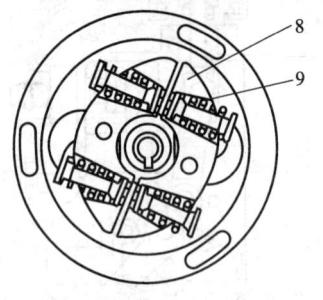

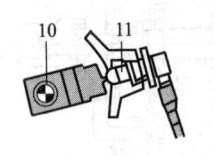

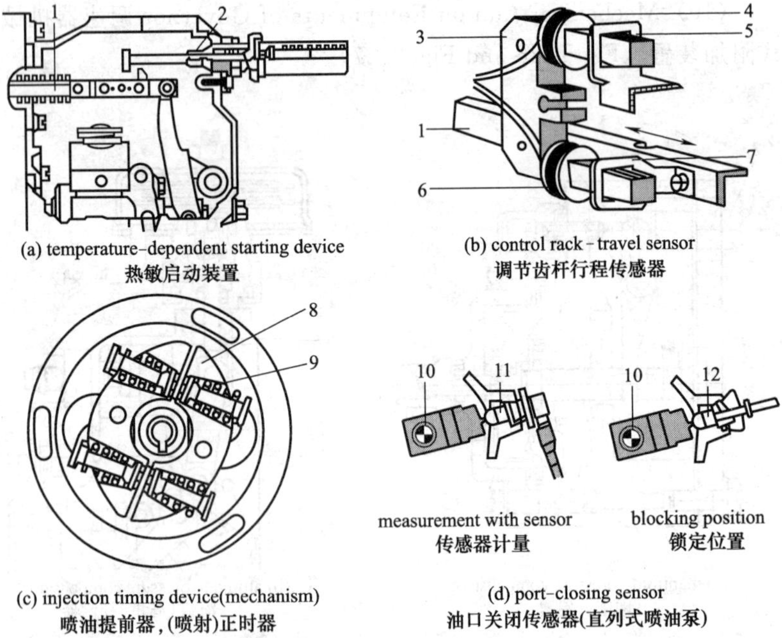

1. control rack 调节齿杆
2. start-quantity stop with expansion element 带膨胀元件的启动油量限制器
3. laminated (iron) core 层叠铁芯
4. reference coil 参照线圈
5. fixed short-circuiting ring 固定短路环
6. measuring coil 测量线圈
7. moving short-circuiting ring 移动短路环
8. flyweight, timer flyweight 提前器飞锤
9. advance device spring 提前器弹簧
10. fuel injection pump camshaft 喷油泵凸轮轴
11. sensor 传感器
12. blocking pin 锁定销

(11) Diesel Electronic Control System 柴油机电子控制系 (Fig. 2. 28)

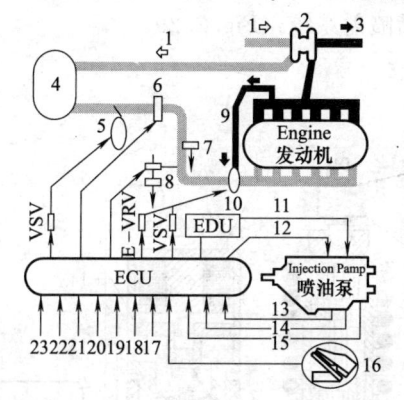

Fig. 2. 28 Diesel electronic control system 柴油机电子控制系

1　intake air flow 进气气流
2　T/C：turbocharger 涡轮增压器
3　exhaust gas flow 排气气流
4　I/C：intercooler 中冷器
5　intake shutter 进气活门
6　intake (air) heater 进气加热器，预热器，glow plug 电热塞
7　intake air temperature sensor 进气温度传感器
8　atmosphere pressure sensor 大气压力传感器
9　EGR flow 排气再循环气流
10　EGR valve EGR 阀，排气再循环阀
11　injected volume 喷射体积，喷油量
12　injected timing 喷射正时
13　revolution pulse 转动脉冲
14　combustion temperature 燃烧温度
15　PROM＝programmable read only memory（corrective information）可编程只读存储器（校正信息）
16　accelerator sensor 加速踏板传感器
17　crank angle sensor，CKP sensor＝crankshaft position sensor 曲轴转角（位置）传感器
18　other sensor signals 其他传感器信号
19　intake air temperature 进气温度
20　atmospheric pressure 大气压力
21　water temperature 水温
22　vehicle speed 车速
23　pressure sensor 压力传感器
ECU　electronic control unit 电子控制模块
EDU　electronic drive unit 电子驱动模块
E-VRV　electronic-vacuum regulator valve 电子真空调节阀
VSV　vacuum switching valve 真空开关（转换）阀

(12) **Electronically Controlled Unit-Injector Injection System**
电子控制泵-喷嘴喷射系统 (Fig. 2.29)

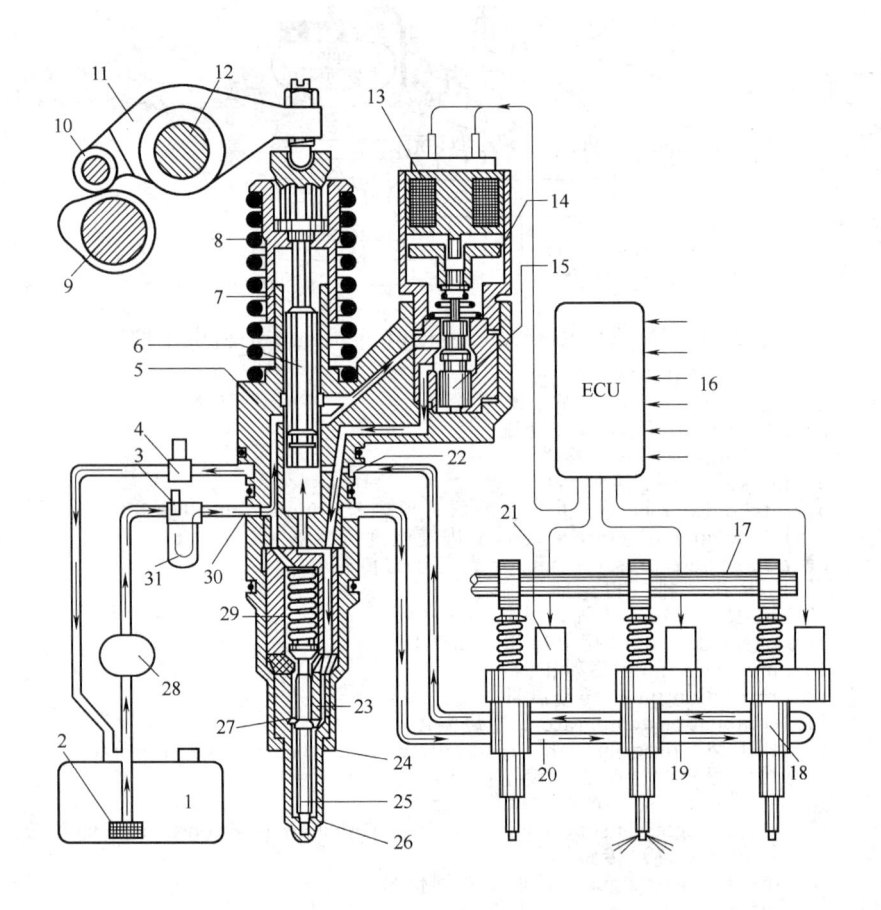

Fig. 2.29 Electronically controlled unit-injector injection system
电子控制泵-喷嘴喷射系统

1　fuel tank 燃油箱
2　primary gauze filter 初级滤网式过滤器
3　hand pump 手压泵，手动泵

4 overflow valve 回油阀，溢流阀

5 plunger body 柱塞体，pump body 泵体

6 plunger 柱塞

7 plunger support guide 柱塞支承导管

8 return spring （柱塞）回位弹簧

9 camshaft 凸轮轴

10 roller 滚子

11 rocker-arm 摇臂

12 rocker-shaft 摇臂轴

13 spill solenoid 溢流电磁线圈

14 disc armature 衔铁盘

15 solenoid-valve needle 电磁阀针阀，spill control valve 溢流控制阀

16 sensor 传感器

17 camshaft 凸轮轴

18 unit injector，pump/injector unit 泵喷嘴

19 overflow gallery 溢流油道

20 fuel feed gallery 燃油供给油道

21 solenoid spill valve 电磁溢流阀

22 bleed port 排出口

23 feed hole 供油孔

24 cap nut 盖形螺母

25 needle valve 针阀

26 nozzle body 针阀体

27 fuel gallery 油道

28 gear feed pump 齿轮式输油泵

29 control spring 控制弹簧

30 feed port 供油口

31 fuel filter 燃油滤清器

ECU electronic control unit 电子控制装置

(13) Electronically Controlled Unit Injector Common-Rail Injection System 电子控制式泵-喷嘴共轨喷射系统 (Fig. 2.30)

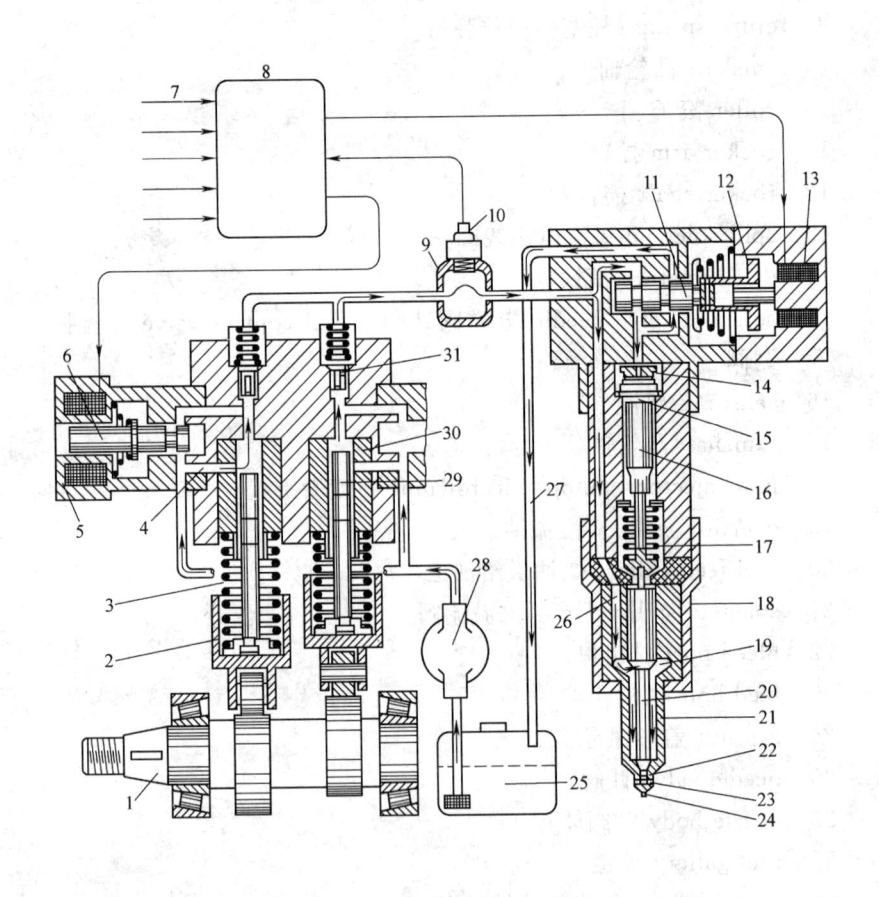

Fig. 2.30 Electronically controlled unit injector common-rail injection system 电子控制式泵-喷嘴共轨喷射系统

1　camshaft of high-pressure pump 高压泵凸轮轴

2　tappet，tappet follower 挺柱
3　return spring 回位弹簧
4　inlet port 进口
5　control solenoid（高压泵）控制电磁线圈
6　plunger armature 柱塞衔铁
7　input signal 输入信号
8　ECU 电子控制模块
9　common rail 共轨，共用油轨
10　pressure sensor 压力传感器
11　injector control valve 喷油器控制阀
12　disc armature 衔铁盘
13　injector control solenoid 喷油器控制电磁线圈
14　one way orifice 单向孔
15　control chamber 控制室
16　control plunger 控制柱塞
17　control spring 控制弹簧
18　cap nut 盖形螺母
19　fuel gallery 油道
20　needle-valve 针阀
21　needle body 针阀体
22　sack 袋
23　spray hole 喷孔
24　nozzle tip 喷油嘴尖端
25　fuel tank 燃油箱
26　feed hole 供油孔
27　return pipe 回油管
28　feed pump 输油泵，primer pump 初级泵
29　plunger 柱塞
30　barrel 柱塞套
31　delivery valve 出油阀

57

（14）Common-Rail（Fuel）Injection System（Accumulator Concept）共轨燃油喷射系统（蓄压气原理）(Fig. 2.31)

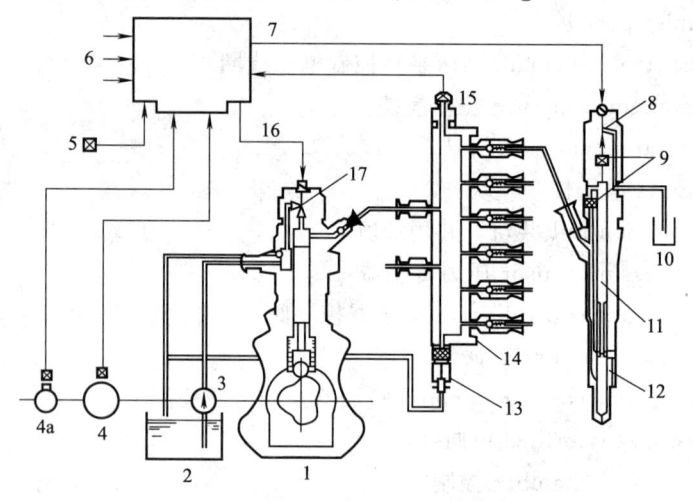

Fig. 2.31　Common-rail (fuel) injection system (accumulator concept) 共轨燃油喷射系统（蓄压气原理）

1　high-pressure pump 高压泵，supply pump 供油泵
2　fuel tank 燃油箱
3　primer pump 初级泵
4　engine speed and crank position sensor 发动机转速和曲轴位置传感器
4a　CPS＝camshaft position sensor 凸轮轴位置传感器，cylinder ID sensor＝cylinder identification sensor，cylinder detector 汽缸识别传感器
5　engine load 发动机负荷
6　additional information 辅助信息
7　command pulse 指令脉冲
8　solenoid valve 电磁阀，injector solenoid valve 喷油器电磁阀，two way valve 双通阀
9　orifice 量孔
10　leak 泄漏回油
11　hydraulic piston 液压柱塞
12　conventional nozzle 普通喷嘴
13　pressure relief (release, reduction) valve 释压阀
14　fuel rail, fuel manifold, distributor rail 燃油轨，common rail 共轨，共用油轨
15　pressure sensor 压力传感器
16　pump control pulse 泵控制脉冲
17　pump control valve 泵控制阀

(15) Injector for Common Rail Injection System 共轨燃油喷射系统喷油器 (Fig. 2.32)

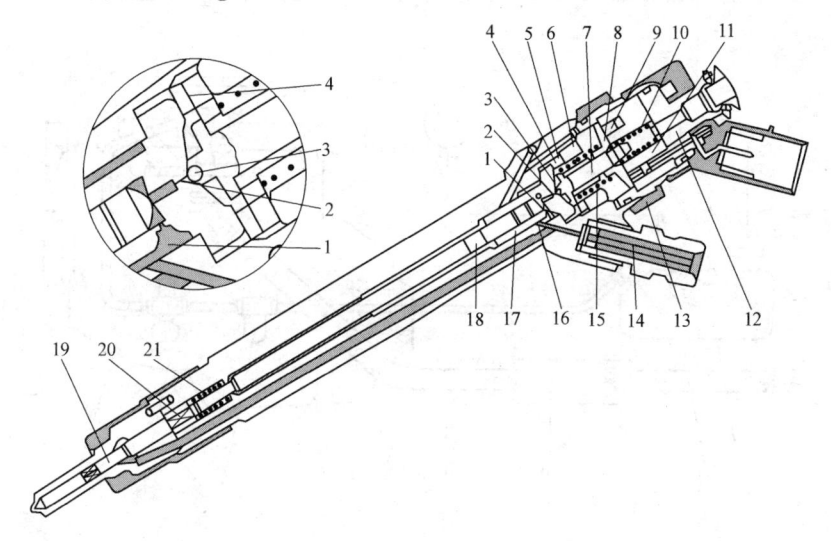

Fig. 2.32 Injector for common rail injection system
共轨燃油喷射系统喷油器

1　Z-throttle Z形节流
2　A-throttle A形节流
3　valve ball 阀球
4~6　adjusting disk 调节板
7　anchor bolt 锚定螺栓，固定螺栓
8　armature plate 衔铁板
9　solenoid coil 电磁线圈，solenoid valve 电磁阀
10　solenoid valve spring 电磁阀弹簧
11　magnet core 磁铁芯
12　drain fitting 回油接头
13　tensioning nut（电磁阀）紧固螺母
14　edge-type filter 缝隙式滤清器
15　spring 弹簧
16　high-pressure sealing ring 高压密封
17　valve part 阀零件
18　valve plunger 阀柱塞
19　nozzle pintle 喷油嘴轴针
20　thrust part 承推部件
21　nozzle spring 喷油嘴弹簧

59

2.4.2 Gasoline Engine Fuel System 汽油机供油系

(1) Gasoline Engine Fuel System 汽油机供油系 (Fig. 2.33)

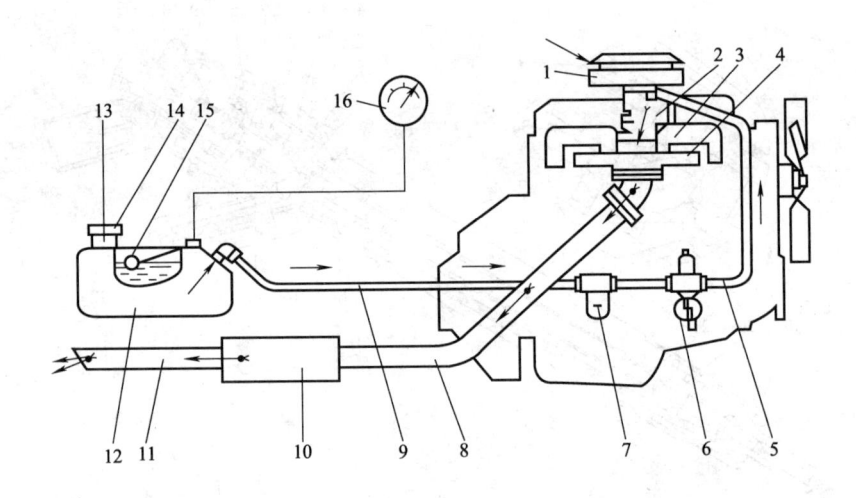

Fig. 2.33 Gasoline engine fuel system 汽油机供油泵

1 air cleaner 空气滤清器
2 carburetor 化油器
3 intake tube 进气管
4,8 exhaust pipe 排气管
5,9 pipe 油管
6 fuel pump 燃油泵
7 fuel filter 燃油滤清器
10 rear muffler 后消声器
11 tailpipe 尾管
12 fuel tank 汽油箱
13 tank filler 油箱加注口
14 tank cup 油箱盖
15 float 浮子
16 gasoline gauge (meter) 汽油表

(2) Schematic for a Carburetor Fuel System 化油器式供给系统简图 (Fig. 2.34)

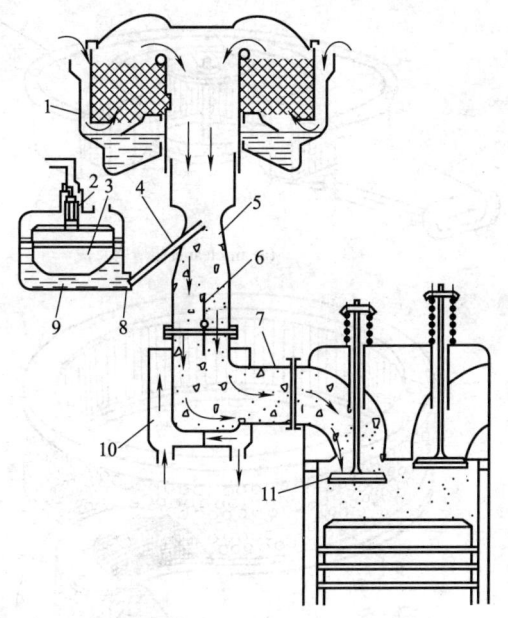

Fig. 2.34 Schematic for a carburetor fuel system
化油器式供给系统简图

1　air cleaner 空气滤清器
2　needle valve 针阀
3　float 浮子
4　main discharge nozzle 主喷管
5　diffuser, venturi 喉管
6　throttle valve 节气门
7　intake manifold 进气歧管
8　main jet 主量孔
9　float chamber (float bowl [美]) 浮子室
10　air intake heater 进气加热器
11　intake valve 进气门

(3) Air Cleaner 纸质空气滤清器（空气滤清器）(Fig. 2.35)

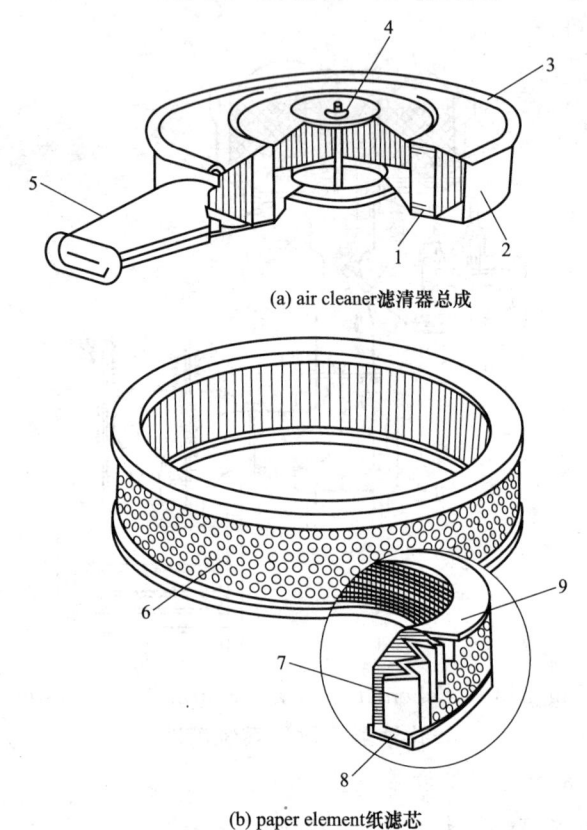

(a) air cleaner 滤清器总成

(b) paper element 纸滤芯

Fig. 2.35　Air cleaner 纸质空气滤清器（空气滤清器）

1　element 滤芯
2　air filter bowl (box, housing) 空气滤清器壳
3　air cleaner housing cover, air cleaner cap (cover) 空气滤清器盖
4　butterfly nut 翼形螺母
5　air inlet 空气进口
6　metal screen 金属网
7　filter 滤纸
8,9　air cleaner cap gasket 空气滤清器盖衬垫

（4）Fuel System-gasoline Injection 汽油喷射式燃油系统
(Fig. 2.36)

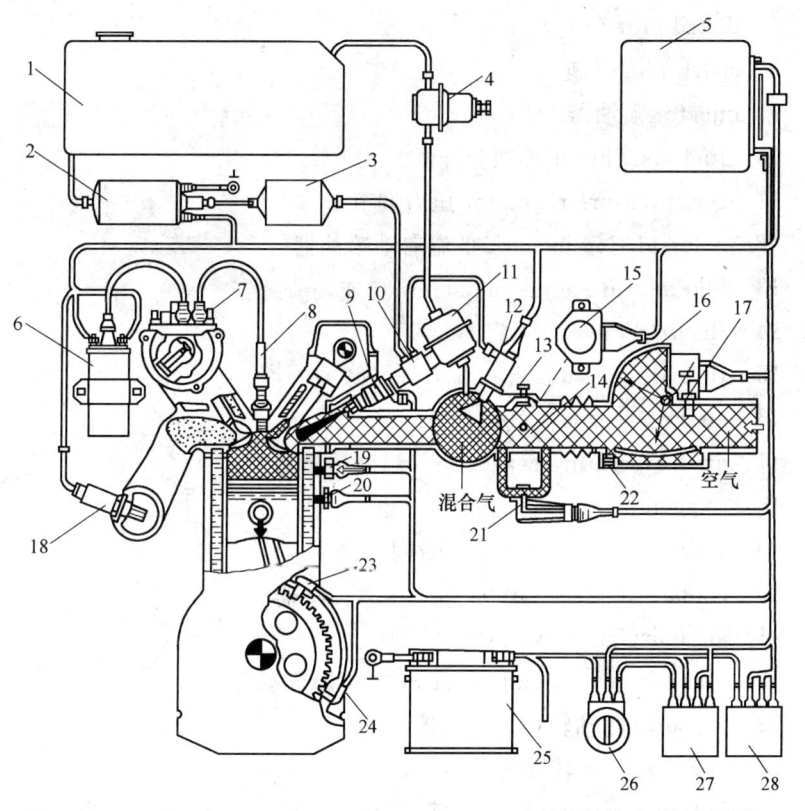

混合气

空气

Fig. 2.36 Fuel system-gasoline injection 汽油喷射式燃油系统

1　fuel tank 汽油箱
2　electric fuel pump 电动燃油泵
3　fuel filter 燃油滤清器
4　shock absorber 缓冲器
5　ECU（electronic control unit）电控单元
6　ignition coil 点火线圈
7　distributor 分电器
8　spark plug 火花塞
9　injector 喷油器
10　fuel distributor 燃油分配器
11　fuel pressure regulator 压力调节器
12　cold-starting injector 低温启动喷油器
13　idle-mixture adjusting screw 怠速调节螺钉
14　throttle valve 节气门
15　throttle position switch 节气门开关
16　airflow sensor 空气流量计
17　air-temperature sensor 空气温度传感器
18　oxygen sensor 氧传感器
19　thermo time switch 温度时间开关
20　coolant-temperature sensor 水温传感器
21　auxiliary air valve 辅助空气阀
22　idle-mixture adjusting screw 怠速调节螺钉
23　sensor（曲轴转角）传感器
24　speed sensor 转速传感器
25　battery（accumulator）蓄电池
26　ignition switch 点火开关
27　main relay 主继电器
28　pump relay 泵继电器

(5) Injector 喷油器 (Fig. 2.37)

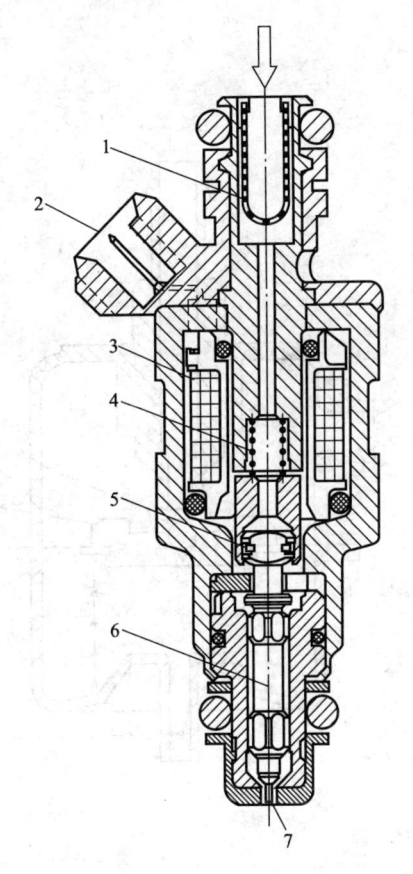

Fig. 2.37　Injector 喷油器

1　filter 滤清器
2　electrical connection 电插头
3　solenoid winding 电磁开关线圈
4　return spring 回位弹簧
5　solenoid plunger 电磁铁芯
6　needle 针阀
7　pintle 轴针

（6）Fuel Pressure Regulator 燃油压力调节器 (Fig. 2.38)

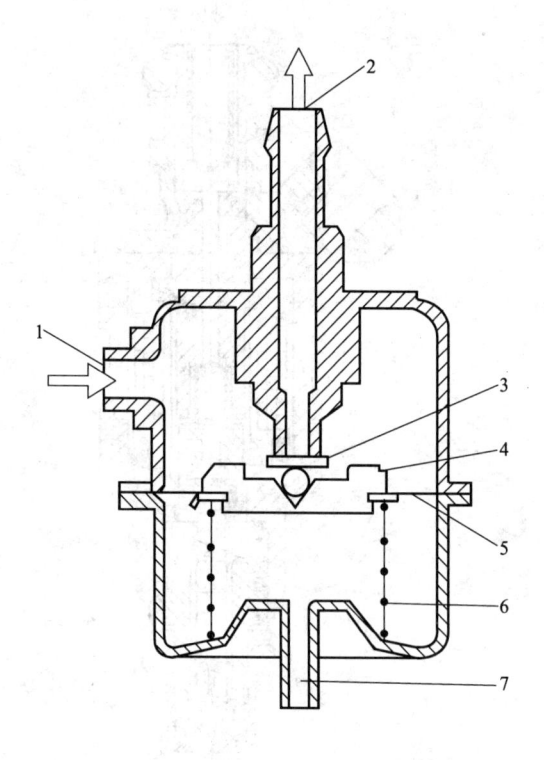

Fig. 2.38　Fuel pressure regulator 燃油压力调节器
1　fuel inlet 进油口
2　fuel return to tank 至燃油箱的回油
3　valve 阀门
4　valve holder 阀门保持器
5　diaphragm 膜片
6　spring 弹簧
7　intake-manifold connection 进气歧管接头

2.5 Spark-Ignition System 火花塞点火系统

2.5.1 Classical（Conventional）Ignition System 传统线圈点火系统（Fig. 2.39）

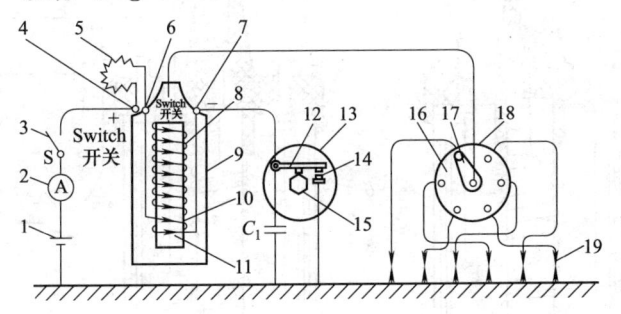

Fig. 2.39 Classical (conventional) ignition system
传统线圈点火系统

1　battery（accumulator）蓄电池
2　ampere meter 电流表
3　ignition switch 点火开关
4,6,7　low-voltage terminal, primary terminal 低压接线柱
5　ballast resistor, external resistor 附加电阻
8　secondary winding 次级绕组
9　coil, ignition coil 点火线圈
10　primary winding 初级绕组
11　iron core 铁芯
12　support 支撑板
13　contact breaker 断电器
14　contact 触点
15　distributor cam 分电器凸轮
16　distributor cap 分电器盖
17　distributor rotor 分火头
18　ignition distributor 分电器
19　sparking plug 火花塞

2.5.2 Ignition Coil 点火线圈 (Fig. 2.40)

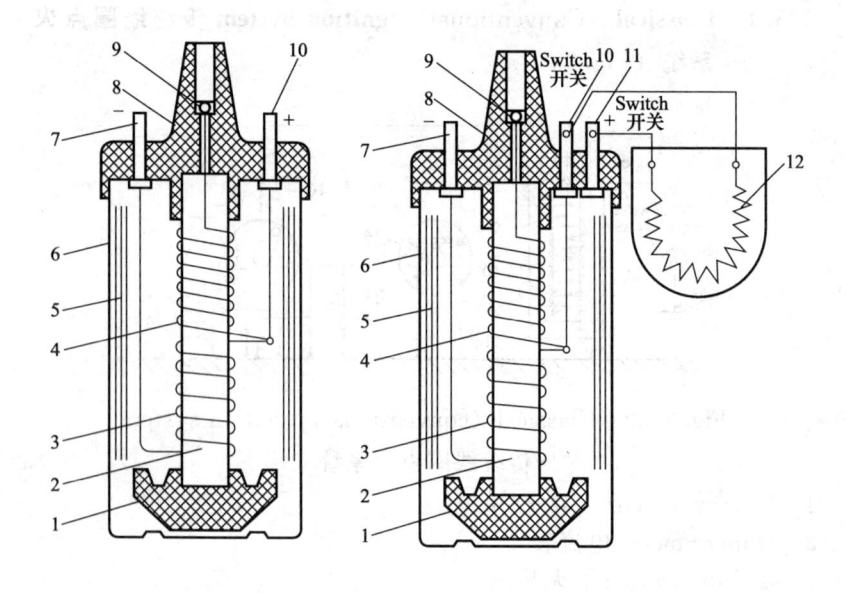

Fig. 2.40　Ignition coil 点火线圈

1　insulator 绝缘子
2　magnetic core 铁芯
3　primary winding 初级线圈
4　secondary winding 次级线圈
5　metal plate jacketing 金属板套
6　housing 外壳
7,10,11　low-voltage terminal, primary terminal 低压接线柱
8　insulating cap 绝缘盖
9　high voltage terminal 高压接线柱
12　ballast resistor, external resistor 附加电阻

2.5.3 Spark(ing) Plug 火花塞 (Fig. 2.41)

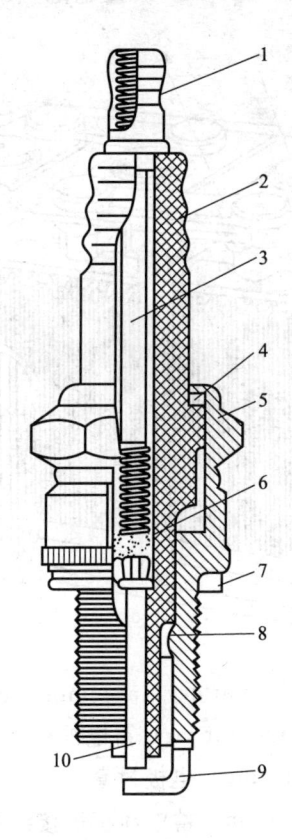

Fig. 2.41 Spark(ing) plug 火花塞

1 high-voltage connector 高压线接头
2 insulator 绝缘体
3 metal rod 金属杆
4,7,8 captive gasket 密封垫
5 shell 外壳
6 conductive glass 导体玻璃
9 ground electrode 旁电极
10 center electrode 中心电极

2.5.4 Battery（Accumulator）蓄电池 (Fig. 2.42)

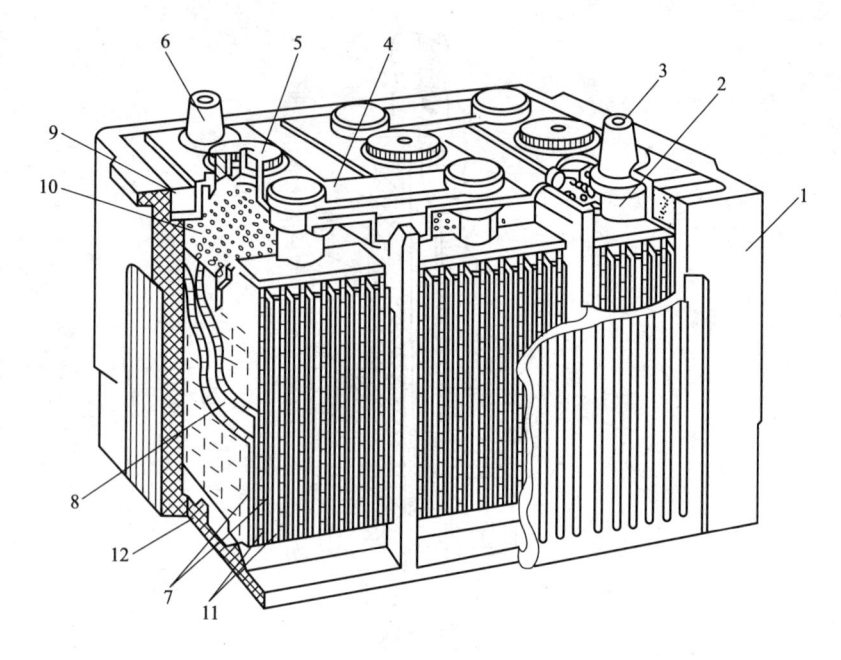

Fig. 2.42　Battery (accumulator) 蓄电池

1　battery jar (accumulator jar) 蓄电池外壳
2　electric pole bush (ing) 电极衬套
3　battery positive terminal 蓄电池正极接线柱
4　cell connector 连接条
5　cell filler plug 加液孔盖
6　battery negative terminal 负极接线柱
7　negative plate 负极板
8　separator 隔板
9　material seal 封料
10　cover sheet 护板
11　positive plate 正极板
12　edge, rib 肋条

2.6　Cooling System 冷却系统

2.6.1　Liquid Cooling System 水冷系统（Fig. 2.43）

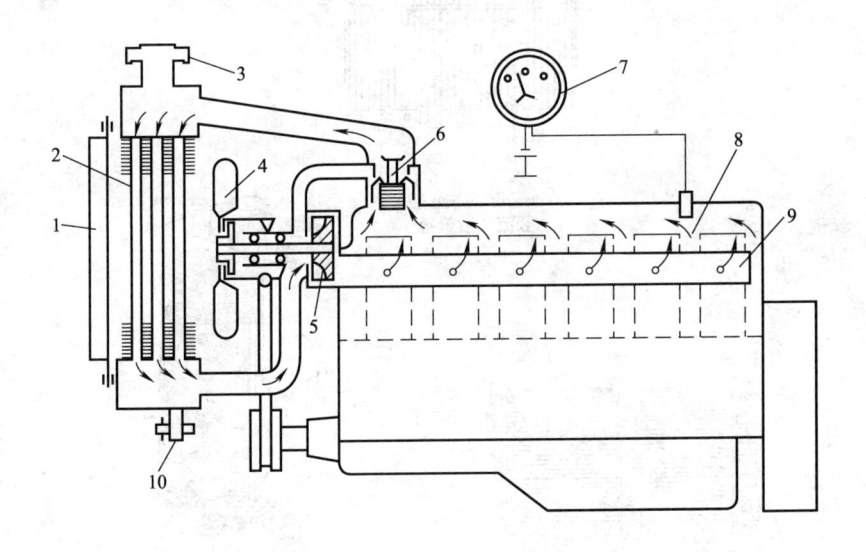

Fig. 2.43　Liquid cooling system 水冷系统

1　radiator shutter 散热器百叶窗
2　radiator 散热器
3　radiator cap 散热器盖
4　fan 风扇
5　water pump, coolant circulation 水泵
6　thermostat 节温器
7　water temperature indicator 水温表
8　water jacket 水套
9　divide the water pipe 分水管
10　drain plug 放水阀

2.6.2 Radiator 散热器 (Fig. 2.44)

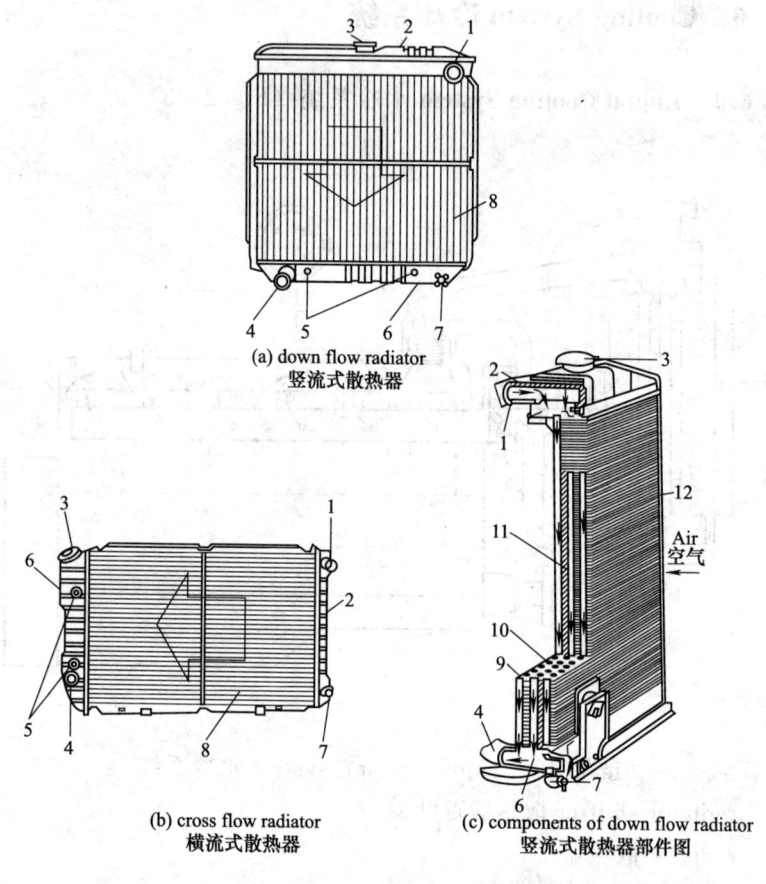

(a) down flow radiator
竖流式散热器

(b) cross flow radiator
横流式散热器

(c) components of down flow radiator
竖流式散热器部件图

Fig. 2.44 Radiator 散热器

1 water inlet 进水口
2 inlet tank 进水室
3 radiator (pressure) cap 散热器盖
4 water outlet 出水口
5 oil cooler-fitting 机油冷却器接头
6 outlet tank 出水室
7 drain plug 放水塞
8 radiator core 散热器芯
9 water passage 水道
10 water-stop sheet 隔水板
11 core 芯部
12 header 端板

2.6.3　Cooling Fan 风扇 (Fig. 2.45)

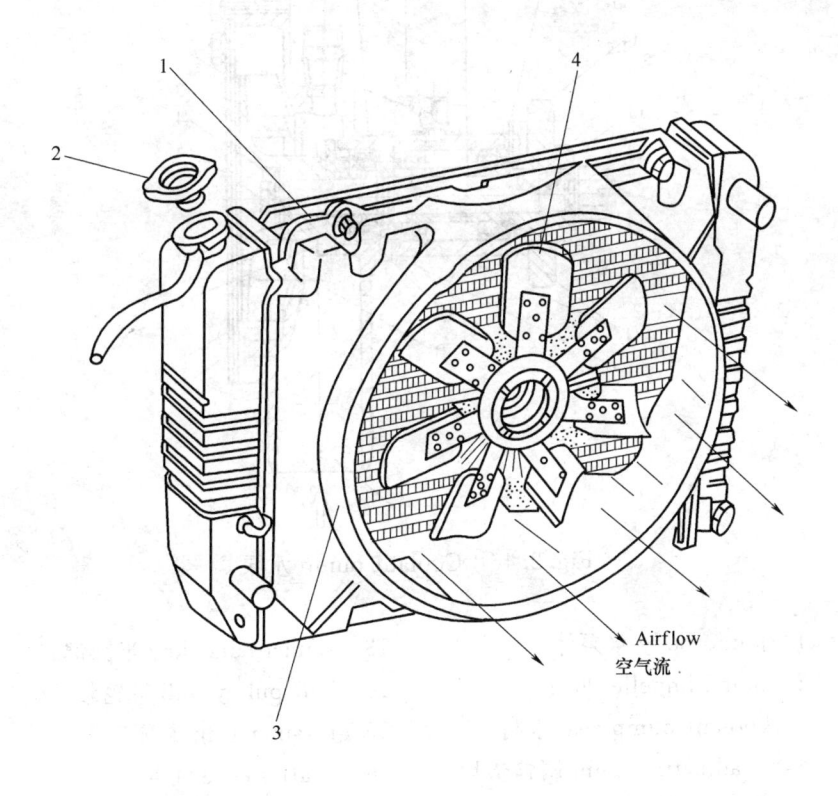

Fig. 2.45　Cooling fan 风扇

1　radiator 散热器
2　radiator (pressure) cap 散热器盖
3　fan shroud 风扇罩
4　fan blade 风扇叶片

2.6.4 Coolant Pump 水泵 (Fig. 2.46)

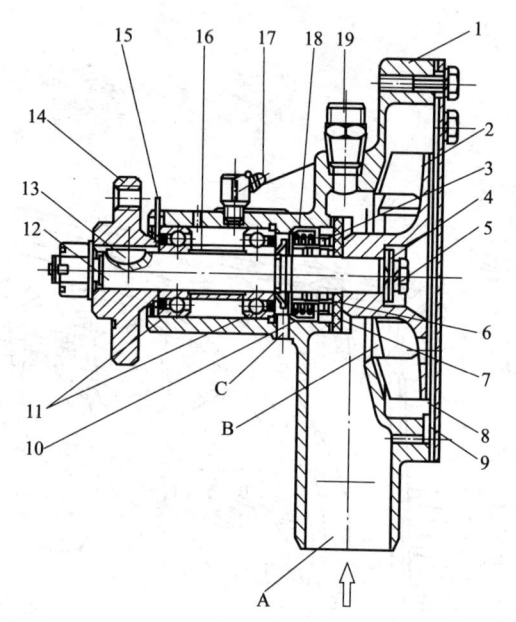

Fig. 2.46　Coolant pump 水泵

1　pump body 水泵体
2　pump impeller 叶轮
3　coolant pump seal 水封
4,8　adjusting shim 调整垫片
5　bolt 螺栓
6　primary seal ring 主密封圈
7　spring 弹簧
9　pump cover 水泵盖
10　cartridge 座圈
11　bearing 轴承
12　pump shaft 水泵轴
13　semicircular key 半圆键
14　belt pulley hub 带轮毂
15　retainer ring 卡环
16　shaft sleeve 轴套
17　lubricator fitting 黄油嘴
18　water thrower ring 甩水圈
19　nipple 管接头
A　water inlet 进水口
B　pump chamber 泵室
C　water outlet 出水口

2.6.5 Viscous Fan Coupling (Clutch) 黏液风扇离合器
(Fig. 2.47)

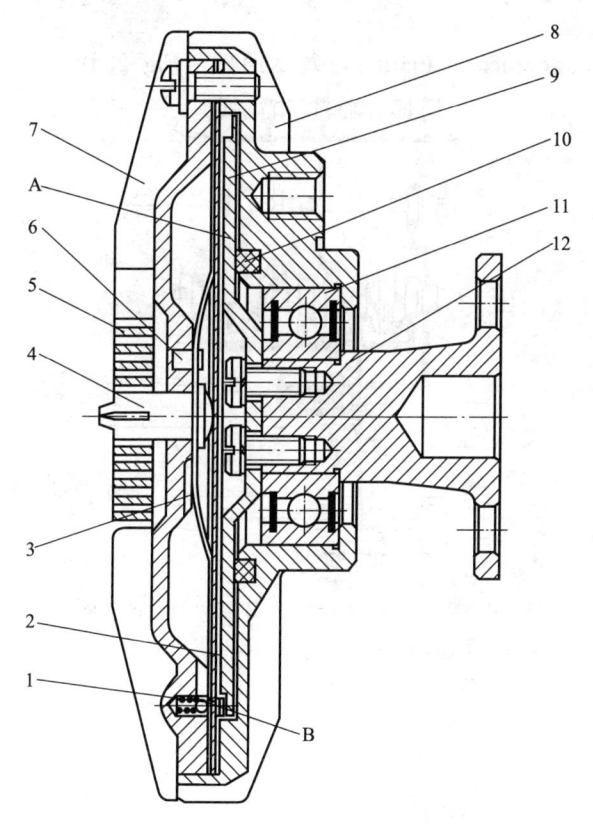

Fig. 2.47 Viscous fan coupling (clutch) 黏液风扇离合器

1. one-way valve 单向阀
2. drive disk 驱动盘
3. bimetallic disk 阀片双金属片
4. shaft（阀片）轴
5. bimetallic coil spring 双金属感温器
6. arresting pin 限位销钉
7. front cover 前盖
8. housing 壳体
9. clutch plate 离合器板
10. seal ring 密封圈
11. bearing 轴承
12. driving shaft 主动轴
A. inlet oil port 进油孔
B. return oil passage 回油道

2.7 Lubrication System 润滑系统

2.7.1 Fundamental Principle 基本原理（Fig. 2.48）

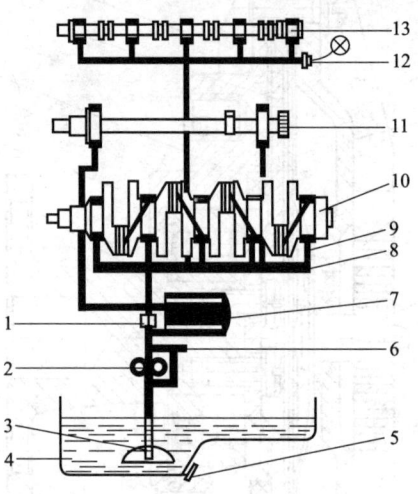

Fig. 2.48 Fundamental principle 基本原理

1 by-pass valve 旁通阀
2 oil pump 机油泵
3 oil strainer 集滤器
4 oil pan 油底壳
5 drain plug 放油螺塞
6 relief valve 溢流阀
7 oil cleaner 机油滤清器
8 main oil gallery (line) 主油道
9 oil duct 油道
10 crankshaft 曲轴
11 connection shaft 中间轴
12 pressure limiting valve 限压阀
13 camshaft 凸轮轴

2.7.2 Oil Pump 机油泵 (Fig. 2.49)

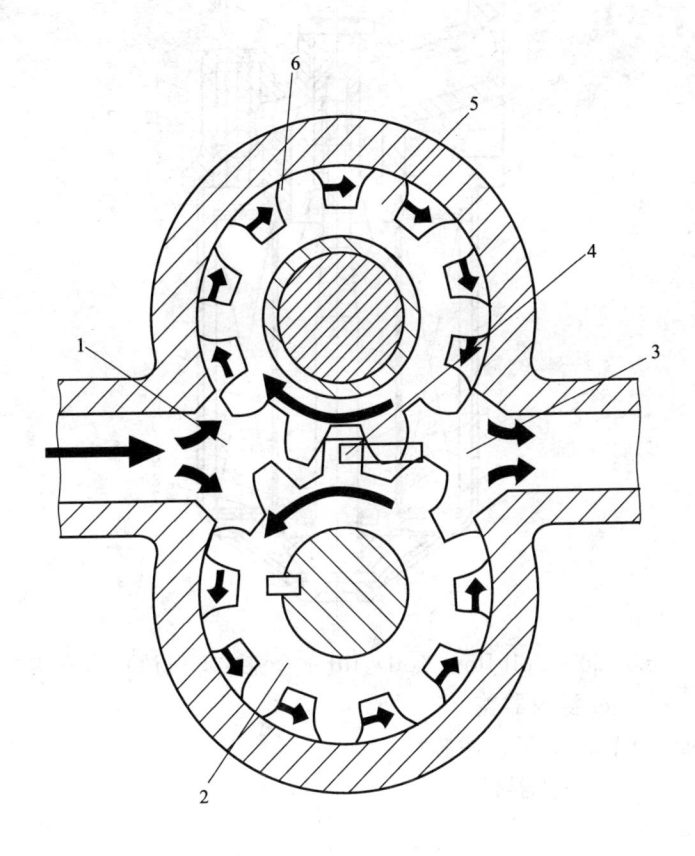

Fig. 2.49 Oil pump 机油泵

1. inlet port 进油口
2. driving gear（机油泵）主动齿轮
3. outlet port 出油口
4. pressure relief groove 卸压槽
5. driven gear（机油泵）从动齿轮
6. pump body 机油泵体

2.7.3 Full-Flow (oil) Filter 全流式（机油）滤清器 (Fig. 2.50)

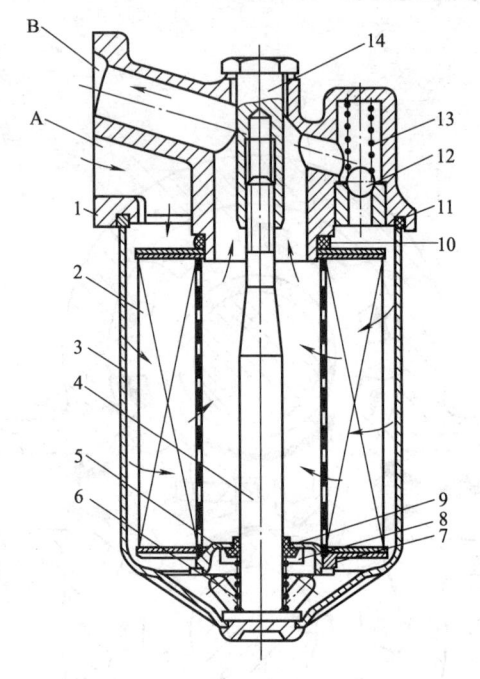

Fig. 2.50 Full-flow (oil) filter 全流式（机油）滤清器

1　filer cover 滤清器盖
2　paper element 纸质滤芯
3　filer bowl 滤清器壳
4　bar 拉杆
5　support plate 支撑板
6,13　spring 弹簧
7,9～11　seal ring 密封圈
8　spring seat 弹簧垫圈
12　by-pass valve 旁通阀
14　bolt 螺栓
A　oil inlet 进油口
B　oil outlet 出油口

2.8 Starting System 启动系统

2.8.1 Gasoline Starting Engine 汽油启动机 (Fig. 2.51)

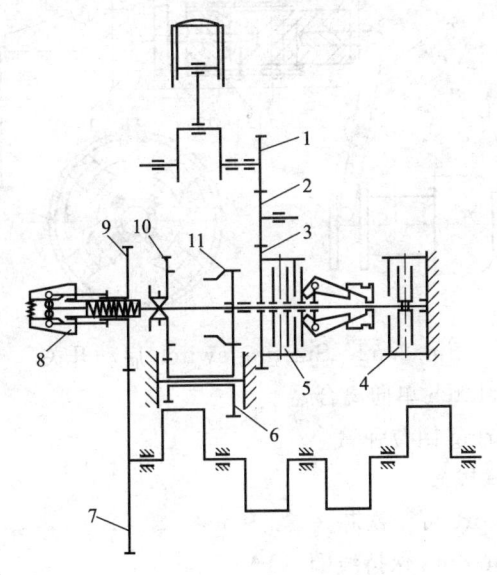

Fig. 2.51 Gasoline starting engine 汽油启动机

1 crankshaft gear 曲轴齿轮
2 middle gear, translating gear, mid-gear 中间齿轮
3 clutch gear 离合器齿轮
4 brake 制动器
5 clutch 离合器
6 middle gear, translating gear, mid-gear (减速器) 中间齿轮
7 flywheel gear ring (主发动机) 飞轮齿圈
8 automatic segregator 自动分离器
9 joint gear 接合齿轮
10 sliding gear (减速器) 滑动齿轮
11 driving gear (减速器) 主动齿轮

2.8.2 Starting Switch 启动开关 (Fig. 2.52)

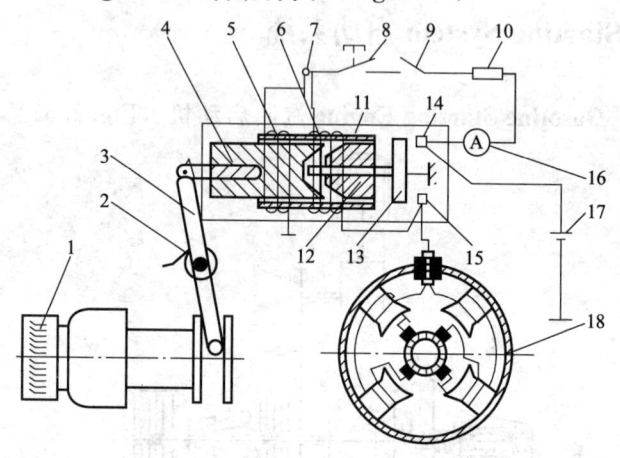

Fig. 2.52 Starting switch 启动开关

1 one-way clutch 单向离合器
2 return spring 回位弹簧
3 shift yoke 拨叉
4 movable core 可动铁芯
5 hold-in winding 保持线圈
6 pull-in winding 吸引线圈
7 terminal 接线柱
8 starting relay 启动继电器
9 starting swith 启动开关
10 safety cut-out 熔断器
11 brass jacket 黄铜套
12 backstop 挡铁
13 contact disc 触板
14,15 primary terminal 主接线柱
16 ampere meter 电流表
17 battery (accumulator) 蓄电池
18 electric starter 启动电机

2.8.3 Starter 启动机 (Fig. 2.53)

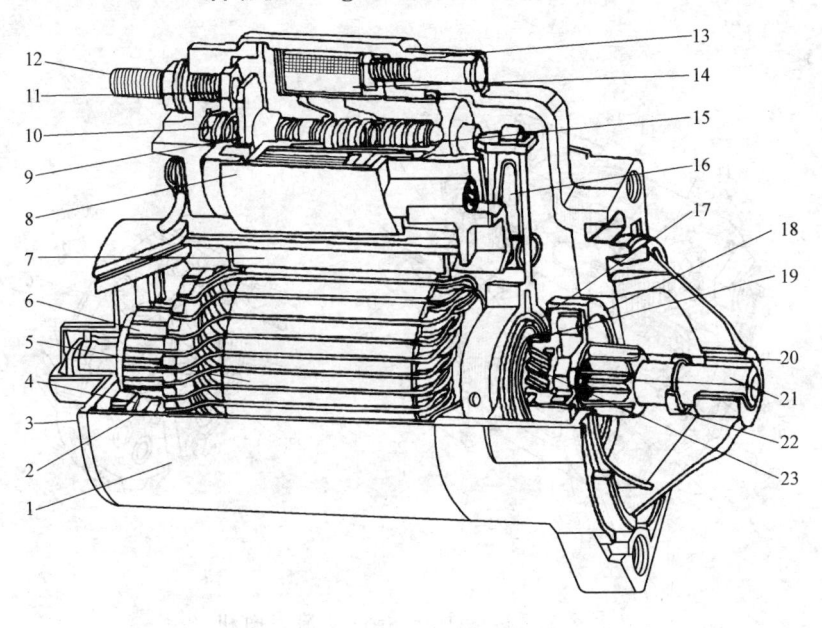

Fig. 2.53 Starter 启动机

1	starter frame 启动机外壳	12	terminal 接线螺栓
2	brush 电刷	13	hold-in winding 保持线圈
3	end cover 后端盖	14	pull-in winding 吸引线圈
4	brush holder 电刷架	16	shift lever 拨叉
5	armature 电枢	17	guide ring 导环
6	commutator 换向器	18	roller-type overruning clutch 滚柱式单向离合器
7	magnetic-pole 磁极		
8	solenoid swith 电磁开关	19	meshing spring 啮合弹簧
9	contact disc; starting swith 电磁开关触板	20	drive gear 驱动齿轮
		21	armature shaft 电枢轴
10,15	return spring 复位弹簧	22	thrust washer 止推垫圈
11	contact 触点	23	helical spline 螺旋花键

81

2.8.4 Alternator 交流发电机 (Fig. 2.54)

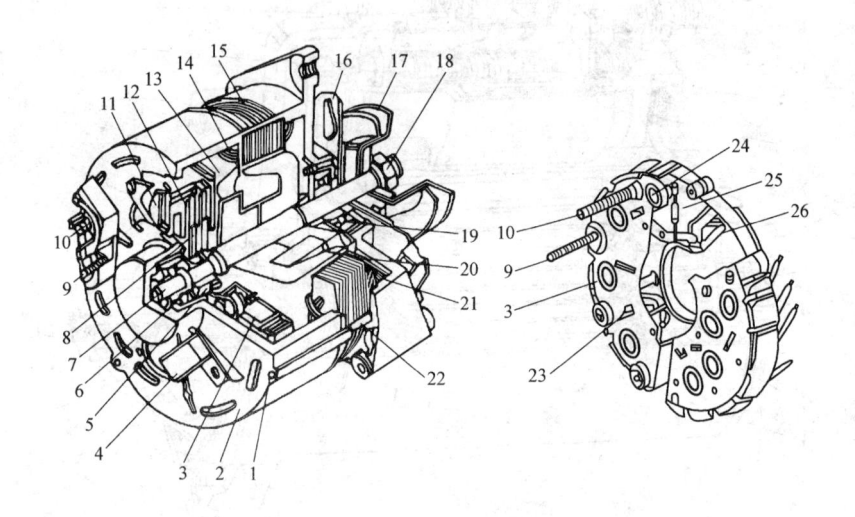

Fig. 2.54 Alternator 交流发电机

1　bolt 螺栓
2　rear end cover 后端盖
3　component card 元件板
4　capacitor 电容器
5　collector ring 集电环
6,19　bearing 轴承
7　rotor shaft 转子轴
8　brush 电刷
9　magnetic-field terminal 磁场接线柱
10　output terminal 输出接线柱
11　voltage regulator 电压调节器
12　brush holder 电刷架
13　magnetic-pole 磁极
14　stator winding 定子绕组
15　stator core 定子铁芯
16　fan 风扇
17　pulley 带轮
18　check nut 锁紧螺母
20　exciting winding 励磁绕组
21　front housing 前端盖
22　stator slot 定子槽
23　condenser bracket 电容器架
24　power diode 功率二极管
25　exciter diode 激励二极管
26　compressing apparatus（电刷架）压紧装置

2.8.5 Heater Plug 电热塞 (Fig. 2.55)

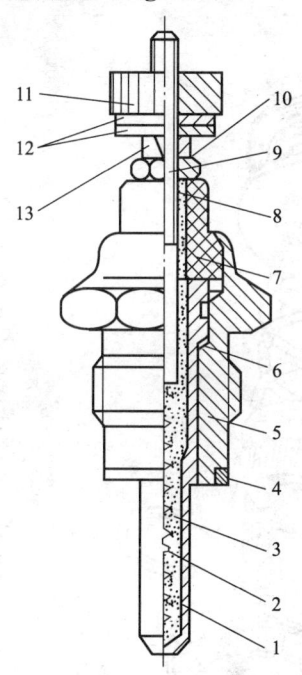

Fig. 2.55 Heater plug 电热塞

1 glow tube 加热管
2 heater and control coil 加热器和控制线圈
3 powder 填充剂
4,6 insulator shim 绝缘垫
5 casing 外壳
7 insulation 绝缘体
8 tackiness agent 胶合剂
9 terminal 端子
10 nut（固定）螺母
11 check nut 锁紧螺母
12 washer 垫圈
13 elastic washer 弹性垫圈

83

2.8.6 Roller-type Overruning Clutch 滚柱式单向离合器 (Fig. 2.56)

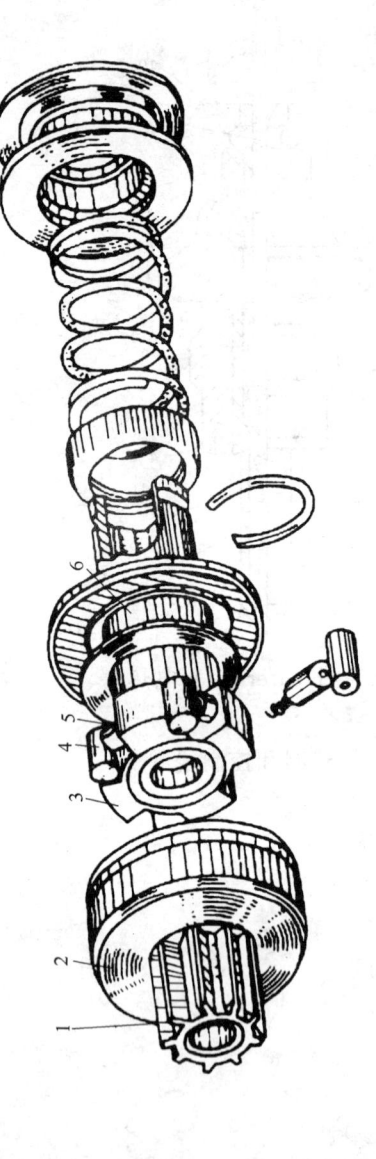

Fig. 2.56 Roller-type overruning clutch 滚柱式单向离合器

1 drive gear 驱动齿轮
2 roller retainer 滚柱保持器
3 roller race 滚柱座圈
4 roller 滚柱
5 lock pin 锁销
6 helical spline 螺旋花键

2.8.7 Multi-disc Overruning Clutch 摩擦片式单向离合器 (Fig. 2.57)

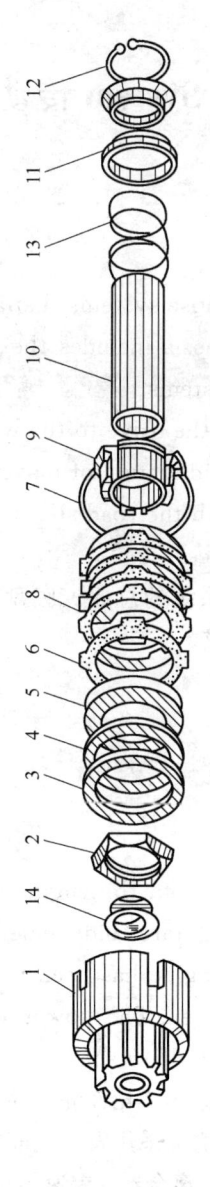

Fig. 2.57 Multi-disc overruning clutch 摩擦片式单向离合器

1 drive gear 驱动齿轮
2 nut 螺母
3 elastic washer 弹性垫圈
4 pressure plate 压盘
5 locating shim 调整垫圈
6 driven plate 从动盘
7 lock ring 卡环
8 driving plate 主动盘
9 splined hub 花键毂
10 sleeve (花键) 套筒
11 shift collar 滑动套
12 lock ring 卡环
13 return spring 回位弹簧
14 stop collar 止动套

Unit 3 Power Train System 传动系统

3.1 General 概述

The chassis is an assembly of those systems that are the major operating parts of a vehicle. The chassis includes the power train, steering, suspension and braking systems.

① Power train system conveys the drive to the wheels.
② Steering system controls the direction of movement.
③ Suspension and wheels absorb the road shocks.
④ Brake slows down the vehicle.

底盘是一个包含车辆主要操作系统的总成。底盘由传动系统、转向系统、悬架系统和制动系统组成。

① 传动系统传递驱动到车轮。
② 转向系统控制运动的方向。
③ 悬架和车轮吸收道路的振动。
④ 制动系减慢车速。

The power train carries power from the engine crankshaft to the vehicle wheels so the wheels rotate and vehicle moves. For many years, on most vehicles the engine has been mounted in the front and the rear wheels were driven. The power train includes transmission, clutch, differential and drive shaft.

从发动机曲轴输出的动力经传动系传递给车轮，使车轮转动，驱动车辆前进。很多年以来，大多数车辆都采用发动机前置后轮驱动的形式。这类车辆的传动系包括变速器、离合器、差速器和传动轴。

3.2 Mechanical Transmission System 机械传动系统 (Fig. 3.1)

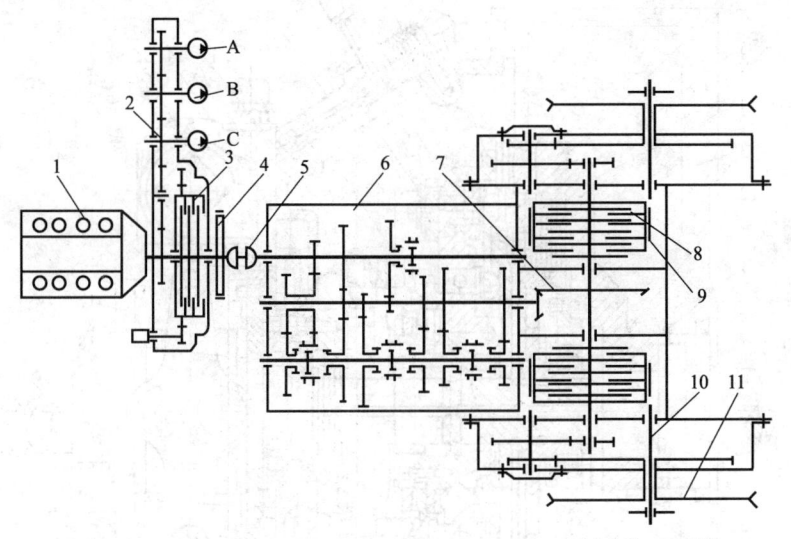

Fig. 3.1 Mechanical transmission system 机械传动系统

1 diesel engine 柴油机
2 transfer case 分动箱
3 main clutch 主离合器
4 parking brake 驻车制动器
5 drive shaft 传动轴
6 transmission case, gear box 变速箱
7 main drive 中央传动
8 steering clutch 转向离合器
9 steering brake 转向制动器
10 final drive 最终传动
11 driving wheel 驱动轮
A work equipment pump 工作装置油泵
B main clutch pump 主离合油泵
C steering pump 转向油泵

3.2.1 Main Clutch 主离合器 (Fig. 3.2)

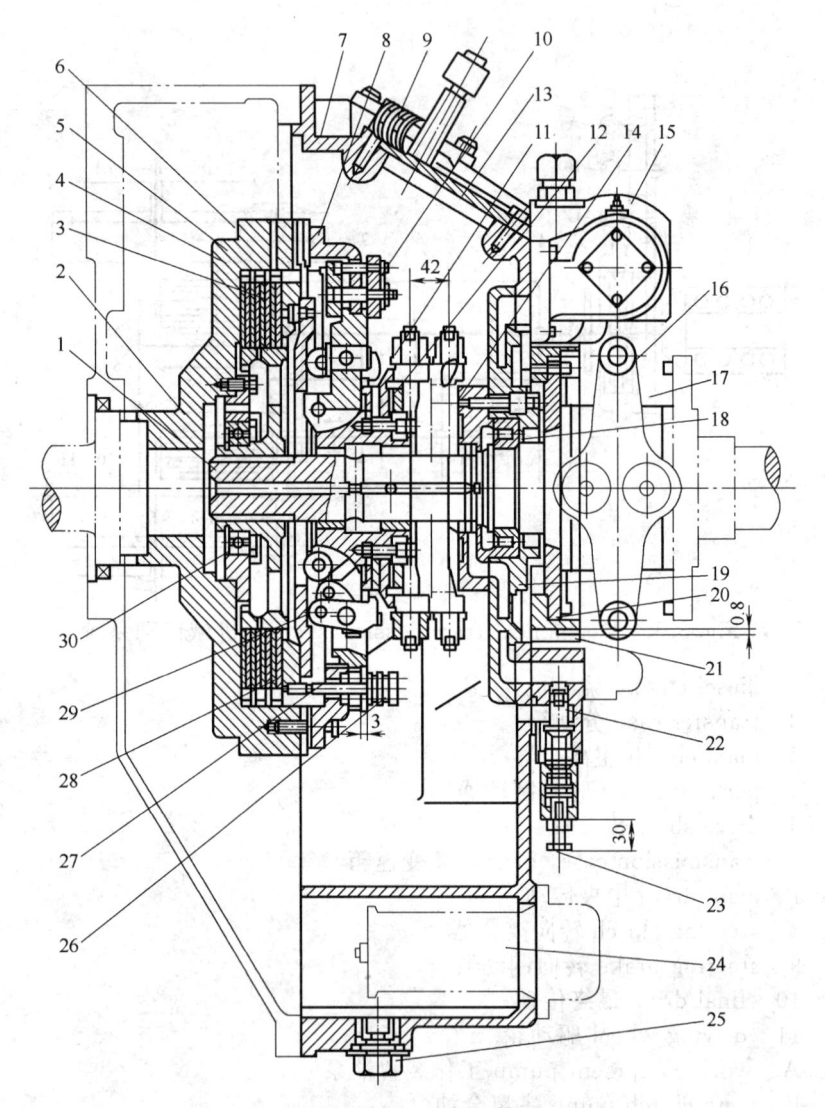

Fig. 3.2 Main clutch 主离合器

1　clutch shaft 离合器轴
2　clutch plate hub 从动轮毂
3　driven plate 从动盘
4　driving plate 主动盘
5　rear pressure plate 后压盘
6　flywheel 飞轮
7　clutch cover 离合器盖
8　flywheel casing 飞轮盖
9　spring 弹簧
10　regulating ring 调整环
11　release sleeve 分离套筒
12　release rim 分离圈
13　cap 盖
14　bearing cap 轴承盖
15　clutch release cylinder 离合器工作缸
16　adapting flange 连接法兰
17　cap 接头盖
18　roller bearing 滚柱轴承
19　bearing seat 轴承座
20　brake drum 制动鼓
21　brakc band 制动带
22　relief valve 溢流阀
23　adjusting screw 调整螺钉
24　coarse filter 粗滤器
25　magnetic (drain) plug 磁性螺塞
26　release spring 分离弹簧
27　lining fork 分离叉
28　pressure plate 压盘
29　centrifugal block 离心块
30　bearing 轴承

(1) Clutch Driven Plate 离合器从动盘 (Fig. 3.3)

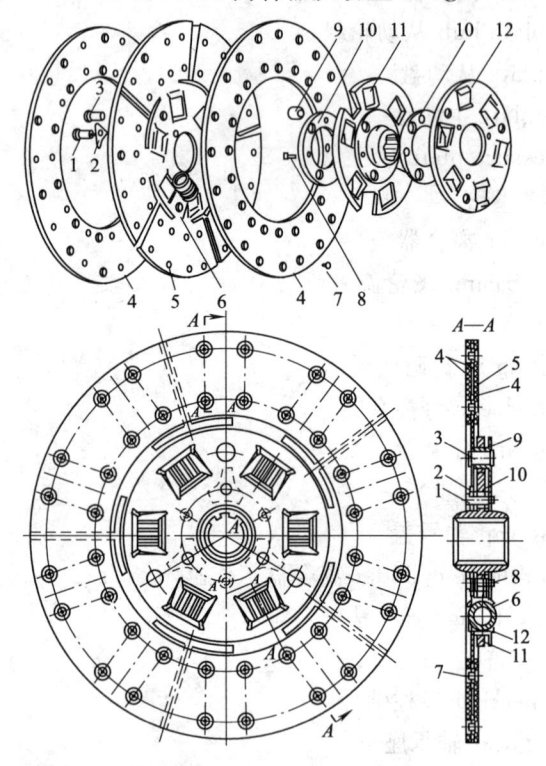

Fig. 3.3 Clutch driven plate 离合器从动盘

1 rivet（扇形弹簧片）铆钉
2 belleville spring 盘形弹簧
3 rivet（从动盘）铆钉
4 friction lining，clutch facing 摩擦片
5 driven plate 从动盘
6 torsional（damping）spring 减振弹簧
7 lining rivet 衬片铆钉
8 rivet（阻尼片）铆钉
9 bushing（铆钉）衬套
10 segmented spring ring 扇形弹簧片
11 driven plate hub 从动轮毂
12 hub flange（从动盘）毂法兰

(2) Clutch Operation 离合器操纵机构 (Fig. 3.4)

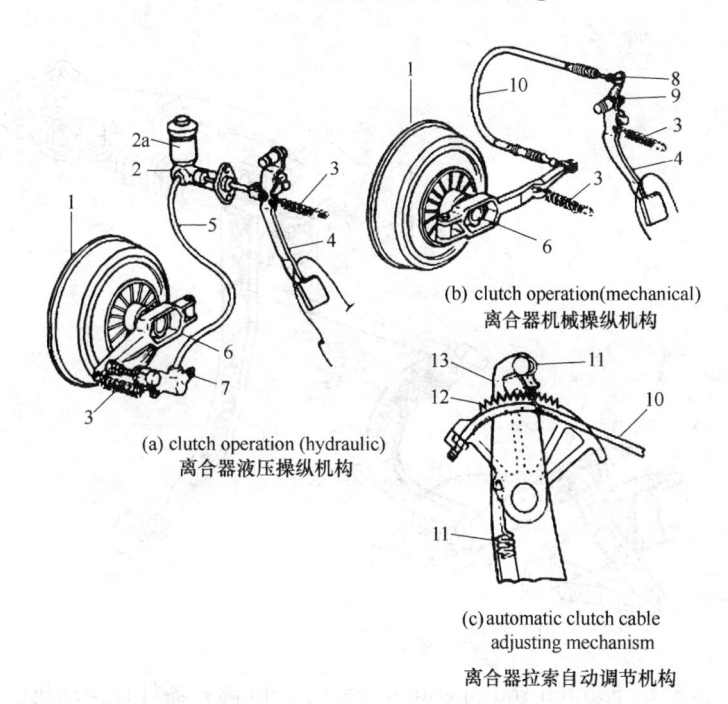

(a) clutch operation (hydraulic)
离合器液压操纵机构

(b) clutch operation (mechanical)
离合器机械操纵机构

(c) automatic clutch cable adjusting mechanism
离合器拉索自动调节机构

Fig. 3.4 Clutch operation 离合器操纵机构

1　clutch cover 离合器盖
2　clutch master cylinder 离合器主缸
2a　reservoir 储液罐
3　return spring 回位弹簧，slave cylinder piston return spring 工作缸活塞回位弹簧
4　clutch pedal 离合器踏板
5　hydraulic line 液压管路，flexible (hydraulic) pipe 连接软管
6　release fork，withdrawal fork，operating fork，clutch fork 分离叉
7　slave cylinder，release cylinder 工作缸，分离缸
8　clutch pedal linkage 离合器踏板拉杆
9　pedal shaft 踏板轴
10　release cable 分离拉索，clutch release cable 离合器分离拉索
11　tension spring 拉伸弹簧
12　toothed segment (quadrant)，notched quadrant 齿扇
13　pawl 棘爪

(3) Clutch Rod-Operated Mechanism 离合器杠杆操纵机构 (Fig. 3.5)

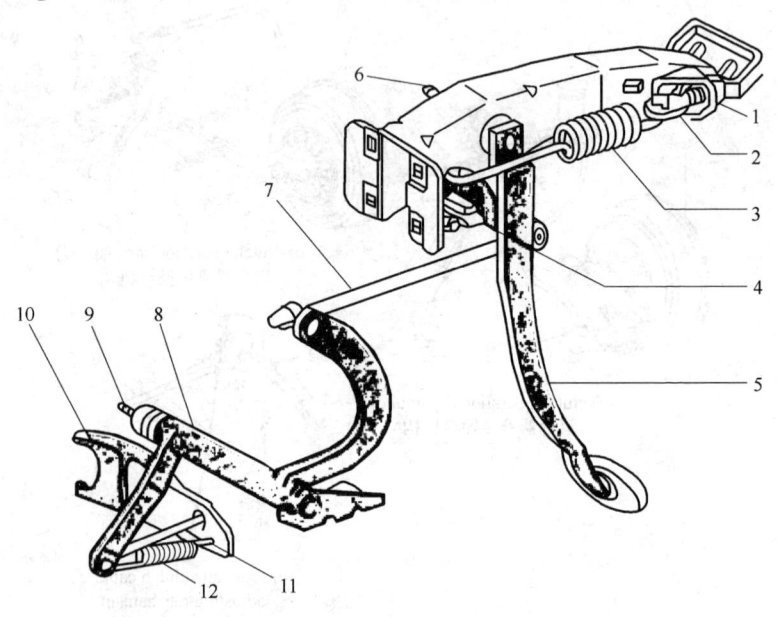

Fig. 3.5 Clutch rod-operated mechanism 离合器杠杆操纵机构
1　link 接头
2　retainer 保持器
3　assist spring 助力弹簧
4　bumper （踏板）缓冲块
5　clutch pedal 离合器踏板
6　bracket 支架
7　pedal-to-equalizer rod 踏板到平衡臂的拉杆
8　equalizer 平衡臂
9　equalizer shaft 平衡臂轴
10　release fork 分离叉
11　release rod 分离杆
12　return spring 回位弹簧

3.2.2 Transmission Case 变速箱 (Fig. 3.6)

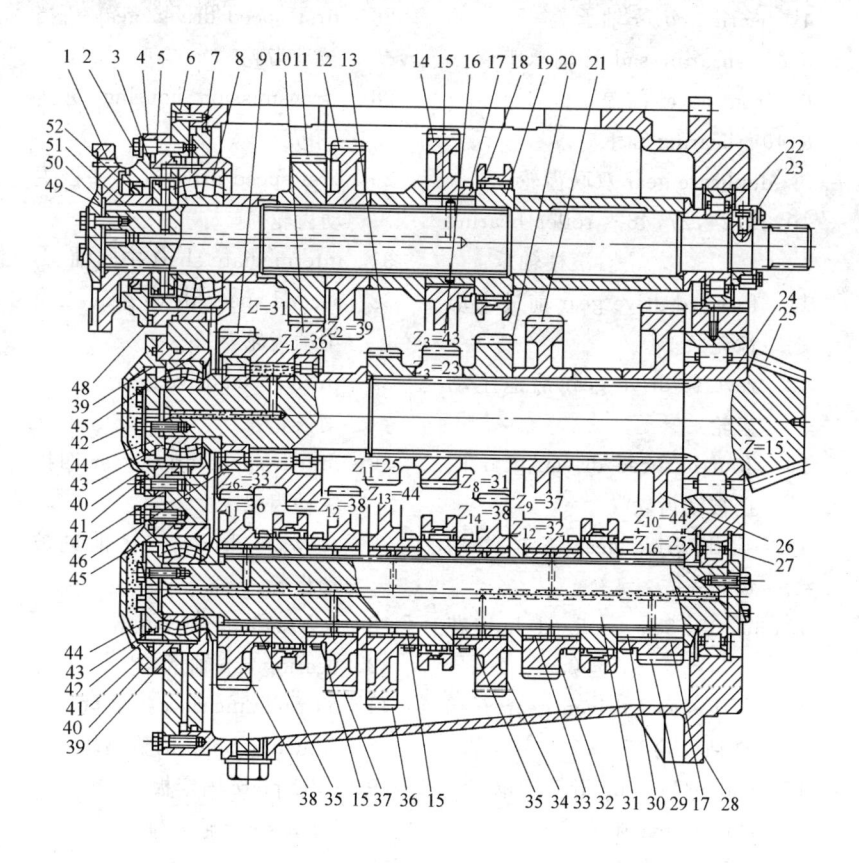

Fig. 3.6 Transmission case 变速箱

1　universal flange 万向节盘
2　baffle plate 挡板
3,7,39,41,43,48　seal ring 密封圈
4　bearing cover 轴承盖
5,45　bearing saddle 轴承座
6　front cover 前盖
8,40　bearing 轴承
9　duplicate gear 双联齿轮
10,22,24,27,46　roller bearing 滚柱轴承
11　forward drive gear 前进主动齿轮
12　reverse drive gear 后退主动齿轮
13　fourth speed driven gear 四挡被动齿轮
14　fifth drive gear 五挡主动齿轮
15,30,33,35　splined hub 花键套
16　fifth speed driven gear 五挡被动齿轮
17　sliding bearing 滑动轴承
18　shift sleeve 啮合套
19　hub 啮合套毂
20　third speed driven gear 三挡被动齿轮
21　second speed driven gear 二挡被动齿轮
23　set nut 定位螺母
25　output shaft 输出轴
26　first speed driven gear 一挡被动齿轮
28　transmission housing 变速箱壳
29　first speed drive gear 一挡主动齿轮
31　intermediate shaft 中间轴
32　second speed drive gear 二挡主动齿轮
34　third speed drive gear 三挡主动齿轮
36　fourth speed drive gear 四挡主动齿轮
37　forward driven gear 前进被动齿轮
38　reverse gear 倒车齿轮
42　bearing cap 轴承盖
44　oil retaining disk 挡油盘
47　adjusting shim 调整垫片
49　solid plate 固定板
50　input shaft 输入轴
51,52　oil seal 油封

(1) Self-Locking and Interlocking Device 自锁和互锁装置 (Fig. 3.7)

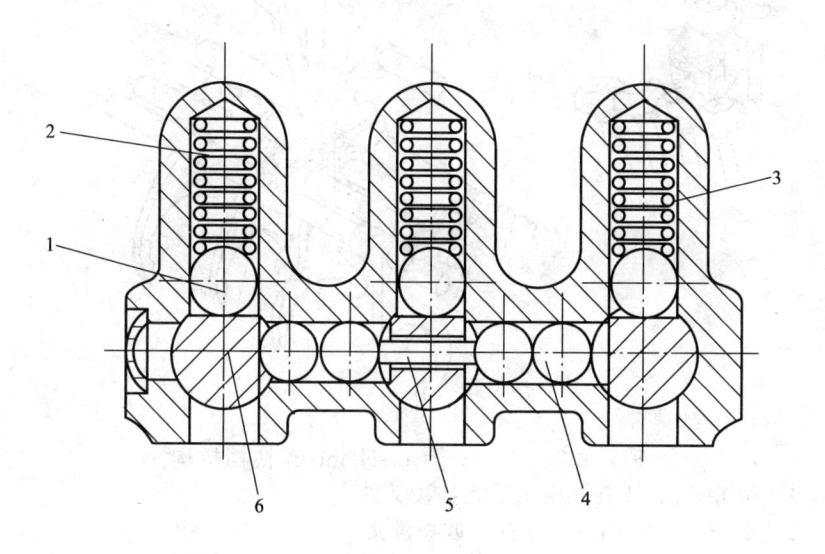

Fig. 3.7 Self-locking and interlocking device 自锁和互锁装置

1　self-lock ball 自锁钢球
2　self-lock spring 自锁弹簧
3　shift lever cover 换挡杆盖
4　interlock ball 互锁钢球
5　interlock plug 互锁销
6　shift fork shaft 拨叉轴

(2) Gearshift Mechanism 换挡机构 (Fig. 3.8)

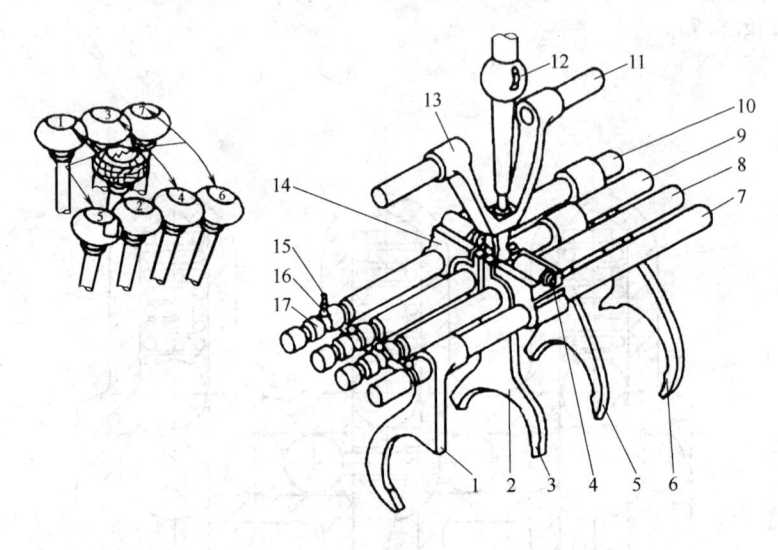

Fig. 3.8 Gearshift mechanism 换挡机构

1　fifth-sixth shift fork 五、六挡拨叉
2　third-fourth shift fork 三、四挡拨叉
3　first-second shift block 一、二挡拨块
4　fifth-sixth shift block 五、六挡拨块
5　first-second shift fork 一、二挡拨叉
6　reverse shift fork 倒挡拨叉
7　fifth-sixth shift fork shaft 五、六挡拨叉轴
8　third-fourth shift fork shaft 三、四挡拨叉轴
9　first-second shift fork shaft 一、二挡拨叉轴
10　reverse shift fork shaft 倒挡拨叉轴
11　shift shaft (换挡) 轴
12　shift lever 变速杆
13　control lever 拨杆
14　reverse shift block 倒挡拨块
15　self-lock spring (自锁) 弹簧
16　self-lock ball 自锁钢球
17　interlock plug 互锁柱销

3.2.3 Propeller Shaft (Drive shaft) 传动轴 (Fig. 3.9)

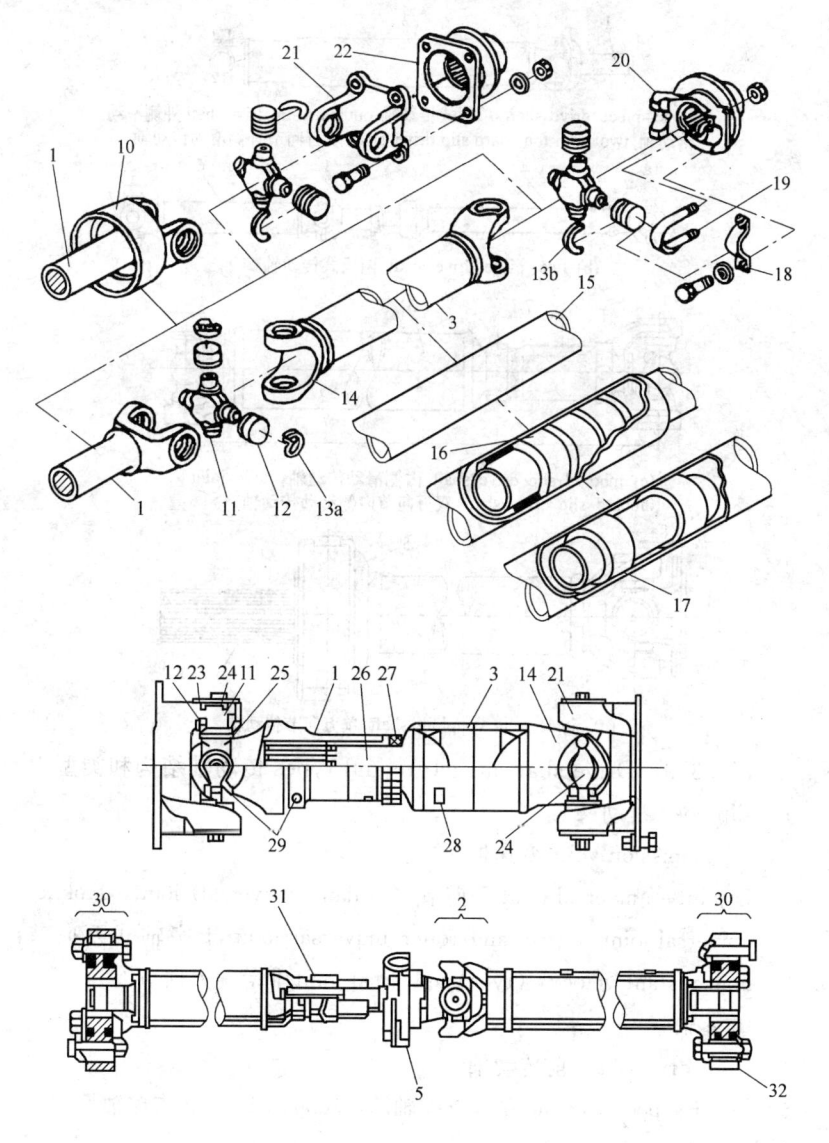

Fig. 3.9

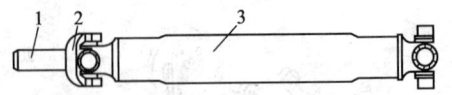

(a) one-piece drive shaft 单根式传动轴, outboard slip drive shaft 外侧滑动传动轴, two-join toutboard slip drive shaft 双万向节外侧滑动传动轴

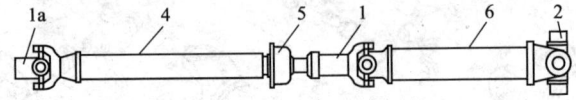

(b) two-piece drive shaft 两段式传动轴

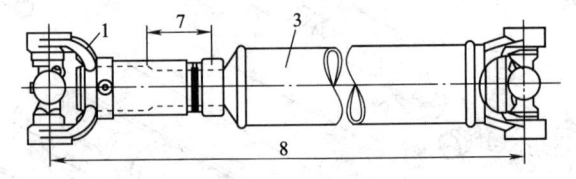

(c) inboard slip drive shaft 内侧滑动传动轴, tow-joint inboard slip drive shaft 双万向节内侧滑动传动轴

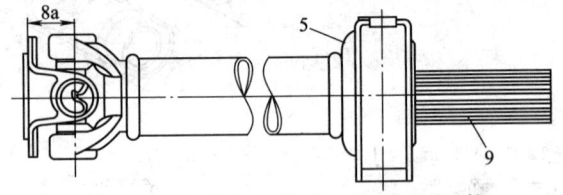

(d) single joint coupling shaft 单万向节传动轴

Fig. 3.9　Drive shaft structure and types 传动轴结构和类型

1　slip yoke 滑动叉

1a　transmission yoke 变速器叉

2　U joint = universal joint 万向节, cardan (universal) joint, Hokke's universal joint, cross and roller universal joint 十字轴式万向节, nonconstant velocity (type) universal joint 非等速万向节

3　tube 轴管

4　front drive shaft 前传动轴

5　center support bearing 中间支撑轴承, support bearing 支撑轴承

6　rear drive shaft 后传动轴

7　slip 允许滑动量

8 drive shaft length 传动轴特征长度

8a over-all length of component 外延长度

9 slip spline 滑动花键

10 torsional damper，vibration absorber 扭振减振器

11 cross，cross spider 十字轴

12 bearing 轴承，needle roller and bearing cup 滚针和轴承杯

11+12 cross assembly 十字轴总成

13 retaining ring 卡环

13a externally locating type 外部定位式

13b internally locating type 内部定位式

14 weld yoke，tube yoke 轴管叉

15 liner 衬管，内衬

16 rubber element 橡胶元件

17 internal vibration absorber 内置式扭振减振器

18 strap 夹板

19 U-bolt U形螺栓

20 end yoke 接头叉

21 flange yoke 凸缘叉

22 companion flange 结合凸缘

23 retainer plate（轴承）保持板

24 lock plate 锁止板

25 bearing seal 轴承油封

26 tube end spline shaft 管端花键轴

27 spline seal 花键油封

28 balance weight 平衡重块

29 lubrication fitting 润滑加注口，黄油嘴

30 flexible universal joint 挠性万向节

31 adjusting nut 调节螺母

32 flexible coupling 挠性联轴节

3.2.4 Drive Axle Assembly 驱动桥总成 (Fig. 3.10)

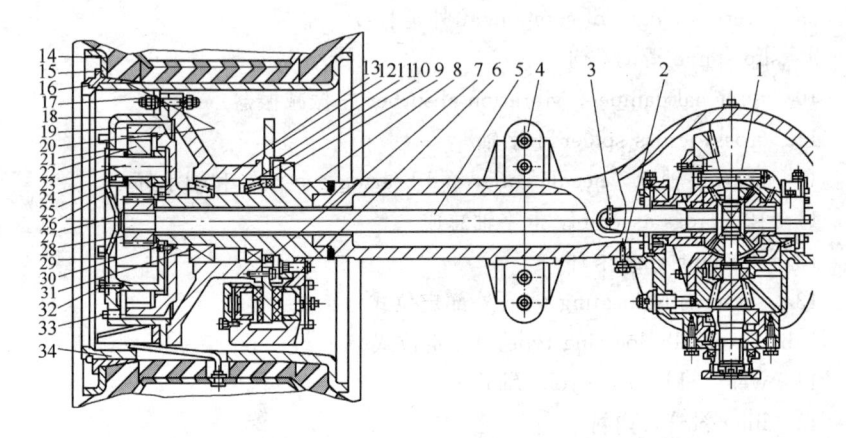

Fig. 3.10 Drive axle assembly 驱动桥总成

1　main drive 主传动
2,4,32　bolt 螺栓
3　vent pipe 透气管
5　axle shaft, half shaft 半轴
6　spot-type disc brake 钳盘式制动器
7　oil seal 油封
8　drive axle housing 驱动桥壳
9　retaining ring 卡环
10,31　bearing 轴承
11　dust helmet 防尘罩
12　brake disc 制动盘
13　wheel hub 轮毂
14　tire 轮胎
15,34　rim 轮辋
16　locking collar 锁环
17　rim bolt 轮辋螺栓
18　planet carrier 行星轮架
19　annular gear 内齿圈
20,27　anti-extrusion ring, retainer 挡圈
21　planetary gear 行星齿轮
22　shim block 垫片
23　planet pin 行星齿轮轴
24　steel ball 钢球
25　needle bearing 滚针轴承
26　end closure 端盖
28　central gear 太阳轮
29　seal washer 密封垫
30　round nut 圆螺母
33　plug screw 螺塞

3.2.5 Main Drive 主传动（Fig. 3.11）

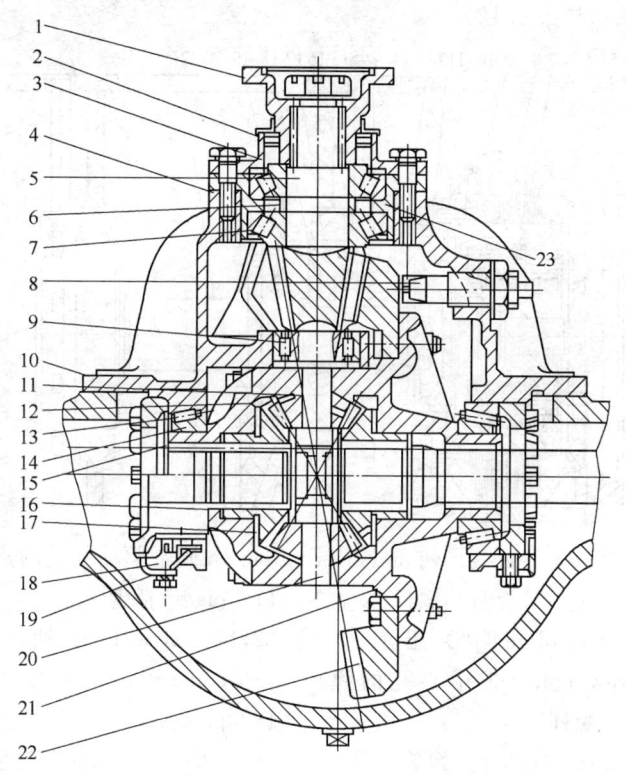

Fig. 3.11 Main drive 主传动

1 pinion flange 主动齿轮法兰
2 oil seal 油封
3 sealing cover 密封盖
4 adjusting shim 调整垫
5 differential bevel pinion 差速器小锥齿轮
6 bearing preload spacer 轴承预紧隔套
7 bearing 轴承
8 catch bolt 止动螺栓
9 bearing 轴承
10 support (ing) bracket 托架
11 thrust washer 止推垫圈
12 planetary gear 行星齿轮
13 adjusting nut 调整螺母
14 bearing 轴承
15,21 differential housing 差速器壳
16 side gear 半轴齿轮
17 thrust washer 止推垫圈
18 bearing saddle 轴承座
19 adjusting nut lock 调整螺母锁片
20 spider 十字轴
22 ring gear 环齿轮
23 locating (adjusting) shim（主动小齿轮）调整垫圈

3.2.6 Track Drive and Steering Clutch 履带驱动与转向离合器

（Fig. 3.12）

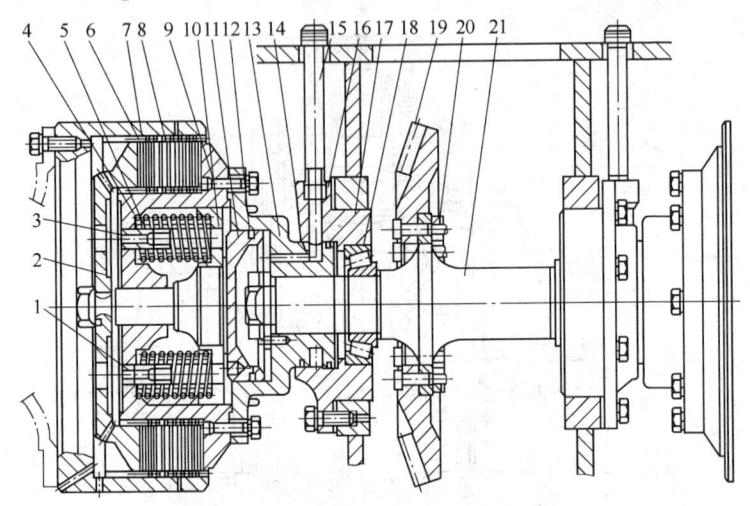

Fig. 3.12 Track drive and steering clutch 履带驱动与转向离合器

1　screw bolt（弹簧）螺杆
2　pressure plate（外）压盘
3　screw bolt（带中心孔的弹簧）螺杆
4　large coil spring 大螺旋弹簧
5　small coil spring 小螺旋弹簧
6　driven plate 从动盘
7　driving disc 主动片
8　clutch plate hub 从动盘毂
9　driving hub 主动毂
10　spring pressure plate 弹簧压盘
11　piston 活塞
12,14　oil seal ring 油封环
13　connecting plate 接合板
15　pipe 油管
16　adjusting shim 调整垫片
17　bearing saddle 轴承座
18　conical bearing 圆锥轴承
19　large bevel gear 大锥齿轮
20　bolt 螺栓
21　cross axle 横轴

3.3 Hydromechanical Transmission System 液力机械传动系统 (Fig. 3.13)

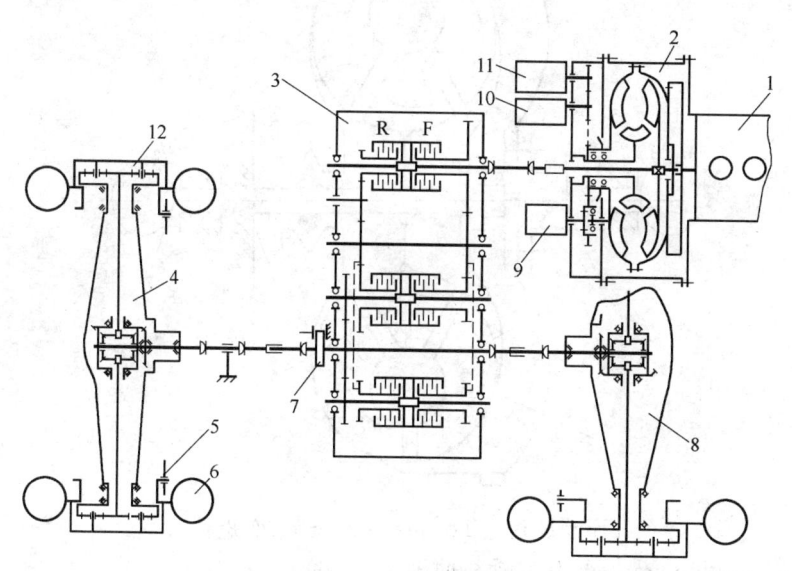

Fig. 3.13 Hydromechanical transmission system 液力机械传动系统

1　engine 发动机
2　torque converter 液力变矩器
3　power shifting transmission case 动力换挡变速箱
4　front axle 前桥
5　caliper disc brake 钳盘式制动器
6　wheel 车轮
7　parking brake 驻车制动器
8　rear axle 后桥
9　variable speed pump 变速油泵
10　steering pump 转向油泵
11　operational pump 工作油泵
12　wheel reductor 轮边减速器

3.3.1 Torque Converter 变矩器 (Fig. 3.14)

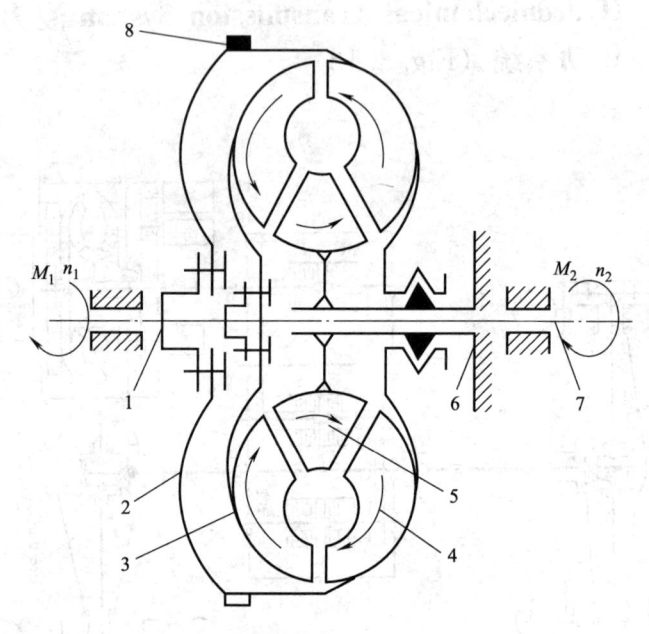

Fig. 3.14 Torque converter 变矩器

1　engine crankshaft 发动机曲轴
2　converter housing 变矩器壳
3　turbine 涡轮
4　pump 泵轮
5　reactor 导轮
6　stator shaft 定子轴
7　output shaft 输出轴
8　starter ring gear 启动齿圈

3.3.2 Power Shifting Transmission Case 动力换挡变速箱 (Fig. 3.15)

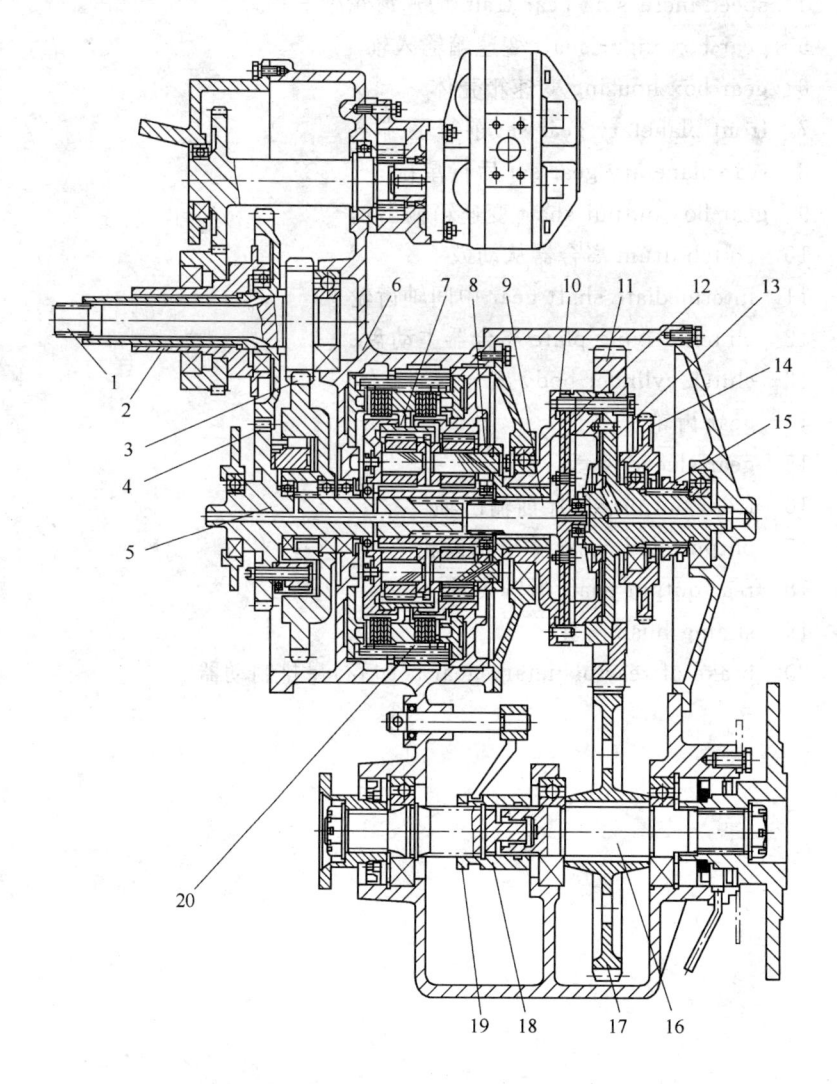

Fig. 3.15 Power shifting transmission case 动力换挡变速箱

105

1,2 torque converter output shaft 变矩器输出轴
3 speed reducing gear pair 减速齿轮副
4 speed increasing gear train 增速齿轮副
5 gear-box input shaft 变速箱输入轴
6 gear-box housing 变速箱壳体
7 front planetary gear set 前行星排
8 rear planetary gear set 后行星排
9 gear-box output shaft 变速箱输出轴
10 clutch drum 离合器从动鼓
11 intermediate shaft gear 中间轴齿轮
12 clutch driving plate 离合器主动盘
13 clutch cylinder body 离合器油缸体
14 gear 齿轮
15 gear sleeve 齿套
16 front output shaft 前输出轴
17 output shaft gear 输出轴齿轮
18 rear output shaft 后输出轴
19 sliding bush 滑套
20 brake of rear planetary gear set 后行星排制动器

3.3.3 Automatic Transmission 自动换挡变速箱 (Fig. 3.16)

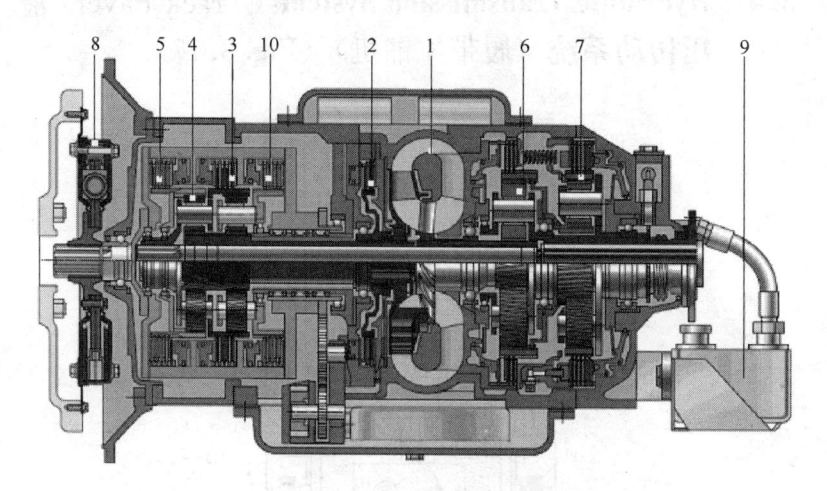

Fig. 3.16 Automatic transmission 自动换挡变速箱

1 counter-rotating torque converter 反转型液力变矩器
2 impeller brake 泵轮制动器
3 lock-up clutch 闭锁离合器
4 differential gear 差速齿轮
5 input clutch 输入端离合器
6 planetary gear set 行星排
7 planetary gear set for reverse gear and retarder 倒挡和减速器行星排
8 torsional vibration damper 扭振减振器
9 heat exchanger 散热器
10 4th gear clutch 第4挡离合器

3.4 Hydraulic Transmission System (Track Paver) 液压传动系统（履带摊铺机）(Fig. 3.17)

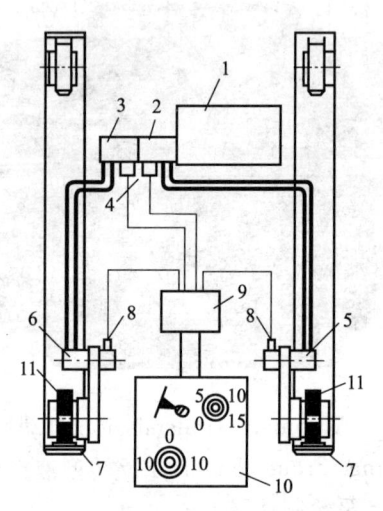

Fig. 3.17 Hydraulic transmission system (track paver)
液压传动系统（履带摊铺机）

1 engine 发动机
2 right variable pump 右变量泵
3 left variable pump 左变量泵
4 proportional speed controller 比例速度控制器
5 right axial plunger motor 右轴向柱塞马达
6 left axial plunger motor 左轴向柱塞马达
7 crawler 履带
8 speed sensor 转速传感器
9 electric control system 电控系统
10 central console 中央控制台
11 driving chain wheel 驱动链轮

Unit 4　Steering System 转向系统

4.1　General 概述

The steering system must deliver precise directional control. And it must do so requiring little driver effort at the steering wheel. Truck steering systems are either manual or power-assisted, with power assist units using either hydraulic or air assist setups to make steering effort easier. In addition to its vital role in vehicle control, the steering system is closely related to front suspension, axle, and wheel/tire components. The key components that make up the steering system are the steering wheel, steering column, steering shaft, steering gear, pitman arm, drag link, steering arm, ball joints and tie-rod assembly.

转向系必须能产生精确的方向控制，且使驾驶员只需要较小的转向操纵力。货车转向系要么是手动转向系，要么是动力助力式转向系。动力助力单元采用液压或空气助力装置来使得转向轻便。转向系除了对车辆控制有着重要的作用外，还与前悬架、车桥、车轮、轮胎等元件有着密切的联系。组成转向系的主要元件有转向盘、转向管柱、转向轴、转向器、转向摇臂、转向直拉杆、转向节臂、球头节和转向横拉杆总成等。

4.2 Wheeled Steering System 轮式转向系统

4.2.1 Steering Types 转向类型 (Fig. 4.1)

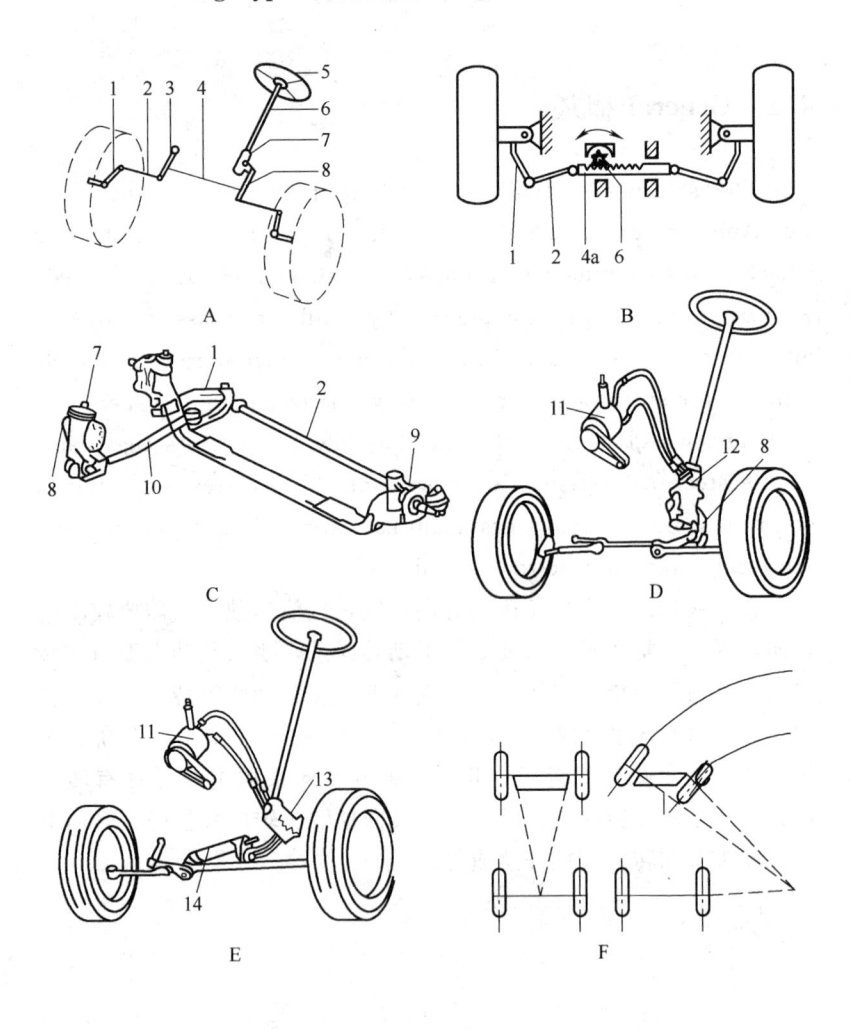

Fig. 4.1 Steering types 转向类型

A~C manual steering system, muscular-energy steering system 人力转向系
A,C parallelogram steering linkage 平行四边形转向传动机构
B rack and pinion steering system 齿轮齿条式转向系, steering system for independent suspension 独立悬架转向系
C steering system for dependent suspension 非独立悬架转向系, steering linkage 转向传动机构, tie rod linkage, Ackerman geometry 梯形机构, single tie rod type tie rod linkage 整体式梯形机构
D,E PS system=power steering system 动力转向系
D integral PS system 整体式动力转向系
E booster type power steering system 助（加）力式动力转向系, semi-integral power steering system 半整体式动力转向系
F Ackerman Jeantaud steering 阿克曼-金特式转向
1 steering (knuckle) arm 转向节臂
2 tie rod（转向）横拉杆
3 idler arm 随动臂; steering idler arm 转向随动臂
4 relay rod, center rod 中继杆
4a steering rack 转向齿条
5 steering wheel 转向盘
6 steering shaft 转向轴
5+6 steering control mechanism 转向操纵机构
7 steering gear, steering gearbox, steering mechanism 转向器
8 pitman arm 转向摇臂
9 steering knuckle, steering (axle) swivel, steering (axle) stub, axle stub 转向节
10 drag link, drag rod 直拉杆
11 PS pump=power steering pump 动力转向油泵
12 integral power steering gear 整体式动力转向器
13 semi-integral power steering gear 半整体式动力转向器
12,13 power steering gear 动力转向器
14 power cylinder 转向动力缸

4.2.2 Steering Linkage (Mechanism) 转向传动机构 (Fig. 4.2)

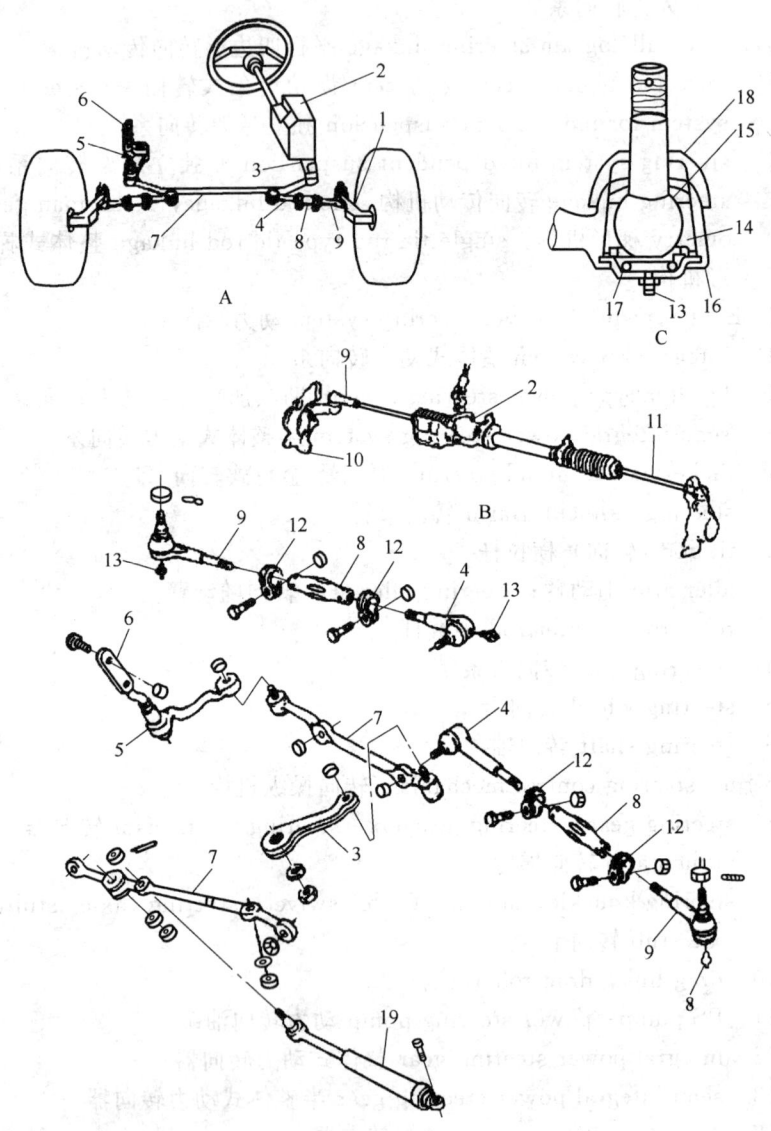

Fig. 4.2 Steering linkage (mechanism) 转向传动机构

A parallelogram steering linkage 平行四边形转向传动机构
B rack and pinion steering linkage 齿轮齿条式转向传动机构
C ball joint 球节
1 steering (knuckle) arm 转向节臂
2 steering gear 转向器
3 pitman arm, drop arm, steering gear arm, steering lever 转向摇臂
4 inner tie rod 内横拉杆, inner tie rod end (joint) 横拉杆内接头
5 idler arm 随动臂
6 bracket (随动臂) 支架, mounting bracket 安装支架
7 relay rod, center link, centre link, connecting rod 中继杆
8 adjusting sleeve, adjuster tube (横拉杆) 调节管
9 outer tie rod 外横拉杆, outer tie rod end (joint) 横拉杆外接头
10 steering knuckle 转向节
11 tie rod, tie bar, track rod 横拉杆, steering tie rod 转向横拉杆
12 tie rod clamp 横拉杆夹
13 grease fitting 滑脂嘴
14 bearing 轴承, ball cup, ball (-stud) socket, ball cap 球碗, 球头座
15 ball stud, ball pivot, ball pin 球头销, "full-ball" stud 全球式球头销
16 joint housing 接头壳
17 compression spring 压缩弹簧
18 dust cover, seal 防尘罩
19 steering shock absorber 转向减振（缓冲）器

4.2.3 Steering Axle 转向桥 (Fig. 4.3)

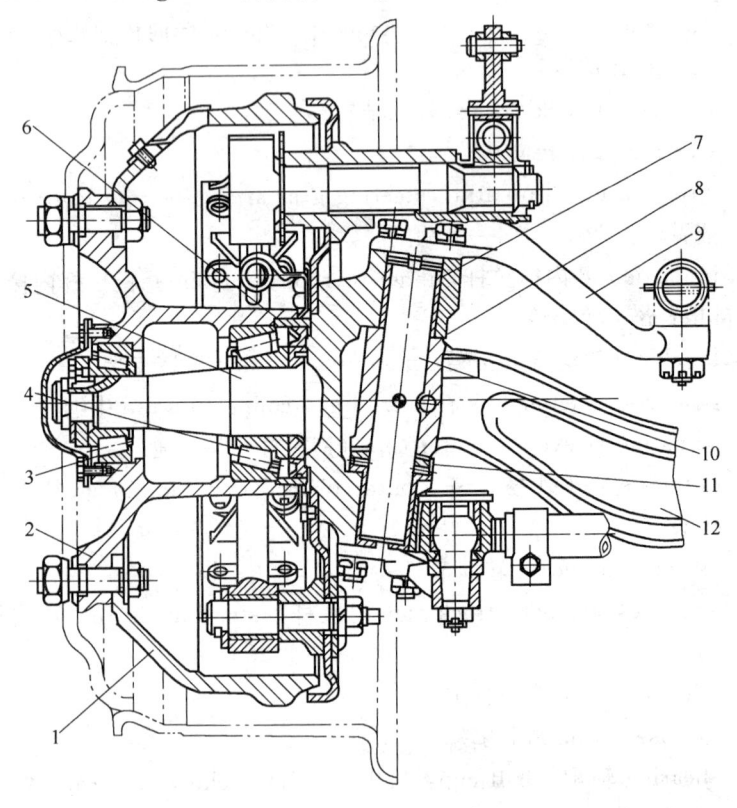

Fig. 4.3 Steering axle 转向桥

1　brake drum 制动鼓
2　wheel hub 轮毂
3,4　conical roller bearing 锥形滚柱轴承
5　steering knuckle 转向节
6　oil seal 油封
7　bushing 衬套
8　adjusting shim 调整垫片
9　steering arm 转向节臂
10　kingpin 转向销
11　thrust bearing 推力轴承
12　front axle beam 前梁

4.2.4 Steering Gear 转向器 (Fig. 4.4)

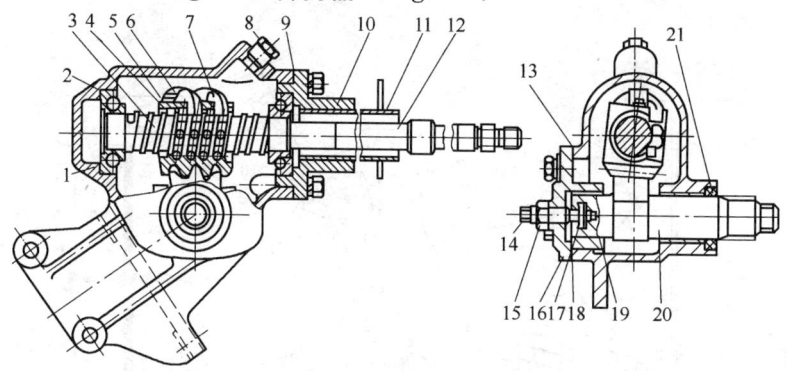

Fig. 4.4 Steering gear 转向器

1 steering gear housing 转向器壳体
2 thrust bearing 推力轴承
3 steering worm 转向蜗杆
4 steering nut 转向螺母
5 steel ball 钢球
6 clamp 固定夹
7 ball guide 钢球导管
8 tapered plug 锥形螺塞
9 adjusting shim 调整垫片
10 steering gear cover 转向器盖
11 steering column 转向柱管
12 steering shaft 转向轴
13 spacer block (转向器侧盖) 衬垫
14 adjusting screw 调整螺钉
15 lock nut 锁紧螺母
16 side cover 侧盖
17 retaining ring 挡圈
18 shim 垫片
19 bushing (摇臂轴) 衬套
20 sector shaft 齿扇轴
21 oil seal 油封

4.2.5 Articulated Steering System 铰接式转向系统 (Fig. 4.5)

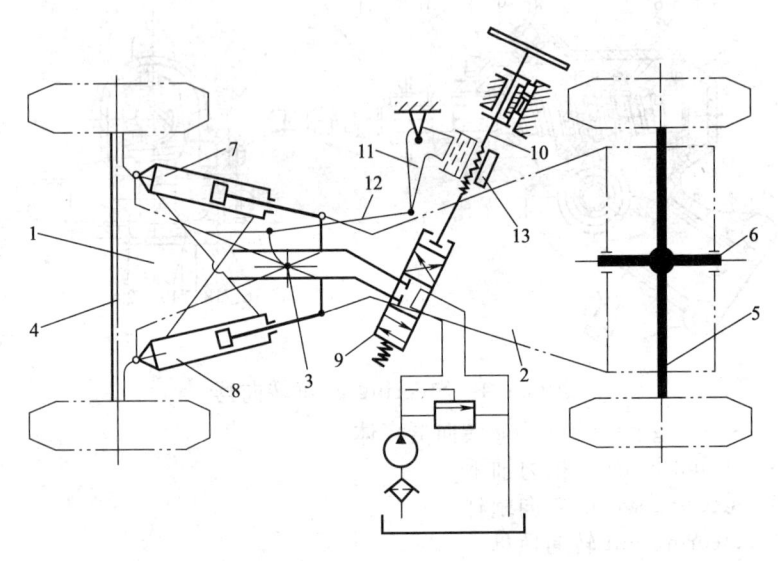

Fig. 4.5 Articulated steering system 铰接式转向系统

1 front frame 前机架

2 rear frame 后机架

3 articulated point 铰接点

4 front axle 前桥

5 rear axle 后桥

6 rear axle oscillating shaft 后桥摆动轴

7 right steering cylinder 右转向油缸

8 left steering cylinder 左转向油缸

9 servo valve 随动阀

10 steering yoke 方向杆

11 pitman arm 转向垂臂

12 follower lever 随动杆

13 rack and sector steering gear 齿条齿扇式转向器

4.2.6 Hydraulic Steering System 液压转向系统 (Fig. 4.6)

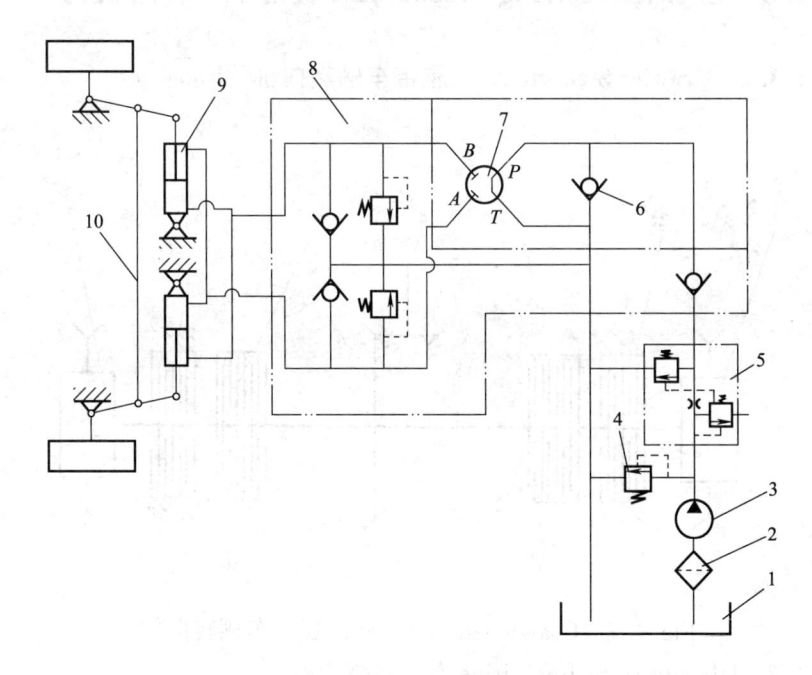

Fig. 4.6 Hydraulic steering system 液压转向系统

1　oil reservoir 油箱
2　filter 滤油器
3　oil pump 油泵
4　relief valve 溢流阀
5　one-way stabilized flow divider valve 单路稳定分流阀
6　one-way valve，non-return valve，check valve 单向阀
7　hydraulic steering control unit 液压转向器
8　combination valves 组合阀块
9　steering cylinder 转向油缸
10　steering trapezium 转向梯形

4.3　Crawler Steering Mechanism 履带车辆转向机构

4.3.1　Crawler Steering Axle 履带车辆转向桥（Fig. 4.7）

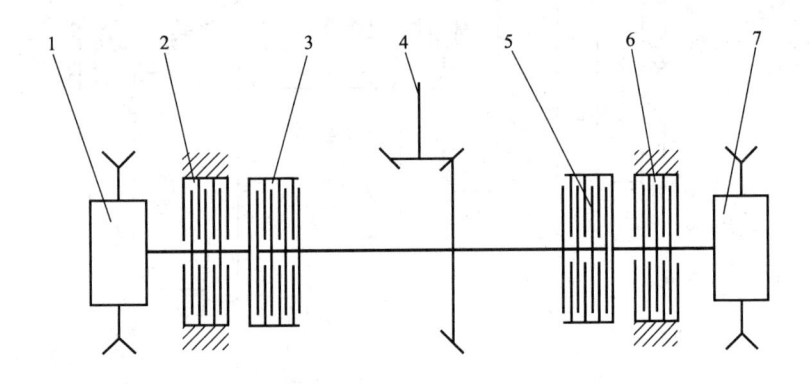

Fig. 4.7　Crawler steering axle 履带车辆转向桥
1,7　left and right final drive 左、右终传动
2,6　left and right disc brake 左、右盘式制动器
3,5　left and right steering clutch 左、右转向离合器
4　main transmission 主传动器

4.3.2 Double Action Steering Clutch 双作用转向离合器 (Fig. 4.8)

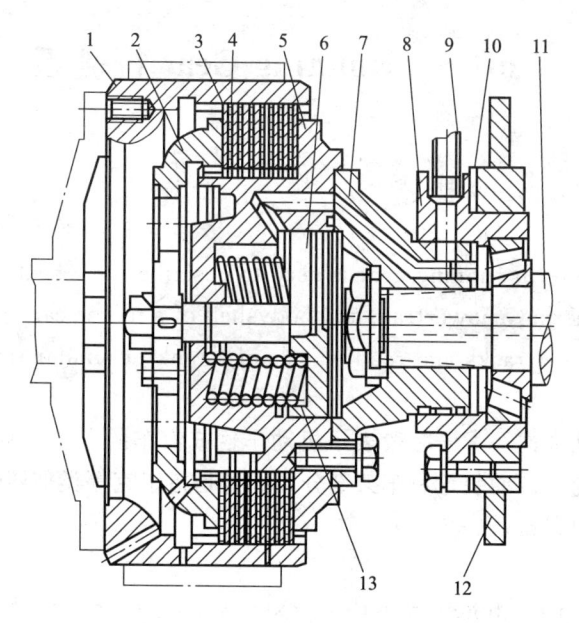

Fig. 4.8 Double action steering clutch 双作用转向离合器

1　clutch plate hub 从动盘毂
2　pressure plate（外）压盘
3　driven plate 从动盘
4　driving disc 主动片
5　driving hub 主动毂
6　piston 活塞
7　coupling flange 连接盘
8　bearing housing 轴承座
9　pipe 油管
10　adjusting shim 调整垫片
11　cross axle 横轴
12　isolating plate 隔板
13　small spring 小弹簧

Unit 5　Running Gear 行驶系

5.1　Overview 概述

The term running gear is used to describe the wheels, suspension, steering, powertrain and bodyshell of a motor-car or automobile, or the tracks and road wheels of a tank or similar tracked vehicle.

行驶系这一术语一般表示机动车辆或汽车的车轮、悬挂装置、转向机构、传动装置和车架部分，或者是指坦克等类似履带车辆的履带机构和轮系。

A wheel, together with an axle overcomes friction by facilitating motion by rolling. In order for wheels to rotate, a moment needs to be applied to the wheel about its axis, either by way of gravity, or by application of another external force.

车轮与轮轴一起，通过滚动克服摩擦力。为使车轮转动，需要依靠重力或运用外力施加给车轮围绕轮轴的力矩。

Suspension is the term given to the system of springs, shock absorbers and linkages that connects a vehicle to its wheels. Suspension systems serve a dual purpose—contributing to the car's handling and braking for good active safety and driving pleasure, and keeping vehicle occupants comfortable and reasonably well isolated from road noise, bumps, and vibrations. The suspension also protects the vehicle itself and any cargo from damage and wear. The design of front and rear suspension of a car may be different.

悬挂装置是关于把车辆连接于自身车轮的弹簧、减振器和连接件组成系统的术语。悬挂系统具有双重作用：提供工作安全、驾驶舒适的车辆操纵和制动性能；保持乘客乘坐舒适性，并使其与道路噪声、冲击和振动具有良好的隔离。悬挂装置也能保护车辆自身与货物免遭损坏和磨损。车辆前悬挂和后悬挂的设计可以不同。

5.2 Wheeled Running Gear 轮式行驶系

5.2.1 Wheeled Running Mechanism 轮式行走机构 (Fig. 5.1)

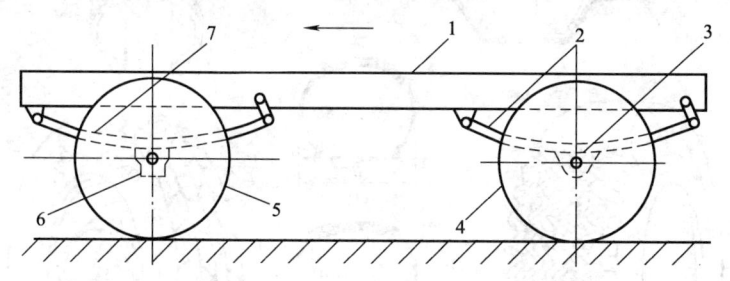

Fig. 5.1 Wheeled running mechanism 轮式行走机构

1　frame 车架
2　rear suspension 后悬架
3　driving axle 驱动桥
4　rear wheel 后轮
5　front wheel 前轮
6　driven axle 从动桥
7　front suspension 前悬架

5.2.2 Tire（Tyre）Type 轮胎类型 (Fig. 5.2)

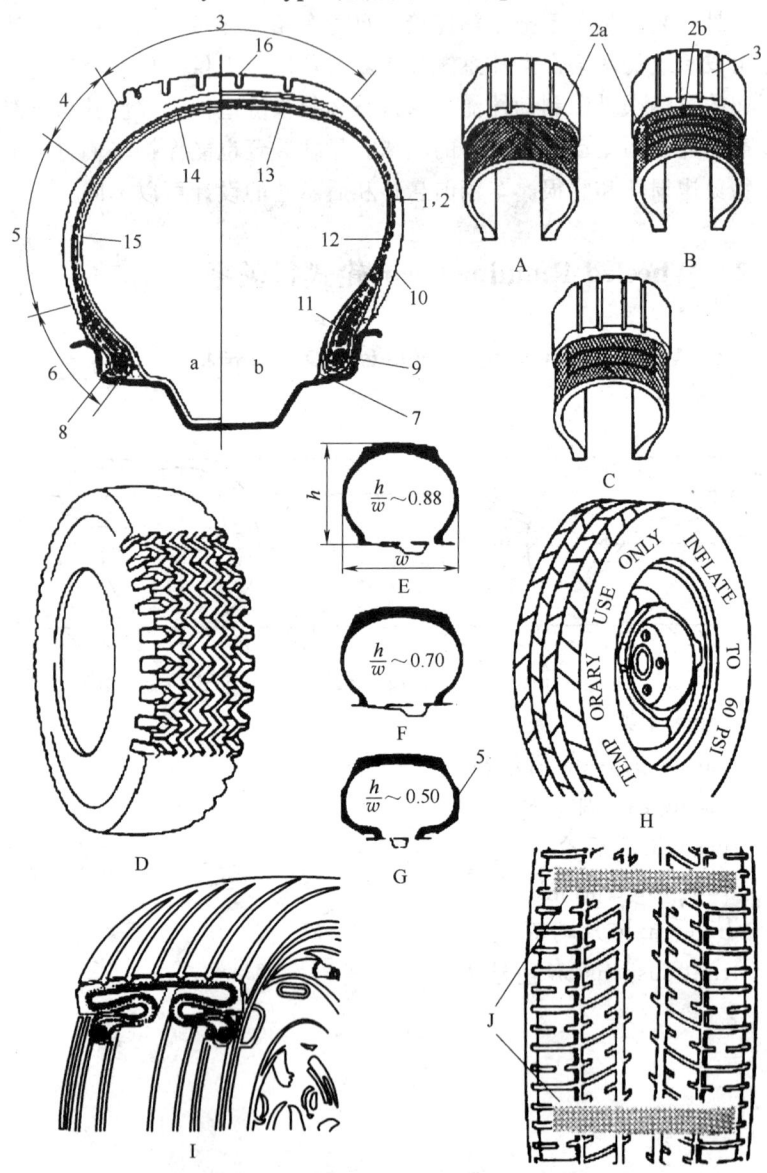

$$\frac{h}{w} \sim 0.88$$

$$\frac{h}{w} \sim 0.70$$

$$\frac{h}{w} \sim 0.50$$

Fig. 5.2 Tire (tyre) type 轮胎类型

A diagonal tire, bias (ply) tire, cross-ply tire 斜交轮胎, bias ply tire with inner tube, bias ply tubed tire 有内胎斜交轮胎
a tubed tire, tube-type tire 有内胎轮胎
B radial (ply) tire 子午线轮胎, belted radial tire 带束子午线轮胎
b tubeless tire 无内胎轮胎
C belted bias (diagonal) tire 带束斜交轮胎
D MS tire=mud and snow tire, all-season tire 泥雪地轮胎, 全天候轮胎
E conventional section tire 普通断面轮
F low section tire 低断面轮胎
G super low section tire 超低断面轮胎
H compact (temporary) spare tire 紧凑型备胎, 应急备胎; high pressure small spare tire 高压小型备胎
h section height 断面高度
w section width 断面宽度
h/w height-to-width ratio, aspect ratio, ratio of cross-section height to width 高宽比
I folding tire 折叠轮胎;
J tread (tire) wear indicator 胎面磨损指示器;
1 cord 帘线
2 cord ply, plies, ply 帘布层
2a carcass plies 胎体帘布层
2b tread plies 胎面帘布层
3 tread, tire tread 胎面
4 shoulder 胎肩, shoulder area 胎肩区
5 sidewall 胎侧
6 bead, tire bead, tyre bead 胎圈, 子口, bead area 胎圈区
7 bead toe 胎趾
8 bead heel 胎踵
9 bead core, bead wire 胎圈芯
10 carcass, carcase, casing 胎体
11 reinforced rubber 增强橡胶
12 inner liner 气密层
13 belt, belt ply, bracing ply, tread belt 带束层
14 breaker 缓冲层
15 inner tube, tube 内胎
16 groove, tread groove, tire groove 花纹沟

5.2.3 Tire Tread 胎面 (Fig. 5.3)

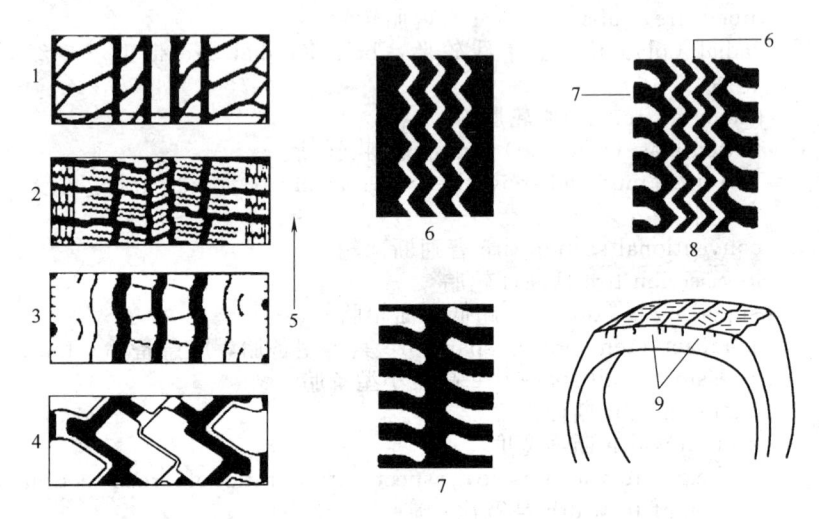

Fig. 5.3 Tire tread 胎面

1 passenger-car tire tread 轿车胎面，乘用车胎面
2 M&S tire tread 泥雪地用胎面
3 commercial-vehicle tire tread 商用车胎面
4 high-traction tread pattern 高牵引力胎面花纹
5 rolling direction 滚动方向
6 circumferential fold line pattern 纵向折线花纹
7 transverse pattern 横向花纹
8 dual purpose tread pattern 混合花纹
9 sipe(s), sipings, sipe cut, traction blades, traction slots 刀槽花纹，细缝花纹

5.2.4 Rim 轮辋 (Fig. 5.4)

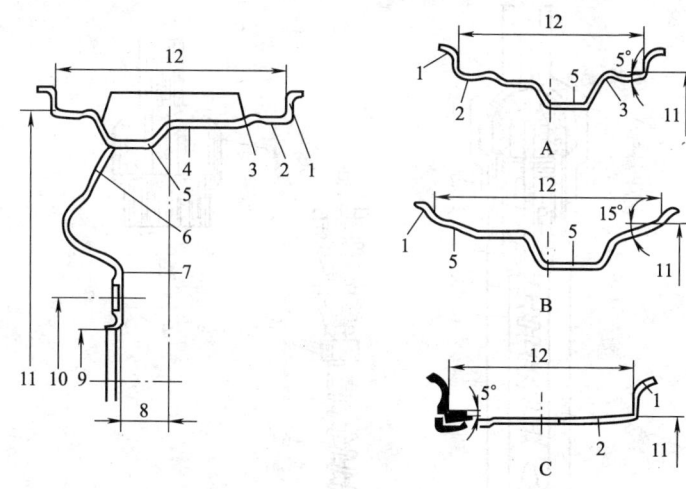

Fig. 5.4 Rim 轮辋

A hump rim 凸峰轮辋
B 15°tapered-bead seat rim 15°斜胎圈轮辋
A,B one (single)-piece rim, normal rim 一件式轮辋，DC rim= drop center rim 深槽轮辋
C 5°tapered-bead seat rim (货车) 5°斜胎圈轮辋，two-piece rim 两件式轮辋，FB rim=flat base rim 平底轮辋；
1 rim flange, flange 轮缘
2 5°tapered (-bead) seat 5°斜胎圈
3 hump 凸峰
4 rim, wheel rim 轮辋
5 drop center 深槽
6 ventilation hole 通风孔
7 wheel disk (disc, spoke, rib) 轮辐
8 rim offset 轮辋偏距
9 center hole 中心孔
10 bolt (hole) circle diameter 螺栓孔圆直径
11 rim diameter 轮辋直径
12 rim width 轮辋宽度

5.2.5 Tire Valve 气门嘴 (Fig. 5.5)

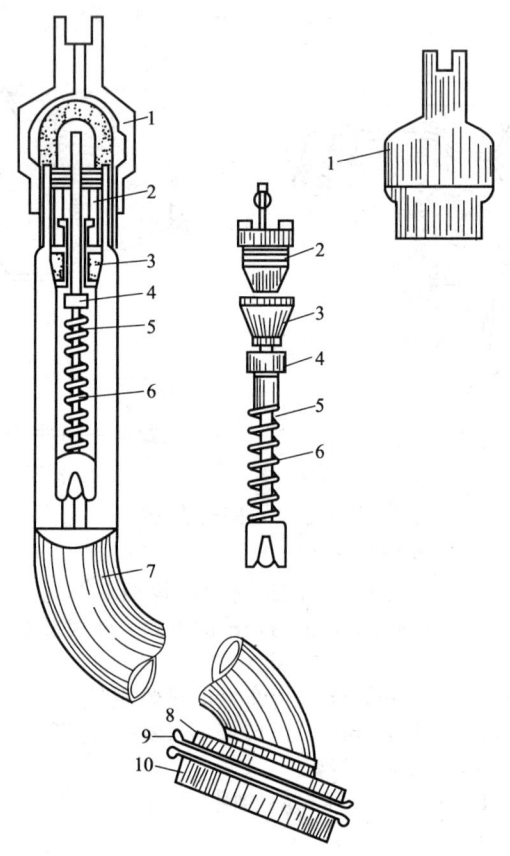

Fig. 5.5 Tire valve 气门嘴

1 cap 盖
2,8 nut 螺母
3 bushing 衬套
4 valve 阀门
5 pin 芯杆
6 return spring 回位弹簧
7 valve body 嘴体
9 washer 垫圈
10 flange 凸缘

5.3 Crawler Unit 履带行走装置

5.3.1 Crawler 履带式车辆（Fig. 5.6）

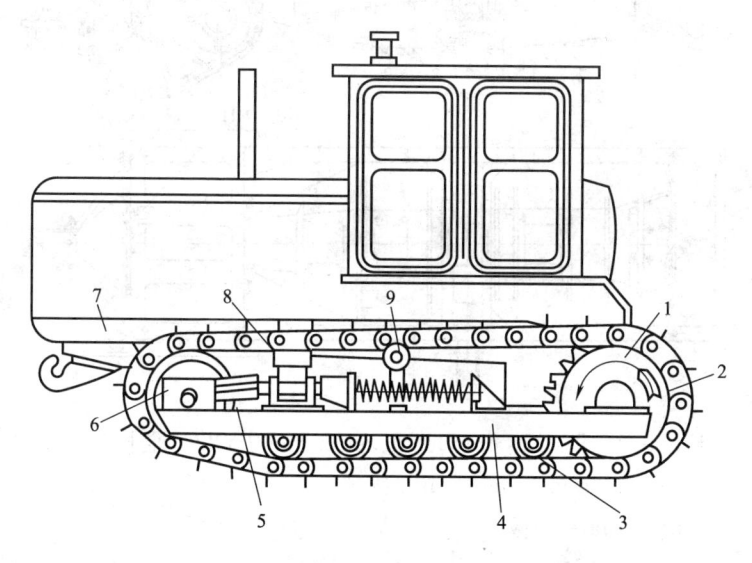

Fig. 5.6 Crawler 履带式车辆

1 drive sprocket 驱动轮
2 caterpillar track, track 履带
3 track roller, track supporting wheel 支重轮
4 supporting carriage 支重台车
5 track adjuster 履带张紧器
6 track idler 引导轮
7 framework 机架
8 suspension 悬架
9 carrier roller 托链轮

5.3.2　Chassis Frame 车架

（1）TY220 Crawler Dozer Frame TY220 推土机机架（Fig. 5.7）

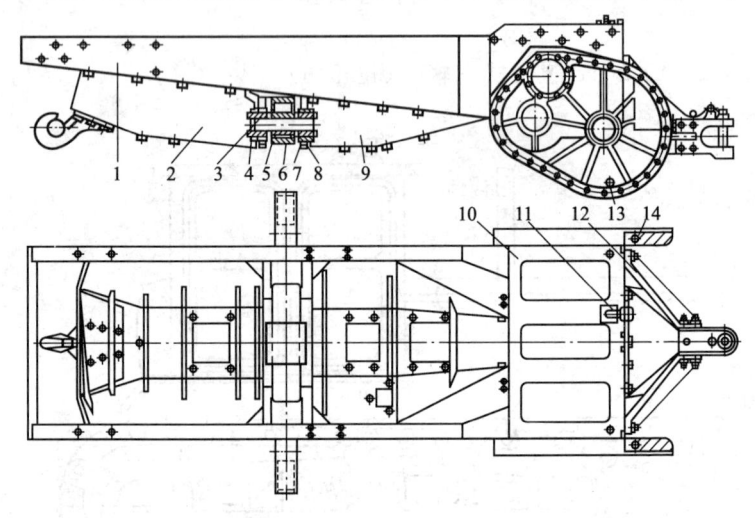

Fig. 5.7　TY220 crawler dozer frame TY220 推土机机架

1　frame side member（rail）纵梁
2　guard plate 护板
3　axis pin 销轴
4　front cover 前盖
5　bushing 衬套
6　equalizer 平衡架
7　rear cover 后盖
8　cross sail 横梁
9　lower back plate 下后板
10　rear axle housing 后桥箱
11　pipe（加）油管
12　tow hook, towing hook, hitch 拖钩
13　oil drain hole 放油孔
14　oil filling port 加油孔

(2) SD7 Crawler Dozer Frame SD7 推土机机架 (Fig. 5.8)

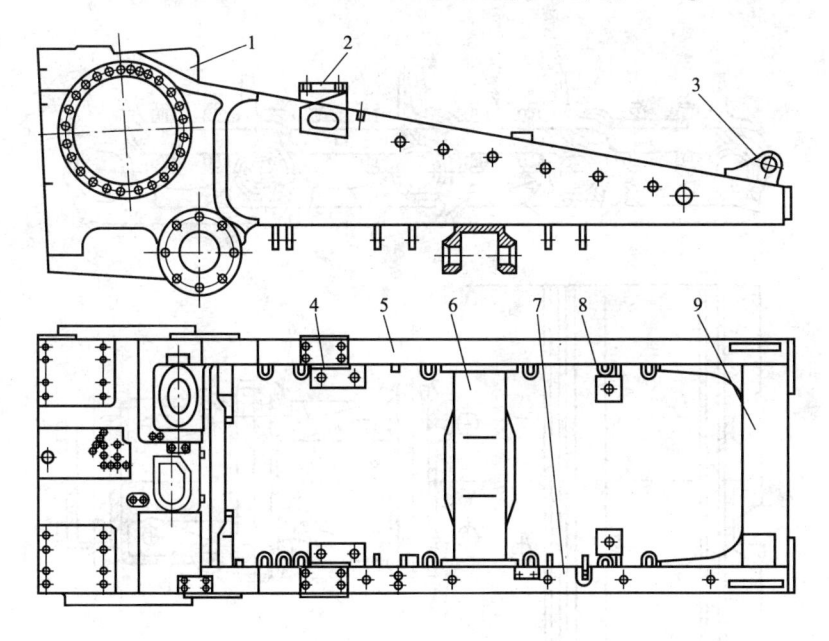

Fig 5.8 SD7 crawler dozer frame SD7 推土机机架

1　rear axle housing 后桥箱体
2　supporting seat（横梁）支座
3　lifting eye，hoisting eye 吊眼
4　engine supporting bracket 发动机支撑架
5,7　frame side member（rail）纵梁
6　equalizing beam 平衡梁
8　engine holding frame 发动机托架
9　front cross member（rail）前横梁

5.3.3 Track Assembly 履带总成 (Fig. 5.9)

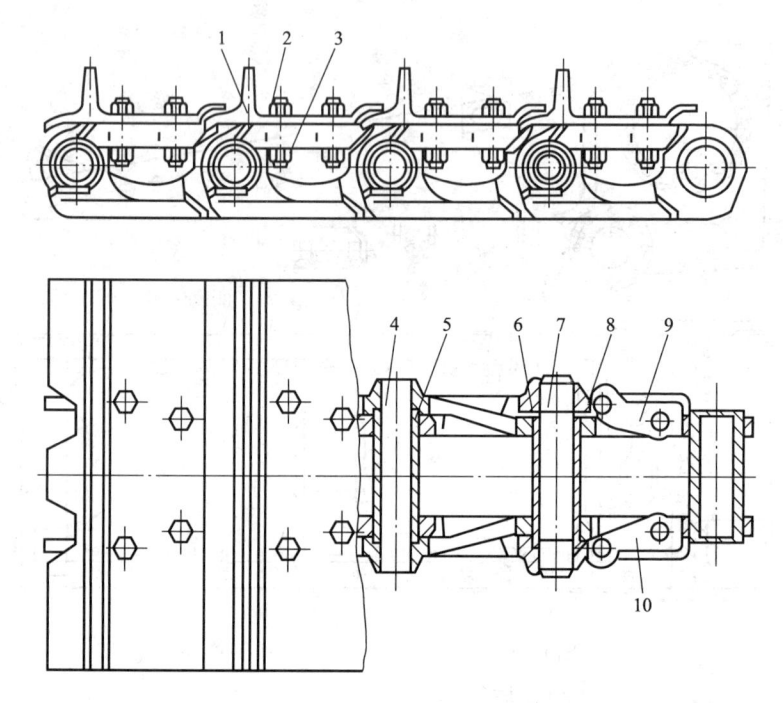

Fig. 5.9 Track assembly 履带总成

1. track shoe 履带板
2. track bolt 履带螺栓
3. track nut 履带螺母
4. track pin 履带销
5. shaft bushing 轴衬
6. washer 垫圈
7. main pin 主销
8. main pin brass 主销铜衬
9. right track link 右链轨节
10. left track link 左链轨节

5.3.4 Track Roller 履带支重轮 (Fig. 5.10)

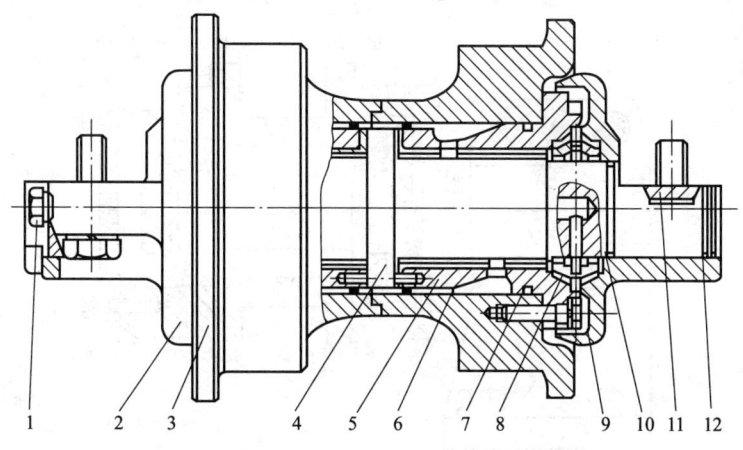

Fig. 5.10 Track roller 履带支重轮

1　oil plug 油塞
2　outer cover （支重轮）外盖
3　wheel hub （支重轮）轮毂
4　wheel shaft （支重轮）轴
5　bearing saddle 轴承座
6　bearing shell 轴瓦
7,10　O-sealing ring O 形密封圈
8　floating oil seal 浮动油封
9　inner cover （支重轮）内盖
11　flat key 平键
12　anti-extrusion ring 挡圈

5.3.5 Carrier Roller 托链轮 (Fig. 5.11)

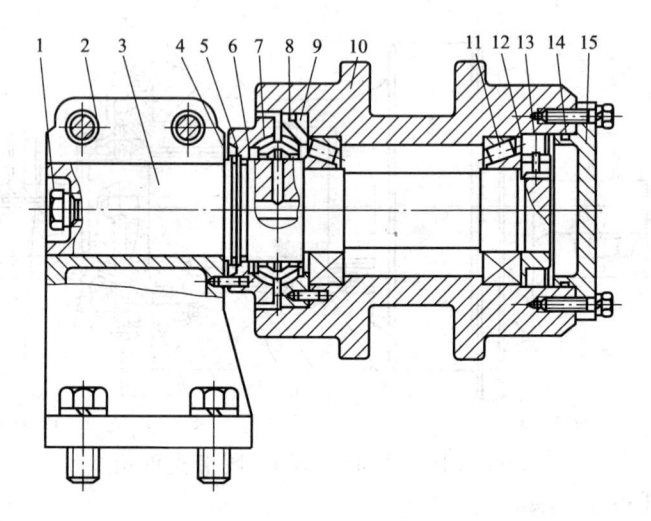

Fig. 5.11 Carrier roller 托链轮

1 oil plug 油塞
2 carrier roller bracket 托轮支架
3 carrier roller shaft 托轮轴
4 anti-extrusion ring 挡圈
5,8,14 O-sealing ring O形密封圈
6 oil sealed cap 油封盖
7 floating oil seal 浮动油封
9 oil sealed seat 油封座
10 carrier roller body 托轮体
11 bearing 轴承
12 lock nut 锁紧螺母
13 spring lock ring 弹性锁圈
15 carrier roller cap 托轮盖

5.3.6 Track Idler 引导轮（Fig. 5.12）

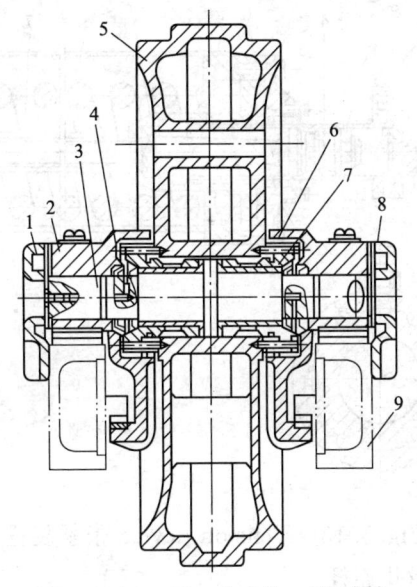

Fig. 5.12 Track idler 引导轮

1　parallel guide cap 导板盖
2　supporting unit 支承装置
3　track idler shaft 引导轮轴
4　floating oil seal 浮动油封
5　track idler body 引导轮体
6　bearing sleeve 轴承衬套
7　bimetallic bearing bush 双金属轴承衬
8　adjusting shim 调整垫片
9　track roller frame 履带台车架

5.3.7 Tension Device 张紧装置 (Fig. 5.13)

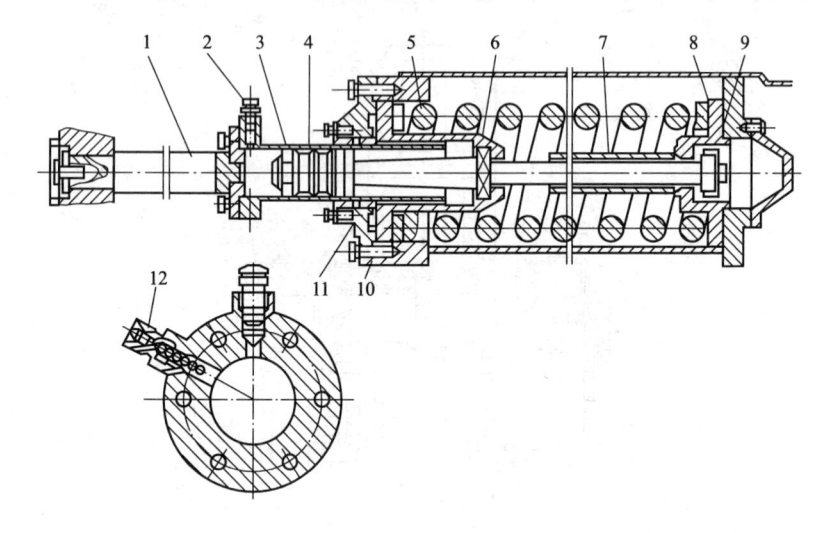

Fig. 5.13 Tension device 张紧装置

1 connecting rod 连杆
2 drain plug 放油塞
3 adjusting device 调整装置
4 piston 活塞
5 tension spring 张紧弹簧
6 sleeve type spring seat 套筒式弹簧座
7 stop tube 止动管
8 spring seat 弹簧座
9 adjusting nut 调整螺母
10 shim 垫片
11 front cover 前盖
12 grease nipple 黄油嘴

5.3.8 Track Frame 台车架（Fig. 5.14）

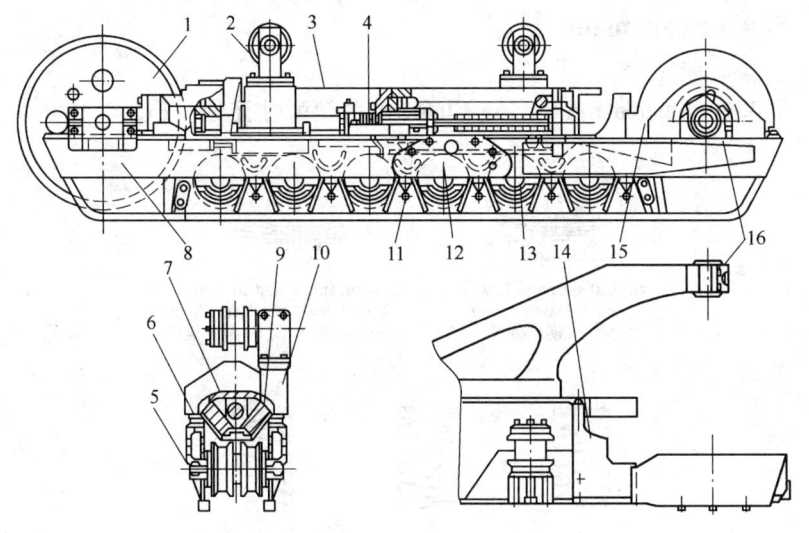

Fig. 5.14　Track frame 台车架

1　track idler 引导轮
2　carrier roller 托链轮
3　center cover （中）罩
4　track adjuster 履带张紧器
5　supporter 托板
6　equalizing beam 平衡梁
7　equalizer 平衡器
8　track roller frame 台车架
9　rubber element （平衡）橡胶元件
10　carrier roller bracket 托轮支架
11　baffle plate 挡板
12　single flange track roller 单边支重轮
13　double flange track roller 双边支重轮
14　rear cover （后）罩
15　drive sprocket cover （驱动轮）罩
16　bearing support 轴承座

5.4 Suspension 悬架

5.4.1 Suspension Spring Element 悬架弹性元件 (Fig. 5.15)

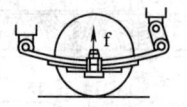

(a) leaf spring 钢板弹簧
multi-leaves spring 多片式钢板弹簧

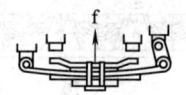

(b) main spring and auxiliary spring, leaf spring and auxiliary spring(载货车)主、副钢板弹簧

tapered end 楔形端

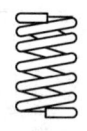

tangential end 正切向端

pig-tail 紧缩端

(c) cylindrical spring 圆柱弹簧

cone spring 锥形弹簧

barrel spring 桶形弹簧

unequally spaced coils spring 不等节矩螺旋弹簧

(d) variable-rate spring 变刚度弹簧

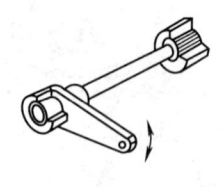

(e) torsion(bar)spring, torsion bar 扭杆弹簧

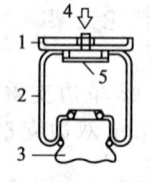

(f) roll bellows 卷翻(膜片)气囊

(g) toroid bellows 环形气囊

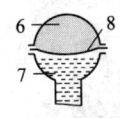

(h) hydraulic diaphragm accumulator 液力膜片式蓄能器

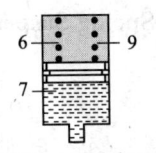

(i) piston accumulator 活塞式蓄能器

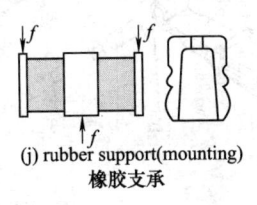

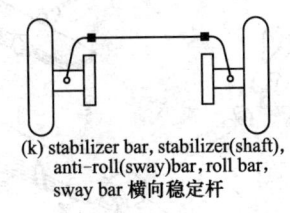

(j) rubber support(mounting) 橡胶支承

(k) stabilizer bar, stabilizer(shaft), anti-roll(sway)bar, roll bar, sway bar 横向稳定杆

Fig. 5.15　Suspension spring element 悬架弹性元件

1　vehicle frame 车架
2　roll bellows 卷翻（膜片）式气囊
3　piston 活塞
4　air supply 气体供给
5　clamping plate 夹板
6　gas 气体
7　fluid 液体
8　diaphragm 膜片
9　steel spring 钢质弹簧

5.4.2 Leaf Spring Suspension 板簧式悬架 (Fig. 5.16)

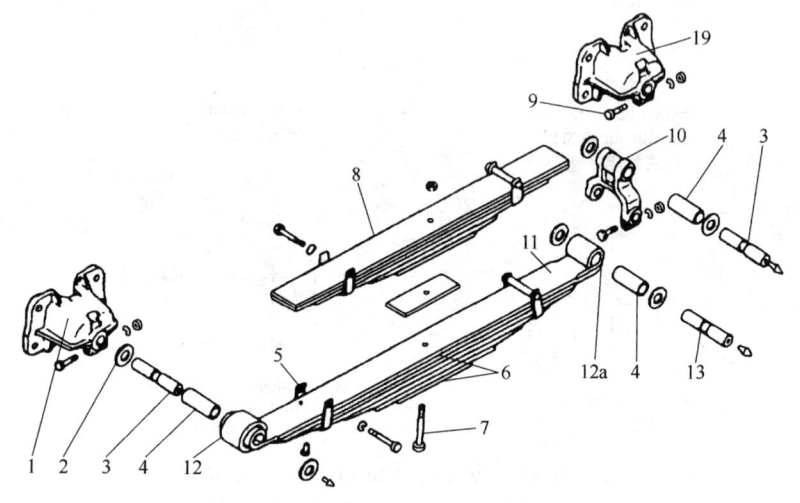

(a) overslung(spring)type, overhung spring type
上置板簧式

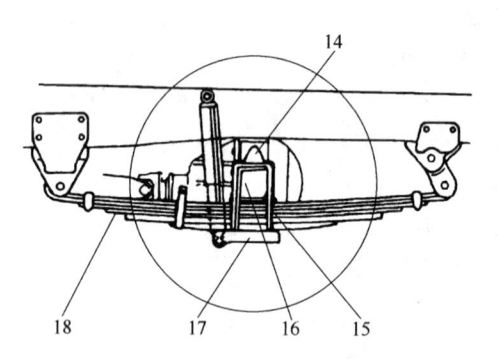

(b) underslung(spring)type, underhung spring type
下置板簧式

(b) Fig. 5.16 Leaf spring suspension 板簧式悬架

138

(a),(b) leaf-spring rear suspension 钢板弹簧式后悬架
1 bracket,hanger,carrier 支架,front bracket 前支架
2 washer 垫圈
3 leaf spring pin,spring pin,spring bolt 钢板弹簧销
4 leaf spring bushing,spring bush(ing)钢板弹簧衬套
5 spring clamp,spring hoop,spring-leaf retainer,spring stirrup 钢板弹簧夹
6 main spring 主钢板弹簧
7 center bolt,centre bolt 中心螺栓
8 auxiliary spring,supplementary (leaf) spring,secondary spring 副钢板弹簧
9 lock bolt(钢板销)锁止螺栓
10 shackle 吊耳
11 main spring leaf 钢板弹簧主片,main leaf 主片 12 spring eye 钢板弹簧卷耳
12a spring free end 钢板弹簧自由(吊耳)端
13 shackle pin 吊耳销
14 bumper,bumper pad,buffer 缓冲块
15 U-bolt,U-clamp U 形螺栓
16 axle housing 桥壳
17 anchor plate 固定底板
18 leaf spring,laminated spring 钢板弹簧
19 rear bracket 后支架

5.4.3 Hydraulic Compensating Axle Suspension 液压平衡悬架 (Fig. 5.17)

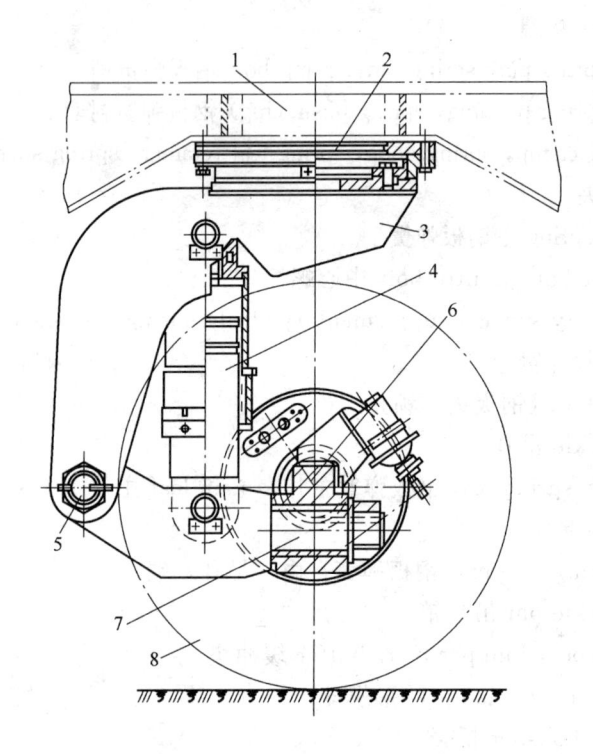

Fig. 5.17 Hydraulic compensating axle suspension 液压平衡悬架
1 supporting beam 支承梁
2 ball bearing turntable 滚珠转盘
3 supporting arm 支承臂
4 suspension cylinder 悬架油缸
5 joint pin 铰销
6 axle 轮轴
7 supporting journal 支承轴颈
8 tyre (tire) 轮胎

5.4.4 Tractor Suspension 拖拉机悬架（Fig. 5.18）

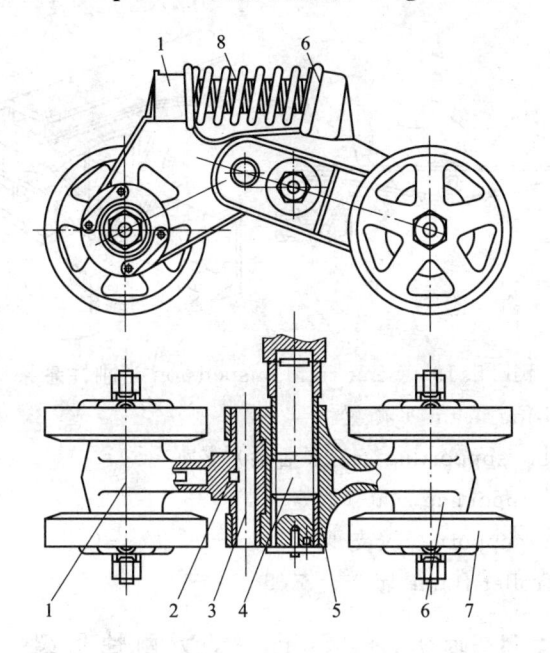

Fig. 5.18　Tractor suspension 拖拉机悬架

1　inside equalizer 内平衡臂
2　pin 销
3　shaft 轴
4　carriage shaft 台车轴
5　bushing，sleeve 衬套
6　outside equalizer 外平衡臂
7　track roller 支重轮
8　suspension spring 悬架弹簧

5.4.5 Semi-rigid Suspension 半刚性悬架 (Fig. 5.19)

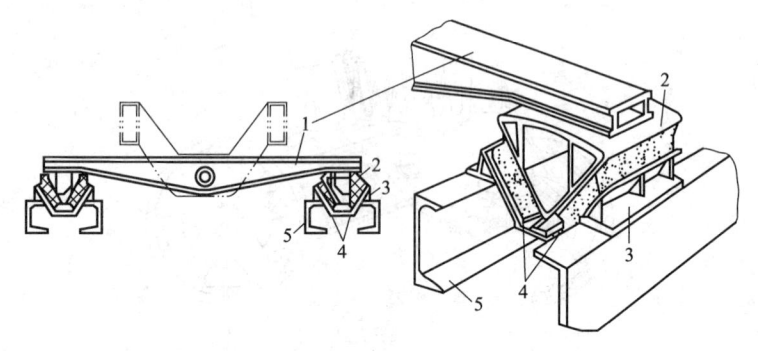

Fig. 5.19 Semi-rigid suspension 半刚性悬架
1　equalizing beam 平衡梁
2　movable supporting seat （活动）支座
3　fixed supporting seat （固定）支座
4　rubber support 橡胶支承
5　track roller frame 履带台车架

5.4.6 Rigid Suspension (Swing Axle) 刚性悬架（摆动桥）(Fig. 5.20)

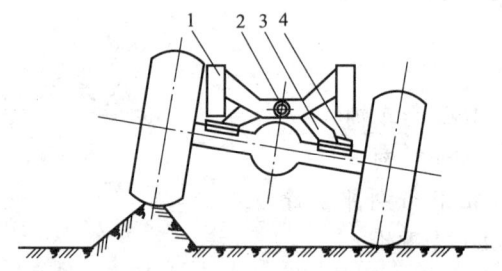

Fig. 5.20 Rigid suspension (swing axle) 刚性悬架（摆动桥）
1　rear frame 后车架
2　axis pin 销轴
3　sub-frame 副车架
4　stop block 限位块

5.4.7 Telescopic Shock Absorber 筒式减振器 (Fig. 5.21)

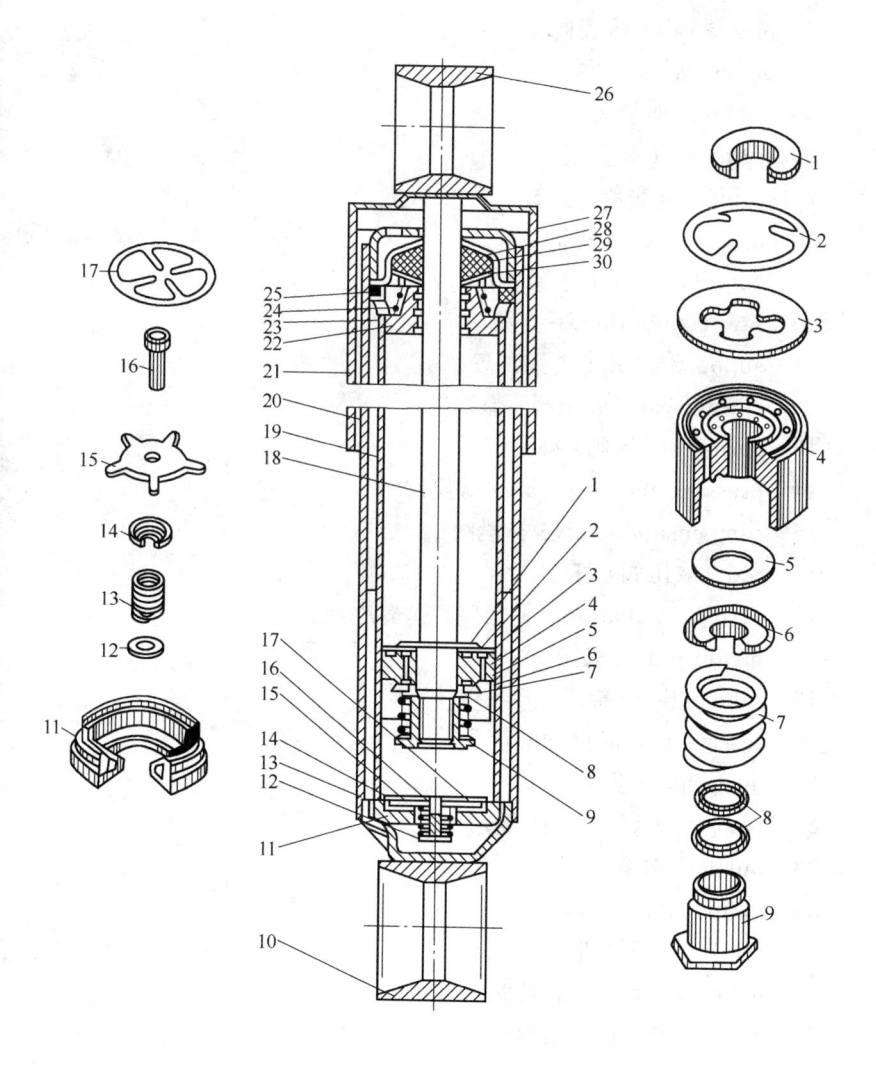

Fig. 5.21 Telescopic shock absorber 筒式减振器

1 spacing collar（流通阀）限位圈
2 spring lamination（流通阀）弹簧片
3 intake valve 流通阀
4 piston 活塞
5 stretcher 伸张器
6 spring seat 弹簧座
7 spring（伸张阀）弹簧
8 adjusting shim 调整垫片
9 compression nut 压紧螺母
10 lower mounting 下支承
11 supporting unit 支承装置
12 spring seat（减压阀）弹簧座
13 spring（减压阀）弹簧
14 pressure-reducing valve 减压阀
15 compensation valve 补偿阀
16 rod（减压阀）杆
17 spring lamination（补偿阀）弹簧片
18 piston rod 活塞杆
19 tube（工作）筒
20 reservoir tube 储油缸筒
21 dust shield 防尘罩
22 rod guide（活塞）杆导管
23 bushing 衬套
24 spring（油封）弹簧
25 seal ring 密封圈
26 upper mounting 上支承
27 nut（储油缸筒）螺母
28 oil seal 油封
29 outer case of seal 油封外壳
30 washer（油封）垫圈

Unit 6 Braking System
制 动 系 统

6.1 General 概述

Vehicle brakes must be able to stop the vehicle, prevent excess speed when coasting, and hold the vehicle in position when stopped on grades. They are designed so that the braking effect can be varied by the driver to keep the vehicle under control. Each vehicle must have two independent brake systems for safety. The main brake system is hydraulically operated and is called the service brake system. The secondary or parking brake system is mechanically operated. The automobile brake systems are divided into three types of service brake combinations: drum brake, disc brakes and disc-drum combinations.

车辆制动器必须能使行驶的车辆停车,防止滑行时的车速过大,并将已停在斜坡上的车辆保持不动。设计的制动器,其制动力要能受驾驶员控制,从而控制车辆。为安全起见,每辆车辆有两套独立的制动系。主制动系是液压制动系,通常称为行车制动系。次制动系或驻车制动系是机械制动系。行车制动系又有三种类型:鼓式制动系、盘式制动系和盘-鼓结合式制动系。

6.2 Types of Brake 制动器类型 (Fig. 6.1)

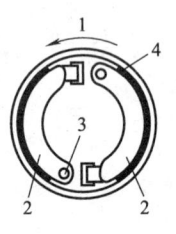

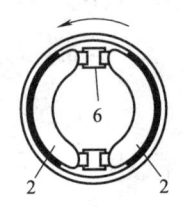

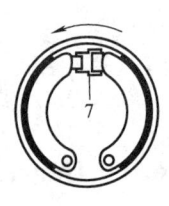

(a) 2LS brake=double(two)-leading shoe brake 双领蹄式制动器,2L式制动器

(b) two trailing shoe brake 双从蹄式制动器,2T式制动器

(c) duo two leading shoe brake with stepped wheel cylinder 双向双领蹄式制动器,D2L式制动器

(d) leading trailing shoe brake with stepped wheel cylinder 带异径轮缸的领从蹄式制动器

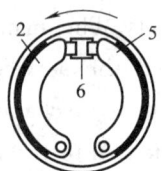

(e) L/TS brake=leading trailing shoe brake 领从蹄式制动器,LT式制动器

(f) US brake=uni-servo brake 单向伺服式制动器,US式制动器

(g) DS brake=duo-servo brake 双向伺服式制动器,DS式制动器

(h) band brake 带式制动器,external contracting drum brake 外收缩型鼓式制动器

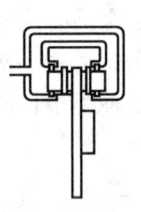

(i) disc(disk) brake with fixed caliper 定钳盘式制动器

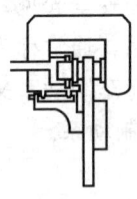

(j) disc(disk) brake with floating caliper 浮钳盘式制动器

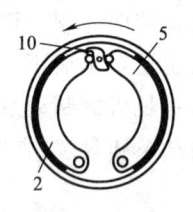

(k) cam(-actuated) brake 凸轮张开式制动器

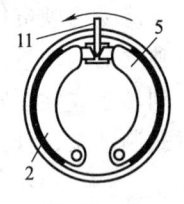

(l) wedge(-actuated, -operated) brake 楔(块作动)式制动器

Fig. 6.1 Types of brake 制动器类型

（a）～（g） internal expanding drum brake 内胀型鼓式制动器，
wheel cylinder brake 轮缸式制动器
（a）～（h） drum brake 鼓式制动器
（i）、（j） caliper disc brake 钳盘式制动器
（a）～（l） friction brake 摩擦片式制动器
1　direction of drum rotation 鼓转动方向
2　leading shoe 领蹄
3　anchor pin 支承销，fixed brake shoe abutment 制动蹄支承
4　friction lining 制动衬片，摩擦片
5　trailing shoe 从蹄
6　wheel cylinder 轮缸，straight-bore wheel cylinder 直筒（双活塞）轮缸
6a　single-piston wheel cylinder 单活塞轮缸
7　stepped wheel cylinder 异径（阶梯形）轮缸
8　brake drum 制动鼓
9　brake band 制动带
10　S-cam S形凸轮
11　wedge 楔块

6.2.1 Drum Type Brake 鼓式（蹄式）制动器

(1) Cam Brake 凸轮张开式制动器 (Fig. 6.2)

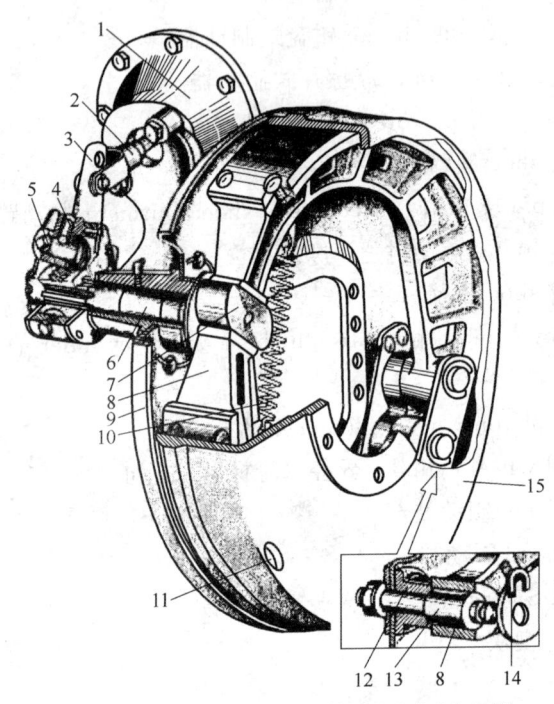

Fig. 6.2 Cam brake 凸轮张开式制动器

1　brake chamber 制动气室
2　push rod 推杆
3　adjusting arm 调整臂
4　worm screw 蜗杆
5　worm gear 蜗轮
6　camshaft 凸轮轴
7　cam 凸轮
8　brake shoe 制动蹄
9　brake base plate 制动底板
10　back spring 回位弹簧
11　inspection hole 检视孔
12　anchor pin pedestal 支承销座
13　off centre anchor pin 偏心支承销
14　brake shoe lock-plate 制动蹄锁片
15　brake drum 制动鼓

(2) Oil Pressure Brake 油压张开式制动器 (Fig. 6.3)

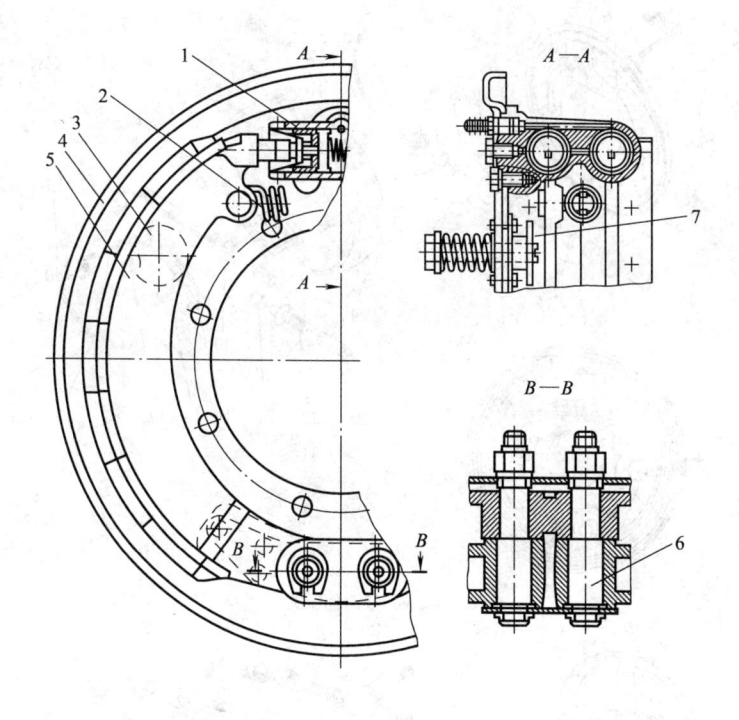

Fig. 6.3　Oil pressure brake 油压张开式制动器

1　wheel braking cylinder 制动轮缸
2　back spring 回位弹簧
3　adjusting cam 调整凸轮
4　brake drum 制动鼓
5　brake shoe 制动蹄
6　off centre anchor pin 偏心支承销
7　additional hold-down mechanism 附加压紧机构

（3）Drum Brake Structural Components 鼓式制动器结构零件 (Fig. 6.4)

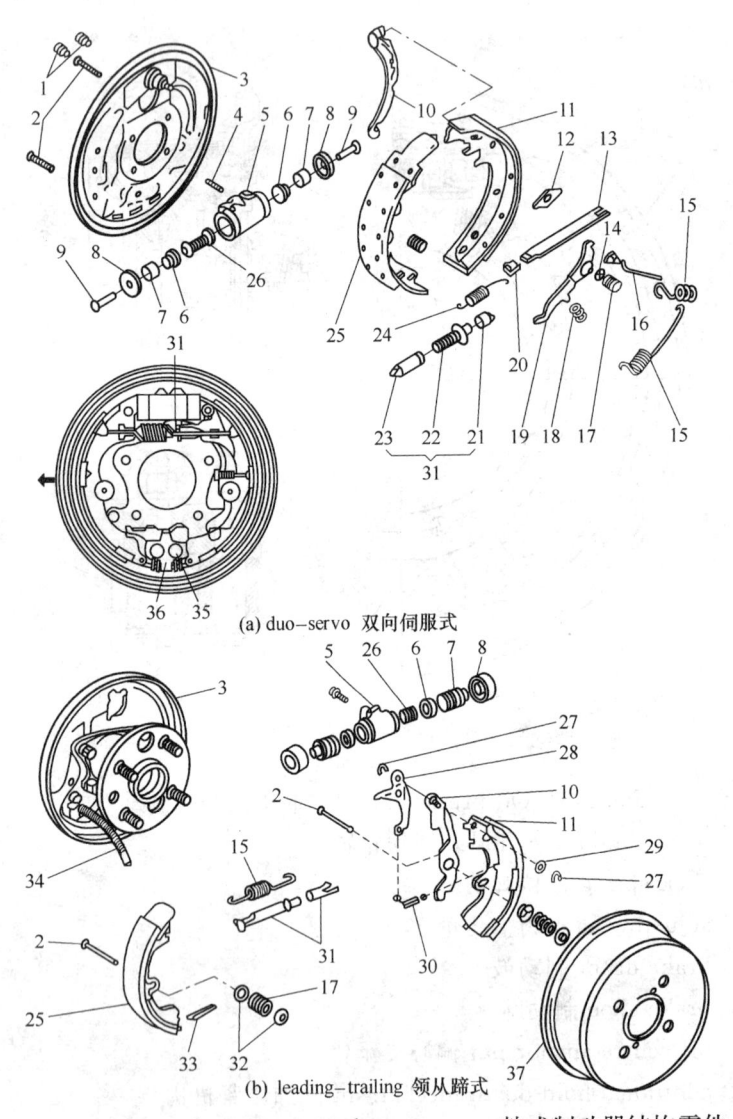

(a) duo-servo 双向伺服式

(b) leading-trailing 领从蹄式

Fig. 6.4 Drum brake structural components 鼓式制动器结构零件

1 bolt 螺栓
2 hold-down pin 限位销，压紧销
3 backing plate, base plate, bottom plate（制动器）底板
4 bleeder valve 放气阀
5 cylinder body 缸筒
6 seal 密封圈，cup 皮碗，皮圈
7 piston 活塞
8 boot 防尘罩
5＋6＋7＋8＋26 wheel cylinder 轮缸
9 cylinder link 轮缸推杆
10 parking brake lever 驻车制动杠杆
11 trailing shoe, secondary shoe 从蹄, trailing shoe and lining, secondary shoe assembly 从蹄总成
12 shoe guide 蹄导板
13 parking brake strut（pushrod）驻车制动推杆
14 lever pivot 作动杠杆支枢
15 return spring（制动蹄）回位弹簧
16 actuator link 作动连杆
17 hold-down spring 限位（压紧）弹簧
18 lever return spring 作动杠杆回位弹簧
19 actuator lever 作动杠杆
20 strut spring 撑杆弹簧
21 socket（调节螺钉）支座
22 adjusting screw（制动蹄间隙）调节螺钉
23 pivot nut 支枢螺母
24 adjusting screw spring 调节螺钉弹簧
25 leading shoe, primary shoe 领蹄, leading shoe and lining, leading shoe assembly 领蹄总成
26 spring（制动轮缸）弹簧
27 C-washer C 形垫圈
28 automating adjusting lever 自动调节杠杆
29 adjusting shim 调节垫片
30 spring（自动调节杠杆）弹簧
31 adjusting（＝21＋22＋23）（制动蹄间隙）调器, adjusting screw assembly 调节螺钉总成, lash adjusting device 间隙调整装置
32 hold-down cup（制动蹄）限位盘，压紧盘
33 anchor spring 支承块弹簧
34 parking brake cable 驻车制动器拉索
35 anchor pin 支承销
36 anchor plate, anchor 支承块，支承板
37 brake drum 制动鼓

6.2.2 Caliper Disk Brake 钳盘式制动器 (Fig. 6.5)

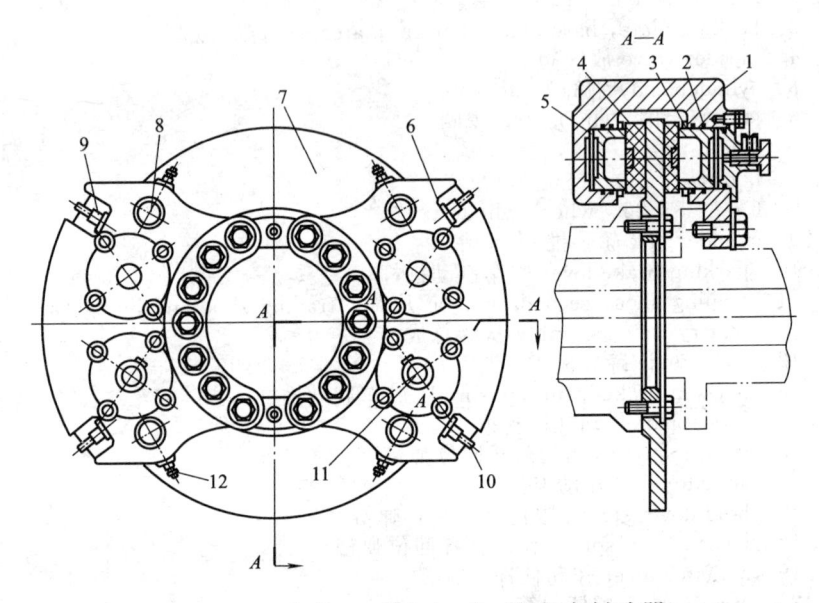

Fig. 6.5 Caliper disk brake 钳盘式制动器

1　caliper 制动钳
2　oil seal ring 油封圈
3　dust ring 防尘圈
4　brake pad 制动衬块
5　oil cylinder piston 油缸活塞
6　washer 垫片
7　brake disk 制动盘
8　guide pin 导向销
9　bleed nipple 放气嘴
10　oil pipe 油管
11　pipe joint 管接头
12　stop screw 止动螺钉

（1）Automatic Clearance Compensator 自动间隙补偿装置 (Fig. 6.6)

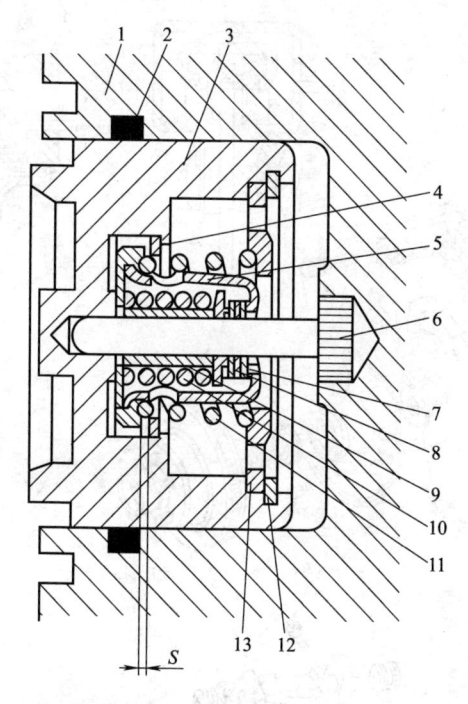

Fig. 6.6 Automatic clearance compensator 自动间隙补偿装置

1　cylinder body 缸体
2　seal ring 密封圈
3　piston 活塞
4　snap ring 卡环
5　casing 罩壳
6　pin rod 销轴
7　friction snap ring 摩擦卡环
8　spring seat 弹簧座
9　bushing 导管
10　spring 弹簧
11　piston back spring 活塞回位弹簧
12　check ring 挡圈
13　cover plate 盖板

（2）Structural Components 结构零件（Fig. 6.7）

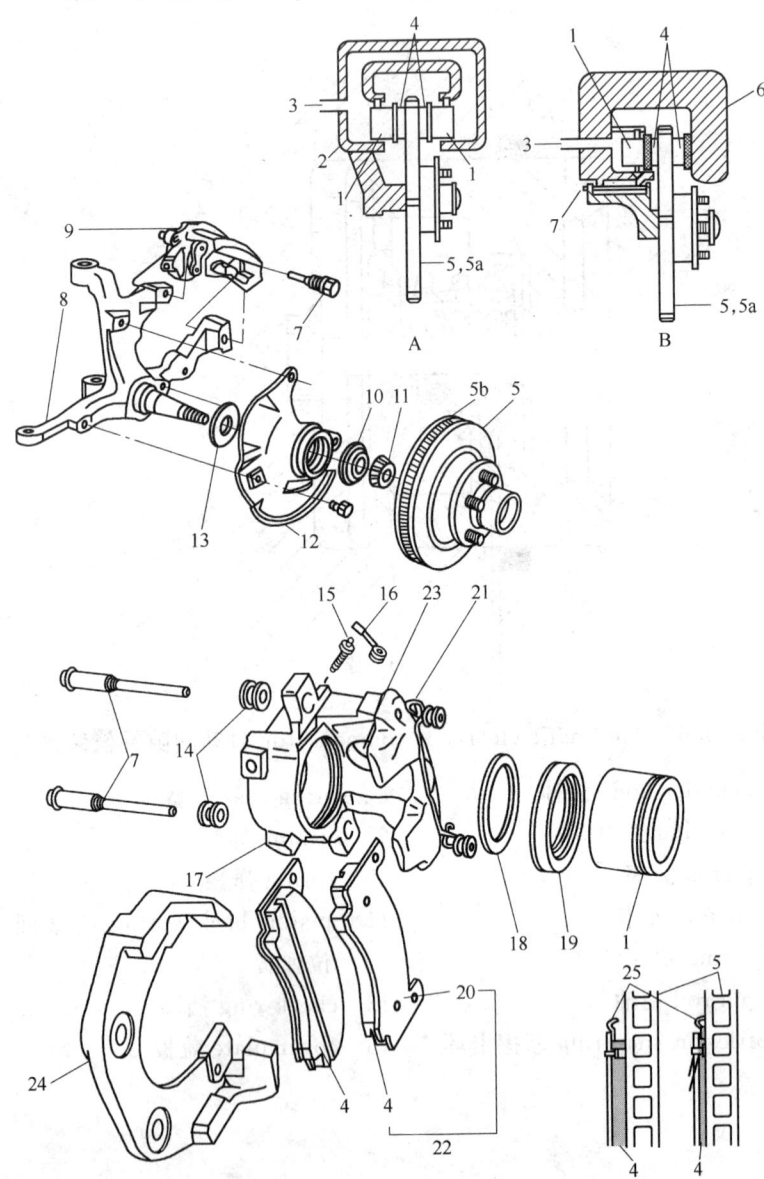

Fig. 6.7 Structural components 结构零件

A fixed (brake) cal (1) iper, stationary cal (1) iper 定钳（式），Two-piston caliper 双活塞式制动钳
B floating (brake) cal (1) iper, movable cal (1) iper, sliding cal (1) iper, moving caliper 浮钳（式），single-piston caliper 单活塞式制动钳
1 piston 活塞
2 fixed caliper 固定钳
3 hydraulic pressure 液压
4 brake pad, brake lining 制动衬块，friction pad 摩擦块
5 brake disc (disc, rotor) 制动盘
5a solid rotor (disc, disk) 整体式制动盘
5b ventilated brake disk (disc), ventilated rotor 通风式制动盘
6 floating caliper 浮钳
7 guide pin, locating pin 导销，sliding pin 滑动销
8 combination spindle and anchor plate 带锚定板的转向节
9 caliper assy 制动钳总成
10 grease retainer 润滑脂保持器
11 inner bearing 内轴承
12 splash shield 防溅罩
13 gasket 垫圈
14 bushing, sleeve 衬套
15 bleeder valve (screw) 放气阀
16 cap (放气阀) 帽
17 brake cal (1) iper body, caliper housing 3
18 seal 密封圈
19 dust boot 防尘罩
20 backing plate (制动衬块) 背板
21 anti-rattle clip 防振夹，anti-squeal (rattle) spring 消声（防啸声）弹簧
22 brake pad assembly 制动衬块总成
23 inspection hole（制动衬块磨损）检查孔
24 anchor bracket, adapter（制动钳）支架，支承板，brake caliper mounting bracket 制动钳安装支架，torque plate 转矩板（丰田公司用法）
25 wear indicator 磨损指示器，brake lining wear sensor 制动衬块磨损传感器

6.2.3 Dry-type Complete Disc Brake 干式全盘式制动器 (Fig. 6.8)

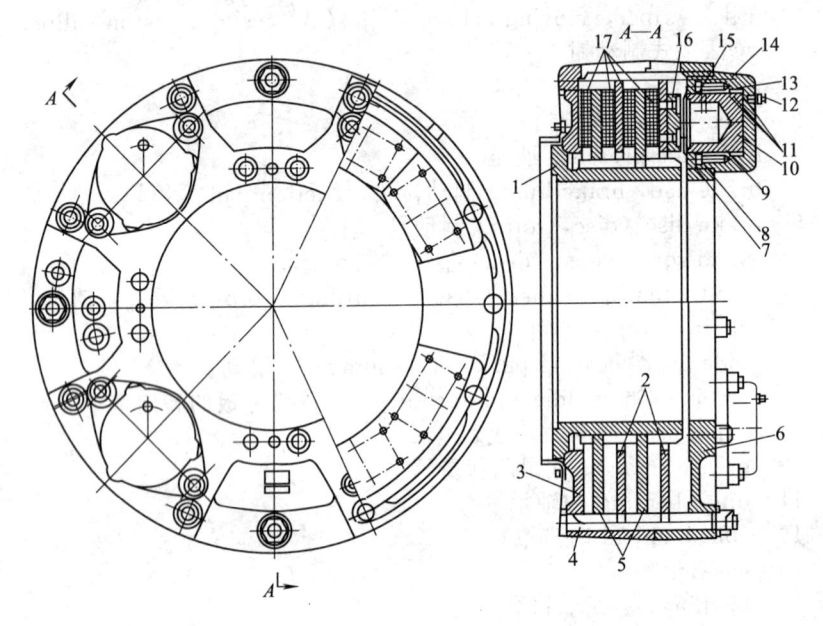

Fig. 6.8 Dry-type complete disc brake 干式全盘式制动器

1 rotating spline drum 旋转花键鼓
2 fixed brake disk 固定制动盘
3 housing 外壳
4 key bolt 带键螺栓
5 rotating brake disk 旋转制动盘
6 inner cap 内盖
7 adjusting thread check ring 调整螺纹挡圈
8 piston back spring 活塞回位弹簧
9 piston sleeve 活塞套筒
10 piston 活塞
11 piston seal ring 活塞密封圈
12 air bleed screw 放气螺钉
13 sleeve seal ring 套筒密封圈
14 cylinder body 油缸缸体
15 spring cap 弹簧座盘
16 cushion block 垫块
17 friction liner 摩擦衬片

6.2.4 Band Brake 带式制动器 (Fig. 6.9 and Fig. 6.10)

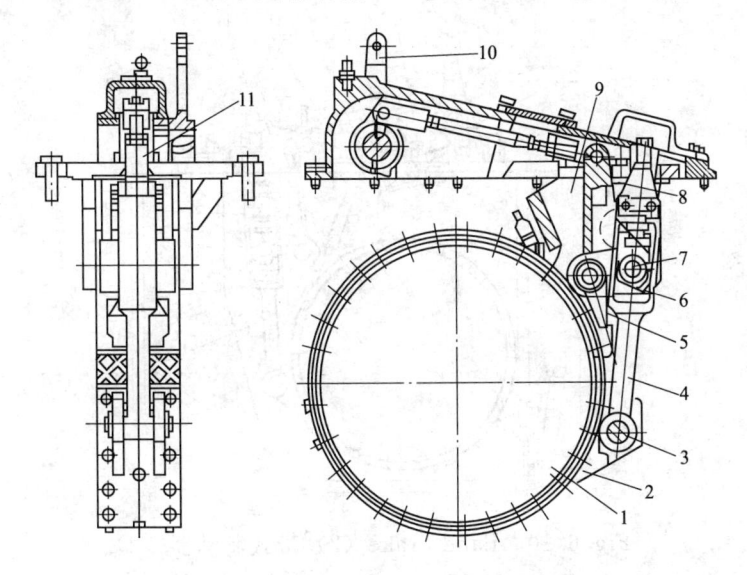

Fig. 6.9 Band brake (1) 带式制动器 (1)

1 brake drum 制动鼓
2 brake band 制动带
3 pin 销子
4 tension rod bar 拉杆
5 carrier rod 顶杆
6 front anchor pin 前支承销
7 rear anchor pin 后支承销
8 bell crank lever 双臂曲柄杆
9 support (bracket) 支架
10 operating lever 操纵杆
11 adjust screw 调整螺钉

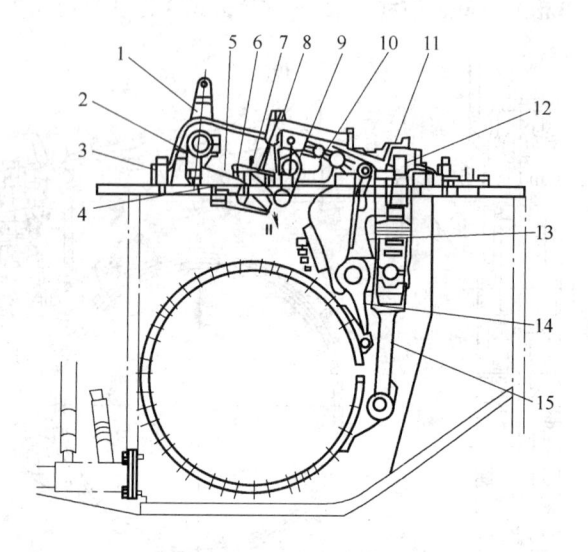

Fig. 6.10　Band brake (2) 带式制动器 (2)

1　upper rocker arm 上摇臂
2　lower rocker arm 下摇臂
3　brake cover 制动器盖
4　slide valve 滑阀
5　spring 弹簧
6　bush 衬套
7　cylinder 油缸
8　piston 活塞
9　rocker arm 摇臂
10　linkage 连接杆
11　spring 弹簧
12　adjusting bolt 调整螺栓
13　lever 杠杆
14　pawl 棘爪
15　adjusting rod 调整杆

6.2.5 Parking Brake 驻车制动器 (Fig. 6.11)

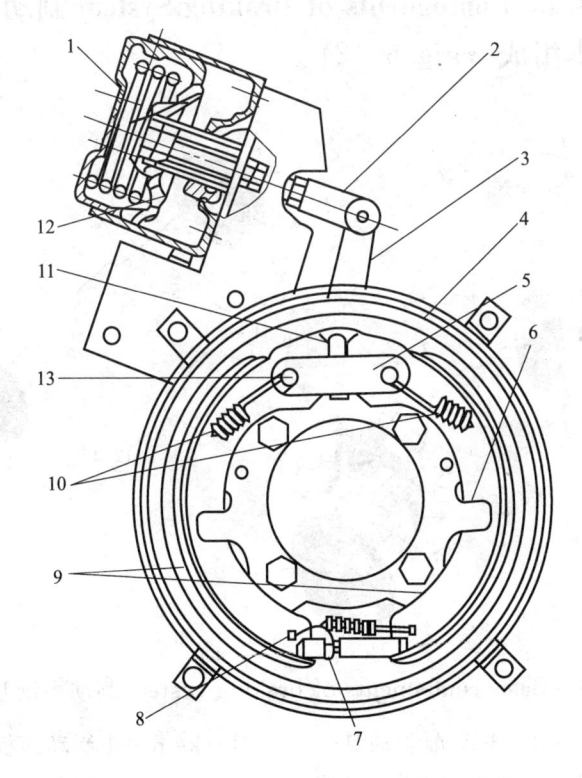

Fig. 6.11　Parking brake 驻车制动器

1　spring 弹簧
2　connecting rod 连杆
3　rocker arm 摇臂
4　brake drum 制动鼓
5　orifice plate 挡板
6　brake base plate 制动底板
7　adjusting rod 调整杆
8　spring 弹簧
9　brake shoe 制动蹄
10　back spring 复位弹簧
11　cam 凸轮
12　piston 活塞
13　anchor pin 支承销

6.3 Basic Components of Braking System 制动系统基本组成（Fig. 6.12）

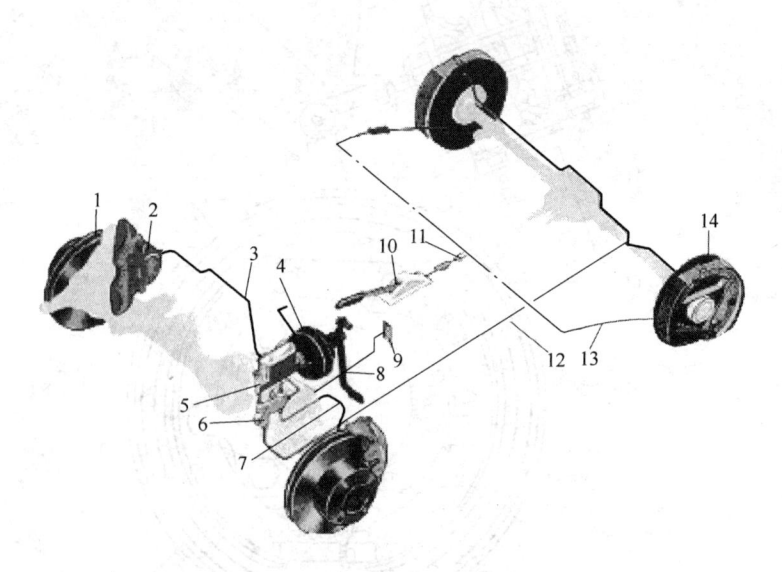

Fig. 6.12 Basic components of braking system 制动系统基本组成

1 front brake disk 前制动盘
2 caliper assembly 制动钳总成
3 brake line, RF 右前制动油管
4 vacuum booster 真空助力器
5 master cylinder assembly 制动主缸总成
6 brake combination valve 组合阀
7 brake line, LF 左前制动油管
8 brake pedal 制动踏板
9 brake warning lamp 报警灯
10 parking brake lever 驻车制动操纵杆
11 equalizer 平衡架
12 rear brake line 后制动油管
13 parking brake cable 驻车制动拉线
14 rear brake assembly 后制动器总成

6.4 Braking Control System 制动操纵系统

6.4.1 Manpower Brake System 人力制动系统 (Fig. 6.13)

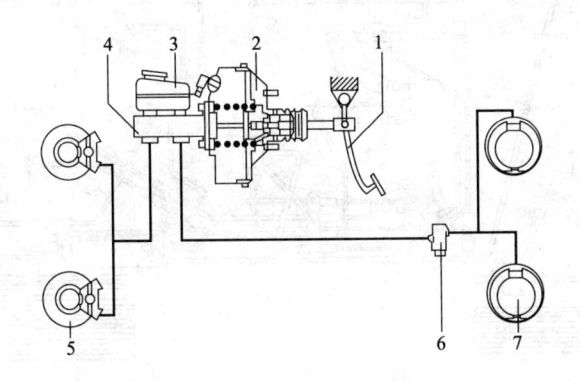

Fig. 6.13 Manpower brake system 人力制动系统

1 brake pedal 制动踏板
2 vacuum booster 真空助力器
3 brake-fluid reservoir 制动油箱
4 tandem master cylinder assembly 串联制动主缸总成
5 disk brake 盘式制动器
6 braking-force regulator 制动力调节器
7 drum brake 鼓式（蹄式）制动器

6.4.2 Typical Air Brake System 典型气制动系统 (Fig. 6.14)

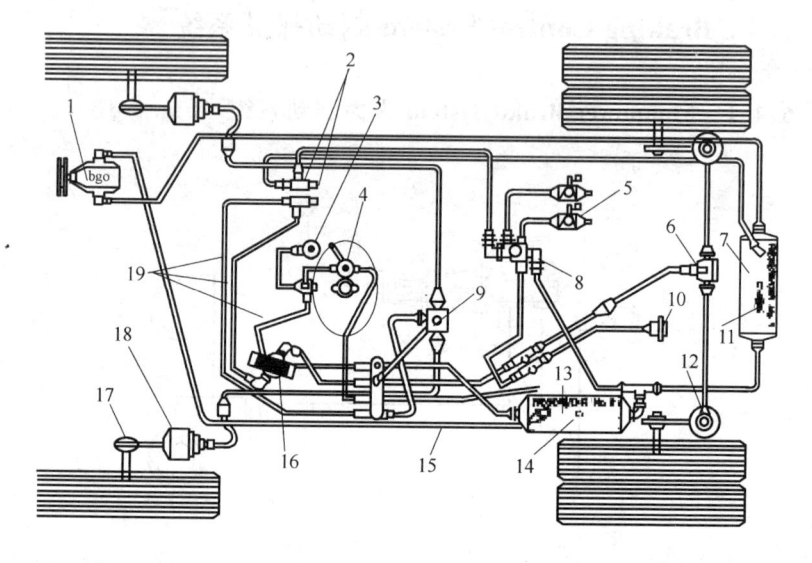

Fig. 6.14 Typical air brake system 典型气制动系统

1 air compressor 空气压缩机
2 two-way valve 二通阀
3 air gauge 气压表
4 hand brake valve 手制动阀
5 service and emergency connection 维护与应急接口
6 quick-release valve 快放阀
7,13 air reservoir 储气筒
8 trailer protection valve 拖车保护阀
9 limiting quick-release valve 极限快放阀
10 stoplight switch 刹车灯开关
11 safety valve 安全阀
12,18 brake chamber 制动气室
14 drain cock 排气阀
15 double check valve 双单向阀
16 foot brake valve 脚制动阀
17 slack adjuster 松紧调节器
19 flexible rubber hose 软胶管

6.4.3 Double Pipeline Air Boost Brake System 双管路空气增压制动系统 (Fig. 6.15)

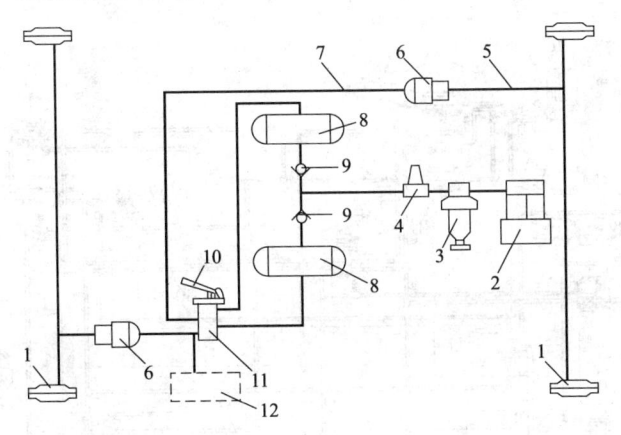

Fig. 6.15 Double pipeline air boost brake system
双管路空气增压制动系统

1 disk brake 盘式制动器
2 air compressor 空气压缩机
3 oil-water separator 油水分离器
4 pressure regulator 压力调节器
5 oil pipe 油管
6 air over hydraulic booster 气顶油加力器
7 compressed air pipe 压缩空气管路
8 air reservoir 储气筒
9 check valve 单向阀
10 brake pedal 制动踏板
11 brake valve 制动阀
12 gearbox control valve 变速箱操纵阀

6.4.4 Electronic Brake System（EBS）电子制动系统 (Fig. 6.16)

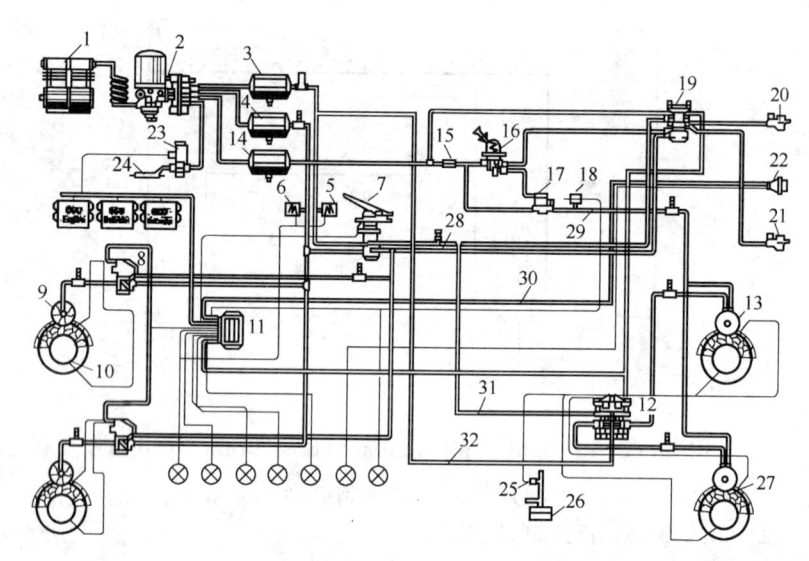

Fig. 6.16 Electronic brake system（EBS）电子制动系统

1　compressor 空气压缩机
2　oil-water separator 油水分离器
3,4,14　air reservoir 储气筒
5,6　pressure switch circuit 压力开关电路
7　foot brake 脚制动器
8,12　EBS channel module 电子制动系统信道组件
9　brake chamber 制动气室
10　sensing ring and speed sensor 感应环与速度传感器
11　ECU 电子控制单元
13　spring brake 弹簧刹车
15　check valve 单向阀
16　hand brake valve 手制动阀
17　relay valve 中继阀
18　pressure switch 压力开关
19　EBS trailer control module EBS 拖车控制模块
20　coupling head supply 拖车制动接头供气
21　coupling head control 车制动接头控制
22　EBS connection EBS 信道连接
23　solenoid valve 电磁阀
24　exhaust braking cylinder 排气制动缸
25　pressure sensor 压力传感器
26　air spring bellow 空气弹簧气囊
27　wear sensor 制动磨损传感器
28　test connector 测试接头
29　parking brake pipeline 驻车制动管路
30　CAN-signal 信号 CAN 总线
31　service brake pipeline 行车制动管路
32　air supply pipeline 制动供气管路

164

6.5 Antilock Brake System（ABS）防抱死制动系统 (Fig. 6.17)

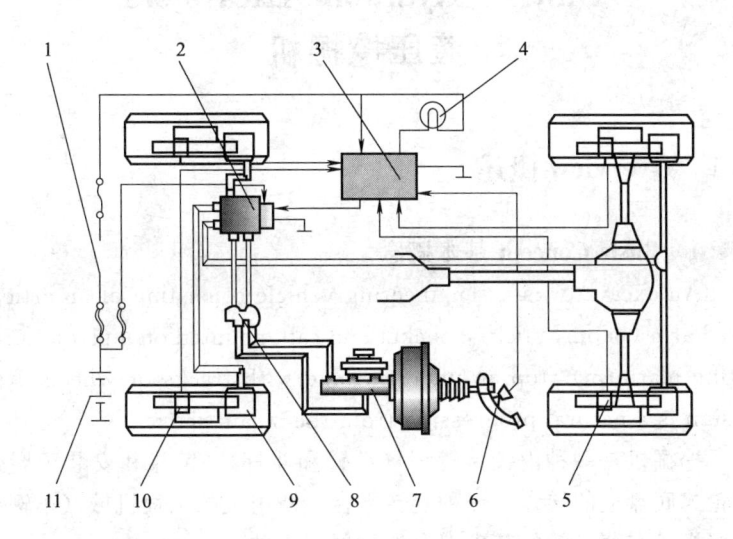

Fig. 6.17 Antilock brake system（ABS）防抱死制动系统

1   ignition switch 点火开关
2   brake pressure regulator 制动压力调节装置
3   electronic control unit（ECU）电子控制单元
4   alarm lamp 报警灯
5   rear wheel speed sensor 后轮速度传感器
6   brake pedal and parking lamp switch 制动踏板与停车灯开关
7   master cylinder 制动主缸
8   proportional distributing valve 比例分配阀
9   wheel braking cylinder 制动轮缸
10   front wheel speed sensor 前轮速度传感器
11   storage battery 蓄电池

Unit 7 Hydraulic Excavators
液压挖掘机

7.1 Overview 概述

7.1.1 Basic Concept 基本概念

An excavator is an engineering vehicle consisting of an articulated arm (boom, stick), bucket and cab mounted on a pivot (a rotating platform) atop an undercarriage with tracks or wheels. It's design is a natural progression from the steam shovel.

挖掘机是一种由铰接臂杆（动臂和斗杆）、铲斗和安装于履带或轮式底盘上的转盘（一种旋转平台）所组成的工程机械（车辆）。挖掘机是在蒸气铲的基础上自然发展起来的。

The history of heavy excavating machinery began in 1835 when the dipper shovel was invented to excavate hard soil and rock and to load trucks. Of course, with the invention of gasoline-and diesel-powered vehicles, construction equipment became even more adaptable. Most construction equipment is powered by diesel engines, although electric-power, battery power, and propane tanks are used on specialized equipment.

重型挖掘机的历史始于1835年，当时发明了拉铲式挖掘机用于开挖坚硬的土石方及装载卡车。当然，随着汽油机和柴油机车辆的发明，工程机械也变得越来越适用。虽然在一些专用设备上使用了电力驱动、蓄电池驱动和丙烷气罐，然而大多数工程机械仍然依靠柴油机驱动。

Design modifications are driven by customer demand. Since 2000, the two primary areas where customers would like to see more improvements are in the ease of operation and the operator's comfort. The need for simple operation is forced by the fact that there are fewer skilled operators in the marketplace. And operations and reliability are both improving because of the continuing integration of electronics, automation, better engine technology, and on-board diagnostics. It is now up to the manufacturers to cost-effectively incorporate improvements.

客户要求推动着设计的改进。自从 2000 年以来，客户所期望改进的两个主要方面为操作的方便性和舒适性。操作简单的要求迫于在市场中很难找到熟练操作人员的事实。由于电子技术、自动化、高性能发动机技术、在线诊断技术的不断集成，操作性和可靠性均得到了不断的改进。目前，制造商在进行各种成本效益方面的改进。

7.1.2　Applications 应用 （Fig. 7.1）

(a) digging and loading 挖掘装载

(b) stonework 石方工程

(c) mining engineering 采掘工程

(d) port operation 港口作业

Fig. 7.1

(e) trench excavation 开挖坑槽

(f) take down old buildings 建筑拆除

(g) rock breaking 岩石破碎

(h) under water operation 水下作业

(i) pipe laying 铺设管道

(j) hoisting heavy object 起吊重物

Fig. 7.1

(k) breaking pavement 破碎路面

(l) clear up side slope 整理边坡

(m) watercourse clearance 疏通水道

(n) removal treatment 清理作业

Fig. 7.1 Applications of excavator 挖掘机的应用

7.1.3 Types 类型（Fig. 7.2）

(a) mini type excavator 微型挖掘机

(b) small type excavator 小型挖掘机

Fig. 7.2

(c) medium type excavator 中型挖掘机

(d) large type excavator 大型挖掘机

(e) wheel excavator 轮式挖掘机

(f) large type shovel(face excavator)
大型正铲挖掘机

(g) ultra high demolition hydraulic excavator
超高层建筑物拆除液压挖掘机

(h) river channel dredging excavator
河道疏浚挖掘机

Fig. 7.2

(i) telescopic boom excavator
伸缩臂式挖掘机

(j) wetlands excavator
湿地挖掘机

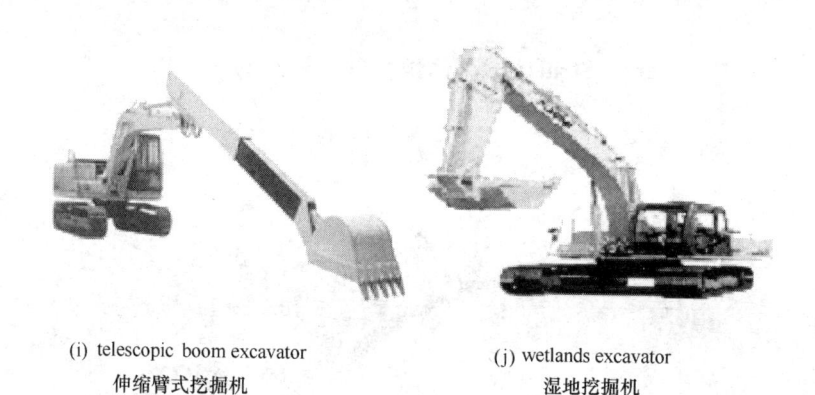

(k) wheel backhoe loader
轮式挖掘装载机

(l) radio controlled excavator
无线控制型挖掘机

Fig. 7.2　Types of excavator 挖掘机的类型

7.2 Components and Features 组成与特点

7.2.1 Overall Structure 总体结构 (Fig. 7.3)

Fig. 7.3 Overall structure 总体结构

1 diesel engine and hydraulic system 柴油机及液压系统
2 undercarriage 行走支承机构
3 swing mechanism 回转机构
4 work equipment assembly 工作装置总成
5 steering and operating system 转向操纵系统

7.2.2 Major Components 主要部件

(1) Diesel Engine and Hydraulic System 柴油机及液压系统 (Fig. 7.4)

Fig. 7.4　Diesel engine and hydraulic system 柴油机及液压系统
1　diesel engine 柴油机
2　hydraulic pump 液压泵

（2）Undercarriage 行走支承机构（Fig. 7.5）

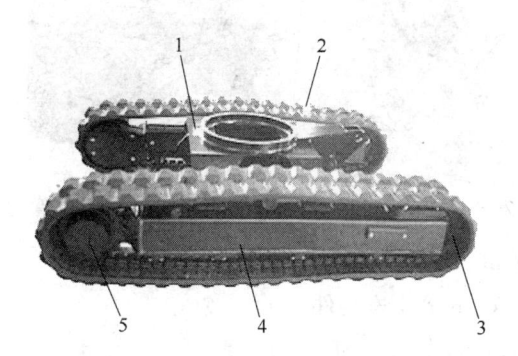

Fig. 7.5　Undercarriage 行走支承机构

1　main frame 主机架
2　track 履带
3　track idler 导向轮
4　track frame 履带台车架
5　final drive（driving motor and drive sprocket）最终传动装置（液压马达与驱动链轮）

(3) Work Equipment Assembly 工作装置总成 (Fig. 7.6)

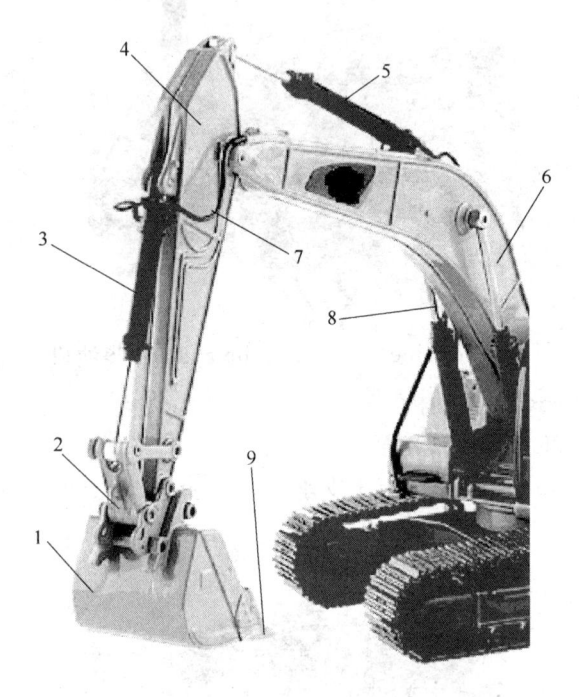

Fig. 7.6 Work equipment assembly 工作装置总成

1　bucket 铲斗
2　bucket linkage 铲斗连接件
3　bucket cylinder 铲斗油缸
4　arm 斗杆
5　arm cylinder 斗杆油缸
6　boom 动臂
7　hydraulic pipeline 液压管路
8　boom cylinder 动臂油缸
9　bucket lip 斗齿

(4) General Purpose Bucket 通用铲斗 (Fig. 7.7)

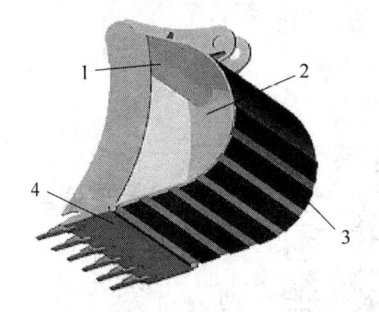

Fig. 7.7　General purpose bucket 通用铲斗
1　anti-torsion pipe fitted for increased strength 抗扭增强钢管
2　two piece side plates 两边侧板
3　wear straps fitted to increase base strength 斗底增强耐磨板条
4　cutting edge 切削刃

(5) Steering and Operating System 转向操纵系统 (Fig. 7.8)

Fig. 7.8　Steering and operating system 转向操纵系统
1　driver's seat 驾驶员座椅　　　5　travel lever 行走操纵杆
2　arm rest 扶手　　　　　　　　6　monitor 工况监视器
3　joystick control 操纵控制手柄　7　console 仪表控制台
4　control pedal 操纵踏板

7.2.3 General Arrangement of Large Type Excavator 大型挖掘机总体布置 (Fig. 7.9)

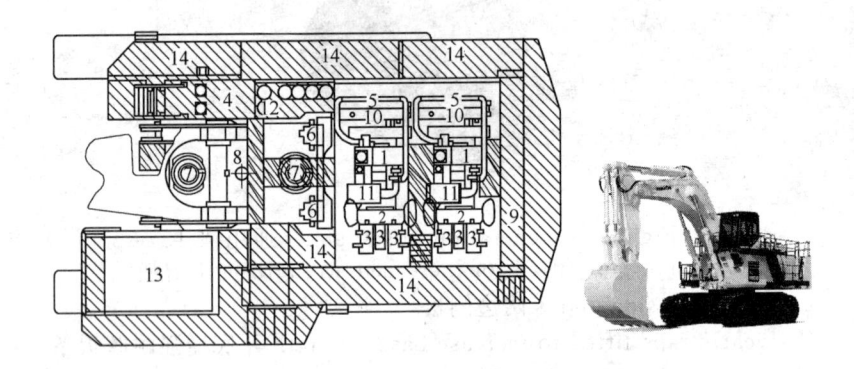

Fig. 7.9 General arrangement of large type excavator
大型挖掘机总体布置

1　engines 发动机
2　PTO 分动箱
3　hydraulic pumps 液压泵
4　hydraulic tank 液压油箱
5　oil coolers 液压油冷却器
6　control valves 控制阀
7　swing motors 回转马达
8　swivel joint 旋转接头
9　fuel tank 燃油箱
10　radiators 散热器
11　air cleaners 空气滤清器
12　hydraulic filters 液压过滤器
13　operator cab 驾驶室
14　walkways 行走通道

7.2.4 Typical Hydraulic System 典型液压系统 (Fig. 7.10)

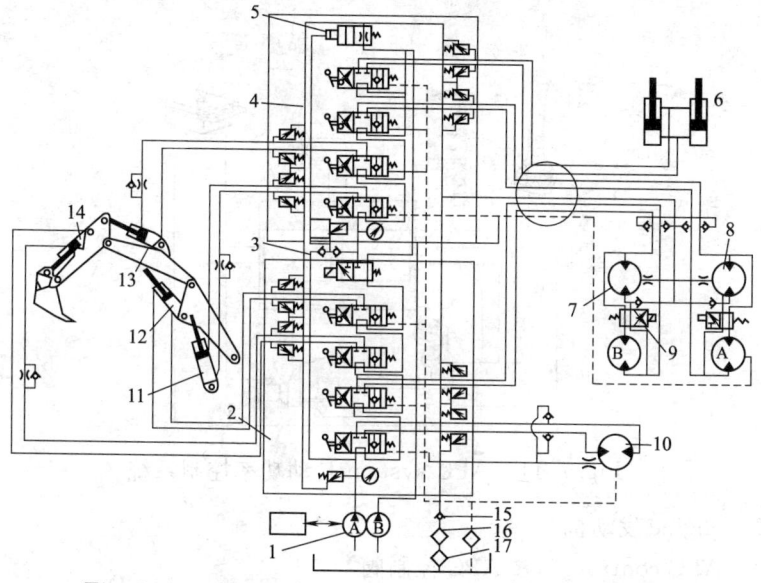

Fig. 7.10 Typical hydraulic system 典型液压系统

1. hydraulic pump 液压泵
2,4. distributing valve group 分配阀组
3. check valve 单向阀
5. speed limit valve 速度限制阀
6. hydraulic cylinder 液压缸
7,8. traveling hydraulic motor 行走液压马达
9. double speed valve 双速阀
10. slewing hydraulic motor 回转液压马达
11. boom cylinder 动臂油缸
12. auxiliary cylinder 辅助油缸
13. arm cylinder 斗杆油缸
14. bucket cylinder 铲斗油缸
15. back pressure valve 背压阀
16. oil cooler 冷却器
17. oil filter 滤油器

7.2.5 APC System 自动功率控制系统 (Fig. 7.11)

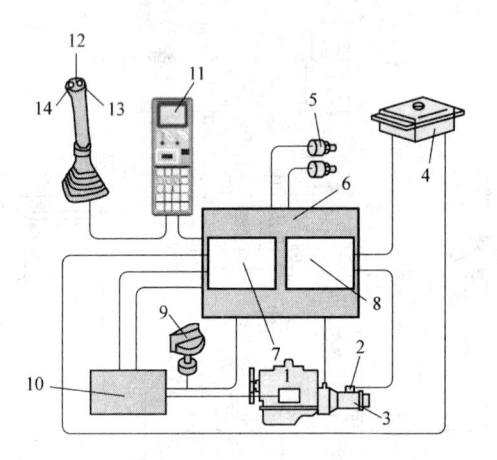

Fig. 7.11 APC system 自动功率控制系统

1 engine 发动机
2 APC control valve APC 控制阀
3 hydraulic pump 液压泵
4 APC & accelerator back up switch APC 与加速器备用开关
5 pressure sensor 压力传感器
6 APC controller APC 控制器
7 accelerator emergency circuit 加速器应急回路
8 APC emergency circuit APC 应急回路
9 accelerator dial 加速器调节刻度盘
10 ECU 电子控制单元
11 combination monitor 综合监视器
12 lever switch 杠杆操纵开关
13 high power switch 大功率开关
14 quick accelerator switch 快速加速开关

7.2.6 Specifications 工作性能

(1) Standard Equipment Specifications 标准装置规格类型与性能参数

① Engine 发动机

Model 型号；

Type：Water-cooled，4 cycle，Direct injection 类型：水冷，四冲程，直喷式；

Aspiration：Turbocharged 充气形式：涡轮增压；

Number of cylinders 汽缸数；

Bore×stroke 缸径×冲程；

Piston displacement 活塞排量；

Governor：Mechanical，all-speed control 调速器：机械式，全程调速；

Net flywheel horsepower 净飞轮功率；

To meet U. S. EPA Tier 3 emissions requirements 符合美国 3 类环保排放标准；

Net flywheel power advertised is the power available at the flywheel when the engine is equipped with fan，air cleaner，muffler and alternator. 所标示的净飞轮功率是指发动机配备风扇、空气滤清器、消声器和发电机时飞轮所能输出的功率。

② Hydraulic System 液压系统

Max. pressure-travel 行走系统最大压力；

Max. pressure-swing 回转系统最大压力；

Hydrau mind system，Closed-center system with load-sensing valves and pressure-compensated valves 智能液压系统，负荷感应阀与压力补偿阀中心闭锁系统；

Selectable working modes 可选工作模式；

Main pump：Variable-displacement piston pump 液压主泵：变量柱塞泵；

Maximum flow 最大流量；

Sub-pump for control circuit 控制回路辅助液压泵；

Travel motors with parking brake 驻车制动型行走液压马达；

Swing motor with swing holding brake 制动型回转液压马达；

Axial piston motor 轴向柱塞马达；
Relief valve setting 安全阀设定；
Implement circuits 执行回路；
Travel circuit 行走回路；
Swing circuit 回转回路；
Pilot circuit 控制回路；
Service valve 操纵阀；
Number of cylinders——bore×stroke 液压缸数量——缸径×行程；
Service valves maximum flow 操纵阀最大流量

③ Drives & Brakes 驱动和制动装置
Steering control：two levers with pedals 转向控制：两组操纵杆和踏板；
Drive method：fully hydrostatic 驱动方式：全静液驱动；
Travel motor：axial piston motor, in-shoe design 行走马达：轴向柱塞马达，滑靴设计；
Reduction system：planetary gear, double-reduction 减速系统：行星减速，双级减速；
Max. drawbar pull 最大牵引力；
Max. travel speed 最大行驶速度；
Service brake：Hydraulic lock 行车制动：液压锁止；
Parking brake：Oil disc brake 驻车制动：湿式盘式制动

④ Swing System 回转系统
Driven by hydraulic motor 液压马达驱动；
Swing reduction 回转减速；
Planetary double reduction 行星双级减速；
Swing circle lubrication：grease-bathed 回转圈润滑：油脂润滑；
Swing lock 回转锁定；
Swing speed 回转速度；

Swing torque 回转力矩

⑤ Undercarriage 下部支承（行走机构）
Center frame：X-frame 中心机架：X形机架；
Track frame：box-section type 履带台车架：箱型截面；
Sealed track 密封型履带；
Track adjuster：hydraulic type 张紧装置：液压型；
No. of shoes 履带板数量；
No. of carrier rollers 托链轮数量；
No. of track rollers 支重轮数量

（2）Dimensions 尺寸规格（Fig. 7. 12）

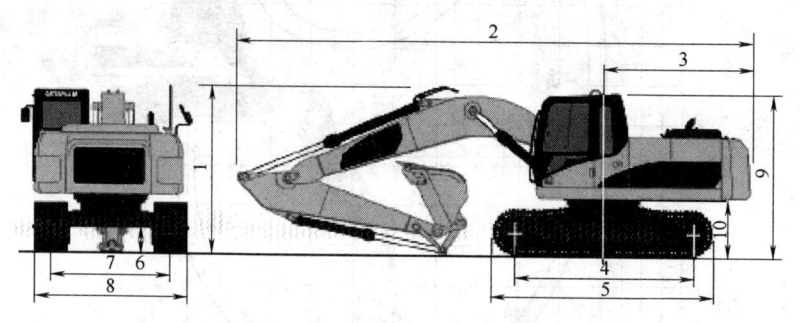

Fig. 7.12　Dimensions 尺寸规格

1　shipping height 海运高度
2　shipping length 海运长度
3　tail swing radius 尾部摆动半径
4　length to center of rollers 滚轮中心距离
5　track length 履带长度
6　ground clearance 离地间隙
7　track gauge 轨距
8　transport width 运输宽度
9　cab height 驾驶室高度
10　counterweight clearance 配重离地间隙

(3) Working Ranges 工作范围 (Fig. 7.13)

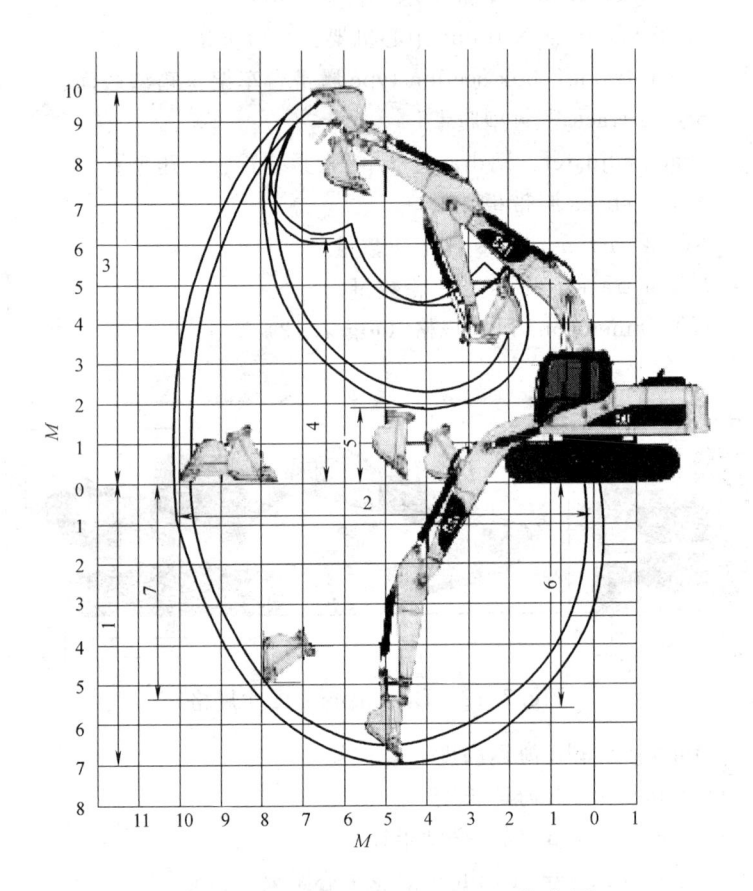

Fig. 7.13 Working ranges 工作范围

1 maximum digging depth 最大挖掘深度
2 maximum reach at ground level 最大水平移动距离
3 maximum cutting height 最大挖掘高度
4 maximum loading height 最大装载高度
5 minimum loading height 最小装载高度
6 maximum depth cut for level bottom 最大水平切削深度
7 maximum vertical wall digging depth 最大垂直挖掘深度

7.2.7 Small Excavator Features 小型挖掘机特点

Fig. 7.14 Small excavator features 小型挖掘机

① Mustang introduces a new bucket series with innovative design improvements that achieve greater bucket volumes, higher breakout forces and improved vertical digging (as shown in 1 of Fig. 7.14).

新型铲斗系列进行了改进设计,具有更大的斗容量、更强的破碎力和更好的垂直挖掘(如图 7.14 中 1 所示)。

② Standard headlights mounted on the boom and at the front of the cab provide excellent nighttime visibility (as shown in 2 of Fig. 7.14).

安装于动臂上和驾驶室前方的标准照明灯提供了最佳的夜间视觉(如图 7.14 中 2 所示)。

③ To help avoiding damage and downtime, mustang securely routes bucket cylinder hoses through the dipper stick. For faster attachment management and parts replacement, we connect boom and arm hoses on the outside of the machine (as shown in 3 of Fig. 7.14).

为避免损坏和停机,沿杆臂安全布置液压缸软管。为快速处理附件和更换零件,在机器外部连接动臂和斗杆软管(如图 7.14 中 3 所示)。

④ Independent right and left boom swing, for offset digging (as shown in 4 of Fig. 7.14).

动臂左、右独立摆动,以适应侧向挖掘(如图 7.14 中 4 所示)。

⑤ Special digging situations call for specialized digging machines, which allow vertical digging even on slopes up to 15° (as shown in 5 of Fig. 7.14).

特殊的挖掘环境需要专业的挖掘机械,即使在 15°的坡道上也可进行垂直挖掘作业(如图 7.14 中 5 所示)。

⑥ Mustang's chassis includes edges reinforced with cast iron——nearly indestructible. This heavy-duty reinforced bumper protects components against accidental collisions (as shown in 6 of Fig. 7.14).

底盘进行了铸铁棱边强化,几乎不可损坏。这种重型保险装置可在碰撞事故中保护机械部件(如图 7.14 中 6 所示)。

7.3 Working Attachments 工作附件（Fig. 7.15）

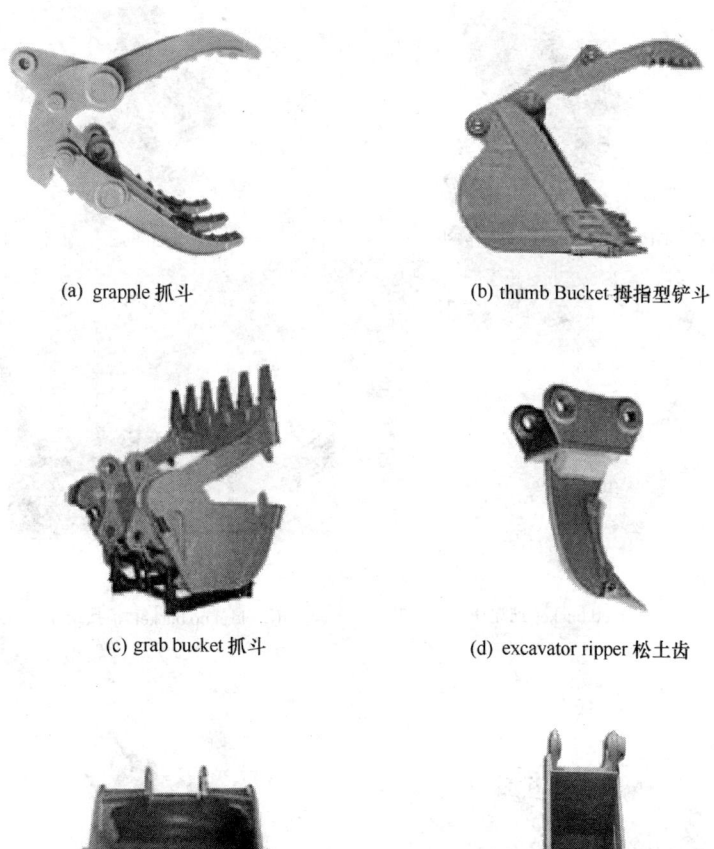

(a) grapple 抓斗

(b) thumb Bucket 拇指型铲斗

(c) grab bucket 抓斗

(d) excavator ripper 松土齿

(e) rock digging 石料铲斗

(f) ditching bucket 挖沟铲斗

Fig. 7.15

(g) tilting bucket 斜挖铲斗

(h) clamshell bucket 蚌壳式抓斗

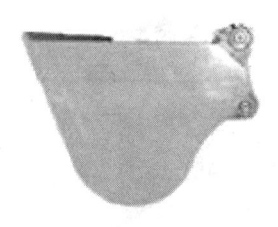

(i) mud bucket 挖泥斗

(j) clean up bucket 清扫铲斗

(k) eliminator manual quick coupler 分离式手动快速连接器

(l) hydraulic crusher 液压破碎器

Fig. 7. 15

(m) universal compaction wheel 万能压实轮

(n) vibro hammer 振动锤

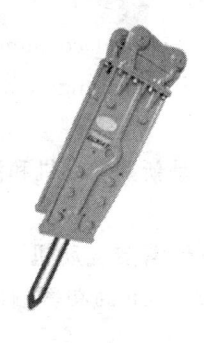

(o) hydraulic breaker 液压破碎锤

(p) skeleton bucket 格栅铲斗

Fig. 7.15 Working attachments 工作附件

7.4 New Technology of Hydraulic Excavator 液压挖掘机新技术

7.4.1 Introduction 简介

The Hitachi ZAXIS-3 series new-generation hydraulic excavators are packed with a host of technological features——clean engine, Hitachi advanced hydraulic technologies, with strong undercarriage and front attachment, plus well matching of power and speed. The ZAXIS-3 series can get the job done with proven productivity, durability and reliability, especially in heavy-duty excavation and quarry operations.

日立 ZAXIS-3 系列新一代液压挖掘机具有一系列技术特点：清洁发动机，先进的日立液压技术，坚固耐用的行走底盘和工作装置附件，以及功率与速度的良好匹配。ZAXIS-3 系列挖掘机所具有的生产率、寿命和可靠性得到了检验证实，特别是在重型挖掘和采石场作业更加适用。

To yield high production yet maintain low fuel consumption, such was the objective of the development of a new engine and hydraulic system.

以较低的燃料消耗获得更大的生产能力是新型发动机和液压系统研究的目标。

7.4.2 New-Generation Clean Engine 新一代清洁发动机

(1) High Power Yet Low Fuel Consumption 高功率输出低燃料消耗

It has 4% increase in output (vs. conventional model). The new clean engine, complying with the emission regulations Tier 3 in US (EPA) and EU Stage Ⅲ, can reduce fuel costs by electronic control.

输出功率增加 4%（与普通型号发动机比较）。新型清洁发动机符合美国环保局 3 级与欧Ⅲ排放标准，并通过电子控制可降低燃料成本。

(2) Common Rail Type Fuel Injection System 共轨型燃油喷射系统 (Fig. 7.16)

Electronic control common rail type fuel injection system drives an integrated fuel pump at an ultrahigh pressure to distribute

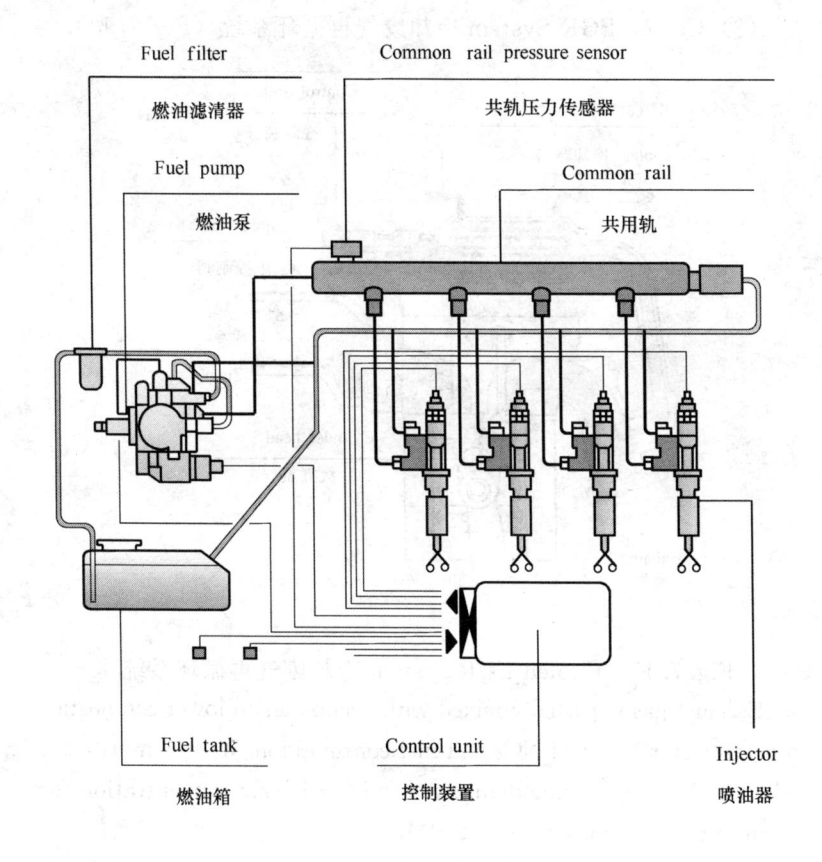

Fig. 7.16　Common rail type fuel injection system
共轨型燃油喷射系统

fuel to each injector per cylinder through a common rail. This enables optimum combustion to generate big horsepower, and reduce PM and fuel consumption.

　　电子控制共轨型燃油喷射系统驱动集成燃油泵，通过一个共用轨以超高压方式将燃油分配给每个气缸的喷油器。这种系统能够使燃烧过程得到优化，从而产生较大的功率，并降低微粒排放和燃料消耗。

(3) Cooled EGR System 冷却废气再循环系统 (Fig. 7.17)

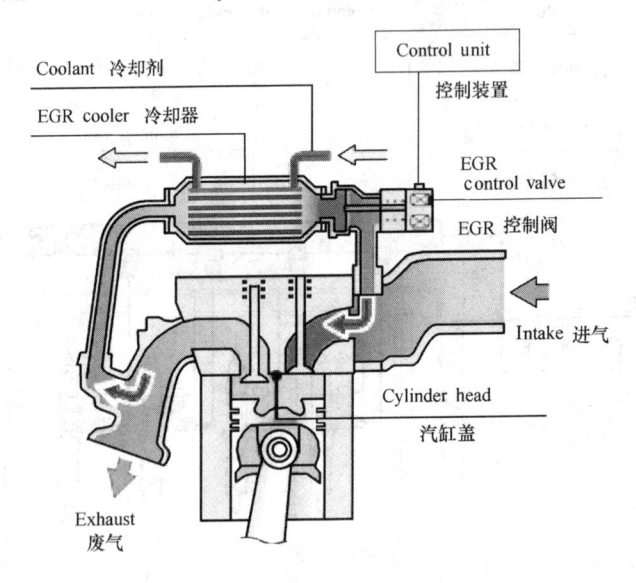

Fig. 7.17　Cooled EGR system 冷却废气再循环系统

Exhaust gas is partially mixed with suction air to lower combustion temperature for reducing NO_x and fuel consumption. What's more, the EGR cooler cools down exhaust gas to increase air concentration for complete combustion, reducing PM.

排放废气与吸入空气进行部分混合以降低燃烧温度，从而减小氮氧化合物 NO_x 与燃油消耗。此外，EGR 冷却器使废气温度降低以增加空气浓度，达到完全燃烧和减少微粒排放的目的。

7.4.3　Advanced Hydraulic Technologies 先进的液压技术

(1) Increased Digging Force 挖掘力增加

7% more bucket digging force and 8% more arm digging force.

铲斗挖掘力增加 7%，杆臂挖掘力增加 8%。

(2) Enhanced Boom Recirculation System 加速型动臂再循环系统 (Fig. 7.18)

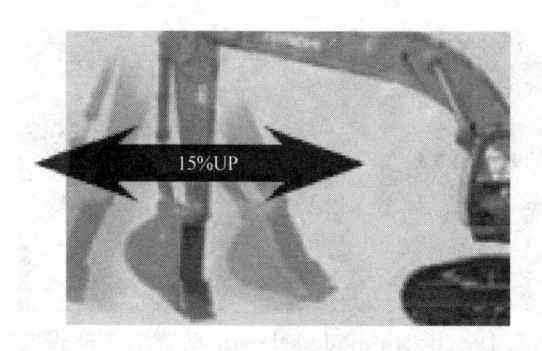

Fig. 7.18 Enhanced boom recirculation system 加速型动臂再循环系统

In combined operation of boom lower and arm, arm speed can be increased by approximately 15% over the conventional. Pressurized oil from boom cylinder bottom side is delivered to boom cylinder rod side to lower the boom, assisted by boom weight. Conventionally, pressurised oil from pump is delivered to boom cylinder rod side to lower the boom. The new system also allows an efficient combined operation of swing and lowering the boom.

动臂下降与杆臂组合作业时，与常规挖掘机相比较，杆臂速度大约可增加15%。动臂油缸底部一端的压力油被输送到动臂油缸的活塞杆一边，以降低动臂，动臂重量加速了降低过程。而在一般情况下，通过使来自液压泵的压力油流入动臂油缸活塞杆一端降低动臂。新系统也可以实现摆动与降低动臂的高效组合作业。

(3) Boom Mode Selector 动臂工作模式选择

The amount the body can be lifted or pulled by the front of machine can be ON or OFF selected (as shown in Fig. 7.19). This helps to provide for more comfortable operation and contributes to longer component service life.

挖掘机前部工装提升或推移机体的力量大小可通过一个 ON/OFF 选择开关进行选择（如图 7.19 所示）。这种选择有助于提高操作舒适性和延长部件工作寿命。

Fig. 7.19　Boom mode selector 动臂工作模式选择

① ON Comfortable mode 舒适工作模式（开关位置 ON）

There is little lifting or pulling of the body so there is less vibration and shock (as shown in Fig. 7.20).

机体几乎没有提升或推移（如图 7.20 所示），因而振动和冲击较小。

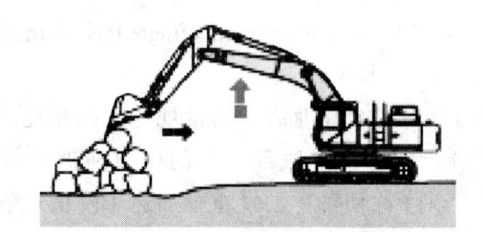

Fig. 7.20　ON comfortable mode 舒适工作模式

② OFF Powerful mode 重型工作模式（开关位置 OFF）

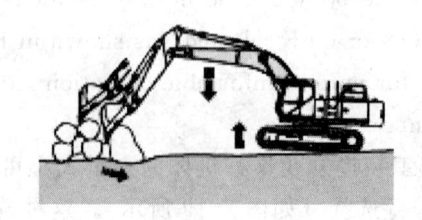

Fig. 7.21　OFF powerful mode 重型工作模式

Much lifting and pulling of the body so there is more vibration and shock (as shown in Fig. 7.21).

机体有较大的抬起和推移（如图 7.21 所示），因而振动和冲击较大。

(4) Larger-Diameter Front Piping 大直径前部管路

Arm piping is increased in diameter to reduce hydraulic loss (theoretically 7%) for speedy front operation.

增加杆臂油管直径以减少液压损失（理论上为 7%），提高作业速度。

(5) Combined Operation of Boom and Arm 动臂与杆臂的组合作业 (Fig. 7.22)

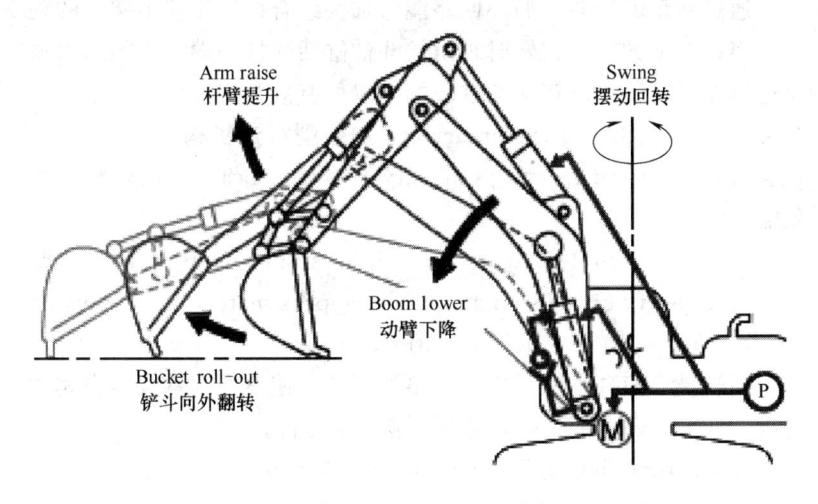

Fig. 7.22 Combined operation of boom and arm
动臂与杆臂的组合作业

In combined operation of swing + boom lower + arm roll-out, or in leveling (boom lower+arm roll-out), arm roll-out speed can be increased greatly. Here's why. A variable throttle, provided in the arm circuit, adjusts the flow when needed to reduce hydraulic loss in combined operation with arm roll-out.

在回转＋动臂下降＋杆臂外伸的组合作业中，或者在平整作业（动臂下降＋杆臂外伸）中，可大大提高杆臂外伸速度。原因在于，在杆臂外伸的组合作业中，当需要减少液压损失时，杆臂回路中的可变节流阀将对流量进行调节。

(6) New Bucket Regenerative System 新型铲斗再循环系统

Swift bucket actions can be done in combined operation for excavation through the new bucket regenerative circuit. When the load to the bucket is light, pressurized oil from bucket cylinder rod side is delivered through a regenerative valve to bucket cylinder bottom side for the effective use of hydraulic energy.

通过新型的铲斗再循环回路能够加快组合挖掘作业中铲斗的动作。当铲斗上的载荷较轻时，由铲斗油缸活塞杆一端产生的压力油通过再循环阀传输到铲斗油缸底端，以便有效利用液压能量。

7.4.4 Strengthened Undercarriage 加强型行走机构

(1) Increased Loading Capacity of Swing Bearing 回转轴承承载能力增强

The swing circle ball bearing ultilizes more balls to boost the loading capacity of the swing circle by approximately 6%, allowing stable swing even in tough operation.

回转循环滚珠轴承采用了更多的滚珠，使滚圈的承载能力大约提高了 6%，即使在重载工况下也能稳定运行。

(2) Strengthened Track Links 强化履带链

The boss diameter of each track link is increased by approximately 19%. The thickness of each track link is also increased by approximately 57%. Thickened track links extend service life.

每一履带链条的凸台直径增加了大约 19%。每一履带链条的厚度也增加了大约 57%。加厚的履带链条延长了使用寿命。

(3) Strengthened Upper Roller Bracket 强化了上托链轮支架

The upper roller bracket wall thickness is increased for higher strength.

增加上托链轮支架壁厚以提高强度。

(4) Full Track Guard Provided Standard 全履带防护装置标准化

On the H-specification machines, full track guards are provided standard. Full track guards protect track links and lower rollers from damage and deformation. Moreover, they also keep out stones, preventing the overload to the undercarriage to reduce wear and damage.

在 H 形挖掘机上，提供了标准的全履带防护装置。全履带防护装置保护了履带链条和支重轮，避免了损坏与变形。而且，履带防护装置也阻止了石块，防止了行走机构的过载，减少了磨损和损坏。

(5) Pressed Master Pins 压力防松主销

The master pin of each track link is pressed, instead of master pin using a pin retention to avoid disengagement.

对每个履带链条主销进行加压，代替了使用钉形销的防松工艺。

(6) Strengthened Idler Pedestal 增强型导向轮支座

The bearing length of the idler pedestal is extended by approximately 67% to increase durability and service life.

导向轮支座支承长度延长了大约 67%，以增加耐久性和寿命。

(7) Strengthened Idler Bracket 增强型导向轮支架

The idler bracket is thickened for rigidity to prevent deformation and increase durability.

增加导向轮支架厚度以提高刚度，防止变形并增加耐久性。

7.4.5 Strengthened Front Components 增强型工作装置

(1) 5% Increase in Strength with Stronger Pin Material 高强度销轴材料强度增加 5%

The strength of pins, used in the arm and boom, is increased by 5%, using harder steel material.

应用高强度钢材,使杆臂和动臂上的销轴强度提高 5%。

(2) Strengthened General-purpose Bucket 增强型通用铲斗(Fig. 7.23)

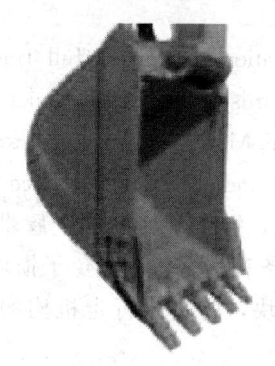

Fig. 7.23　Strengthened general-purpose bucket
　　　　　增强型通用铲斗

Bucket teeth are reshaped as Super-V teeth for smooth penetration and higher production. Bushings are utilized at both ends of a bucket pin to eliminate clearances, preventing jerky operation.

铲斗斗齿改为超级 V 形齿,使铲入平稳、生产率提高。铲斗销轴两端均使用衬套,以便消除间隙,防止急拉式作业。

(3) Strengthened H-bucket for Heavy-Duty H 形重型强化铲斗 (Fig. 7.24)

Fig. 7.24　Strengthened H-bucket for heavy-duty
　　　　　H 形重型强化铲斗

The heavy-duty bucket is reshaped, and bucket parts are strengthened to increase durability.

改进重型铲斗，增强铲斗零件，提高耐久性。

7.4.6 Enhanced Operator Comfort 提高驾驶员舒适性

The spacious cab is ergonomically designed with excellent visibility to reduce operator fatigue and burden.

宽敞的驾驶室符合人机工程学设计，具有最佳的视野，减少了驾驶员工作疲劳与负荷。

(1) Excellent Visibility 最佳的视野

The glass windows are widened for excellent visibility, especially improving right downward view during travel and excavation.

为获得最佳视野，加宽了玻璃窗，特别是改善了行走和挖掘时右下方的视野。

(2) Ample Foot Space 宽敞的足下空间 (Fig. 7.25)

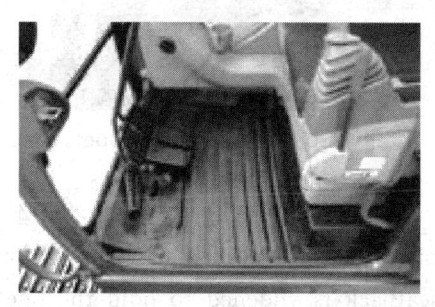

Fig. 7.25 Ample foot space 宽敞的足下空间

Foot space is expanded forward, and pedals are reshaped for pleasant operation.

足下空间向前扩展，改进踏板形式，以保证愉快操作。

(3) Short-stroke Levers 短行程操纵杆

Fingertip control of short-stoke levers, with the help of armrests, allows long, continuous operation with less fatigue (30% reduction in lever control effort).

短行程操纵杆的指尖控制在扶手帮助下,能够长时间进行无疲劳连续操作(操纵杆操作力减小 30%)。

(4) Comfort-designed Operator Seat 设计舒适的驾驶员座椅 (Fig. 7. 26)

Fig. 7. 26　Comfort-designed operator seat
设计舒适的驾驶员座椅

The operator seat is ergonomically designed for long-hour pleasant operation. The seatback is widened to hold the operator securely, and the headrest is reshaped. The operator seat is strengthened to reduce vibration and shocks, and increase durability.

驾驶员座椅依照人机工程学原理设计,以便使驾驶员长时间愉快操作。加宽座椅靠背,使驾驶员操作安全稳固,并且改进了座椅头靠的形状。对座椅进行增强,以减小振动和冲击,并提高耐久性。

(5) Fluid-filled Elastic Mounts 充液弹性支座

The cab rests on fluid-filled elastic mounts that absorb shocks and vibration to enhance operator comfort.

驾驶室安装于充液弹性支座上，从而吸收了冲击和振动，提高了驾驶员工作的舒适性。

（6）Large Multilanguage，Multi Function Monitor 大界面多语言多功能监视器（Fig. 7.27）

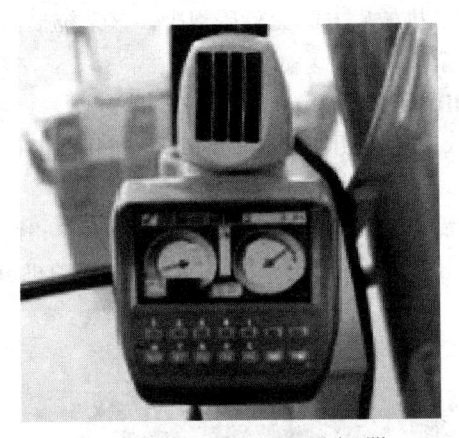

Fig. 7.27　Monitor 监视器

（7）Rear View Camera 后视摄像头（Fig. 7.28）

Fig. 7.28　Rear view camera 后视摄像头

The large color LCD monitor, teamed up with the rear view camera (optional) on the counterweight, gives the operator unobstructed rearward view. This system enhances safety during swing and reversing.

彩色大界面监视器与配重上方的后视摄像头（可选件）组合，为驾驶员提供了机械后方的无障碍视野。该系统提高了挖掘机回转与倒车时的安全性。

7.4.7 Simplified Maintenance 维护简单方便

Focusing on simplified maintenance, including easy inspection, service and cleaning.

维护保养简单，其中包括方便的检查、保养和清洁。

(1) Simplified Cleaning around Engine 发动机清洁简单方便

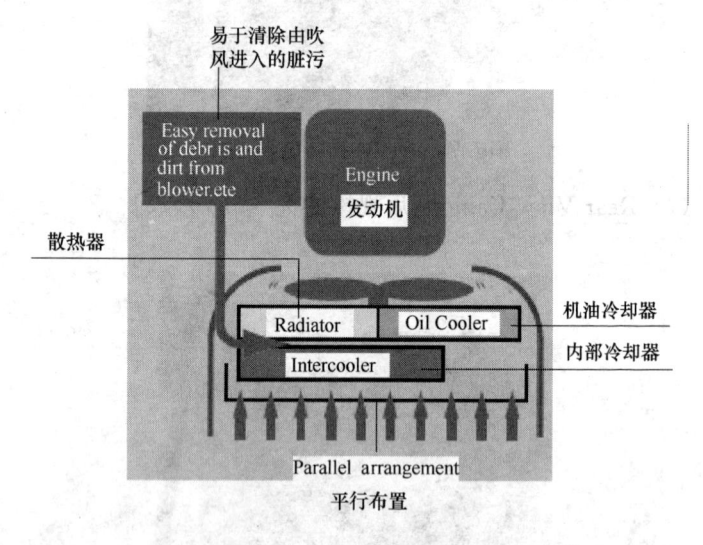

Fig. 7.29 Arrangement of engine 发动机的布置

The radiator and oil cooler are laid out in parallel arrangement for easy demounting, as shown in Fig. 7.29, instead of conventional inline arrangement. This new arrangement significantly helps facilitate cleaning around the radiator and oil cooler.

与传统的内联布置方法不同，对散热器和机油冷却器进行并行布置（如图 7.29 所示），以方便拆卸。这一新型布置极大地方便了散热器和机油冷却器的清洁。

(2) Dual Main Fuel Filters Provided Standard 标准化双主燃油滤清器 (Fig. 7.30)

Fig. 7.30 Dual main fuel filters provided standard 标准化双主燃油滤清器

In addition to a pre-filter, dual main fuel filters are provided standard to reduce clogging of the fuel line to the engine.

除粗滤器外，设置了两个主燃油滤清器以减小发动机油路的堵塞。

(3) Easy Draining 排油方便 (Fig. 7.31)

Fig. 7.31 Easy draining 排油方便

The engine oil pan is fitted with a drain coupler. When draining, an associated drain hose is connected to the drain coupler. Unlike a cock, the drain coupler is reliable, avoiding oil spills and vandalism.

发动机油底壳设置有排油管接头。需要排油时,将排油软管与排油管接头连接。与旋塞不同,这种排油管接头使用可靠,避免了油的泄漏和人为破坏。

(4) Automatic Lubrication 自动润滑

The front attachment is automatically lubricated, except for bucket lubricating points at the top of arm that are repositioned for side lubrication.

前部工作装置采用自动润滑方式,将杆臂顶部的润滑点重新设置在侧面。

(5) Extended Hydraulic Oil Filter Change Intervals 较长的液压油滤清器更换时间间隔

Hydraulic oil filter change intervals are extended from 500 hours to 1000 hours to help reduce running costs.

液压油滤清器更换时间间隔由 500h 延长至 1000h 以降低使用成本。

7.4.8 Environmental Preservation 环境保护

Boarding a clean engine complying with the rigorous emission regulations.

提供符合严格排放标准的清洁发动机。

(1) Environmentally Friendly Designs 环境友好设计

① Boarding Clean Engine 提供清洁发动机

The clean engine complying with the emission regulations Stage Ⅲ in EU and Tier 3 in US (EPA) is boarded to reduce emissions containing nitrogen oxide (NO_x) and particulate matter (PM).

清洁发动机符合欧Ⅲ与美国环保局(EPA)3级排放标准,减少了氮氧化物(NO_x)和微粒(PM)的排放。

② Low Noise Engine 低噪声发动机

Engine noise is reduced by approximately 2 dB with the robust engine. It goes without saying that the engine meets the EU noise regulations.

发动机噪声大约减小了 2dB。不言而喻,该发动机符合欧洲噪声标准。

(2) Variable-Speed Fan 变速风扇

The engine cooling fan is a large 1120mm diameter variable-speed electro-hydraulic fan. This fan automatically starts when temperature comes into the high temperature range, ensuring low noise operation.

发动机冷却风扇为大直径(1120mm)电液控制变速风扇。当温度达到高温区时,风扇自动启动,并保证低噪声运行。

(3) Proven Muffler 合格消声器

A proven large muffler is provided to reduce sound and exhaust emissions greatly.

使用较大规格的消声器,大大降低了噪声与排放。

(4) Marking of Recyclable Parts 标记可再生零件

All resin parts are marked for the sake of recycling. This helps ease the separation of recyclable wastes.

标记树脂材料零件以便再生利用。这种做法有助于再生废料的分拣。

(5) Reducing the Burden to the Environment 减轻环境负担

Lead-free design is achieved through the use of lead-free wire harness covering, radiator, oil cooler and others. No asbestos is used. The use of aluminum radiator, oil cooler and intercooler increases the durability of the machine.

通过使用无铅线束盖、散热器、机油冷却器等实现了无铅化设计。未使用任何石棉物。使用铝制散热器、机油冷却器和内置冷却器提高了机械的耐久性。

(6) Biodegradable Hydraulic Oil 生物可降解液压油

Degradable hydraulic oil is ecological, which is decomposed into water and carbon dioxide in water and ground.

可降解液压油是生态环保性的,在水中和地下可分解为水与二氧化碳。

7.4.9　Enhanced Safety 高安全性

(1) CRES Ⅱ Cab 不锈钢结构驾驶室

The CRES Ⅱ cab is designed to help with "just in case" protection for the operator. Safety in case of tipping is improved. The cab top can withstand nine-fold loading.

CRES Ⅱ形驾驶室设计为驾驶员提供了"以防万一"的保护。倾翻时的安全性得到了改善。驾驶室顶部可承受 9 倍载荷。

(2) H/R Cab　H/R 形驾驶室

The H/R cab utilizes the reinforced front window and FOPS at the roof for protection against falling objects. The front glass window, made of straight-laminated, is fixed to shut out dirt and debris. The cab provided with a full guard satisfies the OPG (Level Ⅱ) cab requirements stipulated by ISO.

H/R 形驾驶室利用增强型前窗和顶部落物保护结构以防下落物的破坏。由多层平面玻璃制作的前窗被固定,防止了污物和碎片的侵入。驾驶室具有完全防护功能,符合 ISO 对于二级 OPG 驾驶室的各项要求。

Fig. 7.32　New pilot control shut-off lever
新型驾驶操纵锁定杆

(3) New Pilot Control Shut-off Lever 新型驾驶操纵锁定杆(Fig. 7.32)

The engine cannot start unless the lock lever is locked completely. This prevents unintended rapid lurching by unintended touching a control lever.

除非将锁杆完全锁定，否则发动机就不能启动。该设置防止了由于无意识碰上操纵杆时所产生的快速晃动。

Unit 8　Loaders
装　载　机

8.1　Overview 概述

8.1.1　Basic Concept 基本概念

A loader is a type of construction equipment (engineering vehicle) machinery that is primarily used to "load" material into another type of machinery (dump truck, conveyor belt, rail-car, etc.). Loaders are used mainly for uploading materials into trucks, laying pipe, clearing rubble, and digging. A loader is not the most efficient machine for digging as it cannot dig very deep below the level of its wheels, like a backhoe can. Their deep bucket can usually store about 3～6 cubic meters of earth. The front loader's bucket capacity is much bigger than a bucket capacity of a backhoe loader. Loaders are not classified as earthmoving machinery, as their primary purpose is other than earthmoving.

装载机是一种主要用于向另一种机械（自卸车、输送皮带、铁路运输车辆等）"装载"物料的建设机械（工程车辆）设备。装载机主要用于向卡车装载物料，以及铺设管道、清理碎石和挖土等工作。用于挖土作业，装载机不是最有效的机械，与挖掘机不同，装载机不适用于轮胎支承面以下较深处的挖掘作业。装载机的深底铲斗一般可装载 3～6m³ 的土壤。铲斗前置装载机的斗容量远大于挖掘装载机的斗容量。装载机不属于铲土运输机械，因其主要用途并非土方运输。

Unlike most bulldozers, most loaders are wheeled and not tracked, although track loaders are common. They are successful where sharp edged materials in construction debris would damage rubber wheels, or where the ground is soft and muddy. Wheels provide better mobility and speed and do not damage paved roads as much as tracks, but provide less traction.

尽管履带式装载机是普遍的,但与大多数推土机不同,大多数装载机是轮式的而并非履带式。履带式装载机适用于棱角锐利的建筑材料会破坏橡胶轮胎的场合,或者在松软泥泞道路上的作业。轮式装载机具有良好的机动性和较高的工作速度,并且不像履带那样破坏铺装路面,但其所能提供的牵引力较小。

Unlike standard tractors fitted with a front bucket, many large loaders do not use automotive steering mechanisms. Instead, they steer by a hydraulically actuated pivot point set exactly between the front and rear axles. This is referred to as "articulated steering" and allows the front axle to be solid, allowing it to carry greater weight. Articulated steering provides better maneuverability for a given wheelbase. Since the front wheels and attachment rotate on the same axis, the operator is able to "steer" his load in an arc after positioning the machine, which can be useful.

与安装前置铲斗的标准拖拉机不同,许多大型装载机不使用汽车转向机构。取而代之,它们通过液压驱动的安装于前、后桥之间的转向铰接装置转向。这种转向称为"铰接转向",它可使前桥固定,并使其承受更大的重量。对于一定的轴距铰接转向提供了较好的机动性。由于前轮与工作装置绕同一车轴旋转,驾驶员在使机械定位后可使铲斗沿弧线"转向",这一点是实用的。

The loader assembly may be a removable attachment or permanently mounted. Often the bucket can be replaced with other devices or tools. For example, many loaders can mount forks to lift heavy pallets or shipping containers, and a hydraulically-opening "clamshell" bucket allows a loader to act as a light dozer or scraper.

装载机的工作装置可以是更换式的或者是固定安装。铲斗常常可用其他装置或工具更换，例如，许多装载机可以安装叉车去提升重型货物或者装运集装箱，装备液压开启式"蛤壳"形铲斗可以使装载机像推土机或铲运机一样作业。

In construction areas loaders are also used to transport building materials, such as bricks, pipe, metal bars, and digging tools, over short distances. Loaders are also used for snow removal, using their bucket or a snowbasket, but usually using a snowplow attachment. They clear snow from streets, highways and parking lots. They sometimes load snow into dump trucks for transport.

在各种建筑工地上，装载机也经常用来近距离转运建筑材料，例如砖块、管材、钢筋、各种挖掘工具等。借助铲斗或除雪铲，装载机也用于除雪作业，但通常使用除雪装置。它们用来清除街道、公路和停车场上的积雪。有时用装载机将积雪装载到自卸车上进行运输。

Front loaders gained popularity during the last two decades, especially in urban engineering projects and small earthmoving works. Many engineering vehicle manufacturers offer a wide range of loaders, the most notable are those of John Deere, Caterpillar, Case, Volvo, Komatsu and Liebherr.

近20年来，特别是在城市建设工程和小型土方运输工程中，装载机获得了普遍的应用。许多工程车辆制造商可生产多种类型的装载机，其中最知名的有约翰迪尔、卡特彼勒、凯斯、沃尔沃、小松和利勃海尔等品牌。

8.1.2 Applications 应用 (Fig. 8.1)

(a) loading materials 装载材料

(b) earthmoving 铲土运输

(c) forestry engineering 林业工程

(d) snow removing 除雪作业

(e) underground work 井下作业

(f) loading and unloading 装卸货

Fig. 8.1

(g) pipe laying 铺设管道

(h) maintain pavement 维修路面

(i) land clearing 场地清理

(j) garden work 园林工作

(k) rolling compaction 碾压路面

(l) tunnel construction 隧道作业

Fig. 8.1　Applications of loader 装载机的应用

8.1.3 Types 类型 (Fig. 8.2)

(a) mini type loader
微型装载机

(b) small type wheel loader
小型轮式装载机

(c) medium type wheel loader
中型轮式装载机

(d) large type wheel loader
大型轮式装载机

(e) track-type loader 覆带式装载机

(f) skid steer loader 滑移转向装载机

Fig. 8.2

(g) underground mining loader
井下作业装载机

(h) multi terrain loader
多功能装载机

(i) wheel backhoe loader
轮式挖掘装载机

(j) side dumping loader
侧卸式装载机

Fig. 8.2　Types of loader 装载机的类型

8.2 Components and Features 组成与特点

8.2.1 Components 组成

(1) Basic Components 基本部件 (Fig. 8.3)

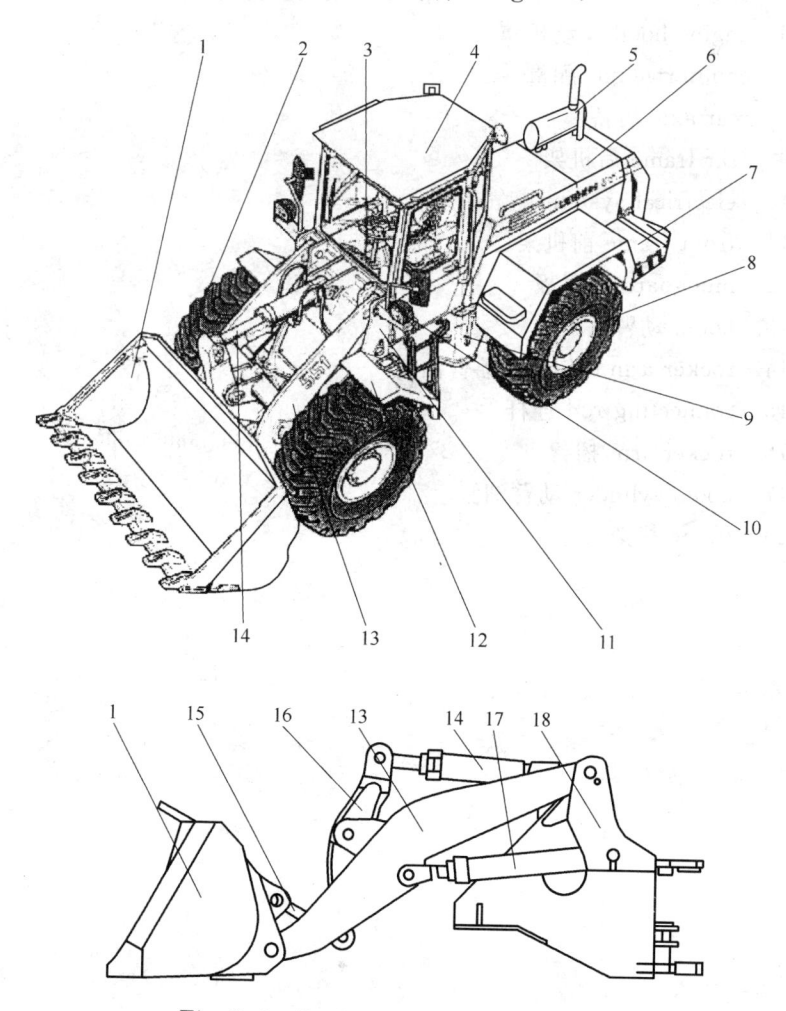

Fig. 8.3 Basic components 基本部件

1　bucket 铲斗
2　front axle 前桥
3　instrumentation console 仪表盘
4　cab and operating system 驾驶室及操作系统
5　engine and transmission system 发动机及传动系统
6　engine hood 发动机罩
7　counterweight 配重
8　rear axle 后桥
9　rear frame 后机架
10　electrical system 电气系统
11　front frame 前机架
12　mudguard 挡泥板
13　boom 动臂
14　rocker arm cylinder 摇臂油缸
15　connecting rod 连杆
16　rocker arm 摇臂
17　boom cylinder 动臂油缸
18　frame 机架

(2) Hydromechanical Transmission System 液力机械传动系统（Fig. 8.4）

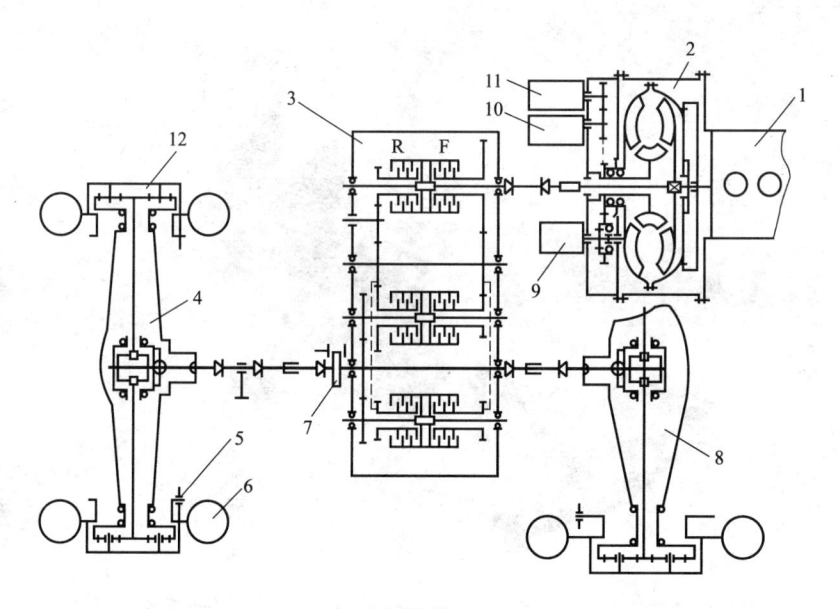

Fig. 8.4 Hydromechanical transmission system 液力机械传动系统
1　engine 发动机
2　torque converter 液力变矩器
3　power shifting transmission box 动力换挡变速箱
4　front axle 前桥
5　caliper disc brake 钳盘式制动器
6　wheel 车轮
7　parking brake 驻车制动器
8　rear axle 后桥
9　gear shift pump 变速油泵
10　steering pump 转向油泵
11　operational pump 工作油泵
12　wheel reductor 轮边减速器

(3) Transmission System Arrangement 传动系统布置 (Fig. 8.5)

Fig. 8.5 Transmission system arrangement 传动系统布置
1　engine 发动机
2　torque converter 液力变矩器
3　power shift transmission box 动力换挡变速箱
4　rear frame 后机架
5　front frame 前机架
6　front axle 前桥
7　transmission shaft 传动轴
8　rear axle 后桥

（4）Torque Converter 液力变矩器（Fig. 8.6）

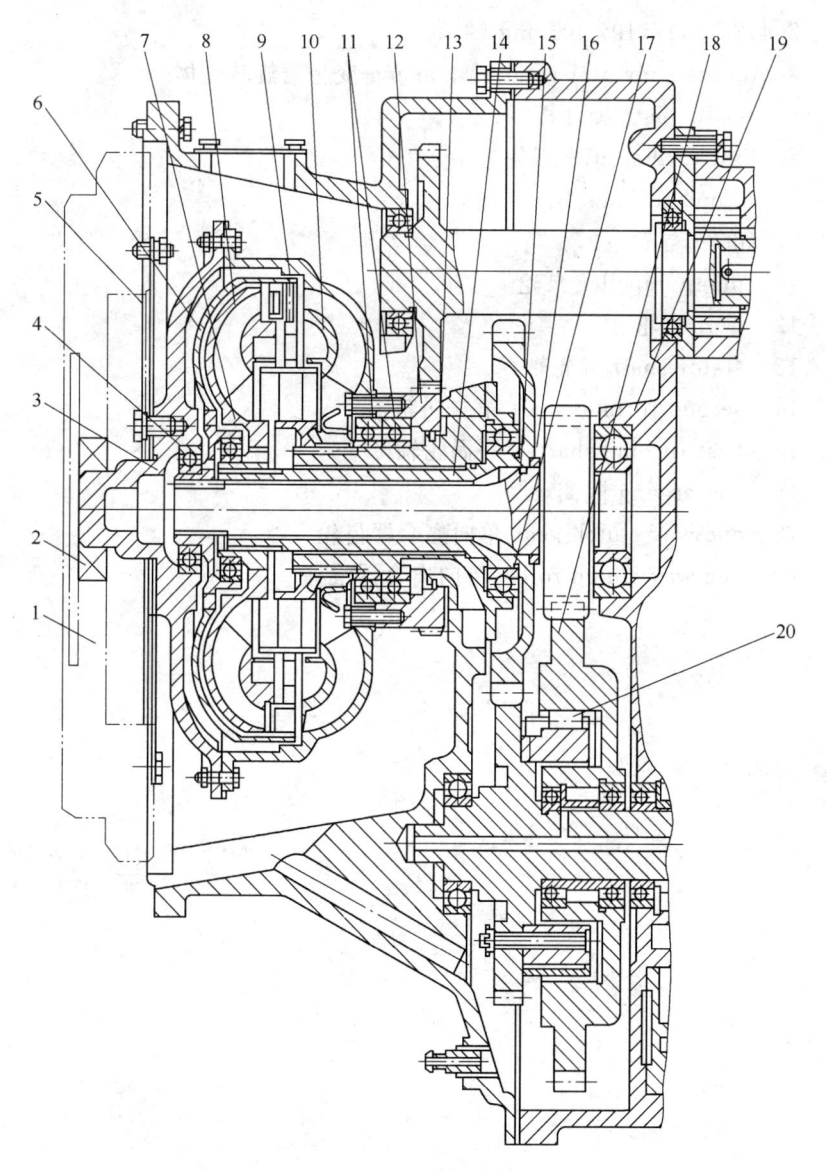

Fig. 8.6　Torque converter 液力变矩器

1   flywheel 飞轮
2,4,7,11,17,19   bearing 轴承
3   torque converter rotation housing 变矩器旋转壳体
5   elastic plate 弹性板
6   first turbine 第一涡轮
8   second turbine 第二涡轮
9   stator 导轮
10   pump impeller 泵轮
12   gear 齿轮
13   stator shaft 导轮轴
14   second turbine shaft 第二涡轮轴
15   first turbine shaft 第一涡轮轴
16   spacer ring 隔离环
18   one-way clutch gear 单向离合器齿轮
20   one-way clutch roller 单向离合器滚柱

8.2.2 Performance Characteristic 工作特性 (Fig. 8.7)

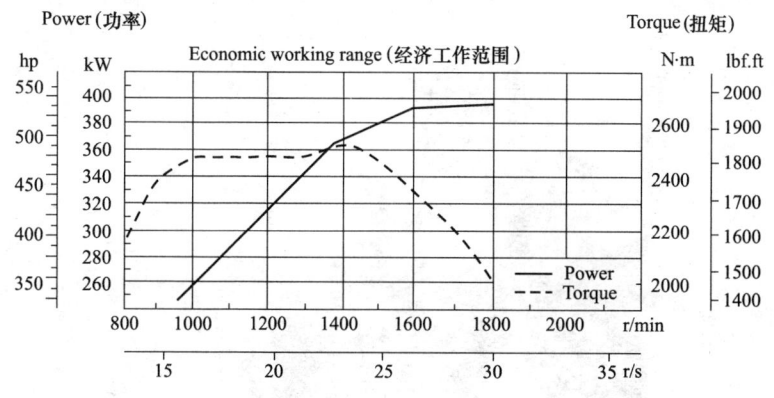

Fig. 8.7 Performance characteristic 工作特性

8.2.3 Hydro-mechanical Series Drive 液压机械组合传动 (Fig. 8.8)

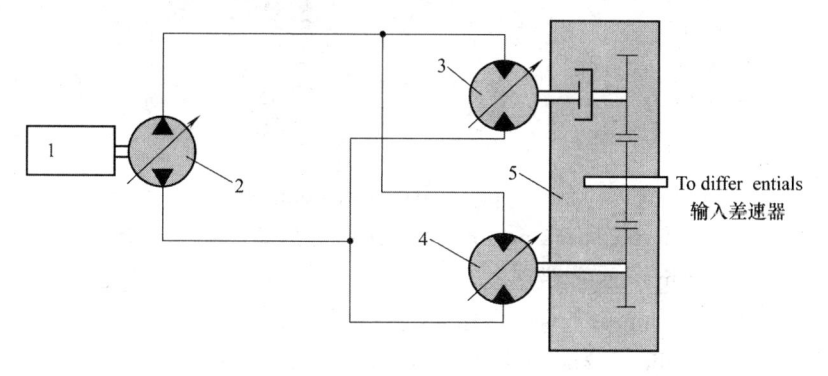

Fig. 8.8 Hydro-mechanical series drive 液压机械组合传动

1 engine 发动机
2 piston pump 柱塞液压泵
3 low speed piston motor 低速柱塞马达
4 high peed piston motor 高速柱塞马达
5 transfer case 分动箱

8.2.4 Hystat Power Train System 静液传动系统（Fig. 8.9）

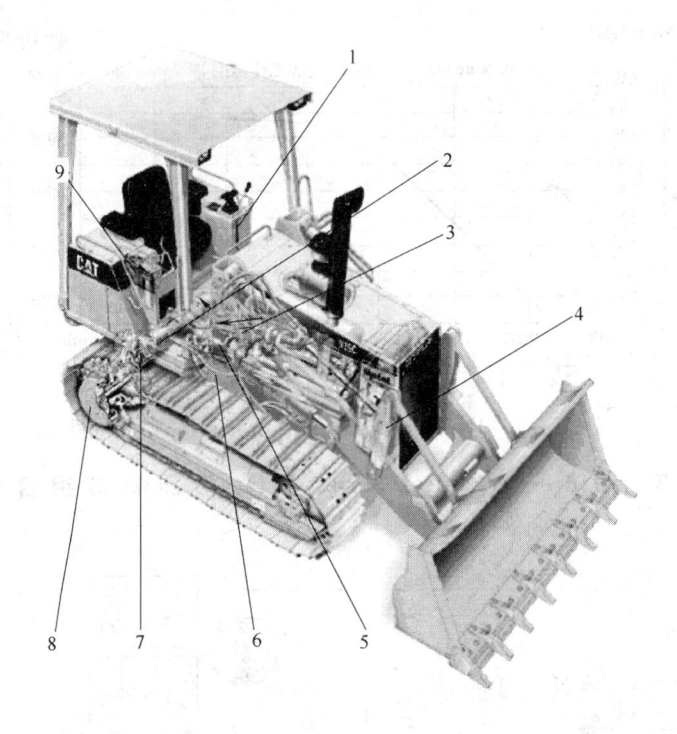

Fig. 8.9　Hystat power train system 静液传动系统
1　neutral-start parking brake lever 空挡启动停车制动手柄
2　track motors 履带驱动马达
3　hystat pumps hoses 液压泵
4　hydraulic oil cooler 液压油冷却器
5　service brakes 行车制动器
6　hoses 液压软管
7　wet，multi-disc parking brakes 湿式、多片停车制动器
8　double reduction planetary final drives 双级行星减速最终驱动装置
9　hydraulic filters 液压滤清器

8.2.5 Operator Station of Track Loader 履带式装载机驾驶员操作台 (Fig. 8.10)

Fig. 8.10 Operator station of track loader
履带式装载机驾驶员操作台

1　neutral-start parking brake lever 空挡启动停车制动手柄
2　track motors 履带驱动马达
3　hystat pumps hoses 液压泵
4　hydraulic oil cooler 液压油冷却器
5　service brakes 行车制动器
6　hoses 液压软管
7　wet, multi-disc parking brakes 湿式、多片停车制动器
8　double reduction planetary final drives 双级行星减速最终驱动装置
9　hydraulic filters 液压滤清器

8.2.6 Standard Equipment Specifications 标准装置规格类型与性能参数

(1) Engine 发动机

Type：Water-cooled, 4-stroke cycle 类型：水冷，四冲程循环；

Aspiration：Turbocharged 充气形式：涡轮增压；

Number of cylinders 汽缸数；

Bore×stroke 缸径×冲程；

Piston displacement 汽缸排量：

Governor：Mechanical, all-speed control 调速器：机械式，全程调速；

Horsepower rating @ 2400r/min（SAE J1349）功率/2400r/min（SAE 标准：J1349）；

Gross horsepower 总功率；

Net horsepower 净功率；

Meets EPA emissions regulations 符合 EPA 排放规范；

Fuel system：Direct injection 供油系：直喷式；

Lubrication system 润滑系；

Method：Gear pump, force-lubrication 方式：齿轮泵，压力润滑；

Filter：Full-flow 滤清器：全流量；

Air cleaner：Dry-type with double elements and dust evacuator, plus dust indicator 空气滤清器：干式，双芯、排尘器、灰尘指示器配置。

(2) Transmission 传动装置

Torque converter：3-element, single-stage, single-phase 变矩器：三元件，单级，单相；

Transmission.：Full power shift, countershaft, automatic 变速器：动力换挡，副传动，自动型。

(3) Axles and Final Drives 驱动桥与终传动

Drive system: Four-wheel drive 传动系统：四轮驱动；

Front: Fixed, semi-floating 前桥：固定式，半浮动轴；

Rear: Center-pin support, semi-floating, 24° total oscillation 后桥：中心铰支承，半浮动轴，总摆动角24°；

Reduction gear: Spiral bevel gear 减速齿轮：螺旋伞齿轮；

Differential gear: Torque proportioning 差速齿轮：转矩比例配合；

Final reduction gear: Planetary gear, single reduction 终减速齿轮：行星齿轮，单级减速

(4) Brakes 制动器

Service brakes: Hydraulically-actuated, wet disc brakes actuate on four wheels 行车制动器：液压驱动，四车轮湿式盘式制动；

Parking brake: Wet, multi-disc brake on transmission output shaft 驻车制动器：变速箱输出轴湿式多片制动。

(5) Steering System 转向系

Type: Articulated type, full-hydraulic power steering 类型：铰接式，全液压动力转向；

Steering angle: 40° each direction 转向角：各个方向40°；

Minimum turning radius at the center of outside tire 外轮中心最小转弯半径。

(6) Boom and Bucket 动臂和铲斗

Z-bar loader linkage is designed for maximum rigidity and offers powerful breakout.

Z形连杆设计提供了最大的刚性和强大的破坏力。

Rap-out loader linkage design enables shock dumping for removing sticky materials.

敲打型连杆设计提供了黏性材料的振动装卸。

Sealed loader linkage pins with dust seals extend greasing intervals. 防尘密封式连接销延长了润滑间隔时间。

The bucket is made of high-tensile strength steel.

铲斗由高抗拉强度钢制作。

(7) Bucket Controls 铲斗控制

The use of a PPC hydraulic control valve offers lighter operating effort for the work equipment control levers.

应用液压程序控制阀使工作装置操纵杆操作轻便。

The reduction in the lever force and travel makes it easy to operate in the work environment.

操纵杆作用力和行程的减小使工作装置的操作变得容易。

 Control positions 位置控制；

 Boom：raise, hold, lower, and float 动臂：提升，保持，下降，浮动；

 Bucket：roll back, hold, and dump 铲斗：后倾翻，保持，倾卸。

(8) Hydraulic System 液压系统

 Capacity (discharge flow) engine-rated rpm 发动机额定转速容量（流量）；

 Loader pump 装载机液压泵；

 Steering pump 转向泵；

 Pilot pump (Gear-type pumps) 引导泵（齿轮泵）；

 Relief valve setting 安全阀设定压力；

 Control valve：2-spool open center type 控制阀：双阀芯开式中心型；

 Hydraulic cylinders：double-acting, piston 液压缸：双作用，活塞；

 Hydraulic cycle time (rated load in bucket)：raise, dump, lower (empty), total cycle time 液压循环时间：提升时间，倾卸时间，下降时间，总循环时间。

8.2.7 Dimensions 尺寸规格

(1) Wheel Loader 轮式装载机 (Fig. 8.11)

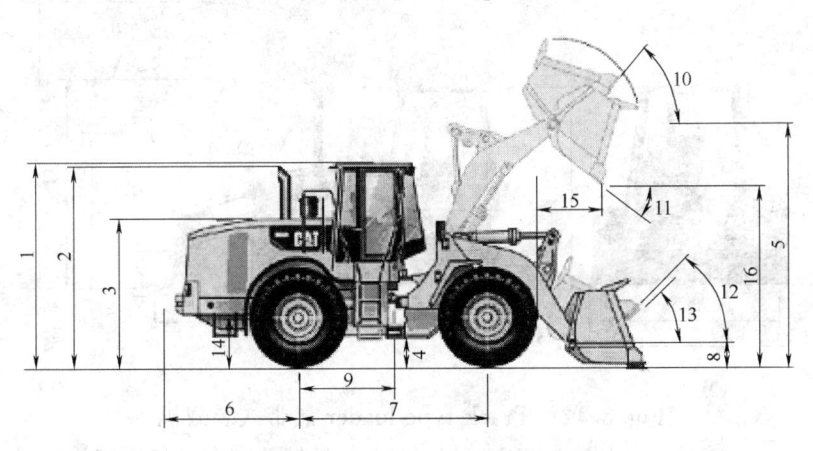

Fig. 8.11　Wheel loader 轮式装载机

1　height to top of ROPS 倾翻保护驾驶室顶部高度
2　height to top of exhaust pipe 发动机排气管道顶部高度
3　height to top of hood 机罩顶部高度
4　ground clearance 离地间隙
5　B-Pin height at max. height 最大铲斗铰点高度
6　center line of rear axle to edge of counterweight 后轴至配重边沿中心距
7　wheelbase 轴距
8　B-Pin height at carry position 铲斗铰点运输高度
9　center line of rear axle to hitch 后轴至车架铰销轴中心距
10　rack back at maximum lift 最大提升高度铲斗后倾角
11　dump angle at maximum lift 最大提升高度铲斗卸载角
12　rack back at carry position 铲斗运输位置后倾角
13　rack back at ground 铲斗地面位置后倾角
14　height to center line of axle 中心轴线高度
15　bucket reach 卸载距离
16　dump clearance at 45° full height 卸载角 45°时的最大卸载高度

（2）Track-Type Loader 履带式装载机（Fig. 8.12）

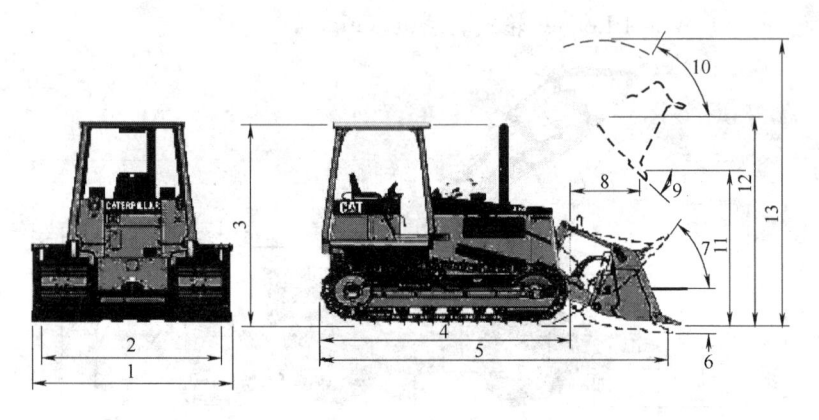

Fig. 8.12　Track-type loader 履带式装载机
1　overall machine width with bucket 机械总宽度（包括铲斗）
2　overall machine width without bucket 机械总宽度（不包括铲斗）
3　machine height to top of cab 机械驾驶室顶部高度
4　length to front of track 履带长度
5　overall machine length 机械总长度
6　digging depth 铲掘深度
7　maximum rollback at carry position 运输位置最大后倾角
8　reach at full lift height 最大高度卸载距离
9　S. A. E. specified dump angle S. A. E. 标准卸载角
10　maximum rollback, fully raised 最大提升高度时的最大后倾角
11　dump clearance at full height and 45° discharge 最大高度45°卸载角时的卸载高度
12　height to bucket hinge pin 铲斗铰销高度
13　overall machine height, bucket fully raised 铲斗最大提升高度时的机械最大高度

8.2.8　Bucket Features 铲斗特点

① Edge steel with extra hardened and toughened wear plates of up to 500 Brinell gives the bucket longer operating life.

铲斗棱边为超硬耐磨钢板，布氏硬度达到 500，具有较长的使用寿命。

② Bucket shell and side plates of up to 400 Brinell to withstand abrasive wear. Reinforced mounting points where the attachment is installed give less wear.

铲斗壳体与侧板的布氏硬度达 400，以抵抗磨料磨损。经强化处理的附件安装铰点减少了磨损。

③ Bucket cutting edges of abrasive-resistant steel of up to 500 Brinell. Replaceable bolt-on wear plates on bucket floor, 500 Brinell.

铲斗切削刀刃为抗磨料磨损钢材，布氏硬度达 500。铲斗底板上安装有耐磨衬板，由螺栓紧固，可更换，布氏硬度为 500。

④ Bolt-on edge savers and segments protect the cutting edge from unnecessary wear.

螺栓紧固的边缘节省块和分段防止了切削刃的不必要磨损。

⑤ Volvo Tooth System with bolt-on or weld-on adapters of up to 515 Brinell gives excellent penetration and less bucket wear.

沃尔沃斗齿系统配备有螺栓紧固型或焊接型连接器，布氏硬度达 515，具有最佳的插入深度和较小的磨损。

8.2.9　Skid-steer Loader Features 滑移装载机特点

① The round-back bucket design is stronger with no angled corners. This configuration makes it easier to fill and dump-improving productivity.

圆弧底铲斗设计更加坚固，没有死角。这种结构使铲斗更加容易装载和倾卸物料，从而提高了生产率。

② The ROPS/FOPS structure protects and shields the operator.

防倾翻/防落物驾驶室结构保护了驾驶员的安全。

③ A total of four exterior lights help to illuminate any job site day or night.

四个外部照明灯设置可在白天或夜晚照亮施工现场。

④ A safety system locks lift, tilt and drive systems when the operator leaves the seat, raises the seat bar, or turns off the ignition switch. The brakes are wet-type multiple discs that require no maintenance.

当驾驶员离开座椅、提起座椅横杆或者关闭启动开关时,安全系统将锁定提升、倾翻和驱动系统。

⑤ Heavy-duty tires are standard-matching the durability of the skid-steer.

使用重型标准轮胎,适应滑移转向的耐久性要求。

⑥ The rugged all-welded unitized frame is constructed of .375-inch gauge steel for years of productivity. Step bushings are placed in all key pivot areas to increase strength and reduce stress.

全焊接整体车架由0.375in工具钢建造,坚固耐用,满足长期生产能力要求。重要枢轴均采用阶梯衬套,以便增加强度和减小应力。

⑦ A wider wheelbase provides for a smooth ride and more balance for stability with heavier loads. A 9-inch ground clearance allows easy maneuverability through mud and other terrain.

较宽的轴距保证了平稳行驶,重载作业更加稳定。

⑧ Hydraulic lines are protected within the loader arm.

液压管路设置于装载机动臂内部受到保护。

⑨ Mustang features a self-leveling vertical lift.

野马牌装载机的特点是具有自找平垂直提升特性。

⑩ The advanced hydraulic system affords longer service intervals and comes with a sight glass for quick and easy fluid level inspections.

先进的液压系统可提供较长的工作时间,并配置了玻璃液面计,以便于检查液压油面高度。

⑪ A drop-down step makes it convenient to check engine and maintenance points.

下落式台阶设置便于发动机和保养点的检查。

8.3　Working Attachments 工作附件

8.3.1　Bucket Types 铲斗类型 （Fig. 8.13）

(a) spade nose rock bucket
中凸式石料铲斗

(b) straight edge rock bucket with teeth
直边有齿石料铲斗

(c) general purpose bucket with teeth
通用有齿铲斗

(d) general purpose bucket with bolt-on-edges
螺栓紧固边刃通用铲斗

(e) light material bucket with bolt-on edges
螺栓紧固边刃轻质材料铲斗

(f) log/sorting grapples
木材堆放抓斗

Fig. 8.13　Bucket types 铲斗类型

8.3.2 Working Attachments of Skid-steer Loader 滑移装载机工作附件 (Fig. 8.14)

(a) cold planer 冷铣刨

(b) pallet fork 货叉

(c) hydraulic breakers 液压破碎锤

(d) angle brooms 转角清扫滚刷

(e) general purpose pick-up broom 通用收集式清扫

(f) brush grapple bucket 刷式抓斗

Fig. 8.14

(g) forked scrap grapple bucket 叉式杂物抓斗

(h) power rake 动力耙

(i) heavy duty scrap grapple bucket 重型杂物抓斗

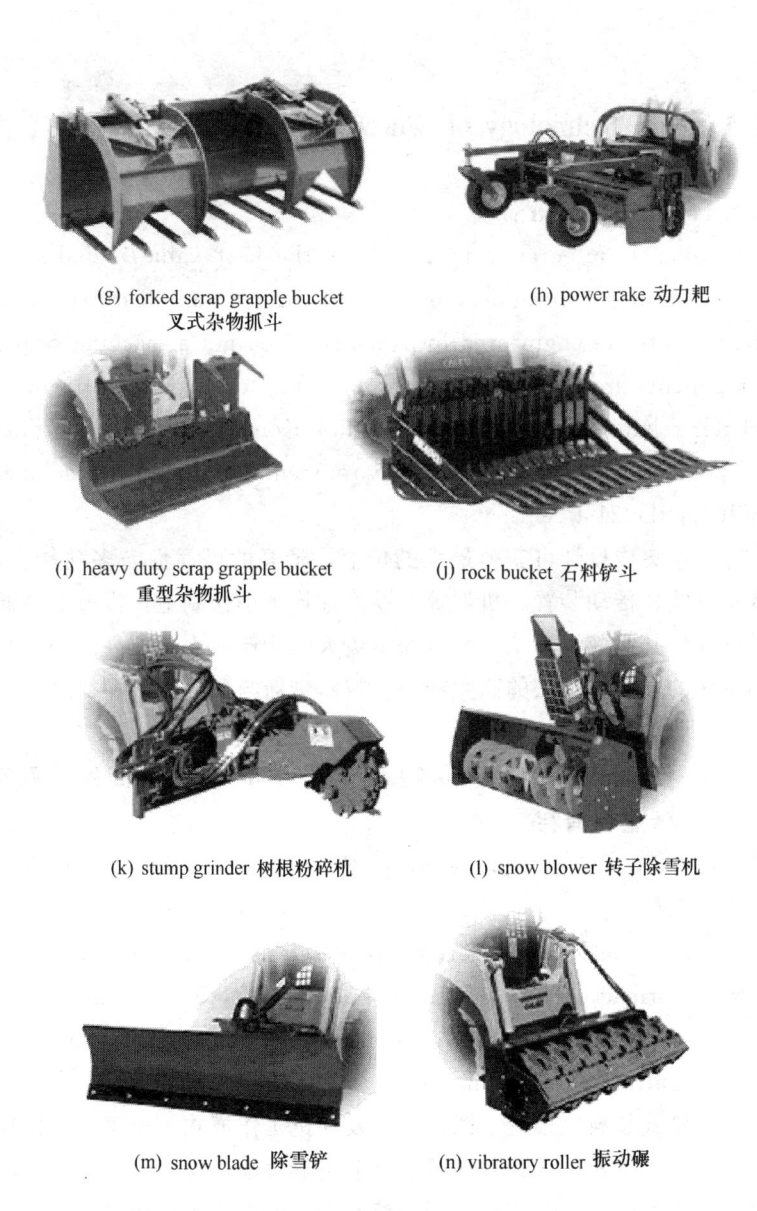

(j) rock bucket 石料铲斗

(k) stump grinder 树根粉碎机

(l) snow blower 转子除雪机

(m) snow blade 除雪铲

(n) vibratory roller 振动碾

Fig. 8.14 Working attachments of skid-steer loader 滑移装载机工作附件

8.4 New Technology of Wheel Loader 轮式装载机新技术

8.4.1 Introduction 简介

Komatsu-integrated design offers the best value, reliability, and versatility. Hydraulics, powertrain, frame and all other major components are engineered by Komatsu. You get a machine whose components are designed to work together for higher production, greater reliability, and more versatility. Komatsu's highly productive, innovative technology, environmentally friendly machines built for the 21st century.

小松集成设计可获得最大的价值、最高的可靠性与多功能性。液压系统、传动装置、机架等主要部件均由小松制造。机械部件通过设计使其共同协调工作,以获得更大的生产能力、更高的可靠性和更多的功能。小松的高生产率、技术创新与环境友好型机械产品为 21 世纪而制造。

8.4.2 High Productivity and Low Fuel Consumption 高生产率与低燃料消耗

(1) Two Mode Engine Power Select System 双模式发动机功率选择系统

This wheel loader offers two selectable engine operating modes-Normal and Power. The operator can adjust the machine's engine performance to match the condition requirements. This system is controlled with a dial on the right side control panel.

本轮式装载机设置了两个可选发动机工作模式——正常工作模式与动力工作模式。驾驶员可以调节机器发动机特性,使其与工况要求相匹配。这一调节系统用右控制台上的旋钮进行控制。

① Normal Mode: provides maximum fuel efficiency for most general loading conditions. 正常工作模式:在大多数负载条件下提

供最大的燃油效率。

② Power Mode: provides maximum power output for hard digging conditions or hill climb operations. 动力工作模式：在坚硬土壤挖掘条件下或在爬坡行驶时提供最大的动力输出。

(2) Automatic Transmission with Four Mode Select System 四工作模式自动变速箱

This operator controlled system allows the selection of manual shifting or three levels of automatic shifting modes (low, medium, and high). The operator can match the machine's operating requirements with optimum performance efficiency. This system is controlled with a dial on the right side of the control panel.

这一由驾驶员控制的系统允许其进行人力换挡或三级（低、中、高）自动换挡模式选择。驾驶员能够使作业要求与最佳性能相匹配。这一系统由控制台上右边的旋钮进行控制。

① Manual: the transmission is fixed to the gear speed and selected with the gear shift lever.

人力换挡模式：变速箱齿轮速度固定并通过变速杆进行选择。

② Auto Low: low mode provides smooth gear shifting at low engine speeds suitable for general excavating and loading while offering reduced fuel consumption.

自动低挡模式：低挡模式保证发动机低速工况下的平稳换挡，适用于普通铲装作业，具有较低的燃油消耗。

③ Auto Medium: medium mode provides gear shifting at mid-range engine speeds required for more aggressive conditions.

自动中挡模式：提供发动机中速范围换挡操作，适用于更加主动的作业工况。

④ Auto High: high mode provides maximum rim pull and fast cycle times by shifting the transmission at high engine speeds. This mode is suitable for hill-climb and load and carry operations.

自动高挡模式：提供发动机高速工况下的换挡操作，可产生最大的铲掘力与快速的作业循环。这一模式适用于爬坡、铲装与转运的循环作业。

(3) Dual-Speed Hydraulic System 双速液压系统

Komatsu's automatic dual-speed hydraulic system increases operational efficiency and productivity by matching the hydraulic demands to the work conditions.

小松自动双速液压系统通过使液压需求与工况相匹配提高了作业效率和生产率。

① Digging Operations 铲装作业 （Fig. 8.15）

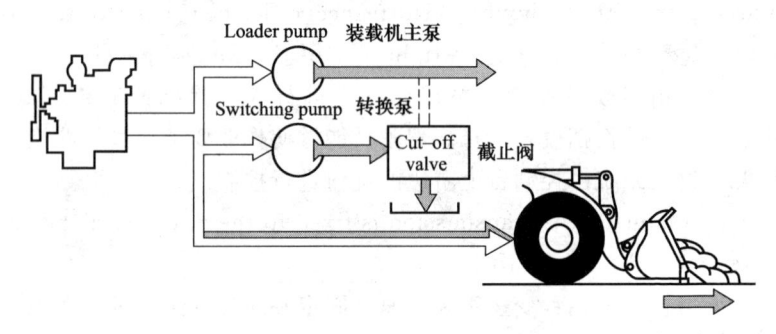

Fig. 8.15　Digging operations 铲装作业

Engine power used to operate the switch pump is transferred to the transmission to provide increased rimpull when digging.

铲装作业时，用来驱动转换泵的发动机功率输入变速箱以增加铲掘力。

② Lifting Operations 提升作业 （Fig. 8.16）

The switch pump assists the loader pump to provide increased lifting speed and power when lifting and loading.

提升装载作业时，转换泵辅助装载机主泵以增加提升速度和功率。

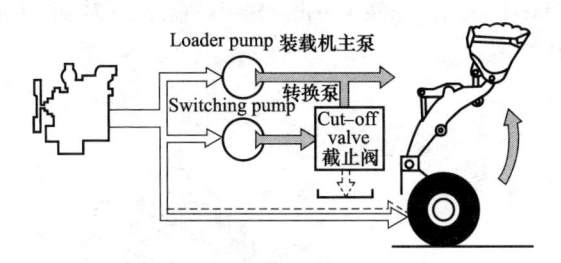

Fig. 8.16　Lifting operations 提升作业

8.4.3　Increased Reliability 提高可靠性

（1）Komatsu Components 小松部件（Fig. 8.17）

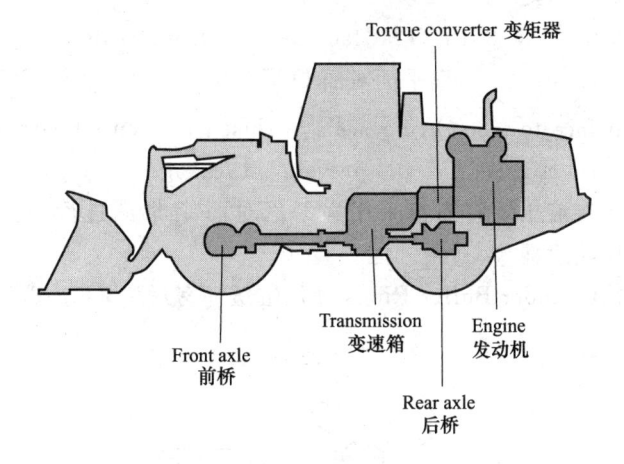

Fig. 8.17　Komatsu components 小松部件

　　Komatsu manufactures the engine, torque converter, transmission, hydraulic units, and electrical parts on this wheel loader. Komatsu loaders are manufactured with an integrated production system under a strict quality control system.

　　该轮式装载机上小松制造了发动机、变矩器、液压装置和电器元件。小松装载机制造采用了严格质量控制下的集成生产系统。

（2）Flat Face-to-Face O-ring Seals 扁平面对面 O 形圈密封（Fig. 8.18）

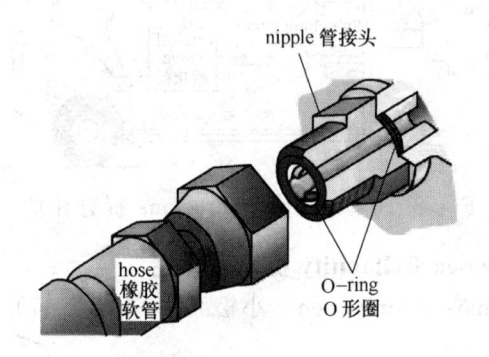

Fig. 8.18　Flat face-to-face O-ring seals
扁平面对面 O 形圈密封

Flat face-to-face O-ring seals are used to securely seal all hydraulic hose connections and prevent oil leakage.

对所有液压软管连接采用扁平面对面 O 形圈进行安全密封，以防液压油泄漏。

（3）Cylinder Buffer Rings 液压缸缓冲密封圈（Fig. 8.19）

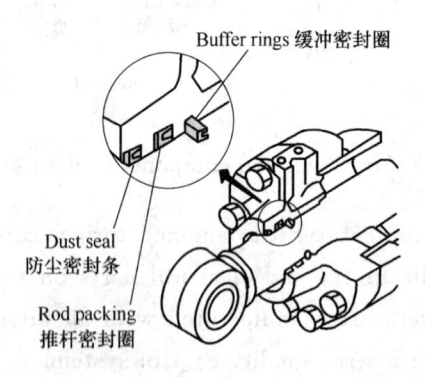

Fig. 8.19　Cylinder buffer rings 液压缸缓冲密封圈

Buffer rings are installed to the head-side of the all-hydraulic cylinders to lower the load on the rod seals, prolong cylinder life by

30% and maximize overall reliability.

缓冲密封圈安装在全液压油缸的头部以降低推杆密封载荷，可延长液压缸寿命 30%，并使总可靠性最大。

(4) Wet multi-disc brakes and fully hydraulic braking system 湿式多片制动器与全液压制动系统 (Fig. 8. 20)

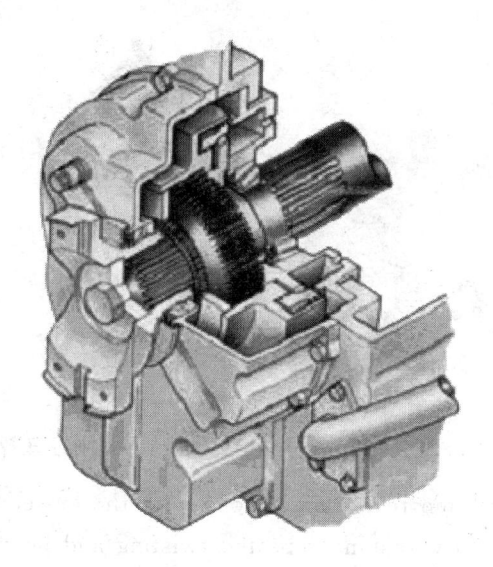

Fig. 8. 20 Wet multi-disc brakes and fully hydraulic braking system 湿式多片制动器与全液压制动系统

The wet disc service and parking brakes are fully sealed and adjustment-free to reduce contamination, wear and maintenance. Added reliability is designed into the braking system by the use of two independent hydraulic circuits providing hydraulic backup should one of the circuits fail. If the brake oil pressure drops, a warning lamp flashes and an alarm sounds intermittently. If the brake pressure continues to drop, the parking brake is automatically applied providing a double safety system.

行车与停车湿式盘式制动器完全密封并无需调节，从而减少了污染、磨损和维护。在制动系统中采用两个独立液压回路，作为当某一液压回路发生故障时的储备，从而增加了系统的可靠性。当制动压力降低时，报警灯闪烁，报警器间歇鸣叫。如果制动压力持续降低，停车制动器将自动启动，形成双安全系统。

（5）High-Rigidity Frames 大刚度车架 (Fig. 8.21)

Fig. 8.21 High-rigidity frames 大刚度车架

The front and rear frames along with the loader linkage have high rigidity to withstand repeated twisting and bending loads to the loader body and linkage. Both the upper and lower center pivot bearings use tapered roller bearings for increased durability.

前、后车架及装载机铰接机构具有较大的刚度，以抵抗重复扭转与弯曲载荷对装载机机身和铰接机构的作用。上、下中心枢轴轴承均采用圆锥滚子轴承以提高寿命。

Unit 9　Motor Graders
自行式平地机

9.1　Overview 概述

9.1.1　Basic Concept 基本概念

A grader, also commonly referred to as a road grader, a blade, a maintainer or a motor grader, is an engineering vehicle with a large blade used to create a flat surface. Typical models have three axles, with the engine and cab situated above the rear axles at one end of the vehicle and a third axle at the front end of the vehicle, with the blade in between.

平地机是一种安装有大型修建平整地面铲刀的工程机械，通常又称为道路平地机、刮铲、养护机械和自行式平地机等。平地机的典型形式为三桥结构，发动机和驾驶室位于机械的两个后桥之上，第三车桥位于机械的前端，铲刀设置在车桥之间。

In civil engineering, the grader's purpose is to "finish grade" (refine, set precisely) the "rough grading" performed by heavy equipment or engineering vehicles such as scrapers and bulldozers. Graders can produce inclined surfaces and surfaces with cambered cross-sections for roads. In some countries, they are used to produce drainage ditches with shallow V-shaped cross-sections on either side of highways.

在土木工程中，平地机的用途是"修饰"（精细修整、精确定型）由重型设备或铲运机和推土机等工程机械建造的"粗糙地面"。

平地机可以修建斜坡和具有拱形断面的路面。在一些国家，通常使用平地机修建道路两侧较浅的 V 形断面排水沟。

Graders are commonly used in the construction and maintenance of dirt roads and gravel roads. In the construction of paved roads they are used to prepare the base course to create a wide flat surface for the asphalt to be placed on. Graders are also used to set native soil foundation pads to finish grade prior to the construction of large buildings.

平地机通常用于建设和维护泥泞与砂石道路。在铺装道路工程中，平地机用来修建路基，以便为沥青混合料的摊铺建造宽广平整的平面。平地机也用于大型建筑施工前土基础的修建。

In some locales such as Canada and places in the United States, graders are often used in municipal and residential snow removal. In scrubland and grassland areas of Australia and Africa, graders are often an essential piece of equipment on ranches, large farms and plantations to make dirt tracks where the absence of rocks and trees means bulldozers are not required. A more recent innovation is the outfitting of graders with GPS technology.

在一些场所和地方，如加拿大和美国，经常使用平地机清除市区和住宅区的积雪。在澳大利亚和非洲的灌木丛林与草原地带，平地机是牧场、大型农场和种植园修建土路的基本机械设备，由于那里缺少砂石和树木而使推土机派不上用场。平地机的最新发展是装备了 GPS 技术。

9.1.2 Applications 应用 (Fig. 9.1)

(a) smooth-riding surface 平整路面

(b) earthmoving 堆移材料

(c) finishing side slope 修整边坡

(d) snow removing 除雪作业

(e) sweeping work 清扫作业

(f) tree farm road construction 林场道路建设

(g) subgrade scarifying 路基翻松

(h) maintain shoulder of road 维修路肩

Fig. 9.1 Applications of grader 平地机的应用

9.1.3 Types 类型 (Fig. 9.2)

(a) hydromechanical transmission motor grader
液力机械传动自行式平地机

(b) full hydraulic drive motor grader
全液压传动自行式平地机

(c) four-wheel drive motor grader
四轮驱动自行式平地机

(d) all wheel drive motor grader
全轮驱动自行式平地机

(e) integrated frame motor grader
整体机架式平地机

(f) articulated frame motor grader
铰接机架式平地机

Fig. 9.2　Types of grader 平地机的类型

9.2 Components and Features 组成与特点

9.2.1 Components 组成

(1) Overall Structure 总体结构 (Fig. 9.3)

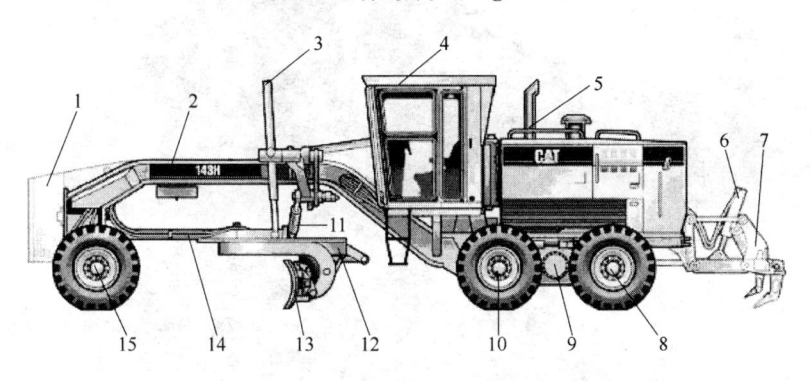

Fig. 9.3 Overall structure 总体结构

1. counterweight 配重
2. front frame 前机架
3. blade hoist cylinder 铲刀升降油缸
4. cab and operating system 驾驶室及操作系统
5. engine 发动机
6. scarifier hoist cylinder 松土器升降油缸
7. scarifier 松土器
8. rear driving axle 后驱动桥
9. power train 传动系
10. middle driving axle 中间驱动桥
11. traction frame moving cylinder 牵引架移动油缸
12. turning circle 回转圈
13. moldboard 铲刀板
14. traction frame 牵引架
15. oscillating steering axle 摆动转向桥

(2) Power Train 传动装置 (Fig. 9.4)

Fig. 9.4　Power train 传动装置

1　torque converter and power shift transmission 变矩器与动力换挡变速箱
2　drive shaft 传动轴
3　drive axle and final reduction gear 驱动桥与终减速器
4　drive hub 驱动轮毂
5　chain drive 链条传动

(3) Operation Mechanism 工作机构 (Fig. 9.5)

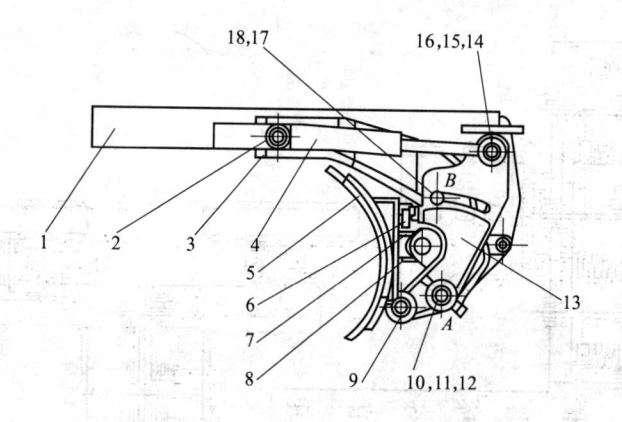

Fig. 9.5 Operation mechanism 工作机构

1　turning circle 回转圈
2　backing plate 垫板
3,11,15　nut 螺母
4　blade angle change cylinder 铲刀角度变换油缸
5　blade 铲刀
6　guide plate 导板
7　bracket 支架
8　blade outstanding cylinder 铲刀外伸油缸
9　bushing block 衬套
10　check ring 挡圈
12　cotter pin 开口销
13　angular position device 角位器
14,17　bolt 螺栓
16　hinge pin 销轴
18　washer 垫片

9.2.2 Typical Drive Line System 典型传动系统 (Fig. 9.6)

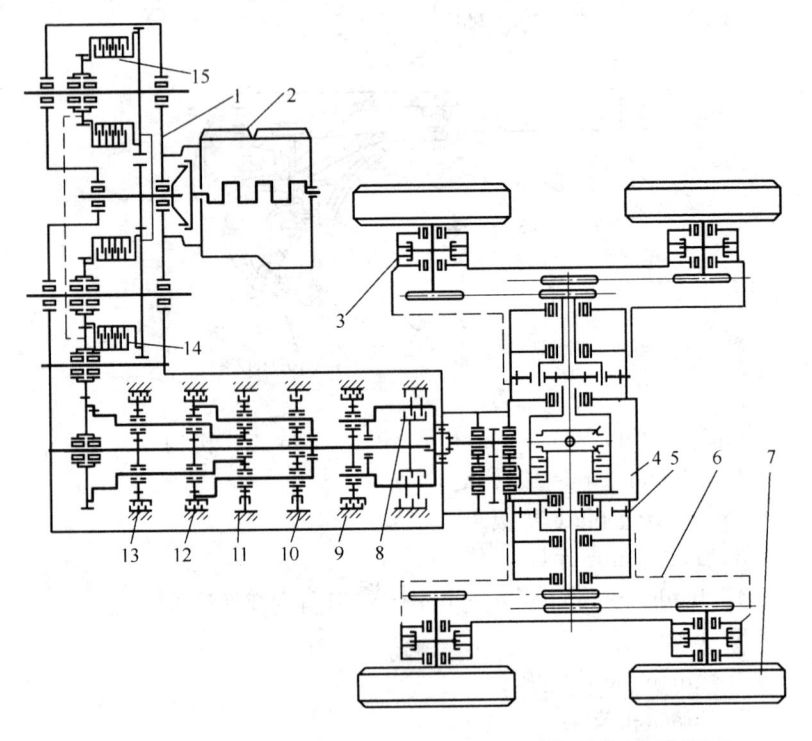

Fig. 9.6 Typical drive line system 典型传动系统

1　power shift transmission 动力换挡变速箱
2　engine 发动机
3　service brake 行车制动器
4　rear axle differential gear 后桥差速器
5　final reduction gear 终减速器
6　chain drive (equilibrium box) 链传动（平衡箱）
7　tire 轮胎
8～13　shift clutch 换挡离合器
14　forward gear shift clutch 前进挡离合器
15　reverse gear shift clutch 倒挡离合器

9.2.3 Typical Hydraulic Control System 典型液压控制系统
(Fig. 9.7)

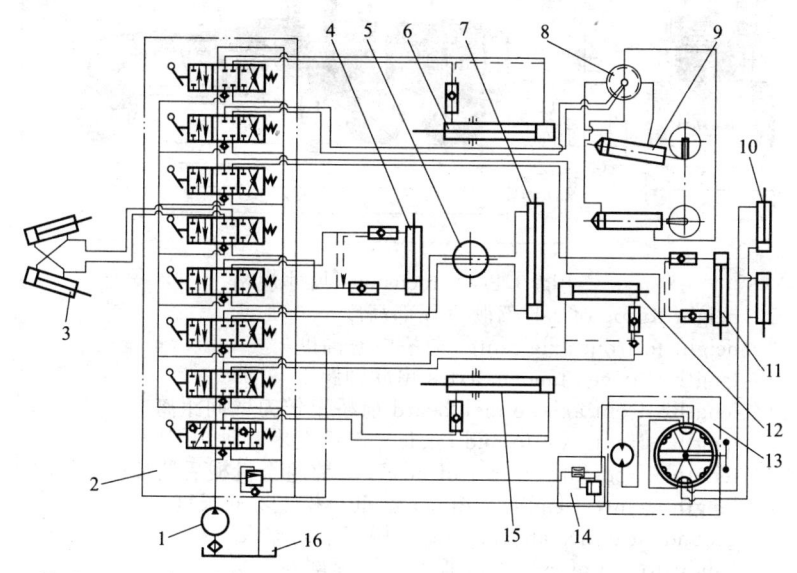

Fig. 9.7 Typical hydraulic control system 典型液压控制系统
1　gear pump 齿轮泵
2　multichannel conversion valve 多路换向阀
3　rear wheel steering cylinder 后轮转向油缸
4　traction frame cylinder 牵引架油缸
5　swivelcoupling 回转接头
6　blade hoist cylinder (left) 铲刀升降油缸（左）
7　blade sidesway cylinder 铲刀侧移油缸
8　revolving valve 回转阀
9　revolving cylinder 回转油缸
10　front wheel steering cylinder 前轮转向油缸
11　front wheel tilt cylinder 前轮倾斜油缸
12　scarifier hoist cylinder 松土器升降油缸
13　diverter 转向器
14　flow control valve 流量控制阀
15　blade hoist cylinder (right) 铲刀升降油缸（右）
16　hydraulic oil tank 液压油箱

9.2.4 Dimensions 尺寸规格 (Fig. 9.8)

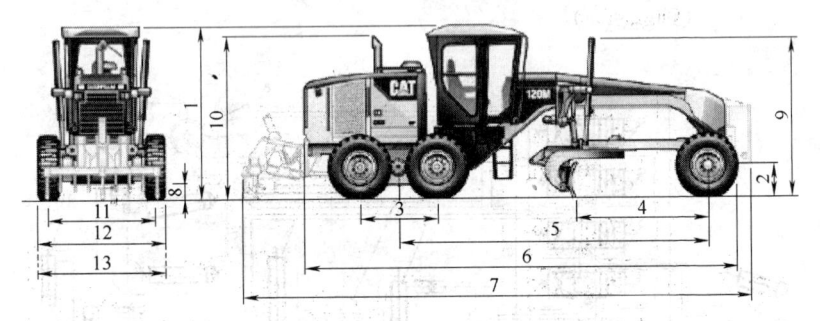

Fig. 9.8 Dimensions 尺寸规格

1 height to top of cab 驾驶室顶部高度
2 height to front axle center 前桥中心高度
3 length between tandem axles 串联轴距
4 length—front axle to moldboard 前桥至铲刀壁间距离
5 length—front axle to mid tandem 前桥至串联轴中间距离
6 length—front tire to rear of machine 前轮至机械后端长度
7 length-counterweight to ripper 配重至松土器间长度
8 ground clearance at rear axle 后桥离地间隙
9 height to top of cylinders 提升油缸顶部高度
10 height to exhaust stack 排烟道高度
11 width-tire center lines 轮距
12 width-outside rear tires 后轮外侧宽度
13 width-outside front tires 前轮外侧宽度

9.2.5 Blade Operating Space 铲刀工作范围 (Fig. 9.9)

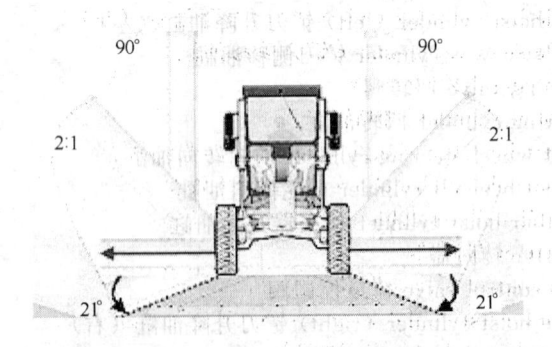

Fig. 9.9 Blade operating space 铲刀工作范围

9.2.6 Activity types 作业类型（Fig. 9.10）

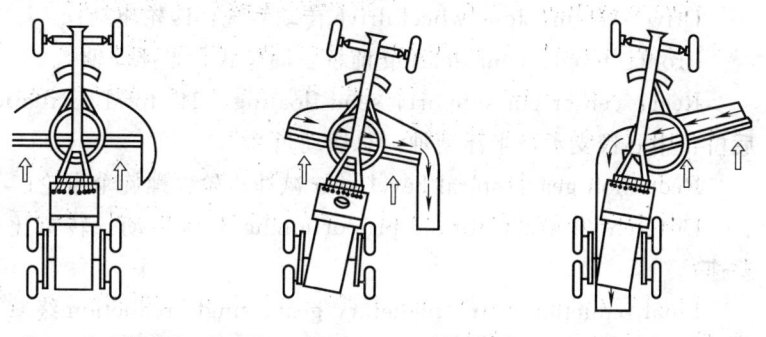

(a) grading work 平整作业　(b) oblique movement work 斜行作业　(c) earth moving 移土作业

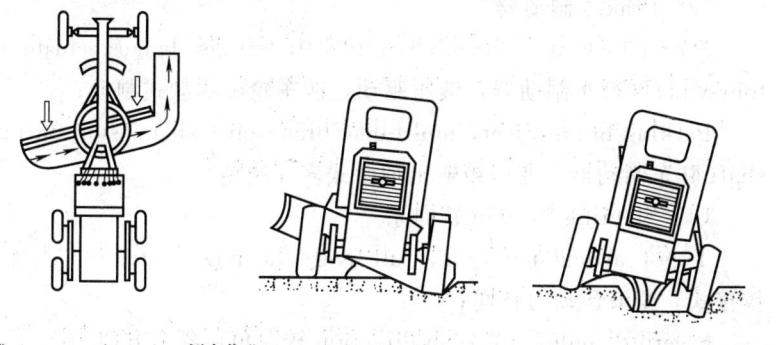

(d) reverse earth moving 倒车作业　(e) ditching 挖沟　(f) to scrape bottom of trench 刮沟底

Fig. 9.10　Activity types 作业类型

9.2.7 Standard Equipment Specifications 标准装置类型与性能参数

（1）Transmission and Torque Converter 变速箱与液力变矩器

Full power shift transmission with integral free wheeling stator torque converter and lock-up 完全动力换挡变速箱，整体式自由导轮液力变矩器与闭锁离合器；

Speeds (at rated engine speed) 行走速度（发动机额定转速条件下）。

(2) Axles and Final Drives 驱动桥与终传动

Drive system: four-wheel drive 传动系统：四轮驱动；

Front: fixed, semi-floating 前桥：固定式，半浮动轴；

Rear: center-pin support, semi-floating, 24° total oscillation 后桥：中心铰支承，半浮动轴，总摆动角 24°；

Reduction gear: spiral bevel gear 减速齿轮：螺旋伞齿轮；

Differential gear: torque proportioning 差速传动：转矩比例差速；

Final reduction gear: planetary gear, single reduction 终减速齿轮：行星齿轮，单级减速。

(3) Brakes 制动器

Service brakes: hydraulically-actuated, wet disc brakes actuate on four wheels 行车制动器：液压驱动，四车轮湿式盘式制动；

Parking brake: wet, multi-disc brake on transmission output shaft 驻车制动器：变速箱输出轴湿式多片制动。

(4) Steering System 转向系

Type: articulated type, full-hydraulic power steering 类型：铰接式，全液压动力转向；

Steering angle: 40° each direction 转向角：各个方向 40°；

Minimum turning radius at the center of outside tire 外轮中心最小转弯半径。

(5) Boom and Bucket 动臂和铲斗

Z-bar loader linkage is designed for maximum rigidity and offers powerful breakout.

Z 形连杆设计提供了最大的刚性和强大的破坏力。

Rap-out loader linkage design enables shock dumping for removing sticky materials.

敲打型连杆设计提供了黏性材料的振动装卸。

Sealed loader linkage pins with dust seals extend greasing intervals.

防尘密封式连接销延长了润滑间隔时间。

The bucket is made of high-tensile strength steel.

铲斗由高抗拉强度钢制作。

(6) Bucket Controls 铲斗控制

The use of a PPC hydraulic control valve offers lighter operating effort for the work equipment control levers.

应用液压程序控制阀使工作装置操纵杆操作轻便。

The reduction in the lever force and travel makes it easy to operate in the work environment.

操纵杆作用力和行程的减小使工作现场操作变得容易。

Control positions 位置控制。

Boom：Raise, hold, lower, and float 动臂：提升，保持，下降，浮动；

Bucket：Roll back, hold, and dump 铲斗：后倾翻，保持，倾卸。

(7) Hydraulic System 液压系统

Capacity (discharge flow) @ engine-rated rpm 发动机额定转速流量

Loader pump 装载机液压泵；

Steering pump 转向泵；

Pilot pump (Gear-type pumps) 引导泵（齿轮泵）；

Relief valve setting 安全阀设定压力；

Control valve：2-spool open center type 控制阀：双阀芯开式中心型；

Hydraulic cylinders：double-acting, piston 液压缸：双作用，活塞；

Hydraulic cycle time (rated load in bucket)：raise, dump, lower (empty), total cycle time 液压循环时间：提升时间，倾卸时间，下降时间，总循环时间。

9.2.8 Laser Grade Control System 激光找平系统（Fig. 9.11）

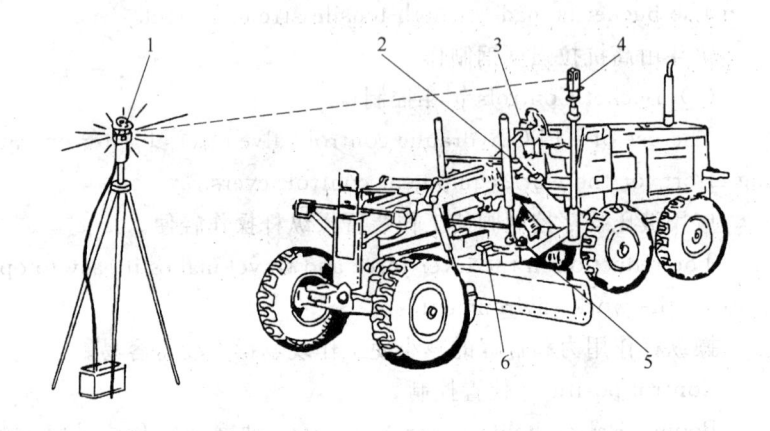

Fig. 9.11 Laser grade control system 激光找平系统

1 generating laser 激光发射器   4 laser pickoff 激光接收器
2 hydraulic tank 液压箱   5 clinometer 倾斜仪
3 controller 控制器   6 rotation sensor 旋转传感器

9.2.9 Volvo Motor Grader Features 沃尔沃平地机特点

（1）Transmission 变速箱（Fig. 9.12）

Fig. 9.12 Transmission 变速箱

The Volvo 8400 transmission is a fully sequential, direct drive, powershift transmission. A single lever controller provides rapid access to eight forward and four reverse evenly stepped speeds to match any job. Evenly proportioned gear ratios deliver the exact power and speed you need to match every grading job.

沃尔沃 8400 变速箱是一种全顺序排列、直接驱动、动力换挡式变速箱。单杆控制器在 8 个前进挡与 4 个后退挡之间提供快速平稳的有级换挡，可与任意作业工况相匹配。比例均匀的传动比可精确传递所需要的功率与速度，以适应每一种平整作业。

（2）Powertrain 传动系（Fig. 9.13）

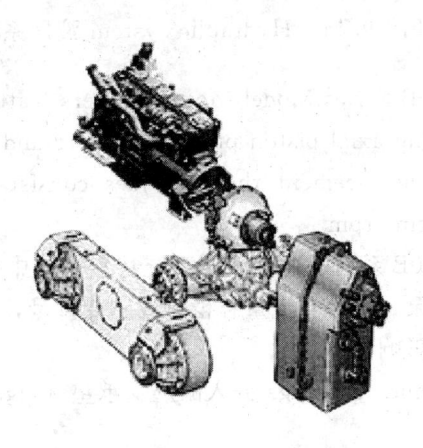

Fig. 9.13　Powertrain 传动系

All Volvo 700B Series Model Motor Graders feature a modular powertrain consisting of an engine, transmission and lock/unlock final drive. A modular powertrain allows the independent removal of any component without affecting other components.

沃尔沃 700B 系列平地机均使用模块化传动系，传动系由发动机、变速箱和闭锁/开锁式终传动所组成。模块化传动系允许任意部件独立移动而不影响其他部件。

(3) Hydraulic System 液压系统 (Fig. 9.14)

Fig. 9.14 Hydraulic system 液压系统

Volvo 700B Series Model Motor Graders feature a closed center, load sensing axial piston pump, pressure and flow compensated, variable displacement that provides consistant response regardless of engine rpm.

沃尔沃700B系列平地机液压系统特点是：中位封闭式、负荷感应轴向柱塞泵、压力与流量补偿方式和变排量，系统一致响应不受发动机转速影响。

(4) Duramide Bearings 嵌入耐磨支承垫 (Fig. 9.15)

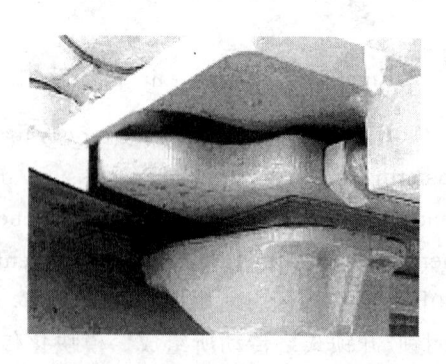

Fig. 9.15 Duramide bearings 嵌入耐磨支承垫

Duramide wear inserts eliminate metal-to-metal contact in all circle turn, blade slide and blade lift areas. Duramide is exclusive to Volvo Motor Graders. Maximum wear life and low cost maintenance.

Duramide 耐磨嵌入支承垫消除了回转、铲刀滑动和提升时结构中金属与金属的接触。Duramide 支承垫是沃尔沃平地机所独有的，具有最大的耐磨寿命和较低的维护成本。

(5) Circle 回转圈 (Fig. 9.16)

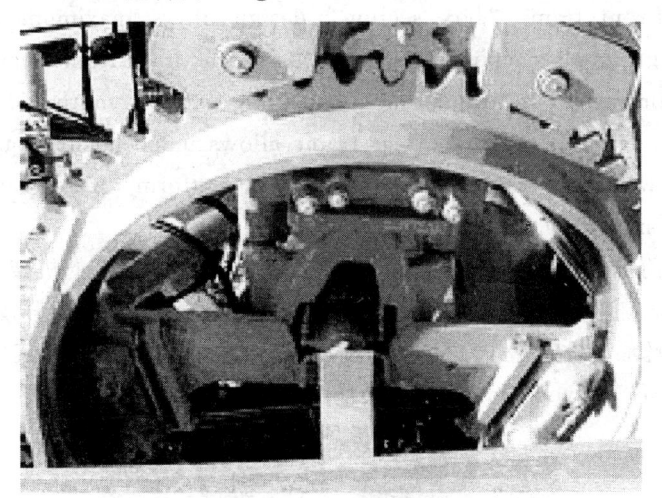

Fig. 9.16 Circle 回转圈

The Volvo circle features hardened teeth cut on the outside of the circle for maximum leverage and minimum wear. The circle is held in place by multiple clamp and guide shoes with replaceable Duramide inserts. A very robust circle turn system with easy, low cost maintainability.

沃尔沃回转圈的特点是具有坚硬的外圈齿，以获得最大的平衡与最小的磨损。回转圈由多层夹板、导向板以及可更换耐磨嵌入元件固定。非常坚固的回转系统维护方便，成本低。

(6) Front Frame 前机架 (Fig. 9.17)

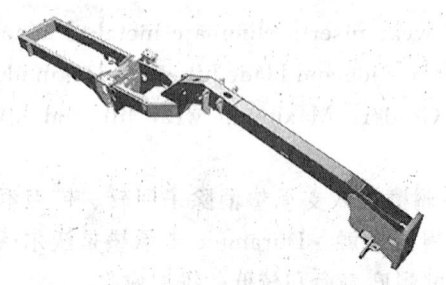

Fig. 9.17　Front frame 前机架

Front frame "box section" design offers maximum frame strength in all machine sizes. The "high arch" front frame section is reinforced by two torque tubes, providing frame strength and flexibility. The full perimeter rear frame allows independent mounting of powertrain components and a robust platform for rear attachment mounting.

前机架"箱型截面"设计在整机范围提供了最大的机架强度。"高拱"前机架部分依靠两个扭力管得到加固,增加了机架强度与韧性。环形后机架允许独立安装传动装置与坚固的后部附件安装平台。

(7) Drive Circle 驱动回转圈 (Fig. 9.18)

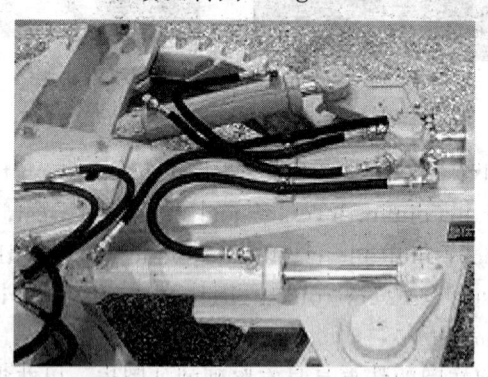

Fig. 9.18　Drive circle 驱动回转圈

The Volvo circle is powered by two hydraulic cylinders, 90 degrees out of phase, providing optimum turning and holding capability. The Volvo circle turn system has the ability to cycle whatever the machine can push.

沃尔沃回转圈由两个液压缸驱动，其相位差为90°，具有最佳的回转和定位能力。沃尔沃回转圈回转系统能够在任何牵引工况下进行回转作业。

（8）Blade Pull 铲刀牵引力

By optimizing blade placement over the drive wheels and over a long blade base and by putting more engine power to the ground, Volvo graders offer a blade pull capability that leads the industry in every weight class.

通过优化铲刀在驱动轮与长刀架上方的位置并向地面提供更多的发动机功率，沃尔沃平地机铲刀牵引能力在各种重量级别上处于领先地位。

（9）Moveable Blade Control System 可移动铲刀控制系统（Fig. 9.19）

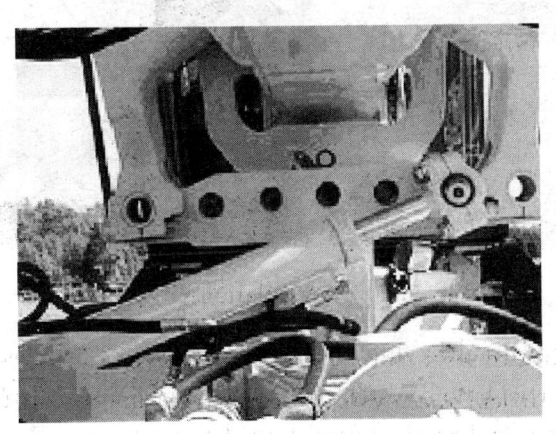

Fig. 9.19 Moveable blade control system
可移动铲刀控制系统

MBCS allows the operator a full range of blade mobilities, achieving any angle up to a full 90 degrees left or right. The MBCS also allows as much as 21 degrees downward angle for ditch cutting and up to a 2∶1 bank slope with the moldboard completely outside of the tire profile.

移动式铲刀控制系统能够使驾驶员进行全方位铲刀移动，实现任意角度直至左右 90°的旋转。该系统还可向下最大旋转 21°进行开沟作业，使铲刀板完全伸出到轮胎外侧进行最大坡度为 2∶1 的边坡作业。

（10）Articulation 铰接连接 （Fig. 9. 20）

Fig. 9. 20　Articulation 铰接连接

Twin hydraulic cylinders articulate frame 22 degrees right and left. The articulation system incorporates an anti drift lock valve that ensures stable operation. Articulation allows optimum blade positioning and short turning radius.

双联液压缸以左、右 22°与机架铰接。铰接系统具有抗偏移保险阀，以确保稳定作业。铰接连接可实现铲刀的最佳定位，减小转弯半径。

(11) Front Axle Mobility 前桥机动性（Fig. 9.21）

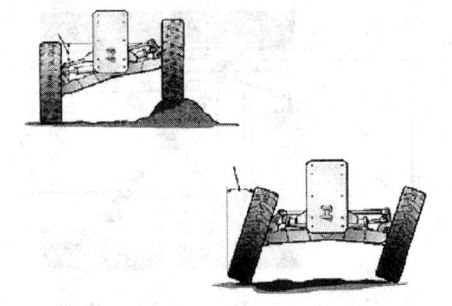

Fig. 9.21　Front axle mobility 前桥机动性

Motor grader front axles have 3 mobilities: Oscillation——16 degrees up and down. Wheel lean——18 degrees to counter the "side draft" which results from cutting material at one end of the moldboard and discharging it at the other. Steering Arc——72 degrees.

平地机前桥有3种运动形式：上、下可摆动16°；车轮可偏斜18°，以平衡铲刀一端切土、另一端卸土时所产生的侧向牵引阻力；可实现72°圆弧转向。

(12) All Wheel Drive 全轮驱动

The Volvo G726B and G746B are the most productive AWD motor graders in the industry. The AWD System functions through speeds up to 32.7 km/h for optimum snow clearing and high speed maintenance activities. For fine grading applications the "Creep Mode" functions at all speeds from 0-3.2 km/h. In "Creep Mode" the machine uses the front drive only. The rear drive is disengaged to eliminate scuffing of the surface.

沃尔沃G726B与G746B是生产能力最强的全轮驱动（AWD）平地机。AWD系统速度可达32.7 km/h，以进行最佳的除雪和快速养护作业。对于精确平整作业，在0～3.2km/h的全速范围内可实施"爬行作业模式"。在"爬行作业模式"中，平地机仅使用前轮驱动。此时，脱开后驱动桥以防地面产生皱褶。

(13) Brakes 制动装置 (Fig. 9.22)

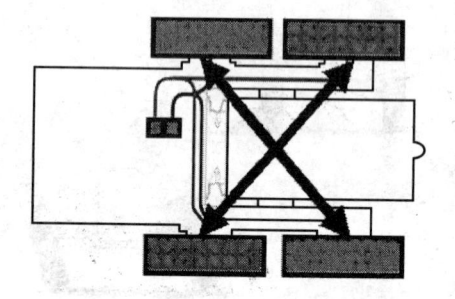

Fig. 9.22　Brakes 制动装置

The brakes feature a "cross-over" plumbing pattern that ensures braking capability to both sides of the machine even in the event of brake line failure. An electrical motor/pump combination supplies full braking power in the event of engine stall or low hydraulic pressure.

制动器具有交叉管路安装方式，即使在制动回路发生故障时也能保证平地机的双侧制动能力。当发动机停机或液压压力降低时，由电马达/泵组合系统提供充足的制动动力。

(14) Controls 操作控制装置 (Fig. 9.23)

Fig. 9.23　Controls 操作控制装置

All of the operator controls are conveniently located within a 90° arc, either on the fully adjustable steering pedestal or in the right hand console. A fully adjustable steering pedestal with adjustable pedestal head allows the operator to mold the steering/control pedestal to whatever position is needed.

所有驾驶员的操纵装置在90°弧度范围设置，安装在完全可调式转向柱上或者是在右操作台上。具有可调头部的完全调节式转向柱使驾驶员可将转向/控制台摆放到任意需要的位置。

(15) Smart Shifter 灵巧变速器（Fig. 9.24）

Fig. 9.24 Smart shifter 灵巧变速器

The exclusive single lever Smart Shifter electronic transmission controller remembers the last forward and reverse gear used to facilitate rapid forward/reverse shifting. Rapid direction changes reduce cycle times.

独特的单杆灵巧变速电子控制器可记忆最后一次前进和后退挡位，以方便快速进行前进/后退方向变换。快速方向变换可缩短工作周期。

9.3　Working Attachments 工作附件（Fig. 9.25）

(a) front scarifier 前置式松土器

(b) reversible snow plow 反转型除雪铲（犁）

(c) one-way snow plow 单向除雪铲（犁）

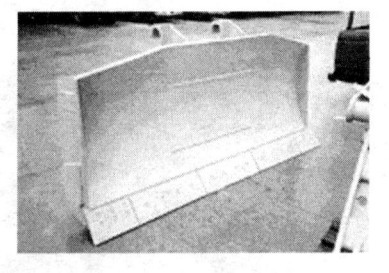

(d) front-mounted straight blade 前置直铲刀

(e) hydraulic snow wing 液压测向除雪铲

(f) broom 清扫滚刷

Fig. 9.25　Working attachments 工作附件

9.4 New Technology of Motor Grader 平地机新技术

9.4.1 Introduction 简介

The 120M motor grader represents a revolution in operational efficiency, visibility, service ease and overall productivity, setting the new standard and building on the legacy of high quality you can trust.

120M 型平地机代表了操作效率、驾驶视野、维护方便性和整机生产率等方面的革命性变革,并且建立了新的标准,在可以信赖的高质量基础上制造。

9.4.2 Power Train 传动系 (Fig. 9.26)

Fig. 9.26 Power train 传动系

An electronically controlled power shift transmission assures smooth shifting and maximum power to the ground. A modular rear axle and hydraulic brakes simplify serviceability and reduce operating costs.

电控动力换挡变速箱保证了平稳换挡和最大的地面动力。模块化后桥与液压制动器简化了维护,降低了使用成本。

(1) Front Axle 前桥 (Fig. 9.27)

Fig. 9.27 Front axle 前桥
1 caterpillar sealed spindle 卡特彼勒密封主轴
2 tapered roller bearing 锥形滚子轴承

The Caterpillar sealed spindle keeps the bearings free from contaminants and lubricated in a light-weight oil.
卡特彼勒密封主轴保护轴承不受污染并由轻质油润滑。

This durable, low-maintenance design reduces your owning and operating costs. Two tapered roller bearings support the wheel spindle.
这种耐久性与低维护设计减少了用户的投资和使用成本。两个锥形滚子轴承支承着车轮主轴。

The Cat "Live Spindle" design places the larger tapered roller bearing outboard where the load is greater, extending bearing life.
卡特"旋转主轴"设计使较大的锥形滚子轴承位于载荷较大的外侧，从而延长了轴承寿命。

(2) Hydraulic Brakes 液压制动器 (Fig. 9.28)

Fig. 9.28　Hydraulic brakes 液压制动器

The oil bathed, multi-disc service brakes are hydraulically actuated, providing smooth predictable braking and lower operating costs.

湿式、多片行车制动器依靠液压驱动，制动平顺，使用成本低。

With brakes located at each tandem wheel, the 120M offers the largest total brake surface area in the industry, delivering dependable stopping power and longer brake life.

在每个串联车轮上设置了制动器，因此，120M型平地机具有最大的制动面积，并传递可靠的刹车动力，延长制动寿命。

An easily accessible brake wear indicator/compensator system maintains consistent brake performance and indicates brake wear without disassembly. This system cuts service time and extends brake service life.

使用方便的制动磨损指示/补偿系统维持着不变的制动性能，无需拆卸即可指示制动磨损情况。该系统减少了维护时间，延长了制动器服务寿命。

(3) Programmable Autoshift 可编程自动换挡

The operator can easily customize various shift parameters through Cat Messenger to match the specific application requirement. This feature automatically shifts the transmission at optimal points, so the operator can focus on the work, improving safety, productivity and ease of operation.

通过卡特信控器驾驶员可以方便地设置各种换挡参数，以满足特殊的使用要求。这一特性可在最佳点自动换挡，从而使驾驶员能够把注意力集中到作业上，提高了安全性、生产率和操作方便性。

9.4.3 Hydraulics 液压系统

The electro-hydraulic load-sensing system provides the foundation for advanced machine controls, enabling superior controllability and precise and predictable hydraulic movements, with the reliability you expect from Caterpillar.

电子液压负荷感应系统为先进的机械控制奠定了基础，具有最佳的控制能力与精确可预测的液压运动，并可从卡特彼勒获得用户所期望的可靠性。

(1) Blade Float 铲刀浮动

The blade float feature allows the blade to move freely under its own weight. By floating both cylinders, the blade can follow the contours of the road when removing snow. Floating only one cylinder permits the toe of the blade to follow a hard surface while the operator controls the slope with the other lift cylinder.

铲刀的浮动特性允许铲刀在自重下自由移动。通过使两个油缸浮动，在除雪作业时铲刀可随路面轮廓移动。浮动单个油缸，在驾驶员用另一个提升油缸控制坡度的同时，可使铲刀刀尖随坚硬表面移动。

(2) Balanced Flow 平衡液流

Hydraulic flow is proportioned to ensure all implements operate simultaneously with little effect on the engine or implement speeds. If demand exceeds pump capacity, all cylinder velocities are reduced by the same ratio. The result is improved productivity in all applications.

液压流量是成比例的,以保证所有元件同时动作而不影响发动机或执行速度。如果需求超过液压泵排量,所有液压缸速度按照相同的比例降低。其结果提高了所有使用工况下的生产率。

(3) Consistent and Predictable Movement 稳定和可预知的运动

PPPC valves have different flow rates for the head and rod ends of the cylinder. This ensures consistent extension and retraction speeds for each cylinder, and gives the operator a consistent and predictable response every time an implement control is moved.

比例优先压力补偿阀对于液压缸头部和活塞杆一端具有不同的流速。这样可保证每个液压缸有相同的外伸与回缩速度,而且,当执行控制时,驾驶员可获得稳定且可预知的响应。

(4) Load Sensing Hydraulics 负荷感应液压系统

The time proven load-sensing system and the advanced Proportional Priority Pressure-Compensating (PPPC) electro-hydraulic valves on the 120M are designed to provide superior implement control and enhanced machine performance in all applications. Continuous matching of hydraulic flow and pressure to power demands creates less heat and reduces power consumption.

在120M平地机上设计了经长期检验的负荷感应系统与先进的比例优先压力补偿(PPPC)电液阀,为各种应用提供良好的执行控制和更好的机械性能。液压流量和压力与功率需求的不断匹配可产生较少的热量和减少功率消耗。

9.4.4 Structures 结构件

(1) Top-Adjust Drawbar Wear Strips 顶部调节牵引架耐磨垫 (Fig. 9.29)

Fig. 9.29 Top-adjust drawbar wear strips
顶部调节牵引架耐磨垫

The patented top-adjust wear strips dramatically reduce drawbar/circle adjustment time. By removing the access plates on top of the drawbar, shims and wear strips can easily be added or replaced. This feature reduces service downtime and lowers overall machine operating costs.

已获专利的顶部调节耐磨垫大大减少了牵引架/回转圈调整时间。卸下牵引架顶部入口压板，可方便地增加或更换垫片与耐磨条。这一特点可减少维护停机时间，降低机械总运行成本。

(2) Shimless Moldboard Retention System 无垫片铲刀板外伸系统 (Fig. 9.30)

Fig. 9.30　Shimless moldboard retention system
无垫片铲刀板外伸系统

The unique shimless moldboard retention system reduces the potential for blade chatter. Vertical and horizontal adjusting screws keep the moldboard's wear strips aligned for precise blade control and dramatic reductions in service time.

独特的无垫片铲刀板外伸系统减少了铲刀潜在的颤动。垂直与水平调整螺纹使牵引架耐磨条保持平整，以便精确控制铲刀，显著减少维护时间。

（3）Circle Construction 回转圈结构

Our one-piece forged steel circle is built to stand up to high stress loads and provide structural durability. The front 240° of circle teeth are hardened to reduce wear and ensure component reliability.

制造整体锻造钢结构回转圈以抵抗大应力载荷，使其具有结构韧性。前部240°的回转圈齿经淬火处理，以减少磨损，确保零件可靠性。

9.4.5　Operator Station 驾驶员操作台

A technologically advanced cab, featuring joystick controls, provides unmatched comfort and visibility.

以操纵杆控制为特点的、技术先进的驾驶室具有最好的舒适性和工作视野。

(1) Cat Comfort Series Seat 卡特舒适型系列驾驶座椅 (Fig. 9.31)

Fig. 9.31 Cat comfort series seat
卡特舒适型系列驾驶座椅

The Cat Comfort Series suspension seat has an ergonomic high-back design, with extra thick contoured cushions and infinitely adjustable lumbar support that evenly distributes the operator's weight. Multiple seat controls and armrests are easy to adjust for optimal support and comfort all day. The optional air suspension seat enhances ride quality for additional comfort.

卡特舒适型系列悬架式驾驶座椅具有人机工程学高靠背设计、超厚波形座垫与可均衡分配驾驶员体重的无限可调的腰部支撑。

(2) Left Joystick Functions 左操纵杆功能 (Fig. 9.32)

The left joystick primarily controls the machine direction and speed.

左操纵杆主要控制机械的方向和速度。

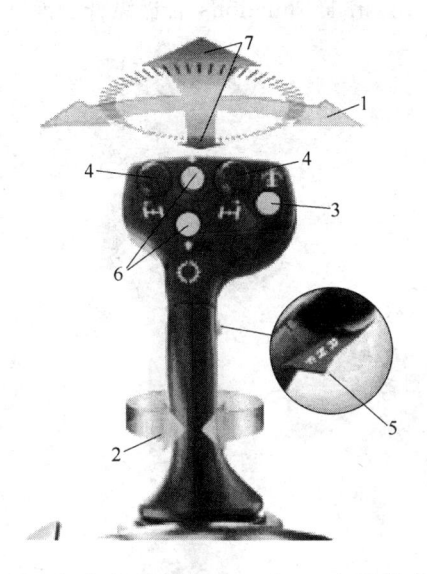

Fig. 9.32 Left joystick functions 左操纵杆功能

1 Steering：lean joystick left and right 转向：向左、右偏摆操纵杆
2 Articulation：twist joystick left and right 铰接回转：左、右扭转操纵杆
3 Articulation Return to Center：yellow thumb button 铰接架回正：黄色拇指按钮
4 Wheel Lean：two black thumb buttons 车轮偏摆：两个黑色拇指按钮
5 Direction：Index trigger shifts transmission to forward, neutral or reverse 行驶方向：通过指示触发开关使变速箱换入前进挡、空挡或倒退挡
6 Gear Selection：two yellow thumb buttons upshift and downshift 挡位选择：通过两个黄色按钮实现升挡和降挡
7 Left moldboard lift cylinder：push joystick to lower, pull joystick to raise 左铲刀板提升油缸：前推操纵杆降低铲刀，后拉操纵杆提升铲刀

(3) Right Joystick Functions 右操纵杆功能 (Fig. 9.33)

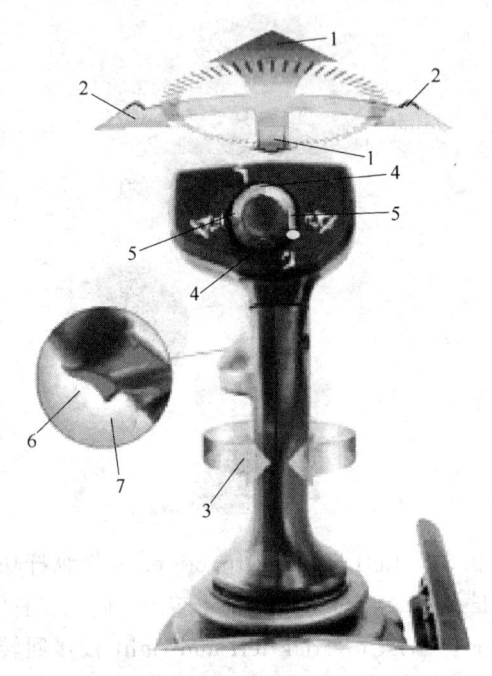

Fig. 9.33 Right joystick functions 右操纵杆功能

1. Right moldboard lift cylinder: push joystick to lower, pull joystick to raise 右铲刀板提升油缸：前推操纵杆降低铲刀，后拉操纵杆提升铲刀

2. Moldboard slide: lean joystick left and right 铲刀滑移：向左、右偏摆操纵杆

3. Circle turn: twist joystick left and right 转动回转圈：左、右扭转操纵杆

4. Moldboard tip: thumb switch fore and aft 铲刀尖倾斜：前、后拇指开关

5. Drawbar center shift: thumb switch left and right 牵引架中心移动：左、右拇指开关

6. Electronic throttle control: trigger switch is resume and decre-

ment 节流阀电子控制：启动和减小触发开关
7 Differential lock/unlock: yellow button 差速器闭锁/开锁：黄色按钮

The right joystick primarily controls the drawbar, circle and moldboard functions.

右操纵杆主要控制牵引架、回转圈和铲刀板的动作。

（4）Visibility 驾驶视野 （Fig. 9. 34）

Fig. 9. 34 Visibility 驾驶视野

The 120M boasts excellent visibility to the work area, made possible with angled cab doors, a tapered engine enclosure and a patented sloped rear window.

120M 型平地机以具有工作区域最佳视野而自豪，这些通过转角驾驶舱门、锥形发动机罩壳与倾斜专利后窗加以保证。

Unit 10　Bulldozer 推土机

10.1　Overview 概述

10.1.1　Basic Concept 基本概念

A bulldozer is a crawler, equipped with a substantial metal plate (known as a blade), used to push large quantities of soil, sand, rubble, etc, during construction work. The term "bulldozer" is often used to mean any heavy engineering vehicle (frequently loaders and in particular track loaders), but precisely, the term refers only to a tractor (usually tracked) fitted with a dozer blade. That is the meaning used here.

推土机是一种安装有坚固金属板（称作铲刀）的履带车辆，其用途为在建设工程中推移大量的土壤、沙砾、碎石等物料。术语 bulldozer 常指各种重型工程车辆（经常指装载机特别是履带式装载机），然而准确地讲，该术语仅指安装有推土铲刀的拖拉机（通常为履带式）。这也是该术语在本文中的含义。

Most often, bulldozers are large and powerful tracked engineering vehicles. The tracks give them excellent ground hold and mobility through very rough terrain. Wide tracks help distribute the bulldozer's weight over large area (decreasing pressure), thus preventing it from sinking in sandy or muddy ground. Extra wide tracks are known as "swamp tracks". Bulldozers have excellent ground hold and a torque divider designed to convert the engine's power into dragging ability, letting the bulldozer use its own weight to push very heavy things and remove obstacles that are stuck in the ground.

在大多数情况下，推土机是一些大型的和功率强大的履带式工程车辆。履带机构使推土机具有极好的地面附着能力和通过颠簸不平地面时的机动性。宽履带有助于在较大面积上分配推土机重量（减小压力），从而防止了推土机在沙滩或泥泞道路上的沉陷。超宽履带称为"湿地履带"。推土机具有极好的地面附着能力和扭矩分配装置，其设计功能为把发动机的功率转化为牵引力，从而使推土机利用自身重量推移重型物品和清除地面障碍物。

Sometimes a bulldozer is used to push another piece of earth-moving equipment known as a "scraper". The towed Fresno Scraper, invented in 1883 by James Porteous, was the first design to enable this to be done economically, removing the soil from the cut and depositing it elsewhere on shallow ground (fill). The bulldozer's primary tools are the blade and the ripper.

有时用推土机去推动另一种称之为"铲运机"的铲土运输机械设备。1833年由詹姆斯·鲍迪斯首先设计发明了经济型的弗雷斯诺托式铲运机，并用其从铲土区运移土壤到另一处低地面（填方）。推土机的主要工作装置是铲刀和松土器。

Bulldozers grew more sophisticated as time passed. Important improvements include more powerful engines, more reliable drive trains, better tracks, raised cabins, and hydraulic (instead of early models' cable operated) arms that enable more precise manipulation of the blade and automated controls. As an option, bulldozers can be equipped with rear ripper claw (s) to loosen rocky soils or to break up pavement. A more recent innovation is the outfitting of bulldozers with GPS technology for precise grade control and "stakeless" construction.

随着时间的推移，推土机发展得更加精密。重要的发展包括发动机功率更加强大、驱动装置更加可靠、履带行走机构更加先进、高级的驾驶室、使铲刀操纵更加精确的液压式（替换旧机型钢索式操纵）顶推杆臂和自动化控制等。作为选择，推土机可安装后置松土爪，用于耙松岩石土壤或破碎路面。最新的发展是为推土机装备了GPS技术以便实施更精确的控制和"无桩化"施工。

The best known maker of bulldozers is probably Caterpillar which earned its reputation for making tough durable reliable machines. There are however other manufacturers of bulldozers for instance Fiat, Komatsu or Allis Chalmers. Although these machines began as modified farm tractors, they became the mainstay for big civil construction projects, and found their way into using by military construction units worldwide. Their best known model, the Caterpillar D9, was also used to clear mines and demolish enemy structures.

最著名的推土机制造商大概要属卡特彼勒公司，制造坚固、耐用和可靠的机械设备为其赢得了荣誉。当然还有其他的推土机制造商，例如菲亚特、小松、艾利斯-查尔莫斯等。最初推土机只是改进的农场拖拉机，现在已成为大型市政建设工程的重要机械装备，并且在世界范围的军事工程部队获得了应用。最著名的卡特D9型推土机也可用于清扫地雷和破坏敌人的设施。

10.1.2 Applications 应用 （Fig. 10.1）

(a) leveling of ground 平整场地　　(b) earthmoving 堆移材料

Fig. 10.1

(c) brush and root out 清理灌木树根

(d) snow removing 除雪作业

(e) stream course clearance 河道清理

(f) dump site work 垃圾场作业

(g) wetlands task 湿地作业

(h) ground cracking 开挖地面

Fig. 10.1 Applications of bulldozer 推土机的应用

10.1.3 Types 类型 (Fig. 10.2)

(a) small crawler dozer (track-type tractor) 小型履带式推土机

(b) medium dozer 中型推土机

(c) large type dozer 大型推土机

(d) supersized dozer 超大型推土机

(e) wet land dozer 湿地推土机

(f) dump area dozer 垃圾场专用推土机

(g) roll-over proofing dozer 防倾翻推土机

(h) wheel dozer 轮胎式推土机

Fig. 10.2 Types of bulldozer 推土机类型

10.2 Components and Features 组成与特点

10.2.1 Components 组成
(1) Overall Structure 总体结构 (Fig. 10.3)

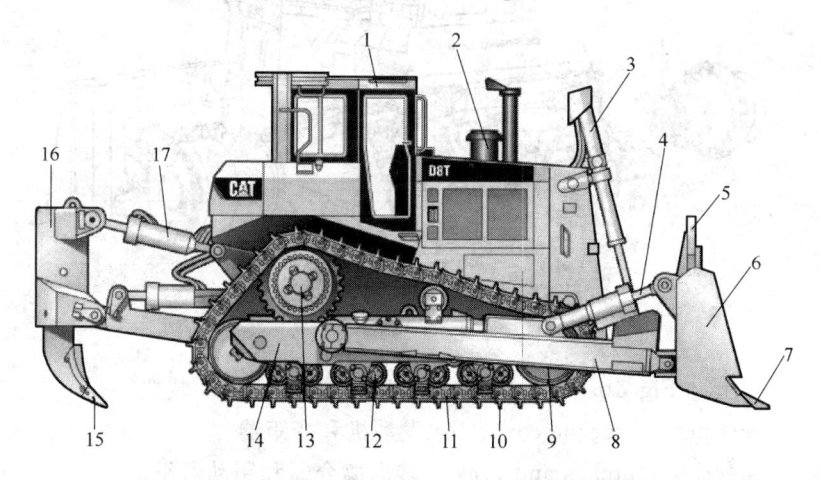

Fig. 10.3 Overall structure 总体结构

1 cab and operating system 驾驶室及操作系统
2 engine 发动机
3 blade hoist cylinder 铲刀升降油缸
4 blade tilting cylinder 铲刀倾斜油缸
5 breast board 挡土板
6 blade 铲刀
7 cutting edge 铲刀刃
8 push frame 顶推架
9 track idler 导向轮
10 grouser 履带齿
11 track 履带
12 track roller 支重轮
13 drive sprocket 驱动链轮
14 track roller frame 台车架
15 ripper tip tooth 松土器齿尖
16 scarifier 松土器
17 scarifier cylinder 松土器油缸

（2）Hydrodynamic Drive 液力传动装置 (Fig. 10.4)

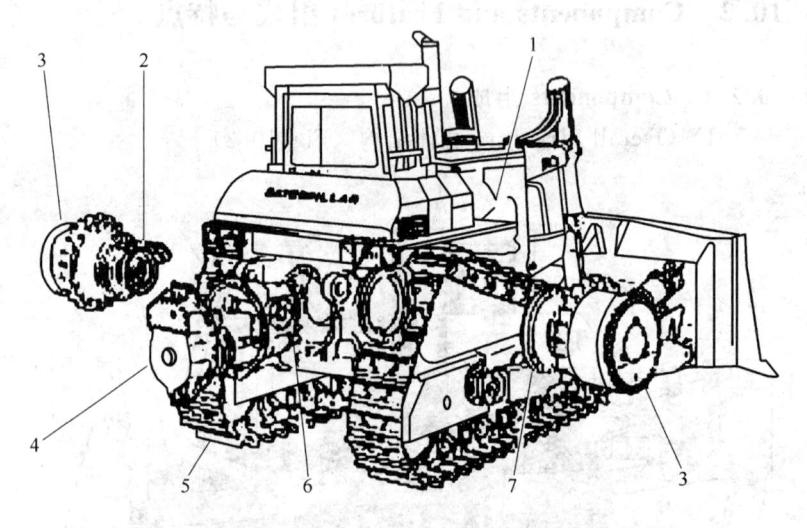

Fig. 10.4　Hydrodynamic drive 液力传动装置

1　engine and torque converter 发动机和变矩器
2　steering clutches and brakes 转向离合器和制动器组
3　final reduction gear 最终传动减速器
4　power shifting transmission 动力换挡变速箱
5　track 履带
6　main bevel gear 主传动锥齿轮
7　planetary reduction gear 行星减速器

(3) Typical Hydrodynamic Drive System 典型液力传动系统 (Fig. 10.5)

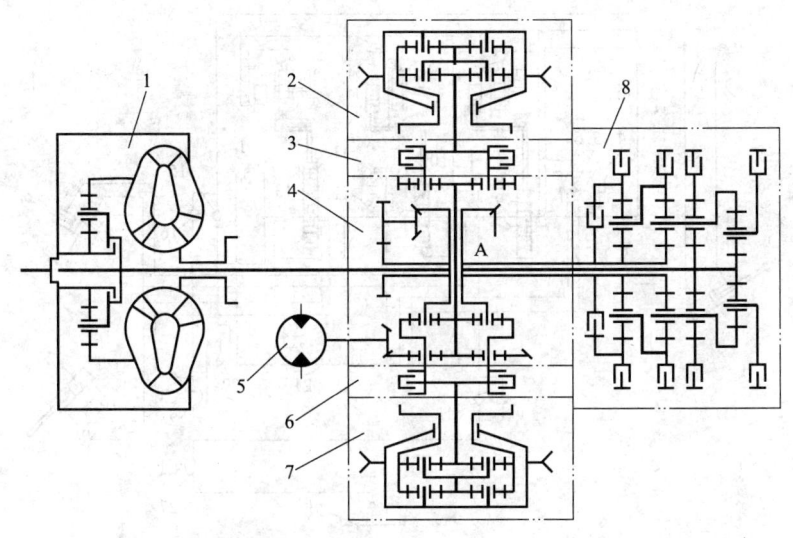

Fig. 10.5 Typical hydrodynamic drive system 典型液力传动系统
1　torque converter 液力变矩器
2　right final reduction gear 右最终传动
3　right brake 右制动器
4　main bevel gear and differential steering drive 中央传动与差速转向传动
5　steering motor 转向马达
6　left brake 左制动器
7　left final reduction gear 左最终传动
8　power shifting transmission 动力换挡变速箱

10.2.2 Typical Hydraulic Control System 典型液压控制系统
(Fig. 10.6)

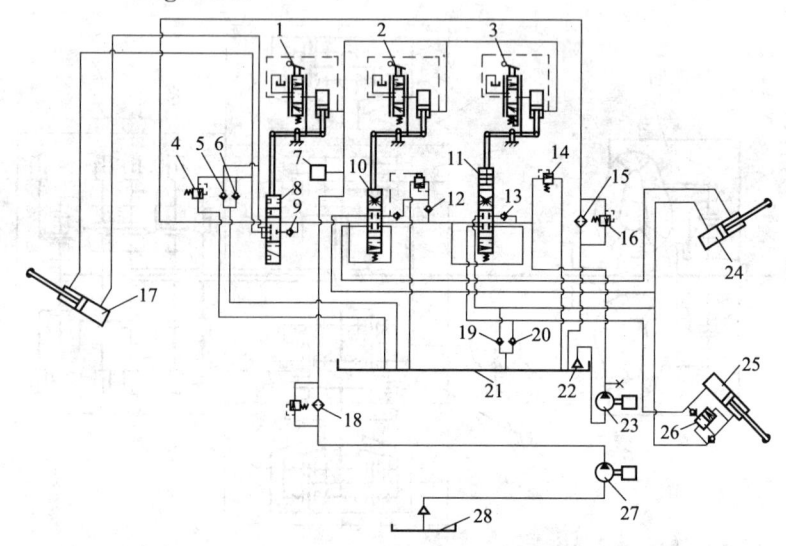

Fig. 10.6 Typical hydraulic control system 典型液压控制系统

1~3　servo valve 伺服阀
4　overload valve 过载阀
5,6,19,20　recharging oil valve 补油阀
7　steering brake valve 转向制动阀
8,10,11　reversing valve 换向阀
9,12,13　check valve 单向阀
14,16　overflow valve 溢流阀
15　strainer filter 粗滤器
17　scarifier cylinder 松土器油缸
18　oil filter 滤油器
21,28　hydraulic oil tank 液压油箱
22　filter screen 过滤网
23　work equipment pump 工作装置液压泵
24　tilt cylinder 倾斜油缸
25　blade hoist cylinder 铲刀提升油缸
26　fast downfall valve 快降阀
27　steering pump 转向液压泵

10.2.3 Hydrostatic Drive Dozer 静液传动推土机 (Fig. 10.7)

Fig. 10.7 Hydrostatic drive dozer 静液传动推土机

1 machine speed and direction control 机械速度和方向控制系统
2 cooling system 冷却系统
3 engine 发动机
4 variable displacement drive pumps and motors 变量驱动泵和马达
5 hydrostatic drive system 静液驱动系统
6 final drives 终传动器

10.2.4 Wheel Dozer Power Train 轮式推土机传动装置 (Fig. 10.8)

Fig. 10.8 Wheel dozer power train 轮式推土机传动装置
1 diesel engine 柴油发动机
2 separated cooling system 分离式冷却系统
3 planetary power shift transmission 行星动力换挡变速箱
4 impeller clutch torque converter 泵轮离合液力变矩器
5 heavy-duty axles 重型驱动桥
6 oil enclosed, multiple disc brakes 封闭湿式多片制动器

10.2.5 Electronic Control System 电控系统 (Fig. 10.9)

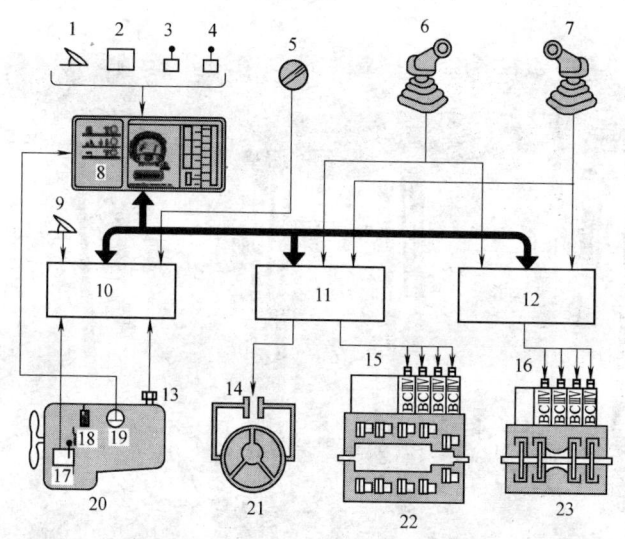

Fig. 10.9 Electronic control system 电控系统

1 brake pedal 制动踏板
2 pitch angle sensor 仰角传感器
3 buzzer cancel switch 蜂鸣消除开关
4 service switch 维护开关
5 fuel control dial 燃料控制旋钮
6 travel control lever 行走操纵手柄
7 blade control lever 铲刀操纵手柄
8 monitor panel 监控仪表盘
9 deceleration pedal 减速踏板
10 engine controller 发动机控制器
11 transmission controller (transmission control, torque converter control) 变速箱控制器（变速箱，液力变矩器控制）
12 steering controller 转向控制器
13 engine speed 发动机转速
14 lockup 闭锁离合器
15 transmission control valve 变速箱控制阀
16 auxiliary valve 辅助阀
17 electrical governor 电子调速器
18 water temperature 水温
19 engine oil pressure 发动机润滑油压
20 engine 发动机
21 torque converter 液力变矩器
22 electronic controlled transmission 电子控制变速箱
23 electronic controlled steering/brake system 电子控制转向/制动系统

10.2.6 Operator Station 驾驶员操作台 (Fig. 10.10)

Fig. 10.10 Operator station 驾驶员操作台

1 steering control 转向控制
2 cat comfort series seat 卡特舒适系列驾驶座
3 adjustable armrests 可调节扶手
4 electronic ripper control 松土器电子控制器
5 electronic, programmable dozer control 推土机可编程电子控制器
6 monitoring display system 监控显示系统
7 wide panoramic view 宽幅全景视野
8 heating and air conditioning 可采暖空调

10.2.7 Monitoring System 监控系统（Fig. 10.11）

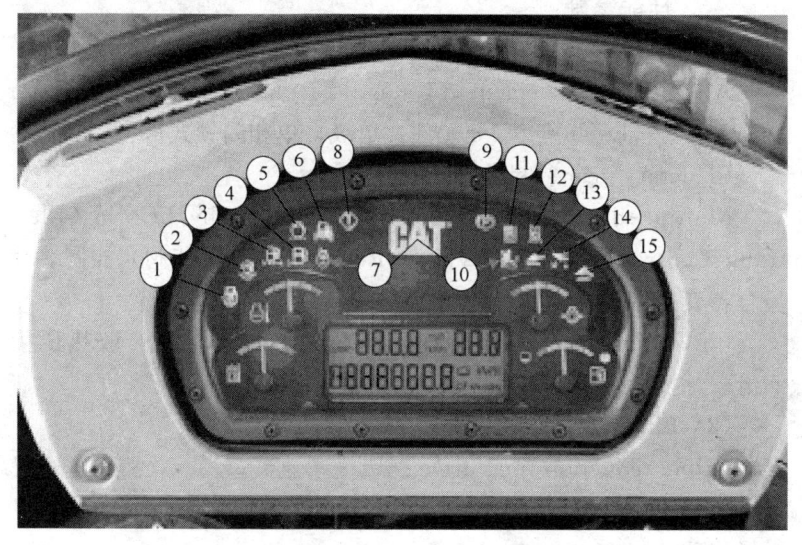

Fig. 10.11 Monitoring system 监控系统

1 reversible fan 双向风扇
2 water separator 水分离器
3 fuel filters plugging 燃油滤清器堵塞
4 fuel level 燃油液面高度
5 engine air filter plugging 发动机空气滤清器堵塞
6 machine security system 机器安全系统
7 ether starting aid 乙醚启动装置
8 warning lamp 报警灯
9 parking brake 驻车制动器
10 operator presence 操作员在场指示
11 hydraulic lockout 液压锁
12 hydraulic oil filter 液压油过滤器
13 bucket float 铲刀浮动
14 lift kickout/lower kickout 提升/下降解除
15 bucket leveler 铲斗调平

10.2.8 Standard Equipment Specifications 标准装置规格类型与性能参数

(1) Torqflow Transmission 液力传动

Air-cooled, 3-element, 1-stage, 1-phase torque converter with lockup clutch 风冷、3元件、单级、单相闭锁式液力变矩器;

Planetary gear 行星传动;

Multiple-disc clutch transmission actuated by ECMV (Electronic Control Modulation Valve) ECMV（电控调节阀）控制多片离合器变速箱;

Force-lubricated for optimum heat dissipation 最佳散热压力润滑。

(2) Final Drives 终传动

Triple-reduction final drive 三级终减速器;

Two-stage spur and single-stage planetary gears 二级直齿单级行星传动;

To minimize transmission of shock to power train components 使传入传动系部件的冲击振动最小;

Segmented sprocket rims 分段式链轮缘;

Bolt-on type for easy in-the-field replacement 螺栓紧固型便于现场更换。

(3) Steering System 转向系统

PCCS lever 手掌控制（PCCS）操纵杆;

Joystick-controlled, wet multiple-disc steering clutches 操纵杆控制湿式多片转向离合器;

Spring-loaded and hydraulically released 弹簧压紧液压松开式;

Pedal controlled steering brakes 踏板控制转向制动器;

Require no adjustment 不需调整;

Steering clutches and brakes are interconnected for easy, responsive steering.

转向离合器与制动器内部联通，以便使转向轻便灵敏。

(4) Undercarriage 台车

Number of shoes (each side) 履带板数量（每边）;
Grouser height 履齿高度;
Shoe width (standard) 履带板宽度（标准型）;
Ground contact area 接地面积;
Ground pressure 接地压力;
Number of track rollers (each side) 支重轮数量（每边）;
Number of carrier rollers (each side) 托链轮数量（每边）;
Suspension: oscillating equalizer bar and pivot shaft;
悬挂方式：摆动式平衡梁和枢轴;
Track roller frame: box-section, high-tensile-strength steel construction;
支重轮支承架：箱型截面，高抗拉强度钢结构;
Rollers and idlers: lubricated track rollers;
支承轮和导轮：润滑型支重轮;
Resilient equalized undercarriage: lubricated track rollers are resiliently mounted to the roller frame with a series of X-type bogies whose oscillating motion is cushioned by rubber pads;
弹性平衡台车：润滑型支重轮以弹性方式安装于装有一系列 X 形支架的台车架上，其摆动由于橡胶垫而得到缓冲;
Extreme service track shoes: lubricated tracks; unique seals prevent entry of foreign abrasives into pin to bushing clearances to provide extended service life. Track tension is easily adjusted with grease gun.

最佳保养履带板：润滑型履带；独特密封防止外部磨料侵入销轴套间隙，延长了使用寿命。履带张紧力可用黄油枪方便调节。

10.2.9 Dimensions 尺寸规格 (Fig. 10.12)

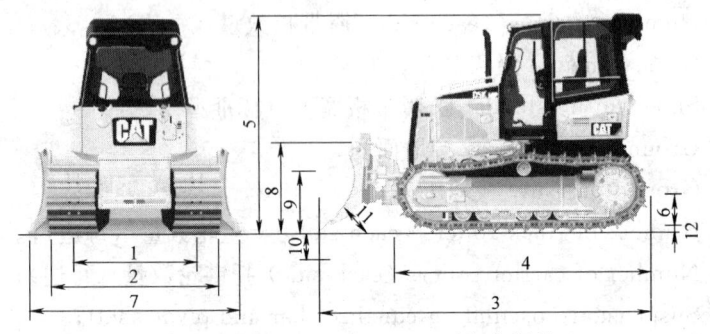

Fig. 10.12　Dimensions 尺寸规格

1　track gauge 轨距
2　width of tractor 推土机（拖拉机底盘）宽度
3　overall length 总长度
4　length of basic tractor 拖拉机底盘长度
5　tractor height 推土机（拖拉机底盘）高度
6　ground clearance 离地间隙
7　blade width 铲刀宽度
8　blade height 铲刀高度
9　blade lift height 铲刀提升高度
10　digging depth 铲掘深度
11　blade cutting edge angle, adjustable 铲刀切削角，可调节
12　grouser height 履带齿高度

10.2.10　Fundamental Operation 基本作业 (Fig. 10.13)

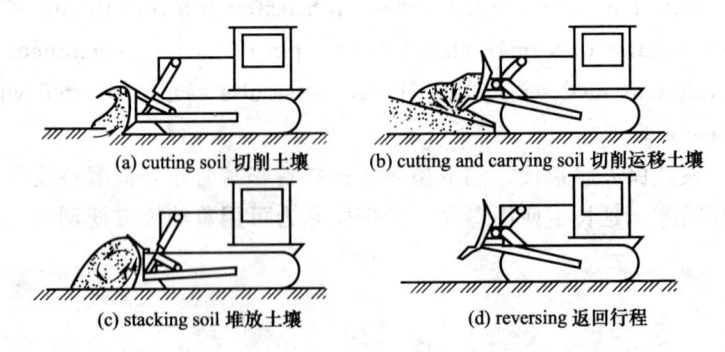

(a) cutting soil 切削土壤
(b) cutting and carrying soil 切削运移土壤
(c) stacking soil 堆放土壤
(d) reversing 返回行程

Fig. 10.13　Fundamental operation 基本作业

10.3 Principal Assembly and Attachments 主要总成与附件 (Fig.10.14)

(a) engine 发动机

(b) planetary power shift transmission 行星动力换挡变速箱

(c) trolley assembly 台车总成

(d) crawler dozer frame 履带推土机机架

(e) wheel dozer frame 轮式推土机机架

(f) crawler dozer operation mechanism 履带推土机工作机构

(g) ripper 松土器

Fig.10.14

(h) wheel dozer operation mechanism
轮式推土机工作机构

(i) pilot seat 驾驶座椅

(j) landfill blade 垃圾填埋铲刀

(k) straight blade 直铲

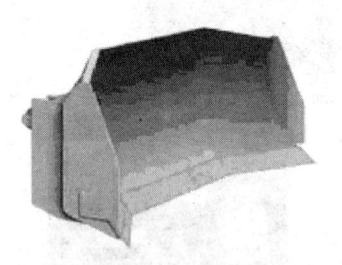

(l) coal U-blades 煤炭推移专用U形铲

(m) semi-U blade 半U形铲

Fig. 10.14　Principal assembly and attachments
主要总成与附件

10.4 New Technology of Crawler Dozer 履带推土机新技术

10.4.1 Power Train Electronic Control System 动力电控系统

(1) ECMV (Electronic Controlled Modulation Valve) Controlled Transmission 电控调节阀控变速箱

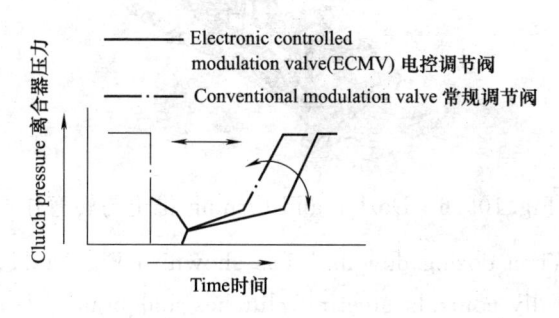

Fig. 10.15 Controller's automatical adjustment 控制器自动调节

Controller automatically adjusts each clutch engagement depending on travel conditions such as gear speed, RPM and shifting pattern, as shovon in Fig. 10.15. This provides shockless, smooth clutch engagement, improved component reliability, improved component life and operator ride comfort.

依据行驶条件，如传动速度、发动机转速和换挡模式等，控制器对每个离合器接合过程进行自动调节，如图10.15所示。这种调节方式提供了离合器的无冲击平顺接合，提高了零部件可靠性，延长了零部件寿命，提高了操作舒适性。

(2) Effect of ECMV Steering Clutches/Brake Control 转向离合器/制动器 ECMV 控制效果

① When dozing and turning (as shown in Fig. 10.16), ECMV automatically controls stroke ratio of steering clutches and brakes depending on degree of load, enabling smooth dozing and turning.

推土与转弯作业时（如图 10.16 所示），ECMV 控制器根据负荷程度自动控制转向离合器与制动器的行程比，确保平稳推土与转弯作业。

Fig. 10.16 Dozing and turning 推土与转弯作业

② When dozing downhill (as shown in Fig. 10.17), ECMV automatically controls steering clutches and brakes depending on incline of machine or degree of load, reducing counter-steering and producing smooth dozing operation.

下坡推土作业时（如图 10.17 所示），ECMV 控制器根据机器倾斜程度或负荷程度自动控制转向离合器与制动器，以减少逆向转弯，保证平稳推土作业。

Fig. 10.17 Dozing downhill 下坡推土作业

(3) Preset Travel Speed Selection Function 行驶速度预置选择功能 (Fig. 10.18)

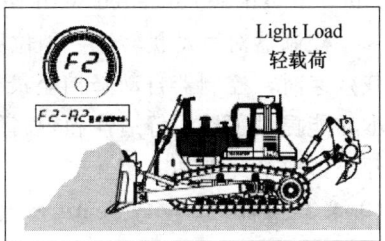

Fig. 10.18 Preset travel speed selection function
行驶速度预置选择功能

Preset travel speed selection function is standard equipment, enabling the operator to select fore and aft travel speed among three preset patterns such as F1-R2, F2-R2 and manual shift.

行驶速度预置选择功能是标准装置，驾驶员可在三个预置模式，即：F1-R2 模式、F2-R2 模式和人力换挡模式之间选择前进与后退行驶速度。

When F1-R2 or F2-R2 preset pattern is selected, and travel control joystick moves to forward/rearward direction, the machine travels forward/reverse with F1-R2 or F2-R2 speed automatically. This function reduces gear shifting time during repeated round-trip operations.

当选择预置 F1-R2 或 F2-R2 工作模式时，在前后方向上推拉行驶控制操纵杆，推土机将自动以 F1-R2 或 F2-R2 挡速度进行前进/后退行驶作业。该项功能可节省重复周期作业期间的换挡时间。

(4) Auto-downshift Function 自动降挡功能

The controller monitors engine speed, travel gear, and travel speed. When load is applied and machine travel speed is reduced, the controller automatically downshifts to optimum gear speed to provide high fuel efficiency. This function provides comfortable operation and high productivity without manual downshifting. This function can be cancelled with the cancel switch.

控制器对发动机转速、挡位和行驶速度实施监控。当推土机加载减速时，控制器自动降挡至最佳挡位，并提供最高的燃油效率。本功能提供了操作舒适性和较高的生产率而无需人力降挡。用消除开关可取消此项功能。

10.4.2　Productivity Features　生产能力特性

（1）Automatic Torque Converter Lockup System 液力变矩器自动闭锁系统（Fig. 10.19）

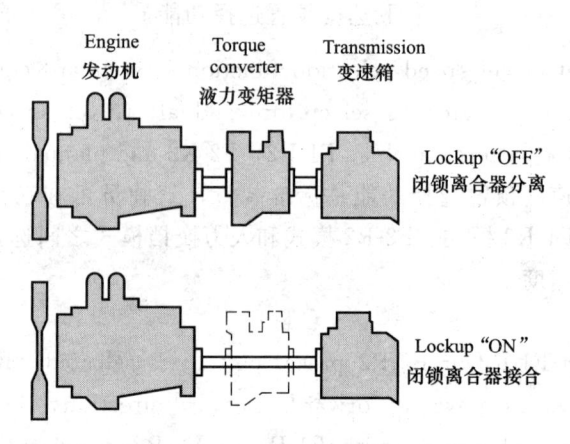

Fig. 10.19　Automatic torque converter lockup system
液力变矩器自动闭锁系统

For greater efficiency during long pushes, the lockup mode allows the system to automatically engage the torque converter lockup clutch.

在长时间推移过程中，为获得更高的效率闭锁模式，允许系统自动接合液力变矩器中的闭锁离合器。

Locking up the torque converter transmits all the engine power directly to the transmission, increasing ground speed and thus achieving efficiencies equal to a direct drive. The results of this efficient use of engine power are less fuel consumption and faster cycle times.

闭锁液力变矩器可将发动机功率全部直接地传递给变速箱，从而提高作业速度，并获得与直接驱动相同的效率。这种有效利用发动机功率的结果降低了燃油消耗，加快了作业循环。

（2）K-bogie Undercarriage System K形台车架行走系统 (Fig. 10.20)

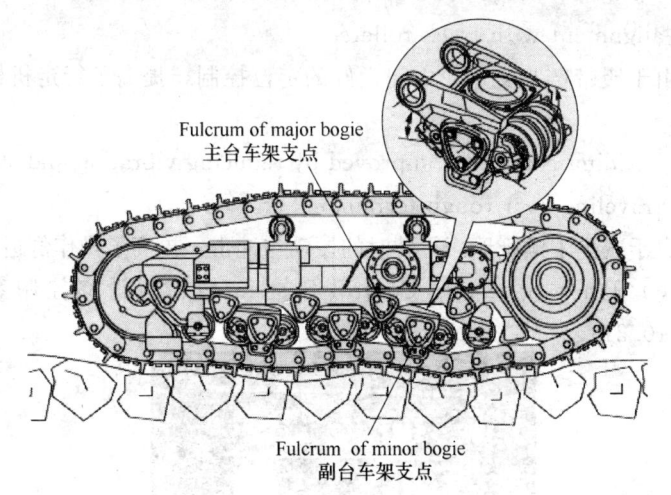

Fig. 10.20 K-bogie undercarriage system K形台车架行走系统

① Effective length of track on ground is consistent. Shoe slippage is minimized, therefore, high traction is obtained.

始终保持履带的有效地面长度。使履带板滑移最小化，因此获得了较大的牵引力。

② The idler does not oscillate under load, providing excellent machine balance. Blade and ripper penetration force remains stable for increased productivity.

导向轮在负荷作用下不发生摆动，保持了最佳的机械平衡。铲刀与松土器插入力保持稳定，以增加生产率。

③ K-bogies oscillate with two fulcrums, and track roller vertical travel is greatly increased. Impact loading to undercarriage components is reduced and durability of components is improved since track rollers are always in contact with track link.

K形台车架随两个支点摆动，大大增加了支重轮的垂直位移。由于支重轮始终与履带链板接触，因而减小了行走机构零部件的冲击载荷，提高了其寿命。

④ Undercarriage life is improved due to better control of track chain alignment with track rollers.

由于履带链与支重轮之间良好的定位控制，提高了行走机构的寿命。

⑤ Riding comfort is improved by reducing vibration and shock when traveling over rough terrain.

由于减少了颠簸地面行驶时的振动与冲击，提高了操作舒适性。

(3) Track Shoe Slip Control System 履带板滑移控制系统 (Fig. 10.21)

Fig. 10.21 Track shoe slip control system
履带板滑移控制系统

① Eliminates the need for the operator to constantly control engine power output with the decelerator while ripping. Operator fatigue is substantially reduced.

松土作业时，驾驶员无需用减速装置不断调整发动机输出功率，大大降低了驾驶员的疲劳程度。

② Maneuverability is improved because the operator is free to focus on the ripping application without having to monitor the track shoe slippage.

驾驶员不需要集中精力监视松土作业时履带板的滑移情况，因而提高了操作机动性。

（4）Rippers 松土器 (Fig. 10.22)

Fig. 10.22　Rippers 松土器

① The variable giant ripper features a long sprocket center-to-ripper point distance, making ripping operation easy and effective while maintaining high penetration force.

巨型可变松土器具有较长的链轮中心——松土器齿尖距离，使松土作业方便有效，同时保持较高的插入力。

② The variable giant ripper is a parallelogram single shank ripper ideal for ripping tough material. The ripping angle is variable, and the depth is adjustable in three stages by a hydraulically controlled pin puller.

巨型可变松土器为平行四边形单耙齿结构，是疏松坚硬材料的理想装置。松土角是可变的，松土深度可通过液压控制式销勾进行三级调节。

③ The multi-shank ripper is a hydraulically controlled parallelogram ripper with three shanks.

多耙齿松土器是一个液压控制平行四边形三耙齿松土器。

10.4.3　Working Environment　工作环境

(1) Hexagonal Pressurized Cab 六边形压力密封驾驶室 (Fig. 10.23)

Fig. 10.23　Hexagonal pressurized cab 六边形压力密封驾驶室

① The cab's new hexagonal design and large tinted glass windows provide excellent front, side, and rear visibility.

驾驶室新型六边形设计与宽敞的遮光玻璃窗具有最佳的前方、侧面和后方工作视野。

② Air filters and a higher internal air pressure combine to prevent dust from entering the cab.

空气过滤器与较高的室内压力相结合防止了灰尘向驾驶室内的侵入。

(2) Comfortable Ride with New Cab Damper Mounting and K-bogie Undercarriage 具有新型驾驶室减振安装形式与K形台车行走机构的舒适型驾驶环境

D375A-5's cab mount uses a new cab damper mounting which fur-

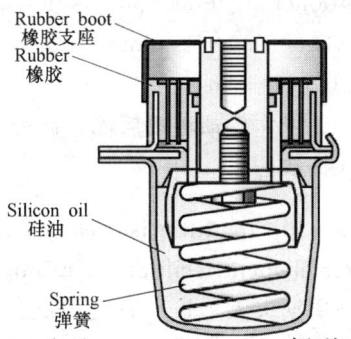

Fig. 10.24 New cab damper mounting 新型减振安装形式

ther improves viscous damper and provides excellent shock and vibration absorption capacity with its long stroke, as showin Fig. 10.24.

D375A-5 型推土机驾驶室安装采用了新型减振安装形式（如图 10.24 所示），该形式进一步改善了黏性阻尼，以其较长的行程提供了最佳的冲击振动吸收能力。

The cab damper mounting, combined with new K-bogie undercarriage, softens shocks and vibrations, while traveling over adverse conditions, that are impossible to absorb with conventional cab mounting methods.

这种驾驶室减振安装形式与新 K 形台车行走机构相结合，减小了不良地面条件下行驶时的冲击和振动，这些冲击和振动采用常规的驾驶室安装方法是不可能被吸收的。

The soft spring cab damper isolates the cab from the machine body, suppressing vibrations and providing a quiet, comfortable operating environment.

这种软弹簧驾驶室减振器使驾驶舱与机身隔离，抑制了振动，从而提供了一个安静、舒适的操作环境。

（3）Fresh Air Intake from Rear of Engine Hood 由发动机罩后部吸入新鲜空气

The air conditioner air intake port is now located at the rear of the engine hood where there is minimal dust. As a result, the air inside the cab is always clean.

将空调进气口设置在发动机罩后部，此处灰尘最少。其结果可使驾驶室内始终保持清洁。

Cleaning interval of the filter is greatly extended, and use of a new structure filter element facilitates cleaning and replacement.

过滤器的清洁周期大大延长，而且，使用新型结构过滤器元件可方便地进行清洁和更换工作。

10.4.4 Easy Maintenance 维护方便容易

Preventative maintenance is the only way to ensure long service life from your equipment. That's why Komatsu designed the D375A-5 dozer with conveniently located maintenance points to make necessary inspections and maintenance quick and easy.

预防性维护是保持设备长久使用寿命的唯一方法。这就是小松为 D375A-5 型推土机设计多个使用方便的维护保养点的原因，使必要的检查与维护工作快速而方便。

(1) Monitor with Self-diagnostic Function 具有自诊断功能的监视器 (Fig. 10.25)

Fig. 10.25 Monitor with self-diagnostic function
具有自诊断功能的监视器

If the monitor finds abnormalities, the corresponding warning lamp blinks and a warning buzzer sounds. When abnormalities occur during operation, user code and service meter are displayed alternately. When a high importance user code is displayed, a caution lamp blinks and warning buzzer sounds to prevent serious problems from developing.

如果监视器发现异常情况，相应的报警灯频闪，报警蜂鸣器鸣叫。当工作中出现异常时，用户代码和维护仪表交替显示。当显示非常重要的用户代码时，警告指示灯频闪，报警蜂鸣器鸣叫，以防止严重的异常情况进一步发展。

(2) Track Link with Wedge Ring 楔形环履带链 （Fig. 10.26）

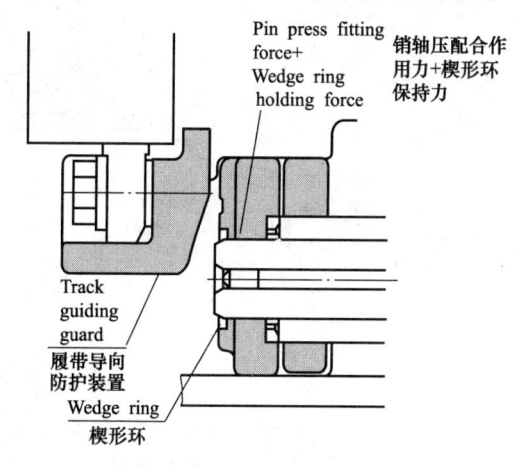

Fig. 10.26 Track link with wedge ring 楔形环履带链

New D375A-5 dozer track links feature reduced press-fit force and a wedge ring. Conventional track pins are retained only with a large press-fit force.

新型 D375A-5 推土机履带链条的特点是降低了压配合作用力并装有楔形环。常规履带链销仅依靠较大的压配合作用力加以固定保持。

This results in easier service with reduced pin damage when turning pins and bushings. This leads to improved undercarriage life and reduced maintenance cost through reduced wear, greater pin reusability, and fewer maintenance man-hours.

由于链销与衬套的转动减少了链销的损坏,新型履带链使维护更加容易。通过减少磨损,提高重复使用性和缩短维护时间,最终将延长行走机构使用寿命,降低维护成本。

(3) VHMS (Vehicle Health Monitoring System) 车辆正常工作状况监视系统 (Fig. 10.27)

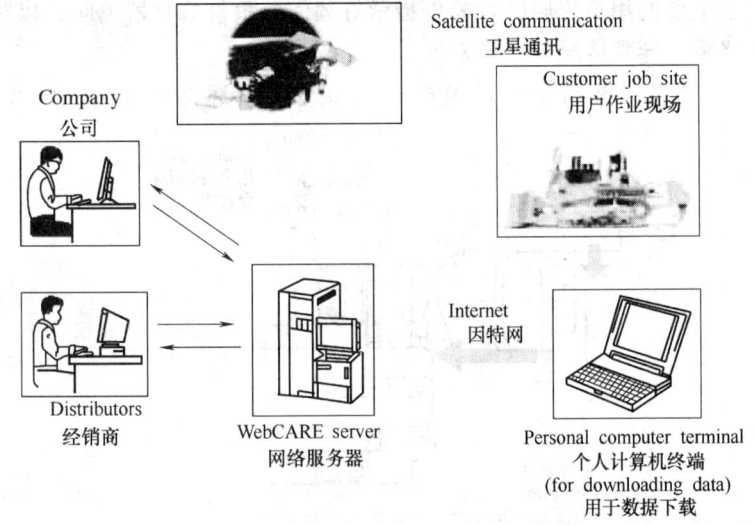

Fig. 10.27 VHMS (Vehicle Health Monitoring System) 车辆正常工作状况监视系统

VHMS controller monitors the health conditions of major components and enables remote analysis of the machine and its operation.

VHMS 控制器可监视主要部件的正常工作状况,并能够对机器及其运行状况进行远距离分析。

This contributes to reduced repair costs and to maintaining maximum availability as the result of proactive service. This process is fully supported by the distributors, factory and design teams.

这将有助于降低维修成本并获得最大的作为主动服务的能力。这一过程受到经销商、制造厂和设计团队的全力支持。

Unit 11 Asphalt Paver
沥青摊铺机

11.1 Overview 概述

11.1.1 Basic Concept 基本概念

Asphalt pavers are special machines for paving asphalt mixture which are mixed by asphalt plants. The primary purpose of the paver is to place the mixed asphalt mixture to the desired width, thickness, and cross slope and to produce a uniform mat texture. The paver should also be able to place the asphalt mixture in a manner that results in improved smoothness of the roadway.

沥青摊铺机是摊铺沥青混合料搅拌设备拌和的沥青混合料的专用机械。摊铺机的主要用途是把搅拌好的沥青混合料摊铺成预定的宽度、厚度和横向坡度，以产生一个均匀的铺层结构。摊铺机也应该能够把沥青混合料摊铺成具有良好平整度的公路路面。

There are two types of pavers—track (crawler) and rubber-tire—which are basically the same and perform similar functions in a paving operation. The track paver offers a high degree of traction when traveling across weak underlying pavement structures by providing an increased area over which to spread the weight of the paver. This type of paver is therefore typically used when paving on a soft or yielding base. A rubber-tire paver is generally used when placing asphalt mixture over well-compacted granular base course layers. In addition, if the paver is to be moved regularly under its own power between paving locations, a rubber-tire paver is generally used because its travel speed is much greater than track paver's.

摊铺机有两种类型——履带式和橡胶轮胎式。在摊铺作业中,这两类摊铺机基本是一样的,并且功能也相似。当通过较软的路面结构时,履带式摊铺机能够通过提供较大的接触面积来分散摊铺机重量,从而提供大的牵引力,因此特别适用于在柔软地面上作业。轮胎式摊铺机一般用于在经过良好压实的粗糙地面上摊铺沥青混合料。另外,如果摊铺机经常在摊铺场地之间依靠自身动力进行转移时,通常会使用轮胎式摊铺机,因为它比履带式摊铺机有更快的行走速度。

The paver consists of two primary parts——the tractor unit and the screed unit. The tractor unit provides the motive power to the paver and pushes the haul truck in front of the paver during the unloading process if the mix is being delivered directly from the truck into the paver hopper. The screed unit, which is towed by the tractor unit, completes the paving sequence and produces the mat in its final state, to the required depth and with the necessary finish and a high degree of initial compaction.

摊铺机的两个主要部件是牵引装置和熨平装置。牵引装置为摊铺机提供运动的动力,并且在卸料过程中,如果混合料从自卸卡车上直接卸入摊铺机料斗时,牵引装置也提供顶推卡车的动力。熨平装置由牵引装置牵引,它完成摊铺工序,并在最后阶段形成铺层,达到要求的厚度,并具有所要求的平整度和较高的初始密实度。

The production process of an asphalt paver is as follows: the rear wheels of reversing dumper contact the push roller of the asphalt paver and dump the asphalt mixture to the hopper of the paver. Asphalt mixture is delivered to the auger conveyer by the drag conveyer which has both left and right individually driven. Asphalt materials are further spread to two sides of the road. Tamper compact them primarily. Screed unit on which there are vibrator, crowning device and screed plate makes the asphalt mixture form positive shape and thickness of mat.

沥青摊铺机的工作过程如下：倒退中的自卸车后轮接触沥青摊铺机的推滚，然后将沥青混合料倾倒在摊铺机的料斗中。沥青混合料由独立驱动的左、右两个刮板输送器输送到螺旋分料器。沥青材料进一步向路面两侧摊铺。振捣夯锤首先将混合料进行夯实。装有振动器、调拱装置和熨平板的熨平装置使沥青混合料形成确定的形状和铺层厚度。

In order to improve smoothness of pavement and reduce segregation of asphalt mixture, the paver was used with material transfer vehicles in modern paving of asphalt roadway. The transfer vehicles deliver asphalt mixture to the paver and allow the paver to operate almost continuously, without stopping between truckloads of mixture, as long as a continuous supply of mixture is available from the asphalt plant.

为了提高摊铺平整度，减少沥青混合料离析，现代沥青路面的铺筑已采用转运车与摊铺机联合工作。转运车为摊铺机供应沥青混合料，可使摊铺机连续作业，只要能够从沥青搅拌设备连续地供应混合料，摊铺机就不会在运料卡车换车之时停止作业。

After nearly eight decades of development, the asphalt paver has been a high-tech product combining mechanical, hydraulic, electronic and other high technology in itself. Now many manufactures can produce a variety of asphalt pavers, of which the most famous includes Dynapac, Vogele, Volvo ABG, Caterpillar and Sumitomo.

沥青摊铺机经过近八十年的发展，已成为集机械技术、液压技术、电子技术等高新技术于一身的高科技产品。目前许多制造商可生产多种类型的沥青摊铺机，最知名的有戴纳派克、福格勒、沃尔沃 ABG、卡特彼勒、住友等品牌。

11.1.2 Application 应用

(1) Routine Paving 常规摊铺 (Fig. 11.1)

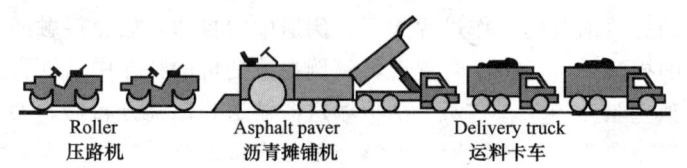

Roller 压路机　　Asphalt paver 沥青摊铺机　　Delivery truck 运料卡车

Fig. 11.1　Routine paving 常规摊铺

(2) Continuous Paving 不间断摊铺 (Fig. 11.2)

Roller 压路机　　Asphalt paver 沥青摊铺机　　Transfer vehicle 转运车　　Delivery truck 运料卡车

Fig. 11.2　Continuous paving 不间断摊铺

11.1.3　Types 类型 (Fig. 11.3)

(a) tracked paver 履带式摊铺机 　　(b) wheeled paver 轮胎式摊铺机

(c) paver with mechanical extension screed 熨平板机械加宽式摊铺机

(d) paver with hydraulic extension screed 熨平板液压伸缩式摊铺机

Fig. 11.3

Paving width＜3.6m

(e) small paver (paving width less than 3.6m)
小型摊铺机(摊铺宽度小于3.6m)

Paving width 4～6m

(f) medium paver (paving width between 4～6m) 中型摊铺机(摊铺宽度4～6m)

Paving width 7～9m

(g) large paver (paving width between 7～9m)
大型摊铺机(摊铺宽度7～9m)

Paving width＞12m

(h) super large paver (paving width more than 12m)
超大型摊铺机(摊铺宽度12m以上)

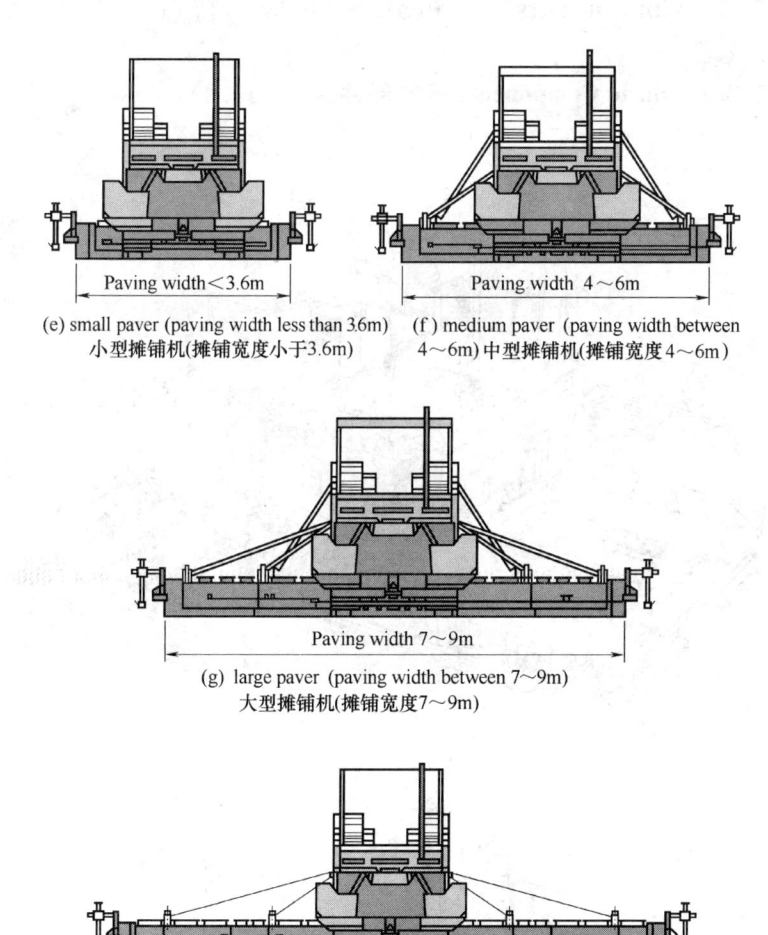

Fig. 11.3　Types of asphalt paver 沥青摊铺机的类型

11.2 Components and Features 组成与特点

11.2.1 Basic Components 基本部件 (Fig. 11.4)

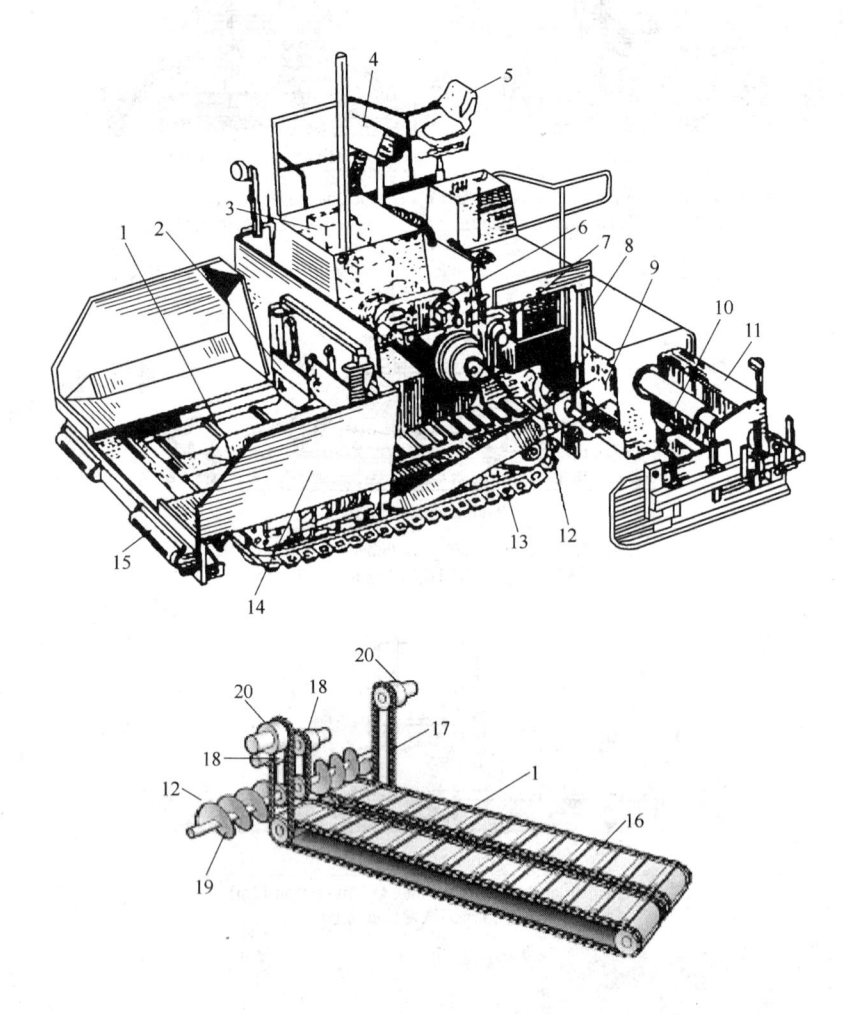

Fig. 11.4

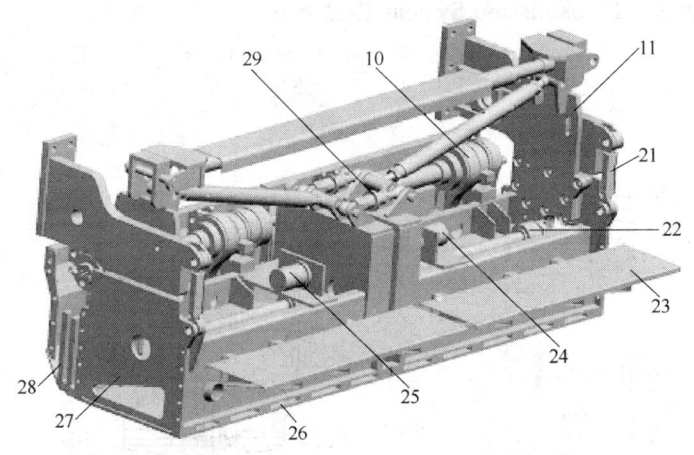

Fig. 11.4 Basic components 基本部件

1 drag conveyers 刮板输送器
2 gate 闸门
3 engine 发动机
4 operator's station 操纵台
5 operator's seat 驾驶座椅
6 transmission system 传动系统
7 frame 机架
8 lifting cylinder 提升油缸
9 towed arm 牵引臂
10 tamper 振捣器
11 screed units 熨平装置
12 auger conveyers 螺旋分料器
13 running gear 行走机构
14 hopper 料斗
15 push roller 推辊
16 drag plate 刮板
17 driving chains 传动链条
18 drag drive motors 刮板驱动马达
19 auger blades 螺旋叶片
20 auger drive motors 螺旋驱动马达
21 depth adjustment 厚度调节装置
22 vibrator 振动器
23 footplate 踏板
24 tamper drive motor 振捣器驱动马达
25 vibrator drive motor 振动器驱动马达
26 screed plate 熨平板底板
27 screed box 熨平板箱体
28 tamper bar 振捣夯锤
29 crown control device 拱度调节装置

11.2.2 Transmission System 传动系统

(1) Mechanical Transmission System 机械式传动系统 (Fig. 11.5)

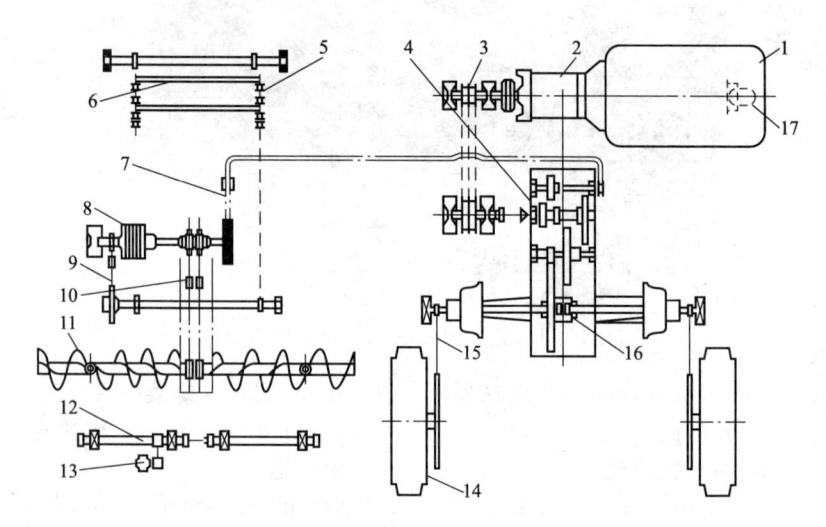

Fig. 11.5 Mechanical transmission system 机械式传动系统

1　engine 发动机
2　main transmission 主变速器
3,5,7,9,10,15　transmission chains 传动链
4　vice transmission 副变速器
6　drag conveyers 刮板输送器
8　clutch 离合器
11　auger conveyers 螺旋分料器
12　tamper eccentric shaft 振捣偏心轴
13　hydraulic motor 液压马达
14　traveling driving wheel 行驶驱动轮
16　differential 差速器
17　pump 油泵

(2) Hydraulic-mechanical Transmission System 液压机械式传动系统 (Fig. 11.6)

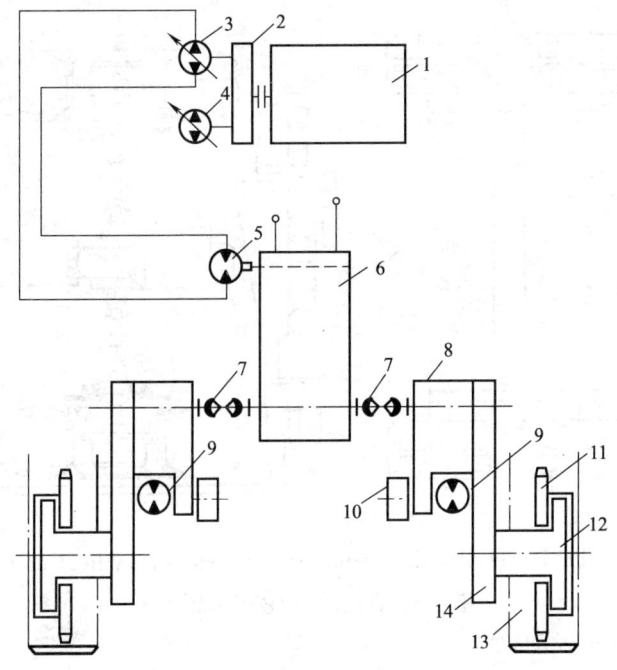

Fig. 11.6 Hydraulic-mechanical transmission system
液压机械式传动系统

1　engine 发动机
2　gear box 齿轮箱
3　traveling variable pump 行走变量泵
4　sterring variable pump 转向变量泵
5　traveling quantitative motor 行走定量马达
6　(four gears) transmission（四挡）变速箱
7　universal driving device 万向传动装置
8　middle transmission gearbox 中间传动齿轮箱
9　steering quantitative motor 转向定量马达
10　brakes 制动器
11　driving wheel 驱动轮
12　wheel-side reducer 轮边减速器
13　crawler 履带
14　transmission chains 传动链

(3) Hydraulic Transmission System (Wheel Paver) 液压传动系统（轮式摊铺机）(Fig. 11.7)

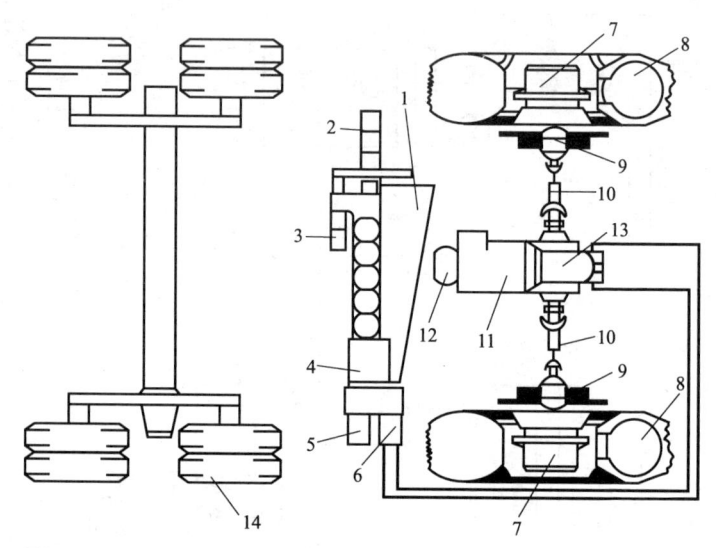

Fig. 11.7　Hydraulic transmission system (wheel paver)
　　　　液压传动系统（轮式摊铺机）

1　engine 发动机
2　right drag and steering triple-link pump 右刮板和转向三联泵
3　left drag and steering double-link pump 左刮板和转向双联泵
4　oil cooler 油冷却器
5，6　axial piston pump 轴向柱塞泵
7　planetary gear reducer 行星齿轮减速器
8　rear wheel 后轮
9　disc brake 盘式制动器
10　universal driving shaft 万向传动轴
11　reducer 减速器
12　brakes 制动器
13　axial plunger motor 轴向柱塞马达
14　front wheel 前轮

(4) Hydraulic Transmission System (Track Paver) 液压传动系统 (履带摊铺机) (Fig. 11.8)

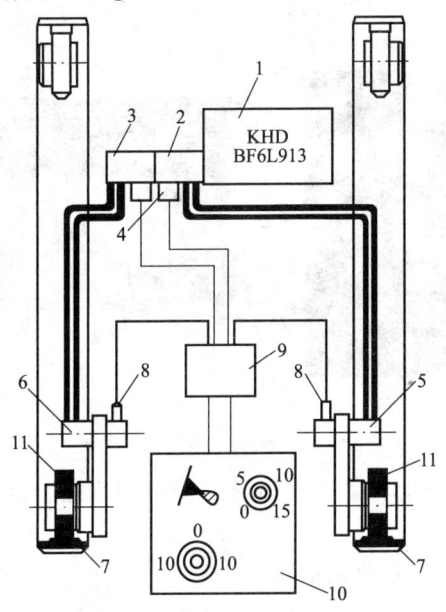

Fig. 11.8 Hydraulic transmission system (track paver)
液压传动系统 (履带摊铺机)

1　engine 发动机
2　right variable pump 右变量泵
3　left variable pump 左变量泵
4　proportional speed controller 比例速度控制器
5　right axial plunger motor 右轴向柱塞马达
6　left axial plunger motor 左轴向柱塞马达
7　crawler 履带
8　speed sensor 速度传感器
9　electric control system 电控系统
10　central console 中央控制台
11　driving chain wheel 驱动链轮

11.2.3　Control Panel 操纵控制台（Fig. 11.9）

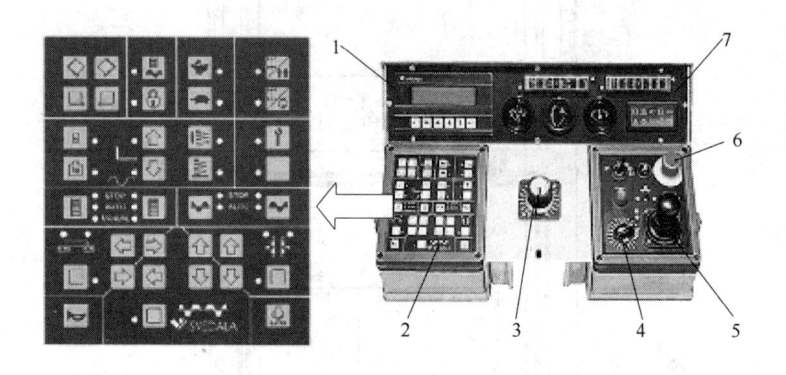

Fig. 11.9　Control panel 操纵控制台

1　LCD panel LCD 显示面板
2　paving operation control keys 摊铺操作控制键
3　direction knob 方向旋钮
4　engine speed indicator 发动机转速指示表
5　paving control handle 摊铺控制手柄
6　emergency brake switch 紧急制动开关
7　engine function indicator 发动机功能指示

11.2.4　Standard Equipment Specifications 标准装置规格类型与性能参数

（1）Engine 发动机

Turbocharged and Air-To-Air Aftercooling（ATAAC）涡轮增压和空气—空气再冷却方式；

Number of cylinders 汽缸数；

Horsepower rating 2200r/min（SAE J1995）功率/2200 r/min（SAE 标准：J1995）；

Gross horsepower 总功率；

Net horsepower 净功率；

Meets European EU Stage Ⅲ engine emissions regulations 符合欧Ⅲ发动机排放标准规范；

Fuel system：HEUI^{TM} fuel injection，Multiple injection fuel delivery 燃油系统：HEUI^{TM} 型燃油喷射，多点喷射燃油输送；

These features allow the engine to have complete control over injection timing, duration and pressure. 这些特点保证了发动机对喷射正时、喷射周期和喷射压力的完全控制；

ADEM A4 electronic control module ADEM A4 电子控制模块；

Cooling system 冷却系统；

Air cleaner 空气滤清器。

（2）Propel System 行走系统

Closed-loop hydrostatic propel system 闭式液压行走系统；

Hydrostatic pumps：Pumps are infinitely variable and electronically controlled for starting and stopping ramps. 液压泵：泵可由电子控制进行无级调速，以适应坡道起步和驻车；

Propulsion control：electro-proportional servo-control 行走控制：电子比例伺服控制。

（3）Screed Units 熨平装置

Paving width 摊铺宽度；

Maximum thickness 最大厚度；

Working speed 工作速度；

Arch degree adjustment 拱度调节；

Electronic ignition 电子点火装置；

Electric heated，LPG hydraulic and mechanical screeds combine the flexibility to match equipment to operator preferences or job requirements 电加热、燃气加热、液压伸缩和机械式熨平板具有广泛的适应性，方便操作，最大满足摊铺工况要求。

(4) Material Handling System 供料系统

Hopper capacity 料斗容量；

Split-segment Ni-hard augers：adjustable height 分段式硬镍螺旋布料器：高度可调；

Conveyors and hopper bottom plate：wear-resisting steel 刮板输送器和料斗底板：耐磨合金钢；

Two feeding conveyors are independently controlled and proportionally driven by two ultrasonic sensors. 两套供料装置采用超声波独立传感器控制，并按比例进行驱动。

(5) Undercarriage 底盘支承系统

Two rubber shoe crawlers：the track-type asphalt paver provides a reliable，smooth ride. The optimum tension of the tracks is assured by a grease piston with a shock absorbing system.

两条橡胶垫板履带：这种驱动形式使履带式沥青混凝土摊铺机性能可靠、行驶平顺。带有减振系统的润滑脂活塞保证了履带获得最佳的张紧度。

Bonded track pads：the track pads contain a special rubber compound in order to provide long life and optimum traction. Pads are attached with four bolts for easy replacement.

粘接式橡胶履带垫板：履带垫板涂有特殊的橡胶黏合剂，以实现长寿命和最佳的牵引性。履带垫板用四根螺栓安装，易于更换。

Two-speed planetary drive：two fixed displacement motors

drive two-speed planetary track drive gearboxes in order to provide infinitely variable speed selection.

双速行星传动：两台定量马达驱动双速履带行走减速器，实现无级变速。

（6）Operator's Station 操作台

Enhanced visibility: both operator seats and console panel are mounted on pivoting pedestals enabling the operator to rotate either to the left or right.

扩大视野：两个操作员座椅和控制台面板都安装在可旋转底座上，使操作员可以向左右两侧旋转。

Control console: the sliding operator's console panel is fully equipped with comprehensive controls allowing the operator to conveniently monitor all machine functions.

控制台：滑动控制台面板配备了全套综合控制装置，使操作员可以轻松监控机器的所有功能。

（7）Brakes 制动系

Closed-loop hydrostatic drive：闭式液压传动：

Safety and parking brakes are mechanical multi-disk spring-applied brakes.

安全和停车制动器为机械式多片弹簧制动器。

Parking brake is automatically applied with the machine in "stand-by" mode.

当机器处于"等待"工作模式时，停车制动器自动制动。

When required the brakes can be released manually.

可以根据需要手动解除停车制动。

（8）Steering 转向系

An electric steering system provides smooth, low effort steering by means of a steering wheel on the console panel.

通过控制台面板上的方向盘电动转向系统控制机器，实现平稳、省力的转向。

11.2.5 Dimensions 尺寸规格

(1) Tracked Pavers 履带式摊铺机 (Fig. 11.10)

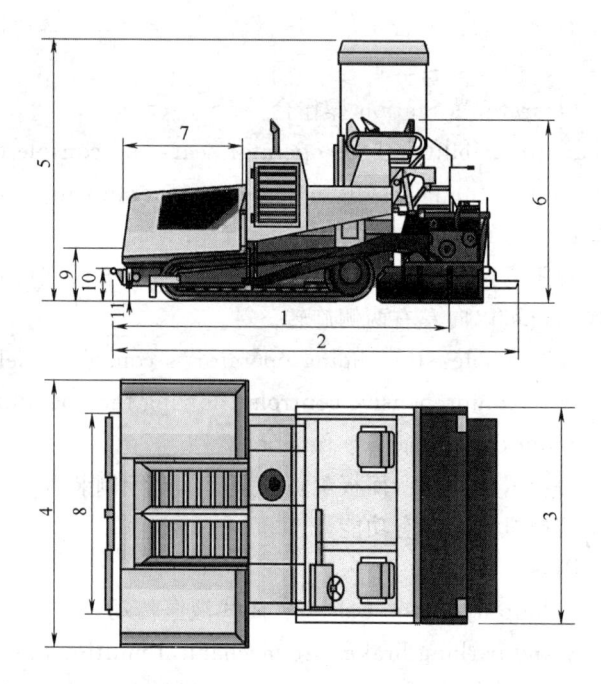

Fig. 11.10 Tracked pavers 履带式摊铺机

1 tractor length with push roller 带推辊时的摊铺机长度
2 length with push roller and screed 带推辊和熨平板时的长度
3 transport width without end gates and screed (hopper raised) 不带端部挡板和熨平板的运输宽度(料斗升起)
4 tractor operating width (hopper lowered) 摊铺机工作宽度(料斗降下)
5 operating height with canopy 带顶棚的工作高度
6 transport height (canopy lowered) 运输高度(顶棚降下)
7 hopper length 料斗长度
8 truck entry width 卸料车入口宽度
9 truck dump height 卸料车倾倒高度
10 push roller height 推辊高度
11 clearance 间隙

(2) Wheeled Pavers 轮胎式摊铺机 (Fig. 11.11)

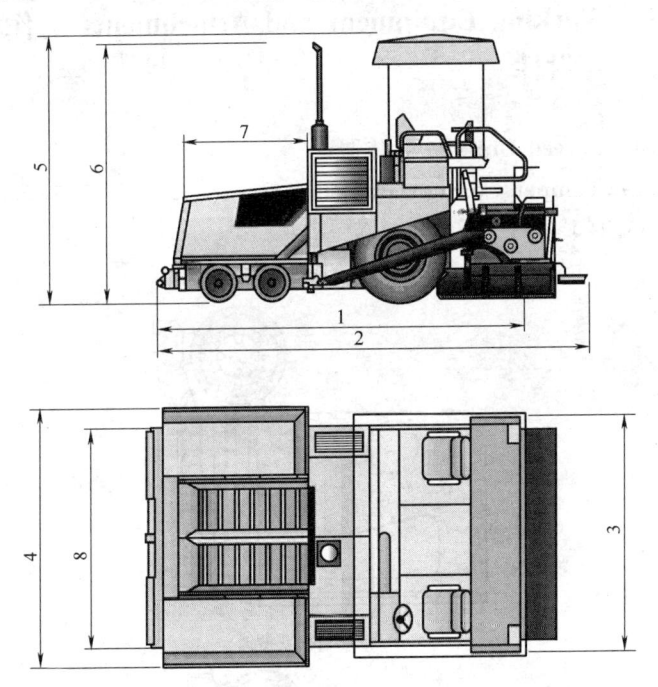

Fig. 11.11 Wheeled pavers 轮胎式摊铺机

1 tractor length with push roller 带推辊时摊铺机的长度
2 length with push roller and screed 带推辊和熨平板时的长度
3 transport width without end gates and screed (hopper raised) 不带端部挡板和熨平板的运输宽度（料斗侧板收拢）
4 tractor operating width (hopper lowered) 摊铺机工作宽度（料斗侧板放平）
5 operating height with canopy 带顶棚的工作高度
6 transport height (no folding exhaust pipe, canopy lowered) 运输高度（顶棚降下）
7 hopper length 料斗长度
8 truck entry width 卸料车入口宽度

11.3 Working Equipment and Attachments 工作装置与附件

11.3.1 Screed Units 熨平装置

(1) Tamper Configuration of Screed Units 熨平板振捣配置 (Fig. 11.12)

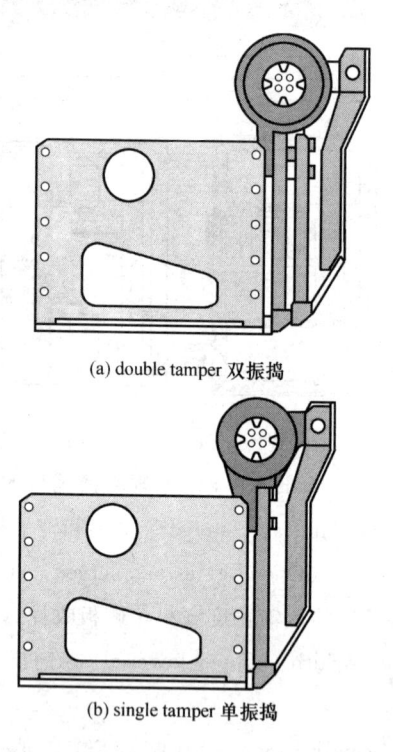

(a) double tamper 双振捣

(b) single tamper 单振捣

Fig. 11.12 Tamper configuration of screed units 熨平板振捣配置

(2) Components of Mechanical Extension Screed 机械加宽式熨平板组成 (Fig. 11.13)

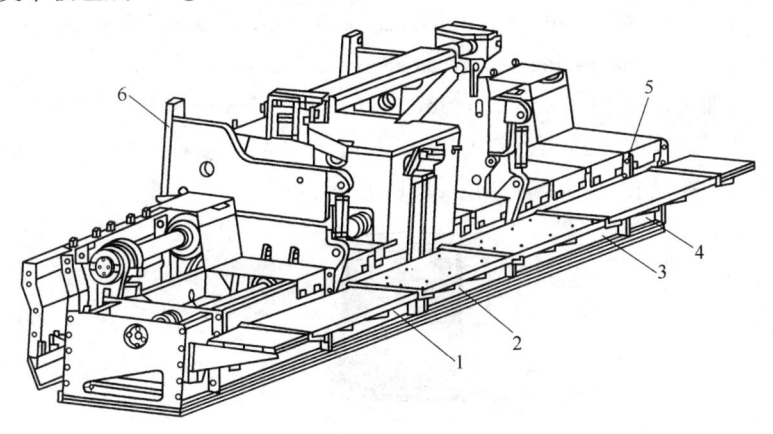

Fig. 11.13 Components of mechanical extension screed
机械加宽式熨平板组成

1　left basic screed 左基本段熨平板
2　right basic screed 右基本段熨平板
3,4　extension screed of different dimension 不同规格的加宽段熨平板
5　joint bolt 连接螺栓
6　towed arm 牵引臂

(3) Features of Mechanical Extension Screed 机械加宽式熨平板特点

① In accordance with the requirements of paving width, mechanical extension screed constitutes by connecting the basic screed and a variety of extension screeds with the bolts.

机械加宽式熨平板是按摊铺宽度要求，用螺栓将基本宽度段熨平板和各种不同尺寸宽度的加宽段熨平板连接而成。

② With the limitation of the traveling and transportation space of vehicles, the width of the basic screed is between 2.5m and 3m.

基本段宽度受车辆行驶及运输空间的限制，一般在2.5～3m之间。

③ Extensions include varies of width such as 0.25m, 0.5m, 1.0m, 1.5m and so on, together with the basic screed, it can be assembled into a variety of width with the difference of 0.25m, to satisfy the requirements of various paving width, as shown in Fig. 11.14.

加宽段包括 0.25m、0.5m、1.0m 和 1.5m 等多种不同的尺寸长度，连同基本段可组装成以 0.25m 为差值的多种宽度，以满足不同的摊铺宽度要求，如图 11.14 所示。

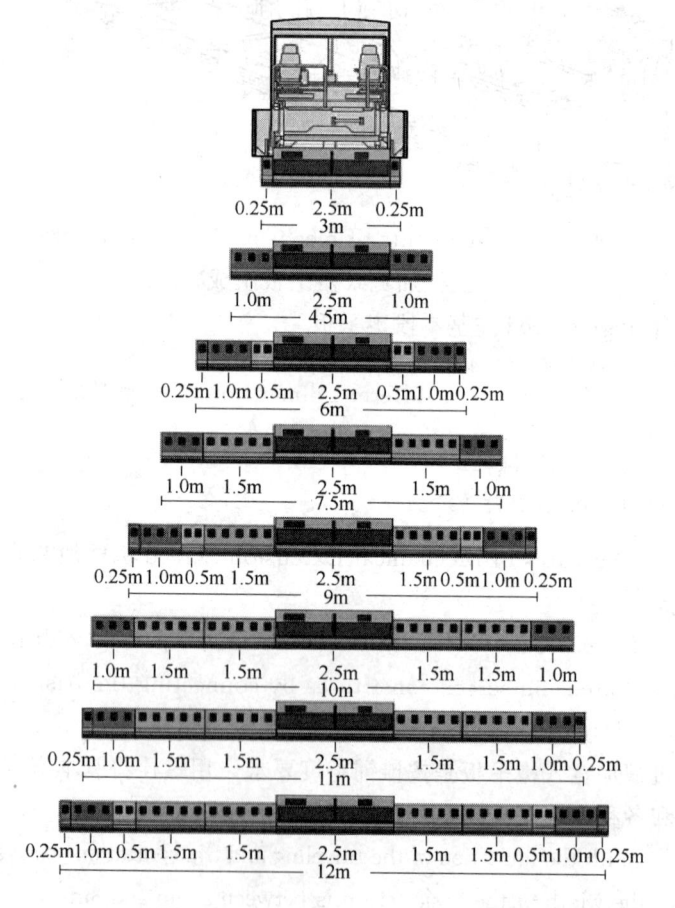

Fig. 11.14 Extensions 加宽段

(4) Components of Hydraulic Extension Screed 液压伸缩式熨平板组成 (Fig. 11. 15)

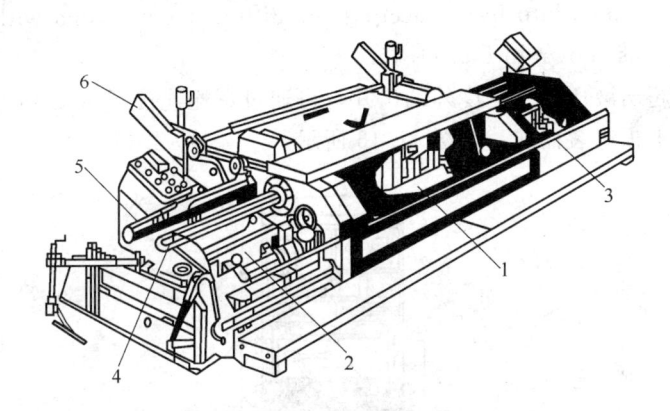

Fig. 11. 15 Components of hydraulic extension screed
液压伸缩式熨平板组成

1 basic screed 基本段熨平板
2 left hydraulic extension screed 左液压伸缩熨平板
3 right hydraulic extension screed 右液压伸缩熨平板
4 telescopic hydraulic cylinder 伸缩液压油缸
5 guide pillar 导柱
6 towed arm 牵引臂

(5) Features of Hydraulic Extension Screed 液压伸缩式熨平板特点

① Hydraulic extension screed adjusts the extended length of the telescopic screed by regulating the hydraulic cylinder, so that it can meet the paving width of the construction requirements.

液压伸缩式熨平板是靠液压油缸伸缩来调整伸缩熨平板的伸出长度，使熨平板达到施工要求的摊铺宽度的。

② When the screed retracts, the rest is the basic width, whose length is between 2.5m and 3m.

伸缩部分缩回时的熨平板为基本宽度段，尺寸一般在2.5～3m

之间。

③ The dimensions beyond the hydraulic telescopic width can be assembled into by connecting the different extensions with the bolts, as shown in Fig. 11.16.

超出液压伸缩宽度外的尺寸，可通过螺栓连接不同尺寸的加宽段熨平板组装而成，如图 11.16 所示。

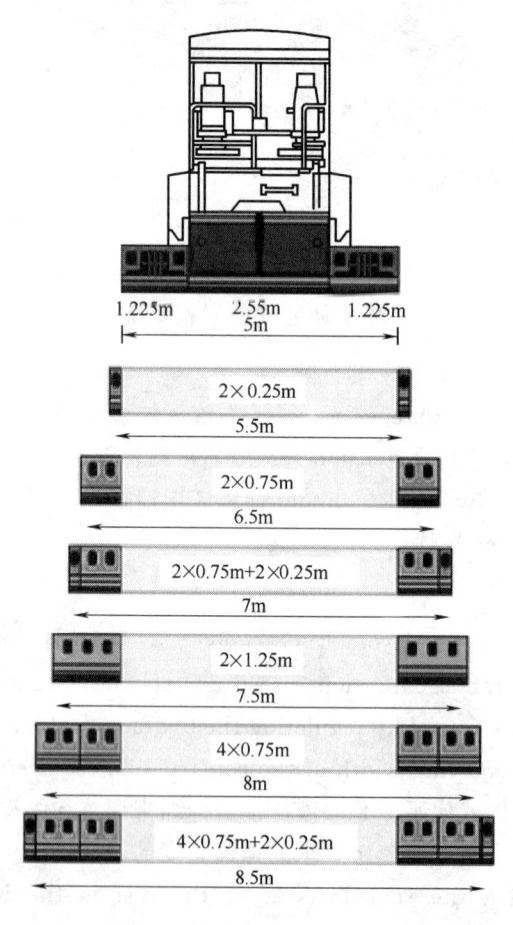

Fig. 11.16　The different extensions with the bolts
不同尺寸的加宽段熨平板

11.3.2 Auto Leveling Device 自动找平装置

(1) Components 组成（Fig. 11.17）

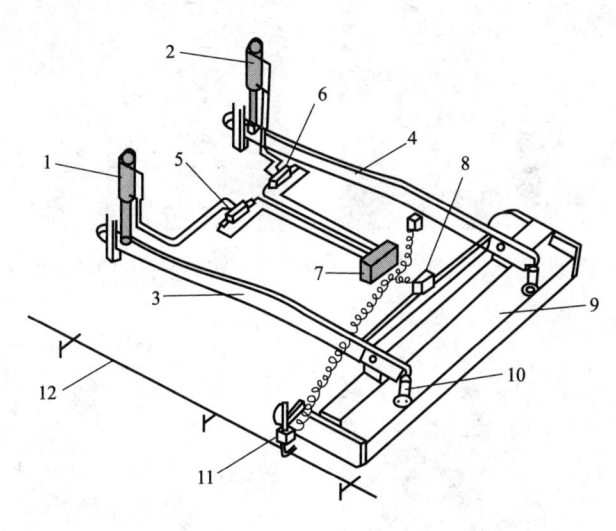

Fig. 11.17 Components of auto leveling device
自动找平装置的组成

1　left leveling cylinder 左调平油缸
2　right leveling cylinder 右调平油缸
3　left towed arm 左牵引臂
4　right towed arm 右牵引臂
5　left electromagnetic valve 左电磁阀
6　right electromagnetic valve 右电磁阀
7　main controller 主控制器
8　cross slope sensor 横坡传感器
9　screed units 熨平板
10　lifting cylinder 提升油缸
11　longitudinal slope sensor 纵坡传感器
12　leveling reference 调平基准

(2) Types 类型 (Fig. 11.18)

(a) erected stringline leveling system
挂线调平系统

(b) mechanical floating averaging beam
机械式浮动平均梁

(c) ultrasonic averaging beam
超声波平均梁

(d) laser leveling system
激光调平系统

Fig. 11.18 Types of auto leveling device 自动找平装置的类型

11.4 New Technology of Asphalt Paver 沥青摊铺机新技术

11.4.1 Introduction 简介

Based upon the industry-proven reputation of the Caterpillar AP-1050B and AP-1055B Asphalt Pavers, the AP-1055D establishes new standards for productivity and reliability in the asphalt paver industry.

在卡特彼勒 AP-1050B 和 AP-1055B 型工业名牌沥青摊铺机的基础上，AP-1055D 在沥青摊铺机工业生产中建立了新的生产率和可靠性标准。

Durable, field proven powertrain, propel system and material handling system along with the world's largest and most dedicated dealer support system ensure the AP-1055D will provide maximum return on investment.

坚固耐久、成熟的传动装置、驱动系统和材料输送系统，以及全球最大和最专业的保障支持系统，将确保AP-1055D产生最大的投资回报。

11.4.2 High Ambient Temperature Cooling System 高温环境下的冷却系统（Fig. 11.19）

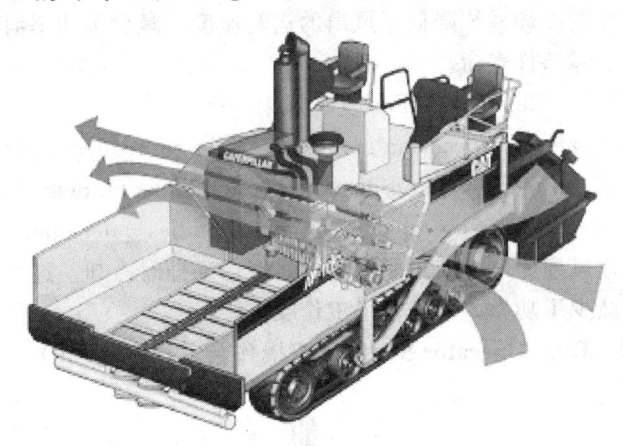

Fig. 11.19 High ambient temperature cooling system
高温环境下的冷却系统

The standard, high-capacity cooling system provides efficient operation in high ambient temperatures. The new system design also provides quiet operation that benefits the operator and the surrounding environment.

标准化大容量冷却系统在高温环境中可保证有效工作。这种新系统的设计也提供了安静的工作环境，从而对操作者和周围环境有利。

(1) Airflow 空气流

The airflow design draws ambient air across the engine compartment and through the radiator. This new design allows the exhaust air to exit the right side of the machine in order to provide a cooler engine compartment and operator platform.

空气流的设计使周围空气经发动机机舱后通过散热器。这种新设计使废气从机器右侧排出，以便使发动机机舱和操作台获得更好的冷却效果。

（2）High Capacity Cooling Package 大容量冷却部件

The high capacity cooling system allows the fan to run slower, reducing power demand while extending component life.

大容量冷却系统降低了风扇的运转速度，减少了功率消耗，同时延长了零部件寿命。

（3）Variable Speed Fan 变速风扇

The variable speed fan is electronically controlled and hydraulically driven to provide on-demand cooling. This on-demand operation reduces engine power demand and provides quiet operation.

变速风扇为电控液压驱动方式，以保证即时冷却。这种即时运行方式减少了功率，并降低了工作噪声。

11.4.3　Dual Operator Stations 双操作台（Fig. 11.20）

Fig. 11.20　Dual operator stations 双操作台

The dual operator stations provide complete control and good visibility from either side of the operating platform.

双操作台为驾驶台两侧提供了完整的控制和良好的视野。

11.4.4 Mobil-trac Undercarriage 移动式履带行走机构 (Fig. 11.21)

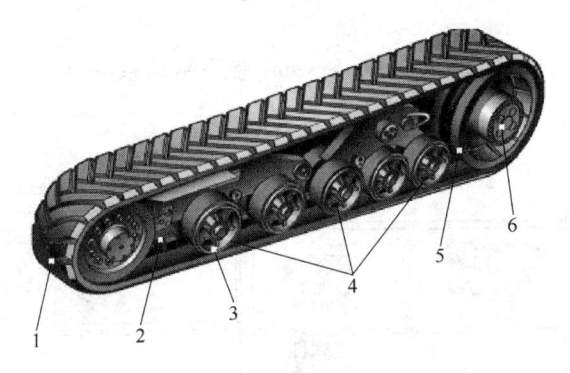

Fig. 11.21 Mobil-trac undercarriage 移动式履带行走机构

1 durable mobil-trac belt 坚韧的移动式履带
2 belt tensioning system 履带张紧系统
3 rubber-coated steel mid-wheel 挂胶中间钢轮
4 fully bogied undercarriage 整体台车式行走机构
5 friction drive wheel 摩擦式驱动轮
6 two-speed planetary 双速行星减速器

11.4.5 Steel Track Undercarriage 钢履带行走机构 (Fig. 11.22)

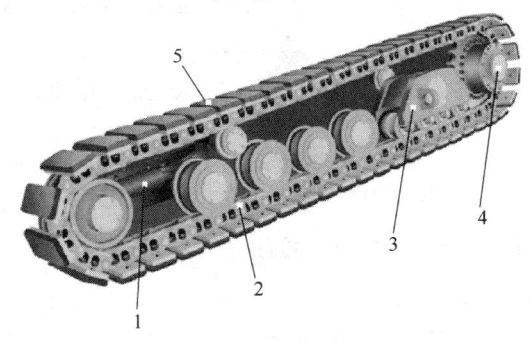

Fig. 11.22 Steel track undercarriage 钢履带行走机构

1　track tension system 履带张紧系统
2　D3 track rails D3（推土机）履带轨
3　quad rear bogie 四边形后台车架
4　single-speed planetary 单速行星减速器
5　bonded track pads 双层履带板

11.4.6　Hydrostatic Drive System 液压驱动系统（Fig. 11.23）

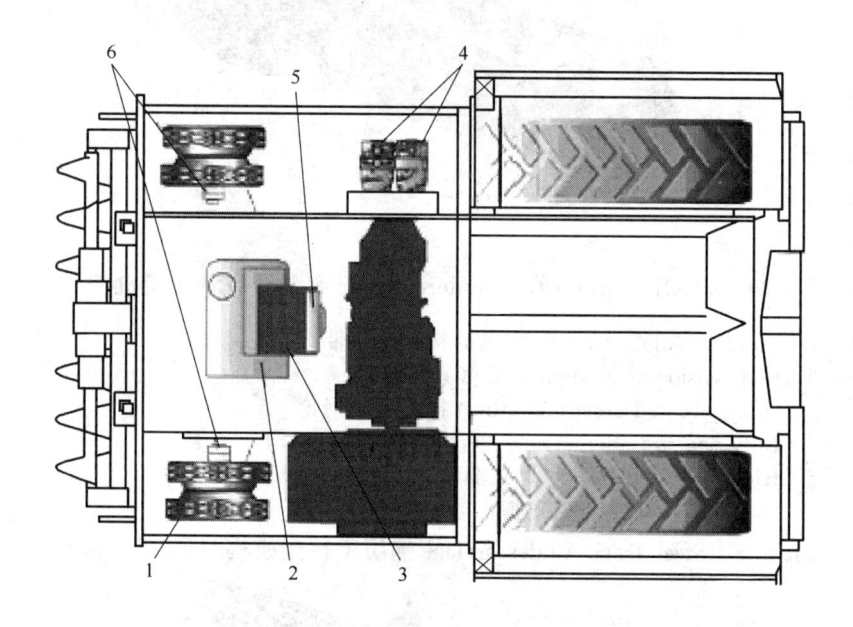

Fig. 11.23　Hydrostatic drive system 液压驱动系统

1　planetary drive 行星传动装置
2　hydraulic oil tank 液压油箱
3　electrical junction box 电子接线盒
4　propel pumps 驱动泵
5　machine controller 机器控制器
6　propel motors 驱动马达

11.4.7 Exclusive Material Delivery System 独特的材料传输系统
（Fig. 11.24）

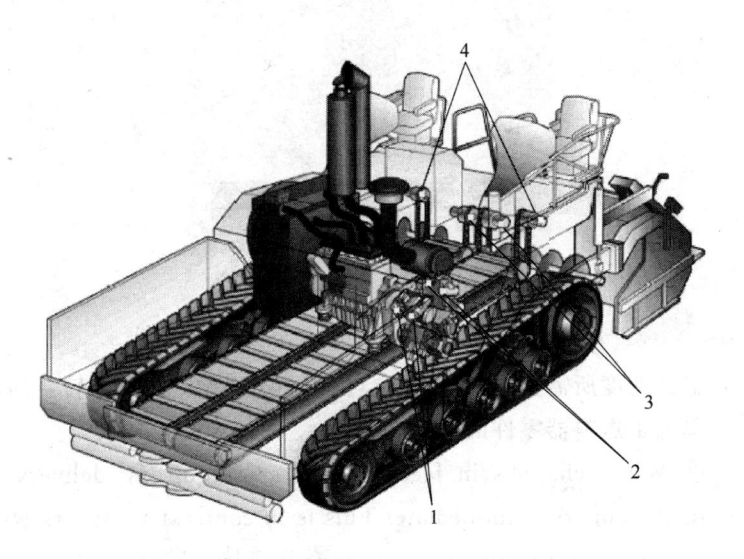

Fig. 11.24 Exclusive material delivery system
独特的材料传输系统

1　right feeder and auger drive pumps 右侧送料器与螺旋器驱动泵
2　left feeder and auger drive pumps 左侧送料器与螺旋器驱动泵
3　auger drive motors 螺旋器驱动马达
4　outboard feeder drive motors 外侧送料器驱动马达

11.4.8　Gateless Feeders 无门送料器 （Fig. 11.25）

① The gateless feeders on the AP-1055D always run full of mix regardless of the speed required to fill the auger chamber. This is typically a slower speed than would be experienced with a paver utilizing feeder gates to control mix delivery rates. By not always having to run at full speed，feeder component wear is significantly reduced.

AP-1055D 摊铺机的无门送料器始终满料运转而不考虑充填螺旋器仓所需要的速度。这一速度明显低于有供料门摊铺机为控制混

Fig. 11.25 Gateless feeders 无门送料器

合料输送速度所需要的供料速度。由于不需要始终全速运转,因而大大降低了送料器零件的磨损。

② When changes in feeder speed are required, delivery of mix to the augers is immediate. This is in contrast to pavers with gates, where any delivery rate change is delayed for the length of time it takes to clear the tunnel of mix from the previous gate setting.

当需要改变送料器速度时,可立即向螺旋器输送混合料。这与有供料门摊铺机形成了鲜明的对比,在有供料门的摊铺机上,任一送料速度的改变均需要延迟一段时间,以便清理先前供料门设置的混合料通道。

③ Running at slower speeds can also help reduce the opportunity for segregation, especially when working with larger stone mixes that have more of a tendency to segregate.

以较低的速度运行还有助于减小材料离析的机会,特别是当摊铺含有大石块混合料时具有更大的离析趋向。

11.4.9 Feeder Design 送料器设计 （Fig. 11.26）

Fig. 11.26 Feeder 送料器

The AP-1055D auger drive assembly is independent of the tractor which allows the distance between the two feeders to be significantly reduced. Keeping the feeders close together allows the flow from both feeders to blend together more easily as they discharge into the auger cavity. The tunnel and auger designs eliminate voids under the chain case to minimize segregation.

AP-1055D 摊铺机的螺旋器驱动装置独立于牵引装置，从而大大减小了两个送料器之间的距离。使两个送料器靠得更加紧密，可使两个送料器料流充入螺旋器空腔时更容易混合。这种通道和螺旋器设计消除了链传动箱下方的空隙，从而使离析达到最小化。

11.4.10　Auger Assembly 螺旋器组件 （Fig. 11.27）

Fig. 11.27　Auger assembly 螺旋器组件

The auger assembly height can be hydraulically adjusted 192mm. The ability to raise the auger assembly simplifies loading and unloading from a transport vehicle. Also, when working with larger stone mixes, segregation can often be eliminated or minimized by raising the augers to allow mix to flow unrestricted under the auger assembly.

螺旋器组件高度可通过液压进行 192mm 的调节。这种提升螺旋器组件的功能使得运输车辆的装载和卸载变得简单容易。而且，当摊铺含有较大石块混合料时，通过提升螺旋器，使混合料在螺旋器组件下方自由流过，常常可消除离析现象或使其最小化。

11.4.11　Electric Heat Screeds 电加热熨平板

（1）Friendly Operating Environment 友好的操作环境

The electric screed plate heating system eliminates the use of diesel fuel burners, creating a user friendly environment.

熨平板电加热系统避免了使用柴油燃烧器，创建了用户友好环境。

（2）Fast Warm-up Time 快速预热

The electric screed provides a warm-up time in 30 minutes or less to 122℃ when ambient temperatures are at or above 22℃.

当环境温度在 22℃ 以上时,电加热熨平板可在 30 分钟内将其预热至 122℃。

(3) Simple Operation 操作简单

The screed control panel incorporates touch-pad technology with high intensity LED's that promote simplified use and diagnostic capability with minimal operator training.

熨平控制面板应用高强度 LED 触摸技术,操作员通过基本培训即可进行简单使用并提高诊断能力。

(4) Multi-Zone Heating Elements 多区域加热元件

The heating elements are mounted to the screed plates in a multi-zone configuration to provide even heat distribution.

加热元件以多区域布局方式安装于熨平板,以提供均匀的热分布。

(5) Thermostatically Controlled 恒温控制

The screed plates incorporate thermostatically controlled temperature sensors in each screed section including the extenders. The temperature sensors provide inputs to the screed controller.

熨平板在每一区域(包括延伸区域)设置有恒温控制温度传感器。温度传感器提供了熨平控制器的输入。

Unit 12　Rollers 压路机

12.1　Overview 概述

12.1.1　Basic Concept 基本概念

Roller is a compactor type engineering vehicle used to compact soil, gravel, concrete or asphalt in the construction of roads and foundations. Rollers compact the material by the pressure exerted by their rolling drums on the surface, which are suitable for most types of road construction, airfields, dam construction, harbour projects and industrial constructions. Rollers are available in several categories: trailer, self-powered and walk-behind, which are available as smooth drum, padded drum and rubber-tyred models; and are further divided into static and vibratory sub-categories.

压路机是压实类工程机械，用于压实道路和基础施工中的土壤、砾石、混凝土或者沥青。压路机通过滚轮对被压实材料表面施加的作用力来完成压实，它适用于各种道路、机场、水坝、港口工程以及工业建设。压路机有不同的类型：拖式、自行式和手扶式；光轮式、凸块式和橡胶轮胎式。压路机可以进一步分为静作用式和振动式。

Static rollers compact asphalt pavements or soils solely by means of their own weight. The weight of the machine applies downward force on the soil, compressing the soil particles and increasing the density of soil. For this type of roller, both the gross weight of the machine and the contact area of the drums with the soil are important in determining the compactive effort applied by the roller to the soil surface. Static rollers have a fairly low penetration but achieve excellent evenness. The only way to change the effective compaction force is by adding or subtracting the weight of the machine. Static smooth drum rollers, pneumatic tyred rollers are two examples of static compaction.

静作用式压路机完全依靠机器自重来压实沥青路面或者土壤。机器重量能够施加给土壤向下的作用力,以压缩土壤颗粒,增加土壤密度。对于这种压路机,影响压实效果的主要因素是整机重量和滚轮与土壤的接触面积。静作用式压路机的压实深度较小,但是有着良好的压实均匀性。改变有效压实力的唯一方法是增加或减小机器的重量。静作用光轮压路机和轮胎压路机是该类压实的两个例子。

Pneumatic tyred rollers are static rollers, meaning that they compact by means of their own weight, although they additionally use the kneading effect generated by tyre deformation. The rolling and kneading effect of the pneumatic tyres produce excellent surfacing sealing results. Their depth of penetration depends on wheel load, tyre pressure and working speed. Pneumatic tyred rollers generally consist of two axles fitted with pneumatic rubber tyres, mounted on a frame. The most popular machines have three tyres in front and four tyres in the rear (a total of seven tyres), or four tyres in fron tand five tyres in the rear (a total of nine tyres). The roller is used to compact asphalt for sealing purposes. It is also used to compact base, sub-base and stabilized soil.

轮胎式压路机尽管采用了轮胎变形所产生的揉搓作用,但属于静作用压路机,这意味着它是通过机器自身重量进行压实的。空气轮胎的滚压和揉搓作用能够产生良好的表面密封效果。它的压实深度取决于轮载、轮胎气压和工作速度。轮胎式压路机一般由安装在车架上的带有充气橡胶轮胎的两轴组成。最流行的轮胎压路机其轮胎分布形式为前三后四（总共七个轮胎），或者是前四后五（总共九个轮胎）。轮胎式压路机用于压实沥青以达到密封表层的目的，它也用于基层、底基层和稳定土的压实。

Vibratory rollers apply two types of compactive effort to the materials-static weight and dynamic (impact) force. The compactive effort derived from the static weight of the roller is caused by the weight of the drums and frame. The compactive effort derived from the dynamic force is produced by a rotating eccentric weight located inside the drum (or drums). The rollers deliver a rapid sequence of blows (impacts) to the surface, thereby affecting the top layers as well as deeper layers. Vibration moves through the material, setting particles in motion and moving them closer together for the highest density possible. The trend is toward vibratory rollers.

振动压路机对材料有两种压实作用力——自身重力和动态冲击力。来自于压路机自身重力的压实力是由钢轮和机架重量产生的。来自动态作用的压实力是由位于钢轮内的偏心块旋转产生。压路机对材料表面提供快速连续的冲击，从而影响了上层以及深层材料。振动在材料中传递，使材料颗粒产生运动，并使它们靠近以达到尽可能高的密实度。振动压路机是发展趋势。

Vibratory rollers come in a variety of configurations. Single drum vibratory rollers feature a single vibrating drum with pneumatic drive wheels. The drum is available as smooth for sub-base or rockfill, or padded for soil compaction. Double drum vibratory rollers are tandem rollers, which are mainly applied to compaction for asphalt road surface. They also can be used for large-scale base, sub-base and embankment fill compaction. Walk behind vibratory rollers are suitable for compacting thin layers on granular soils and asphalt. They are mostly used for small jobs, repair work and compaction in confined areas.

振动压路机有多种配置。单钢轮振动压路机的特点是单个钢轮振动，轮胎驱动。钢轮可以是用于底基层或填石压实的光轮，或者是用于土壤压实的凸块式钢轮。双钢轮振动压路机是串联式压路机，主要用于沥青路面的压实，还可用于大规模基层、底基层和路堤填方的压实。手扶式振动压路机适于粒状土和沥青的薄层压实，该压路机主要用于小型作业、维护以及狭窄区域的压实。

Today many different types and variations of rollers are manufactured and used to meet widely varying soil and field conditions, from granular soils to asphalt concrete. Many compactor manufacturers can produce various types of high-performance rollers, mainly including Bomag, DYNAPAC, AMMANN, Sakai, Hamm, Caterpillar, and so on.

现在已制造出多种不同类型的压路机，可满足从粒状土到沥青混凝土的各种各样的土壤类型和现场条件要求。许多压实机械生产企业已经可以生产出各种类型的高性能压路机，其中，主要有宝马格、戴纳帕克、安迈、酒井、悍马、卡特彼勒等公司。

12.1.2 Application 应用 (Fig. 12.1)

(a) soil compaction 土壤压实

(b) rockfill compaction 堆石压实

(c) asphalt compaction 沥青压实

(d) landfill compaction 垃圾填埋压实

(e) base compaction 基础压实

(f) pavement compaction 路面压实

(g) trench compaction 沟槽压实

(h) slope compaction 斜坡压实

Fig. 12.1 Application of rollers 压路机的应用

12.1.3 Types 类型 (Fig. 12.2)

(a) static smooth drum roller
静作用光轮压路机

(b) pneumatic tyred roller
轮胎压路机

(c) pad foot roller 凸块式压路机

(d) impact roller 冲击式压路机

(e) walk behind single drum vibratory roller
单轮手扶式振动压路机

(f) walk behind double drum vibratory roller
双轮手扶式振动压路机

(g) single drum vibratory roller
单钢轮振动压路机

(h) vibratory pad foot roller
凸块式振动压路机

(i) tandem vibratory roller (double drum)
串联式振动压路机（双钢轮）

(j) combined vibratory roller
组合式振动压路机

Fig. 12.2

(k) towed smooth drum vibratory roller
拖式光轮振动压路机

(l) towed pad foot vibratory roller
拖式凸块振动压路机

Fig. 12.2　Types of roller 压络机的类型

12.2　Components and Features 组成与特点

12.2.1　Components 组成

(1) Basic Components of Single Drum Vibratory Roller 单钢轮振动压路机基本部件 (Fig. 12.3)

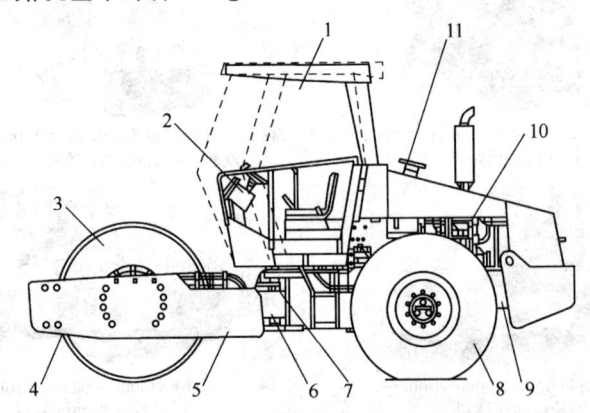

Fig. 12.3　Basic components of single drum vibratory roller
单钢轮振动压路机基本部件

1	driving cab 驾驶室		铰架
2	operating console 操纵台	7	steering cylinder 转向油缸
3	vibratory drum 振动轮	8	driving tire 驱动轮胎
4	scrapers 刮泥板	9	rear frame 后车架
5	front frame 前车架	10	engine 发动机
6	central articulated frame 中心	11	air filter 空气滤清器

(2) Basic Components of Tandem Vibratory Roller 双钢轮振动压路机基本部件（Fig. 12.4）

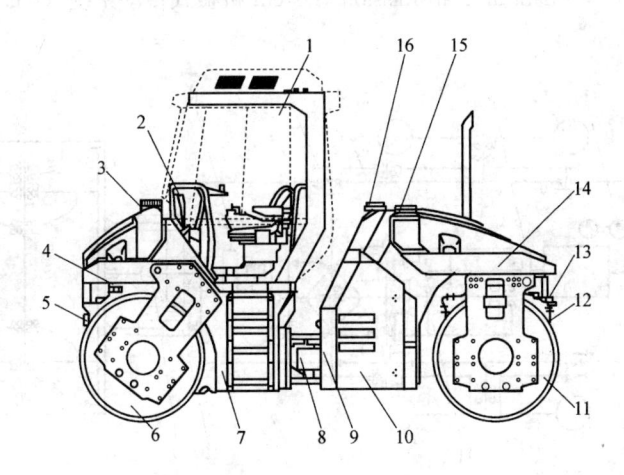

Fig. 12.4 Basic components of tandem vibratory roller
双钢轮振动压路机基本部件

1　driving cab 驾驶室
2　operating console 操纵台
3,15　water tank 水箱
4,13　watering system 喷水系统
5,12　scrapers 刮泥板
6　front drum 前轮
7　front frame 前车架
8　central articulated frame 中心铰接架
9　steering cylinder 转向油缸
10　engine 发动机
11　rear drum 后轮
14　rear frame 后车架
16　air filter 空气过滤器

345

12.2.2 Transmission System of Single Drum Vibratory Roller 单钢轮振动压路机传动系统

(1) Mechanical Transmission System 机械式传动系统 (Fig. 12.5)

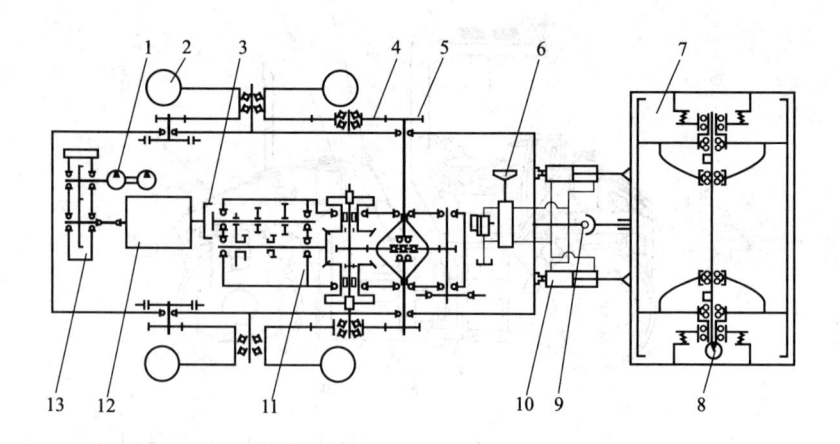

Fig. 12.5 Mechanical transmission system 机械式传动系统

1 double gear pump for steering and vibration 转向及振动用双联齿轮泵
2 driving tire 驱动轮胎
3 main clutch 主离合器
4 side driving gear 侧传动齿轮
5 final reduction pinion 末级减速小齿轮
6 steering device and steering valve 转向器和转向阀
7 vibratory drum 振动轮
8 vibration driving motor 振动驱动马达
9 articulated steering joint 铰接转向节
10 steering cylinder 转向油缸
11 gearbox 变速箱
12 engine 发动机
13 auxiliary gearbox 副齿轮箱

(2) Hydraulic Transmission System (one-wheel drive) 液压式传动系统（单轮驱动）(Fig. 12. 6)

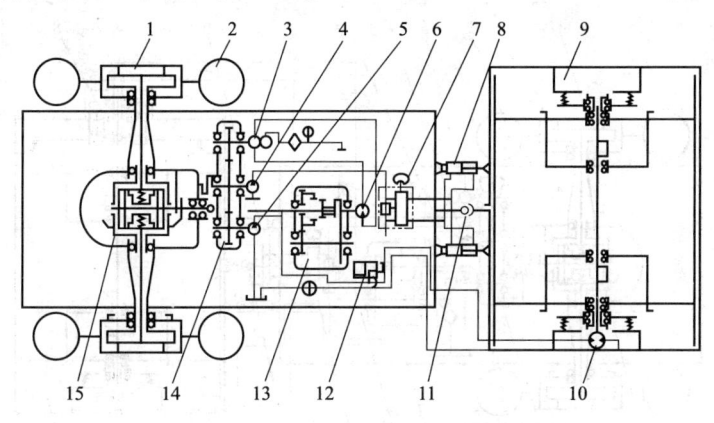

Fig. 12. 6 Hydraulic transmission system (one-wheel drive)
液压式传动系统（单轮驱动）

1　wheel reduction gear 轮边减速器
2　driving tire 驱动轮胎
3　travel driving pump 行走驱动泵
4　steering pump 转向泵
5　vibration driving pump 振动驱动泵
6　travel driving motor 行走驱动马达
7　hydraulic steering device 液压转向器
8　steering cylinder 转向油缸
9　vibratory drum 振动轮
10　vibration driving motor 振动驱动马达
11　articulated steering joint 铰接转向节
12　vibration valve 起振阀
13　gearbox 变速箱
14　transfer case 分动箱
15　driving axle 驱动桥

(3) Hydraulic Transmission System (two-wheel drive) 液压式传动系统（双轮驱动）(Fig. 12.7)

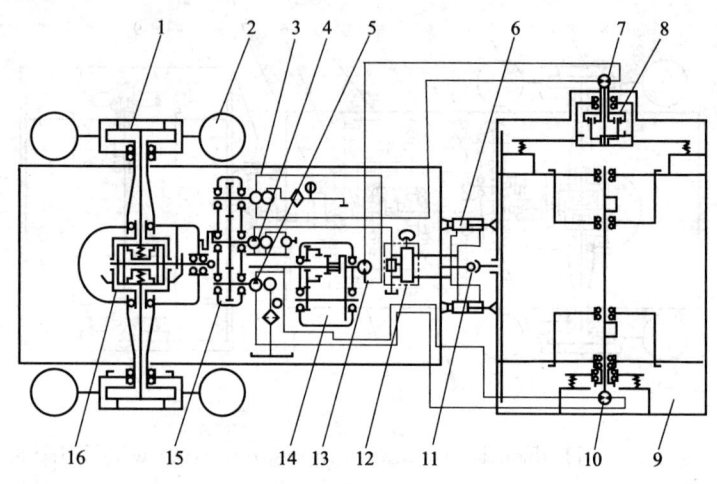

Fig. 12.7　Hydraulic transmission system (two-wheel drive)
液压式传动系统（双轮驱动）

1　wheel reduction gear 轮边减速器
2　driving tire 驱动轮胎
3　travel driving pump 行走驱动泵
4　steering pump 转向泵
5　vibration driving pump 振动驱动泵
6　steering cylinder 转向油缸
7　vibratory drum travel driving motor 振动轮行走驱动马达
8　planetary reduction gear 行星减速器
9　vibratory drum 振动轮
10　vibration driving motor 振动驱动马达
11　articulated steering joint 铰接转向节
12　hydraulic steering device 液压转向器
13　travel driving motor 行走驱动马达
14　gearbox 变速箱
15　transfer case 分动箱
16　driving axle 驱动桥

12.2.3 Hydraulic Transmission System of Tandem Vibratory Roller 双钢轮振动压路机液压传动系统

(1) Hydraulic Traveling System 行走液压系统 (Fig. 12.8)

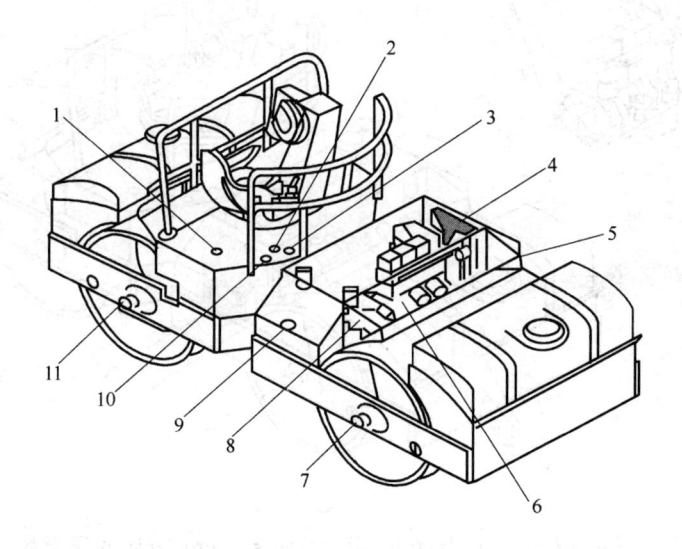

Fig. 12.8 Hydraulic traveling system 行走液压系统

1 brake valve 制动阀
2 hand pump 手动泵
3 pressure gauge 压力计
4 oil cooler 油冷却器
5 hydraulic tank 液压油箱
6 traveling suction strainer 行走吸滤器
7 drum traveling motor 滚轮行走马达
8 traveling pump 行走泵
9 loop flush valve 环形冲洗阀
10 dump valve 卸荷阀
11 drum traveling motor 滚轮行走马达

(2) Hydraulic Vibration System 振动液压系统（Fig. 12.9）

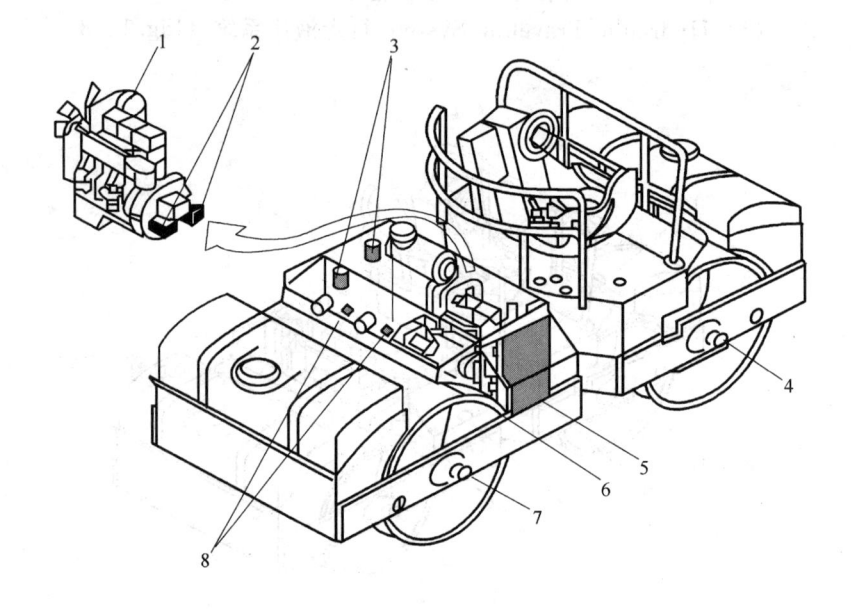

Fig. 12.9 Hydraulic vibration system 振动液压系统

1 engine 发动机
2 vibration pumps 振动泵
3 vibration filters 振动过滤器
4 vibration motor 振动马达
5 oil cooler 油冷却器
6 hydraulic tank 液压油箱
7 vibration motor 振动马达
8 vibration suction strainers 振动吸滤器

(3) Hydraulic Steering System 转向液压系统 (Fig. 12.10)

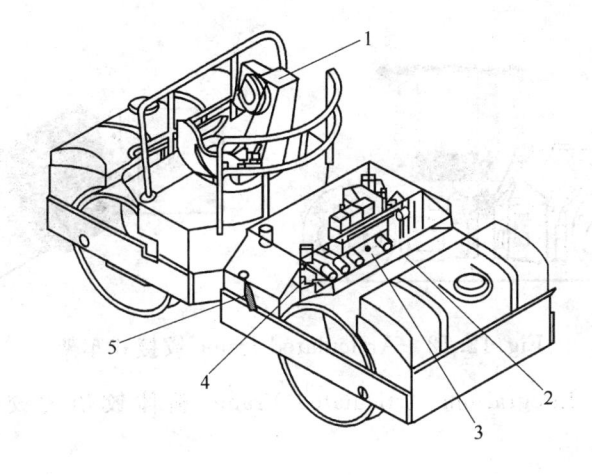

Fig. 12.10　Hydraulic steering system 转向液压系统

1　steering valve 转向阀
2　hydraulic tank 液压油箱
3　steering suction strainer 转向吸滤器
4　steering pump 转向泵
5　steering cylinder 转向油缸

12.2.4　Frame 车架

(1) Types 类型

① Rigid Frame 刚性（整体式）车架 (Fig. 12.11)

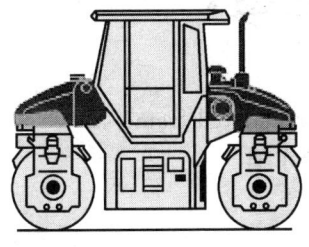

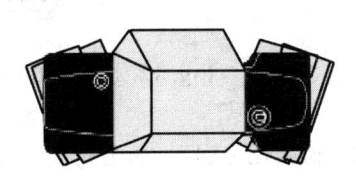

Fig. 12.11　Rigid frame 刚性（整体式）车架

② Articulated Frame 铰接式车架 (Fig. 12.12)

Fig. 12.12 Articulated frame 铰接式车架

(2) Integral-pin Articulated Frame 整体铰销式铰接车架 (Fig. 12.13)

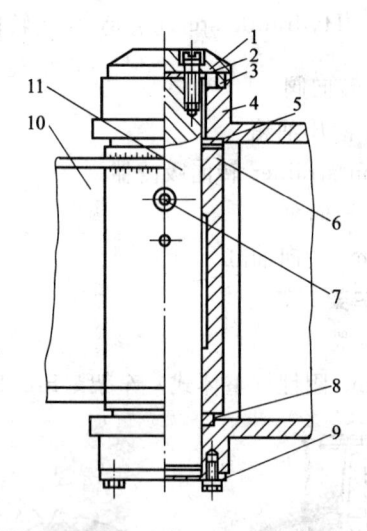

Fig. 12.13 Integral-pin articulated frame 整体铰销式铰接车架

1　pressure plate 压力盘
2　adjusting shim 调整垫片
3　seal ring 密封圈

4   rear frame 后车架
5   adjusting shim 调整垫片
6   pin bracket 销轴套
7   grease fitting 黄油嘴
8   seal ring 密封圈
9   lower cover 下盖
10 front frame 前车架
11 pin pivot 铰销轴

(3) Two-pins Articulated Frame 双铰销式铰接架 (Fig. 12.14)

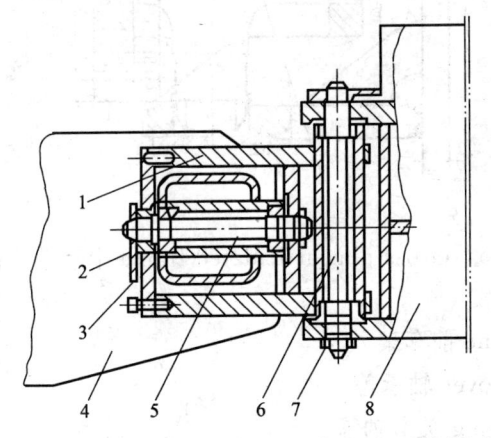

Fig. 12.14 Two-pins articulated frame 双铰销式铰接架

1   articulated joint shell 铰接架壳体
2   locating plate 定位板
3   joint bearing 关节轴承
4   front frame 前车架
5   horizontal pin 水平销轴
6   vertical pin 垂直销轴
7   lock nut 锁紧螺母
8   rear frame 后车架

（4）Cross-pins Articulated Frame 十字轴式铰接车架（Fig. 12.15）

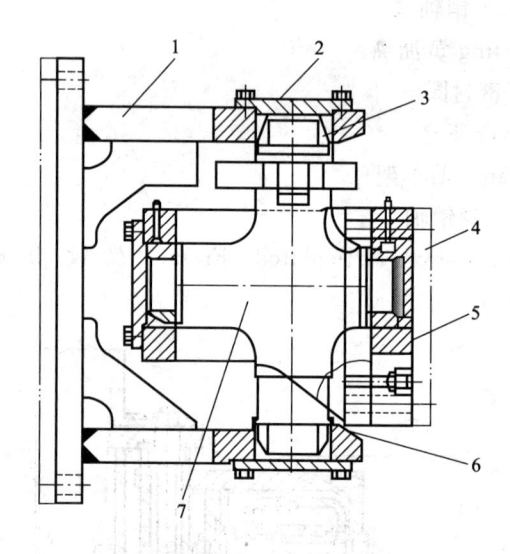

Fig. 12.15 Gross-pins articulated frame 十字轴式链接车架

1 front frame 前车架
2 bearing cover 轴承盖
3 joint bearing 关节轴承
4 rear frame 后车架
5 pin bracket 销轴套
6 seal ring 密封圈
7 cross-pins pivot 十字轴

12.2.5 Vibratory Drum 振动轮

(1) None Drive Mode 非驱动型 (Fig. 12.16)

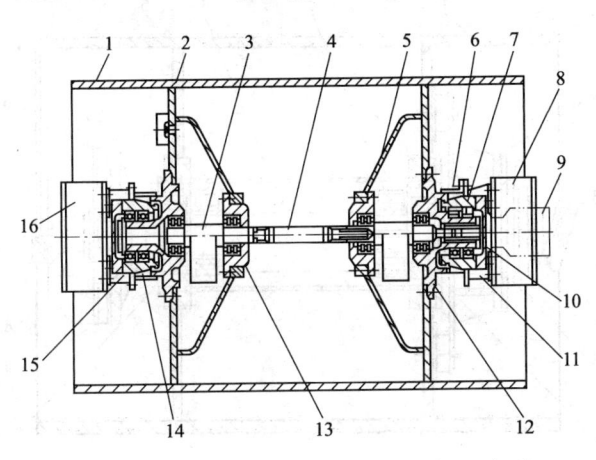

Fig. 12.16 None drive mode 非驱动型

1. drum shell 轮圈
2. spoke plate 轮辐板
3. eccentric shaft 偏心轴
4. middle driving shaft 中间传动轴
5. vibration bearing 振动轴承
6. right junction bracket 右连接支架
7. frame bearing 车架轴承
8. right junction plate 右连接板
9. vibration motor 振动马达
10. splined hub 花键套
11. shock absorber 减振器
12. outer bearing housing 外轴承座
13. inner bearing housing 内轴承座
14. left junction bracket 左连接支架
15. shock absorber 减振器
16. left junction plate 左连接板

(2) Drive Mode 驱动型 (Fig. 12.17)

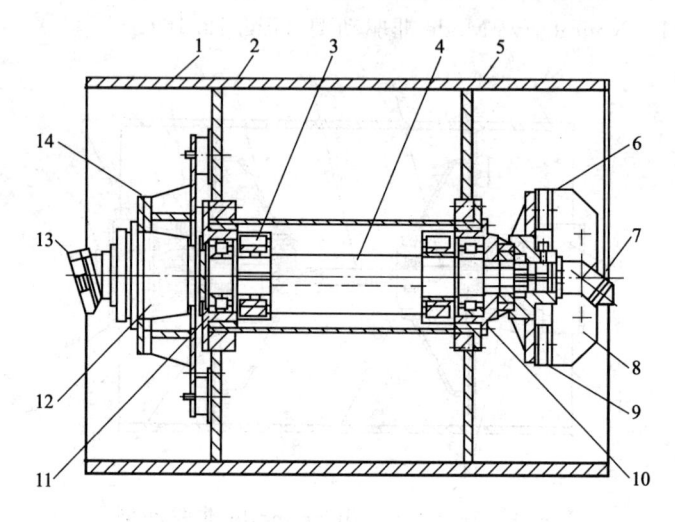

Fig. 12.17 Drive mode 驱动型

1 drum shell 轮圈
2 shock absorber 减振器
3 amplitude adjusting mechanism 调幅机构
4 eccentric shaft 偏心轴
5 spoke plate 轮辐板
6 shock absorber 减振器
7 vibration motor 振动马达
8 right junction plate 右连接板
9 right junction bracket 右连接支架
10 bearing cover 轴承端盖
11 vibration bearing 振动轴承
12 reducer 减速器
13 travel motor 行走马达
14 left junction bracket 左连接支架

12.2.6 Amplitude Adjusting Mechanism 调幅机构

(1) Dual Amplitude Mechanism of Reversible Eccentric Weight 逆转偏心块式双幅机构 (Fig. 12.18)

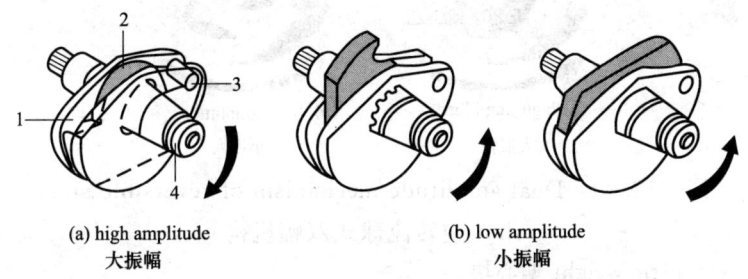

(a) high amplitude
大振幅

(b) low amplitude
小振幅

Fig. 12.18 Dual amplitude mechanism of reversible eccenric weight 逆转偏心块式双幅机构

1　fixed eccentric weight 固定偏心块
2　free eccentric weight 活动偏心块
3　stopping pin 挡销
4　vibratory shaft 振动轴

Reversing the direction of a rotating shaft changes the position of the eccentric weights and results in a change of amplitude and centrifugal force.

振动轴反转可以改变偏心块位置，从而改变振幅和离心力。

(2) Dual Amplitude Mechanism of Reversible Steel Shot 逆转流球式双幅机构 (Fig. 12.19)

Amplitude selection is determined by the position of the steel shot inside the hollow eccentric weight. The rotational direction of the vibratory shaft determines the amplitude level.

调整振幅是通过改变空心偏心块内钢球的位置来实现的，振动轴的旋转方向决定着振幅的大小。

(3) Five Amplitude Vibratory System 5 振幅振动系统 (Fig. 12.20)

(a) high amplilude
大振幅

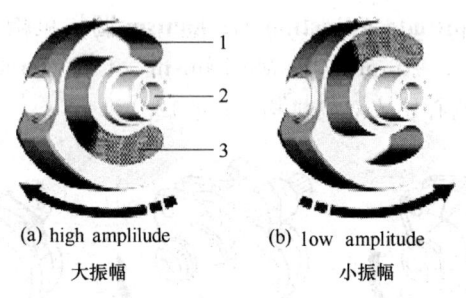

(b) low amplitude
小振幅

Fig. 12.19　Dual amplitude mechanism of reversible steel shot 逆转流球式双幅机构

1　eccentric weight 偏心块
2　vibratory shaft 振动轴
3　steel shot 钢球

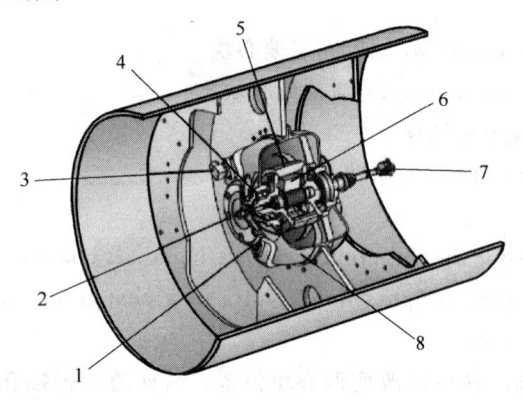

Fig. 12.20　Five amplitude vibratory system 5 振幅振动系统

1　oil level sight gauge 油面观测计
2　amplitude selection wheel 振幅选择轮
3　oil drain 放油口
4　eccentric weight shaft bearings 偏心轴轴承
5　fixed eccentric Weight 固定偏心块
6　5-position counterweight 5 位置平衡块
7　weight drive shaft to motor 传动轴（连接马达）
8　eccentric weight housing 偏心块壳体

12.2.7 Control Panel 操纵控制台 (Fig. 12.21)

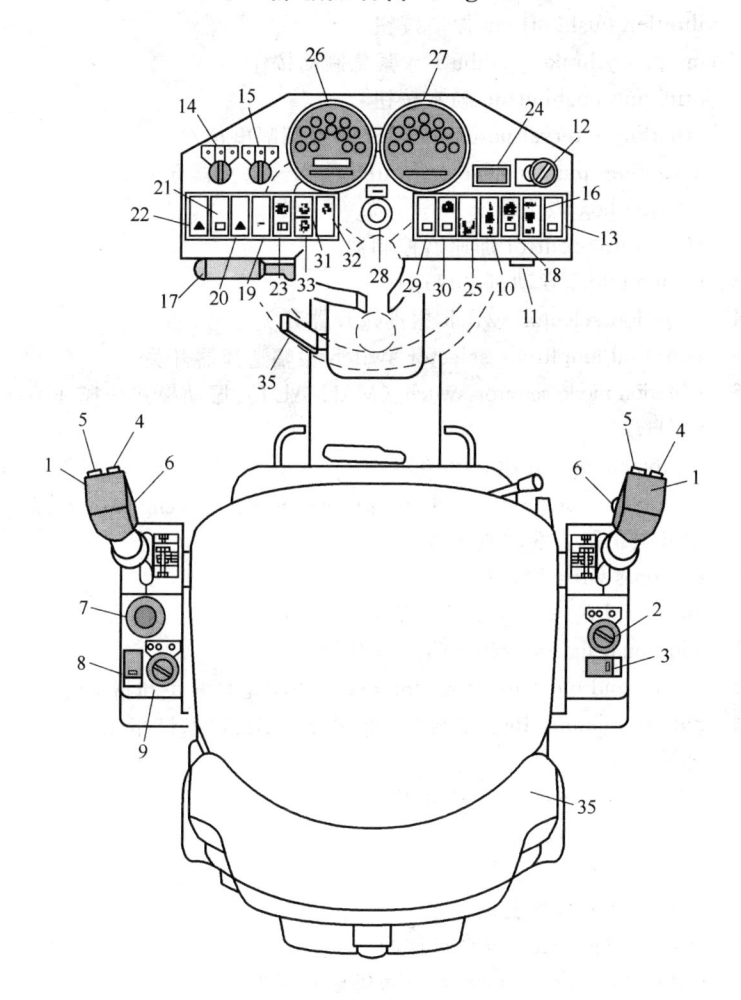

Fig. 12.21 Control panel 操纵控制台

1 travel controls 行驶控制器
2 speed potentiometer 速度电位器
3 pushbutton for mode of soft starting to move and stopping to move 开始移动和停止移动模式按钮
4 pushbutton for CRAB mode-right 横向模式按钮-右侧

359

5	pushbutton for CRAB mode-left 横向模式按钮-左侧	
6	vibration pushbuttons 振动按钮	
7	emergency brake pushbutton 紧急制动按钮	
8	sprinkling pushbutton 喷水按钮	
9	sprinkling interval potentiometer 喷水间隔电位器	
10	sprinkling pumps selector switch 喷水泵选择器开关	
11	ignition box 点火器	
12	accelerator control 加速器控制器	
13	engine idling 发动机怠速运行	
14	vibration selector switch 振动选择器开关	
15	vibration amplitude selector switch 振幅选择器开关	
16	vibration mode selector switch (MAN/AUT) 振动模式选择开关（手动/自动）	
17	combined switch 组合开关	
18	switch for constant speed and protection against engine overload 恒速开关，防止发动机过载	
19	beacon switch 警示灯开关	
20	alarm lights switch 报警灯开关	
21	additional lights switch 附加灯开关	
22	switch and indicator lamp for rear lights 尾灯开关和指示灯	
23	indicator lamps for lights (dipped/distance) 车灯指示灯（近光/远光）	
24	infrared thermometer 红外温度计	
25	spreader 喷洒器	
26	LH cluster 左仪表盘	
27	RH cluster 右仪表盘	
28	engine diagnostics 发动机诊断	
29	engine diagnostics switch 发动机诊断开关	
30	troubleshooting switch 故障排除开关	
31	red lamp (engine diagnostics) 红灯（发动机诊断）	
32	yellow lamp (engine diagnostics) 黄灯（发动机诊断）	
33	engine heating 发动机加热	
34	steering wheel position adjustment 方向盘位置调整	
35	operator seat 操作员座位	

12.2.8 Water Spray System 喷水系统 (Fig. 12.22)

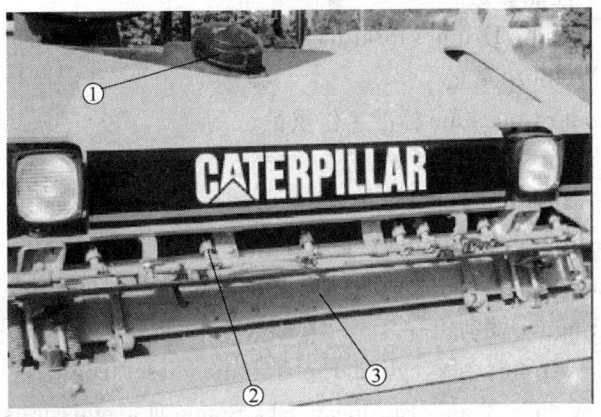

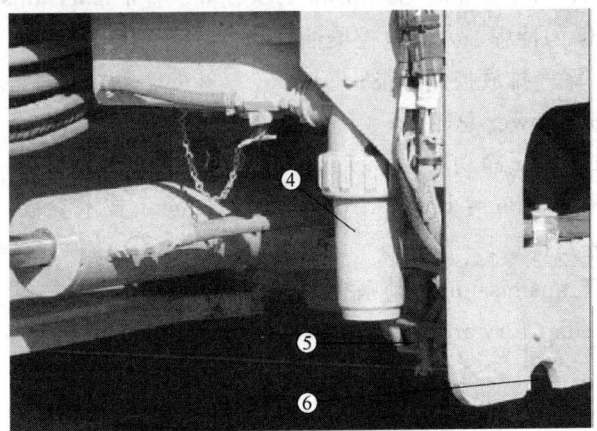

Fig. 12.22 Water spray system 喷水系统

1　single water fill port 单一加水口
2　spray nozzle with filter 过滤型喷咀
3　water distribution mat 配水垫板
4　water filter 水过滤器
5　water pumps 水泵
6　single water tank drain 单一水箱排水口

12.2.9 Standard Equipment Specifications 标准装置规格类型与性能参数

(1) Single Drum Vibratory Rollers 单钢轮振动压路机

① Weights 重量

Standard machine 标准工作重量；

At front drum 前桥处；

At rear drum 后桥处；

Maximum machine 机器最大工作重量；

Static linear load (at drum) 线性静压力（振动钢轮处）。

② Engine 发动机

Four-stroke, six cylinder electronic diesel engine, it meets U.S. EPA Tier 3 and European EU Stage Ⅲa emissions control standards 四冲程、六缸电控柴油发动机，满足美国 EPA Tier3 和欧洲Ⅲa 尾气排放控制标准；

Gross power 总功率；

Net power 净功率；

Specifications: bore, stroke, displacement 技术参数：缸体内径，行程，排量。

③ Transmission 传动系统

Speeds (forward and reverse) low range, high range 速度（前进及后退）低速范围，高速范围；

Two variable displacement piston pump 两个变排量柱塞泵；

Two dual displacement piston motors 两个双行走柱塞马达。

④ Steering 转向

Minimum turning radius 最小回转半径；

Inside drum edge 内转弯半径；

Outside drum edge 外转弯半径；

Steering angles 转向角；

Oscillation angle 摆角；

Hydraulic system: a gear-type pump 液压系统：一个齿轮泵。

⑤ Brakes 制动器
Service brake features 行车制动器特点：
Closed-loop hydrostatic drive system provides dynamic braking during machine operation.
闭式静液压驱动系统可在机器工作期间提供动态制动。
Secondary brake features 停车制动器特点：
Spring-applied/hydraulically released brake 弹簧制动/液压释放制动器；
Gear reducer 齿轮减速器；
A brake interlock system helps prevent driving through the secondary brake.
一个连锁制动系统在停车制动过程中辅助制动。
⑥ Frame 机架
The frame is joined to the drum yoke at the articulation pivot. Articulation area is structurally reinforced and joined by hardened steel pins. One vertical pin provides a steering angle of $\pm 34°$ and a horizontal pin allows frame oscillation of $\pm 15°$.
机架在铰接枢轴处连接到钢轮处。铰接区域被加固，并由硬质钢销连接在一起。垂直钢销提供±34°转向角，水平钢销提供±15°的摆动。
⑦ Instrumentation 仪表盘
Warning system 警报系统：action alarm and lamp 警报器和警报灯；
Low engine oil pressure 发动机液压油压力过低；
High engine coolant temperature 发动机冷却液温度过高；
High hydraulic oil temperature 发动机液压油温度过高；
An alternator malfunction light 交流发电机故障灯；
Check engine/electrical fault 发动机/电器故障检测；
Service hour meter and fuel gauge 工作小时表和燃油表。
⑧ Vibratory System 振动系统
Frequency 频率；

Nominal amplitude 名义振幅；

Centrifugal force 离心力。

(2) Tandem Vibratory Rollers 双钢轮振动压路机

① Weights 重量

Standard machine 标准工作重量；

At front drum 前桥处；

At rear drum 后桥处；

Maximum machine 机器最大工作重量；

Static linear load (at drum) 线性静压力（振动钢轮处）。

② Transmission 传动系统

Speeds (forward and reverse) low, high 速度（前进及后退）低、高挡；

Variable displacement piston pump 变排量柱塞泵；

Two-speed hydraulic motors 双速液压马达；

Planetary gearboxes 行星变速箱。

③ Steering 转向

Minimum turning radius 最小回转半径；

Inside drum edge 内转弯半径；

Outside drum edge 外转弯半径；

Steering angles 转向角。

Priority-demand hydraulic power-assist steering system provides smooth, firm machine handling. The automotive-type steering wheel and column are integral with the operator's swivel platform and allow steering from multiple positions.

优化的液压助力转向系统提供平稳的机器操纵，方向盘和控制台与可旋转的驾驶座椅构成一体，可在多个位置上进行转向操作。

④ Brakes 制动器

Service brake features 行车制动器特点：

Closed-loop hydrostatic drive system provides dynamic braking during machine operation.

闭式静液压驱动系统可在机器工作期间提供动态制动。

Secondary brake features 停车制动器特点：

Spring-applied/hydraulically released brake on front and rear drums. Actuated by switch on console or automatically when pressure is lost in brake circuit or when the engine is shut off.

前、后振动钢轮上的弹簧制动/液压释放制动器,由控制台上的开关启动,当制动回路中的压力释放或发动机关闭时自动启动。

⑤ Frame 机架

The frame is joined at the articulation pivot. 50% of the machine is rear of the articulation pivot and 50% is in front of the pivot. The two sections are joined by two hardened steel pins that are supported by heavy-duty roller bearings. A vertical pin provides a ±40° steering angle and the frame/yoke provides ±4° oscillation for a smooth ride, uniform drum loading and no maintenance interval.

机架在铰接枢轴处连接。机器的50%在铰接枢轴后部,50%在枢轴前部。两部分通过两个重型滚柱轴承支撑的硬质钢销连接在一起。垂直钢销提供±40°转向角,机架/拨叉提供±4°的摆动,使机器行驶平稳,振动钢轮负荷均衡,不需要定期保养。

⑥ Instrumentation 仪表盘

Speedometer 速度计;

Vibe tachometer 振动指示表;

Vibration mode selector 振动模式选择开关;

Light switches 照明开关;

Hour meter 小时表;

Alternator indicator light 交流发电机指示灯;

Fuel gauge 燃油表;

Water tank gauge and warning lights 水箱水位表和警告灯。

An audible alarm sounds and a warning light illuminates if abnormal conditions occur in engine oil pressure, engine coolant temperature or charge pressure.

如果发动机机油压力、发动机冷却液温度或充气压力出现异常,将发出报警声并点亮警告灯。

⑦ Vibratory system 振动系统

Dual amplitude and dual frequency vibratory system 双幅双频振动系统;

Frequency 频率;

Nominal amplitude 名义振幅;

Centrifugal force per drum 单轮离心力。

12.2.10 Dimensions 尺寸规格

(1) Single Drum Vibratory Rollers 单钢轮振动压路机 (Fig. 12.23)

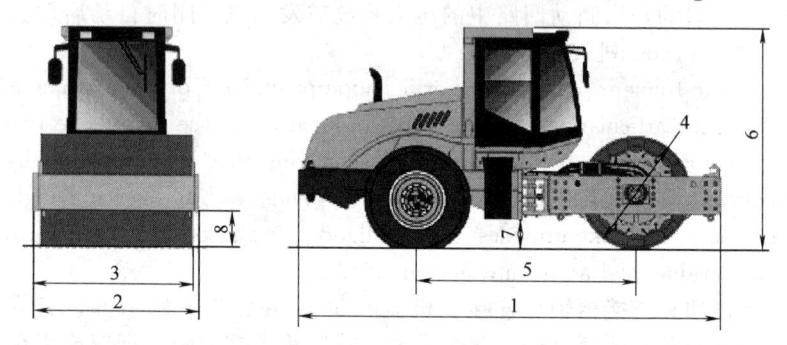

Fig. 12.23 Single drum vibratory rollers 单钢轮振动压路机

1 overall length 总长
2 overall width 总宽度
3 drum width 振动钢轮宽度
4 drum diameter 振动轮直径
5 wheelbase 轴距
6 height to top of cab 驾驶室顶部高度
7 ground clearance 最小离地间隙
8 curb clearance 轮边通过高度

(2) Tandem Vibratory Rollers 双钢轮振动压路机 (Fig. 12.24)

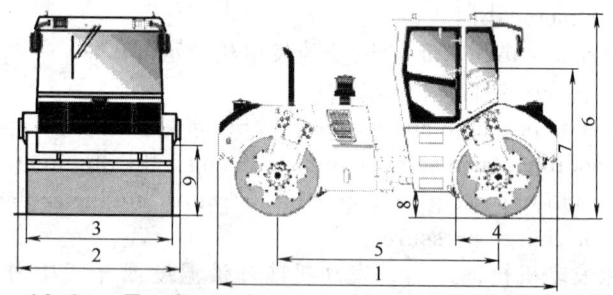

Fig. 12.24 Tandem vibratory rollers 双钢轮振动压路机

1 overall length 总长
2 overall width 总宽度
3 drum width 振动钢轮宽度
4 drum diameter 振动轮直径
5 wheelbase 轴距
6 height to top of cab 驾驶室顶部高度
7 height at steering wheel 方向盘处高度
8 ground clearance 最小离地间隙
9 curb clearance 轮边通过高度

12.3 Automatic Amplitude Compaction System 自动调幅压实系统

(1) Single Drum Vibratory Rollers 单钢轮振动压路机 (Fig. 12.25)

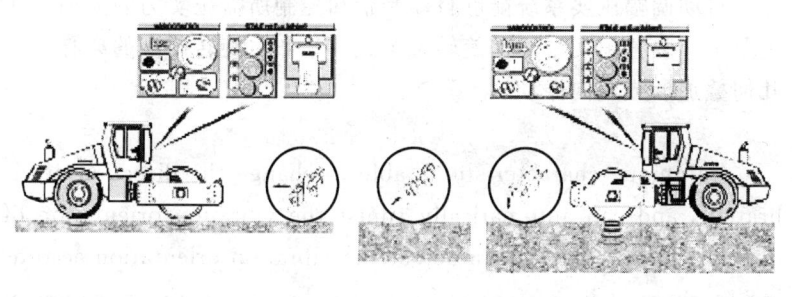

(a) amplitude=min
小振幅

(b) amplitude=max
大振幅

Fig. 12.25　Single drum vibratory rollers 单钢轮振动压路机

(2) Tandem Vibratory Rollers 双钢轮振动压路机 (Fig. 12.26)

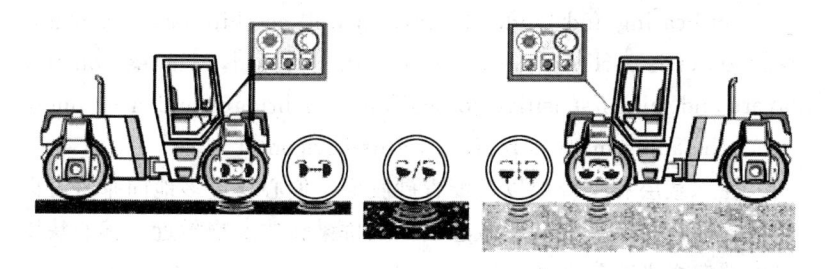

(a) amplitude=min
小振幅

(b) amplitude=max
大振幅

Fig. 12.26　Tandem vibratory rollers 双钢轮振动压路机

Automatic amplitude compaction system is able to automatically determine and control the size of the required compaction energy. It's mainly composed of two reverse rotation axis, and rotating centrifugal force generated while working formed the directional vibration.

自动调幅压实系统能够自动判别和控制所需压实力的大小，其主要工作装置由两根反向旋转轴组成，工作时旋转产生的离心力经几何叠加形成定向振动。

Its unique characteristic is able to change the direction of vibration, and can automatically adjust the vibration orientation of directional vibration. It can adjust the vibration orientation according to changes in surface stiffness or changes in the direction of roller travel during the compaction process, so that it can achieve the purpose of adjusting the amplitude.

该系统的特点是振动方向可变化，它能自动调节定向振动的施振方向，在压实过程中可根据压实面刚度的变化或压路机行驶方向的变化调节施振方向，从而达到调节振幅的目的。

On bearing and binder layers, as well as chip mastic asphalt, the exciter is inclined more towards the vertical, whereas on thin layers and mixes sensitive to scuffing, on bridges and near buildings, the adjustment is more towards horizontal.

在承载层和结合层以及沥青砂胶层，偏心块更多地向垂直方向倾斜；而在薄层、混合料敏感层以及桥梁和建筑物附近，偏心块则更多地向水平方向调整。

12.4 Oscillation Compaction Technology 振荡压实技术

12.4.1 Components of Oscillation Roller 振荡轮结构 (Fig. 12.27)

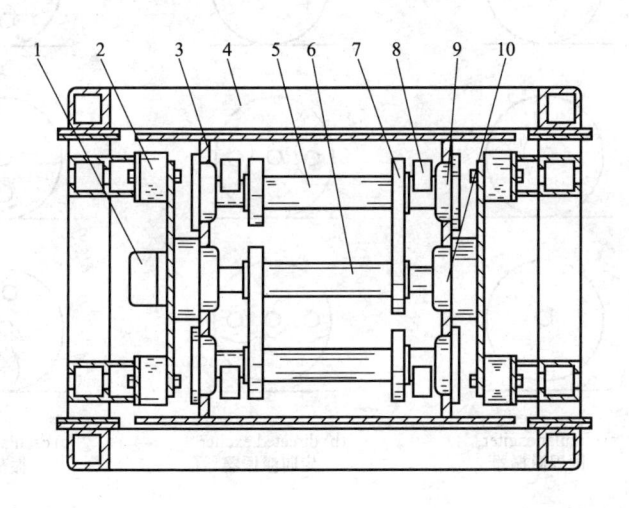

Fig. 12.27 Components of oscillation roller 振荡轮结构

1　oscillation motor 振荡马达
2　shock absorber 减振器
3　oscillating drum 振荡滚筒
4　frame 机架
5　eccentric shaft 偏心轴
6　center shaft 中心轴
7　synchronous cog belt 同步齿形带
8　eccentric weight 偏心块
9　bearing housing of eccentric shaft 偏心轴轴承座
10　bearing housing of center axle 中心轴轴承座

12.4.2 The principle of Oscillation Compaction 振荡压实原理
(Fig. 12.28)

90°

180°

(a) circular exciter
圆周激振器

(b) directed exciter
定向激振器

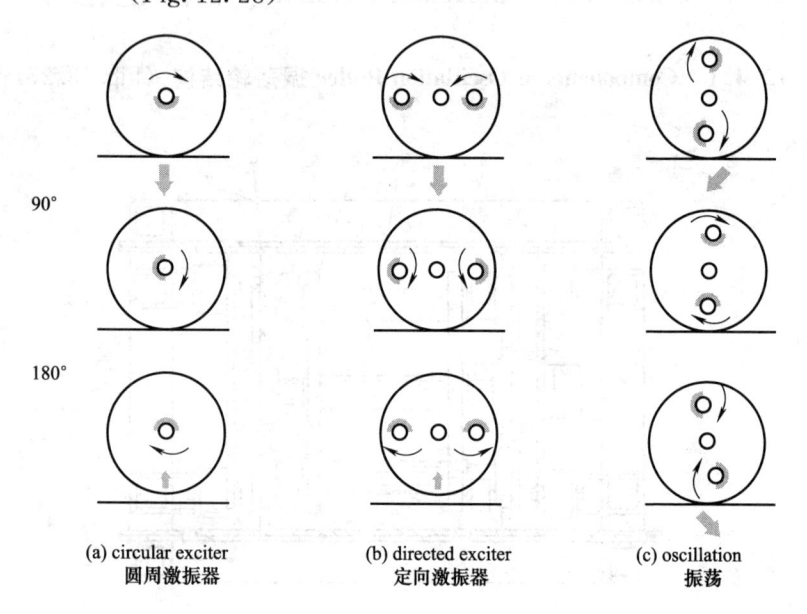

(c) oscillation
振荡

Fig. 12.28 The principle of oscillation compaction 振荡压实原理

To replace vibration, an oscillatory system has been developed, which works with two synchronously rotating weights in the drum. These create shearing forces directed forwards and backwards on the road surface, rather than up and down, at the same time, a motion generates inside the drum by two eccentric shafts that turn in the same direction and cause movement around the drum axle.

为取代振动，开发了一种振荡系统，该系统的振动轮内有两个同步旋转质量块，可对路面产生前后剪切力，而不是上下冲击。同时，通过两根偏心轴同向旋转并引起绕钢轮轴的运动，从而在振荡轮内部产生了某种运动。

Oscillatory technology creates better compaction effort by

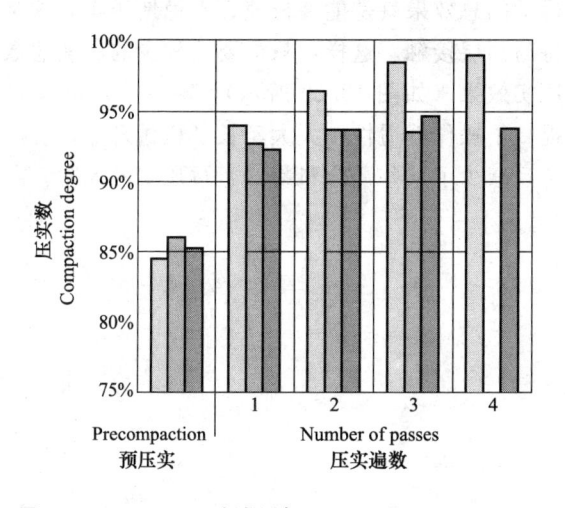

Fig. 12.29　The compaction level 压实效果

means of generating forces that move out into the asphalt in a horizontal direction, compared to the vertical forces created by a conventional vibratory system.

与传统振动压实系统中的垂直压实力相比较,振荡压实技术通过产生水平方向压实沥青的作用力可达到更好的压实效果。

The overall effect of the oscillatory motion is faster, gentler compaction, because the drum remains in constant contact with the mat. This translates into higher compaction levels in fewer passes (as shown in Fig. 12.29), reduced damage to the pavement and surrounding areas, increased operator comfort, significantly longer machine life, the ability to compact at lower temperatures, and reduced risk of over compacting certain mixes.

振荡运动的总效果就是能够快速、平稳地压实，这是因为振荡轮始终保持与面层接触。这样，只需要比较少的压实遍数，就能达到很好的压实效果（如图 12.29 所示），减少了对铺层和周围环境的破坏，提高了操作舒适性，大大延长了机械寿命，提高了低温工作性能，并且减少了某些混合料易产生过压实的风险。

Unit 13 Asphalt Mixing Plant
沥青混合料搅拌设备

13.1 Overview 概述

13.1.1 Basic Concept 基本概念

Asphalt mixture is widely used in the road making. It is a high grade material of road surface. At present producing of asphalt mixture is mechanized. Its productive equipment is called asphalt mixing plant where aggregates are blended, heated, dried, and mixed with asphalt to produce a homogeneous asphalt mixture that meets specified requirements.

沥青混合料广泛应用于道路建设，它是一种高等级路面材料。目前，沥青混合料的生产已经机械化，其生产设备称为沥青混合料搅拌设备，它将骨料混合、加热、烘干，并且与沥青一起搅拌，从而生产出满足具体要求的拌和均匀的沥青混合料。

Asphalt mixing plant can be classified by the period of operation and the area serviced, asphalt mixing plants can be subdivided into stationary and mobile; by their productive process, forced batch plant and continuous drum plant. Both types serve the same ultimate purpose, and the asphalt mixture should be essentially similar regardless of the type of plant used to manufacture it.

沥青混合料搅拌设备按照施工的时间和地点分为固定式和移动式，按照生产工艺分为间歇强制式和连续滚筒式。这两种类型搅拌设备有着相同的目标，并且，无论使用何种类型搅拌设备，所生产的沥青混合料在本质上应该是相似的。

Movable asphalt plant is usually applied on small scale site and temporary occasion, stationary asphalt mixing plant is reverse of the mobile. Batch plants get their name because they produce asphalt mixture in batches; one batch at a time, one after the other. The size of a batch varies according to the capacity of the plant mixer. Batch plants are distinguished from continuous-type plants, which produce asphalt mixture in a steady flow.

移动式沥青混合料搅拌设备通常用于工程量小以及工程周期短的施工场合,而固定式设备刚好相反。间歇式搅拌设备的命名是因为它们是分批地生产沥青混合料,一次生产一批,一批生产完再生产下一批。根据搅拌器的不同生产能力,搅拌设备一批所生产的混合料量是不一样的。连续式搅拌设备是连续稳定地生产沥青混合料,其不同于间歇式搅拌设备。

The production process of a batch plant is as follows: the aggregates supplied from the cold feed unit are dried in a direct-fired drum and heated to the temperature for their further treatment. The dried and heated aggregates are then carried up to the screen by the hot elevator. The screen reclassifies the aggregates and feeds them into appropriate hot bins. The proper amount of aggregates and asphalt is weighed in their respective weigh hopper or bucket and discharged into the mixer. When mixing has been completed, the mixed material is discharged into the haul vehicle or into a conveying device that carries the material to the storage silo.

间歇式搅拌设备的生产过程如下:由冷骨料供料系统供给的骨料在直接加热的滚筒内进行烘干,并加热到所需的工作温度。干燥后的热骨料经热料提升机送入筛分机。筛分机将骨料重新分级,并将其送入合适的热料仓。骨料和沥青在各自的称量斗内称重后投入搅拌器。搅拌结束后,成品料被卸入运输车辆,或卸入输送装置,由其将料送至成品料仓。

The mixing drum for which the plant is named is very similar in appearance to the batch plant dryer drum. The difference between the two is that in a drum-mix plant the aggregate is not only dried and heated within the drum, but it is also mixed with the asphalt. In a continuous drum plant, there is no gradation screen, hot bins, weigh hopper or mixer. Aggregate gradation is controlled at the cold feed.

以滚筒得名的滚筒式搅拌设备,其滚筒在外观上与间歇式搅拌设备的烘干滚筒非常相似。两者的区别在于,在滚筒式搅拌设备中,骨料在烘干筒中不仅仅要烘干和加热,而且还要与沥青一起进行搅拌。连续滚筒式搅拌设备无需筛分机、热料仓、骨料称量斗和搅拌器。骨料的级配控制是由冷料供给来完成的。

Comparing with the forced batch mixing plant, the ease of setup and operation of the continuous drum mixing plant makes it the ideal machine and has been widely used in some countries. However, due to the limitation of aggregate specifications, 95% of the asphalt mixing plant in China is the forced batch mixing plant.

与间歇强制式搅拌设备相比,连续滚筒式搅拌设备易于安装和操作,使其成为理想的施工设备,并且在一些国家获得了广泛应用。然而在我国,由于受骨料规格标准的限制,95%的沥青搅拌设备为间歇强制式搅拌设备。

At present, the asphalt mixing plant is an assembly of mechanical, computerized, electronic equipment which can realize automatic production according to the productivity and mix of the materials. Many construction machinery manufacturers offer a wide range of mixing plants, the most well-known are those of ASTEC of the United States, AMMANN of Switzerland, BENNINGHOVEN of Germany, MARINI of Italy and NIKKO of Japan.

目前，沥青混合料搅拌设备集机械、计算机和电气于一体，能够根据混合料的产量和配比实现自动化生产。许多工程机械制造企业可生产多种类型的搅拌设备，其中最知名的有美国的爱斯泰克，瑞士的安迈，德国的边宁荷夫，意大利的玛连尼以及日本的日工。

13.1.2 Types 类型（Fig. 13.1）

(a) batch forced mixing plant (stationary)
间歇强制式搅拌设备(固定式)

(b) batch forced mixing plant (movable)
间歇强制式搅拌设备(移动式)

(c) continuous drum mixing plant (stationary)
连续滚筒式搅拌设备(固定式)

(d) continuous drum mixing plant (movable)
连续滚筒式搅拌设备(移动式)

Fig. 13.1 Types of asphalt mixing plant
沥青混合料搅拌设备的类型

13.1.3 Productive Processes 生产工艺

(1) Batch Forced Mixing Plant 间歇强制式搅拌设备（Fig. 13.2）

(2) Continuous Drum Mixing Plant 连续滚筒式搅拌设备（Fig. 13.3）

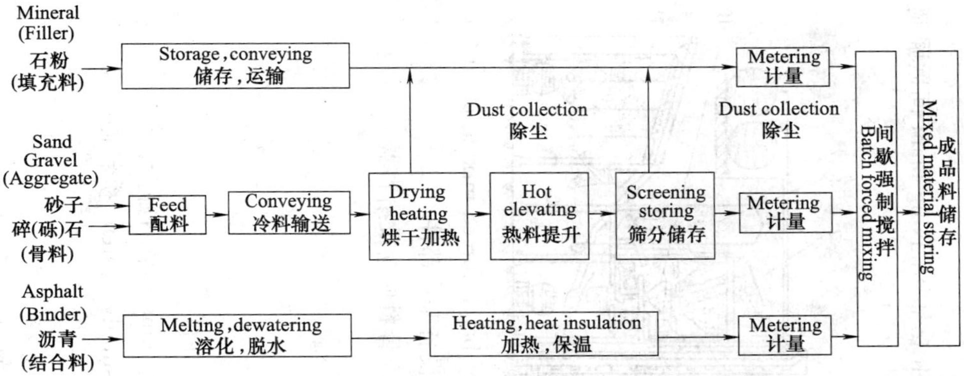

Fig. 13.2 Productive processes of batch forced mixing plant 间歇强制式搅拌设备的生产工艺

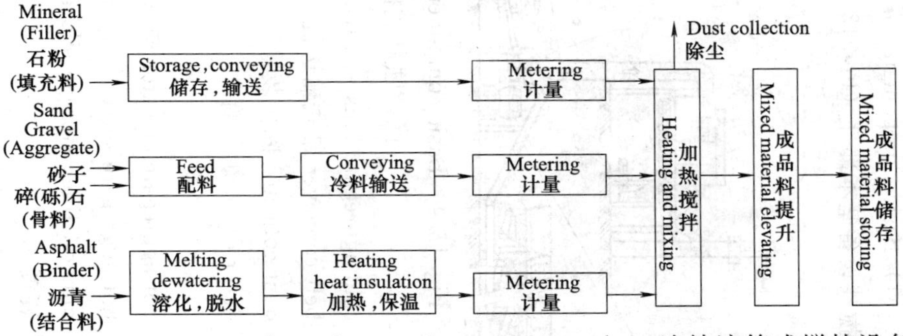

Fig. 13.3 Productive processes of continuous drum mixing plant 连续滚筒式搅拌设备的生产工艺

13.2 Components and Features 组成与特点

13.2.1 Components 组成

(1) Basic Components of batch forced mixing plant 间歇强制式搅拌设备基本部件（Fig. 13.4）

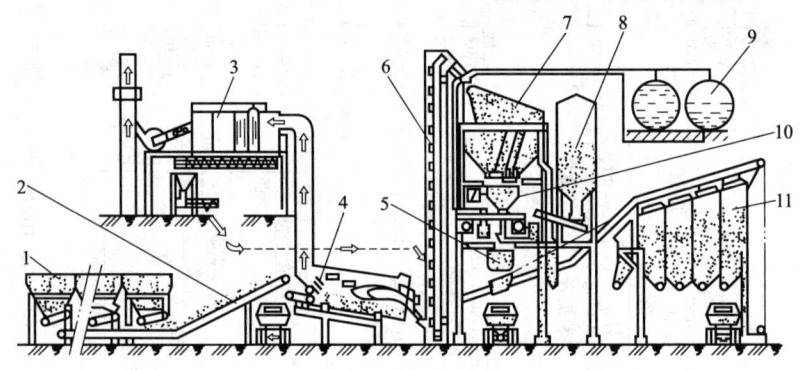

Fig. 13.4 Basic components of batch forced mixing plant
间歇强制式搅拌设备基本部件

1. cold aggregate bins and feeder 冷骨料储仓及给料器
2. belt conveyer 带式输送机
3. dust collector 除尘装置
4. dryer drum 烘干筒
5. mixer 搅拌器
6. hot aggregate elevator 热骨料提升机
7. hot aggregate screen and storage bins 热骨料筛分及储仓
8. mineral filler storage silo and supply system 粉料储仓及供给装置
9. asphalt supply system 沥青供给系统
10. hot aggregate weigh hopper 热骨料计量装置
11. mixed material storage silo 成品料储仓

(2) Basic Components of Continuous Drum Mixing Plant 连续滚筒式搅拌设备基本部件（Fig. 13.5）

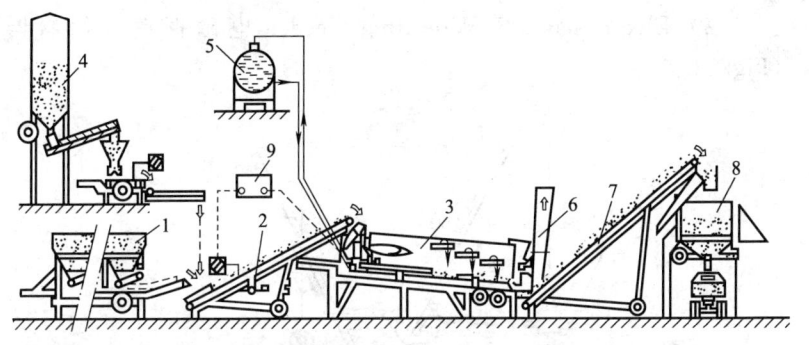

Fig. 13.5 Basic components of continuous drum mixing plant
连续滚筒式搅拌设备基本部件

1　cold aggregate bins and feeder 冷骨料储存和给料器
2　cold aggregate belt conveyer and weighing system 冷骨料带式输送机及称量系统
3　dryer-mixer drum 干燥搅拌筒
4　mineral filler storage silo and supply system 粉料储仓及供给装置
5　asphalt supply system 沥青供给系统
6　dust collector 除尘装置
7　mixed material conveyer 成品料输送机
8　mixed material storage silo 成品料储仓
9　control system 控制系统

13.2.2　Cold aggregate Feed System 冷骨料供给系统

（1）Reciprocating Feeder 往复式给料器 (Fig. 13.6)

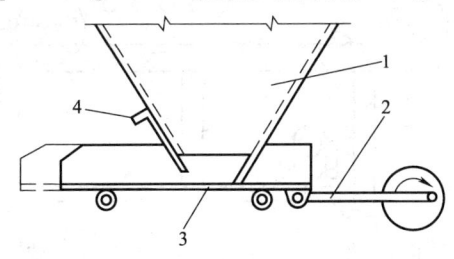

Fig. 13.6　Reciprocating feeder 往复式给料器

1　cold bins 料斗
2　crank link mechanism 曲柄连杆机构
3　discharge chute 卸料槽
4　cold feed gate 闸门

(2) Electromagnetic Vibrating Feeder 电磁振动式给料器 (Fig. 13.7)

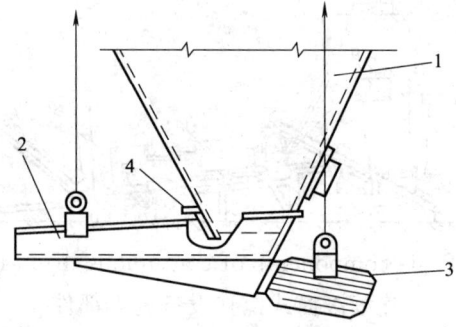

Fig. 13.7 Electromagnetic vibrating feeder 电磁振动式给料器
1　cold bins 料斗
2　discharge chute 卸料槽
3　electromagnetic vibrator 电磁振动器
4　cold feed gate 闸门

(3) Belt Feeder 带式给料器 (Fig. 13.8)

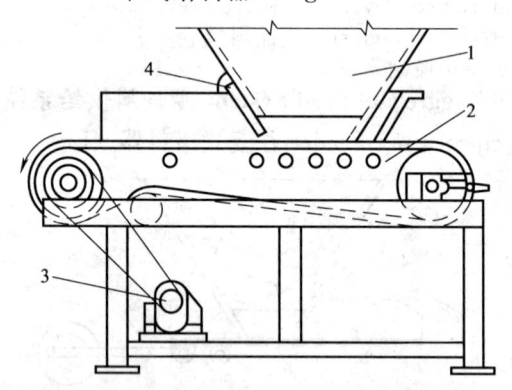

Fig. 13.8　Belt feeder 带式给料器
1　cold bins 料斗
2　belt conveyer 带式输送机
3　electrical motor 电机
4　cold feed gate 闸门

(4) Slat Feeder 板式给料器 (Fig. 13.9)

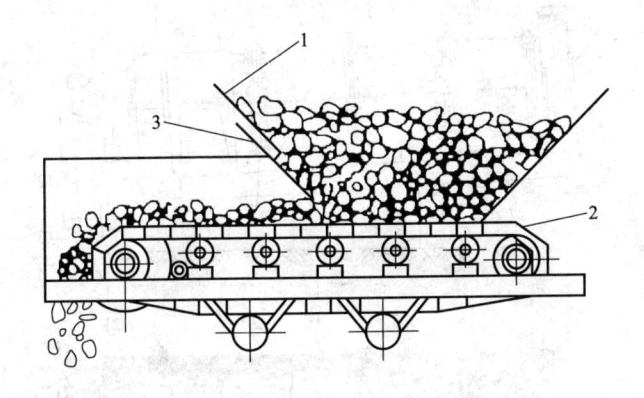

Fig. 13.9 Slat feeder 板式给料器

1　cold bins 料斗
2　slat conveyor 链板输送机
3　cold feed gate 闸门

13.2.3 Dryer drum 干燥滚筒

(1) Forced Batch Mixing Plant 强制间歇式搅拌设备 (Fig. 13.10)

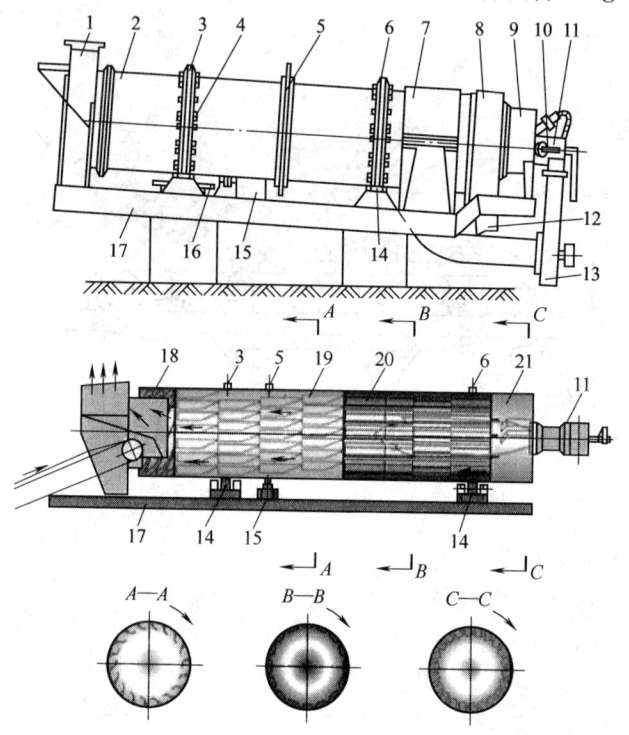

Fig. 13.10 Forced batch mixing plant 强制间歇式搅拌设备

1　feeder box 加料箱
2　drum 滚筒体
3,6　rolling ring 滚圈
4　compensator 胀缩件
5　driving gear ring 传动齿圈
7　cooling jacket 冷却罩
8　discharge box 卸料箱
9　fire box 火箱
10　ignition nozzle 点火喷头
11　burner 燃烧器
12　discharge chute 卸料槽
13　blower 鼓风机
14　supporting roller 支承滚轮
15　driving unit 驱动装置
16　thrust roller 挡滑滚轮
17　frame 机架
18　feeding zone flights 进料区叶片
19　drying zone flights 干燥区叶片
20　combustion zone flights 燃烧区叶片
21　discharging zone flights 卸料区叶片

(2) Continuous Drum Mixing Plant 连续滚筒式搅拌设备 (Fig. 13. 11)

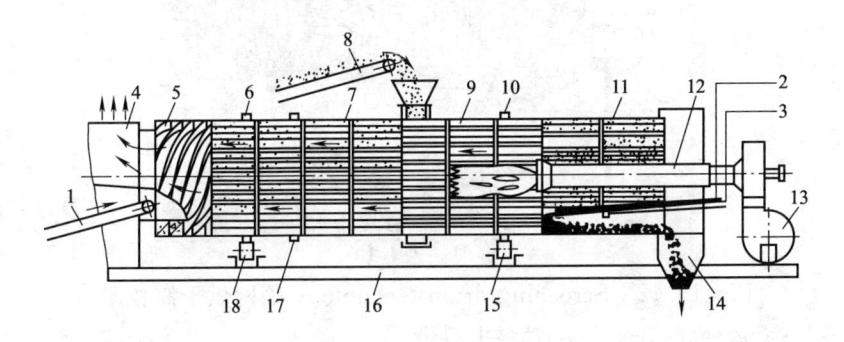

Fig. 13. 11 Continuous drum mixing plant 连续滚筒式搅拌设备

1 aggregate charging belt 骨料上料带
2 asphalt spray pipe 沥青喷管
3 filler supply system 粉料供给装置
4 smoke exhaust box 排烟箱
5 feeding zone flights 进料区叶片
6,10 rolling ring 滚圈
7 drying zone flights 干燥区叶片
8 reclaimed material charging belt 回收料上料带
9 combustion zone flights 燃烧区叶片
11 mixing zone flights 搅拌区叶片
12 burner 燃烧器
13 blower 鼓风机
14 discharge box 卸料箱
15,18 supporting roller 支承滚轮
16 frame 支架
17 driving chain wheel 传动链轮

(3) Screening Drum Technology 筛网烘干筒技术 (Fig. 13.12)

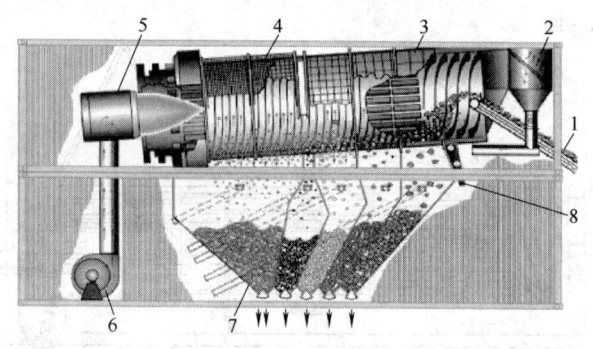

Fig. 13.12　Screening drum technology 筛网烘干筒技术

1　aggregate feed belt 骨料上料带
2　primary dust collector 一级除尘系统
3　dryer drum 烘干滚筒
4　screen system 筛分系统
5　burner 燃烧器
6　blower 鼓风机
7　hot aggregate storage silo 热料仓
8　over-sized aggregate discharge chute 过大料溢料管道

The screening drum combines the heating and screening of the minerals in a single process unit thus eliminating process heat loss due to material transportation.

筛网烘干筒把矿料的加热和筛分合并在一个装置中，因此消除了由于物料输送所引起的沿途热量损失。

Only cold material is conveyed to the top of the plant. The flow of hot material follows the natural way-from top to bottom. So the plant eliminates the hot elevator associated with other tower plants.

仅仅是冷骨料被输送到搅拌设备上部，热料是以自然的方式自上而下流动。因此，该搅拌设备节省了其他塔式搅拌设备所需的热料提升机。

(4) Driving Type of Drum 干燥滚筒驱动形式 (Fig. 13.13)

(a) gear drive 齿轮驱动　　(b) chain wheel drive 链轮驱动　　(c) friction wheel drive 摩擦轮驱动

Fig. 13.13　Driving type of drum 干燥滚筒驱动形式

(5) Burner 燃烧器 (Fig. 13.14)

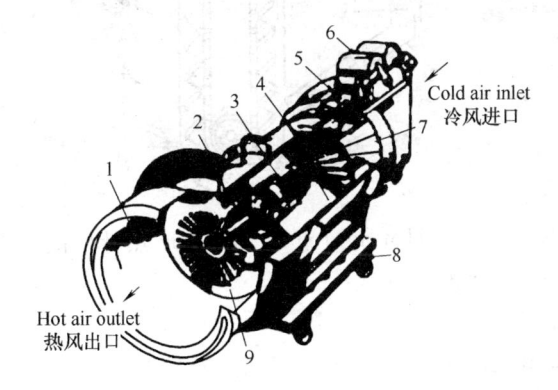

Fig. 13.14　Burner 燃烧器

1　reaction chamber 反应室
2　nozzle 喷嘴
3　electric motor 电动机
4　blower 鼓风机
5　oil quantity controlling valve 油量控制阀
6　oil gas ratio controlling valve 油气比控制阀

7　shutter 进风门
8　frame 支架
9　volution guide vane 涡旋导流板

13.2.4　Hot Aggregate Elevator（only for batch forced mixing plant）热骨料提升机（仅用于间歇强制式搅拌设备）(Fig. 13.15)

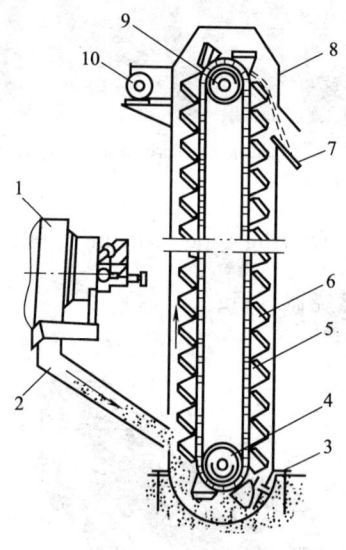

Fig. 13.15　Hot aggregate elevator 热骨料提升机

1　dryer drum 干燥滚筒
2　chute 料槽
3　stone bolt 地脚螺栓
4　driven chain wheel 从动链轮
5　chain 链条
6　bucket 料斗
7　discharge chute 溜料槽
8　encloser 罩壳
9　driving chain wheel 主动链轮
10　driving device 驱动装置

13.2.5 Vibrating Screen (only for batch forced mixing plant) 振动筛（仅用于间歇强制式搅拌设备）

(1) Underneath Vibrator 下置式振动器 (Fig. 13.16)

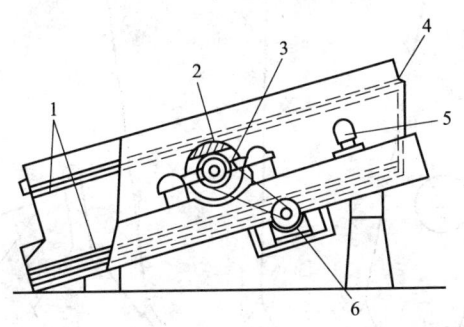

Fig. 13.16 Underneath vibrator 下置式振动器

1 screen deck 筛网
2 vibrator 振动器
3 driving belt 传动带
4 screen box 筛箱
5 damping spring 减振弹簧
6 electric motor 电动机

(2) Overhead Vibrator 上置式振动器 (Fig. 13.17)

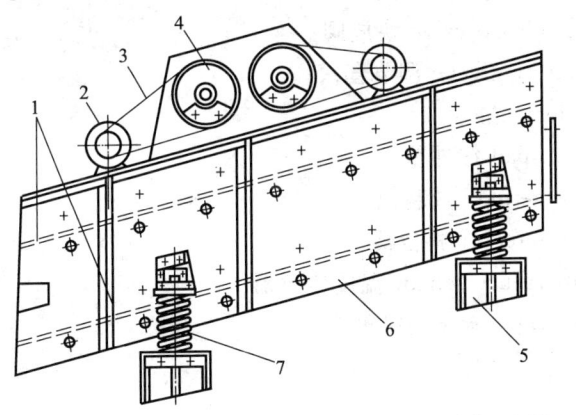

Fig. 13.17 Overhead vibrator 上置式振动器

1 screen deck 筛网
2 electric motor 电动机
3 driving belt 传动带
4 vibrator 振动器
5 supporting seat 支座
6 screen box 筛箱
7 damping spring 减振弹簧

13.2.6 Hot Aggregate Bins 热骨料储仓 (Fig. 13.18)

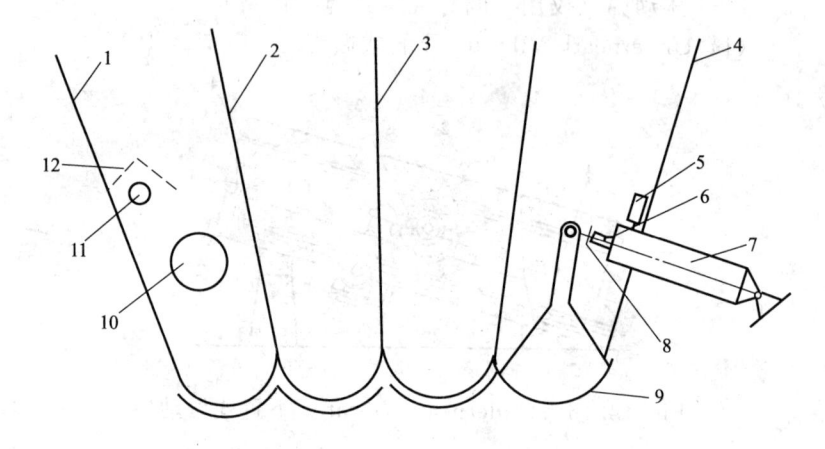

Fig. 13.18　Hot aggregate bins 热骨料储仓

1,4　side plate 壁板
2,3　isolating plate 隔板
5　quick release valve 快放阀
6　regulating sleeve 调节套
7　cylinder 汽缸
8　cushion pad 缓冲垫
9　discharge gate 放料门
10　level detector 料位器
11　temperature sensor 温度传感器
12　stop angle iron 挡料角钢

13.2.7 Filler Storage and Conveying Device 粉料储存和输送装置（Fig. 13.19）

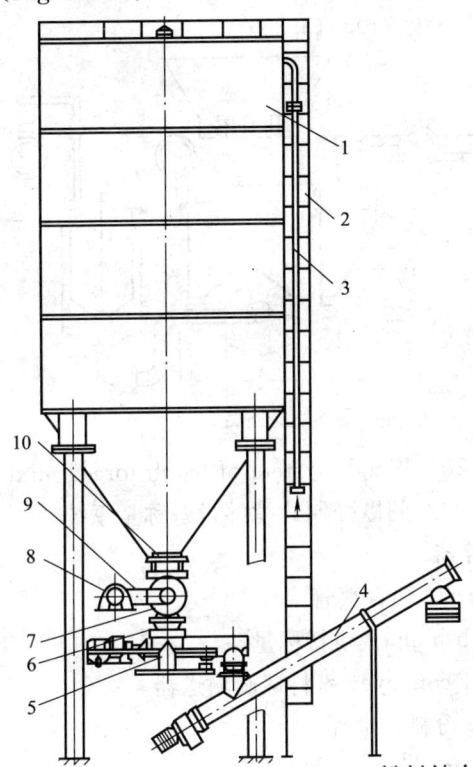

Fig. 13.19 Filler storage and conveying device 粉料储存和输送装置

1　filler storage silo 料仓
2　ladder stand 爬梯
3　filler input pipe 粉料输入管
4　auger conveyer 螺旋送料机
5　auger electronic scale 螺旋电子秤
6　connecting hose 连接管
7　revolving plow reclaimer 叶轮给料机
8　speed reducer 减速机
9　belt 带
10　butterfly gate 闸门

13.2.8 Weigh System 称量系统

(1) Weigh System of Batch Forced Mixing Plant 间歇强制式搅拌设备称量系统 (Fig. 13.20)

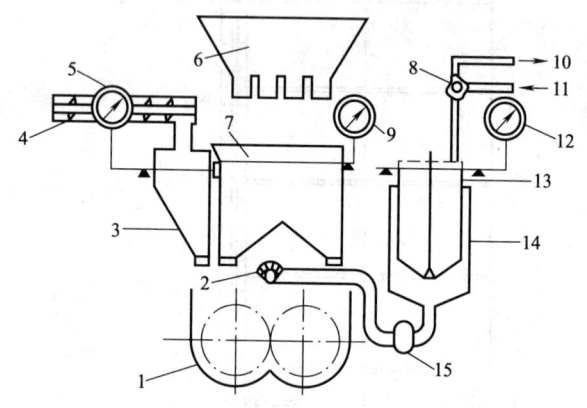

Fig. 13.20 Weigh system of batch forced mixing plant
间歇强制式搅拌设备称量系统

1　mixer 搅拌器
2　asphalt nozzle 沥青喷管
3　filler weigh hopper 粉料称量斗
4　filler auger conveyer 粉料螺旋输送器
5　filler scale 粉料计量秤
6　hot aggregate bins 热骨料储仓
7　aggregate weigh hopper 骨料称量斗
8　tripple valve 三通阀
9　aggregate scale 骨料计量秤
10　asphalt return pipe 沥青回油管
11　asphalt inlet pipe 沥青进油管
12　asphalt scale 沥青计量秤
13　asphalt weigh bucket 沥青称量桶
14　asphalt bucket 沥青桶
15　asphalt injection pump 沥青喷射泵

（2）Positive Displacement Asphalt Weigh System 容积式沥青称量装置 (Fig. 13.21)

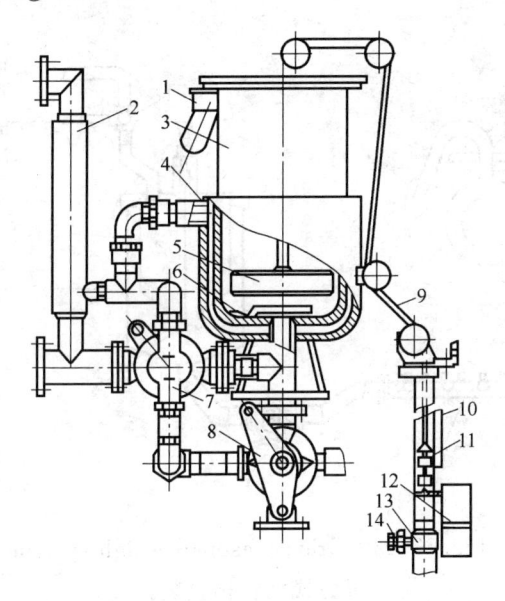

Fig. 13.21 Positive displacement asphalt weigh system
容积式沥青称量装置

1	overflow pipe 溢流管	8	asphalt discharge valve 沥青排放阀
2	asphalt injection pipe 沥青注入管	9	soft cable 软钢绳
3	weigh bucket 量桶	10	staff gauge 标尺
4	insulating jacket 保温套	11	weight 重块
5	floater 浮子	12	sensor 传感器
6	baffle plate 挡板	13	collet 夹头
7	asphalt injection valve 沥青注入阀	14	adjusting screw 调整螺钉

(3) Gravity Asphalt Weigh System 重力式沥青称量装置 (Fig. 13.22)

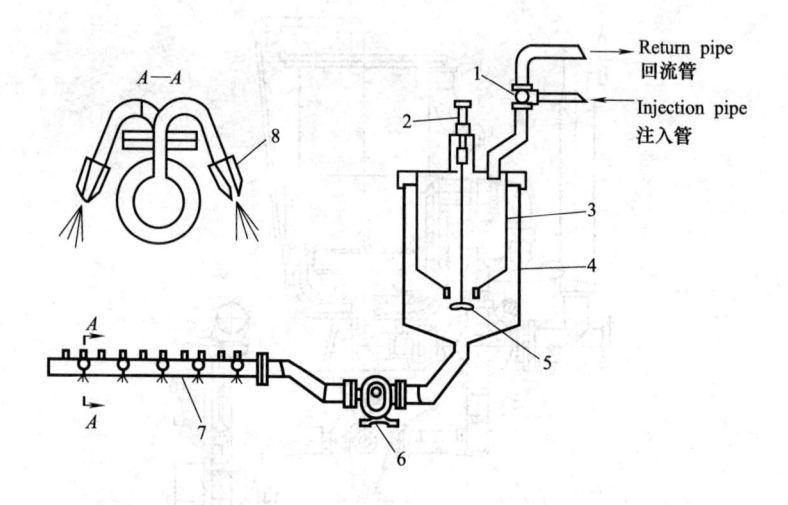

Fig. 13.22 Gravity asphalt weigh system
重力式沥青称量装置

1　tripple valve 三通阀
2　tension sensor 拉力传感器
3　asphalt weigh bucket 沥青称量桶
4　asphalt bucket 沥青桶
5　tapered foot valve 锥形底阀
6　asphalt injection pump 沥青喷射泵
7　spray pipe 喷管
8　nozzle 喷嘴

13.2.9 Mixer 搅拌器

(1) Low Speed Side Synchronous 低速端同步式 (Fig. 13.23)

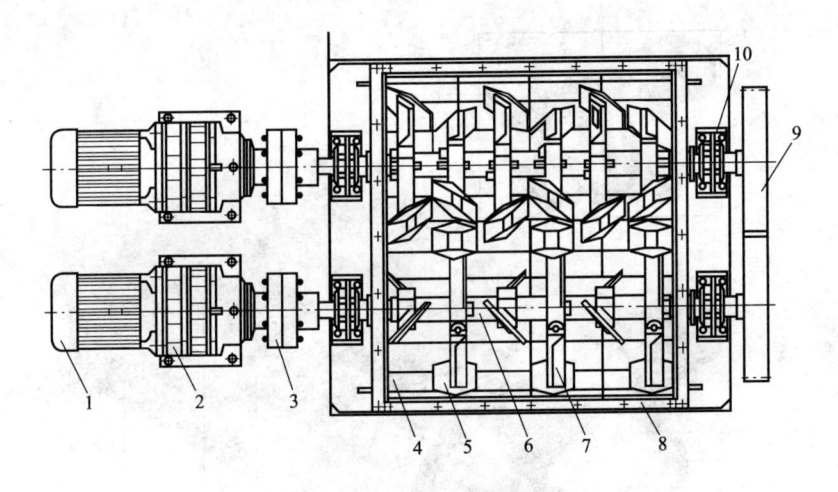

Fig. 13.23　Low speed side synchronous mixer
低速端同步式搅拌器

1　driving motor 驱动电机

2　speed reducer 减速器

3　coupling 联轴器

4　lining plate 衬板

5　mixing paddle 搅拌桨叶

6　mixing shaft 搅拌轴

7　mixing arm 搅拌臂

8　mixing trough 搅拌筒体

9　synchronizing gear 同步齿轮

10　bearing assembly 轴承

(2) High Speed Side Synchronous 高速端同步式 (Fig. 13.24)

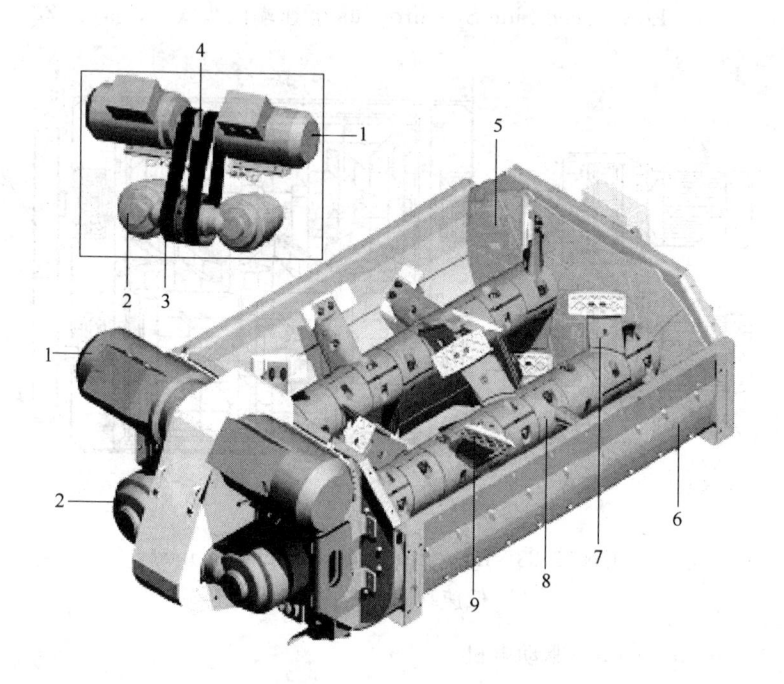

Fig. 13.24　High speed side synchronous mixer
　　　　　　高速端同步式搅拌器

1　driving motor 驱动电机
2　speed reducer 减速器
3　belt drive unit 带传动装置
4　coupling 联轴器
5　lining plate 衬板
6　mixing trough 搅拌筒体
7　mixing arm 搅拌臂
8　mixing shaft 搅拌轴
9　mixing paddle 搅拌桨叶

13.2.10 Mixed Material Storage Silo 成品料储仓

(1) Underneath 底置式 (Fig. 13.25)

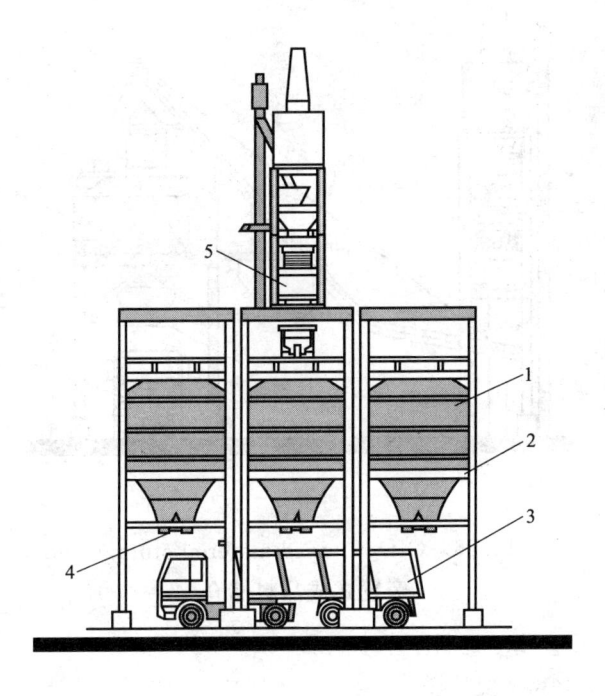

Fig. 13.25 Underneath mixed material storage silo
底置式成品料储仓

1 mixed material storage silo 成品料储仓
2 frame 支架
3 transport truck 运输卡车
4 discharge gate 卸料闸门
5 mixing tower 搅拌楼

(2) Offset 旁置式（Fig. 13.26）

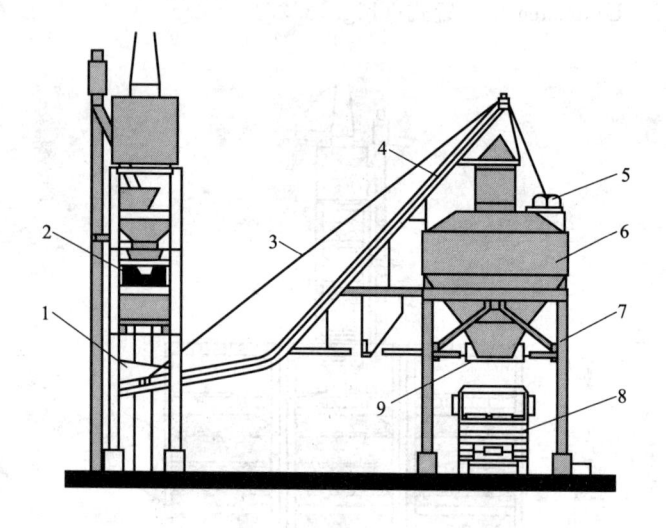

Fig. 13.26 Offset mixed material storage silo
旁置式成品料储仓

1　conveying skip 运料小车
2　mixing tower 搅拌楼
3　steel cable 钢索
4　track 轨道
5　driving mechanism 驱动机构
6　mixed material storage silo 成品料储仓
7　frame 支架
8　transport truck 运输卡车
9　discharge gate 卸料闸门

13.2.11 Dust Collectors 除尘装置

(1) Cyclone Dust Filter 旋风式除尘器 (Fig. 13.27)

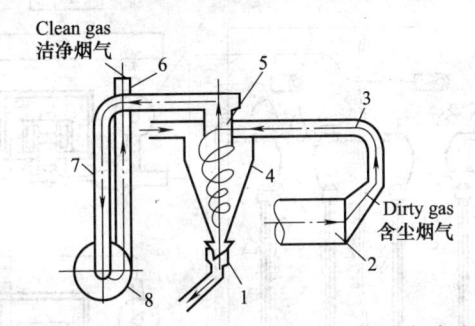

Fig. 13.27 Cyclone dust filter 旋风式除尘器

1 discharge gate 卸尘闸门
2 dryer drum 干燥滚筒
3 air pipe 风管
4 cyclone dust collection collector 旋风集尘筒
5 air draft tube 吸风小筒
6 stack 烟囱
7 exhaust tube 抽风管
8 exhaust fan 抽风机

(2) Venturi Scrubbing Dust Filter 文丘里除尘器 (Fig. 13.28)

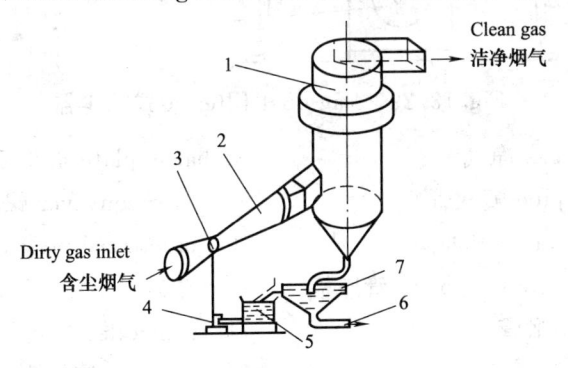

Fig. 13.28 Venturi scrubbing dust filter 文丘里除尘器

1 gas liquid separating tank 气液分离罐
2 venturi scrubber 文丘里洗涤器
3 venturi nozzle 文丘里喷嘴
4 pressured water pump 加压水泵
5 clean water reservoir 清水池
6 drain pipe 排水管
7 sedimentation reservoir 沉淀池

(3) Bag Dust Filter 袋式除尘器 (Fig. 13.29)

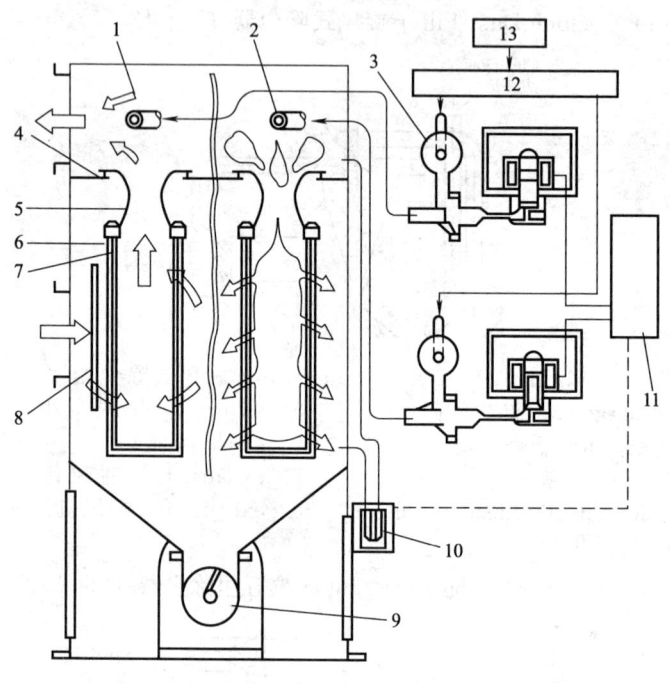

Fig. 13.29 Bag dust filter 袋式除尘器

1 clean gas 净气
2 blow pipe 喷吹管
3 pulse valve 脉冲阀
4 pipe mounting plate 管座板
5 throat 喉管
6 filter bag 滤袋
7 bag cages 袋骨架
8 baffle plate 折流板
9 auger conveyer 螺旋输送机
10 differential pressure gage 压差计
11 controller 控制器
12 air tank 储气罐
13 air compressor 压缩机

13.3 Standard Equipment Specifications 标准装置规格类型与性能参数

(1) Cold Feed System 冷骨料供料系统
Hopper capacity 冷料仓体容积;
Dump width 上料宽度;
Dump height 上料高度;
Hopper vibrator 砂仓振动器;
Metering range mechanically adjustable in 3 stages 机械调节料门,分3级控制;
Hopper discharge belt 料斗供料带;
Belt width 带宽度;
Distance between conveyor centres 滚轮中心距;
Hopper discharge belt with drive, corrugated side wall belt, galvanized belt frame, flow control via inductive aggregate starvation switch and flag. 带驱动装置的料斗卸料带、波形侧壁带、镀锌支架、设有断料报警开关和标记的料流控制器。

(2) Collection and Transfer belt 收集及输送带机
Conveying capacity 输送能力;
Distance between conveyor centers 滚轮中心距;
Belt width 带宽度;
Belt quality 带型号;
Belt conveyor fitted with emergency stop and hand guards. 带配有紧急停止和安全装置。

(3) Dryer Drum 烘干筒
Drum cylinder with running rings, flights and lifters 干燥滚筒(带驱动圈、载料片和提升片);
Diameter 直径;
Length 长度;

Wall thickness 壁厚；

Insulation with rock wool and aluminum cover 岩棉保温层和铝皮外罩；

Insulation thickness 保温层厚度；

Insulation density 保温层密度；

Friction drive with carrier rollers and guide rollers 摩擦驱动装置，配驱动轮和导向轮；

Manufacturer's assembly of burner and fuel pump 制造商燃烧器和燃油泵集成装配；

Low pressure burner 低压燃烧器；

Max. burner capacity 燃烧器最大功率；

Integrated ventilator with silencer 带消声装置的鼓风机；

Flow volume 鼓风机风量；

Negative pressure sensor system in dryer drum burner wall 负压传感器位于烘干筒燃烧器一侧；

Aggregate temperature measuring system in the drum outlet 温度传感器位于烘干滚筒出口。

(4) Hot Elevator 热料提升机

Capacity 提升能力；

Head station consisting of a housing with inspection flaps and removable hood, drive shaft with external roller bearings, drive unit and three sided maintenance platform with stairs from the roof of the screen box. 热料提升顶部包括带检查口的机体外壳，可移动的顶部罩，驱动轴轴承外置，驱动电机和三面维修平台，并带有可通向振动筛箱体顶部的梯子。

(5) Screening Machine 振动筛

Driven by 2 external eccentric shafts 外置式双偏心轴驱动；

Max. aggregate temperature 最高工作温度；

Total screen area 总筛分面积；

Area of sand deck 砂仓筛分面积；

Drive 驱动功率;
Mesh sizes according to customers' requests. 筛孔尺寸根据用户要求设定;
Insulation thickness for screen box 保温层厚度。
(6) Hot Storage Silo 热料储仓
Content 容积;
Insulation for hot mineral silo 热骨料仓保温层;
Insulation thickness 保温层厚度;
Insulation density 保温层密度;
Dosing unit with electro-pneumatically operated flaps 电气动配料仓门;
Number of flaps 配料仓门数目;
Flap operation through cylinders for coarse and fine dosage 配料仓门采用汽缸驱动,实现粗计量和精称量;
Continuous level sensor in component bin 各仓设连续料位传感器;
Mineral temperature sensor for bypass bin 旁通仓设石料温度传感器。
(7) Filler Supply System 粉料供给系统
Double filler elevator 双粉料提升机;
Capacity 输送能力;
Filler silo 粉料罐;
Reclaimed filler silo 回收石粉罐;
Content 容量;
Diameter 直径。
(8) Asphalt Supply System 沥青供给系统
Asphalt tank 沥青罐;
Horizontal 卧式;
Volume 容量;
Diameter 直径。
(9) Weighing and Mixing System 称重和搅拌系统

Steel construction to bear the aggregates of the mixing and weighing level 钢结构支撑；

Max. Batch 最大称重量；

Number of load cells 称重传感器数量；

Weighing container, resting on load cells, with lining protecting from wear and tear, fabric compensator, electro-pneumatically operated bottom flaps and mechanical device to hold standard weights needed to adjust the scale. 称重容器置于称重传感器上，采用耐磨设计，软连接部件，底部电气控制卸料门和石料秤校正器；

Asphalt scale with bottom discharge 底卸式沥青秤；

Max. batch quantity 最大搅拌量；

Min. batch quantity 最小搅拌量；

Drive 驱动功率；

Twin shaft compulsory mixer, driven through V-belt and synchromesh transmission 双卧轴强制式搅拌锅，由V形带同步驱动；

Mixer trough with electro-pneumatically operated outlet flap 电气控制阀门控制搅拌锅卸料槽；

Lining consisting of staggered and screwed wearing plates 由错落排列螺栓固定的耐磨衬板所组成的内衬；

Stirring arms with honeycomb shovels. Mixer shafts with antifriction bearings and labyrinth sealing 搅拌臂配有蜂巢式搅拌桨，搅拌轴带配有耐磨轴承及机械密封。

(10) Dust Collection System 除尘系统

Primary collector 一级除尘；

Secondary collector 二级除尘；

Extraction volume in working 除尘器工作引风量；

Number of filter bags 除尘袋数量；

Filter area 除尘面积；

Number of cleaning compartments 除尘室数目；

Number of cleaning mechanisms 反吹装置数目；
Max. dust burden onto plant 最大入口含尘量；
Max. emission of dry particulate 最大出口排放量；
Filter type 除尘器型号；
Max continuous temperature 最大设计连续工作温度；
Max. peak temperature 最大设计瞬间温度；
Stack height 烟囱高度。

13.4 Double Barrel Dryer/drum Mixer Technology 双滚筒拌和技术

13.4.1 Brief Introduction 简介

The Double Barrel dryer/drum mixer combines the functions of a dryer and a continuous-process mixer in one compact, efficient system. Drying of the virgin aggregate is the first step in the process and takes place in the inner drum. Mixing of aggregate and other ingredients follows, which happens in the outer, stationary shell.

双滚筒将干燥筒和连续搅拌器的功能综合为一个紧凑、有效的系统。新骨料的烘干作为第一步，是在内滚筒中进行的。骨料和添加的其他材料在外壳固定的外滚筒中进行搅拌。

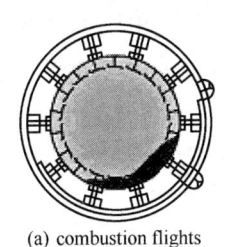

(a) combustion flights
燃烧区叶片

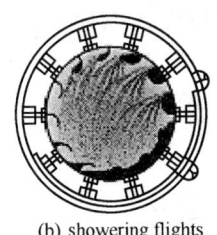

(b) showering flights
料帘区叶片

(c) conditioning flights
调整叶片

Fig. 13.30 Three different types of flights 三种不同类型的叶片

Three different types of flights move the material through the drying chamber (as shown in Fig. 13. 30). They are especially designed for three separate functions. Conditioning flights break up any clumps or sticky material as the aggregate enters. Showering flights make sure that the material is veiled evenly through the hot gas stream. Combustion zone flights prevent aggregate from impinging on the flame while spreading the material to maximize radiant heat transfer. Mixing paddles in the outer shell ensure that liquid asphalt cement thoroughly coat all of the aggregate.

三种不同类型的叶片推动物料并使其在干燥室中流动（如图 13.30 所示）。这三种叶片根据各自不同的功能进行了专门设计。当骨料进入时，调整区叶片能够粉碎任何块状或黏性物料，料帘区叶片确保物料均匀撒落并通过热气流。燃烧区叶片能够在撒布物料以获得最大辐射热传递时，防止骨料与火焰撞击。在外筒内的搅拌桨叶确保液态沥青充分地裹覆骨料。

RAP enters directly into the mixing chamber and does not contact the hot gas stream of the dryer. This is an important advantage because the atmosphere in the mixing chamber minimizes emissions. The Double Barrel dryer/drum mixer runs clean, even at 50% RAP.

回收料（RAP）直接进入搅拌室，并且不会与烘干筒的热气接触。由于搅拌室减少了废气排放，所以这是一大优点。双滚筒运行清洁，甚至能添加 50% 的回收料。

13.4.2 Basic Structure 基本结构 (Fig. 13.31)

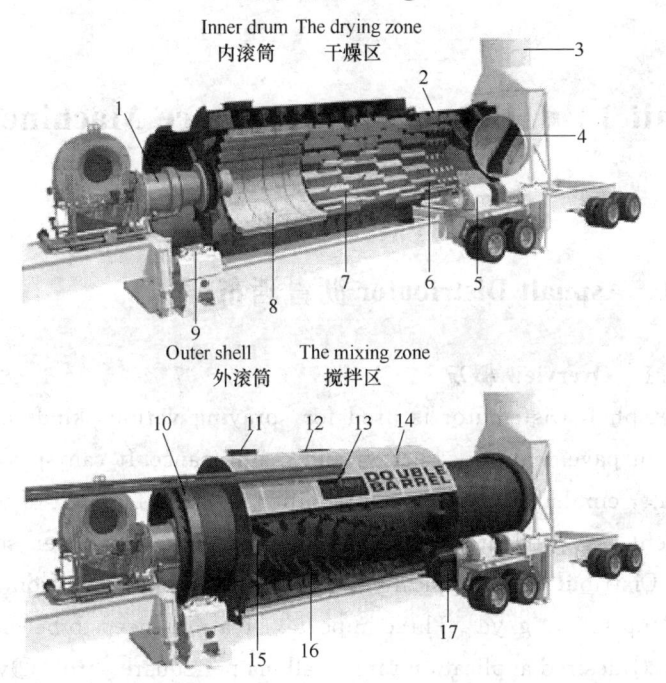

Fig. 13.31 Basic structure 基本结构

1　burner 燃烧器
2　inner drum 内滚筒
3　smoke outlet 排烟口
4　aggregate inlet 骨料进口
5　driving device 驱动装置
6　conditioning flights 调整叶片
7　showering flights 料帘区叶片
8　combustion flights 燃烧区叶片
9　supporting roller 支承滚轮
10　rolling ring 滚圈
11　reclaimed material inlet 回收料入口
12　filler inlet 粉料入口
13　asphalt inlet 沥青入口
14　outer shell 外筒
15　hot aggregate outlet 热骨料出口
16　mixing paddles 搅拌桨叶
17　mixed material outlet 成品料出口

Unit 14　Highway Maintenance Machinery
公路养护机械

14.1　Asphalt Distributor 沥青洒布车

14.1.1　Overview 概况

Asphalt Distributor is used for spraying various kinds of asphalt in pavement construction and maintenance. It can spray hot asphalt, emulsified asphalt and modified asphalt. The unit of measurement for product "on the ground" is in gallons per square yard. Distributors are typically used to apply applications from 0.05 g/yd^2 up to 1.0 g/yd^2. Three important features need to be considered: ①desired application rate, gallons per square yard; ②width of spray, feet; ③forward ground speed, feet per minute.

沥青洒布车用于在路面施工和养护作业中喷洒不同类型的沥青。它能够喷洒热态沥青、乳化沥青和改性沥青。该机械"向地面上"洒布沥青的测量单位是 g/yd^2。沥青洒布车的典型洒布量为 $0.05 \sim 1.0 g/yd^2$。沥青洒布车的应用需要考虑三个重要特点：①所需要的洒布量，g/yd^2；②洒布宽度，in；③地面前进速度，in/min。

14.1.2 Application 应用 (Fig. 14.1)

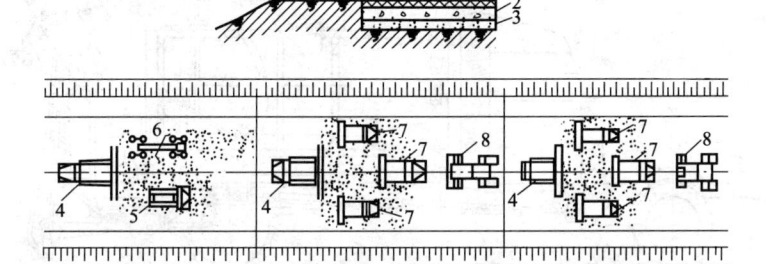

Fig. 14.1 Application of highway maintenance machinery
公路养护机械的应用

1　surface 面层
2　subbase 基层
3　under layer 底基层
4　asphalt distributor 沥青洒布车
5　dump truck 自卸车
6　grader 平地机
7　chips spreader 石屑洒布车
8　roller 压路机

14.1.3　Components 组成（Fig. 14.2）

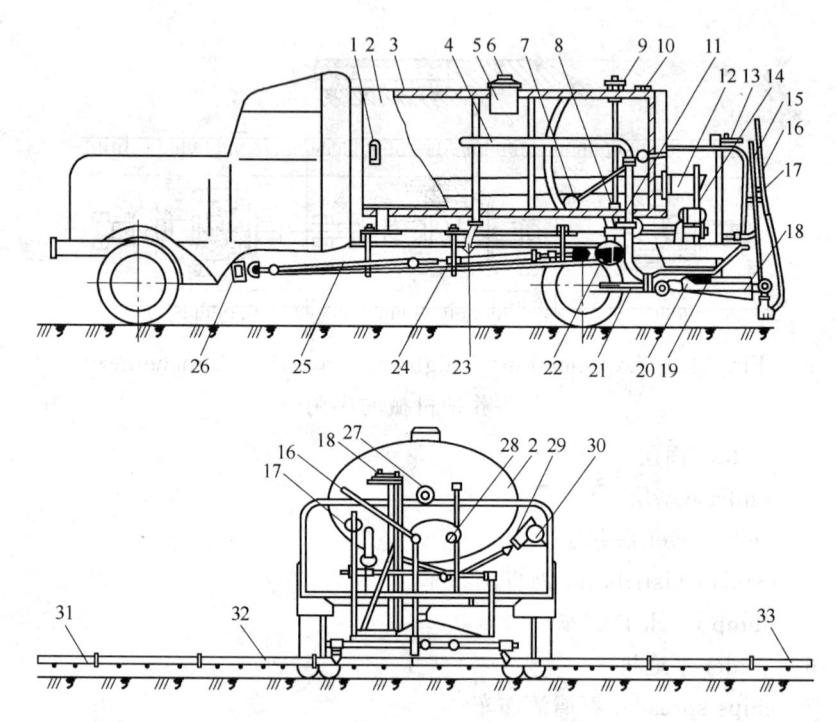

Fig. 14.2　Components of highway maintenance machinery
公路养护机械的组成

1　thermometer 温度计
2　asphalt storage tank 沥青储箱
3　insulating layer (glass wool) 保温隔热层（玻璃棉）
4　supply pipe 进料管
5　strainer 滤网
6　charging opening 装料口
7　ball float opening 浮球口
8　fuel tank switch 油箱开关
9　fuel tank switch hand wheel 油箱开关手轮
10　smoke outlet 排烟口

11　large asphalt triple valve 沥青大三通阀
12　blow lamp shade 喷灯罩
13　small pipeline triple valve control handle 管路小三通阀操纵手柄
14　heating system 加热系统
15　asphalt spray pipe lifter rod 洒沥青管升降杆
16　asphalt spraying pipe nozzle adjusting handle 洒沥青管喷嘴角度调节手柄
17　a：sphalt spraying pipe lifter control handle 洒沥青管升降操纵手柄
18　spherical connecting pipe 球状连接管
19　asphalt discharging pipe 放沥青管
20　small triple valve 小三通阀
21　cyclic flow pipe 循环流动管道
22　asphalt pump 沥青泵
23　overflow pipe 溢流管
24　driving shaft seat 传动轴座
25　driving shaft 传动轴
26　transfer case 分动箱
27　asphalt capacity indicator 沥青容量指示器
28　blow lamp 加热火焰喷灯
29　asphalt suction pipe 吸沥青管
30　fuel tank 燃料箱
31～33　left、middle、right asphalt spraying pipe 左、中、右洒沥青管

(1) Asphalt Storage Tank 沥青箱 (Fig. 14.3)

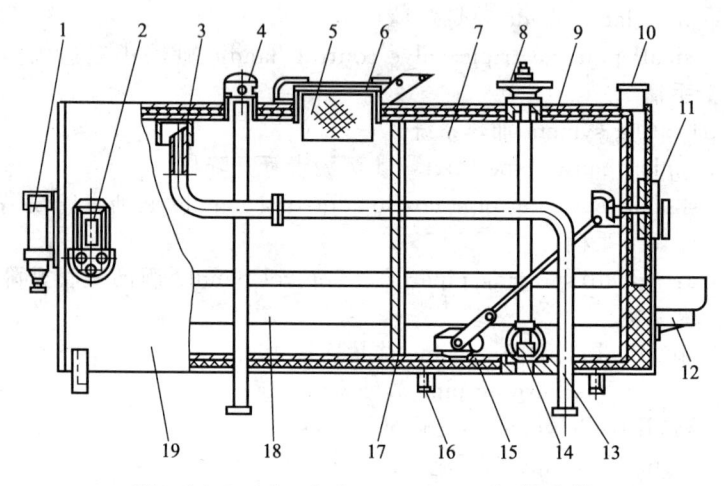

Fig. 14.3 Asphalt storage tank 沥青箱

1 extinguisher 灭火器
2 thermometer 温度计
3 overflow pipe 溢流管
4 exhaust cover 排气盖
5 charging strainer 进料滤网
6 charging cover 进料口盖
7 asphalt storage tank 沥青箱体
8 total valve hand wheel 总阀门手轮
9 glass wool 玻璃绒
10 smoke outlet 排烟口
11 dial plate 刻度盘
12 fixed blow lamp 固定喷灯
13 oil inlet pipe 进油管
14 total valve 总阀门
15 buoyage 浮标
16 tank mounting frame 箱体固定架
17 isolating plate 隔板
18 heating fire tube 加热火管
19 asphalt tank outer cover 沥青箱外罩

（2）Heating System 加热系统（Fig. 14.4）

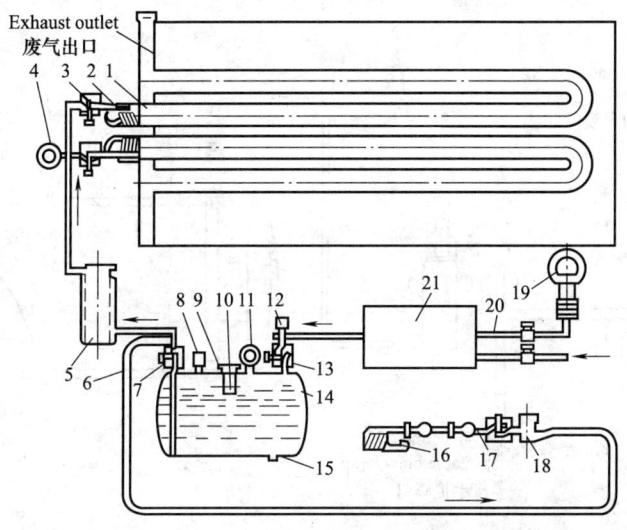

Fig. 14.4　Heating system 加热系统

1　fire tube 火管
2　burner 燃烧器
3　oil inlet valve 进油阀门
4　pressure meter 压力表
5　filter 滤清器
6　flexible pipe 软管
7　oil outlet switch 出油开关
8,12　relief valve 安全阀
9　fuel tank cap 油箱盖
10,18　strainer 滤网
11　oil pressure gauge 油压表
13　air inlet switch 进气开关
14　fuel tank 燃油箱
15　drain plug 放油螺塞
16　portable blow lamp 手提式喷灯
17　blow lamp switch 喷灯开关
19　air compressor 空气压缩机
20　air pipe 气管
21　air reservoir 储气筒

（3）Fuel Tank 燃料箱 (Fig. 14.5)

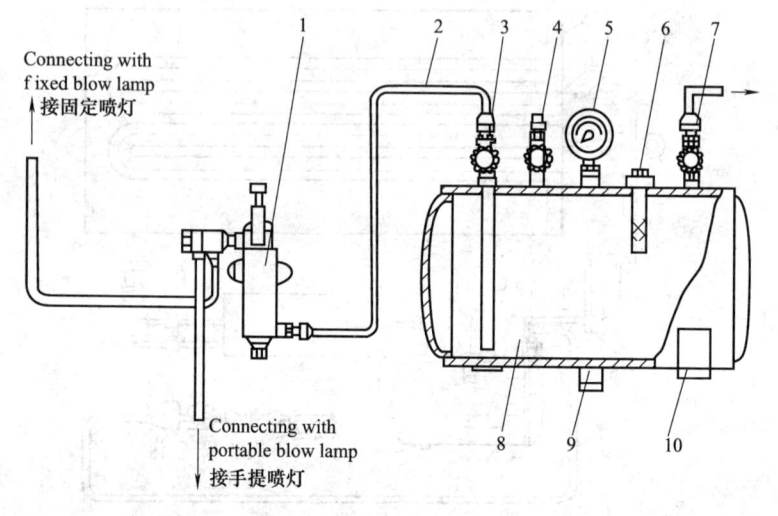

Fig. 14.5 Fuel tank 燃料箱

1　filter 滤清器
2　oil outlet pipe 出油管
3　oil outlet switch 出油开关
4　air deflation switch 放气开关
5　air pressure gauge 气压表
6　oil filler 加油口
7　air inlet switch 进气开关
8　tank body 箱体
9　drain plug 放油塞
10　fixed foot stand 固定脚架

(4) Circulating and Distributing System 循环、洒布系统
(Fig. 14.6)

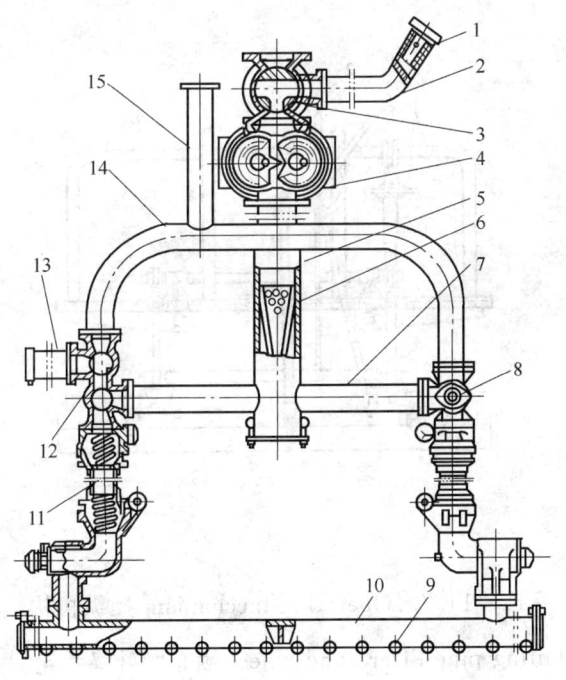

Fig. 14.6 Circulating and distributing system 循环、洒布系统

1,6 strainer 滤网
2   heating pipe 加热管
3   main triple valve 主三通阀
4   asphalt pump 沥青泵
5   main delivery pipe 输油总管
7   horizontal pipe 横管
8   right horizontal pipe triple valve 右横管三通阀
9   nozzle 喷嘴
10 distributing pipe 洒布管
11 spherical hinge connecting pipe 球铰式连接管
12 left horizontal pipe triple valve 左横管三通阀
13 oil outlet pipe 放油管
14 circulating pipe 循环管
15 oil inlet pipe 进油管

(5) Operating Mechanism 操纵机构 (Fig. 14.7)

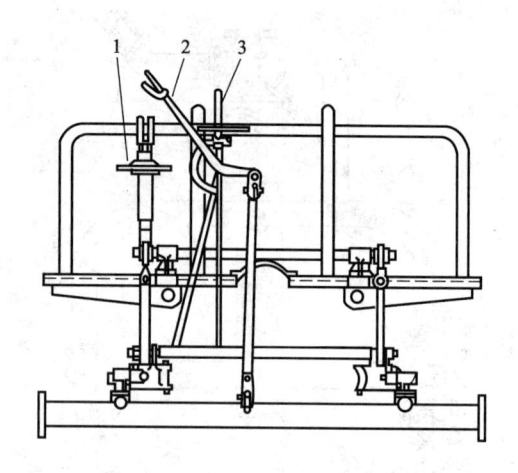

Fig. 14.7　Operating mechanism 操纵机构

1　distributing pipe lifter hand wheel 洒布管升降手轮
2　spraying angle adjusting handle 洒布管喷洒角度调整手柄
3　left and right swing push rod 洒布管左右摆动推杆

(6) Asphalt Pump 沥青泵 (Fig. 14.8)

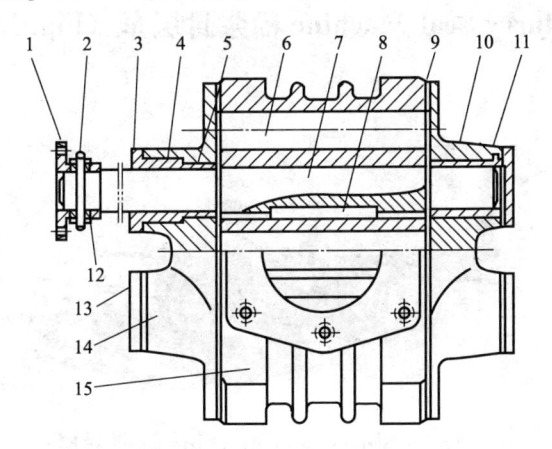

Fig. 14.8　Asphalt pump 沥青泵

1　coupling 联轴节
2　pin cotter 横销
3　cap 封盖
4　asbest rope stuffing 石棉绳填料
5，11　shaft sleeve 轴套
6　gear 齿轮
7　driving shaft 主动轴
8　key 键
9　shim 垫片
10　rear cover of pump body 泵体后盖
12　pin sleeve 销子垫套
13　cover board 盖板
14　front cover of pump body 泵体前盖
15　pump case 泵壳

14.2 Slurry Seal Machine 稀浆封层车（Fig. 14.9）

Fig. 14.9　Slurry seal machine 稀浆封层车

14.2.1　Overview 概况

The slurry seal machine is an universal machine for micro-surfacing and the production of slurries, designed for all types of urban, road and motorway works.

稀浆封层车是进行道路表面微处理和生产稀浆的通用设备，其设计适用于城市、道路和高速公路的各种作业。

According to the different methods of construction work, the slurry seal machine is divided into intermittent and continuous slurry seal types; by traveling in different ways, it is divided into self-propelled-style and trailer slurry seal types. At present, the slurry seal machine at home and abroad are mainly self-propelled type.

稀浆封层车按施工方式不同，分为间断式作业稀浆封层车和连续式稀浆封层车；按行驶方式不同，分为自行式稀浆封层车和拖挂式稀浆封层车。目前，国内外的稀浆封层车主要采用自行式。

14.2.2 Components 组成 (Fig. 14.10)

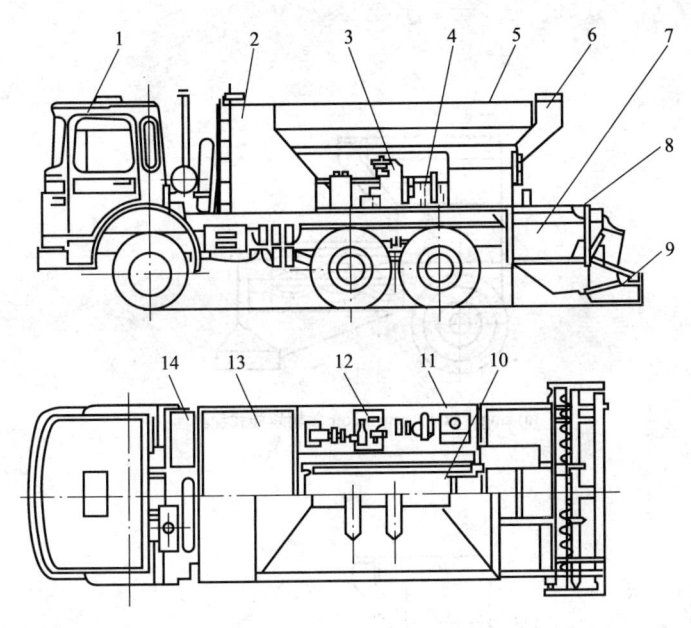

Fig. 14.10 Components of slurry seal machine 稀浆封层车的组成

1 traveling system 行驶系统
2 water tank 水箱
3 diesel engine for working unit 作业用柴油机
4 mechanical transmission system 机械传动系统
5 aggregate bin 骨料仓
6 filler bin 填料仓
7 mixer 搅拌箱
8 control console 操作台
9 speader 摊铺器
10 belt conveyer 带式运输机
11 additive box 添加剂箱
12 fluid control system 流控系统
13 emulsion box 乳液箱
14 cleaning diesel box 清洗柴油箱

417

(1) Mixing System 拌和系统 (Fig. 14.11)

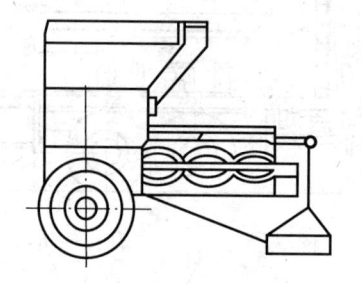

(a) single axle screw mixer 单轴螺旋式搅拌器

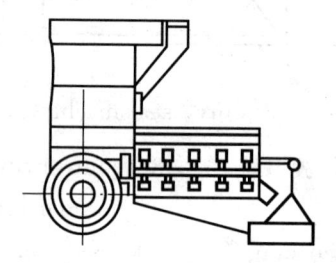

(b) double shaft paddle mixer 双轴浆叶式搅拌器

Fig. 14.11　Mixing system 拌和系统

（2）Spreader Box 摊铺箱（Fig. 14.12）

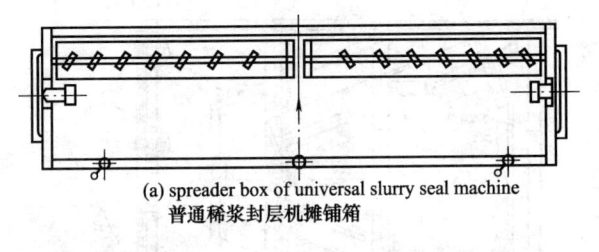

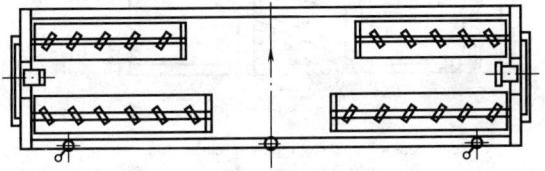

(a) spreader box of universal slurry seal machine
普通稀浆封层机摊铺箱

(b) spreader box of polymer modification slurry seal machine
聚合物改性稀浆封层摊铺箱

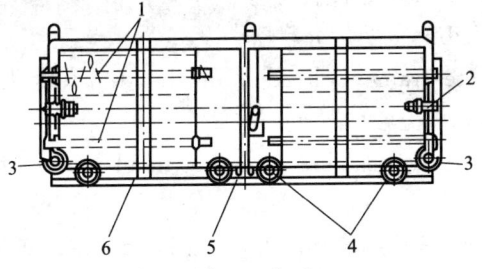

(c) rectangle spreader box
矩形路面封层摊铺箱

1　screw distributor 螺旋分料器
2　distributer motor 分料器马达
3　distributer screw ground clearance adjusting hand wheel 分料器螺旋离地高度调节手轮
4　spreading thickness fine adjusting hand wheel 摊铺厚度微调手轮
5　crown adjustor 路拱调节器
6　spreader box frame 摊铺箱框架

Fig. 14.12

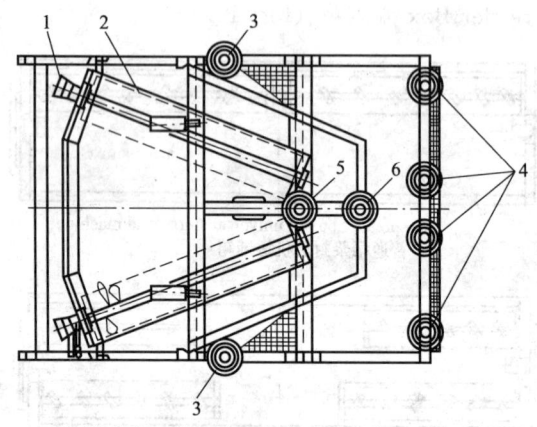

(d) V-shaped tracking repair spreader box
V形车辙修复摊铺箱

1　distributor motor 分料器马达
2　screw distributor 螺旋分料器
3,6　aggregate framework adjusting hand wheel 集料框架调节手轮
4　spreading thickness fine adjusting hand wheel 摊铺厚度微调手轮
5　spreading thickness main adjusting hand wheel 铺层厚度主调节手轮

Fig. 14.12　Spreader box 摊铺箱

14.3 Pavement Recyclers 道路再生机

14.3.1 Hot-in-place Recycling Train 就地热再生机组 (Fig. 14.13)

Fig. 14.13 Hot-in-place recycling train 就地热再生机组

(1) Overview 概况

The hot-in-place recycling train comprises one preheater, one preheater/miller, and one postheater/dryer/mixer, which operate in tandem with a conventional paver and rollers. If desired, extra preheaters may be added to increase operating speed and depth.

就地热再生机组包括一台预加热机、预加热/铣刨机和一台后加热/烘干/搅拌机，这一机组与普通的摊铺机和压路机一起形成串联作业。如果需要，可增加预加热机以便提高作业速度和深度。

The train recycles all types of asphalt pavement on-site in a continuous, one-lane operation and produces asphalt that is fully compliant with end-product specifications for conventional hot-mix asphalt and Superpave.

再生机组可在一个车道上对各种沥青路面连续进行再生作业，所生产的沥青路面完全符合常规热拌沥青混合料和超级路面的各种最终产品性能要求。

（2）Preheater 预加热机

① Concentrated combustion preheater 集中燃烧式加热机 (Fig. 14.14)

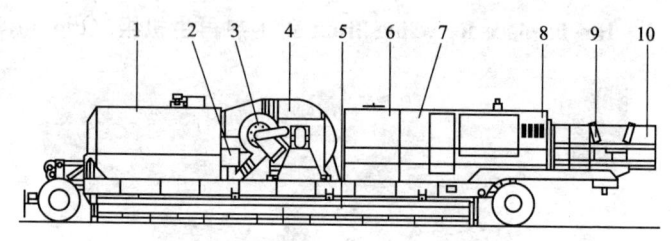

Fig. 14.14 Concentrated combustion preheater 集中燃烧式加热机

1　combustion chamber 燃烧室
2　burner system 燃烧系统
3　combustion air turbo blower 燃气涡轮鼓风机
4　recirculating hot air blower 热风再循环鼓风机
5　heating plenum 加热室
6　diesel fuel tank 柴油箱
7　hydraulic oil tank 液压油箱
8　diesel engine 柴油发动机
9　control panel 控制面板
10　operator station 操作台

② Decentralized combustion preheater 分散燃烧式加热机 (Fig. 14.15)

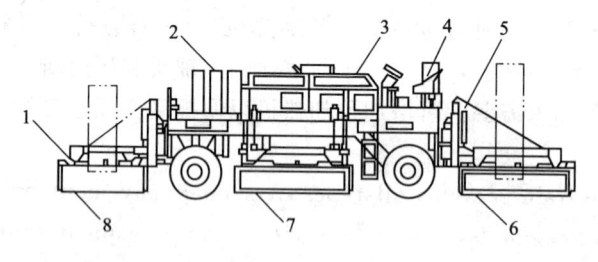

Fig. 14.15 Decentralized combustion preheater 分散燃烧式加热机

1　nozzle 喷嘴
2　fuel tank 燃料箱
3　engine 发动机
4　seat 座椅
5　lifting gear 升降装置
6~8　heating plenum 加热室

(3) Preheater/Miller 加热/铣刨机 (Fig. 14.16)

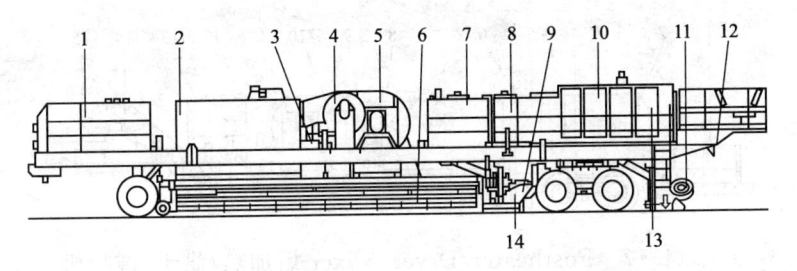

Fig. 14.16 Preheater/Miller 加热/铣刨机

1 diesel fuel tank 柴油箱
2 combustion chamber 燃烧室
3 burner system 燃烧系统
4 combustion air turbo blower 燃气涡轮鼓风机
5 recirculating hot air blower 热风再循环鼓风机
6 heating plenum 加热室
7 regenerator tank 再生剂储罐
8 hydraulic oil tank 液压油箱
9 left and right milling drum 左右铣刨鼓
10 diesel engine 柴油发动机
11 center milling drum 中间铣刨鼓
12 operator station 操作台
13,14 milling depth control 铣刨深度控制装置

（4）Postheater/Dryer/Mixer 后加热/烘干/搅拌机（Fig. 14.17）

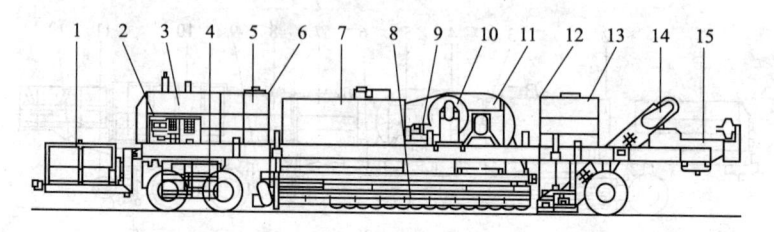

Fig. 14.17　Postheater/Dryer/Mixer 后加热/烘干/搅拌机

1　add-mix hopper 添加混合料料斗
2　control panel 控制面板
3　diesel engine 柴油发动机
4　operator station 操作台
5　hydraulic oil tank 液压油箱
6　spreading auger 布料螺旋
7　combustion chamber 燃烧室
8　heating plenum with mixing device 带有搅拌装置的加热室
9　burner system 燃烧系统
10　combustion air turbo blower 燃气涡轮鼓风机
11　recirculating hot air blower 热风再循环鼓风机
12　aggregate auger 集料螺旋
13　diesel fuel tank 柴油箱
14　drag slat conveyor 拖挂板式输送机
15　twin-shaft mixer 双轴搅拌器

（5）Basic Operation Process 基本作业过程
① Preheating pavement. 路面预加热。
② Preheating and milling pavement、adding regenerator. 加热铣刨路面、加再生剂。
③ Adding new mix, postheating、drying and mixing recycling material, paving. 添加新混合料，加热、烘干并搅拌再生料，摊铺。

④ Rolling. 碾压成型。

(6) Heating System 加热系统 (Fig. 14.18)

Fig. 14.18　Heating system 加热系统

This pre-heating is achieved by the combination of forced hot-air with low-level radiant heat. Air is heated to about 700℃ in a diesel-fuelled combustion chamber. Jets of high-velocity hot-air are blown onto the pavement through thousands of small holes in a heating plenum.

预加热由压力热空气与低辐射热组合而形成。空气在柴油燃烧室中被加热到700℃。高速热空气流透过加热室内数千个小孔被吹到路面上。

The combination of forced hot-air with the low-level radiant heat generated by the heating plenum effectively results in uniform and controlled heating of the wearing course of the asphalt pavement. Used hot-air is vacuumed for reheating, which minimizes heat loss and reduces fuel consumption.

压力热空气与加热室产生的低辐射热组合对磨损的沥青路面形成了均匀有效与可控的加热。使用过的热空气被抽吸进行重新加热,从而最大程度地减少了热损失,并降低了燃油消耗。

14.3.2 Hot-in-place Remixer 就地热再生重铺机 (Fig. 14.19)

Fig. 14.19 Hot-in-place remixer 就地热再生重铺机

(1) Overview 概况

The remixer is a self-propelled compact machine for recycling and relaying bituminous road pavements. The pavement material is rehabilitated either by shaping the existing pavement and overlaying it with a new layer, or by mixing in admix material and relaying the mix.

重铺机是一种用于沥青路面再生和重铺的自行式综合机组。该机组通过对现有路面进行修整并在其上铺设新面层,或者通过搅拌所添加的混合料并将其重铺来改善路面材料。

(2) Operating Principle 工作原理 (Fig. 14.20)

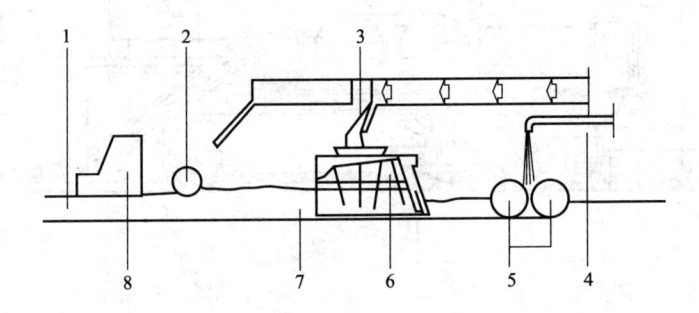

Fig. 14.20 Operating principle of hot-in-place remixer
就地热再生重铺机工作原理

1　remixed wearing course 再生磨耗层
2　distributor auger 螺旋分料器
3　material flow 材料流
4　asphalt spraying 沥青喷洒
5　scarifier 翻松器
6　mixer 搅拌器
7　recycled mix 再生混合料
8　paving screed 摊铺熨平板

(3) Components 组成 (Fig. 14.21)

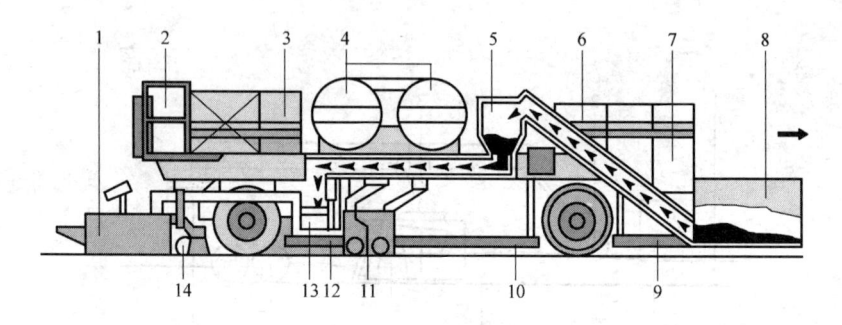

Fig. 14.21　Components of hot-in-place remixer
就地热再生重铺机的组成

1　paving screed 摊铺熨平板
2　operator station 操作台
3　diesel engine 柴油发动机
4　gas tank 燃气罐
5　intermediate proportioning bin 中间配料仓
6　diesel tank 柴油箱
7　additive tank 添加剂料箱
8　receiving hopper 接料斗
9，10，12　heating system 加热系统
11　variable scarifying device 宽度可变式翻松器
13　mixer 搅拌器
14　spreading auger 螺旋分料器

14.3.3 Cold-in-place Recycler 就地冷再生机 (Fig. 14.22)

Fig. 14.22 Cold-in-place recycler 就地冷再生机

(1) Overview 概况

The cold-in-place recycler is capable of tackling all cold recycling projects. The machine scarifies the existing pavement by milling, mixes it with binding agents in the integrated mixer, and immediately places the recycled material. The biggest plus point of the cold recycler is that the recycled, homogeneous material mix is distributed evenly across the entire working width by a spreading auger, and then paved and pre-compacted by a paving screed. This method produces high-quality base layers in one single work step, which can be immediately used by traffic.

就地冷再生机能够满足各种冷再生工程的需要。该机器通过铣刨将现有路面翻松，然后在集成的搅拌机中将其与结合料一起搅拌，并且对再生料立即进行摊铺。就地冷再生机最大的优势就是螺旋分料器能够将再生、匀质的混合料均匀地分布在整个工作宽度上，然后由熨平板对其摊铺和预压实。这种再生可以在一个工序内修建出高质量的基层，使得交通能够立即开放。

(2) Components 组成 (Fig. 14.23)

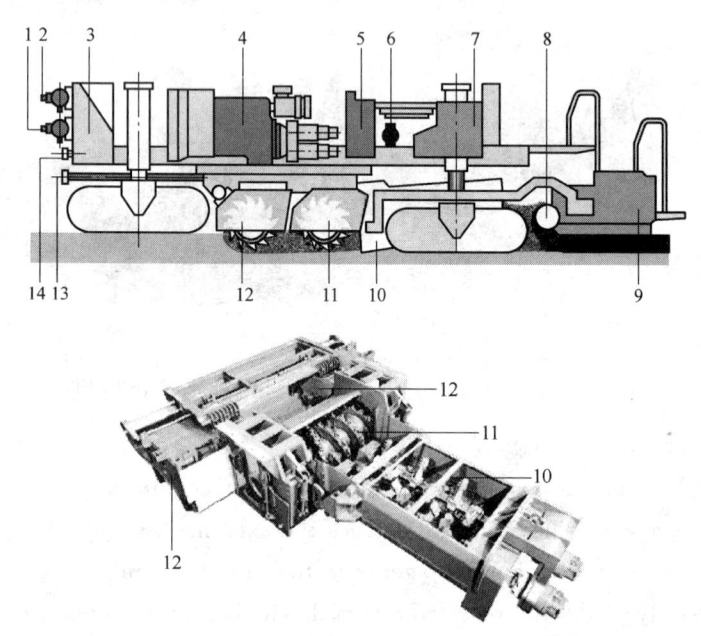

Fig. 14.23　Components of cold-in-place recycler
就地冷再生机的组成

1　injection system for emulsified asphalt 乳化沥青喷洒系统
2　water injection system 喷水系统
3　water tank 水箱
4　drive unit with two diesel engines 双柴油发动机驱动装置
5　hydraulic oil tank 液压油箱
6　generator for hot asphalt system 热沥青系统电机
7　diesel tank 柴油箱
8　spreading auger 螺旋分料器
9　variable width screed 变宽度熨平板
10　twin-shaft mixer 双轴搅拌器
11　fixed milling drum 固定铣刨鼓
12　two-side variable width milling drum 双边变宽度铣刨鼓
13　hot asphalt injection system 热沥青喷洒系统
14　cement slurry injection system 水泥稀浆喷洒系统

(3) Components of the Milling Drum 铣刨转子的组成 (Fig. 14.24)

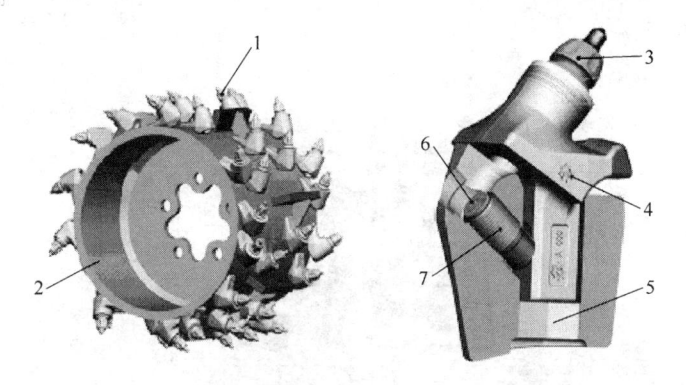

Fig. 14.24 Components of the milling drum 铣刨转子的组成

1 milling tool 铣刀
2 milling drum 铣刨鼓
3 tool bit 刀头
4 tool clamp 刀夹
5 tool holder 刀座
6 protective plug 保护塞
7 bolt 螺栓

(4) Components of the Twin-shaft Mixer 双轴搅拌器的组成 (Fig. 14.25)

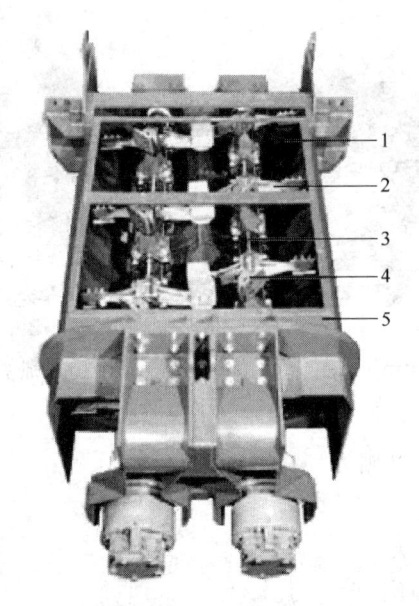

Fig. 14.25　Components of the twin-shaft mixer
双轴搅拌器的组成

1　lining plate 衬板
2　mixing arm 搅拌臂
3　mixing shaft 搅拌轴
4　mixing paddle 搅拌桨叶
5　mixing trough 搅拌筒体

(5) Operating Principle 工作原理 (Fig. 14.26)

| Damaged asphalt course 破损沥青路面 | Variable milling drums 可变铣刨鼓 | Fixed milling drum 固定铣刨鼓 | Twin-shaft mixer 双轴搅拌器 | Processed material mixture 混合料摊铺处理 |

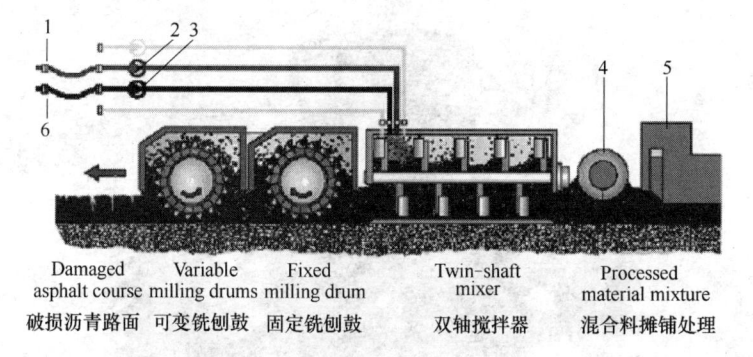

Fig. 14.26 Operating principle 工作原理

1 hose connection on the water tanker truck 水罐车软管连接
2 microprocessor-controlled pump for the water injection 微机控制喷水泵
3 microprocessor-controlled pump for the emulsified asphalt injection 微机控制乳化沥青喷洒泵
4 spreading auger 螺旋分料器
5 variable width screed 变宽度熨平板
6 hose connection on the emulsified asphalt tanker 乳化沥青罐车软管连接

(6) Basic Operation Process 基本作业过程 (Fig. 14.27)

| Water delivery 供水 | Emulsified asphalt delivery 乳化沥青供给 | Milling, mixing, paving, pre-compacting 铣刨，拌和，摊铺，预压 |

Fig. 14.27 Basic operation process 基本作业过程

14.3.4　Stabilizer/Recycler 稳拌/再生机（Fig. 14.28）

Fig. 14.28　Stabilizer/Recycler 稳拌/再生机

(1) Overview 概况

The stabilizer/recycler is the solution for universal use on the stabilization of low load bearing soils and the recycling of road pavements. This high performance stabilizer/recycler continues to prove its capabilities on a wide range of construction sites. The high quality mix results achieved with this unit are consistent regardless of the soil condition or the additive type.

稳拌/再生机广泛用于解决轻载土壤稳定和路面再生问题。高性能的稳拌/再生机在各种建设工程中不断显示着自身的适用性。该机械所达到的高质量拌和效果均匀一致，不受土壤条件或添加剂类型的影响。

For soil stabilization, the stabilizer/recycler is used to improve and strengthen existing soils by mixing in lime, fly ash or cement. In recycling applications the machine is used to cut and pulverize old, damaged surfaces and road pavements. Here the complete road construction, including the bearing course, is treated. The pulverized material is then mixed with a binder "In-Place" and reused as a new bound bearing course.

对于土壤稳定工作，稳拌/再生机用来使石灰、粉煤灰或水泥与土壤混合，从而改善和增强现有土壤的承载能力。再生作业中，稳拌/再生机用于切削与粉碎旧的破损面层和路面。这种作业中，整个道路结构包括承重层均得到改造处理。粉碎的道路材料与黏结剂"就地"拌和并用作新的承重层。

（2）Components 组成 （Fig. 14.29）

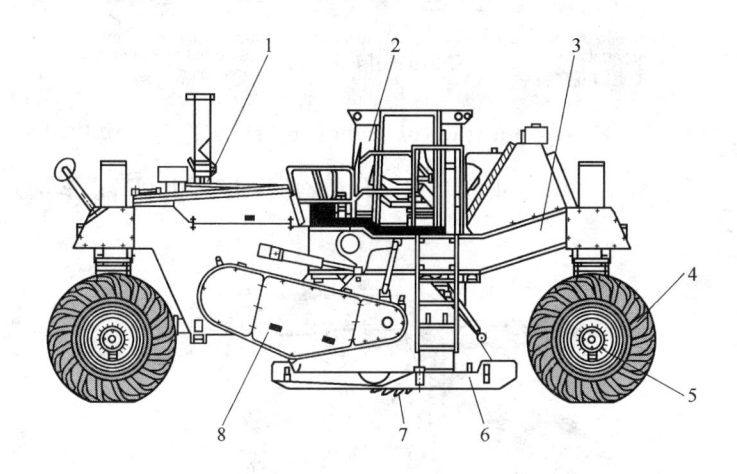

Fig. 14.29 Components of stabilizer/recycler 稳拌/再生机的组成

1 diesel engine 柴油发动机
2 cab and operator station 驾驶室与操作台
3 frame 机架
4 deep-tread tire 深胎面花纹轮胎
5 drive motor 驱动马达
6 rotor encloser 拌和转子罩壳
7 cutters and rotor assembly 刀具与拌和转子组件
8 rotor transmission case 拌和转子传动箱

(3) Application of Stabilizing Soils 稳定土壤功用 (Fig. 14.30)

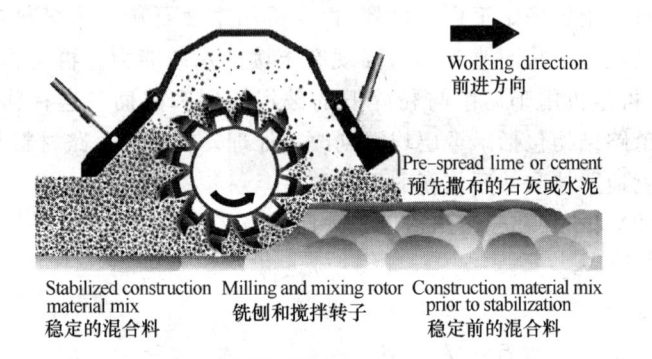

Fig. 14.30 Application of stabilizing soils 稳定土壤功用

(4) Application of Cold Recycling 冷再生功用 (Fig. 14.31)

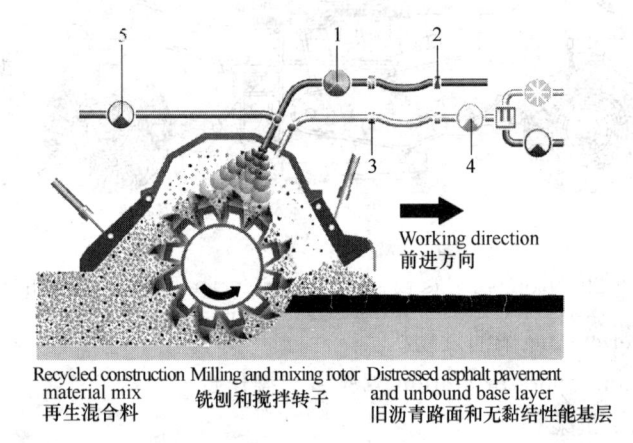

Fig. 14.31 Application of cold recycling 冷再生功用

1 microprocessor-controlled pump for injecting hot asphalt 微机控制热态沥青喷洒泵
2 hose connection of the asphalt tank 沥青罐车的软管连接
3 hose connection to slurry mixer 与稀浆搅拌器的软管连接
4 microprocessor-controlled pump for injecting the cement-water slurry 微机控制水泥稀浆喷洒泵
5 microprocessor-controlled pump for injecting water 微机控制喷水泵

（5）Micro-processor Control For the Injection Systems 喷洒系统微机控制（Fig. 14.32）

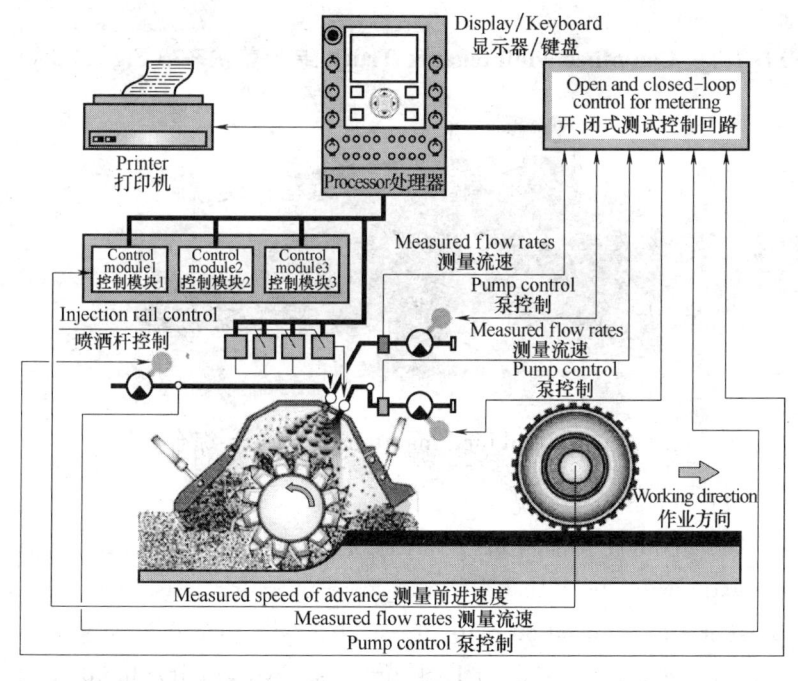

Fig. 14.32 Micro-processor control for the injection systems 喷洒系统微机控制

（6）Basic Operation Process 基本作业过程（Fig. 14.33）

Fig. 14.33 Basic operation process 基本作业过程

1　cement truck 水泥运输车
2　water truck 运水车
3　bitumen tank truck 沥青罐车
4　stabilizer/recycler 稳拌/再生机
5　roller 压路机

14.4 Pothole Patcher 坑槽修补车

14.4.1 Combined Maintenance Truck 综合养护车 (Fig. 14.34)

Fig. 14.34 Combined maintenance truck 综合养护车

(1) Overview 概况

The pothole patcher has a variety of features that provide safety and the extra production capabilities that lower operating costs. Its pavement breaker and compaction plate are strategically placed for easy handling to reduce the risk of back injuries. Two gravity dump spoils bins, rear and curbside-mounted, save time and provide extra storage.

坑槽修补车具有多种特点，可提供安全和超额的生产能力，因而具有较低的使用成本。所配备的路面破碎镐和平板夯使用方便，减小了背部损伤的风险。两个设置在后部和靠路边侧部的废料箱可节省时间，并且提供了更大的仓储空间。

A screw conveyor feeds the patching mix from the hopper into the pothole through a rear-mounted chute. The hopper agitator assures a constant supply of mix to the screw conveyor. The full length of the hopper is insulated and electrically heated with thermostatically controlled electric heating elements — used during working and non-working hours to keep the mix at the right temperature.

螺旋输送器通过一后置式卸料槽将修补混合料从料仓送入坑槽。料仓振动器确保将混合料连续供给螺旋输送器。对料仓全长进行绝热，并由自动温控电加热元件进行加热。加热可在工作和非工作时间进行，以保持混合料所需要的正常温度。

（2）Components 组成（Fig. 14.35）

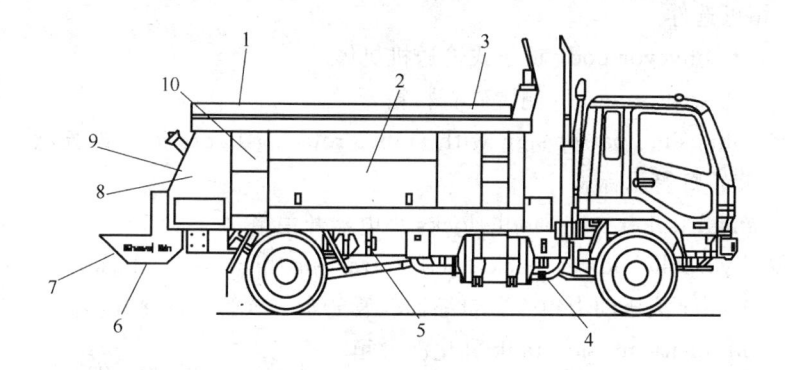

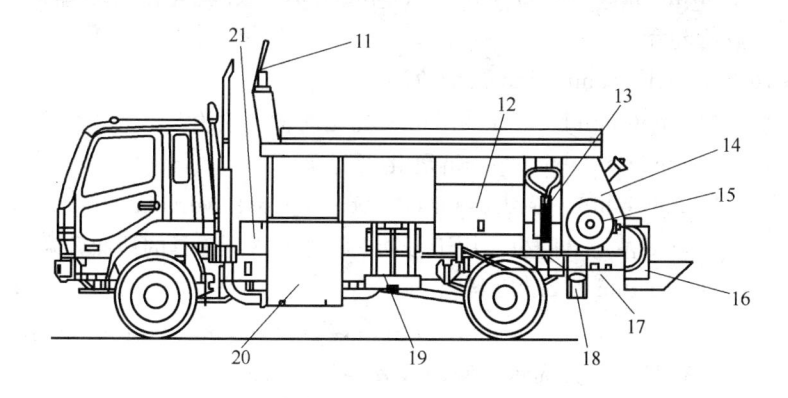

Fig. 14.35 Components of combined maintenance truck
综合养护车的组成

1　rear sand/grit bin 后置砂石料箱
2　large locker and paddle locks 大电路开关箱
3　front sand/grit bin 前置砂石料箱
4　isolate heating valve 隔离式加热阀
5　water hose reel 软水管卷盘
6　bottom of shovel bin 铁铲工具箱底部
7　shovel bin 铁铲工具箱
8　water tank or optional second emulsion tank 水箱或第二乳化剂箱可选件
9　slat conveyor body 板条式输送机机体
10　side grit/sand bin 侧置砂石料箱
11　collapsible patrol sign with amber rotating lights 折叠式黄色旋转灯警示标志
12　small locker and paddle locks 小电器开关箱
13　hydraulic power pack, self retracting hose reel, hose, oil cooler 液压动力组件,自缩回软管卷盘,软管,油冷却器
14　bitumen emulsion tank 乳化沥青箱
15　bitumen emulsion self retracting hose reel 乳化沥青自缩回软管卷盘
16　shovel cleaning bin 铁铲清洁箱
17　bitumen emulsion hand lance 乳化沥青手喷枪
18　bitumen emulsion pump 乳化沥青泵
19　hydraulic lifter used to lower vibe plate and hydraulic tools to the ground 液压升降机,用于振动平板夯和液压工具的地面升降
20　spoil rubbish bin 废料箱
21　sign storage tray, emulsion tank, side tipping spoil bin 标志存放托盘,乳化剂箱,侧卸式废料箱

14.4.2 Spray Patching Road Maintenance Machinery 喷射修补式道路养护机械

(1) Overview 概况

Spray pothole patching is the breakthrough process of filling a pothole or sealing and filling a damaged road surface by blowing liquid asphalt and aggregate into the void.

喷射式坑槽修补是一个突入式坑槽填充过程，或者是通过把液态沥青和骨料射入地面空穴以封闭和充填破损路面的过程。

The major appeal of this technology is its simplicity. Pothole patching using the spray patching method will increase the strength and life of the patch while also decreasing the time involved in patching and patching costs.

这一技术的主要吸引力在于其简单性。应用喷射式修补方法修补坑槽将提高修补强度和寿命，同时也将减小修补时间和降低维修成本。

(2) Spray Patching Road Maintenance Vehicle 喷射式道路修补车 (Fig. 14.36)

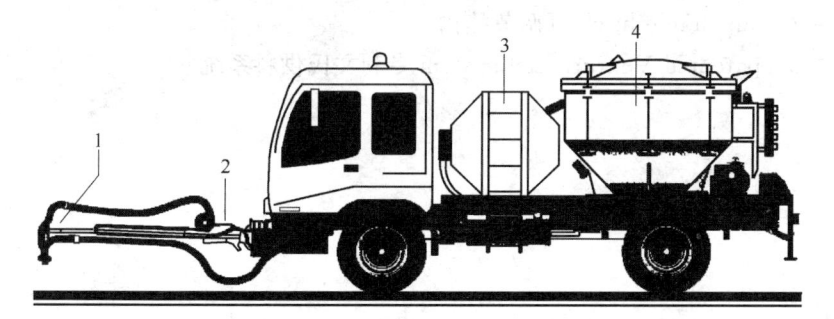

Fig. 14.36 Spray patching road maintenance vehicle
喷射式道路修补车

1　spray nozzle 喷嘴　　　　3　emulsion hopper 乳化沥青仓
2　swing boom 回转式吊杆　　4　aggregate hopper 骨料仓

(3) Trailer-mounted Pothole Patcher 拖挂喷射式坑槽修补机 (Fig. 14.37)

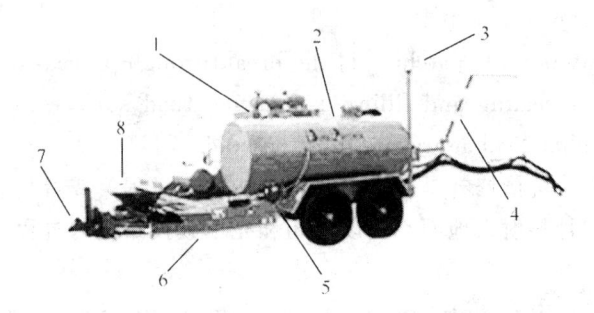

Fig. 14.37　Trailer-mounted pothole patcher 拖挂喷射式坑槽修补机

1　power with sound-suppressed engine enclosures 装有坚固发动机罩壳的动力装置
2　emulsion tank 乳化沥青罐
3　safety strobe light 安全频闪灯
4　tri-flex no fatigue boom 三维无疲劳吊杆
5　electric overnight heating 通宵电加热器
6　heavy duty trailer 重型拖挂装置
7　adjustable hitch 可调节挂钩
8　patented Venturi feed system 专利文氏供料系统

（4）Working Procedure 作业工序（Fig. 14.38）

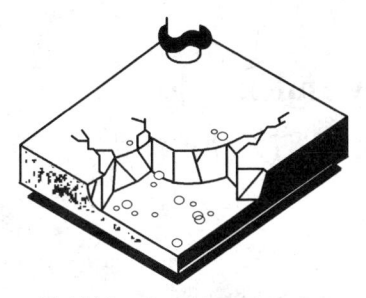

(a) A high-volume blower is used to clean out the hole or crack.
应用大容量鼓风机清理坑槽或裂缝

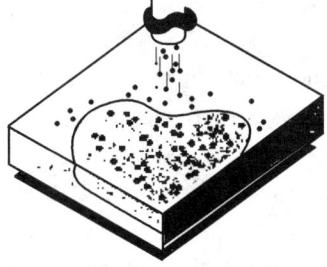

(b) A tack coat of hot asphalt emulsion is applied
喷洒形成热乳化沥青黏结层

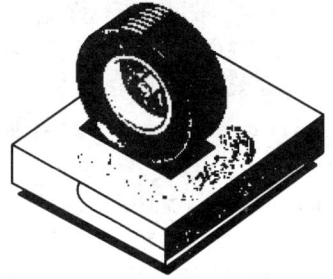

(c) A mixture of aggregate and hot asphalt emulsion are shot into the hole.
将骨料与热乳化沥青混合物喷入坑槽

(d) A top coat of aggregate is applied. Traffic can flow immediately.
喷洒形成骨料罩面层。交通可立即开放

Fig. 14.38　Working procedure 作业工序

Vocabulary Index
词汇索引(英中对照)

15°tapered-bead seat rim 15°斜胎圈轮辋 125
45°angle joint 45°切口 32
4th gear clutch 第4挡离合器 107
5-position counterweight 5位置平衡块 358
5°tapered (-bead) seat 5°斜胎圈 125
5°tapered-bead seat rim 5°斜胎圈轮辋 125

A

accelerator control 加速器控制器 360
accelerator dial 加速器调节刻度盘 178
accelerator emergency circuit 加速器应急回路 178
accelerator sensor 加速踏板传感器 53
Ackerman Jeantaud steering 阿克曼-金特式转向 111
actuator lever 作动杠杆 151
actuator link 作动连杆 151
adapting flange 连接法兰 89

additional hold-down mechanism 附加压紧机构 149
additional lights switch 附加灯开关 360
additive box 添加剂箱 417
additive tank 添加剂料箱 428
add-mix hopper 添加混合料料斗 424
adjustable armrest 可调节扶手 286
adjustable hitch 可调节挂钩 442
adjusting 调节器 151
adjusting arm 调整臂 148
adjusting bolt 调整螺栓 158
adjusting cam 调整凸轮 149
adjusting device 调整装置 134
adjusting disk 调节板 59
adjusting nut 调节螺母,调整螺母 99,101,134
adjusting nut lock 调整螺母锁片 101
adjusting rod 调整杆 158,159
adjusting screw 调整螺钉 39,41,43,44,45,89,115,151,157,391
adjusting screw assembly 调节螺钉

总成　151

adjusting screw spring　调节螺钉弹簧　151

adjusting shim　调整垫片　74,94,101,102,114,115,119,133,144,151,352,353

adjusting sleeve, adjuster tube　（横拉杆）调整管　113

adjusting speed bolt　调速螺栓　50

adjusting spring　调节弹簧　50

adjusting thread check ring　调整螺纹挡圈　156

adjusting washer　调节垫片　51

advance device spring　提前器弹簧　52

aggregate auger　集料螺旋　424

aggregate bin　骨料仓　417

aggregate charging belt　骨料上料带　383

aggregate feed belt　骨料上料带　384

aggregate framework adjusting hand wheel　集料框架调节手轮　420

aggregate hopper　骨料仓　441

aggregate inlet　骨料进口　405

aggregate scale　骨料计量秤　390

aggregate weigh hopper　骨料称量斗　390

air bleed screw　放气螺钉　156

air brake system　气制动系统　162

air cleaner　空气滤清器　26,60,61,62,176

air cleaner cap gasket　空气滤清器盖衬垫　62

air cleaner housing cover, air cleaner cap(cover)　空气滤清器盖　62

air compressor　空气压缩机　162,163,398,411

air deflation switch　放气开关　412

air draft tube　吸风小筒　397

air filter bowl (box, housing)　空气滤清器壳　62

air filter　空气滤清器,空气过滤器　344,345

airflow sensor　空气流量计　64

air gauge　气压表　162

air inlet　空气进口　62

air inlet switch　进气开关　411,412

air intake heater　进气加热器　61

air leg hand-hold rock drill　气腿手持式凿岩机　5

air-leg rock drill　气腿式凿岩机　5

air over hydraulic booster　气顶油加力器　163

air pipe　风管　397,411

air pressure gauge　气压表　412

air reservoir　储气筒　162,163,164,411

air spring bellow　空气弹簧气囊　164

air supply　气体供给　137

air supply pipeline　制动供气管路　164

air tank　储气罐　398

air-temperature sensor　空气温度传感器　64

alarm lamp 报警灯 165
alarm lights switch 报警灯开关 360
all terrain crane 全路起重机 8
all wheel drive motor grader 全轮驱动自行式平地机 242
alternator 交流发电机 82
altitude-pressure connection 大气压力接头 51
ampere meter 电流表 67,80
amplitude adjusting mechanism 调幅机构 356
amplitude selection wheel 振幅选择轮 358
anchor bolt 锚定螺栓,固定螺栓 59
anchor bracket,adapter （制动钳）支架,支承板 155
anchor pin pedestal 支承销座 148
anchor pin 支承销 147,151,159
anchor plate 固定底板 139
anchor plate,anchor 支承块,支承板 151
anchor spring 支承块弹簧 151
angle broom 转角清扫滚刷 230
angular position device 角位器 245
annular gear 内齿圈 100
annular oil groove 环形油槽 35
anti-extrusion ring, retainer 挡圈 100
anti-extrusion ring 挡圈 131,132
Antilock Brake System（ABS） 防抱死制动系统 165
anti-rattle clip 防振夹 155
anti-squeal(rattle) spring 消声（防啸声)弹簧 155
anti-torsion pipe fitted for increased strength 抗扭增强钢管 175
APC & accelerator back up switch APC与加速器备用开关 178
APC controller APC控制器 178
APC control valve APC控制阀 178
APC emergency circuit APC应急回路 178
APC system 自动功率控制系统 178
architectural engineering 建筑工程 3
armature 电枢 81
armature plate 衔铁板 59
armature shaft 电枢轴 81
arm 斗杆 174
arm cylinder 斗杆油缸 174,177
arm rest 扶手 175
arresting pin 限位销钉 75
articulated frame motor grader 铰接机架式平地机 242
articulated frame 铰接式车架 352
articulated joint shell 铰接架壳体 353
articulated point 铰接点 116
articulated steering joint 铰接转向节 346,347,348
articulated truck 铰接式自卸车 4

asbest rope stuffing 石棉绳填料 415

asphalt bucket 沥青桶 390,392

asphalt capacity indicator 沥青容量指示器 409

asphalt discharge valve 沥青排放阀 391

asphalt discharging pipe 放沥青管 409

asphalt distributor 沥青洒布车 13,407

asphalt emulsion plant 乳化沥青设备 7

asphalt heating tank 沥青加热罐 7

asphalt injection pipe 沥青注入管 391

asphalt injection pump 沥青喷射泵 390,392

asphalt injection valve 沥青注入阀 391

asphalt inlet 沥青入口 405

asphalt inlet pipe 沥青进油管 390

asphalt melting equipment 沥青脱筒设备 7

asphalt mixing plant 沥青搅拌设备 7

asphalt mixture transfer vehicle 沥青混合料转运车 7

asphalt nozzle 沥青喷管 390

asphalt pavement combined maintenance vehicle 沥青路面综合养护车 11

asphalt pavement heater 沥青路面加热机 12

asphalt pavement-hot-in-place recycling machine set 沥青路面就地热再生机组 12

asphalt paver 沥青摊铺机 7,308

asphalt pump 沥青泵 409,413,415

asphalt return pipe 沥青回油管 390

asphalt scale 沥青计量秤 390

asphalt slurry seal machine 稀浆封层机 11

asphalt spray pipe 沥青喷管 383

asphalt spray pipe lifter rod 洒沥青管升降杆 409

asphalt spraying 沥青喷洒 427

asphalt spraying pipe lifter control handle 洒沥青管升降操纵手柄 409

asphalt spraying pipe nozzle adjusting handle 洒沥青管喷嘴角度调节手柄 409

asphalt storage tank 沥青储箱,沥青箱,沥青箱体 408,410

asphalt suction pipe 吸沥青管 409

asphalt supply system 沥青供给系统 378,379

asphalt tank outer cover 沥青箱外罩 410

asphalt weigh bucket 沥青称量桶 390,392

assist spring 助力弹簧 92

447

A-throttle　A形节流　59
atmospheric pressure　大气压力　53
atmosphere pressure sensor　大气压力传感器　53
auger blades　螺旋叶片　311
auger conveyer　螺旋输送机　389,398
auger conveyers　螺旋分料器　311,312
auger drive motors　螺旋驱动马达　311,333
auger electronic scale　螺旋电子秤　389
automatic clearance compensator　自动间隙补偿装置　153
automatic clutch cable adjusting mechanism　离合器拉索自动调节机构　91
automatic segregator　自动分离器　79
automatic transmission　自动换挡变速箱　107
automating adjusting lever　自动调节杠杆　151
autothermic piston　热膨胀自动调节式活塞(此时镶片为低碳钢)　31
auxiliary air valve　辅助空气阀　64
auxiliary cylinder　辅助油缸　177
auxiliary gearbox　副齿轮箱　346
auxiliary idle spring　怠速辅助弹簧　49
auxiliary spring, supplementary (leaf) spring, secondary spring

副钢板弹簧　139
auxiliary valve　辅助阀　285
axial piston pump　轴向柱塞泵　314
axial plunger motor　轴向柱塞马达　314
axial-radial spring expander　轴向-径向弹簧式胀簧　34
axis pin　销轴　128,142
axle　轮轴　140
axle housing　桥壳　139
axle shaft, half shaft　半轴　100

B

back end collar　后端凸缘　37
backing plate　(制动衬块)背板,垫板　155,245
backing plate, base plate, bottom plate　(制动器)底板　151
back pressure valve　背压阀　177
back spring　回(复)位弹簧　148,149,159
backstop　挡铁　80
baffle plate　挡板,折流板　94,135,391,398
bag cages　袋骨架　398
bag dust filter　袋式除尘器　398
balance weight　平衡重块　37,99
ball bearing turntable　滚珠转盘　140
ball cup, ball(-stud) socket, ball cap　球碗,球头座　113
ball float opening　浮球口　408
ball guide　钢球导管　115

ball joint 球节 113
ball stud, ball pivot, ball pin 球头销 113
ballast resistor, external resistor 附加电阻 67,68
barrel 柱塞套 45,48,57
barrel spring 桶形弹簧 136
barrell(ed) face ring 桶面环 34
bar 拉杆 78
basic screed 基本段熨平板 325
batch forced mixing plant 间歇强制式搅拌设备 376
battery(accumulator) 蓄电池 64,67,70,80
battery jar (accumulator jar) 蓄电池外壳 70
battery negative terminal 负极接线柱 70
battery positive terminal 蓄电池正极接线柱 70
beacon switch 警示灯开关 360
bead area 胎圈区 123
bead core, bead wire 胎圈芯 123
bead heel 胎踵 123
bead, tire bead, tyre bead 胎圈, 子口 123
bead toe 胎趾 123
bearing 轴承 23,45,74,75,82,89,94,99,100,101,113,132,218
bearing assembly 轴承 393
bearing bush 轴瓦 22
bearing cap （曲轴）轴承盖 22,89,94

bearing cover 轴承端盖 94,354,356
bearing housing 轴承座 119
bearing housing of center axle 中心轴轴承座 369
bearing housing of eccentric shaft 偏心轴轴承座 369
bearing preload spacer 轴承预紧隔套 101
bearing saddle 轴承座 94,101,102,131
bearing seal 轴承油封 99
bearing seat 轴承座 89
bearing shell 轴瓦 131
bearing sleeve 轴承衬套 133
bearing support 轴承座 135
bell crank lever 双臂曲柄杆 157
belleville spring 盘形弹簧 90
belt 带 389
belt, belt ply, bracing ply, tread belt 带束层 123
belt conveyer 带式输送机 378,380,417
belt drive unit 带传动装置 394
belted bias(diagonal) tire 带束斜交轮胎 123
belted radial tire 带束子午线轮胎 123
belt feeder 带式给料器 380
belt pulley hub 带轮毂 74
belt tensioning system 履带张紧系统 331
bevel 斜角 29

449

beveled joint, diagonal joint 斜切口 32
bevelled edge oil control ring 倒角油环 34
bias ply tire with inner tube, bias ply tubed tire 有内胎斜交轮胎 123
big end, bottom end （连杆）大头 35
bimetallic bearing bush 双金属轴承衬 133
bimetallic coil spring 双金属感温器 75
bimetallic disk 阀片双金属片 75
bitumen emulsion hand lance 乳化沥青手喷枪 440
bitumen emulsion pump 乳化沥青泵 440
bitumen emulsion self retracting hose reel 乳化沥青自缩回软管卷盘 440
bitumen emulsion tank 乳化沥青箱 440
bitumen tank truck 沥青罐车 437
blade 铲刀 245,279
blade angle change cylinder 铲刀角度变换油缸 245
blade control lever 铲刀操纵手柄 285
blade hoist cylinder 铲刀升降油缸 243,279,282
blade hoist cylinder(left) 铲刀升降油缸（左） 247
blade hoist cylinder(right) 铲刀升降油缸（右） 247
blade outstanding cylinder 铲刀外伸油缸 245
blade sidesway cylinder 铲刀侧移油缸 247
blade tilting cylinder 铲刀倾斜油缸 279
bleeder valve (screw) 放气阀 151,155
bleed nipple 放气嘴 152
bleed port 排出口 55
blocking pin 锁定销 52
blow lamp 加热火焰喷灯 409
blow lamp shade 喷灯罩 409
blow lamp switch 喷灯开关 411
blow pipe 喷吹管 398
blower 鼓风机 382,383,384,385
bolt 螺栓 23,27,36,41,74,78,82,100,102,151,245,431
bolt(hole) circle diameter 螺栓孔圆直径 125
bonded track pad 双层履带板 332
boom 动臂 174,214
boom cylinder 动臂油缸 174,177,214
boost feed fuel stroke 增压供油行程 51
boost pressure connection 增压进气压力接头 51
boot 防尘罩 151
bottom of shovel bin 铁铲工具箱底部 440
bottom rib （活塞裙部）底肋 29

bottom ring 下环片 34
bowl cap 碗形盖 41
brake 制动器 79,313,314
bracket （随动臂）支架 92,
113,245
bracket, hanger, carrier 支架 139
brake band 制动带 89,147,157
brake base plate 制动底板
148,159
brake caliper mounting bracket 制
动钳安装支架 155
brake cal(l)iper body, caliper housing
seal 密封圈 155
brake chamber 制动气室 148,
162,164
brake combination valve 组合阀
160
brake cover 制动器盖 158
brake disc(disc, rotor) 制动盘
100,152,155
brake drum 制动鼓 89,114,147,
148,149,151,157,159
brake-fluid reservoir 制动油箱
161
brake line, LF 左前制动油管 160
brake line, RF 右前制动油管 160
brake lining wear sensor 制动衬块
磨损传感器 155
brake of rear planetary gear set 后
行星排制动器 106
brake pad 制动衬块 152
brake pad assembly 制动衬块总成
155

brake pad, brake lining 制动衬块
155
brake pedal 制动踏板 160,161,
163,285
brake pedal and parking lamp switch
制动踏板与停车灯开关 165
brake pressure regulator 制动压力
调节装置 165
brake shoe 制动蹄 148,149,159
brake shoe lock-plate 制动蹄锁片
148
brake system 制动系统 15
brake valve 制动阀 163,349
brake warning lamp 报警灯 160
braking-force regulator 制动力调节
器 161
brass jacket 黄铜套 80
breaker 缓冲层 123
breast board 挡土板 279
breather tube 通风管 23
bridge and tunnel machinery 桥梁和
隧道机械 10
bridge girder erection equipment 架
桥机 10
bridge inspection vehicle 桥梁检测
车 10
broom 清扫滚刷 262
broom sweeper 滚刷式清扫车 12
brush 电刷 81,82
brush grapple bucket 刷式抓斗
230
brush holder 电刷架 81,82
bucket cylinder 铲斗油缸 174,177

451

bucket float 铲刀浮动 287
bucket leveler 铲斗调平 287
bucket linkage 铲斗连接件 174
bucket lip 斗齿 174
bucket 铲斗,料斗 174,214,386
built-up crankshaft 组合式曲轴 37
bumper （踏板）缓冲块 92
bumper, bumper pad, buffer 缓冲块 139
buoyage 浮标 410
burner 燃烧器 382,383,384,385,405,411
burner system 燃烧系统 422,423,424
bush 衬套 158
bushing,sleeve 衬套 141,155
bushing 衬套,导管 90,114,115,126,128,144,153
bushing block 衬套 245
butt joint 平切口 32
butterfly gate 闸门 389
butterfly nut 翼形螺母 62
buzzer cancel switch 蜂鸣消除开关 285
by-pass valve 旁通阀 76,78

C

cab and operating system 驾驶室及操作系统 214,243,279
cab and operator station 驾驶室与操作台 435
caliper 制动钳 152

caliper assembly 制动钳总成 155,160
caliper disc brake 钳盘式制动器 103,147,152,215
cam brake 凸轮张开式制动器 148
cam 凸轮 38,45,148,159
cam disc, plate cam, disk cam 凸轮盘 47
cam shaft 凸轮轴 22,26,39,45,55,76,148
camshaft bearing cap 凸轮轴轴承盖 22
camshaft of high-pressure pump 高压泵凸轮轴 56
CAN 总线 164
CAN-signal 信号 164
cap 盖,接头盖,封盖,(放气阀)帽 89,126,155,415
cap nut 盖形螺母 55,57
capacitor 电容器 82
captive gasket 密封垫 69
carburetor 化油器 23,60
carburetor fuel system 化油器式供给系统简图 61
carcass,carcase,casing 胎体 123
carcass plies 胎体帘布层 123
carriage shaft 台车轴 141
carrier rod 顶杆 157
carrier roller 托链轮 16,127,132,135
carrier roller body 托轮体 132
carrier roller bracket 托轮支架 132,135

carrier roller cap 托轮盖 132

carrier roller shaft 托轮轴 132

cartridge 座圈 74

casing 外壳,罩壳 83,153

casoline engine 汽油机 20

cat comfort series seat 卡特舒适系列驾驶座 286

catch bolt 止动螺栓 101

caterpillar track, track 履带 127

cell connector 连接条 70

cell filler plug 加液孔盖 70

cement slurry injection system 水泥稀浆喷洒系统 430

cement truck 水泥运输车 437

center bolt, centre bolt 中心螺栓 139

center cover 罩 135

center electrode 中心电极 69

center hole 中心孔 125

center milling drum 中间铣刨鼓 423

center shaft 中心轴 369

center support bearing 中间支撑轴承 98

central articulated frame 中心铰(接)架 344,345

central console 中央控制台 108,315

central gear 太阳轮 100

centrifugal block 离心块 89

chain 链条 386

chain drive(equilibrium box) 链传动(平衡箱) 244,246

chain wheel drive 链轮驱动 385

chamfer 圆角,倒角 29

charging cover 进料口盖 410

charging opening 装料口 408

charging strainer 进料滤网 410

check nut 锁紧螺母 39,82,83

check ring 挡圈 153,245

check valve 单向阀 31,163,164,177,282

chips spreader 石屑洒布车 407

chromium-plated rail 镀铬的环片 34

chromium-plated ring, chrome-plated ring, chromed (piston) ring 表面镀铬气环 34

chute 料槽 386

circle 回转圈 255

circular exciter 圆周激振器 370

circulating pipe 循环管 413

circumferential fold line pattern 纵向折线花纹 124

clamp 固定夹 115

clamping plate 夹板 137

clamshell bucket 蚌壳式抓斗 186

classical(conventional)ignition system 传统线圈点火系统 67

clean gas 净气 398

clean up bucket 清扫铲斗 186

clean water reservoir 清水池 397

cleaning diesel box 清洗柴油箱 417

clinometer 倾斜仪 252

closed ring 工作状态环 32

453

clutch 离合器 79,312
clutch cover 离合器盖 89,91
clutch cylinder body 离合器油缸体 106
clutch driven plate 离合器从动盘 90
clutch driving plate 离合器主动盘 106
clutch drum 离合器从动鼓 106
clutch gear 离合器齿轮 79
clutch master cylinder 离合器主缸 91
clutch operation 离合器操纵机构 91
clutch operation(hydraulic) 离合器液压操纵机构 91
clutch operation(mechanical) 离合器机械操纵机构 91
clutch pedal 离合器踏板 91,92
clutch pedal linkage 离合器踏板拉杆 91
clutch plate 离合器板 75
clutch plate hub 从动盘(轮)毂 89,102,119
clutch release cable 离合器分离拉索 91
clutch release cylinder 离合器工作缸 89
clutch rod-operated mechanism 离合器杠杆操纵机构 92
clutch shaft 离合器轴 89
coal U-blade 煤炭推移专用 U 形铲 292

coarse filter 粗滤器 89
coarse oil filter 机油粗滤器 26
coated fully faced ring 表面全镀环 34
coated ring 有镀层环 34
coil,ignition coil 点火线圈 67
coil spring loaded beveled edge oil control ring 螺旋弹簧加压倒角油环 34
coil spring loaded double beveled oil control ring 螺旋弹簧加压双倒角油环 34
coil(spring) loaded slotted oil control ring 螺旋弹簧加压开槽油环 34
cold aggregate belt conveyer and weighing system 冷骨料带式输送机及称量系统 379
cold aggregate bins and feeder 冷骨料储仓及给料器 378,379
cold bin 料仓 379,380,381
cold feed gate 闸门 379,380,381
cold planer 冷铣刨 230
cold-starting injector 低温启动喷油器 64
collapsible patrol sign with amber rotating lights 折叠式黄色旋转灯警示标志 440
collector ring 集电环 82
collet 夹头 391
column crane(tower crane) 塔式起重机 8
combination monitor 综合监视器 178

combination spindle and anchor plate 带锚定板的转向节 155
combination valves 组合阀块 117
combined switch 组合开关 360
combined vibratory roller 组合式振动压路机 343
combustion air turbo blower 燃气涡轮鼓风机 422,423,424
combustion chamber 燃烧室 422,423,424
combustion flight 燃烧区叶片 403,405
combustion temperature 燃烧温度 53
combustion zone flight 燃烧区叶片 382,383
command pulse 指令脉冲 58
commercial-vehicle tire tread 商用车胎面 124
common-rail(fuel)injection system 共轨燃油喷射系统(蓄压气原理) 58
common rail 共轨,共用油轨 57,58
commutator 换向器 81
compactor 压实机械 6
compact(temporary) spare tire 紧凑型备胎,应急备胎 123
companion flange 结合凸缘 99
compensation valve 补偿阀 144
compensator 胀缩件 382
component card 元件板 82
compressed air pipe 压缩空气管路 163
compressing apparatus (电刷架)压紧装置 82
compression bolt 压紧螺栓 23
compression nut 压紧螺母 144
compression spring 压缩弹簧 113
compressor 空气压缩机 164
concave head(top,crown,roof) 凹顶 31
concentrated combustion preheater 集中燃烧式加热机 422
concrete machinery 混凝土机械 13
concrete mixer truck 混凝土搅拌车 14
concrete mixing plant 混凝土搅拌设备 14
concrete placing boom 混凝土布料机 14
condenser bracket 电容器架 82
conditioning flight 调整叶片 405,403
conductive glass 导体玻璃 69
cone crusher 圆锥式碎石机 5
cone spring 锥形弹簧 136
conformable rail 贴合环片 34
conical bearing 圆锥轴承 102
conical roller bearing 锥形滚柱轴承 114
connecting hose 连接管 389
connecting plate 接合板 102
connecting rod 连杆 22,26,35,134,159,214

455

connecting rod bearing cap 连杆盖 22

connecting rod bearing shell 连杆轴瓦 23,35

connecting rod bolt 连杆螺栓 35

connecting rod cap 连杆大头盖 35

connecting rod nut 连杆螺母 35

connecting rod shank 连杆杆身 35

connection shaft 中间轴 76

console 仪表控制台 175

contact 触点 67,81

contact breaker 断电器 67

contact disc 触板 80

contact disc, starting swith 电磁开关触板 81

continuous drum mixing plant 连续滚筒式搅拌设备 376,383

continuous flight auger drilling machine 长螺旋钻机 9

continuous wall grab 连续墙抓斗 9

contour head (top, crown, roof) 异形顶 31

control arm 调节臂 48

control chamber 控制室 57

control console 操作台 417

control fork 调节叉 48

controller 控制器 252,398

control lever 拨杆,控制杆,控制杠杆 47,49,50,96

control panel 控制面板 422,424

control pedal 操纵踏板 175

control pinion 调节齿圈 45,48

control plunger 控制柱塞 57

control rack （供油量）调节齿杆 45,48,49,50,51,52

control rod 调节拉杆 48

control sleeve （油量）调节套筒,控制套筒 45,47,48

control solenoid （高压泵）控制电磁线圈 57

control spring 控制弹簧 55,57

control system 控制系统 379

control valve 控制阀 176

conventional nozzle 普通喷嘴 58

conventional section tire 普通断面轮 123

converter housing 变矩器壳 104

conveying skip 运料小车 396

coolant pump seal 水封 74

coolant pump 水泵 74

coolant-temperature sensor 水温传感器 64

cooling fan 风扇 73

cooling gallery, cooling passage 冷却槽（通道） 31

cooling jacket 冷却罩 382

cooling system 冷却系统 71,283

cord ply, plies, ply 帘布层 123

cord 帘线 123

core 芯部 72

cotter pin 开口销 245

counter-rotating torque converter 反转型液力变矩器 107

counterweight 配重 214,243

coupling 联轴器,联轴节 393,

394,415
coupling flange 连接盘 119
coupling head control 车制动接头控制 164
coupling head supply 拖车制动接头供气 164
cover board 盖板 415
cover plate 盖板 153
cover sheet 护板 70
CPS=Camshaft Position Sensor 凸轮轴位置传感器 58
crack pouring machine 灌缝机 11
crank 曲柄 37
crank angle sensor, CKP sensor = Crankshaft Position Sensor 曲轴转角(位置)传感器 53
crank connecting rod mechanism 曲柄连杆机构 27
crank link mechanism 曲柄连杆机构 379
crank pin 曲柄销 37
crank pulley 曲轴带轮 22
crankshaft front end 曲轴前端 37
crankshaft gear 曲轴齿轮 79
crankshaft pulley 曲轴带轮 37
crankshaft timing pulley 曲轴定时带轮 22
crank shaft 曲轴 22,26,36,76
crank web 曲柄臂 37
crawler crane 覆带起重机 8
crawler dozer frame 推土机机架 128,129,291
crawler dozer operation mechanism 履带推土机工作机构 291
crawler hydraulic drill rig 覆带式全液压凿岩钻车 5
crawler steering axle 履带车辆转向桥 118
crawler 履带,履带式车辆 108,127,313,315
cross, cross spider 十字轴 99
cross-pins pivot 十字轴 354
cross assembly 十字轴总成 99
cross axle 横轴 102,119
cross sail 横梁 128
cross slope sensor 横坡传感器 327
crown adjustor 路拱调节器 419
crown control device 拱度调节装置 311
crushing & screening equipment 联合碎合设备 6
cup 皮碗,皮圈 151
cup depth 杯深 31
cup(dish)head(top,crown,roof) 杯形顶 31
cushion block 垫块 156
cushion pad 缓冲垫 388
cutters and rotor assembly 刀具与拌和转子组件 435
cutting edge 切削刃,铲刀刃 175,279
C-washer C形垫圈 151
cyclic flow pipe 循环流动管道 409
cyclone dust collection collector 旋

风集尘筒 397
cyclone dust filter 旋风式除尘器 397
cylinder 油缸,汽缸 158,388
cylinder block 汽缸体,机体 22,26
cylinder body 缸筒,缸体,油缸缸体 151,153,156
cylinder head 汽缸盖 22,26
cylinder head cover 汽缸盖罩,气门室罩 23,26
cylinder head gasket 汽缸衬垫 23
cylinder ID sensor=cylinder identification sensor,cylinder detector 汽缸识别传感器 58
cylinder liner(cylinder sleeve) 汽缸套 27
cylinder liner 汽缸套 26
cylinder link 轮缸推杆 151
cylindrical spring 圆柱弹簧 136

D

D3 track rails D3(推土机)履带轨 332
damping spring 减振弹簧 387
DC rim=Drop Center rim 深槽轮辋 125
deceleration pedal 减速踏板 285
decentralized combustion preheater 分散燃烧式加热机 422
deep-tread tire 深胎面花纹轮胎 435
delivery truck 运料卡车 308
delivery valve,check valve 出油阀 47
delivery valve flute 出油阀切槽 46
delivery valve holder 出油阀紧座 45,46
delivery valve seat 出油阀座 45,46
delivery valve spring 出油阀弹簧 45,46
delivery valve volume reducer 减容体 46
delivery valve 出油阀 45,46,57
depth adjustment 厚度调节装置 311
diagonal tire,bias(ply)tire,cross-ply tire 斜交轮胎 123
dial plate 刻度盘 410
diaphragm 膜片 51,66,137
diesel electronic control system 柴油机电子控制系 53
diesel engine 柴油机,柴油发动机 24,87,173,284,422,423,424,428,435
diesel fuel tank 柴油箱 422,423,424
diesel tank 柴油箱 428,430
differential 差速器 312
differential bevel pinion 差速器小锥齿轮 101
differential gear 差速齿轮 107
differential housing 差速器壳 101
differential pressure gage 压差计 398
diffuser,venturi 喉管 61

directed exciter 定向激振器 370
direction knob 方向旋钮 316
direction of drum rotation 鼓转动方向 147
disc armature 衔铁盘 55,57
disc brake 盘式制动器 314
discharge box 卸料箱 382,383
discharge chute 卸(溜)料槽 379,380,382,386
discharge gate 放料门,卸料(尘)闸门 388,395,396,397
discharging zone flights 卸料区叶片 382
dish piston 皿形(顶)活塞 31
disk brake 盘式制动器 161,163
distributer motor 分料器马达 419
distributer screw ground clearance adjusting hand wheel 分料器螺旋离地高度调节手轮 419
distributing pipe lifter hand wheel 洒布管升降手轮 414
distributing pipe 洒布管 413
distributing valve group 分配阀组 177
distributor auger 螺旋分料器 427
distributor cam 分电器凸轮 67
distributor cap 分电器盖 67
distributor motor 分料器马达 420
distributor plunger, distributor-pump 分配柱塞 47
distributor rotor 分火头 67
distributor-type injection pump 分配式喷油泵 47

distributor 分电器 23,64
ditching bucket 挖沟铲斗 185
diverter 转向器 247
divide the water pipe 分水管 71
double action steering clutch 双作用转向离合器 119
double check valve 双单向阀 162
double drum vibratory compactor (tandem vibratory roller) 双钢轮振动压路机(串联式振动压路机) 6
double flange track roller 双边支重轮 135
double gear pump for steering and vibration 转向及振动用双联齿轮泵 346
double pipeline air boost brake system 双管路空气增压制动系统 163
double reduction planetary final drive 双级行星减速最终驱动装置 220,221
double shaft paddle mixer 双轴浆叶式搅拌器 418
double speed valve 双速阀 177
drag conveyer 刮板输送器 311,312
drag drive motor 刮板驱动马达 311
drag link, drag rod 直拉杆 111
drag plate 刮板 311
drag rod, drag link, pull-rod 拉杆 50

drag slat conveyor　拖挂板式输送机　424
drain cock　排气阀　162
drain fitting　回油接头　59
drain pipe　排水管　397
drain plug　放水阀（塞），放油（螺）塞　71,72,76,134,411,412
drain pulley　放油螺塞　23,26,27
drive axle　驱动桥　244
drive axle housing　驱动桥壳　100
drive circle　驱动回转圈　256
drive disk　驱动盘　75
drive gear　驱动齿轮　81,84,85
drive hub　驱动轮毂　244
drive motor　驱动马达　435
driven axle　从动桥　121
driven chain wheel　从动链轮　386
driven gear　（机油泵）从动齿轮　77
driven plate　从动盘　85,89,90,102,119
driven plate hub　从动轮毂　90
driver's seat　驾驶员座椅　175
drive shaft length　传动轴特征长度　99
drive shaft　驱动轴，传动轴　47,87,244
drive sprocket　驱动（链）轮　16,127,279
drive sprocket cover　（驱动轮）罩　135
drive unit with two diesel engines　双柴油发动机驱动装置　430
driving axle　驱动桥　121,347,348

driving belt　传动带　387
driving cab　驾驶室　344,345
driving chain　传动链条　311
driving chain wheel　（传）驱动链轮，主动链轮　108,315,383,386
driving device　驱动装置　386,405
driving disc　主动片　102,119
driving gear　（机油泵,减速器）主动齿轮　77,79
driving gear ring　传动齿圈　382
driving hub　主动毂　102,119
driving mechanism　驱动机构　396
driving motor　驱动电机　393,394
driving plate　主动盘　85,89
driving shaft　主动轴,传动轴　75,409,415
driving shaft seat　传动轴座　409
driving tire　驱动轮胎　344,346,347,348
driving unit　驱动装置　382
driving wheel　驱动轮　87,313
drop center　深槽　125
drum　滚筒体　382
drum brake　鼓式（蹄式）制动器　147,150,161
drum shell　轮圈　355,356
drum traveling motor　滚轮行走马达　349
dry sleeve(liner)type　干式缸套　27
dry-type complete disc brake　干式全盘式制动器　156
dryer drum　烘干（滚）筒,干燥滚筒　378,384,386,397

dryer-mixer drum 干燥搅拌筒 379
drying zone flights 干燥区叶片 382,383
dual purpose tread pattern 混合花纹 124
dumparea dozer 垃圾场专用推土机 278
dump truck 自卸车 407
dump valve 卸荷阀 349
duplicate gear 双联齿轮 94
durable mobil-trac belt 坚韧的移动式履带 331
duramide bearing 嵌入耐磨支承垫 254
dust boot 防尘罩 155
dust collector 除尘装置 378,379
dust cover,seal 防尘罩 113
dust helmet 防尘罩 100
dust ring 防尘圈 152
dust shield 防尘罩 144

E

eaf spring bushing, spring bush(ing) 钢板弹簧衬套 139
earthmoving machinery 铲土运输机械 4
earthmoving work 土方工程 2
EBS channel module 电子制动系统信道组件 164
EBS connection EBS 信道连接 164
EBS trailer control module EBS 拖车控制模块 164
eccentric shaft 偏心轴 355,356,369
eccentric weight 偏心块 358,369
eccentric weight housing 偏心块壳体 358
eccentric weight shaft bearing 偏心轴轴承 358
ECU(Electronic Control Unit) 电(子)控(制)单元 57,64,164,178
edge, rib 肋条 70
edge-type filter 缝隙式滤清器 59
edge filter 缝隙式滤清器 43,44
EGR flow 排气再循环气流 53
EGR valve EGR 阀,排气再循环阀 53
elastic plate 弹性板 218
elastic washer 弹性垫圈 83,85
electrical connection 电插头 65
electrical governor 电子调速器 285
electrical junction box 电子接线盒 332
electrical motor 电机 380
electrical system 电气系统 214
electric control system 电控系统 108,315
electric fuel pump 电动燃油泵 64
electric motor 电动机 385,387
electric overnight heating 通宵电加热器 442
electric pole bush(ing) 电极衬套 70

electric starter 启动电机 80
electromagnetic vibrating feeder 电磁振动式给料器 380
electromagnetic vibrator 电磁振动器 380
electronically controlled unit injector common-rail injection system 电子控制式泵-喷嘴共轨喷射系统 56
electronically controlled unit-injector injection system 电子控制泵-喷嘴喷射系统 54
Electronic Brake System(EBS) 电子制动系统 164
electronic control system 电控系统 285
Electronic Control Unit(ECU) 电子控制单元,电子控制模块 53,55,165
electronic controlled steering/brake system 电子控制转向/制动系统 285
electronic controlled transmission 电子控制变速箱 285
electronic drive unit 电子驱动模块 53
electronic, programmable dozer control 推土机可编程电子控制器 286
electronic ripper control 松土器电子控制器 286
electronic-vacuum regulator valve 电子真空调节阀 53

element 滤芯 62
eliminator manual quick coupler 分离式手动快速连接器 186
emergency brake pushbutton 紧急制动按钮 360
emergency brake switch 紧急制动开关 316
emulsion box 乳液箱 417
emulsion hopper 乳化沥青仓 441
emulsion tank 乳化沥青罐 442
encloser 罩壳 386
end closure 端盖 100
end cover 后端盖 81
end yoke 接头叉 99
engine 发动机 103,108,176,178,215,216,219,243,246,279,283,285,291,311,312,313,314,315,344,345,346,350,422
engine air filter plugging 发动机空气滤清器堵塞 287
engine and torque converter 发动机和变矩器 280
engine and transmission system 发动机及传动系统 214
engine assembly 发动机总成 14
engine blok, block 汽缸体 27
engine controller 发动机控制器 285
engine crankshaft 发动机曲轴 104
engine diagnostics 发动机诊断 360
engine diagnostics switch 发动机诊断开关 360

engine function indicator 发动机功能指示 316
engine heating 发动机加热 360
engine holding frame 发动机托架 129
engine hood 发动机罩 214
engine idling 发动机怠速运行 360
engine load 发动机负荷 58
engine oil pressure 发动机润滑油压 285
engine speed and crank position sensor 发动机转速和曲轴位置传感器 58
engine speed 发动机转速 285
engine speed indicator 发动机转速指示表 316
engine supporting bracket 发动机支撑架 129
environmental engineering 环境工程 3
equalizer 平衡臂,平衡架(器) 92,128,138,160
equalizer shaft 平衡臂轴 92
equalizing beam 平衡梁 129,135,142
erected stringline leveling system 挂线调平系统 328
ether starting aid 乙醚启动装置 287
excavator ripper 松土齿 185
exciter diode 激励二极管 82
exciting winding 励磁绕组 82
exhaust braking cylinder 排气制动缸 164
exhaust cover 排气盖 410
exhaust fan 抽风机 397
exhaust gas flow 排气气流 53
exhaust outlet 废气出口 411
exhaust pipe 排气管 23,26,60
exhaust tube 抽风管 397
exhaust valve 排气门 22,38
expander 衬簧 34
expander/segment oil control ring, composite type oil control ring, steel strip composite type oil ring 钢片组合式油环,胀簧刮片式油环 34
expander-spacer 轴向-径向胀簧 34
externally locating type 外部定位式 99
extinguisher 灭火器 410

F

fan 风扇 22,26,71,82
fan blade 风扇叶片 73
fan shroud 风扇罩 73
fast downfall valve 快降阀 282
FB rim = Flat Base rim 平底轮辋 125
feed hole 供油孔 55,57
feed increment direction 增加供给方向 51
feed port 供油口 55
feed pump 输油泵 57
feeder box 加料箱 382

463

feeding zone flights　进料区叶片　382,383

fiber reinforced metal　纤维增强金属　31

fifth drive gear　五挡主动齿轮　94

fifth-sixth shift block　五、六挡拨块　96

fifth-sixth shift fork shaft　五、六挡拨叉轴　96

fifth-sixth shift fork　五、六挡拨叉　96

fifth speed driven gear　五挡被动齿轮　94

filer bowl　滤清器壳　78

filer cover　滤清器盖　78

filler auger conveyer　粉料螺旋输送器　390

filler bin　填料仓　417

filler cap　（机油）加油口盖　22

filler inlet　粉料入口　405

filler input pipe　粉料输入管　389

filler scale　粉料计量秤　390

filler storage silo　料仓　389

filler supply system　粉料供给装置　383

filler weigh hopper　粉料称量斗　390

filter　滤纸，滤清器　62,65,117,411,412

filter bag　滤袋　398

filter screen　过滤网　282

final drive　最终传动装置,终传动器　16,87,173,283

final reduction gear　终减速器,最终传动减速器　244,246,280

final reduction pinion　末级减速小齿轮　346

fire box　火箱　382

fire tube　火管　411

first-second shift block　一、二挡拨块　96

first-second shift fork shaft　一、二挡拨叉轴　96

first-second shift fork　一、二挡拨叉　96

first speed drive gear　一挡主动齿轮　94

first speed driven gear　一挡被动齿轮　94

first turbine shaft　第一涡轮轴　218

first turbine　第一涡轮　218

fixed blow lamp　固定喷灯　410

fixed brake disk　固定制动盘　156

fixed brake shoe abutment　制动蹄支承　147

fixed caliper　固定钳　155

fixed eccentric weight　固定偏心块　357,358

fixed foot stand　固定脚架　412

fixed milling drum　固定铣刨鼓　430

fixed short-circuiting ring　固定短路环　52

fixed supporting seat　（固定）支座　142

flange　凸缘　126

flange yoke 凸缘叉 99
flat head (top, crown, poof) 平顶 31
flat key 平键 131
flexible coupling 挠性联轴节 99
flexible (hydraulic) pipe 连接软管,软管 91,411
flexible rubber hose 软胶管 162
flexible universal joint 挠性万向节 99
float 浮子 60,61
float chamber (float bowl[美]) 浮子室 61
floater 浮子 391
floating caliper 浮钳 155
floating lever 浮动杠杆 50
floating oil seal 浮动油封 131,132,133
flow control valve 流量控制阀 247
fluid control system 流控系统 417
flyweight 提前器飞锤,飞锤 49,50
flyweight, centrifugal weight 提前器飞锤,离心重块 47
flyweight, timer flyweight 提前器飞锤 52
flywheel 飞轮 23,26,37,89,218
flywheel casing 飞轮盖 89
flywheel gear ring (主发动机)飞轮齿圈 36,79
folding tire 折叠轮胎 123
follower lever 随动杆 116
foot brake 脚制动器 164
foot brake valve 脚制动阀 162
footplate 踏板 311
forced batch mixing plant 强制间歇式搅拌设备 382
fork control mechanism 拨叉式油量调节机构 48
forked scrap grapple bucket 叉式杂物抓斗 231
forward drive gear 前进主动齿轮 94
forward driven gear 前进被动齿轮 94
forward gear shift clutch 前进挡离合器 246
(four gears) transmission （四挡）变速箱 313
fourth speed drive gear 四挡主动齿轮 94
fourth speed driven gear 四挡被动齿轮 94
four-wheel drive motor grader 四轮驱动自行式平地机 242
frame 车架,机架,支架 121,214,311,369,382,383,386,395,396,435
frame and suspension system 车架与悬挂系统 15
frame bearing 车架轴承 355
frame side member (rail) 纵梁 128,129
framework 机架 127
free eccentric weight 活动偏心块 357

465

free ring, unstressed ring 自由状态环 32
friction brake 摩擦片式制动器 147
friction drive wheel 摩擦式驱动轮 331
friction liner 摩擦衬片 156
friction lining, clutch facing 摩擦片 90
friction lining 制动衬片,摩擦片 147
friction pad 摩擦块 155
friction snap ring 摩擦卡环 153
friction wheel drive 摩擦轮驱动 385
front anchor pin 前支承销 157
front axle 前桥 15,103,116,214,215,216
front axle beam 前梁 114
front bracket 前支架 139
front brake disk 前制动盘 160
front cover 前盖 75,94,128,134
front cover of pump body 泵体前盖 415
front cross member (rail) 前横梁 129
front drive shaft 前传动轴 98
front drum 前轮 345
front frame 前车架,前机架 116,214,216,243,256,344,345,353,354
front housing 前端盖 82
front-mounted straight blade 前置直铲刀 262
front output shaft 前输出轴 106
front planetary gear set 前行星排 106
front sand/grit bin 前置砂石料箱 440
front scarifier 前置式松土器 262
front suspension 前悬架 121
front wheel 前轮 121,314
front wheel speed sensor 前轮速度传感器 165
front wheel steering cylinder 前轮转向油缸 247
front wheel tilt cylinder 前轮倾斜油缸 247
fuel control dial 燃料控制旋钮 285
fuel distributor 燃油分配器 64
fuel feed gallery 燃油供给油道 55
fuel feed pump 输油泵 26,42
fuel filter plugging 燃油滤清器堵塞 287
fuel filter 燃油滤清器 55,60,64
fuel fine 柴油细滤器 42
fuel gallery 油道 55,57
fuel injection pump camshaft 喷油泵凸轮轴 52
fuel inlet 进油口 66
fuel level 燃油液面高度 287
fuel pressure regulator 压力(燃油)调节器 64,66
fuel pump 燃油泵 60
fuel rail, fuel manifold, distributor rail

燃油轨　58
fuel return to tank　至燃油箱的回油　66
fuel shutoff solenoid　电磁断油阀　47
fuel supply　燃油供给　47
fuel system-gasoline injection　汽油喷射式燃油系统　63
fuel system　供油系统　42
fuel tank　汽油箱,燃料箱　42,54,57,58,60,64,176,409,411,412,422
fuel tank cap　油箱盖　411
fuel tank switch　油箱开关　408
fuel tank switch hand wheel　油箱开关手轮　408
full-ballstud　全球式球头销　113
full-flow(oil)filter　全流式(机油)滤清器　78
full hydraulic drive motor grader　全液压传动自行式平地机　242
full-load stop　全负荷限制器　49
full-skirt piston　全裙式活塞　31
full slipper piston,slipper (-skirt) piston　全拖板式活塞　29
fully bogied undercarriage　整体台车式行走机构　331

G

gap adjuster　(气门)间隙调节器　23
gas　气体　137
gas tank　燃气罐　428

gas liquid separating tank　气液分离罐　397
gasket　衬垫,密封垫　27,155
gasoline engine fuel system　汽油机供油泵　60
gasoline gauge(meter)　汽油表　60
gasoline starting engine　汽油启动机　79
gate　闸门　311
gear　齿轮　106,218,415
gearbox　变速箱　346,347,348
gearbox control valve　变速箱操纵阀　163
gear-box housing　变速箱壳体　106
gear-box input shaft　变速箱输入轴　106
gear-box output shaft　变速箱输出轴　106
gear box　齿轮箱　313
gear drive　齿轮驱动　385
gear feed pump　齿轮式输油泵　55
gear pump　齿轮泵　247
gear ring　齿圈　37
gearshift mechanism　换挡机构　96
gear shift pump　变速油泵　215
gear sleeve　齿套　106
general purpose bucket　通用铲斗　175
general purpose bucket with bolt-on-edge　螺栓紧固边刃通用铲斗　229
general purpose bucket with teeth　通用有齿铲斗　229

general purpose pick-up broom 通用收集式清扫 230
generating laser 激光发射器 252
generator for hot asphalt system 热沥青系统电机 430
glass wool 玻璃绒 410
glow plug 电热塞 53
glow tube 加热管 83
governor 调速器 42
governor drive 调速器驱动装置 47
governor lever mechanism (drive) 调速器杠杆机构 47
governor spring 调速(器)弹簧 47,49,50
grab bucket 抓斗 185
grader 平地机 407
grapple 抓斗 185
grease fitting, grease nipple 滑脂嘴,黄油嘴 113,134,353
grease retainer 润滑脂保持器 155
groove-bottom diameter 槽底直径 29
groove depth, depth of groove (活塞环)槽深 29
groove, tread groove, tire groove 花纹沟 123
groove width (活塞)槽高 29
grooving machine 开槽机 11
gross-pins articulated frame 十字轴式链接车架 354
ground electrode 旁电极 69
grouser 履带齿 279

guard plate 护板 128
guide 导向体 46
guide lever 导向杠杆 50
guide pillar 导柱 325
guide pin, locating pin 导销,导向销 152,155
guide plate 导板 245
guide ring 导环 81

H

half keystone ring 半梯(楔)形环 33
half-slipper piston 半拖板式活塞 31
hammer crusher 锤式碎石机 5
hand brake valve 手制动阀 162,164
hand pump 手压泵,手动泵 54,349
head, crown, top, roof 顶(部),头(部) 29
header 端板 72
heat dam 热坝,隔热槽 29
heat exchanger 散热器 107
heater and control coil 加热器和控制线圈 83
heater plug 电热塞 83
heating and air conditioning 可采暖空调 286
heating fire tube 加热火管 410
heating pipe 加热管 413
heating plenum 加热室 422,423
heating plenum with mixing device

带有搅拌装置的加热室　424
heating system　加热系统　409,411,428
heat-proof slot　隔热槽　31
heavy-duty axle　重型驱动桥　284
heavy duty dump truck　重型自卸车　4
heavy duty scrap grapple bucket　重型杂物抓斗　231
heavy duty trailer　重型拖挂装置　442
helical spline　螺旋花键　81,84
high peed piston motor　高速柱塞马达　219
high power switch　大功率开关　178
high pressure pipe connection　高压油管接头　43
high-pressure pump　高压泵　58
high-pressure sealing ring　高压密封　59
high pressure small spare tire　高压小型备胎　123
high-traction tread pattern　高牵引力胎面花纹　124
high-voltage connector　高压线接头　69
high voltage terminal　高压接线柱　68
hinge pin　销轴　245
hoisting machinery　起重机械　8
hold-down cup　(制动蹄)限位盘,压紧盘　151

hold-down pin　限位销,压紧销　151
hold-down spring　限位(压紧)弹簧　151
hold-in winding　保持线圈　80,81
hole type nozzle　孔式喷嘴　43
home head　圆顶　31
home height　圆顶高度,凸高　31
hopper　料斗　311
horizontal directional drilling machine　水平定向钻机　9
horizontal pin　水平销轴　353
horizontal pipe　横管　413
horizontal slot　水平切槽　29
hose connection on the emulsified asphalt tanker　乳化沥青罐车软管连接　433
hose connection on the water tanker truck　水罐车软管连接　433
hose　液压软管　220,221
hot aggregate bin　热骨料储仓　388,390
hot aggregate elevator　热骨料提升机　378,386
hot aggregate outlet　热骨料出口　405
hot aggregate screen and storage bin　热骨科筛分及储仓　378
hot aggregate storage silo　热料仓　384
hot aggregate weigh hopper　热骨料计量装置　378
hot asphalt injection system　热沥青

喷洒系统 430
housing 外壳,壳体 68,75,156
hub 啮合套毂 94
hub flange （从动盘）毂法兰 90
hump 凸峰 125
hump head (top, crown, roof), convex head(top, crown, roof), hump(convex)piston head (top, crown, roof) 凸顶 31
hump rim 凸峰轮辋 125
hydraulic breaker 液压破碎锤 187,230
hydraulic compensating axle suspension 液压平衡悬架 140
hydraulic crusher 液压破碎器 186
hydraulic cylinder 液压缸 177
hydraulic diaphragm accumulator 液力膜片蓄能器 137
hydraulic filter 液压过滤器 176, 220,221
hydraulic lifter 液压升降机 440
hydraulic line 液压管路 91
hydraulic lockout 液压锁 287
hydraulic motor 液压马达 312
hydraulic oil cooler 液压油冷却器 220,221
hydraulic oil filter 液压油过滤器 287
hydraulic oil tank 液压油箱 247, 282,332,422,423,424,430
hydraulic pile-driver 全液压打桩机 9
hydraulic pipeline 液压管路 174

hydraulic piston 液压柱塞 58
hydraulic power pack, self retracting hose reel, hose, oil cooler 液压动力组件,自缩回软管卷盘,软管,油冷却器 440
hydraulic pressure 液压 155
hydraulic pump 液压泵 173,176, 177,178
hydraulic snow wing 液压测向除雪铲 262
hydraulic steering control unit 液压转向器 117
hydraulic steering device 液压转向器 347,348
hydraulic system 液压系统 15,254
hydraulic tank 液压（油）箱 176, 252,349,350,351
hydromechanical transmission motor grader 液力机械传动自行式平地机 242
hydromechanical transmission system 液力机械传动系统 103
hydrostatic drive system 静液驱动系统 283
hydrostatic pressure pile drive 液压静力压桩机 10
hystat power train system 静液传动系统 220
hystat pumps hose 液压泵 220,221

I

I/C: intercooler 中冷器 53

idle-mixture adjusting screw　怠速调节螺钉　64,64
idler arm　随动臂　111,113
idle spring, idling spring　怠速弹簧　50
ignition box　点火器　360
ignition coil　点火线圈　64,68
ignition distributor　分电器　67
ignition nozzle　点火喷头　382
ignition switch　点火开关　64,67,165
impact crusher　反击式碎石机　5
impact roller　冲击式压路机　343
impacting rammer　冲击夯　6
impeller brake　泵轮制动器　107
impeller clutch torque converter　泵轮离合液力变矩器　284
inboard slip drive shaft　内侧滑动传动轴　98
indicator lamps for light(dipped/distance)　车灯指示灯(近光/远光)　360
infrared thermometer　红外温度计　360
injected timing　喷射正时　53
injected volume　喷射体积,喷油量　53
injection pump　喷油泵　26,42
injection-pump camshaft　喷油泵凸轮　50,49
injection system for emulsified asphalt　乳化沥青喷洒系统　430
injection timing device　喷油提前器　42

injector　喷油器　26,42,64,65
injector control solenoid　喷油器控制电磁线圈　57
injector control valve　喷油器控制阀　57
injector for common rail injection system　共轨燃油喷射系统喷油器　59
injector solenoid valve　喷油器电磁阀　58
inlaid ring　填充环　34
inlet adaptor　进油管接头　43,44
inlet oil port　进油孔　75
inlet port　进(油)口　57,77
inlet tank　进水室　72
inner bearing　内轴承　155
inner bearing housing　内轴承座　355
inner cap　内盖　156
inner cover　(支重轮)内盖　131
inner drum　内滚筒　405
inner liner　气密层　123
inner tie rod　内横拉杆　113
inner tie rod end(joint)　横拉杆内接头　113
inner tube, tube　内胎　123
input clutch　输入端离合器　107
input shaft　输入轴　94
input signal　输入信号　57
inside and outside edges chamfered ring　内外棱倒角环　34
inside edges chamfered ring　内棱倒

471

角环 34
inside equalizer 内平衡臂 141
inspection hole （制动衬块磨损）检查孔,检视孔 148,155
instrumentation console 仪表盘 214
insulating cap 绝缘盖 68
insulating jacket 保温套 391
insulating layer (glass wool) 保温隔热层(玻璃棉) 408
insulation 绝缘体 83
insulator 绝缘子,绝缘体 68,69
insulator shim 绝缘垫 83
intake(air) heater 进气加热器,预热器 53
intake air flow 进气气流 53
intake air temperature 进气温度 53
intake air temperature sensor 进气温度传感器 53
intake-manifold connection 进气歧管接头 66
intake manifold 进气歧管 61
intake shutter 进气活门 53
intake tube 进气管 23,26,60
intake valve 进气门,流通阀 22,38,61,144
integral-pin articulated frame 整体铰销式铰接车架 352
integral power steering gear 整体式动力转向器 111
integrated frame motor grader 整体机架式平地机 242

interlock ball 互锁钢球 95
interlock plug 互锁销,互锁柱销 95,96
intermediate proportioning bin 中间配料仓 428
intermediate shaft 中间轴 94
intermediate shaft gear 中间轴齿轮 106
internal bevel bottom ring 内上棱阶梯切槽环 34
internal bevel top ring 内上棱斜切环 34
internal expanding drum brake 内胀型鼓式制动器 147
internally locating type 内部定位式 99
internal step bottom ring 内下棱阶梯切槽环 34
internal step top ring 内上棱阶梯槽环 34
internal vibration absorber 内置式扭振减振器 99
in-the-hole drill 潜孔钻机 5
invar insert 恒范钢镶片,殷钢镶片 31
invar strut piston 恒范钢镶片活塞 31
iron core 铁芯 67
isolate heating valve 隔离式加热阀 440
isolating plate 隔板 119,388,410

J

jaw crusher 鄂式碎石机 5

jerk fuel injection pump 柱塞式喷油泵 45
jet grouting drilling machine 旋喷钻机 9
joint bearing 关节轴承 353,354
joint bolt 连接螺栓 323
joint gear 接合齿轮 79
joint housing 接头壳 113
joint pin 铰销 140
joint slack 联轴器 45
joint with internal notch 带内切口开口 34
joint with side notch 带侧切口开口 34
joystick control 操纵控制手柄 175

K

key 键 415
key bolt 带键螺栓 156
keystone ring, wedge section ring, full keystone ring 梯（楔）形环 33
kingpin 转向销 114

L

ladder stand 爬梯 389
laminated(iron) core 层叠铁芯 52
land clearance 岸隙 29
land diameter, ring land diameter 环岸直径 29
landfill blade 垃圾填理铲刀 292
large asphalt triple valve 沥青大三通阀 409
large bevel gear 大锥齿轮 102
large coil spring 大螺旋弹簧 102
large locker and paddle locks 大电路开关箱 440
large paver 大型摊铺机 309
large type dozer 大型推土机 278
large type excavator 大型挖掘机 170
large type shovel(face excavator) 大型正铲挖掘机 170
large type wheel loader 大型轮式装载机 211
laser grade control system 激光找平系统 252
laser leveling system 激光调平系统 328
laser pickoff 激光接收器 252
lash adjusting device 间隙调整装置 151
LCD panel LCD显示面板 316
leading shoe, primary shoe 领蹄 151,147
leading shoe and lining, leading shoe assembly 领蹄总成 151
leaf soring 钢板弹簧 136
leaf spring, laminated spring 钢板弹簧 139
leaf spring pin, spring pin, spring bolt 钢板弹簧销 139
leaf-spring rear suspension 钢板弹簧式后悬架 139
leaf spring suspension 板簧式悬架

138

leak 泄漏回油 58
leak-off connection 回油接头 43,44
leak-off pipe 溢流回油管 42
left and right disc brake 左、右盘式制动器 118
left and right final drive 左、右终传动 118
left and right milling drum 左右铣刨鼓 423
left and right steering clutch 左、右转向离合器 118
left and right swing push rod 洒布管左右摆动推杆 414
left axial plunger motor 左轴向柱塞马达 108,315
left basic screed 左基本段熨平板 323
left brake 左制动器 281
left drag and steering double-link pump 左刮板和转向双联泵 314
left electromagnetic valve 左电磁阀 327
left feeder and auger drive pump 左侧送料器与螺旋器驱动泵 333
left final reduction gear 左最终传动 281
left horizontal pipe triple valve 左横管三通阀 413
left hydraulic extension screed 左液压伸缩熨平板 325
left junction bracket 左连接支架 355,356
left junction plate 左连接板 355
left leveling cylinder 左调平油缸 327
left steering cylinder 左转向油缸 116
left towed arm 左牵引臂 327
left track link 左链轨节 130
left variable pump 左变量泵 108,315
level detector 料位器 388
leveling reference 调平基准 327
lever 杠杆 158
lever arm 杠杆臂 51
lever pivot 作动杠杆支枢 151
lever return spring 作动杠杆回位弹簧 151
lever switch 杠杆操纵开关 178
LH cluster 左仪表盘 360
lift kickout/lower kickout 提升/下降解除 287
lifting cylinder 提升油缸 311,327
lifting eye, hoisting eye 吊眼 129
lifting gear 升降装置 422
light material bucket with bolt-on edges 螺栓紧固边刃轻质材料铲斗 229
limiting quick-release valve 极限快放阀 162
liner 衬管,内衬 99
lining fork 分离叉 89
lining plate 衬板 393,394,432
lining rivet 衬片铆钉 90

link 接头 92
linkage 连接杆 158
liquid cooling system 水冷系统 71
locating (adjusting) shim （主动小齿轮）调整垫圈 101
locating pin(plug) 定位销 22,35,37,43
locating plate 定位板 353
locating screw 定位螺钉 45
locating shim 调整垫圈 85
lock bolt （钢板销）锁止螺栓 139
lock nut 锁紧螺母 115,132,353
locknut 锁止螺母 41
lock pin 锁销 84
lock plate 锁片 37,99
lock ring 卡环 85
locking collar 锁环 100
locking lip, locating lug (tang) 定位凸键 35
lock-up clutch 闭锁离合器 107
lockup 闭锁离合器 285
log/sorting grapple 木材堆放抓斗 229
longitudinal slope sensor 纵坡传感器 327
loop flush valve 环形冲洗阀 349
lorry-mounted crane 随车起重机 8
low section tire 低断面轮胎 123
low speed piston motor 低速柱塞马达 219
lower back plate 下后板 128
lower cover 下盖 353

lower mounting 下支承 144
lower rocker arm 下摇臂 158
low-voltage terminal, primary terminal 低压接线柱 67,68
lubrication fitting 润滑加注口,黄油嘴 99
lubrication system 润滑系统 76
lubricator fitting 黄油嘴 74

M

machine controller 机器控制器 332
machine security system 机器安全系统 287
magnet core 磁铁芯 59
magnetic core 铁芯 68
magnetic(drain)plug 磁性放油塞 27,89
magnetic-field terminal 磁场接线柱 82
magnetic-pole 磁极 81,82
main bearing shell(upper, lower) 主轴承(上、下)轴瓦 36
main bevel gear 主传动锥齿轮 280
main clutch 主离合器 87,88,346
main clutch pump 主离合油泵 87
main controller 主控制器 327
main delivery pipe 输油总管 413
main discharge nozzle 主喷管 61
main drive 中央传动,主传动 87,100
main frame 主机架 16,173

main jet 主量孔 61
main journal 主轴颈 37
main leaf 主片 139
main oil gallery (channel,line) 主油道 31,76
main pin 主销 130
main pin brass 主销铜衬 130
main relay 主继电器 64
mainshaft bearing cap 主轴承盖 36
main spring and auxiliary spring,leaf spring and auxiliary spring （载货车）主、副钢板弹簧 136
main spring leaf 钢板弹簧主片 139
main spring 主钢板弹簧 139
main transmission 主传动器,主变速器 118,312
main triple valve 主三通阀 413
major thrust face 主承推面 29
manpower brake system 人力制动系统 161
master cylinder 制动主缸 165
master cylinder assembly 制动主缸总成 160
material flow 材料流 427
material seal 封料 70
maximum-speed stop 最高转速限制器 49
measuring coil 测量线圈 52
mechanical floating averaging beam 机械式浮动平均梁 328
mechanical shutoff device 机械式断油装置 47
mechanical transmission system 机械传动系统 87,417
medium dozer 中型推土机 278
medium paver 中型摊铺机 309
medium type excavator 中型挖掘机 170
medium type wheel loader 中型轮式装载机 211
meshing spring 啮合弹簧 81
metal plate jacketing 金属板套 68
metal rod 金属杆 69
metal screen 金属网 62
microprocessor-controlled pump for the emulsified asphalt injection 微机控制乳化沥青喷洒泵 433
microprocessor-controlled pump for the water injection 微机控制喷水泵 433
middle driving axle 中间驱动桥 243
middle driving shaft 中间传动轴 355
middle gear, translating gear, mid-gear （减速器）中间齿轮 79
middle transmission gearbox 中间传动齿轮箱 313
milling depth control 铣刨深度控制装置 423
milling drum 铣刨鼓 431
milling tool 铣刀 431
mineral filler storage silo and supply system 粉料储仓及供给装置

378,379

mini type excavator 微型挖掘机 169

mini type loader 微型装载机 211

minor thrust face 次承推面(传递小侧压力面) 29

mixed material conveyer 成品料输送机 379

mixed material outlet 成品料出口 405

mixed material storage silo 成品料储仓 378,379,395,396

mixer 搅拌器 378,390,427,428,417

mixing arm 搅拌臂 393,394,432

mixing paddle 搅拌桨叶 393,394,405,432

mixing shaft 搅拌轴 393,394,432

mixing system 拌和系统 418

mixing tower 搅拌楼 395,396

mixing trough 搅拌筒体 393,394,432

mixing zone flight 搅拌区叶片 383

mobile crane 汽车起重机 8

moldboard 铲刀板 243

molybdenum-filled inlay ring, molybdenum coated ring, molybedeum ring 表面填(镶)钼环,喷钼环 34

monitor 工况监视器 175

monitor panel 监控仪表盘 285

monitoring display system 监控显示系统 286

monitoring system 监控系统 287

mounting bracket 安装支架 113

movable core 可动铁芯 80

movable supporting seat （活动）支座 142

moving short-circuiting ring 移动短路环 52

MS tire＝Mud and Snow tire, all-season tire 泥雪地轮胎,全天候轮胎 123

M&S tire tread 泥雪地用胎面 124

mud bucket 挖泥斗 186

mudguard 挡泥板 214

multichannel conversion valve 多路换向阀 247

multifunctional vehicle 多功能工程车 12

multi-leaves soring 多片式钢板弹簧 136

multi-piece oil ring 多件式油环 34

multi-piece oil-cooled piston 多件式油冷活塞 31

multi terrain loader 多功能装载机 212

N

Napier ring, Napier scraper ring 鼻型环、纳尔比环 33

needle 针阀 44,65

needle bearing 滚针轴承 100

needle body 针阀体 57

477

needle roller and bearing cup　滚针和轴承杯　99
needle valve　喷油器针阀,针阀　43,55,57,61
negative plate　负极板　70
negative twist type　反扭曲型　34
neutral-start parking brake lever　空挡启动停车制动手柄　220,221
nipple　管接头　74
Ni-resist insert　耐蚀高镍铸铁镶圈　31
nozzle　喷嘴　385,392,413,422
nozzle body　针阀体　43,44,55
nozzle holder　喷油器体　43,44
nozzle holder body　喷油嘴体　43
nozzle pintle　喷油嘴轴针　59
nozzle(retaining)nut　喷油嘴固定螺母　43,44
nozzle spring　喷油嘴弹簧　59
nozzle tip　喷油嘴尖端　57
nut　螺母,(储油缸筒)螺母,(固定)螺母　36,41,83,85,126,144,245

O

off centre anchor pin　偏心支承销　148,149
oil baffle　挡油罩板,挡油圈　23,37
oil cleaner　机油滤清器　26,76
oil(control) ring　油环　32
oil cooler-fitting　机油冷却器接头　72
oil cooler　液压油冷却器,(油)冷却器　176,177,314,349,350
oil cylinder piston　油缸活塞　152
oil drain　放油口　358
oil drain hole　放油孔　128
oil drain (return) hole, oil return passage　回油孔　29
oil duct　油道　76
oil enclosed, multiple disc brake　封闭湿式多片制动器　284
oil filler　加油口　412
oil filling port　加油孔　128
oil filter　滤油器　177,282
oil gallery　油道　41
oil gas ratio controlling valve　油气比控制阀　385
oil hole　油孔　35
oil inlet　进油口　78
oil inlet pipe　进油管　410,413
oil inlet valve　进油阀门　411
oil level sight gauge　油面观测计　358
oil nozzle　机油喷嘴　31
oil outlet　出油口　78
oil outlet pipe　出油管　412,413
oil outlet switch　出油开关　411,412
oil pan　油底壳　23,26,27,76
oil pipe　油管　152,163
oil plug　油塞　22,131,132
oil pressure brake　油压张开式制动器　149
oil pressure gauge　油压表　411
oil pump　(机)油泵　23,26,76,77,117

oil quantity controlling valve 油量控制阀 385
oil reservoir 油箱 117
oil retaining disk 挡油盘 94
oil ring 油环 23
oil ring groove(slot) 油环槽 28
oil rule 油标尺 23
oil seal 油封 40,41,94,100,101,114,115,144
oil seal ring 油封环 102,152
oil sealed cap 油封盖 132
oil sealed seat 油封座 132
oil strainer （机油）集滤器 23,26,76
oil-water separator 油水分离器 163,164,42
one-piece drive shaft 单根式传动轴 98
one(single)-piece rim, normal rim 一件式轮辋 125
one-way clutch 单向离合器 80
one-way clutch gear 单向离合器齿轮 218
one-way clutch roller 单向离合器滚柱 218
one way orifice 单向孔 57
one-way snow plow 单向除雪铲（犁） 262
one-way stabilized flow divider valve 单路稳定分流阀 117
one-way valve, non-return valve, check valve 单向阀 75,117
operating console 操纵台 344,345

operating lever 操纵杆 157
operational pump 工作油泵 103,215
operator cab 驾驶室 176
operator's seat 驾驶座椅 311
operator's station 操纵台 311
operator presence 操作员在场指示 287
operator seat 操作员座位 360
operator station 操作台 286,422,423,424,428
orifice 量孔 58
orifice plate 挡板 159
oscillating drum 振荡滚筒 369
oscillating steering axle 摆动转向桥 243
oscillation 振荡 370
oscillation motor 振荡马达 369
oscillation roller 振荡轮 369
O-sealing ring O形密封圈 131,132
other sensor signal 其他传感器信号 53
outboard feeder drive motor 外侧送料器驱动马达 333
outboard slip drive shaft 外侧滑动传动轴 98
outer bearing housing 外轴承座 355
outer case of seal 油封外壳 144
outer cover （支重轮）外盖 131
outer shell 外筒 405
outer tie rod 外横拉杆 113

479

outer tie rod end(joint) 横拉杆外接头 113
outlet port 出油口 77
outlet tank 出水室 72
output shaft 输出轴 94,104
output shaft gear 输出轴齿轮 106
output terminal 输出接线柱 82
outside edges chamfered ring 外棱倒角环 34
outside equalizer 外平衡臂 141
over-all length of component 外延长度 99
overflow gallery 溢流油道 55
overflow pipe 溢流管 391,409,410
overflow throttle 溢流节流孔 47
overflow valve 回油阀,溢流阀 55,282
overhead vibrator 上置式振动器 387
overload valve 过载阀 282
over-sized aggregate discharge chute 过大料溢料管道 384
overslung (spring) type, overhung spring type 上置板簧式 138
oxygen sensor 氧传感器 64

P

pad foot roller 凸块式压路机 343
paint line marker 划线机 11
pallet fork 货叉 230
paper element 纸质滤芯 78
parallel guide cap 导板盖 133

parallelogram steering linkage 平行四边形转向传动机构 113
parking brake 驻车制动器 87,103,159,215,287
parking brake cable 驻车制动器拉索(线) 151,160
parking brake lever 驻车制动杠杆,驻车制动操纵杆 151,160
parking brake pipeline 驻车制动管路 164
parking brake strut(pushrod) 驻车制动推杆 151
passenger-car tire tread 轿车胎面,乘用车胎面 124
patented Venturi feed system 专利文氏供料系统 442
pavement breaker 路面破碎机 13
pavement heating repairing vehicle 路面加热修补车 11
pavement high pressure cleaning vehicle 路面高压清洗车 13
pavement machinery 路面机械 7
pavement maintenance machinery 路面养护机械 11
pavement recycler 道路再生机 421
pavement repairing vehicle 路面修补车 11
paver with hydraulie extension screed 熨平板液压伸缩式摊铺机 308
paver with mechanical extension screed 熨平板机械加宽式摊铺机 308

paving control handle 摊铺控制手柄 316
paving operation control key 摊铺操作控制键 316
paving screed 摊铺熨平板 427,428
pawl 棘爪 91,158
pedal shaft 踏板轴 91
pedal-to-equalizer rod 踏板到平衡臂的拉杆 92
pig-tail 紧缩端 136
pile driving machinery 桩工机械 9
pilot seat 驾驶座椅 292
pin 销,销子,芯杆 126,141,157
pin boss 活塞销孔凸台 29
pin bracket 销轴套 353,354
pin cotter 横销 415
pin hole,gudgeon(piston,wrist)hole 活塞销孔 29
pinion flange 主动齿轮法兰 101
pin pivot 铰销轴 353
pin rod 销轴 153
pin sleeve 销子垫套 415
pintle type nozzle 轴针式喷嘴 44
pintle 轴针 65
pipe （加）油管 60,102,119,128
pipe joint 管接头 152
pipe mounting plate 管座板 398
piston 活塞 102,119,134,137,144,151,153,155,156,158,159,22,26,28
piston accumulator 活塞式蓄能器 137

piston back spring 活塞回位弹簧 153,156
piston head 活塞顶 29
piston head with combustion chamber 带燃烧室的活塞顶 31
piston insert 活塞环槽镶圈 31
piston pin 活塞销 22
piston pin bush(ing) 活塞销衬套 35
piston pin,gudgeon pin,wrist pin,pin 活塞销 29
piston pump 柱塞液压泵 219
piston relief 活塞凹坑 31
piston rod 活塞杆 144
piston seal ring 活塞密封圈 156
piston skirt 活塞裙部 28
piston sleeve 活塞套筒 156
pitch angle sensor 仰角传感器 285
pitman arm,drop arm,steering gear arm,steering lever 转向摇臂 113
pitman arm 转向摇臂,转向垂臂 111,116
pivot nut 支枢螺母 151
planet carrier 行星轮架 100
planet pin 行星齿轮轴 100
planetary drive 行星传动装置 332
planetary gear 行星齿轮 100,101
planetary gear reducer 行星齿轮减速器 314
planetary gear set 行星排 107
planetary gear set for reverse gear

481

and retarder 倒挡和减速器行星排 107
planetary power shift transmission 行星动力换挡变速箱 284,291
planetary reduction gear 行星减速器 280,348
plug screw 螺塞 100
plunger 柱塞 45,48,55,57
plunger armature 柱塞衔铁 57
plunger body 柱塞体 55
plunger spring 柱塞弹簧 45
plunger support guide 柱塞支承导管 55
pneumatic tire compactor (pneumatic tyred roller) 轮胎压路机 6
pneumatic tyred roller 轮胎压路机 343
polymer modified asphalt plant 聚合物改性沥青设备 7
porous-chrome ring 多孔镀铬环 34
portable blow lamp 手提式喷灯 411
positive plate 正极板 70
positive twist type 正扭曲型 34
postheater/dryer/mixer 后加热/烘干/搅拌机 424
powder 填充剂 83
power cylinder 转向动力缸 111
power diode 功率二极管 82
power rake 动力耙 231
power shift transmission 动力换挡变速箱 246

power shifting transmission box 动力换挡变速箱 215
power shifting transmission case 动力换挡变速箱 103,105,280,281,216
power steering gear 动力转向器 111
power train 传动系 243,254
power train system 传动系统 15
preheater/miller 加热/铣刨机 423
pressure capsule 压力膜盒 51
pressure-adjusting shim 调压垫片 43
pressure-control valve 压力调节阀 47
pressure-reducing valve 减压阀 144
pressure gauge 压力计 349
pressure limiting valve 限压阀 76
pressure meter 压力表 411
pressure pipe 高压油管 42
pressure plate （外）压盘,压力盘 85,89,102,119,352
pressure regulator 压力调节器 163,42
pressure relief valve 释压阀 58
pressure relief groove 卸压槽 77
pressure sensor 压力传感器 53,57,58,164,178
pressure spring 调压弹簧 43,44
pressure switch 压力开关 164
pressure switch circuit 压力开关电路 164

pressured water pump 加压水泵 397
primary dust collector 一级除尘系统 384
primary gauze filter 初级滤网式过滤器 54
primary seal ring 主密封圈 74
primary terminal 主接线柱 80
primary winding 初级绕组,初级线圈 67,68
primer pump 初级泵 57,58
PROM = Programmable Read Only Memory(corrective information) 可编程只读存储器(校正信息) 53
propel motor 驱动马达 332
propel pump 驱动泵 332
propeller shaft(drive shaft) 传动轴 97
proportional distributing valve 比例分配阀 165
proportional speed controller 比例速度控制器 108,315
protective cap 保护帽 45
protective nut 保护螺母 43,44
protective plug 保护塞 431
protective sleeve 保护套 43
PS pump = power steering pump 动力转向油泵 111
PTO 分动箱 176
pull-in winding 吸引线圈 80,81
pulley 带轮 82
pulse valve 脉冲阀 398

pump 泵轮,油泵 104,314
pump body 泵体,水泵体,机油泵体 45,55,74,77
pump case 泵壳 415
pump chamber 泵室 74
pump control pulse 泵控制脉冲 58
pump control valve 泵控制阀 58
pump cover 水泵盖 74
pump impeller 叶轮,泵轮 74,218
pump plunger 柱塞 49
pump relay 泵继电器 64
pump shaft 水泵轴 74
pushbotton for CRAB mode-left 横向模式按钮-左侧 360
pushbutton for CRAB mode-right 横向模式按钮-右侧 360
push frame 顶推架 279
push rod 推杆 148,26,39,51
push roller 推辊 311

Q

quad rear bogie 四边形后台车架 332
quick accelerator switch 快速加速开关 178
quick-release valve 快放阀 162,388

R

rack and pinion steering linkage 齿轮齿条式转向传动机构 113

483

rack and sector steering gear　齿条齿扇式转向器　116
rack control machanism　齿杆式油量调节机构　48
radial(ply) tire　子午线轮胎　123
radiator　散热器　71,72,73,176
radiator cap　散热器盖　71,72,73
radiator core　散热器芯　72
radiator shutter　散热器百叶窗　71
radio controlled excavator　无线控制型挖掘机　171
RAD minimum-maximum-speed governor　RAD型两极式减速器　50
reaction chamber　反应室　385
reactor　导轮　104
rear anchor pin　后支承销　157
rear axle　后桥　15,103,116,214,215,216
rear axle differential gear　后桥差速器　246
rear axle housing　后桥箱体　128,129
rear axle oscillating shaft　后桥摆动轴　116
rear bracket　后支架　139
rear brake assembly　后制动器总成　160
rear brake line　后制动油管　160
rear cover　后盖,(后)罩　128,135
rear cover of pump body　泵体后盖　415
rear drive shaft　后传动轴　98
rear driving axle　后驱动桥　243
rear drum　后轮　345
rear end cover　后端盖　23,82
rear frame　后车架,后机架　116,142,214,216,344,345,353,354
rear muffler　后消声器　60
rear output shaft　后输出轴　106
rear planetary gear set　后行星排　106
rear pressure plate　后压盘　89
rear sand/grit bin　后置砂石料箱　440
rear suspension　后悬架　121
rear wheel　后轮　121,314
rear wheel speed sensor　后轮速度传感器　165
rear wheel steering cylinder　后轮转向油缸　247
receiving hopper　接料斗　428
recharging oil valve　补油阀　282
reciprocating feeder　往复式给料器　379
recirculating hot air blower　热风再循环鼓风机　422,423,424
reclaimed material charging belt　回收料上料带　383
reclaimed material inlet　回收料入口　405
rectangle spreader box　矩形路面封层摊铺箱　419
rectangular ring,plain(piston) ring　矩形环　33
recycled mix　再生混合料　427
red lamp(engine diagnostics)　红灯

484

（发动机诊断） 360
reducer 减速器 314,356
reference coil 参照线圈 52
regenerator tank 再生剂储罐 423
regulating ring 调整环 89
regulating sleeve 调节套 388
reinforced rubber 增强橡胶 123
relay rod, center link, centre link, connecting rod, center rod 中继杆 111,113
relay valve 中继阀 164
release cable 分离拉索 91
release fork, withdrawal fork, operating fork, clutch fork 分离叉 91,92
release rim 分离圈 89
release rod 分离杆 92
release sleeve 分离套筒 89
release spring 分离弹簧 89
relief valve 溢流阀,安全阀 76,89,117,411
remixed wearing course 再生磨耗层 427
reservoir 储液罐 91
reservoir tube 储油缸筒 144
retainer 保持器 92
retainer oil seal groove 挡油环油槽 37
retainer plate （轴承）保持板 99
retainer ring 卡环 74
retaining bolt 固定螺栓 37
retaining member 锁紧件,锁止装置 35
retaining ring 挡圈,卡环 41,99,100,115
retraction piston 减压环带 46
return line to fuel tank 至燃油箱的回油管 47
return oil passage 回油道 42,57,75
return spring 复位弹簧 81
return spring （制动蹄,柱塞）回位弹簧 55,57,65,80,85,91,92,126,151
reverse circulation drilling rig 反循环钻机 10
reverse drive gear 后退主动齿轮 94
reverse gear 倒车齿轮 94
reverse gear shift clutch 倒挡离合器 246
reverse shift block 倒挡拨块 96
reverse shift fork 倒挡拨叉 96
reverse shift fork shaft 倒挡拨叉轴 96
reversible fan 双向风扇 287
reversible snow plow 反转型除雪铲（犁） 262
reversing valve 换向阀 282
revolution pulse 转动脉冲 53
revolving cylinder 回转油缸 247
revolving plow reclaimer 叶轮给料机 389
revolving valve 回转阀 247
RH cluster 右仪表盘 360
right axial plunger motor 右轴向柱

485

塞马达 108,315
right basic screed 右基本段熨平板 323
right brake 右制动器 281
right drag and steering triple-link pump 右刮板和转向三联泵 314
right electromagnetic valve 右电磁阀 327
right feeder and auger drive pumps 右侧送料器与螺旋器驱动泵 333
right final reduction gear 右最终传动 281
right horizontal pipe triple valve 右横管三通阀 413
right hydraulic extension screed 右液压伸缩熨平板 325
right junction bracket 右连接支架 355,356
right junction plate 右连接板 355,356
right leveling cylinder 右调平油缸 327
right steering cylinder 右转向油缸 116
right towed arm 右牵引臂 327
right track link 右链轨节 130
right variable pump 右变量泵 108,315
rigid frame 刚性(整体式)车架 351
rigid suspension(swing axle) 刚性悬架(摆动桥) 142
rim,wheel rim 轮辋 100,125

rim bolt 轮辋螺栓 100
rim diameter 轮辋直径 125
rim flange,flange 轮缘 125
rim offset 轮辋偏距 125
rim width 轮辋宽度 125
ring belt,ring zone 活塞环(分布)带 29
ring clearance 环间隙 32
ring face,ring periphery,ring working face 环(工作)表面,环外表面 32
ring gear (飞轮)齿圈,环齿轮 23,26,101
ring groove bottom 槽底 29
ring-groove pad 环槽加厚部,环槽基底 29
ring-groove side 环槽侧面 29
ripper 松土器 291
ripper tip tooth 松土器齿尖 279
river channel dredging excavator 河道疏浚挖掘机 170
rivet (从动盘,扇形弹簧片,阻尼片)铆钉 90
road stabilizer/reclaimer 稳定土拌和/道路再生机 12
rock bucket 石料铲斗 231
rock digging 石料铲斗 185
rocker arm 摇臂 23,26,38,39,41,55,158,159,214
rocker arm cylinder 摇臂油缸 214
rocker-arm mounting structure 摇臂支架结构 41
rocker-arm spring 定位弹簧 41

rocker-arm support 摇臂轴座 41
rocker bush(ing) 摇臂衬套 41
rocker shaft 摇臂轴 39,41,55
rocker support screw 摇臂轴座螺杆 41
rock machinery 石方机械 5
rod （减压阀）杆 144
rod guide （活塞）杆导管 144
roll bellow 卷翻（膜片）气囊 136,137
roll-over proofing dozer 防倾翻推土机 278
roller 滚子,滚轮,滚柱,压路机 45,55,84,308,407,437
roller bearing 滚柱轴承 89,94
roller pin 滚轮销 45
roller race 滚柱座圈 84
roller retainer 滚柱保持器 84
roller tappet 滚轮式挺柱 45
roller-type overruning clutch 滚柱式单向离合器 81
rolling bearing 滚动轴承 37
rolling direction 滚动方向 124
rolling ring 滚圈 382,383,405
rotating brake disk 旋转制动盘 156
rotating spline drum 旋转花键鼓 156
rotation sensor 旋转传感器 252
rotor encloser 拌和转子罩壳 435
rotor shaft 转子轴 82
rotor transmission case 拌和转子传动箱 435

round nut 圆螺母 100
RQ minimum-maximum-speed governor RQ型两极式调速器 49
RSV variable-speed governor RSV型全程式调速器 49
rubber-coated steel mid-wheel 挂胶中间钢轮 331
rubber element （平衡）橡胶元件 99,135
rubber support(mountiong) 橡胶支承 137,142
runnel construction 隧道工程 3
running gear 行走机构 311

S

sack 袋 57
safety cut-out 熔断器 80
safety strobe light 安全频闪灯 442
safety valve 安全阀 162
salt-sand spreader 盐沙防滑材料洒布机 12
S-cam S形凸轮 147
scarifier 翻松器,松土器 243,279,427
scarifier cylinder 松土器油缸 279,282
scarifier hoist cylinder 松土器升降油缸 243,247
scraper 刮泥板 344,345
screed box 熨平板箱体 311
screed plate 熨平板底板 311
screed unit 熨平装置,熨平板

487

311,327
screen box 筛箱 387
screen deck 筛网 3877
screen system 筛分系统 384
screw bolt 螺杆 102
screw distributor 螺旋分料器 419,420
seal ring 密封圈,密封垫 46,75, 78,94,144,153,352,353,354
seal washer 密封垫 100
seal 密封圈 151
sealing cone 密封锥面 46
sealing cover 密封盖 101
sealing element 密封件 22
seat 座椅 422
secondary filter 机油细滤器 26
secondary winding 次级绕组,次级线圈 67,68
second(compression) ring,2nd(compression) ring, lower compression ring 第二道气环,第二道压缩环 32
second(No.2)land 第二环岸 29
second(No.2)ring groove(slot) 第二道环槽 28
second speed drive gear 二挡主动齿轮 94
second speed driven gear 二挡被动齿轮 94
second turbine 第二涡轮 218
second turbine shaft 第二涡轮轴 218
sector shaft 齿扇轴 115

sedimentation reservoir 沉淀池 397
segment 挂片 3
segmented spring ring 扇形弹簧片 90
self-lock ball 自锁钢球 95,96
self-locking and interlocking device 自锁和互锁装置 95
self-lock spring （自锁）弹簧 95,96
self-propelled construction machinery 自行工程机械 14
self-propelled grader(motor grader) 自行式平地机 4
self-propelled scraper(motor scraper) 自行式铲运机 4
semicircular key 半圆键 74
semi-inlaid(filled)ring 两半填充环 34
semi-integral power steering gear 半整体式动力转向器 111
semi-rigid suspension 半刚性悬架 142
semi-U blade 半U形铲 292
sensing ring and speed sensor 感应环与速度传感器 164
sensor 传感器 52,55,64,391
separated cooling system 分离式冷却系统 284
separator 隔板 70
serrated joint 锯齿式切口 35
service and emergency connection 维护与应急接口 162

service brake 行车制动器 220,221,246
service brake pipeline 行车制动管路 164
service switch 维护开关 285
servo valve 随动阀,伺服阀 116,282
set nut 定位螺母 94
shackle 吊耳 139
shackle pin 吊耳销 139
shaft bushing 轴衬 130
shaft sleeve 轴套 74,415
shaft 轴 75,141
shell 外壳 69
shift clutch 换挡离合器 246
shift collar 滑动套 85
shift fork shaft 拨叉轴 95
shift lever 变速杆,拨叉 81,96
shift lever cover 换挡杆盖 95
shift shaft (换挡)轴 96
shift sleeve 啮合套 94
shift yoke 拨叉 80
shim 垫片 43,115,134,415
shim block 垫片 100
shock absorber 缓冲器,减振器 64,355,356,369
shoe guide 蹄导板 151
shoulder 胎肩 123
shoulder area 胎肩区 123
shovel bin 铁铲工具箱 440
shovel cleaning bin 铁铲清洁箱 440
showering flight 料帘区叶片 403,405
shutter 进风门 386
side cover 侧盖 115
side driving gear 侧传动齿轮 346
side dumping loader 侧卸式装载机 212
side gear 半轴齿轮 101
side grit/sand bin 侧置砂石料箱 440
side plate 壁板 388
side rail 侧环片 34
sidewall 胎侧 123
sign storage tray, emulsion tank, side tipping spoil bin 标志存放托盘,乳化剂箱,侧卸式废料箱 440
single axle screw mixer 单轴螺旋式搅拌器 418
single drum vibratory roller 单钢轮振动压路机 6,343,367
single flange track roller 单边支重轮 135
single joint couping shaft 单万向节传动轴 98
single overhead camshaft 单顶置凸轮轴 38
single-piston wheel cylinder 单活塞轮缸 147
single-speed planetary 单速行星减速器 332
single water fill port 单一加水口 361
single water tank drain 单一水箱排水口 361

sipe（s）,sipings,sipe cut,traction blades,traction slots 刀槽花纹,细缝花纹 124
skeleton bucket 格栅铲斗 187
skid steer loader 滑移转向装载机 211
skirt relief 裙部凹口 29
skirt ring groove(slot) （活塞）裙部环槽 29
slack adjuster 松紧调节器 162
slat conveyor 链板输送机 381
slat conveyor body 板条式输送机机体 440
slat feeder 板式给料器 381
slave cylinder piston return spring 工作缸活塞回位弹簧 91
slave cylinder,release cylinder 工作缸,分离缸 91
sleeve （花键）套筒 85
sleeve seal 缸套密封圈 27
sleeve seal ring 套筒密封圈 156
sleeve type spring seat 套筒式弹簧座 134
slewing hydraulic motor 回转液压马达 177
slide valve 滑阀 158
sliding bearing 滑动轴承 94
sliding bush 滑套 106
sliding gear （减速器）滑动齿轮 79
sliding pin 滑动销 155
sliding rod 滑动杆 49
slight pressure chamber 低压油腔 45

slip-form concrete paver 滑模水泥摊铺机 7
slipper,slipper skirt （活塞）拖板,滑座 29
slip spline 滑动花键 99
slip yoke 滑动叉 98
slotted oil ring 开槽油环 33
slurry seal machine 稀浆封层车 416
small coil spring 小螺旋弹簧 102
small crawler dozer(track-type tractor) 小型履带式推土机 278
small end,top end （连杆）小头 35
small locker and paddle lock 小电器开关箱 440
small paver 小型摊铺机 309
small pipeline triple valve control handle 管路小三通阀操纵手柄 409
small spring 小弹簧 119
small triple valve 小三通阀 409
small type excavator 小型挖掘机 169
small type wheel loader 小型轮式装载机 211
small wheel cold planer 小型轮式冷铣刨机 13
smoke exhaust box 排烟箱 383
smoke outlet 排烟口 405,408,410
snap ring 卡环 153
snow blade 除雪铲 231
snow blower 转子除雪机 231
snow plough 犁式除雪机 12

socket （调节螺钉）支座 151
soft cable 软钢绳 391
solenoid coil 电磁线圈 59
solenoid plunger 电磁铁芯 65
solenoid spill valve 电磁溢流阀 55
solenoid swith 电磁开关 81
solenoid valve 电磁阀 58,59,164
solenoid-valve needle 电磁阀针阀 55
solenoid valve spring 电磁阀弹簧 59
solenoid winding 电磁开关线圈 65
solid plate 固定板 94
solid rotor(disc,disk) 整体式制动盘 155
spacer block （转向器侧盖）衬垫 115
spacer ring 隔离环 218
spacing collar （流通阀）限位圈 144
spade nose rock bucket 中凸式石料铲斗 229
spark(ing) plug 火花塞 23,64,67,69
speader 摊铺器 417
speed control lever, adjusting speed lever 调速杠杆 50
speed-control lever （发动机）转速控制杆 47
speed increasing gear train 增速齿轮副 106
speed limit valve 速度限制阀 177

speed potentiometer 速度电位器 359
speed reducer 减速器 389,393,394
speed reducing gear pair 减速齿轮副 106
speed sensor 速度传感器 64,108,315
spherical connecting pipe 球状连接管 409
spherical hinge connecting pipe 球铰式连接管 413
spider 十字轴 101
spill control valve 溢流控制阀 55
spill ring 溢流环 47
spill solenoid 溢流电磁线圈 55
splash shield 防溅罩 155
splined hub 花键毂,花键套 85,94,355
spline seal 花键油封 99
spoil rubbish bin 废料箱 440
spoke plate 轮辐板 355,356
spot-type disc brake 钳盘式制动器 100
spray hole 喷孔 57
spraying angle adjusting handle 洒布管喷洒角度调整手柄 414
spray nozzle 喷嘴 441
spray nozzle with filter 过滤型喷咀 361
spray pipe 喷管 392
spreader box frame 摊铺箱框架 419

491

spreader box of polymer modification slurry seal machine 聚合物改性稀浆封层摊铺箱 419
spreader box of universal slurry seal machine 普通稀浆封层机摊铺箱 419
spreader box 摊铺箱 419
spreader 喷洒器 360
spreading auger 布料螺旋,螺旋分料器 424,428,430,433
spreading thickness fine adjusting hand wheel 摊铺厚度微调手轮 419,420
spreading thickness main adjusting hand wheel 铺层厚度主调节手轮 420
spring 弹簧 51,59,66,74,78,89,144,151,153,158,159
spring brake 弹簧刹车 164
spring cap 弹簧座盘 156
spring clamp, spring hoop, spring-leaf retainer, spring stirrup 钢板弹簧夹 139
spring eye 钢板弹簧卷耳 139
spring free end 钢板弹簧自由(吊耳)端 139
spring lamination (补偿阀,流通阀)弹簧片 144
spring lock ring 弹性锁圈 132
spring pressure plate 弹簧压盘 102
spring seat 弹簧垫圈,弹簧座 45,78,134,144,153

spring washer 弹簧垫圈 41
sprinkling interval potentiometer 喷水间隔电位器 360
sprinkling pumps selector switch 喷水泵选择器开关 360
sprinkling pushbutton 喷水按钮 360
stabilized soil mixing plant 稳定土厂拌设备 7
stabilizer bar, stabilizer(shaft), anti-roll(sway)bar, roll bar, sway bar 横向稳定杆 137
stabilizer 稳定土拌和机 7
stack 烟囱 397
staff gauge 标尺 391
starter frame 启动机外壳 81
starter ring gear 启动齿圈 104
starting jaw 启动爪 37
starting relay 启动继电器 80
start(ing) spring 启动弹簧 49
starting switch 启动开关 80
start-quantity stop with expansion element 带膨胀元件的启动油量限制器 52
static smooth drum roller 静作用光轮压路机 343
stator 导轮 218
stator core 定子铁芯 82
stator shaft 导轮轴 218,104
stator slot 定子槽 82
stator winding 定子绕组 82
steel ball 钢球 100,115
steel cable 钢索 396

steel insert 钢镶片 31
steel piston insert 活塞钢镶片 31
steel shot 钢球 358
steel spring 钢质弹簧 137
steering and operating system 转向操纵系统 15,16,175
steering arm 转向节臂 114
steering axle 转向桥 114
steering brake valve 转向制动阀 282
steering brake 转向制动器 87
steering clutch 转向离合器 87
steering clutches and brakes 转向离合器和制动器组 280
steering column 转向柱管 115
steering control 转向控制 286
steering control mechanism 转向操纵机构 111
steering controller 转向控制器 285
steering cylinder 转向油缸 117,344,345,346,347,348,351
steering device and steering valve 转向器和转向阀 346
steering gear cover 转向器盖 115
steering gear housing 转向器壳体 115
steering gear, steering gearbox, steering mechanism 转向器 111,113,115
steering idler arm 转向随动臂 111
steering (knuckle) arm 转向节臂 111,113
steering knuckle, steering (axle) swivel, steering (axle) stub, axle stub 转向节 111,113,114
steering motor 转向马达 281
steering nut 转向螺母 115
steering pump 转向(液压,油)泵 87,103,215,282,347,348,351
steering quantitative motor 转向定量马达 313
steering rack 转向齿条 111
steering shaft 转向轴 111,115
steering shock absorber 转向减振(缓冲)器 113
steering suction strainer 转向吸滤器 351
steering tie rod 转向横拉杆 113
steering trapezium 转向梯形 117
steering valve 转向阀 351
steering wheel 转向盘 111
steering wheel position adjustment 方向盘位置调整 360
steering worm 转向蜗杆 115
steering yoke 方向杆 116
step head(top,crown,roof) 台阶顶 31
step joint 阶梯状切口 32
stepped scraper ring 阶梯状切口刮油环 33
stepped wheel cylinder 异径(阶梯形)轮缸 147
step-type bridge erection equipment 步履式架桥机 10

step-type hydraulic pile driving machine 液压步履式桩机 9
step-type multi-fuction hydraulic driller 液压步履式多功能钻机 9
sterring variable pump 转向变量泵 313
stone bolt 地脚螺栓 386
stone chip spreader 碎石洒布机 12
stop angle iron 挡料角钢 388
stop block 限位块 142
stop collar 止动套 85
stop or idle stop 断油或怠速限制器 49
stop screw 止动螺钉 152
stop tube 止动管 134
stoplight switch 刹车灯开关 162
stopping pin 挡销 357
storage battery 蓄电池 165
straight blade 直铲 292
straight-bore wheel cylinder 直筒(双活塞)轮缸 147
straight edge rock bucket with teeth 直边有齿石料铲斗 229
strainer 滤网 408,411,413
strainer filter 粗滤器 282
strap 夹板 99
stretcher 伸张器 144
strip inserts for expansion control 控制膨胀镶片 31
stroke adjusting screw 行程调节螺钉 50
strut spring 撑杆弹簧 151

stump grinder 树根粉碎机 231
sub-frame 副车架 142
subbase 基层 407
super large paver 超大型摊铺机 309
super low section tire 超低断面轮胎 123
supersized dozer 超大型推土机 278
supply pipe 进料管 408
supply pump 供油泵 58
support,support plate 支撑板,支架 67,78,157
support bearing 支撑轴承 98
support lever 支承杆 50
supporter 托板 135
supporting arm 支承臂 140
supporting beam 支承梁 140
support(ing) bracket 托架 101
supporting carriage 支重台车 127
supporting journal 支承轴颈 140
supporting point 支点 51
supporting roller 支承滚轮 382,383,405
supporting seat (横梁)支座 129,387
supporting unit 支承装置 133,144
surface 面层 407
suspension 悬架 127
suspension cylinder 悬架油缸 140
suspension spring 悬架弹簧 141
suspension spring element 悬架弹性元件 137

swing boom　回转式吊杆　441
swing motor　回转马达　176
switch and indicator lamp for rear light　尾灯开关和指示灯　360
swivelcoupling　回转接头　247
swivel joint　旋转接头　176
synchronizing gear　同步齿轮　393
synchronous chip seal vehicle　同步碎石封层车　11
synchronous cog belt　同步齿形带　369

T

tackiness agent　胶合剂　83
tailpipe　尾管　60
tamper　振捣器　311
tamper bar　振捣夯锤　311
tamper drive motor　振捣器驱动马达　311
tamper eccentric shaft　振捣偏心轴　312
tandem master cylinder assembly　串联制动主缸总成　161
tandem vibratory roller(doubie drum)　串联式振动压路机(双钢轮)　343
tandem vibratory roller　双钢轮振动压路机　367
tangential end　正切向端　136
tank body　箱体　412
tank cup　油箱盖　60
tank filler　油箱加注口　60
tank mounting frame　箱体固定架　410

tapered end　楔形端　136
tapered foot valve　锥形底阀　392
tapered plug　锥形螺塞　115
taper faced ring　锥面环　34
tappet, tappet follower　挺柱,挺杆　26,39,43,44,57
T/C：turbocharger　涡轮增压器　53
telescopic boom excavator　伸缩臂式挖掘机　171
telescopic crawler crane　伸缩臂履带起重机　8
telescopic hydraulic cylinder　伸缩液压油缸　325
telescopic shock absorber　筒式减振器　143
temperature sensor　温度传感器　388
tension device　张紧装置　134
tensioning nut　(电磁阀)紧固螺母　59
tension rod bar　拉杆　157
tension sensor　拉力传感器　392
tension spring　拉伸弹簧,张紧弹簧　91,134
terminal　接线柱,端子,接线螺栓　80,81,83
test connector　测试接头　164
thermo time switch　温度时间开关　64
thermometer　温度计　408,410
thermostat　节温器　71
third-fourth shift fork　三、四挡拨叉

495

96
third-fourth shift fork shaft 三、四挡拨叉轴 96
third land 第三环岸 29
third speed drive gear 三挡主动齿轮 94
third speed driven gear 三挡被动齿轮 94
three piece oil ring 三件式油环 34
throat 喉管 398
throttle position switch 节气门开关 64
throttle valve 节气门 61,64
thrust bearing 推力轴承 114,115
thrust bearing shell 止推轴瓦 23
thrust part 承推部件 59
thrust roller 挡滑滚轮 382
thrust washer 止推垫圈 101,36,81
thumb bucket 拇指型铲斗 185
tie rod clamp 横拉杆夹 113
tie rod, tie bar, track rod 横拉杆 111,113
tightening screw 紧固螺钉 45,48
tilt cylinder 倾斜油缸 282
tilting bucket 斜挖铲斗 186
timing belt cover 定时齿带罩 22
timing belt pulley 定时带轮 22
timing device, timing control, injection advance mechanism(device) 喷油提前器,正时装置 47
timing gear 正时齿轮 36
timing sleeve(collar) 正时套筒 47

tire 轮胎 100,246
tire tread 胎面 124
tire valve 气门嘴 126
tool bit 刀头 431
tool clamp 刀夹 431
tool holder 刀座 431
toothed belt 齿形带 22
toothed segment (quadrant), notched quadrant 齿扇 91
top(No.1)land,fire(head)land 第一环岸,火力岸 29
top(No.1)ring groove(slot) 第一道环槽 28
top ring insert 头道环槽镶圈 31
top ring 上环片 34
top (upper) compression ring, top ring, No.1 compression ring 第一道气环,上压缩环 32
toroid bellow 环形气囊 136
torque-control spring 转矩控制弹簧 49
torque converter and power shift transmission 变矩器与动力换挡变速箱 244
torque converter output shaft 变矩器输出轴 106
torque converter rotation housing 变矩器旋转壳体 218
torque converter 液力变矩器 103,104,215,216,281,285
torque plate 转矩板(丰田公司用法) 155
torsional damper, vibration absorber

扭振减振器 99
torsional(damping)spring 减振弹簧 90
torsional vibration damper 扭振减振器 107
torsion(bar)spring,torsion bar 扭杆弹簧 136
total valve 总阀门 410
total valve hand wheel 总阀门手轮 410
towed arm 牵引臂 311,323,325
towed pad foot vibratory roller 拖式凸块振动压路机 344
towed smooth drum vibratory roller 拖式光轮振动压路机 344
tow hook,towing hook,hitch 拖钩 128
tow-joint inboard slip drive shaft 双万向节内侧滑动传动轴 98
track 履带,轨道 16,173,279,280,396
track adjuster 履带张紧器 127,135
track assembly 履带总成 130
track bolt 履带螺栓 130
track bulldozer(crawler bulldozer) 覆带式推土机 4
track cold milling machine,track cold planer 履带式冷铣刨机 12
track drive and steering clutch 履带驱动与转向离合器 102
track dump truck(crawler dump truck) 履带式自卸车 4

tracked chassis 履带底盘 14,16
tracked paver 履带式摊铺机 108,308
track frame 台车架 135,173
track hydrulic excavator 履带式液压挖掘机 4
track idler 引导轮,导向轮 16,127,133,135,173,279
track idler body 引导轮体 133
track idler shaft 引导轮轴 133
track motor 履带驱动马达 220,221
track nut 履带螺母 130
track pin 履带销 130
track rail 履带轨 332
track roller frame 台车架 16,133,135,142,279
track roller,track supporting wheel 支重轮 16,127,131,141,279
track rotary drilling rig 履带式旋挖钻机 9
track shoe 履带板 130
track tension system 履带张紧系统 332
track-type loader 覆带式装载机 211
traction frame 牵引架 243
traction frame cylinder 牵引架油缸 247
traction frame moving cylinder 牵引架移动油缸 243
tractor suspension 拖拉机悬架 141

497

trailer concrete pump 混凝土拖泵 14
trailer protection valve 拖车保护阀 162
trailer-type scraper 拖式铲运机 4
trailing shoe, secondary shoe 从蹄 147,151
transfer case 分动箱 219,347, 348,409,87
transfer vehicle 转运车 308
transmission case, gear box, transmission 变速箱 87,93,252
transmission chain 传动链 312,313
transmission control valve 变速箱控制阀 285
transmission controller 变速箱控制器 285
transmission housing 变速箱壳 94
transmission shaft 传动轴 216
transmission system 传动系统 311
transmission yoke 变速器叉 98
transport truck 运输卡车 395,396
transporting girder vehicle 运梁车 10
transverse pattern 横向花纹 124
travel control 行驶控制器 359
travel control lever 行走操纵手柄 285
travel driving motor 行走驱动马达 347,348
travel driving pump 行走驱动泵 347,348
travel lever 行走操纵杆 175
travel motor 行走马达 356
traveling driving wheel 行驶驱动轮 312
traveling hydraulic motor 行走液压马达 177
traveling pump 行走泵 349
traveling quantitative motor 行走定量马达 313
traveling suction strainer 行走吸滤器 349
traveling system 行驶系统 417
traveling variable pump 行走变量泵 313
tread, tire tread 胎面 123
tread plie 胎面帘布层 123
tread(tire) wear indicator 胎面磨损指示器 123
tri-flex no fatigue boom 三维无疲劳吊杆 442
tripple valve 三通阀 390,392
trolley assembly 台车总成 291
troubleshooting switch 故障排除开关 360
truck-mounted concrete line pump 混凝土车载泵 14
truck-mounted concrete pump 混凝土泵车 14
T-slot, T-shaped slot T形槽 29
T-slot piston T形槽活塞 29
tube 轴管,筒 98,144
tube end spline shaft 管端花键轴

99
tubed tire,tube-type tire　有内胎轮胎　123
tubeless tire　无内胎轮胎　123
tunnel borer,tunnel boring machine　隧道掘进机　10
tunnel shield machine　盾构机　10
turbine　涡轮　104
turning circle　回转圈　243,245
twin-shaft mixer　双轴搅拌器　424,430,432
twist(torsional)ring　扭曲型　34
two-join toutboard slip drive shaft　双万向节外侧滑动传动轴　98
two-piece drive shaft　两段式传动轴　98
two-piece rim　两件式轮辋　125
two piece side plates　两边侧板　175
two-pins articulated frame　双铰销式铰接架　353
two-side variable width milling drum　双边变宽度铣刨鼓　430
two-speed planetary　双速行星减速器　331
two-way valve　二通阀,双通阀　58,162
tyre(tire)　轮　140

U

U-bolt, U-clamp　U形螺栓　139
ultra high demolition hydraulic excavator　超高层建筑物拆除液压挖掘机　170
ultrasonic averaging beam　超专长波平均梁　328
uncoated ring　无镀层环　33
under layer　底基层　407
undercarriage　行走支承机构　173
underground mining loader　井下作业装载机　212
underneath camshaft overhead valve　下置凸轮轴顶置式气门　39
underneath vibrator　下置式振动器　387
underslung(spring)type,underhung spring rype　下置板簧式　138
unequally spaced coils spring　不等节矩螺旋弹簧　136
unit　作业用柴油机　417
unit injector,pump/injector unit　泵喷嘴　55
universal compaction wheel　万能压实轮　187
universal driving device　万向传动装置　313
universal driving shaft　万向传动轴　314
universal flange　万向节盘　94
upper mounting　上支承　144
upper rocker arm　上摇臂　158
U-slot　U形槽　29

V

vacuum booster　真空助力器　160,161

499

vacuum switching valve 真空开关
（转换）阀 53
valve 气门，阀门 26，39，40，
66，126
valve ball 阀球 59
valve body 嘴体 126
valve collet 气门锁夹 39，40
valve guide 气门导管 22，39，40
valve holder 阀门保持器 66
valve part 阀零件 59
valve plunger 阀柱塞 59
valve relief （活塞上防干涉）气门凹
坑 31
valve seat 气门座 39
valve spring 气门弹簧 22，39，40
valve spring retainer 气门弹簧座
22，39，40
vane-type supply pump 滑片式输油
泵 47
variable displacement drive pumps
变量驱动泵和马达 283
variable-rate spring 变刚度弹簧
136
variable scarifying device 宽度可变
式翻松器 428
variable speed pump 变速油泵
103
variable width screed 变宽度熨平板
430，433
vehicle frame 车架 137
ventilated brake disk(disc)，ventilated
rotor 通风式制动盘 155
vent pipe 透气管 100

ventilation hole 通风孔 125
venturi nozzle 文丘里喷嘴 397
venturi scrubber 文丘里洗涤器
397
venturi scrubbing dust filter 文丘里
除尘器 397
vertical pin 垂直销轴 353
vertical slot 直槽 29
vibrating screen 振动筛 6
vibration amplitude selector switch
振幅选择器开关 360
vibration bearing 振动轴承
355，356
vibration driving motor 振动驱动马
达 346，347，348
vibration driving pump 振动驱动泵
347，348
vibration filters 振动过滤器 350
vibration mode selector switch
（MAN/AUT） 振动模式选择开
关（手动/自动） 360
vibration motor 振动马达 350，
355，356
vibration pump 振动泵 350
vibration pushbutton 振动按钮
360
vibration selector switch 振动选择
器开关 360
vibration suction strainer 振动吸滤
器 350
vibration valve 起振阀 347
vibrator 振动器 311，387
vibrator drive motor 振动器驱动马

达 311
vibratory drum 振动轮 344,346,347,348
vibratory drum travel driving motor 振动轮行走驱动马达 348
vibratory pad foot roller 凸块式振动压路机 343
vibratory plate 振动平板夯 6
vibratory roller 振动碾 231
vibratory shaft 振动轴 357,358
vibro hammer 振动锤 187
vice transmission 副变速器 312
viscous fan coupling(clutch) 黏液风扇离合器 75
voltage regulator 电压调节器 82
volution guide vane 涡旋导流板 386
V-shaped tracking repair spreader box V形车辙修复摊铺箱 420

W

walk behind doubie drum vibratory roller 双轮手扶式振动压路机 343
walk behind roller 手扶压路机 6
walk behind single drum vibratory roller 单轮手扶式振动压路机 343
walkway 行走通道 176
warning lamp 报警灯 287
washer 垫片,垫圈 27,41,43,44,83,126,130,139,144,152,245
water distribution mat 配水垫板 361
water filter 水过滤器 361
water hose reel 软水管卷盘 440
water injection system 喷水系统 430
water inlet 进水口 72,74
water jacket 水套 27,71
water outlet 出水口 72,74
water passage 水道 72
water pump, coolant circulation 水泵 26,71,361
water separator 水分离器 287
water spray system 喷水系统 361
water-stop sheet 隔水板 72
water tank or optional second emulsion tank 水箱或第二乳化剂箱可选件 440
water tank 水箱 345,417,430
water temperature indicator 水温表 71
water thrower ring 甩水圈 74
water truck 运水车 437
watering system 喷水系统 345
wear indicator 磨损指示器 155
wear sensor 制动磨损传感器 164
wear straps fitted to increase base strength 斗底增强耐磨板条 175
wedge 楔块 147
weigh bucket 量桶 391
weight 重块 391
weight drive shaft to motor 传动轴（连接马达） 358

weld yoke, tube yoke 轴管叉 99
wet land dozer 湿地推土机 278
wetlands excavator 湿地挖掘机 171
wet, multi-disc parking brake 湿式、多片停车制动器 220,221
wet sleeve (liner) typer 湿式缸套 27
wheel 车轮 103,215
wheel backhoe loader 轮式挖掘装载机 171,212
wheel braking cylinder 制动轮缸 149,165
wheel cylinder 轮缸 147,151
wheel cylinder brake 轮缸式制动器 147
wheel disk (disc, spoke, rib) 轮辐 125
wheel dozer 轮胎式推土机 278
wheel dozer frame 轮式推土机机架 291
wheel dozer operation mechanism 轮式推土机工作机构 292
wheeled chassis 轮式底盘 14,15
wheeled chassis travel system 轮式底盘行走系统 15
wheeled paver 轮胎式摊铺机 308
wheeled running mechanism 轮式行走机构 121
wheel excavator 轮式挖掘机 170
wheel hub 轮毂 100,114,131
wheel loader 轮胎式装载机 4
wheel reductor 轮边减速器 103,215
wheel reduction gear 轮边减速器 347,348
wheel shaft (支重轮)轴 131
wheel-side reducer 轮边减速器 313
wide panoramic view 宽幅全景视野 286
work equipment assembly 工作装置总成 14,174
work equipment pump 工作装置油泵,工作装置液压泵 87,282
worm gear 蜗轮 148
worm screw 蜗杆 148

Y

yellow lamp (engine diagnostics) 黄灯(发动机诊断) 360

Z

Z-throttle Z形节流 59

Vocabulary Index
词汇索引(中英对照)

15°斜胎圈轮辋　15°tapered-bead seat rim　125
45°切口　45° angle joint　32
5°斜胎圈　5° tapered (-bead) seat　125
5°斜胎圈轮辋　5° tapered-bead seat rim　125

A

A形节流　A-throttle　59
阿克曼-金特式转向　Ackerman Jeantaud steering　111
安全阀　safety valve, relief valve　162,411
安全频闪灯　safety strobe light　442
安装支架　mounting bracket　113
岸隙　land clearance　29
凹顶　concave head　31

B

摆动转向桥　oscillating steering axle　243
板簧式悬架　leaf spring suspension　138
板式给料器　slat feeder　381
板条式输送机机体　slat conveyor body　440
半刚性悬架　semi-rigid suspension　142
半梯(楔)形环　half keystone ring　33
半拖板式活塞　half-slipper piston　31
半U形铲　semi-U blade　292
半圆键　semicircular key　74
半整体式动力转向器　semi-integral power steering gear　111
半轴　axle shaft, half shaft　100
半轴齿轮　side gear　101
拌和系统　mixing system　418
拌和转子传动箱　rotor transmission case　435
拌和转子罩壳　rotor encloser　435
蚌壳式抓斗　clamshell bucket　186
保持板　retainer plate　99
保持器　retainer　92
保持线圈　hold-in winding　80,81
保护螺母　protective nut　43,44
保护帽　protective cap　45

503

保护塞 protective plug 431
保护套 protective sleeve 43
保温隔热层（玻璃棉） insulating layer (glass wool) 408
保温套 insulating jacket 391
报警灯 brake warning lamp, alarm lamp, warning lamp 160,165,287
报警灯开关 alarm lights switch 360
杯深 cup depth 31
杯形顶 cup(dish) head(top, crown, roof) 31
背压阀 back pressure valve 177
背板 backing plate 155
泵继电器 pump relay 64
泵壳 pump case 415
泵控制阀 pump control valve 58
泵控制脉冲 pump control pulse 58
泵轮 pump, pump impeller 104,218
泵轮离合液力变矩器 impeller clutch torque converter 284
泵轮制动器 impeller brake 107
泵喷嘴 unit injector, pump/injector unit 55
泵室 pump chamber 74
泵体 pump body 45,55
泵体后盖 rear cover of pump body 415
泵体前盖 front cover of pump body 415
鼻型环、纳尔比环 Napier ring, Na-
pier scraper ring 33
比例分配阀 proportional distributing valve 165
比例速度控制器 proportional speed controller 108,315
闭锁离合器 lock-up clutch 107,285
壁板 side plate 388
变刚度弹簧 variable-rate spring 136
变矩器 torque converter 104
变矩器壳 converter housing 104
变矩器输出轴 torque converter output shaft 106
变矩器旋转壳体 torque converter rotation housing 218
变矩器与动力换挡变速箱 torque converter and power shift transmission 244
变宽度熨平板 variable width screed 430,433
变量驱动泵和马达 variable displacement drive pump 283
变速杆 shift lever 96
变速器叉 transmission yoke 98
变速箱 transmission case, transmission, gearbox 87,252,346,347,348
变速箱操纵阀 gearbox control valve 163
变速箱壳 transmission housing 94
变速箱壳体 gear-box housing 106
变速箱控制阀 transmission control

valve 285
变速箱控制器（变速箱，液力变矩器控制） transmission controller (transmission control, torque converter control) 285
变速箱输出轴 gear-box output shaft 106
变速箱输入轴 gear-box input shaft 106
变速油泵 variable speed pump, gear shift pump 103, 215
标尺 staff gauge 391
标志存放托盘，乳化剂箱，侧卸式废料箱 sign storage tray, emulsion tank, side tipping spoil bin 440
表面镀铬气环 chromium-plated ring, chrome-plated ring, chromed (piston) ring 34
表面全镀环 coated fully faced ring 34
表面填(镶)钼环，喷钼环 molybdenum-filled inlay ring, molybdenum coated ring, molybedeum ring 34
拨叉 shift yoke 80, 81
拨叉式油量调节机构 fork control mechanism 48
拨叉轴 shift fork shaft 95
拨杆 control lever 96
玻璃绒 glass wool 410
补偿阀 compensation valve 144
补油阀 recharging oil valve 282
不等节矩螺旋弹簧 unequally spaced coils spring 136
布料螺旋 spreading auger 424
步履式架桥机 step-type bridge erection equipment 10

C

C形垫圈 C-washer 151
材料流 material flow 427
参照线圈 reference coil 52
操纵杆 operating lever 157
操纵控制手柄 joystick control 175
操纵踏板 control pedal 175
操纵台 operator's station, operating console, control console, operator station 311, 344, 345, 417, 422, 423, 424, 428
操作员在场指示 operator presence 287
操作员座位 operator seat 360
槽底 ring groove bottom 29
槽底直径 groove-bottom diameter 29
侧传动齿轮 side driving gear 346
侧盖 side cover 115
侧环片 side rail 34
侧卸式装载机 side dumping loader 212
侧置砂石料箱 side grit/sand bin 440
测量线圈 measuring coil 52
测试接头 test connector 164
层叠铁芯 laminated(iron) core 52
叉式杂物抓斗 forked scrap grapple

bucket 231
差速齿轮 differential gear 107
差速器 differential 312
差速器壳 differential housing 101
差速器小锥齿轮 differential bevel pinion 101
柴油发动机 diesel engine 284,422,423,424,428,435
柴油机 diesel engine 24,87,173
柴油机电子控制系 diesel electronic control system 53
柴油细滤器 fuel fine 42
柴油箱 diesel fuel tank 422,423,424
柴油箱 diesel tank 428,430
铲刀 blade 245,279
铲刀板 moldboard 243
铲刀操纵手柄 blade control lever 285
铲刀侧移油缸 blade sideway cylinder 247
铲刀浮动 bucket float 287
铲刀角度变换油缸 blade angle change cylinder 245
铲刀倾斜油缸 blade tilting cylinder 279
铲刀刃 cutting edge 279
铲刀升降油缸 blade hoist cylinder 243,279
铲刀升降油缸(右) blade hoist cylinder(right) 247
铲刀升降油缸(左) blade hoist cylinder(left) 247
铲刀提升油缸 blade hoist cylinder 282
铲刀外伸油缸 blade outstanding cylinder 245
铲斗 bucket 174,214
铲斗调平 bucket leveler 287
铲斗连接件 bucket linkage 174
铲斗油缸 bucket cylinder 174,177
铲土运输机械 earthmoving machinery 4
长螺旋钻机 continuous flight auger drilling machine 9
超大型摊铺机 super large paver 309
超大型推土机 supersized dozer 278
超低断面轮胎 super low section tire 123
超高层建筑物拆除液压挖掘机 ultra high demolition hydraulic excavator 170
超专长波平均梁 ultrasonic averaging beam 328
车灯指示灯(近光/远光) indicator lamps for lights(dipped/distance) 360
车架 frame,vehicle frame 121,137
车架与悬挂系统 frame and suspension system 15
车架轴承 frame bearing 355
车轮 wheel 103,215
车速 vehicle speed 53
车制动接头控制 coupling head con-

trol 164
沉淀池 sedimentation reservoir 397
衬板 lining plate 393,394,432
衬垫 gasket,spacer block 27,115
衬管,内衬 liner 99
衬簧 expander 34
衬片铆钉 lining rivet 90
衬套 bush,bushing,bushing block, bushing,sleeve 90,114,115,126, 128,141,144,155,158,245
撑杆弹簧 strut spring 151
成品料出口 mixed material outlet 405
成品料储仓 mixed material storage silo 378,379,395,396
成品料输送机 mixed material conveyer 379
承推部件 thrust part 59
齿杆式油量调节机构 rack control machanism 48
齿轮 gear 106,218,415
齿轮泵 gear pump 247
齿轮齿条式转向传动机构 rack and pinion steering linkage 113
齿轮驱动 gear drive 385
齿轮式输油泵 gear feed pump 55
齿轮箱 gear box 313
齿圈 gear ring,ring gear 23,26,37
齿扇 toothed segment(quadrant), notched quadrant 91
齿扇轴 sector shaft 115

齿套 gear sleeve 106
齿条齿扇式转向器 rack and sector steering gear 116
齿形带 toothed belt 22
冲击夯 impacting rammer 6
冲击式压路机 impact roller 343
抽风管 exhaust tube 397
抽风机 exhaust fan 397
出水口 water outlet 72,74
出水室 outlet tank 72
出油阀 delivery valve,check valve 45,46,47,57
出油阀弹簧 delivery valve spring 45,46
出油阀紧座 delivery valve holder (carrier,support) 46
出油阀切槽 delivery valve flute 46
出油阀压紧座 delivery valve holder 45
出油阀座 delivery valve seat 45,46
出油管 oil outlet pipe 412
出油开关 oil outlet switch 411,412
出油口 outlet port,oil outlet 77,78
初级泵 primer pump 57,58
初级滤网式过滤器 primary gauze filter 54
初级绕组 primary winding 67
初级线圈 primary winding 68
除尘装置 dust collector 378,379
除雪铲 snow blade 231

储气罐　air tank　398
储气筒　air reservoir　162，163，164，411
储液罐　reservoir　91
储油缸筒　reservoir tube　144
触板　contact disc　80
触点　contact　67,81
传动齿圈　driving gear ring　382
传动带　driving belt　387
传动链　transmission chain　312,313
传动链轮　driving chain wheel　383
传动链条　driving chain　311
传动系　power train　243,254
传动系统　power train system, transmission system　15,311
传动轴　drive shaft, drive shaft, driving shaft, propeller shaft (drive shaft), transmission shaft, weight drive shaft to motor　87,97,216,244,358,409
传动轴特征长度　drive shaft length　99
传动轴座　driving shaft seat　409
传感器　sensor　52,55,64,391
传统线圈点火系统　classical (conventional) ignition system　67
串联式振动压路机（双钢轮）　tandem vibratory roller (doubie drum)　343
串联制动主缸总成　tandem master cylinder assembly　161
垂直销轴　vertical pin　353

锤式碎石机　hammer crusher　5
磁场接线柱　magnetic-field terminal　82
磁极　magnetic-pole　81,82
磁铁芯　magnet core　59
磁性放油塞　magnetic (drain) plug　27
磁性螺塞　magnetic (drain) plug　89
次承推面（传递小侧压力面）　minor thrust face　29
次级绕组　secondary winding　67
次级线圈　secondary winding　68
从动齿轮　driven gear　77
从动链轮　driven chain wheel　386
从动轮毂　clutch plate hub, driven plate hub　89,90
从动盘　driven plate　85,89,90,102,119
从动盘毂　clutch plate hub　102,119
（从动盘）毂法兰　hub flange　90
从动桥　driven axle　121
从蹄　trailing shoe　147
从蹄总成　trailing shoe and lining, secondary shoe assembly　151
粗滤器　coarse filter, strainer filter　89,282

D

大电路开关箱　large locker and paddle lock　440
大功率开关　high power switch　178

大螺旋弹簧　large coil spring　102
大气压力传感器　atmosphere pressure sensor　53
大气压力接头　altitude-pressure connection　51
大型轮式装载机　large type wheel loader　211
大型摊铺机　large paver　309
大型推土机　large type dozer　278
大型挖掘机　large type excavator　170
大型正铲挖掘机　large type shovel (face excavator)　170
大直径　major diameter　29
大锥齿轮　large bevel gear　102
带　belt　389
带侧切口开口　joint with side notch　34
带传动装置　belt drive unit　394
带键螺栓　key bolt　156
带轮　pulley　82
带轮毂　belt pulley hub　74
带锚定板的转向节　combination spindle and anchor plate　155
带内切口开口　joint with internal notch　34
带膨胀元件的启动油量限制器　start-quantity stop with expansion element　52
带燃烧室的活塞顶　piston head with combustion chamber　31
带式给料器　belt feeder　380
带式输送机,带式运输机　belt conveyer　378,380,417
带束层　belt, belt ply, bracing ply, tread belt　123
带束斜交轮胎　belted bias (diagonal) tire　123
带束子午线轮胎　belted radial tire　123
带有搅拌装置的加热室　heating plenum with mixing device　424
怠速弹簧　idle spring, idling spring　50
怠速调节螺钉　idle-mixture adjusting screw　64
怠速辅助弹簧　auxiliary idle spring　49
袋　sack　57
袋骨架　bag cage　398
袋式除尘器　bag dust filter　398
单边支重轮　single flange track roller　135
单顶置凸轮轴　single overhead camshaft　38
单钢轮振动压路机　single drum vibratory roller　6,343,367
单根式传动轴　one-piece drive shaft　98
单活塞轮缸　single-piston wheel cylinder　147
单路稳定分流阀　one-way stabilized flow divider valve　117
单轮手扶式振动压路机　walk behind single drum vibratory roller　343

509

单速行星减速器 single-speed planetary 332

单万向节传动轴 single joint couping shaft 98

单向除雪铲（犁） one-way snow plow 262

单向阀 one-way valve, non-return valve, check valve 31, 75, 117, 163, 164, 177, 282

单向孔 one way orifice 57

单向离合器 one-way clutch 80

单向离合器齿轮 one-way clutch gear 218

单向离合器滚柱 one-way clutch roller 218

单一加水口 single water fill port 361

单一水箱排水口 single water tank drain 361

单轴螺旋式搅拌器 single axle screw mixer 418

挡板 baffle plate, orifice plate 94, 135, 159, 391

挡滑滚轮 thrust roller 382

挡料角钢 stop angle iron 388

挡泥板 mudguard 214

挡圈 anti-extrusion ring, check ring, retainer, retaining ring 41, 100, 115, 131, 132, 152, 245

挡铁 backstop 80

挡土板 breast board 279

挡销 stopping pin 357

挡油环油槽 retainer oil seal groove 37

挡油盘 oil retaining disk 94

挡油圈,挡油罩板 oil baffle 23, 37

刀槽花纹,细缝花纹 sipe(s), sipings, sipe cut, traction blades, traction slots 124

刀夹 tool clamp 431

刀具与拌和转子组件 cutter and rotor assembly 435

刀头 tool bit 431

刀座 tool holder 431

导板 guide plate 245

导板盖 parallel guide cap 133

导管 bushing 153

导环 guide ring 81

导轮 reactor, stator 104, 218

导轮轴 stator shaft 218

导体玻璃 conductive glass 69

导向杠杆 guide lever 50

导向轮 track idler 173, 279

导向体 guide 46

导向销 guide pin 152

导销 guide pin, locating pin 155

导柱 guide pillar 325

倒车齿轮 reverse gear 94

倒挡拨叉 reverse shift fork 96

倒挡拨叉轴 reverse shift fork shaft 96

倒挡拨块 reverse shift block 96

倒挡和减速器行星排 planetary gear set for reverse gear and retarder 107

倒挡离合器 reverse gear shift

clutch 246

倒角油环 bevelled edge oil control ring 34

道路再生机 pavement recycler 421

低断面轮胎 low section tire 123

低速柱塞马达 low speed piston motor 219

低温启动喷油器 cold-starting injector 64

低压接线柱 low-voltage terminal, primary terminal 67,68

低压油腔 slight pressure chamber 45

底板 backing plate, base plate, bottom plate 151

底肋 bottom rib 29

底基层 under layer 407

地脚螺栓 stone bolt 386

第4挡离合器 4th gear clutch 107

第二道环槽 second (No.2) ring groove(slot) 28

第二道气环,第二道压缩环 second (compression) ring, 2nd (compression) ring, lower compression ring 32

第二环岸 second(No.2)land 29

第二涡轮 second turbine 218

第二涡轮轴 second turbine shaft 218

第三环岸 third land 29

第一道环槽 top(No.1) ring groove (slot) 28

第一道气环,上压缩环 top(upper) compression ring, top ring, No.1 compression ring 32

第一环岸,火力岸 top(No.1)land, fire(head)land 29

第一涡轮 first turbine 218

第一涡轮轴 first turbine shaft 218

点火开关 ignition switch 64, 67,165

点火喷头 ignition nozzle 382

点火器 ignition box 360

点火线圈 coil, ignition coil 64, 67,68

电插头 electrical connection 65

电磁断油阀 fuel shutoff solenoid 47

电磁阀 solenoid valve 58,59,164

电磁阀弹簧 solenoid valve spring 59

电磁阀针阀 solenoid-valve needle 55

电磁开关 solenoid swith 81

电磁开关触板 contact disc; starting swith 81

电磁开关线圈 solenoid winding 65

电磁铁芯 solenoid plunger 65

电磁线圈 solenoid coil 59

电磁溢流阀 solenoid spill valve 55

电磁振动器 electromagnetic vibrator 380

电磁振动式给料器 electromagnetic vibrating feeder 380

511

电动机　electric motor　385,387
电动燃油泵　electric fuel pump　64
电机　electrical motor　380
电极衬套　electric pole bush(ing)　70
电控单元　ECU(Electronic Control Unit)　64,165
电控系统　electric control system　108,285,315
电流表　ampere meter　67,80
电气系统　electrical system　214
电热塞　glow plug, heater plug　53,83
电容器　capacitor　82
电容器架　condenser bracket　82
电枢　armature　81
电枢轴　armature shaft　81
电刷　brush　81,82
电刷架　brush holder　81,82
电压调节器　voltage regulator　82
电子调速器　electrical governor　285
电子接线盒　electrical junction box　332
电子控制泵-喷嘴喷射系统　electronically controlled unit-injector injection system　54
电子控制变速箱　electronic controlled transmission　285
电子控制单元　ECU　57,164,178
电子控制模块　electronic control unit　53
电子控制式泵-喷嘴共轨喷射系统　electronically controlled unit injector common-rail injection system　56
电子控制转向/制动系统　electronic controlled steering/brake system　285
电子控制装置　electronic control unit　55
电子驱动模块　electronic drive unit　53
电子真空调节阀　electronic-vacuum regulator valve　53
电子制动系统　Electronic Brake System(EBS)　164
电子制动系统信道组件　EBS channel module　164
垫板　backing plate　245
垫块　cushion block　156
垫片　shim, shim block, washer　43,100,115,134,152,245,415
垫圈　washer, gasket　27,41,43,44,83,126,130,139,155
吊耳　shackle　139
吊耳销　shackle pin　139
吊眼　lifting eye, hoisting eye　129
顶(部), 头(部)　head, crown, top, roof　29
顶杆　carrier rod　157
顶推架　push frame　279
定时齿带罩　timing belt cover　22
定时带轮　timing bett puller　22
定位板　locating plate　353
定位弹簧　rocker-arm spring　41

定位螺钉　locating screw　45
定位螺母　set nut　94
定位凸键　locking lip, locating lug (tang)　35
定位销　locating pin(plug)　22,35,37,43
定向激振器　directed exciter　370
定子槽　stator slot　82
定子绕组　stator winding　82
定子铁芯　stator core　82
定子轴　stator shaft　104
动臂　boom　174,214
动臂油缸　boom cylinder　174,177,214
动力换挡变速箱　power shifting transmission case　103,105,215,216,246,280,281
动力耙　power rake　231
动力转向器　power steering gear　111
动力转向油泵　PS pump = Power Steering pump　111
斗齿　bucket lip　174
斗底增强耐磨板条　wear straps fitted to increase base strength　175
斗杆　arm　174
斗杆油缸　arm cylinder　174,177
镀铬的环片　chromium-plated rail　34
端板　header　72
端盖　end closure　100
端子　terminal　83
断电器　contact breaker　67

断油或怠速限制器　stop or idle stop　49
盾构机　tunnel shield machine　10
多功能工程车　multifunctional vehicle　12
多功能装载机　multi terrain loader　212
多件式油环　multi-piece oil ring　34
多件式油冷活塞　multi-piece oil-cooled piston　31
多孔镀铬环　porous-chrome ring　34
多路换向阀　multichannel conversion valve　247
多片式钢板弹簧　multi-leaves soring　136

E

鄂式碎石机　jaw crusher　5
二挡被动齿轮　second speed driven gear　94
二挡主动齿轮　second speed drive gear　94
二通阀　two-way valve　162

F

发动机　engine　103,108,176,178,215,216,219,243,246,279,283,285,291,311,312,313,314,315,344,345,346,350,422
发动机怠速运行　engine idling　360
发动机负荷　engine load　58

513

发动机功能指示 engine function indicator 316
发动机和变矩器 engine and torque converter 280
发动机及传动系统 engine and transmission system 214
发动机加热 engine heating 360
发动机空气滤清器堵塞 engine air filter plugging 287
发动机控制器 engine controller 285
发动机曲轴 engine crankshaft 104
发动机润滑油压 engine oil pressure 285
发动机托架 engine holding frame 129
发动机罩 engine hood 214
发动机诊断 engine diagnostics 360
发动机诊断开关 engine diagnostics switch 360
发动机支撑架 engine supporting bracket 129
发动机转速 engine speed 285
发动机转速和曲轴位置传感器 engine speed and crank position sensor 58
发动机转速指示表 engine speed indicator 316
发动机总成 engine assembly 14
阀零件 valve part 59
阀门 valve 66,126
阀门保持器 valve holder 66

阀片双金属片 bimetallic disk 75
阀球 valve ball 59
阀柱塞 valve plunger 59
翻松器 scarifier 427
反击式碎石机 impact crusher 5
反扭曲型 negative twist type 34
反循环钻机 reverse circulation drilling rig 10
反应室 reaction chamber 385
反转型除雪铲（犁） reversible snow plow 262
反转型液力变矩器 counter-rotating torque converter 107
方向杆 steering yoke 116
方向盘位置调整 steering wheel position adjustment 360
方向旋钮 direction knob 316
防抱死制动系统 Antilock Brake System (ABS) 165
防尘圈 dust ring 152
防尘罩 boot,dust boot,dust cover, seal, dust helmet, dust shield 100,113,144,151,155
防溅罩 splash shield 155
防倾翻推土机 roll-over proofing dozer 278
防振夹 anti-rattle clip 155
放沥青管 asphalt discharging pipe 409
放料门 discharge gate 388
放气阀 bleeder valve (screw) 151,155
放气阀帽 cap 155

放气开关　air deflation switch　412
放气螺钉　air bleed screw　156
放气嘴　bleed nipple　152
放水阀(塞)　drain plug　71,72
放油管　oil outlet pipe　413
放油孔　oil drain hole　128
放油口　oil drain　358
放油螺塞　drain pulley,drain plug　23,26,27,76,411
放油塞　drain plug　134,412
飞轮　flywheel　23,26,37,89,218
飞轮齿圈　flywheel gear ring　36,79
飞轮盖　flywheel casing　89
废料箱　spoil rubbish bin　440
废气出口　exhaust outlet　411
分电器　distributor,ignition distributor　23,64,67
分电器盖　distributor cap　67
分电器凸轮　distributor cam　67
分动箱　PTO, transfer case　87,176,219,347,348,409
分火头　distributor rotor　67
分离叉　lining fork, release fork, withdrawal fork, operating fork, clutch fork,release fork　89,91,92
分离弹簧　release spring　89
分离杆　release rod　92
分离拉索　release cable　91
分离圈　release rim　89
分离式冷却系统　separated cooling system　284
分离式手动快速连接器　eliminator manual quick coupler　186
分离套筒　release sleeve　89
分料器螺旋离地高度调节手轮　distributer screw ground clearance adjusting hand wheel　419
分料器马达　distributer motor　419,420
分配阀组　distributing valve group　177
分配式喷油泵　Distributor-type injection pump　47
分配柱塞　distributor plunger, distributor-pump　47
分散燃烧式加热机　Decentralized combustion preheater　422
分水管　divide the water pipe　71
粉料称量斗　filler weigh hopper　390
粉料储仓及供给装置　mineral filler storage silo and supply system　378,379
粉料供给装置　filler supply system　383
粉料计量秤　filler scale　390
粉料螺旋输送器　filler auger conveyer　390
粉料入口　filler inlet　405
粉料输入管　filler input pipe　389
风管　air pipe　397
风机　blower　383
风扇　fan, cooling fan　22,26,71,73,82
风扇叶片　fan blade　73

515

风扇罩　fan shroud　73
封闭湿式多片制动器　oil enclosed, multiple disc brakes　284
封盖　cap　415
封料　material seal　70
蜂鸣消除开关　buzzer cancel switch　285
缝隙式滤清器　edge filter, edge-type filter　43, 44, 59
扶手　arm rest　175
浮标　buoyage　410
浮动杠杆　floating lever　50
浮动油封　floating oil seal　131, 132, 133
浮钳　floating caliper　155
浮球口　ball float opening　408
浮子　float, floater　60, 61, 391
浮子室　float chamber (float bowl [美])　61
辅助阀　auxiliary valve　285
辅助空气阀　auxiliary air valve　64
辅助油缸　auxiliary cylinder　177
负极板　negative plate　70
负极接线柱　battery negative terminal　70
附加灯开关　additional lights switch　360
附加电阻　ballast resistor, external resistor　67, 68
附加压紧机构　additional hold-down mechanism　149
复位弹簧　return spring, back spring　81, 159

副变速器　vice transmission　312
副车架　sub-frame　142
副齿轮箱　auxiliary gearbox　346
副钢板弹簧　auxiliary spring, supplementary (leaf) spring, secondary spring　139
覆带起重机　crawler crane　8
覆带式全液压凿岩钻车　crawler hydraulic drill rig　5
覆带式推土机　track bulldozer (crawler bulldozer)　4
覆带式装载机　track-type loader　211

G

盖　cap　89, 126
盖板　cover plate, cover board　153, 415
盖形螺母　cap nut　55, 57
干式缸套　dry sleeve(liner) type　27
干式全盘式制动器　Dry-type complete disc brake　156
干燥滚筒　dryer drum　386, 397
干燥搅拌筒　dryer-mixer drum　379
干燥区叶片　drying zone flights　382, 383
杆　rod　144
杆导管　rod guide　144
感应环与速度传感器　sensing ring and speed sensor　164
刚性悬架(摆动桥)　Rigid suspension(swing axle)　142

刚性（整体式）车架　Rigid Frame　351
钢板弹簧　leaf soring, leaf spring, laminated spring　136,139
钢板弹簧衬套　eaf spring bushing, spring bush(ing)　139
钢板弹簧夹　spring clamp, spring hoop, spring-leaf retainer, spring stirrup　139
钢板弹簧卷耳　spring eye　139
钢板弹簧式后悬架　leaf-spring rear suspension　139
钢板弹簧销　leaf spring pin, spring pin, spring bolt　139
钢板弹簧主片　main spring leaf　139
钢板弹簧自由（吊耳）端　spring free end　139
钢片组合式油环,胀簧刮片式油环　expander/segment oil control ring, composite type oil control ring, steel strip composite type oil ring　34
钢球　steel ball, steel shot　100,115,358
钢球导管　ball guide　115
钢索　steel cable　396
钢镶片　steel insert　31
钢质弹簧　steel spring　137
缸套密封圈　sleeve seal　27
缸筒,缸体　cylinder body　151,153
杠杆　lever　158
杠杆臂　lever arm　51

杠杆操纵开关　lever switch　178
高牵引力胎面花纹　high-traction tread pattern　124
高速柱塞马达　high peed piston motor　219
高压泵　high-pressure pump　58
高压泵凸轮轴　camshaft of high-pressure pump　56
高压接线柱　high voltage terminal　68
高压密封　high-pressure sealing ring　59
高压线接头　high-voltage connector　69
高压小型备胎　high pressure small spare tire　123
高压油管　pressure pipe　42
高压油管接头　high pressure pipe connection　43
格栅铲斗　skeleton bucket　187
隔板　separator, isolating plate　70,119,388,410
隔离环　spacer ring　218
隔离式加热阀　isolate heating valve　440
隔热槽　heat-proof slots　31
隔水板　water-stop sheet　72
工况监视器　monitor　175
工作缸,分离缸　slave cylinder, release cylinder　91
工作缸活塞回位弹簧　slave cylinder piston return spring　91
工作筒　tube　144

517

工作油泵 operational pump 103,215
工作装置液压泵 work equipment pump 282
工作装置油泵 work equipment pump 87
工作装置总成 work equipment assembly 14,174
工作状态环 closed ring 32
功率二极管 power diode 82
供油泵 supply pump 58
供油孔 feed hole 55,57
供油口 feed port 55
供油系统 fuel system 42
拱度调节装置 crown control device 311
共轨,共用油轨 common rail 57,58
共轨燃油喷射系统喷油器 injector for common rail injection system 59
共轨燃油喷射系统(蓄压气原理) common-rail(fuel)injection system 58
骨料仓 aggregate bin, aggregate hopper 417,441
骨料称量斗 aggregate weigh hopper 390
骨料计量秤 aggregate scale 390
骨料进口 aggregate inlet 405
骨料上料带 aggregate charging belt,aggregate feed belt 383,384
毂法兰 hubflange 90

鼓风机 blower 382,384,385
鼓式(蹄式)制动器 drum brake 147,150,161
鼓转动方向 direction of drum rotation 147
固定板 solid plate 94
固定底板 anchor plate 139
固定短路环 fixed short-circuiting ring 52
固定夹 clamp 115
固定脚架 fixed foot stand 412
固定螺栓 retaining bolt 37
固定喷灯 fixed blow lamp 410
固定偏心块 fixed eccentric weight 357,358
固定钳 fixed caliper 155
固定铣刨鼓 fixed milling drum 430
固定支座 fixed supporting seat 142
固定制动盘 fixed brake disk 156
故障排除开关 troubleshooting switch 360
刮板 drag plate 311
刮板驱动马达 drag drive motors 311
刮板输送器 drag conveyers 311,312
刮泥板 scrapers 344,345
挂胶中间钢轮 rubber-coated steel mid-wheel 331
挂片 segment 34
挂线调平系统 erected stringline

leveling system 328
关节轴承 joint bearing 353,354
管端花键轴 tube end spline shaft 99
管接头 nipple,pipe joint 74,152
管路小三通阀操纵手柄 small pipeline triple valve control handle 409
管座板 pipe mounting plate 398
灌缝机 crack pouring machine 11
轨道 track 396
滚动方向 rolling direction 124
滚动轴承 rolling bearing 37
滚轮 roller 45
滚轮式挺柱 roller tappet 45
滚轮销 roller pin 45
滚轮行走马达 drum traveling motor 349
滚圈 rolling ring 382,383,405
滚刷式清扫车 broom sweeper 12
滚筒体 drum 382
滚针和轴承杯 needle roller and bearing cup 99
滚针轴承 needle bearing 100
滚珠转盘 ball bearing turntable 140
滚柱 roller 84
滚柱保持器 roller retainer 84
滚柱式单向离合器 roller-type overruning clutch 81
滚柱轴承 roller bearing 89,94
滚柱座圈 roller race 84
滚子 roller 55

过大料溢料管道 over-sized aggregate discharge chute 384
过滤网 filter screen 282
过滤型喷咀 spray nozzle with filter 361
过载阀 overload valve 282

H

河道疏浚挖掘机 river channel dredging excavator 170
恒范钢镶片活塞 invar strut piston 31
恒范钢镶片,殷钢镶片 invar insert 31
横管 horizontal pipe 413
横拉杆 tie rod,tie bar, track rod 111,113
横拉杆夹 tie rod clamp 113
横拉杆内接头 inner tie rod end (joint) 113
横拉杆外接头 outer tie rod end (joint) 113
横梁 cross sail 128
横坡传感器 cross slope sensor 327
横向花纹 transverse pattern 124
横向模式按钮-右侧 pushbutton for CRAB mode-right 360
横向模式按钮-左侧 pushb Hon for CRAB mode-left 360
横向稳定杆 stabilizer bar,stabilizer (shaft),anti-roll (sway) bar,roll bar,sway bar 137

519

横销 pin cotter 415
横轴 cross axle 102,119
烘干滚筒 dryer drum 384
烘干筒 dryer drum 378
红灯(发动机诊断) red lamp(engine diagnostics) 360
红外温度计 infrared thermometer 360
喉管 diffuser, venturi, throat 61,398
后车架 rear frame 142,344,345,353,354
后传动轴 rear drive shaft 98
后端盖 rear end cover, end cover 81,82
后端凸缘 back end collar 37
后盖 rear cover 128
后机架 rear frame 116,214,216
后加热/烘干/搅拌机 postheater/dryer/mixer 424
后轮 rear wheel, rear drum 121,314,345
后轮速度传感器 rear wheel speed sensor 165
后轮转向油缸 rear wheel steering cylinder 247
后桥 rear axle 103,116,15,214,215,216
后桥摆动轴 rear axle oscillating shaft 116
后桥差速器 rear axle differential gear 246
后桥箱(体) rear axle housing 128,129
后驱动桥 rear driving axle 243
后输出轴 rear output shaft 106
后退主动齿轮 reverse drive gear 94
后消声器 rear muffler 60
后行星排 rear planetary gear set 106
后行星排制动器 brake of rear planetary gear set 106
后悬架 rear suspension 121
后压盘 rear pressure plate 89
后支承销 rear anchor pin 157
后支架 rear bracket 139
后制动器总成 rear brake assembly 160
后制动油管 rear brake line 160
后置砂石料箱 rear sand/grit bin 440
厚度调节装置 depth adjustment 311
互锁装置 inter locking derice 95
互锁钢球 interlock ball 95
互锁销,互锁柱销 interlock plug 95,96
护板 cover sheet, guard plate 70,128
花键毂 splined hub 85,355,94
花键油封 spline seal 99
花纹沟 groove, tread groove, tire groove 123
滑动叉 slip yoke 98
滑动齿轮 sliding gear 79

滑动杆　sliding rod　49
滑动花键　slip spline　99
滑动套　shift collar　85
滑动销　sliding pin　155
滑动轴承　sliding bearing　94
滑阀　slide valve　158
滑模水泥摊铺机　slip-form concrete paver　7
滑片式输油泵　vane-type supply pump　47
滑套　sliding bush　106
滑移转向装载机　skid steer loader　211
滑脂嘴　grease fitting　113
化油器　carburetor　23,60
化油器式供给系统　carburetor fuel system　61
划线机　paint line marker　11
环岸直径　land diameter,ring land diameter　29
环槽侧面　ring-groove side　29
环槽加厚部,环槽基底　ring-groove pad　29
环齿轮　ring gear　101
环(工作)表面,环外表面　ring face, ring periphery, ring working face　32
环间隙　ring clearance　32
环形冲洗阀　loop flush valve　349
环形气囊　toroid bellow　136
环形油槽　annular oil groove　35
缓冲层　breaker　123
缓冲垫　cushion pad　388

缓冲块　bumper, bumper pad, buffer　92,139
缓冲器　shock absorber　64
换挡杆盖　shift lever cover　95
换挡机构　gearshift mechanism　96
换挡离合器　shift clutch　246
换挡轴　shift shaft　96
换向阀　reversing valve　282
换向器　commutator　81
黄灯(发动机诊断)　yellow lamp(engine diagnostics)　360
黄铜套　brass jacket　80
黄油嘴　grease nipple, grease fitting, lubricator fitting　74,134,353
回收料入口　reclaimed material inlet　405
回收料上料带　reclaimed material charging belt　383
回位弹簧　return spring, back spring　55,57,65,80,85,91,92,126,148,149,151
回油道　return oil passage　75
回油阀,溢流阀　overflow valve　55
回油管　return pipe　42,57
回油接头　leak-off connection, drain fitting　43,44,59
回油孔　oil drain (return) hole, oil return passage　29
回转阀　revolving valve　247
回转接头　swivelcoupling　247
回转马达　swing motor　176
回转圈　turning circle, circle　243,

521

245,255
回转式吊杆　swing boom　441
回转液压马达　slewing hydraulic motor　177
回转油缸　revolving cylinder　247
混合花纹　dual purpose tread pattern　124
混凝土泵车　truck-mounted concrete pump　14
混凝土布料机　concrete placing boom　14
混凝土车载泵　truck-mounted concrete line pump　14
混凝土机械　concrete machinery　13
混凝土搅拌车　concrete mixer truck　14
混凝土搅拌设备　concrete mixing plant　14
混凝土拖泵　trailer concrete pump　14
活动偏心块　free eccentric weight　357
活动支座　movable supporting seat　142
活塞　piston　22,26,28,102,119,134,137,144,151,153,155,156,158,159
活塞凹坑　piston relief (recess)　31
活塞顶　piston head (crown, top, roof)　29
活塞杆　piston rod　144
活塞钢镶片　steel piston insert　31
活塞环槽镶圈　piston insert　31
活塞环(分布)带　ring belt, ring zone　29
活塞回位弹簧　piston back spring　153,156
活塞密封圈　piston seal ring　156
活塞裙部　piston skirt (body, barrel)　28
活塞式蓄能器　piston accumulator　137
活塞套筒　piston sleeve　156
活塞销　piston pin, gudgeon pin, wrist pin, pin　22,29
活塞销衬套　piston pin bush (ing)　35
活塞销孔　pin hole, gudgeon (piston, wrist) hole　29
活塞销孔凸台　pin boss　29
火管　fire tube　411
火花塞　spark plug, sparking plug　23,64,67,69
火箱　fire box　382
货叉　pallet fork　230

J

机架　frame, framework　127,214,311,369,382,435
机器安全系统　machine security system　287
机器控制器　machine controller　332
机体　cylinder block　26
机械传动系统　mechanical transmis-

sion system 87,417
机械式断油装置 mechanical shutoff device 47
机械式浮动平均梁 mechanical floating averaging beam 328
机油泵 oil pump 23,26,76,77
机油泵体 pump body 77
机油粗滤器 coarse oil filter 26
机油集滤器 oil strainer 23,26
机油冷却器接头 oil cooler-fitting 72
机油滤清器 oil cleaner 26,76
机油喷嘴 oil nozzle 31
机油细滤器 secondary filter 26
基本段熨平板 basic screed 325
基层 subbase 407
激光调平系统 laser leveling system 328
激光发射器 generating laser 252
激光接收器 laser pickoff 252
激光找平系统 laser grade control system 252
激励二极管 exciter diode 82
极限快放阀 limiting quick-release valve 162
棘爪 pawl 158,91
集电环 collector ring 82
集料框架调节手轮 aggregate framework adjusting hand wheel 420
集料螺旋 aggregate auger 424
集滤器 oil strainer 76
集中燃烧式加热机 concentrated

combustion preheater 422
加料箱 feeder box 382
加热管 glow tube, heating pipe 83,413
加热火管 heating fire tube 410
加热火焰喷灯 blow lamp 409
加热器和控制线圈 heater and control coil 83
加热室 heating plenum 422,423
加热/铣刨机 preheater/miller 423
加热系统 heating system 409, 411,428
加速器备用开关 accelerator back up switch 178
加速器调节刻度盘 accelerator dial 178
加速器控制器 accelerator control 360
加速器应急回路 accelerator emergency circuit 178
加速踏板传感器 accelerator sensor 53
加压水泵 pressured water pump 397
加液孔盖 cell filler plug 70
加油孔 oil filling port 128
加油口 oil filler 412
加油口盖 filler cap 22
夹板 strap, clamping plate 99,137
夹头 collet 391
驾驶室 operator cab, driving cab 176,344,345
驾驶室及操作系统 cab and operat-

ing system 214,243,279
驾驶员操作台 operator station 286
驾驶员座椅 driver's seat, pilot seat, operator's seat 175,292,311
架桥机 bridge girder erection equipment 10
坚韧的移动式履带 durable mobil-trac belt 331
间隙调节器 gap adjuster 23
间隙调整装置 lash adjusting device 151
间歇强制式搅拌设备 batch forced mixing plant 376
监控系统 monitoring system 287
监控显示系统 monitoring display system 286
监控仪表盘 monitor panel 285
检视孔,检查孔 inspection hole 148,155
减容体 delivery valve volume reducer 46
减速齿轮副 speed reducing gear pair 106
减速器(机) reducer, speed reducer 314,356,389,393,394
减速踏板 deceleration pedal 285
减压阀 pressure-reducing valve 144
减压环带 retraction piston 46
减振弹簧 torsional (damping) spring 90,387
减振器 shock absorber 355,356,369
键 key 415
交流发电机 alternator 82
胶合剂 tackiness agent 83
角位器 angular position device 245
铰接点 articulated point 116
铰接机架式平地机 articulated frame motor grader 242
铰接架壳体 articulated joint shell 353
铰接式车架 articulated frame 352
铰接式自卸车 articulated truck 4
铰接转向节 articulated steering joint 346,347,348
铰销 joint pin 140
铰销轴 pin pivot 353
脚制动阀 foot brake valve 162
脚制动器 foot brake 164
搅拌臂 mixing arm 393,394,432
搅拌桨叶 mixing paddle 393,394,405,432
搅拌楼 mixing tower 395,396
搅拌器 mixer 378,390,427,428
搅拌区叶片 mixing zone flights 383
搅拌筒体 mixing trough 393,394,432
搅拌箱 mixer 417
搅拌轴 mixing shaft 393,394,432
轿车胎面,乘用车胎面 passenger-car tire tread 124
阶梯状切口 step joint 32

阶梯状切口刮油环　stepped scraper ring　33
接合板　connecting plate　102
接合齿轮　joint gear　79
接料斗　receiving hopper　428
接头　link　92
接头叉　end yoke　99
接头盖　cap　89
接头壳　joint housing　113
接线螺栓　terminal　81
接线柱　terminal　80
节气门　throttle valve　61,64
节气门开关　throttle position switch　64
节温器　thermostat　71
结合凸缘　companion flange　99
金属板套　metal plate jacketing　68
金属杆　metal rod　69
金属网　metal screen　62
紧凑型备胎,应急备胎　compact (temporary) spare tire　123
紧固螺钉　tightening screw　45,48
紧固螺母　tensioning nut　59
紧急制动按钮　emergency brake pushbutton　360
紧急制动开关　emergency brake switch　316
紧缩端　pig-tail　136
进风门　shutter　386
进口　inlet port　57
进料管　supply pipe　408
进料口盖　charging cover　410
进料滤网　charging strainer　410

进料区叶片　feeding zone flight　382,383
进气管　intake tube　23,26,60
进气活门　intake shutter　53
进气加热器,预热器　(air)intake heater　53,61
进气开关　air inlet switch　411,412
进气门　intake valve　22,38,61
进气歧管　intake manifold　61
进气歧管接头　intake-manifold connection　66
进气气流　intake air flow　53
进气温度　intake air temperature　53
进气温度传感器　intake air temperature sensor　53
进水口　water inlet　72,74
进水室　inlet tank　72
进油阀门　oil inlet valve　411
进油管　oil inlet pipe　410,413
进油管接头　inlet adaptor　43,44
进油孔　inlet oil port　75
进油口　fuel inlet,oil inlet　66,77,78
井下作业装载机　underground mining loader　212
警示灯开关　beacon switch　360
净气　clean gas　398
静液传动系统　hystat power train system　220
静液驱动系统　hydrostatic drive system　283
静作用光轮压路机　static smooth

525

drum roller 343

矩形环 rectangular ring, plain (piston) ring 33

矩形路面封层摊铺箱 rectangle spreader box 419

锯齿式切口 serrated joint 35

聚合物改性沥青设备 polymer modified asphalt plant 7

聚合物改性稀浆封层摊铺箱 spreader box of polymer modification slurry seal machine 419

卷翻(膜片)式气囊 roll bellow 136,137

绝缘垫 insulator shim 83

绝缘盖 insulating cap 68

绝缘体,绝缘子 insulator, insulation 68,69,83

K

卡环 lock ring, retaining ring, retainer ring, snap ring 74,85,99,100,153

卡特舒适系列驾驶座 cat comfort series seat 286

开槽机 grooving machine 11

开槽油环 slotted oil ring 33

开口销 cotter pin 245

抗扭增强钢管 anti-torsion pipe fitted for increased strength 175

壳体 housing 75

可编程只读存储器(校正信息) PROM = Programmable Read Only Memory (corrective information) 53

可采暖空调 heating and air conditioning 286

可调节扶手 adjustable armrest 286

可调节挂钩 adjustable hitch 442

可动铁芯 movable core 80

刻度盘 dial plate 410

空挡启动停车制动手柄 neutral-start parking brake lever 220,221

空气弹簧气囊 air spring bellow 164

空气过滤器 air filter 345

空气进口 air inlet 62

空气流量计 airflow sensor 64

空气滤清器 air cleaner, air filter 26,60,61,176,344

空气滤清器盖 air cleaner housing cover, air cleaner cap(cover) 62

空气滤清器盖衬垫 air cleaner cap gasket 62

空气滤清器壳 air filter bowl (box, housing) 62

空气温度传感器 air-temperature sensor 64

空气压缩机 air compressor, compressor 162,163,164,411

孔式喷嘴 hole type nozzle 43

控制电磁线圈 control solenoid 57

控制弹簧 control spring 55,57

控制阀 control valve 176

控制阀 APC control valve APC 178

控制杆　control lever　47
控制杠杆　control lever　49,50
控制面板　control panel　422,424
控制膨胀镶片　strip inserts for expansion control　31
控制器　controller　252,398
控制器APC　controller APC　178
控制室　control chamber　57
控制套筒　control sleeve　47,48
控制系统　control system　379
控制柱塞　control plunger　57
快放阀　quick-release valve　162,388
快降阀　fast downfall valve　282
快速加速开关　quick accelerator switch　178
宽度可变式翻松器　variable scarifying device　428
宽幅全景视野　wide panoramic view　286

L

垃圾场专用推土机　dumparea dozer　278
垃圾填埋铲刀　landfill blade　292
拉杆　bar, drag rod, drag link, pullrod, tension rod bar　50,78,157
拉力传感器　tension sensor　392
拉伸弹簧　tension spring　91
肋条　edge, rib　70
冷骨料储仓及给料器　cold aggregate bins and feeder　378,379
冷骨料带式输送机及称量系统　cold aggregate belt conveyer and weighing system　379
冷却槽（通道）　cooling gallery, cooling passage　31
冷却器　oil cooler　177
冷却系统　cooling system　71,283
冷却罩　cooling jacket　382
冷铣刨　cold planer　230
离合器　clutch　312,79
离合器板　clutch plate　75
离合器操纵机构　clutch operation　91
离合器齿轮　clutch gear　79
离合器从动鼓　clutch drum　106
离合器从动盘　clutch driven plate　90
离合器分离拉索　clutch release cable　91
离合器盖　clutch cover　89,91
离合器杠杆操纵机构　clutch rod-operated mechanism　92
离合器工作缸　clutch release cylinder　89
离合器机械操纵机构　clutch operation(mechanical)　91
离合器拉索自动调节机构　automatic clutch cable adjusting mechanism　91
离合器踏板　clutch pedal　91,92
离合器踏板拉杆　clutch pedal linkage　91
离合器液压操纵机构　clutch operation(hydraulic)　91

离合器油缸体　clutch cylinder body　106
离合器轴　clutch shaft　89
离合器主动盘　clutch driving plate　106
离合器主缸　clutch master cylinder　91
离心块　centrifugal block　89
犁式除雪机　snow plough　12
励磁绕组　exciting winding　82
沥青泵　asphalt pump　409,413,415
沥青称量桶　asphalt weigh bucket　390
沥青储箱　asphalt storage tank　408
沥青大三通阀　large asphalt triple valve　409
沥青供给系统　asphalt supply system　378,379
沥青罐车　bitumen tank truck　437
沥青回油管　asphalt return pipe　390
沥青混合料转运车　asphalt mixture transfer vehicle　7
沥青计量秤　asphalt scale　390
沥青加热罐　asphalt heating tank　7
沥青搅拌设备　asphalt mixing plant　7
沥青进油管　asphalt inlet pipe　390
沥青量桶　asphalt weigh bucket　392
沥青路面加热机　asphalt pavement heater　12
沥青路面就地热再生机组　asphalt pavement-hot-in-place recycling machine set　12
沥青路面综合养护车　asphalt pavement combined maintenance vehicle　11
沥青排放阀　asphalt discharge valve　391
沥青喷管　asphalt spray pipe, asphalt nozzle　383,390
沥青喷洒　asphalt spraying　427
沥青喷射泵　asphalt injection pump　390,392
沥青容量指示器　asphalt capacity indicator　409
沥青入口　asphalt inlet　405
沥青洒布车　asphalt distributor　13,407
沥青摊铺机　asphalt paver　7,308
沥青桶　asphalt bucket　390,392
沥青脱筒设备　asphalt melting equipment　7
沥青箱　asphalt storage tank　410
沥青箱外罩　asphalt tank outer cover　410
沥青注入阀　asphalt injection valve　391
沥青注入管　asphalt injection pipe　391
连杆　connecting rod　22,26,35,134,159,214,

连杆大头盖　connecting rod cap　35
连杆盖　connecting rod bearing cap　22
连杆杆身　connecting rod shank　35
连杆螺母　connecting rod nut　35
连杆螺栓　connecting rod bolt　35
连杆轴瓦　connecting rod bearing shell　23,35
连接法兰　adapting flange　89
连接杆　linkage　158
连接管　connecting hose　389
连接螺栓　joint bolt　323
连接盘　coupling flange　119
连接软管　flexible(hydraulic) pipe　91
连接条　cell connector　70
连续滚筒式搅拌设备　continuous drum mixing plant　376,383
连续墙抓斗　continuous wall grab　9
帘布层　cord ply,plies,ply　123
帘线　cord　123
联合碎合设备　crushing & screening equipment　6
联轴节　coupling　393,394,415
联轴器　joint slack　45
链板输送机　slat conveyor　381
链传动(平衡箱)　chain drive(equilibrium box)　246
链轮驱动　chain wheel drive　385
链条　chain　386
链条传动　chain drive　244
两半填充环　semi-inlaid(filled)ring　34
两边侧板　two piece side plates　175
两段式传动轴　two-piece drive shaft　98
两件式轮辋　two-piece rim　125
量孔　orifice　58
量桶　weigh bucket　391
料仓　filler storage silo　389
料槽　chute　386
料斗　bucket,cold bins,hopper　311,379,380,381,386
料帘区叶片　showeing flight　403,405
料位器　level detector　388
领蹄　leading shoe,primary shoe　147,151
领蹄总成　leading shoe and lining,leading shoe assembly　151
溜料槽　discharge chute　386
流控系统　fluid control system　417
流量控制阀　flow control valve　247
流通阀　intake valve　144
路拱调节器　crown adjustor　419
路面高压清洗车　pavement high pressure cleaning vehicle　13
路面机械　pavement machinery　7
路面加热修补车　pavement heating repairing vehicle　11
路面破碎机　pavement breaker　13
路面修补车　pavement repairing vehicle　11

529

路面养护机械　pavement maintenance machinery　11
滤袋　filter bag　398
滤清器　filter　411,412,65
滤清器盖　filer cover　78
滤清器壳　filer bowl　78
滤网　strainer　408,411,413
滤芯　element　62
滤油器　filter, oil filter　117,177,282
滤纸　filter　62
履带　crawler, caterpillar track, track　16,108,127,173,279,280,313,315
履带板　track shoe　130
履带车辆转向桥　crawler steering axle　118
履带齿　grouser　279
履带底盘　tracked chassis　14,16
履带机　track rail　332
履带螺母　track nut　130
履带螺栓　track bolt　130
履带驱动马达　track motor　220,221
履带驱动与转向离合器　track drive and steering clutch　102
履带式车辆　crawler　127
履带式冷铣刨机　track cold milling machine,track cold planer　12
履带式摊铺机　tracked paver,track paper　108,308
履带式旋挖钻机　track rotary drilling rig　9

履带式液压挖掘机　track hydrulic excavator　4
履带式自卸车　track dump truck (crawler dump truck)　4
履带台车架　track roller frame, track frame　133,142,173
履带推土机工作机构　crawler dozer operation mechanism　291
履带推土机机架　crawler dozer frame　291
履带销　track pin　130
履带张紧器　track adjuster　127,135
履带张紧系统　belt(track) tensioning system　331,332
履带支重轮　track roller　131
履带总成　track assembly　130
轮　tyre(tire)　140
轮边减速器　wheel reductor,wheel-side reducer,wheel reduction gear　103,215,313,347,348
轮辐　wheel disk(disc,spoke,rib)　125
轮辐板　spoke plate　355,356
轮缸　wheel cylinder,straight-bore wheel cylinder　147,151
轮缸式制动器　wheel cylinder brake　147
轮缸推杆　cylinder link　151
轮毂　wheel hub　100,114
轮圈　drum shell　355,356
轮式底盘　wheeled chassis　14,15
轮式底盘行走系统　wheeled chassis

travel system 15
轮式推土机工作机构 wheel dozer operation mechanism 292
轮式推土机机架 wheel dozer frame 291
轮式挖掘机 wheel excavator 170
轮式挖掘装载机 wheel backhoe loader 171,212
轮式行走机构 wheeled running mechanism 121
轮胎 tire 100,246
轮胎式摊铺机 wheeled paver 308
轮胎式推土机 wheel dozer 278
轮胎式装载机 wheel loader 4
轮胎压路机 pneumatic tire compactor,pneumatic tyred roller 6,343
轮毂 whell hub 131
轮辋 rim,wheel rim 100,125
轮辋宽度 rim width 125
轮辋螺栓 rim bolt 100
轮辋偏距 rim offset 125
轮辋直径 rim diameter 125
轮缘 rim flange,flange 125
轮轴 axle 140
螺杆 screw bol 102
螺母 nut 36,41,83,85,126,144,245
螺塞 plug screw 100
螺栓 bolt 23,27,36,41,74,78,82,100,102,151,245,431
螺栓紧固边刃轻质材料铲斗 light material bucket with bolt-on edges 229

螺栓紧固边刃通用铲斗 general purpose bucket with bolt-on-edges 229
螺旋弹簧加压倒角油环 coil spring loaded beveled edge oil control ring 34
螺旋弹簧加压开槽油环 coil (spring) loaded slotted oil control ring 34
螺旋弹簧加压双倒角油环 coil spring loaded double beveled oil control ring 34
螺旋电子秤 auger electronic scale 389
螺旋分料器 auger conveyers,screw distributor, distributor auger, spreading auger 311,312,419,420,427,428,430,433
螺旋花键 helical spline 81,84
螺旋器驱动泵 auger drive pump 333
螺旋驱动马达 auger drive motor 311,333
螺旋输送机 auger conveyer 389,398
螺旋叶片 auger blade 311

M

脉冲阀 pulse valve 398
铆钉 rivet 90
锚定螺栓,固定螺栓 anchor bolt 59
煤炭推移专用U形铲 coal U-blades

密封垫　captive gasket, gasket, seal ring, seal washer　27,46,69,100
密封盖　sealing cover　101
密封件　sealing element　22
密封圈　brake cal(l)iper body, caliper housing seal, seal, seal ring　75,78,94,144,151,153,155,352,353,354
密封锥面　sealing cone　46
面层　surface　407
灭火器　extinguisher　410
皿形(顶)活塞　dish piston　31
膜片　diaphragm　137,51,66
摩擦衬片　friction liner　156
摩擦卡环　friction snap ring　153
摩擦块　friction pad　155
摩擦轮驱动　friction wheel drive　385
摩擦片　friction lining, clutch facing　90
摩擦片式制动器　friction brake　147
摩擦式驱动轮　friction drive wheel　331
磨损指示器　wear indicator　155
末级减速小齿轮　final reduction pinion　346
拇指型铲斗　thumb bucket　185
木材堆放抓斗　log/sorting grapple　229

N

耐蚀高镍铸铁镶圈　Ni-resist insert　31
挠性联轴节　flexible coupling　99
挠性万向节　flexible universal joint　99
内部定位式　internally locating type　99
内侧滑动传动轴　inboard slip drive shaft　98
内齿圈　annular gear　100
内盖　inner cap, inner cover　131,156
内滚筒　inner drum　405
内横拉杆　inner tie rod　113
内棱倒角环　inside edges chamfered ring　34
内平衡臂　inside equalizer　141
内上棱阶梯切槽环　internal bevel bottom ring, internal step top ring　34
内上棱斜切环　internal bevel top ring　34
内胎　inner tube, tube　123
内外棱倒角环　inside and outside edges chamfered ring　34
内下棱阶梯切槽环　internal step bottom ring　34
内胀型鼓式制动器　internal expanding drum brake　147
内置式扭振减振器　internal vibration absorber　99
内轴承　inner bearing　155
内轴承座　inner bearing housing　355

泥雪地轮胎,全天候轮胎　MS tire＝Mud and Snow tire,all-season tire　123

泥雪地用胎面　M&S tire tread　124

黏液风扇离合器　viscous fan coupling(clutch)　75

啮合弹簧　meshing spring　81

啮合套　shift sleeve　94

啮合套毂　hub　94

扭杆弹簧　torsion(bar) spring,torsion bar　136

扭曲型　twist(torsional)ring　34

扭振减振器　torsional damper,vibration absorber,torsional vibration damper　99,107

O

O形密封圈　O-sealing ring　131,132

P

爬梯　ladder stand　389

排出口　bleed port　55

排气阀　drain cock　162

排气盖　exhaust cover　410

排气管　exhaust pipe　23,26,60

排气门　exhaust valve　22,38

排气气流　exhaust gas flow　53

排气再循环阀,EGR阀　EGR valve　53

排气再循环气流　EGR flow　53

排气制动缸　exhaust braking cylinder　164

排水管　drain pipe　397

排烟口　smoke outlet　405,408,410

排烟箱　smoke exhaust box　383

盘式制动器　disk brake　161,163,314

盘形弹簧　belleville spring　90

旁电极　ground electrode　69

旁通阀　by-pass valve　76,78

配水垫板　water distribution mat　361

配重　counterweight　214,243

喷吹管　blow pipe　398

喷灯开关　blow lamp switch　411

喷灯罩　blow lamp shade　409

喷管　spray pipe　392

喷孔　spray hole　57

喷洒器　spreader　360

喷射体积,喷油量　injected volume　53

喷射正时　injected timing　53

喷水按钮　sprinkling pushbutton　360

喷水泵选择器开关　sprinkling pumps selector switch　360

喷水间隔电位器　sprinkling interval potentiometer　360

喷水系统　watering system,water spray system,water injection system　345,361,430

喷油泵　injection pump　26,42

喷油泵凸轮　injection-pump cam-

shaft 50
喷油泵凸轮轴 （fuel）injection-pump camshaft 49,52
喷油器 injector 26,42,64,65
喷油器电磁阀 injector solenoid valve 58
喷油器控制电磁线圈 injector control solenoid 57
喷油器控制阀 injector control valve 57
喷油器体 nozzle holder 43,44
喷油器针阀 needle valve 43
喷油提前器 injection timing device 42
喷油提前器,正时装置 timing device, timing control, injection advance mechanism(device) 47
喷油嘴弹簧 nozzle spring 59
喷油嘴固定螺母 nozzle(retaining) nut 43,44
喷油嘴尖端 nozzle tip 57
喷油嘴体 nozzle holder body 43
喷油嘴轴针 nozzle pintle 59
喷嘴 nozzle, spray nozzle 385, 392,411,413,422
皮碗,皮圈 cup 151
偏心块 eccentric weight 358,369
偏心块壳体 eccentric weight housing 358
偏心支承销 off centre anchor pin 148,149
偏心轴 eccentric shaft 355, 356,369

偏心轴轴承 eccentric weight shaft bearing 358
偏心轴轴承座 bearing housing of eccentric shaft 369
平底轮辋 FB rim = Flat Base rim 125
平地机 grader 407
平顶 flat head (top, crown, poof) 31
平衡臂 equalizer 92
平衡臂轴 equalizer shaft 92
平衡架 equalizer 128,160
平衡梁 equalizing beam 129, 135,142
平衡器 equalizer 135
平衡质量,平衡重块 balance weight 37,99
平键 flat key 131
平切口 butt joint 32
平行四边形转向传动机构 parallelogram steering linkage 113
铺层厚度主调节手轮 spreading thickness main adjusting hand wheel 420
普通断面轮 conventional section tire 123
普通喷嘴 conventional nozzle 58
普通稀浆封层机摊铺箱 spreader box of universal slurry seal machine 419

Q

气顶油加力器 air over hydraulic

booster 163
气管 air pipe 411
气门 valve 26,39,40
气门凹坑 valve relied 31
气门弹簧 valve spring 22,39,40
气门弹簧座 valve spring retainer 22,39,40
气门导管 valve guide 22,39,40
气门室罩 cylinder head cover 26
气门锁夹 valve collet 39,40
气门嘴 tire valve 126
气门座 valve seat 39
气密层 inner liner 123
气体 gas 137
气体供给 air supply 137
气腿式凿岩机 air-leg rock drill 5
气腿手持式凿岩机 air leg hand-hold rock drill 5
气压表 air gauge,air pressure gauge 162,412
气液分离罐 gas liquid separating tank 397
气制动系统 air brake system 162
汽车起重机 mobile crane 8
汽缸 cylinder 388
汽缸衬垫 cylinder head gasket 23
汽缸盖 cylinder head 22,26
汽缸盖罩 cylinder head cover 23
汽缸识别传感器 cylinder ID sensor＝cylinder identification sensor,cylinder detector 58
汽缸套 cylinder liner (cylinder sleeve) 26,27

汽缸体 engine blok,block,cylinder block 22,27
汽油表 gasoline gauge(meter) 60
汽油机 casoline engine 20
汽油机供油泵 gasoline engine fuel system 60
汽油喷射式燃油系统 fuel system-gasoline injection 63
汽油启动机 gasoline starting engine 79
汽油箱 fuel tank 60,64
启动齿圈 starter ring gear 104
启动弹簧 start(ing) spring 49
启动电机 electric starter 80
启动机外壳 starter frame 81
启动继电器 starting relay 80
启动开关 starting swith 80
启动爪 starting jaw 37
起振阀 vibration valve 347
起重机械 hoisting machinery 8
牵引臂 towed arm 311,323,325
牵引架 traction frame 243
牵引架移动油缸 traction frame moving cylinder 243
牵引架油缸 traction frame cylinder 247
前车架 front frame 344,345,353,354
前传动轴 front drive shaft 98
前端盖 front housing 82
前盖 front cover 75,94,128,134
前横梁 front cross member (rail) 129

535

前机架 front frame 116,214,216,243,256
前进被动齿轮 forward driven gear 94
前进挡离合器 forward gear shift clutch 246
前进主动齿轮 forward drive gear 94
前梁 front axle beam 114
前轮 front wheel,front drum 121,314,345
前轮倾斜油缸 front wheel tilt cylinder 247
前轮速度传感器 front wheel speed sensor 165
前轮转向油缸 front wheel steering cylinder 247
前桥 front axle 15,103,116,214,215,216
前输出轴 front output shaft 106
前行星排 front planetary gear set 106
前悬架 front suspension 121
前支承销 front anchor pin 157
前支架 front bracket 139
前制动盘 front brake disk 160
前置砂石料箱 front sand/grit bin 440
前置式松土器 front scarifier 262
前置直铲刀 front-mounted straight blade 262
钳盘式制动器 spot-type disc brake,caliper disc brake 100,103,147,152,215
潜孔钻机 in-the-hole drill 5
嵌入耐磨支承垫 duramide bearing 254
强制间歇式搅拌设备 forced batch mixing plant 382
桥壳 axle housing 139
桥梁工程 bridge work 2
桥梁和隧道机械 bridge and tunnel machinery 10
桥梁检测车 bridge inspection vehicle 10
切削刃 cutting edge 175
倾斜仪 clinometer 252
倾斜油缸 tilt cylinder 282
清扫铲斗 clean up bucket 186
清扫滚刷 broom 262
清水池 clean water reservoir 397
清洗柴油箱 cleaning diesel box 417
球铰式连接管 spherical hinge connecting pipe 413
球节 ball joint 113
球头销 ball stud,ball pivot,ball pin 113
球碗,球头座 ball cup,ball(-stud) socket,ball cap 113
球状连接管 spherical connecting pipe 409
曲柄 crank 37
曲柄臂 crank web 37
曲柄连杆机构 crank connecting rod mechanism,crank link mechanism

27,379
曲柄销 crank pin 37
曲轴 crank shaft 22,26,36,76
曲轴齿轮 crankshaft gear 79
曲轴带轮 crank pulley,crankshaft pulley 22,37
曲轴定时带轮 crankshaft timing pulley 22
曲轴前端 crankshaft front end 37
曲轴转角(位置)传感器 crank angle sensor,CKP sensor = crankshaft position sensor 53
驱动泵 propel pump 332
驱动齿轮 drive gear 81,84,85
驱动电机 driving motor 393,394
驱动回转圈 drive circle 256
驱动机构 driving mechanism 108,396
驱动链轮 driving chain wheel,drive sprocket 16,279,315
驱动轮 driving wheel,drive sprocket 87,127,313
驱动轮毂 drive hub 244
驱动轮胎 driving tire 344,346, 347,348
驱动轮罩 drive sprocket cover 135
驱动马达 propel motor,drive motor 332,435
驱动盘 drive disk 75
驱动桥 driving axle 121,244, 347,348
驱动桥壳 drive axle housing 100
驱动轴 drive shaft 47

驱动装置 driving device,driving unit 382,386,405
全负荷限制器 full-load stop 49
全流式(机油)滤清器 full-flow(oil) filter 78
全路起重机 all terrain crane 8
全轮驱动自行式平地机 all wheel drive motor grader 242
全球式球头销 full-ball stud 113
全裙式活塞 full-skirt piston 31
全拖板式活塞 full slipper piston, slipper(-skirt) piston 29
全液压传动自行式平地机 full hydraulic drive motor grader 242
全液压打桩机 hydraulic pile-driver 9
裙部凹口 skirt relief 29
裙部环槽 skirt ring groove(slot) 29

R

RAD型两极式减速器 RAD minimum-maximum-speed governor 50
RQ型两极式调速器 RQ minimum-maximum-speed governor 49
RSV型全程式调速器 RSV variable-speed governor 49
燃料控制旋钮 fuel control dial 285
燃料箱 fuel tank 409,412,422
燃气罐 gas tank 428
燃气涡轮鼓风机 combustion air

turbo blower 422,423,424

燃烧器 burner 382,383,384,385,405,411

燃烧区叶片 combustion zone flight, combustion flight 382,383,403,405

燃烧室 combustion chamber 422,423,424

燃烧系统 burner system 422,423,424

燃油泵 fuel pump 60

燃油分配器 fuel distributor 64

燃油供给 fuel supply 47

燃油供给油道 fuel feed gallery 55

燃油轨 fuel rail, fuel manifold, distributor rail 58

燃油滤清器 fuel filter 55,60,64

燃油滤清器堵塞 fuel filter plugging 287

燃油箱 fuel tank 42,54,57,58,176,411

燃油压力调节器 fuel pressure regulator 66

燃油液面高度 fuel level 287

热坝,隔热槽 heat dam 29

热风再循环鼓风机 recirculating hot air blower 422,423,424

热骨科筛分及储仓 hot aggregate screen and storage bin 378

热骨料出口 hot aggregate outlet 405

热骨料储仓 hot aggregate bin 388,390

热骨料计量装置 hot aggregate weigh hopper 378

热骨料提升机 hot aggregate elevator 378,386

热沥青喷洒系统 hot asphalt injection system 430

热沥青系统电机 generator for hot asphalt system 430

热料仓 hot aggregate storage silo 384

热膨胀自动调节式活塞(此时镶片为低碳钢) autothermic piston 31

人力制动系统 manpower brake system 161

熔断器 safety cut-out 80

乳化沥青泵 bitumen emulsion pump 440

乳化沥青仓 emulsion hopper 441

乳化沥青罐 emulsion tank 442

乳化沥青罐车软管连接 hose connection on the emulsified asphalt tanker 433

乳化沥青喷洒系统 injection system for emulsified asphalt 430

乳化沥青设备 asphalt emulsion plant 7

乳化沥青手喷枪 bitumen emulsion hand lance 440

乳化沥青箱 bitumen emulsion tank 440

乳化沥青自缩回软管卷盘 bitumen emulsion self retracting hose reel 440

乳液箱　emulsion box　417
软钢绳　soft cable　391
软管　flexible pipe　411
软胶管　flexible rubber hose　162
软水管卷盘　water hose reel　440
润滑加注口,黄油嘴　lubrication fitting　99
润滑系统　lubrication system　76
润滑脂保持器　grease retainer　155

S

S形凸轮　S-cam　147
洒布管　distributing pipe　413
洒布管喷洒角度调整手柄　spraying angle adjusting handle　414
洒布管升降手轮　distributing pipe lifter hand wheel　414
洒布管左右摆动推杆　left and right swing push rod　414
洒沥青管喷嘴角度调节手柄　asphalt spraying pipe nozzle adjusting handle　409
洒沥青管升降操纵手柄　a:sphalt spraying pipe lifter control handle　409
洒沥青管升降杆　asphalt spray pipe lifter rod　409
三挡被动齿轮　third speed driven gear　94
三件式油环　three piece oil ring　34
三、四挡拨叉　third-fourth shift fork　96
三、四挡拨叉轴　third-fourth shift

fork shaft　96
三通阀　tripple valve　390,392
三维无疲劳吊杆　tri-flex no fatigue boom　442
散热器　heat exchanger, radiator　71,72,73,107,176
散热器百叶窗　radiator shutter　71
散热器盖　radiator (pressure) cap　71,72,73
散热器芯　radiator core　72
刹车灯开关　stoplight switch　162
筛分系统　screen system　384
筛网　screen deck　387
筛箱　screen box　387
扇形弹簧片　segmented spring ring　90
商用车胎面　commercial-vehicle tire tread　124
上环片　top ring　34
上摇臂　upper rocker arm　158
上支承　upper mounting　144
上置板簧式　overslung (spring) type, overhung spring type　138
上置式振动器　overhead vibrator　387
伸缩臂履带起重机　telescopic crawler crane　8
伸缩臂式挖掘机　telescopic boom excavator　171
伸缩液压油缸　telescopic hydraulic cylinder　325
伸张器　stretcher　144
深槽　drop center　125

深槽轮辋　DC rim＝Drop Center rim　125

深胎面花纹轮胎　deep-tread tire　435

升降装置　lifting gear　422

湿地推土机　wet land dozer　278

湿地挖掘机　wetlands excavator　171

湿式、多片停车制动器　wet, multi-disc parking brakes　220,221

湿式缸套　wet sleeve (liner) typer　27

十字轴　spider, cross, cross spider, cross-pins pivot　99,101,354

十字轴式链接车架　gross-pins articulated frame　354

十字轴总成　cross assembly　99

石方机械　rock machinery　5

石料铲斗　rock digging, rock bucket　185,231

石棉绳填料　asbest rope stuffing　415

石屑洒布车　chips spreader　407

释压阀　pressure relief (release, reduction) valve　58

手动泵　hand pump　349

手扶压路机　walk behind roller　6

手提式喷灯　portable blow lamp　411

手压泵,手动泵　hand pump　54

手制动阀　hand brake valve　162,164

输出接线柱　output terminal　82

输出轴　output shaft　104,94

输出轴齿轮　output shaft gear　106

输入端离合器　input clutch　107

输入信号　input signal　57

输入轴　input shaft　94

输油泵　fuel feed pump, feed pump　26,42,57

输油总管　main delivery pipe　413

树根粉碎机　stump grinder　231

刷式抓斗　brush grapple bucket　230

甩水圈　water thrower ring　74

双臂曲柄杆　bell crank lever　157

双边变宽度铣刨鼓　two-side variable width milling drum　430

双边支重轮　double flange track roller　135

双层履带板　bonded track pads　332

双柴油发动机驱动装置　drive unit with two diesel engines　430

双单向阀　double check valve　162

双钢轮振动压路机　tandem vibratory roller　367

双钢轮振动压路机(串联式振动压路机)　double drum vibratory compactor(tandem vibratory roller)　6

双管路空气增压制动系统　double pipeline air boost brake system　163

双级行星减速最终驱动装置　double reduction planetary final drive　220,221

双铰销式铰接架　two-pins articulated frame　353

双金属感温器　bimetallic coil spring　75

双金属轴承衬　bimetallic bearing bush　133

双联齿轮　duplicate gear　94

双轮手扶式振动压路机　walk behind doubie drum vibratory roller　343

双速阀　double speed valve　177

双速行星减速器　two-speed planetary　331

双通阀　two way valve　58

双万向节内侧滑动传动轴　tow-joint inboard slip drive shaft　98

双万向节外侧滑动传动轴　two-join toutboard slip drive shaft　98

双向风扇　reversible fan　287

双轴浆叶式搅拌器　double shaft paddle mixer　418

双轴搅拌器　twin-shaft mixer　424,430,432

双作用转向离合器　double action steering clutch　119

水泵　water pump, coolant circulation, coolant pump　26

水泵盖　pump cover　74

水泵体　pump body　74

水泵轴　pump shaft　74

水道　water passage　72

水分离器　water separator　287

水封　coolant pump seal　74

水罐车软管连接　hose connection on the water tanker truck　433

水过滤器　water filter　361

水冷系统　liquid cooling system　71

水泥稀浆喷洒系统　cement slurry injection system　430

水泥运输车　cement truck　437

水平定向钻机　horizontal directional drilling machine　9

水平切槽　horizontal slot　29

水平销轴　horizontal pin　353

水套　water jacket　27,71

水温　water temperature　285,53

水温表　water temperature indicator　71

水温传感器　coolant-temperature sensor　64

水箱　water tank　345,417,430

水箱或第二乳化剂箱可选件　water tank or optional second emulsion tank　440

四边形后台车架　quad rear bogie　332

四挡被动齿轮　fourth speed driven gear　94

四挡变速箱　four gears transmission　313

四挡主动齿轮　fourth speed drive gear　94

四轮驱动自行式平地机　four-wheel drive motor grader　242

伺服阀　servo valve　282

松紧调节器　slack adjuster　162

541

松土齿　excavator ripper　185
松土器　scarifier, ripper　243, 279, 291
松土器齿尖　ripper tip tooth　279
松土器电子控制器　electronic ripper control　286
松土器升降油缸　scarifier hoist cylinder　243, 247
松土器油缸　scarifier cylinder　279, 282
速度传感器　speed sensor　315
速度电位器　speed potentiometer　359
速度限制阀　speed limit valve　177
随车起重机　lorry-mounted crane　8
随动臂　idler arm　111, 113
随动阀　servo valve　116
随动杆　follower lever　116
碎石洒布机　stone chip spreader　12
隧道掘进机　tunnel borer, tunnel boring machine　10
锁定销　blocking pin　52
锁环　locking collar　100
锁紧件,锁止装置　retaining member　35
锁紧螺母　check nut, lock nut　39, 82, 83, 115, 132, 353
锁片　lock plate　37
锁销　lock pin　84
锁止螺栓　lock bolt　139
锁止板　lock plate　99

锁止螺母　locknut　41

T

T形槽　T-slot, T-shaped slot　29
T形槽活塞　T-slot piston　29
弹簧　spring　51, 59, 66, 74, 78, 89, 144, 153, 158, 159
弹簧垫圈　spring washer, spring seat　41, 78
弹簧刹车　spring brake　164
弹簧压盘　spring pressure plate　102
弹簧座　spring seat　45, 134, 144, 153
弹簧座盘　spring cap　156
弹性板　elastic plate　218
弹性垫圈　elastic washer　83, 85
弹性锁圈　spring lock ring　132
弹簧片　spring lamination　144
套筒　sleeve　85
调幅机构　amplitude adjusting mechanism　356
调节板　adjusting disk　59
调节臂　control arm　48
调节叉　control fork　48
调节齿杆　control rack　45, 48, 49, 50, 51, 52
调节齿圈　control pinion　45, 48
调节管　adjusting sleeve, adjuster tube　113
调节弹簧　adjusting spring　50
调节垫片　adjusting washer, adjusting shim　51, 151

调节拉杆　control rod　48
调节螺钉　adjusting screw　45,151
调节螺钉弹簧　adjusting screw spring　151
调节螺钉总成　adjusting screw assembly　151
调节螺母　adjusting nut　99
调节器　adjusting　151
调节套筒　control sleeve　45
调节套　regulating sleeve　388
调平基准　leveling reference　327
调速弹簧　governor spring　49,50
调速杠杆　speed control lever, adjusting speed lever　50
调速螺栓　adjusting speed bolt　50
调速器　governor　42
调速器弹簧　governor spring　47
调速器杠杆机构　governor lever mechanism(drive)　47
调速器驱动装置　governor drive　47
调压弹簧　pressure spring　43,44
调压垫片　pressure-adjusting shim　43
调整臂　adjusting arm　148
调整垫　adjusting shim　101
调整垫片　adjusting shim　74,94,102,114,115,119,133,144,352,353
调整垫圈　locating shim　85,101
调整杆　adjusting rod　158,159
调整环　regulating ring　89
调整螺钉　adjust screw, adjusting screw　39,41,43,44,89,115,157,391
调整螺母　adjusting nut　101,134
调整螺母锁片　adjusting nut lock　101
调整螺栓　adjusting bolt　158
调整螺纹挡圈　adjusting thread check ring　156
调整凸轮　adjusting cam　149
调整叶片　conditioning flinghts　403
调整叶片　conditioning flights　405
调整装置　adjusting device　134
塔式起重机　column crane(tower crane)　8
踏板　footplate　311
踏板到平衡臂的拉杆　pedal-to-equalizer rod　92
踏板轴　pedal shaft　91
胎侧　sidewall　123
胎肩　shoulder　123
胎肩区　shoulder area　123
胎面　tread,tire tread　123,124
胎面帘布层　tread plies　123
胎面磨损指示器　tread(tire) wear indicator　123
胎圈区　bead area　123
胎圈芯　bead core,bead wire　123
胎圈,子口　bead,tire bead,tyre bead　123
胎体　carcass,carcase,casing　123
胎体帘布层　carcass plies　123
胎趾　bead toe　123

543

胎踵　bead heel　123
台车架　track roller frame, track frame　16,135,279
台车轴　carriage shaft　141
台车总成　trolley assembly　291
台阶顶　step head(top,crown,roof)　31
太阳轮　central gear　100
摊铺操作控制键　paving operation control keys　316
摊铺厚度微调手轮　spreading thickness fine adjusting hand wheel　419,420
摊铺控制手柄　paving control handle　316
摊铺器　speader　417
摊铺箱　spreader box　419
摊铺箱框架　spreader box frame　419
摊铺熨平板　paving screed　427,428
套筒密封圈　sleeve seal ring　156
套筒式弹簧座　sleeve type spring seat　134
梯(楔)形环　keystone ring, wedge section ring,full keystone ring　33
提前器弹簧　advance device spring　52
提前器飞锤　flyweight, timer flyweight　49,50,52
提前器飞锤,离心重块　flyweight, centrifugal weight　47
提升/下降解除　lift kickout/lower kickout　287
提升油缸　lifting cylinder　311,327
蹄导板　shoe guide　151
添加混合料料斗　add-mix hopper　424
添加剂料箱　additive tank　428
添加剂箱　additive box　417
填充环　inlaid ring　34
填充剂　powder　83
填料仓　filler bin　417
贴合环片　conformable rail　34
铁铲工具箱　shovel bin　440
铁铲工具箱底部　bottom of shovel bin　440
铁铲清洁箱　shovel cleaning bin　440
铁芯　iron core, magnetic core　67,68
停止　stop　49
挺柱,挺杆　tappet,tappet follower　26,39,43,44,57
通风管　breather tube　23
通风孔　ventilation hole　125
通风式制动盘　ventilated brake disk (disc),ventilated rotor　155
通宵电加热器　electric overnight heating　442
通用铲斗　General purpose bucket　175
通用收集式清扫　general purpose pick-up broom　230
通用有齿铲斗　general purpose bucket with teeth　229

同步齿轮 synchronizing gear 393

同步齿形带 synchronous cog belt 369

同步碎石封层车 synchronous chip seal vehicle 11

桶面环 barrell(ed) face ring 34

桶形弹簧 barrel spring 136

筒式减振器 telescopic shock absorber 143

头道环槽镶圈 top ring insert 31

透气管 vent pipe 100

凸顶 hump head, convex head, hump(convex) piston head 31

凸峰 hump 125

凸峰轮辋 hump rim 125

凸块式压路机 pad foot roller 343

凸块式振动压路机 vibratory pad foot roller 343

凸轮 cam 148,159,38,45

凸轮盘 cam disc, plate cam, disk cam 47

凸轮张开式制动器 cam brake 148

凸轮轴 camshaft 22,26,39,45,55,55,76,148

凸轮轴位置传感器 CPS＝Camshaft Position Sensor 58

凸轮轴轴承盖 camshaft bearing cap 22

凸缘 flange 126

凸缘叉 flange yoke 99

推杆 push rod, pushrod 26,39,51,148

推辊 push roller 311

推力轴承 thrust bearing 114,115

推土机机架 crawler dozer frame 128,129

推土机机架 crawler dozer frame 129

推土机可编程电子控制器 electronic, programmable dozer control 286

托板 supporter 135

托架 support(ing) bracket 101

托链轮 carrier roller 16,127,132,135

托轮盖 carrier roller cap 132

托轮体 carrier roller body 132

托轮支架 carrier roller bracket 132,135

托轮轴 carrier roller shaft 132

拖板,滑座 slipper, slipper skirt 29

拖车保护阀 trailer protection valve 162

拖车控制模块 trailer control module 164

拖车制动接头供气 coupling head supply 164

拖钩 tow hook, towing hook, hitch 128

拖挂板式输送机 drag slat conveyor 424

拖拉机悬架 Tractor suspension 141

拖式铲运机 trailer-type scraper 4

拖式光轮振动压路机 towed smooth drum vibratory roller 344

545

拖式凸块振动压路机 towed pad foot vibratory roller 344

U

U形槽 U-slot 29
U形螺栓 U-bolt, U-damp, Ubolt 99,139

V

V形车辙修复摊铺箱 V-shaped tracking repair spreader box 420

W

挖沟铲斗 ditching bucket 185
挖泥斗 mud bucket 186
外部定位式 externally locating type 99
外侧滑动传动轴 outboard slip drive shaf 98
外侧送料器驱动马达 outboard feeder drive motor 333
外盖 outer cover 131
外横拉杆 outer tie rod 113
外壳 casing, housing, shell 68,69, 83,156
外棱倒角环 outside edges chamfered ring 34
外平衡臂 outside equalizer 141
外筒 outer shell 405
外轴承座 outer bearing housing 355
碗形盖 bowl cap 41

万能压实轮 universal compaction wheel 187
万向传动轴 universal driving shaft 314
万向传动装置 universal driving device 313
万向节盘 universal flange 94
往复式给料器 reciprocating feeder 379
微机控制喷水泵 microprocessor-controlled pump for the water injection 433
微机控制乳化沥青喷洒泵 microprocessor-controlled pump for the emulsified asphalt injection 433
微型挖掘机 mini type excavator 169
微型装载机 mini type loader 211
维护开关 service switch 285
维护与应急接口 service and emergency connection 162
位置平衡块 position counterweight 358
尾灯开关和指示灯 switch and indicator lamp for rear light 360
尾管 tailpipe 60
温度传感器 temperature sensor 388
温度计 thermometer 408,410
温度时间开关 thermo time switch 64
文丘里除尘器 Venturi scrubbing dust filter 397

文丘里喷嘴　venturi nozzle　397
文丘里洗涤器　Venturi scrubber　397
稳拌/再生机　stabilizer/recycler　7,437
稳定土拌和/道路再生机　road stabilizer/reclaimer　12
稳定土厂拌设备　stabilized soil mixing plant　7
涡轮　turbine　104
涡轮增压器　turbocharger　53
涡旋导流板　volution guide vane　386
蜗杆　worm screw　148
蜗轮　worm gear　148
无镀层环　uncoated ring　33
无内胎轮胎　tubeless tire　123
无线控制型挖掘机　radio controlled excavator　171
五挡被动齿轮　fifth speed driven gear　94
五挡主动齿轮　fifth drive gear　94
五、六挡拨叉　fifth-sixth shift fork　96
五、六挡拨叉轴　fifth-sixth shift fork shaft　96
五、六挡拨块　fifth-sixth shift block　96

X

吸风小筒　air draft tube　397
吸沥青管　asphalt suction pipe　409
吸引线圈　pull-in winding　80,81

稀浆封层机　asphalt slurry seal machine　11,416
铣刀　milling tool　431
铣刨鼓　milling drum　431
铣刨深度控制装置　milling depth control　423
铣刨转子　milling drum　431
下盖　lower cover　353
下后板　lower back plate　128
下环片　bottom ring　34
下摇臂　lower rocker arm　158
下支承　lower mounting　144
下置板簧式　underslung(spring) type,underhung spring rype　138
下置式振动器　underneath vibrator　387
下置凸轮轴顶置式气门　underneath camshaft overhead valve　39
纤维增强金属　fiber reinforced metal　31
衔铁板　armature plate　59
衔铁盘　disc armature　55,57
显示面板　LCD panel　316
限位块　stop block　142
限位盘,压紧盘　hold-down cup　151
限位销钉　arresting pin　75
限位销,压紧销　hold-down pin　151
限位(压紧)弹簧　hold-down spring　151
限压阀　pressure limiting valve　76
箱体　tank body　412

箱体固定架　tank mounting frame　410
橡胶元件　rubber element　99,135
橡胶支承　rubber support（mountiong）　137,142
消声（防啸声）弹簧　anti-squeal（rattle）spring　155
销　pin　141
销轴　axis pin, hinge pin, pin rod　128,142,153,245
销轴套　pin bracket　353,354
销子　pin　157
销子垫套　pin sleeve　415
小弹簧　small spring　119
小电器开关箱　small locker and paddle locks　440
小螺旋弹簧　small coil spring　102
小三通阀　small triple valve　409
小型履带式推土机　small crawler dozer（track-type tractor）　278
小型轮式冷铣刨机　small wheel cold planer　13
小型轮式装载机　small type wheel loader　211
小型摊铺机　small paver　309
小型挖掘机　small type excavator　169
楔块　wedge　147
楔形端　tapered end　136
斜交轮胎　diagonal tire, bias（ply）tire, cross-ply tire　123
斜角　bevel　29
斜切口　beveled joint, diagonal joint　32
斜挖铲斗　tilting bucket　186
泄漏回油　leak　58
卸尘闸门　discharge gate　397
卸荷阀　dump valve　349
卸料槽　discharge chute　379,380,382
卸料区叶片　discharging zone flights　382
卸料箱　discharge box　382,383
卸料闸门　discharge gate　395,396
卸压槽　pressure relief groove　77
芯部　core　72
芯杆　pin　126
信道连接　EBS connection　164
信号　CAN-signal　164
行车制动管路　service brake pipeline　164
行车制动器　service brake　220,221,246
行程调节螺钉　stroke adjusting screw　50
行驶控制器　travel control　359
行驶驱动轮　traveling driving wheel　312
行驶系统　traveling system　417
行星齿轮　planetary gear　100,101
行星齿轮减速器　planetary gear reducer　314
行星齿轮轴　planet pin　100
行星传动装置　planetary drive　332
行星动力换挡变速箱　planetary power shift transmission　284,291

行星减速器　planetary reduction gear　280,348
行星轮架　planet carrier　100
行星排　planetary gear set　107
行走泵　traveling pump　349
行走变量泵　traveling variable pump　313
行走操纵杆　travel lever　175
行走操纵手柄　travel control lever　285
行走定量马达　traveling quantitative motor　313
行走机构　running gear　311
行走马达　travel motor　356
行走驱动泵　travel driving pump　347,348
行走驱动马达　travel driving motor　347,348
行走通道　walkway　176
行走吸滤器　traveling suction strainer　349
行走液压马达　traveling hydraulic motor　177
行走支承机构　undercarriage　173
蓄电池　battery(accumulator), storage battery　64,67,70,80,165
蓄电池外壳　battery jar (accumulator jar)　70
蓄电池正极接线柱　battery positive terminal　70
悬架　suspension　127
悬架弹簧　suspension spring　141
悬架弹性元件　suspension spring element　137
悬架油缸　suspension cylinder　140
旋风集尘筒　cyclone dust collection collector　397
旋风式除尘器　cyclone dust filter　397
旋喷钻机　jet grouting drilling machine　9
旋转传感器　rotation sensor　252
旋转花键鼓　rotating spline drum　156
旋转接头　swivel joint　176
旋转制动盘　rotating brake disk　156
循环管　circulating pipe　413
循环流动管道　cyclic flow pipe　409

Y

压差计　differential pressure gage　398
压紧螺母　compression nut　144
压紧螺栓　compression bolt　23
压紧装置　compressing apparatus　82
压力表　pressure meter　411
压力传感器　pressure sensor　53,57,58,164,178
压力调节阀　pressure-control valve　47
压力调节器　pressure regulator　42,163
压力调节器　fuel pressure regulator

549

64

压力计　pressure gauge　349

压力开关　pressure switch　164

压力开关电路　pressure switch circuit　164

压力膜盒　pressure capsule　51

压力盘　pressure plate　352

压路机　roller　308,407,437

压盘　pressure plate　85,89,102,119

压实机械　compactor　6

压缩弹簧　compression spring　113

压缩机　air compressor　398

压缩空气管路　compressed air pipe　163

烟囱　stack　397

盐沙防滑材料洒布机　salt-sand spreader　12

仰角传感器　pitch angle sensor　285

氧传感器　oxygen sensor　64

摇臂　rocker arm, rocker-arm　23,26,38,39,41,55,158,159,214

摇臂衬套　rocker bush(ing)　41

摇臂油缸　rocker arm cylinder　214

摇臂支架结构　Rocker-arm mounting structure　41

摇臂轴　rocker shaft　39,41,55

摇臂轴座　rocker-arm support　41

摇臂轴座螺杆　rocker support screw　41

叶轮　pump impeller　74

叶轮给料机　revolving plow reclai-

mer　389

液力变矩器　torque converter　103,215,216,281,285

液力机械传动系统　hydromechanical transmission system　103

液力机械传动自行式平地机　hydromechanical transmission motor grader　242

液力膜片蓄能器　hydraulic diaphragm accumulator　137

液压　hydraulic pressure　155

液压泵　hydraulic pump, hystat pumps hose　173,176,177,178,220,221

液压步履式多功能钻机　step-type multi-fuction hydraulic driller　9

液压步履式桩机　step-type hydraulic pile driving machine　9

液压测向除雪铲　hydraulic snow wing　262

液压动力组件,自缩回软管卷盘,软管,油冷却器　hydraulic power pack, self retracting hose reel, hose, oil cooler　440

液压缸　hydraulic cylinder　177

液压管路　hydraulic line, hydraulic pipeline　91,174

液压过滤器　hydraulic filter　176

液压静力压桩机　hydrostatic pressure pile drive　10

液压滤清器　hydraulic filter　220,221

液压马达　hydraulic motor　312

550

液压平衡悬架　hydraulic compensating axle suspension　140
液压破碎锤　hydraulic breaker, hydraulic crusher　186,187,230
液压软管　hose　220,221
液压升降机　hydraulic lifter　440
液压锁　hydraulic lockout　287
液压系统　hydraulic system　15,254
液压箱　hydraulic tank　252
液压油过滤器　hydraulic oil filter　287
液压油冷却器　hydraulic oil cooler, oil cooler　176,220,221
液压油箱　hydraulic tank, hydraulic oil tank　176,247,282,332,349,350,351,422,423,424,430
液压柱塞　hydraulic piston　58
液压转向器　hydraulic steering control unit, hydraulic steering device　117,347,348
一挡被动齿轮　first speed driven gear　94
一挡主动齿轮　first speed drive gear　94
一、二挡拨叉　first-second shift fork　96
一、二挡拨叉轴　first-second shift fork shaft　96
一、二挡拨块　first-second shift block　96
一级除尘系统　primary dust collector　384

一件式轮辋　one(single)-piece rim, normal rim　125
仪表控制台　console　175
仪表盘　instrumentation console　214
移动短路环　moving short-circuiting ring　52
乙醚启动装置　ether starting aid　287
异径(阶梯形)轮缸　stepped wheel cylinder　147
异形顶　contour head　31
溢流电磁线圈　spill solenoid　55
溢流阀　relief valve, overflow valve　76,89,117,282
溢流管　overflow pipe　391,409,410
溢流环　spill ring　47
溢流回油管　leak-off pipe　42
溢流节流孔　overflow throttle　47
溢流控制阀　spill control valve　55
溢流油道　overflow gallery　55
翼形螺母　butterfly nut　62
引导轮　track idler　16,127,133,135
引导轮体　track idler body　133
引导轮轴　track idler shaft　133
应急回路　emergency circuit　178
油泵　oil pump, pump　117,312
油标尺　oil rule　23
油道　fuel gallery, oil gallery, oil duct　41,55,57,76
油底壳　oil pan　23,26,27,76

551

油封　oil seal　40,41,94,100,101,114,115,144
油封盖　oil sealed cap　132
油封环　oil seal ring　102,152
油封外壳　outer case of seal　144
油封座　oil sealed seat　132
油缸　cylinder　158
油缸缸体　cylinder body　156
油缸活塞　oil cylinder piston　152
油管　pipe,oil pipe　60,102,119,128,152,163
油环　oil ring,oil(control) ring　23,32
油环槽　oil ring groove(slot)　28
油孔　oil hole　35
油冷却器　oil cooler　314,349,350
油量控制阀　oil quantity controlling valve　385
油面观测计　oil level sight gauge　358
油气比控制阀　oil gas ratio controlling valve　385
油塞　oil plug　131,132,22
油水分离器　oil-water separator　42,163,164
油箱　oil reservoir　117
油箱盖　tank cup, fuel tank cap　60,411
油箱加注口　tank filler　60
油箱开关　fuel tank switch　408
油箱开关手轮　fuel tank switch hand wheel　408
油压表　oil pressure gauge　411

油压张开式制动器　oil pressure brake　149
有镀层环　coated ring　34
有内胎轮胎　tubed tire, tube-type tire　123
有内胎斜交轮胎　bias ply tire with inner tube, bias ply tubed tire　123
右变量泵　right variable pump　108,315
右侧送料器与螺旋器驱动泵　right feeder and auger drive pump　333
右电磁阀　right electromagnetic valve　327
右调平油缸　right leveling cylinder　327
右刮板和转向三联泵　right drag and steering triple-link pump　314
右横管三通阀　right horizontal pipe triple valve　413
右基本段熨平板　right basic screed　323
右连接板　right junction plate　355,356
右连接支架　right junction bracket　355,356
右链轨节　right track link　130
右牵引臂　right towed arm　327
右前制动油管　brake line, RF　160
右液压伸缩熨平板　right hydraulic extension screed　325
右仪表盘　RH cluster　360
右制动器　right brake　281
右轴向柱塞马达　right axial plunger

motor 108,315
右转向油缸 right steering cylinder 116
右最终传动 right final reduction gear 281
元件板 component card 82
圆顶 home head 31
圆顶高度,凸高 home height 31
圆角,倒角 chamfer 29
圆螺母 round nut 100
圆周激振器 circular exciter 370
圆柱弹簧 cylindrical spring 136
圆锥式碎石机 cone crusher 5
圆锥轴承 conical bearing 102
允许滑动量 slip 98
运梁车 transporting girder vehicle 10
运料卡车 delivery truck 308
运料小车 conveying skip 396
运输卡车 transport truck 395,396
运水车 water truck 437
熨平板 screed units 327
熨平板底板 screed plate 311
熨平板机械加宽式摊铺机 paver with mechanical extension screed 308
熨平板箱体 screed box 311
熨平板液压伸缩式摊铺机 paver with hydraulic extension screed 308
熨平装置 screed unit 311

Z

Z形节流 Z-throttle 59

再生混合料 recycled mix 427
再生剂储罐 regenerator tank 423
再生磨耗层 remixed wearing course 427
增加供给方向 feed increment direction 51
增强橡胶 reinforced rubber 123
增速齿轮副 speed increasing gear train 106
增压供油行程 boost feed fuel stroke 51
增压进气压力接头 boost pressure connection 51
闸门 gate, cold feed gate, butterfly gate 311,379,380,381,389
张紧弹簧 tension spring 134
张紧装置 tension device 134
胀缩件 compensator 382
罩 rear cover 135
罩壳 casing, encloser 153,386
折叠轮胎 folding tire 123
折叠式黄色旋转灯警示标志 collapsible patrol sign with amber rotating lights 440
折流板 baffle plate 398
针阀 needle, needle valve 44,55,57,61,65
针阀体 nozzle body, needle body 43,44,55,57
真空开关(转换)阀 vacuum switching valve 53
真空助力器 vacuum booster 160,161

553

振荡 oscillation 370
振荡滚筒 oscillating drum 369
振荡轮 oscillation roller 369
振荡马达 oscillation motor 369
振捣夯锤 tamper bar 311
振捣偏心轴 tamper eccentric shaft 312
振捣器 tamper 311
振捣器驱动马达 tamper drive motor 311
振动按钮 vibration pushbuttons 360
振动泵 vibration pump 350
振动锤 vibro hammer 187
振动过滤器 vibration filter 350
振动轮 vibratory drum 344,346,347,348
振动轮行走驱动马达 vibratory drum travel driving motor 348
振动马达 vibration motor 350,355,356
振动模式选择开关(手动/自动) vibration mode selector switch (MAN/AUT) 360
振动碾 vibratory roller 231
振动平板夯 vibratory plate 6
振动器 vibrator 311,387,387
振动器驱动马达 vibrator drive motor 311
振动驱动泵 vibration driving pump 347,348
振动驱动马达 vibration driving motor 346,347,348

振动筛 vibrating screen 6
振动吸滤器 vibration suction strainer 350
振动选择器开关 vibration selector switch 360
振动轴 vibratory shaft 357,358
振动轴承 vibration bearing 355,356
振幅选择轮 amplitude selection wheel 358
振幅选择器开关 vibration amplitude selector switch 360
整体机架式平地机 integrated frame motor grader 242
整体铰销式铰接车架 integral-pin articulated frame 352
整体式动力转向器 integral power steering gear 111
整体式制动盘 solid rotor(disc,disk) 155
整体台车式行走机构 fully bogied undercarriage 331
正极板 positive plate 70
正扭曲型 positive twist type 34
正切向端 tangential end 136
正时齿轮 timing gear 36
正时套筒 timing sleeve(collar) 47
支撑板 support,support plate 67,78
支撑轴承 support bearing 98
支承臂 supporting arm 140
支承杆 support lever 50
支承滚轮 supporting roller 382,

支承块弹簧　anchor spring　151
支承块,支承板　anchor plate,anchor　151,155
支承梁　supporting beam　140
支承销　anchor pin　151,159
支承销座　anchor pin pedestal　148
支承轴颈　supporting journal　140
支承装置　supporting unit　133,144
支点　supporting point　51
支架　hanger,carrier,support,bracket,frame　92,113,139,157,245,383,386,395,396
支枢螺母　pivot nut　151
支销　anchor pin　147
支重轮　track roller, track supporting wheel　16,127,141,279
支重台车　supporting carriage　127
支座　socket,supporting seat　129,151,387
直边有齿石料铲斗　straight edge rock bucket with teeth　229
直槽　vertical slot　29
直铲　straight blade　292
直拉杆　drag link,drag rod　111
止动管　stop tube　134
止动螺钉　stop screw　152
止动螺栓　catch bolt　101
止动套　stop collar　85
止推垫圈　thrust washer　36,81,101
止推轴瓦　thrust bearing shell　23
纸质空气滤清器(空气滤清器)　air cleaner　62
纸质滤芯　paper element　78
指令脉冲　command pulse　58
至燃油箱的回油　fuel return to tank　66
至燃油箱的回油管　return line to fuel tank　47
制动衬块　brake pad, brake lining　152,155
制动衬块磨损传感器　brake lining wear sensor　155
制动衬块总成　brake pad assembly　155
制动衬片,摩擦片　friction lining　147
制动带　brake band　147,157,89
制动底板　brake base plate　148,159
制动阀　brake valve　163,349
制动供气管路　air supply pipeline　164
制动鼓,制动毂　brake drum　89,114,147,148,149,151,157,159
制动力调节器　braking-force regulator　161
制动轮缸　wheel braking cylinder　149,165
制动磨损传感器　wear sensor　164
制动盘　brake disc(disk,rotor)　100,152,155
制动气室　brake chamber　148,162,164
制动器　brake　79,313,314

制动器盖　brake cover　158

制动钳　caliper　152

制动钳安装支架　brake caliper mounting bracket　155

制动钳总成　caliper assy, caliper assembly　155, 160

制动踏板　brake pedal　160, 161, 163, 285

制动踏板与停车灯开关　brake pedal and parking lamp switch　165

制动蹄　brake shoe　148, 149, 159

制动蹄锁片　brake shoe lock-plate　148

制动蹄支承　fixed brake shoe abutment　147

制动系统　brake system　15

制动压力调节装置　brake pressure regulator　165

制动油箱　brake-fluid reservoir　161

制动主缸　master cylinder　165

制动主缸总成　master cylinder assembly　160

中继阀　relay valve　164

中继杆　relay rod, center rod, center link, centre link, connecting rod　111, 113

中间齿轮　middle gear, translating gear, mid-gear　79

中间传动齿轮箱　middle transmission gearbox　313

中间传动轴　middle driving shaft　355

中间配料仓　intermediate proportioning bin　428

中间驱动桥　middle driving axle　243

中间铣刨鼓　center milling drum　423

中间支撑轴承　center support bearing　98

中间轴　connection shaft, intermediate shaft　76, 94

中间轴齿轮　intermediate shaft gear　106

中冷器　intercooler　53

中凸式石料铲斗　spade nose rock bucket　229

中心电极　center electrode　69

中心铰架　central articulated frame　344

中心铰接架　central articulated frame　345

中心孔　center hole　125

中心螺栓　center bolt, centre bolt　139

中心轴　center shaft　369

中心轴轴承座　bearing housing of center axle　369

中型轮式装载机　medium type wheel loader　211

中型摊铺机　medium paver　309, 278

中型挖掘机　medium type excavator　170

中央传动　main drive　87

中央控制台 central console 108,315
中罩 center cover 135
终传动器 final drive 283
终减速器 final reduction gear 244,246
重块 weight 391
重型驱动桥 heavy-duty axles 284
重型拖挂装置 heavy duty trailer 442
重型杂物抓斗 heavy duty scrap grapple bucket 231
重型自卸车 heavy duty dump truck 4
轴 shaft, wheel shaft 75,131,141
轴衬 shaft bushing 130
轴承 bearing 23,45,74,75,82,89,94,99,100,101,113,132,218,393
轴承衬套 bearing sleeve 133
轴承端盖,轴承盖 bearing cover, bearing cap 22,89,94,354,356
轴承油封 bearing seal 99
轴承预紧隔套 bearing preload spacer 101
轴承座 bearing housing, bearing seat, bearing saddle, bearing support 89,94,101,102,119,131,135
轴管 tube 98
轴管叉 weld yoke, tube yoke 99
轴套 shaft sleeve 74,415
轴瓦 bearing bush, bearing shell 22,131
轴向-径向弹簧式胀簧 axial-radial spring expander 34
轴向-径向胀簧 expander-spacer 34
轴向柱塞泵 axial piston pump 314
轴向柱塞马达 axial plunger motor 314
轴针 pintle 65
轴针式喷嘴 Pintle type nozzle 44
主变速器 main transmission 312
主承推面 major thrust face 29
主传动 main drive 100
主传动器 main transmission 118
主传动锥齿轮 main bevel gear 280
主动齿轮 driving gear 77,79
主动齿轮法兰 pinion flange 101
主动毂 driving hub 102,119
主动链轮 driving chain wheel 386
主动盘 driving plate 85,89
主动片 driving disc 102,119
主动轴 driving shaft 75,415
主、副钢板弹簧 main spring and auxiliary spring, leaf spring and auxiliary spring 136
主钢板弹簧 main spring 139
主机架 main frame 16,173
主继电器 main relay 64
主接线柱 primary terminal 80
主控制器 main controller 327
主离合器 main clutch 87,88,346
主离合油泵 main clutch pump 87

557

主量孔　main jet　61
主密封圈　primary seal ring　74
主喷管　main discharge nozzle　61
主片　main leaf　139
主三通阀　main triple valve　413
主销　main pin　130
主销铜衬　main pin brass　130
主油道　main oil gallery　31,76
主轴承盖　mainshaft bearing cap　36
主轴承(上、下)轴瓦　main bearing shell(upper,lower)　36
主轴颈　main journal　37
助力弹簧　assist spring　92
驻车制动操纵杆　parking brake lever　160
驻车制动杠杆　parking brake lever　151
驻车制动管路　parking brake pipeline　164
驻车制动拉线　parking brake cable　160
驻车制动器　parking brake　87,103,159,215,287
驻车制动器拉索　parking brake cable　151
驻车制动推杆　parking brake strut (pushrod)　151
柱塞,柱塞弹簧　plunger,pump plunger,plunger spring　45,48,49,55,185
柱塞式喷油泵　jerk fuel injection pump　45

柱塞套　barrel　45,48,57
柱塞体　plunger body　55
柱塞衔铁　plunger armature　57
柱塞液压泵　piston pump　219
柱塞支承导管　plunger support guide　55
抓斗　grapple,grab bucket　185
专利文氏供料系统　patented Venturi feed system　442
转动脉冲　revolution pulse　53
转角清扫滚刷　angle broom　230
转矩板(丰田公司用法)　torque plate　155
转矩控制弹簧　torque-control spring　49
转速传感器　speed sensor　64,108
转速控制杆　speed-control lever　47
转向泵　steering pump　347,348,351
转向变量泵　sterring variable pump　313
转向操纵机构　steering control mechanism　111
转向操纵系统　steering and operating system　15,16,175
转向齿条　steering rack　111
转向垂臂　pitman arm　116
转向定量马达　steering quantitative motor　313
转向动力缸　power cylinder　111
转向阀　steering valve　346,351
转向横拉杆　steering tie rod　113
转向及振动用双联齿轮泵　double

转向器齿轮泵 gear pump for steering and vibration 346

转向减振(缓冲)器 steering shock absorber 113

转向节 steering knuckle, steering (axle) swivel, steering (axle) stub, axle stub 111,113,114

转向节臂 steering (knuckle) arm 111,113,114

转向控制 steering control 286

转向控制器 steering controller 285

转向离合器 steering clutch 87

转向螺母 steering nut 115

转向马达 steering motor 281

转向盘 steering wheel 111

转向器 steering gear, diverter, steering gear box, steering mechanism 111,113,115,247,346

转向器盖 steering gear cover 115

转向器壳体 steering gear housing 115

转向桥 steering axle 114

转向随动臂 steering idler arm 111

转向梯形 steering trapezium 117

转向蜗杆 steering worm 115

转向吸滤器 steering suction strainer 351

转向销 kingpin 114

转向摇臂 pitman arm, drop arm, steering gear arm, steering lever 111,113

转向油泵,转向液压泵 steering pump 87,103,215,282

转向油缸 steering cylinder 117,344,345,346,347,348,351

转向制动阀 steering brake valve 282

转向制动器 steering brake 87

转向轴 steering shaft 111,115

转向柱管 steering column 115

转运车 transfer vehicle 308

转子除雪机 snow blower 231

转子轴 rotor shaft 82

桩工机械 pile driving machinery 9

装料口 charging opening 408

锥面环 taper faced ring 34

锥形弹簧 cone spring 136

锥形底阀 tapered foot valve 392

锥形滚柱轴承 conical roller bearing 114

锥形螺塞 tapered plug 115

子午线轮胎 radial(ply) tire 123

自动调节杠杆 automating adjusting lever 151

自动分离器 automatic segregator 79

自动功率控制系统 APC system 178

自动换挡变速箱 automatic transmission 107

自动间隙补偿装置 automatic clearance compensator 153

自锁弹簧 self-lock spring 95,96

自锁钢球 self-lock ball 95,96

559

自锁装置 self-locking device 95
自卸车 dump truck 407
自行工程机械 self-propelled construction machinery 14
自行式铲运机 self-propelled scraper(motor scraper) 4
自行式平地机 self-propelled grader (motor grader) 4
自由状态环 free ring, unstressed ring 32
纵梁 frame side member (rail) 128,129
纵坡传感器 longitudinal slope sensor 327
纵向折线花纹 circumferential fold line pattern 124
总阀门 total valve 410
总阀门手轮 total valve hand wheel 410
总线 CAN 164
综合监视器 combination monitor 178
组合阀 brake combination valve 160
组合阀块 combination valves 117
组合开关 combined switch 360
组合式曲轴 built-up crankshaft 37
组合式振动压路机 combined vibratory roller 343
嘴体 valve body 126
最高转速限制器 maximum-speed stop 49

最终传动,最终传动装置 final drive 16,87,173
最终传动减速器 final reduction gear 280
左变量泵 left variable pump 108,315
左侧送料器 left feeder 333
左电磁阀 left electromagnetic valve 327
左调平油缸 left leveling cylinder 327
左刮板和转向双联泵 left drag and steering double-link pump 314
左横管三通阀 left horizontal pipe triple valve 413
左基本段熨平板 left basic screed 323
左连接板 left junction plate 355
左连接支架 left junction bracket 355,356
左链轨节 left track link 130
左牵引臂 left towed arm 327
左前制动油管 brake line, LF 160
左液压伸缩熨平板 left hydraulic extension screed 325
左仪表盘 LH cluster 360
左、右盘式制动器 left and right disc brake 118
左右铣刨鼓 left and right milling drum 423
左、右终传动 left and right final drive 118
左、右转向离合器 left and right

steering clutch 118

左制动器 left brake 281

左轴向柱塞马达 left axial plunger motor 108,315

左转向油缸 left steering cylinder 116

左最终传动 left final reduction gear 281

作动杠杆 actuator lever 151

作动杠杆回位弹簧 lever return spring 151

作动杠杆支枢 lever pivot 151

作动连杆 actuator link 151

作业用柴油机 diesel engine for working unit 417

座圈 cartridge 74

座椅 seat 422

参 考 文 献

[1] 陈作江,王占运. 汉英机械工程词典. 北京:海洋出版社,1999.
[2] 王锦俞,闵思鹏. 图解英汉技术词典. 北京:机械工业出版社,2002.
[3] 曹元寿. 英汉农业机械工程词典. 北京:中国农业出版社,1995.
[4] 葛贤康. 英汉图文对照汽车技术词典. 上海:上海科学技术文献出版社,2000.
[5] 沈希瑾,李京生,张文杰. 英汉图解汽车工程词典. 北京:北京理工大学出版社,2001.
[6] 吴社强. 汽车构造. 上海:上海科学技术出版社,2003.
[7] 李俊玲,罗永革. 汽车工程专业英语. 北京:机械工业出版社,2005.
[8] 马林才. 汽车实用英语. 北京:人民交通出版社,2005.
[9] 蔡安薇,崔永春. 汽车专业英语. 北京:北京理工大学出版社,1998.
[10] 粟利萍,黄秋平. 汽车实用英语. 北京:电子工业出版社,2005.
[11] 陈家瑞. 汽车构造. 第 2 版. 北京:机械工业出版社,2005.
[12] 郁录平. 工程机械底盘设计. 北京:人民交通出版社,2004.
[13] 车胜创. 奥迪系列轿车维修技术. 济南:山东科学技术出版社,2000.
[14] 陈新轩,展朝勇,郑忠敏. 现代工程机械发动机与底盘构造. 北京:人民交通出版社,2002.
[15] 唐经世. 工程机械底盘学. 成都:西南交通大学出版社,1999.
[16] 周一鸣. 汽车拖拉机学发动机构造. 北京:中国农业大学出版社,2000.
[17] 王健. 工程机械构造. 北京:中国铁道出版社,1995.
[18] 何挺继,展朝勇. 现代公路施工机械. 北京:人民交通出版社,1999.
[19] 张世英,陈元基. 筑路机械工程. 北京:机械工业出版社,1998.
[20] 何挺继,朱文天,邓世新. 筑路机械手册. 北京:人民交通出版社,1998.
[21] 吴永平,姚怀新. 工程机械设计. 北京:人民交通出版社,2005.

欢迎订阅工程机械类图书

小松挖掘机构造原理及拆装维修	56.00元
现代挖掘机构造原理及拆装维修	56.00元
工程机械液压、液力系统故障诊断与维修	58.00元
挖掘机液压原理与拆装维修	59.00元
最新挖掘机液压和电路图册	68.00元
工程机械构造与设计	48.00元
工程起重机结构与设计	49.00元
起重机操作工培训教程	29.00元
叉车操作工培训教程	26.00元
挖掘机操作工培训教程	26.00元
装载机操作工培训教程	24.00元
液压挖掘机维修速查手册	68.00元
工程机械液压系统及故障维修	39.00元
工程机械设计与维修丛书-电器、电子控制与安全系统	32.00元
工程机械设计与维修丛书-轮式装载机	48.00元
工程机械设计与维修丛书-内燃机	49.00元
工程机械设计与维修丛书-金属结构	42.00元
工程机械设计与维修丛书-现代起重运输机械	38.00元
工程机械设计与维修丛书-振动压路机	29.00元
工程机械设计与维修丛书-现代设计技术	32.00元
工程机械设计与维修丛书-钻井与非开挖机械	40.00元
工程机械设计与维修丛书-推土机与平地机	24.00元
工程机械设计与维修丛书-液压挖掘机	22.00元
工程机械结构与维护检修技术	39.00元
建筑与养护路机械——原理、结构与设计	31.00元
破碎与筛分机械设计选用手册	95.00元
运输机械设计选用手册 上册	98.00元
运输机械设计选用手册 下册	90.00元
管道物料输送与工程应用	45.00元
现代物流设备设计与选用	49.00元
电动滚筒设计与选用手册	48.00元
叉车维修与养护实例	38.00元

以上图书由**化学工业出版社　机械·电气分社**出版。如要以上图书的内容简介和详细目录，或者更多的专业图书信息，请登录 www.cip.com.cn。如要出版新著，请与编辑联系。

地址：北京市东城区青年湖南街 13 号（100011）
编辑：010-64519276，jiana@cip.com.cn
购书咨询：010-64519685（传真：010-64519686）